Burning Images

1968_02_16_USA-SC:
Governor McNair

1979_02_18_Iran: Uncle Sam

2001_12_30_USA-FL:
Osama bin Laden

2010_11_08_India:
US President Obama

2016_11_09_USA-CA:
President elect Trump

Florian Göttke

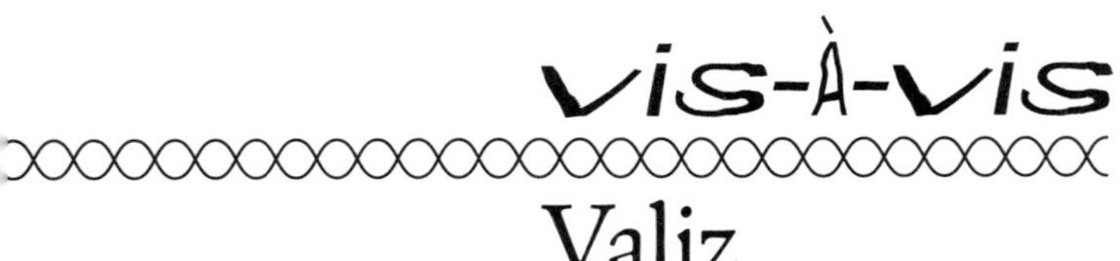

Valiz

Burning Images

A History of Effigy Protests

Contents

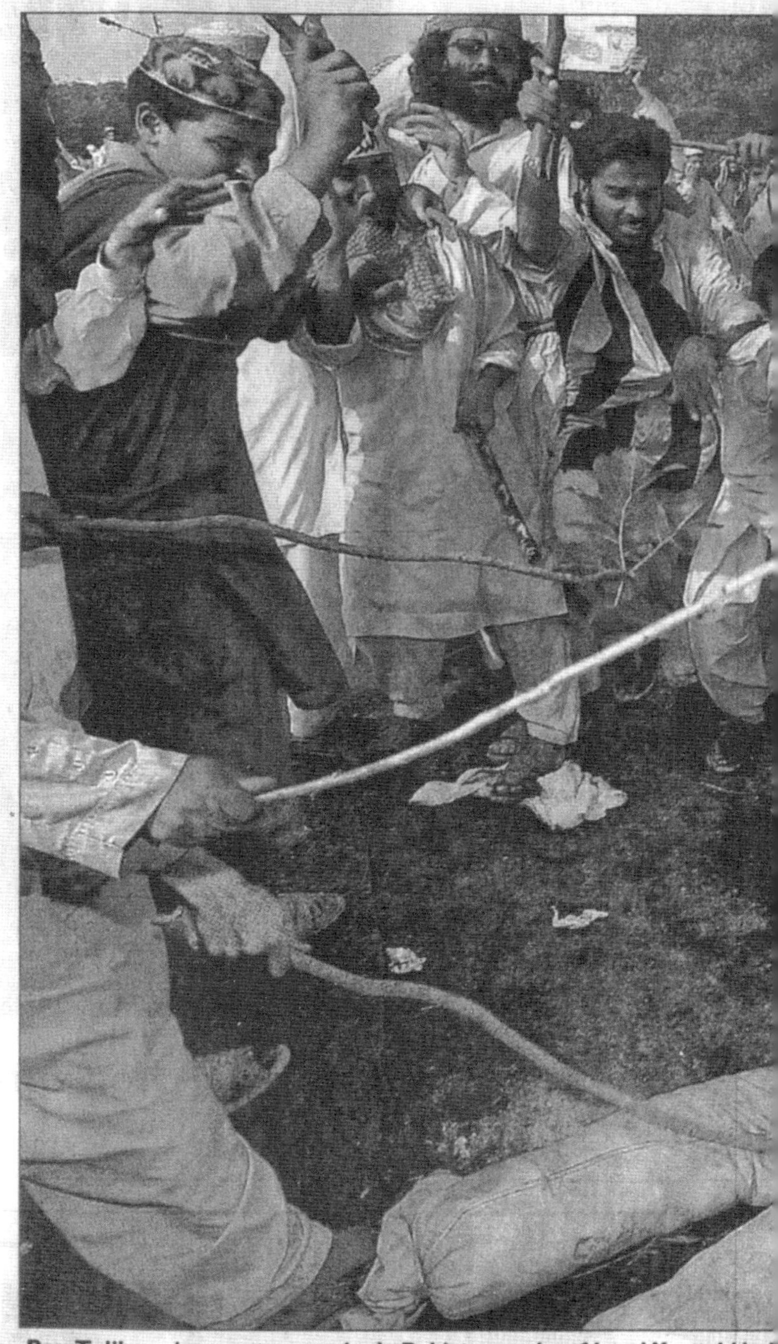

Pro-Taliban-demonstranten in de Pakistaanse hoofdstad Karachi ha[...]

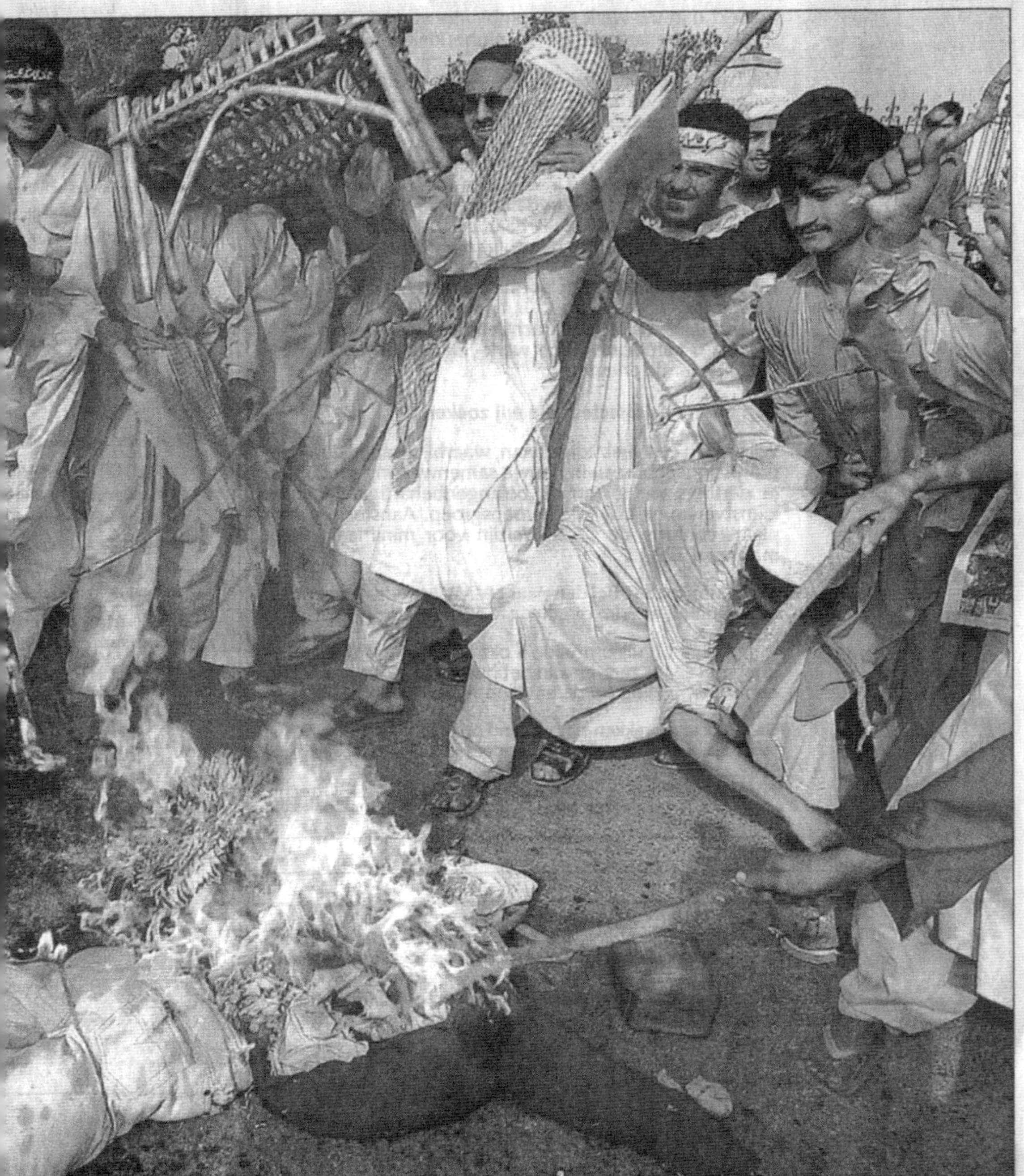

2001_09_22_Pakistan: US President Bush; Pro-Taliban-
demonstrators in the Pakistan capital Karachi hack away at a
burning doll representing President Bush of the United States.

Burning Questions

It was 2001, in an issue of Dutch newspaper *de Volkskrant,*
that I first saw an effigy being burned in a political protest.
The photograph taken in Pakistan less than two weeks after
the September 11 attacks in New York, showed a throng of
young men beat and burn a stuffed version of President of the
United States George W. Bush. The protesters responded to
Bush's threat to invade neighboring Afghanistan, if the
Taliban government didn't extradite Osama bin Laden, who
the US deemed responsible for the attacks.

While my clipping of this image has yellowed, it has not
lost its appeal. One can sense the chaotic expression of communal anger, captured so well by the photographer in far-
away Pakistan; the crowd's energy is palpable to Western-
European readers. Excitement shows on the young men's
faces, who take part in the symbolic punishment of the US
leader who is made responsible for the neglectful politics and
the resulting injustices in their country. While searching for
images for the work *Toppled,*[1] I came across many more
images of Bush effigies being burned in protests against the

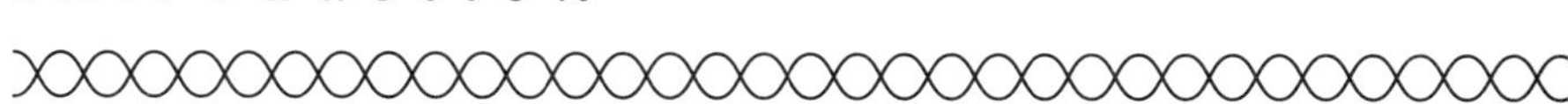

1   The book *Toppled* developed
from a series of image lectures
investigating what happened to
the statues of Saddam Hussein,
which were toppled during the
Iraq War of 2003. Florian
Göttke, *Toppled* (Rotterdam:
Post Editions, 2003).

Iraq War in Iraq itself, as well as in Pakistan, Afghanistan, India, and many Western countries.

In 2011, I saw effigies appear in reports from the Arab Uprisings in Egypt, Libya, Syria, and Yemen. In February, activists in Tahrir Square staged mock trials of President Hosni Mubarak, his effigy standing in as the accused – six months later, the real Mubarak was wheeled into a Cairo courthouse to stand trial. That same month, protesters in the Yemeni capital Sanaa hanged effigies of President Ali Abdullah Saleh – by April he had promised to step down, and after eight months of delay tactics finally did. Also in February, protesters in Benghazi, Libya, hanged and mutilated effigies of Colonel Muammar Gaddafi. In October, Gaddafi was captured and killed. Images of his corpse, exhibited for four days in a walk-in freezer in a market, circulated widely in the news.

The connection between the actual punishments of these leaders, and the staged burning of their effigies, seemed strangely prescient. I became intrigued and began searching for effigy protests more systematically and found an overwhelming number of reports and images from across the globe and extending far back in time. From these many instances, the picture of a curious protest practice emerged: a paradoxical visual form in which protesters create an image just to destroy it during their demonstration. An archaic material practice with roots in traditions and rituals, it nevertheless seemed to have survived many changes in the way societies communicate and function perfectly within the framework of the global digital news media. Based on image research as it is part of my practice as a visual artist, I embarked on research across different academic fields, which led to a PhD at the Amsterdam School for Cultural Analysis at the University of Amsterdam.

My work has affinity with artists, theorists and curators like Eyal Weizman, Rabih Mroué, or Ariella Azoulay, who work in between academia, art and activism and who combine modes of artistic or architectural practice with academic research. Trained as an architect, Eyal Weizman established the research agency Forensic Architecture in 2010 at Goldsmiths University of London with a team of researchers assembled from multiple disciplines. Forensic Architecture has primarily an activist agenda, and conducts research "on behalf of international prosecutors, human rights organizations and political and environmental justice groups."[2] Forensic Architecture applies visual methods from architectural practice, 3D modeling and animation, to enhance and contextualize fragmented audio-visual material of critical moments in highly politicized conflicts to be used as evidence in human rights court cases. That their visually compelling documentary presentations are also in demand in the art context and presented in exhibitions, publications, etc. is secondary. Nevertheless, their prominence in the art world validates their work, enhances their public profile and credibility, and furthers their activist agenda.

The Lebanese artist, performer and theater maker Rabih Mroué mixes reality and fiction, often using documentary and archival material for his discursive works. For his 2012 video "The Pixelated Revolution," he collected video-footage of the Syrian civil war from the internet made by activists documenting the war with mobile phone cameras. Because of their image making, these activists were targeted by the regime and in a number of cases recorded their own deaths. Mroué reflects on the moments when the viewfinder of the camera and the scope of the rifle align. For a fraction of a moment, the rifle is aimed at the viewer of the video before the video image breaks apart and the viewer is left

2　See Forensic Architecture (website), forensic-architecture. org/project/.

3   Rabih Mroué, "Oppressive Regimes Wage War Against Cellphone Video – Rabih Mroué," interview with Rabih Mroué, San Francisco Museum of Modern Art, July 9, 2018, youtube.com/watch?v=zRsNSmRpKmg.

4   Ariella Azoulay, "Unlearning the Origins of Photography," Fotomuseum Winterthur (website), September 6, 2018, fotomuseum.ch/en/explore/still-searching/authors/10605_ariella_azoulay.

5   Ariella Azoulay, "The Family of Man: A Visual Universal Declaration of Human Rights," in *The Human Snapshot*, ed. Thomas Keenan and Tirdad Zolghadr (Berlin: Sternberg Press, 2013), 20.

to imagine the violence that occurred.[3]

Ariella Azoulay is a theorist of photography and visual culture and Professor of Comparative Literature and Modern Culture and Media. She attempts to radically rethink photography's relation to the political and make visible photography's grounding in colonial rule and state power.[4] Azoulay is also a curator and filmmaker. She uses archival material in videos or installations combined with discursive text to visually and argumentatively demonstrate her theoretical analysis. The installation *The Body Politic* builds on Edward Steichen's famous photography exhibition *The Family of Man,* which Azoulay proposes as a "visual proxy of the United Nations 1948 Universal Declaration of Human Rights."[5] She complements Steichen's collection with photographs from the same period that document concrete instances where people make rights claims in strikes and presents the arrangement of images with a discursive text.

In this work I want to avoid making the distinction between artistic work and academic research, and rather integrate artistic modes of research into academic research and integrate academic research into the work of art. This book then, is one form of the work, appropriate in the academic context, adhering to but also stretching the conventions that apply. What I present in an art exhibition, while still combining both visual and textual elements, takes on a different form. Here the visual part – the image montages described later in this introduction – have the leading role. Text is added in a rather fragmentary way as annotations, hand-outs, audio-tracks, and/or in some other form.

Given the long history and topicality of this protest practice in recent geopolitics, it came as a surprise to me at the outset of this study that it had not previously been taken up as a topic of academic research. The only substantial work on effigies is ethnographer and art historian Wolfgang Brückner's *Bildnis und Brauch: Studien zur Bildfunktion der Effigies* (Portrait and Custom – Studies of the Image Function of Effigies) from 1966, in which he examines effigy punishment and the use of images in formal law in European history.[6] While he acknowledges that formal effigy punishment developed from traditional ritual effigy practices through political use, he dismisses the study of the many modern examples in political contexts.

Effigy protests are mentioned in some studies of rituals and folklore in relation to traditional effigy practices like public shaming or Guy Fawkes Day celebrations.[7] They appear anecdotally in books and weblogs about early us history and in studies about nineteenth-century rioting in England and the us.[8] American anthropologist Mériam N. Belli devotes a chapter of her book *An Incurable Past: Nasser's Egypt Then and Now* (2013) to effigy protests during the first half of the twentieth century, which over time turned into a carnivalesque festival in Port Said, Egypt.[9] Performance scholar Joseph Roach proposes "effigy" as a conceptual category that signifies the prescribed roles of social actors.[10] But there is virtually no text that aims to understand the practice as a genre of political protest. Effigy hanging and burning seem to have remained out of sight for any academic discipline, perhaps too infrequent to be really relevant to the histories of riots and political protests, and too unspecific for anthropology. It might also have been too uncommon for performance studies and possibly too violent for progressive political protest studies. More closely related to folklore than high art, this image practice remained equally invisible to the field of art history.[11]

Effigy protests comprise an image practice central to which is the production, manipulation, and dissemination of

13

6 Wolfgang Brückner, *Bildnis und Brauch: Studien zur Bildfunktion der Effigies* (Berlin: Erich Schmidt Verlag, 1966), 169.

7 Edward Muir, *Ritual in Early Modern Europe* (Cambridge: Cambridge University Press, 1997), 111; E. P. Thompson, "Rough Music Reconsidered," *Folklore* 103, no. 1 (1992): 16–18; Mike Jay, "Bonfire Night in Lewes," in *Gunpowder Plots* (London: Penguin, 2005), 128–32.

8 Stephen H. Norwood, *Strikebreaking and Intimidation: Mercenaries and Masculinity in Twentieth-Century America* (Chapel Hill, NC: University of North Carolina Press, 2002), 41, 43, 92, 214; Charles Tilly, *Contentious Performances* (Cambridge: Cambridge University Press, 2008), 117, 140.

9 Mériam N. Belli, *An Incurable Past: Nasser's Egypt Then and Now* (Gainesville: University Press of Florida, 2013), 75–162.

10 Joseph Roach, *Cities of the Dead: Circum-Atlantic Performance* (New York: Columbia University Press, 1996), 36–41.

11 Georges Didi-Huberman wrote about a similar archaic kind of image practice, the votive image. It has a lot of similar characteristics, formally as well as functionally. But in contrast to effigies the votive hardly plays a role in contemporary culture or politics. Georges Didi-Huberman, "Ex-Voto: Image, Organ, Time," *L'Esprit Créateur* 47, no. 3 (2007): 7–16.

12 Marcel Finke, "Materialtäten und Praktiken," in *Bild: Ein Interdisziplinäres Handbuch*, ed. Stephan Günzel and Dieter Mersch (Stuttgart: Verlag J. B. Metzler, 2014), 28.

13 James Elkins, for instance, names W. J. T. Mitchell, Nicholas Mirzoeff, Gottfried Boehm, Marie-José Mondzain, Hans Belting, and Horst Bredekamp. James Elkins, "Afterword," in *Image Operations: Visual Media and Political Conflict*, ed. Jens Eder and Charlotte Klonk (Manchester: Manchester University Press, 2017), Kindle edition.

14 Eder and Klonk, "Introduction."

images[12]: the effigies as well as the photographs produced during their performance. The images are tools of a practice that communicates through mass media; they are used for impact. In the interaction, images acquire agency: they become "operative" and influence social and political relations beyond the control of human actors. Many visual culture scholars have worked more or less explicitly with the notion of "image operation."[13] In their 2017 book *Image Operations: Visual Media and Political Conflict*, Jens Eder and Charlotte Klonk collect a number of different approaches to the term and consider the role of images as both tools and agents from an interdisciplinary perspective, especially in the context of political conflict. Relevant to my study is that images can "influence the development of social discourses, the distribution of knowledge and power and the formation of social organizations."[14]

There are five different aspects of effigy practice that can be described as operations:

1   Effigies are images that are used as props in protest performances, as tools to demean and insult the depicted.

2   Their specific qualities, namely their grotesque aesthetics, contribute to this aforementioned operation of denigration and declassification.

3   During performances, protesters often interact with effigies as if the dolls possess a life of their own. Effigies seem animated in these interactions and operate with some agency.

4   Protesters stage performances with an image – the effigy – to produce news media images and thereby communicate with a wider public and influence the social and political constellations of their community. The media images are used as tools to operate in the social and political realm.

5   As it becomes detached from the specific event in the process of mediation, both actors and mediators lose control of the media image's relevance and meaning. It can affect social and political relations beyond the intention of any actor involved in its creation. The media image becomes operational on its own.

Images and the effects they have in the social and political arena are at the center of this study. Working from the images toward theory and back to images I venture into the fields of history, art history, anthropology, performance studies, photography theory, iconology, image studies, and political philosophy. The protest practice as it becomes visible in the images, poses some fundamental questions that concern these disciplines: what are the genealogies of effigy protests in these different countries? What are the mechanisms of transfer between different places and over time? How does this trans-historical and trans-local image practice function in the contemporary global media environment? How does it operate as an image practice in so many different political constellations? What kind of politics does this protest practice promote?

Collecting Images

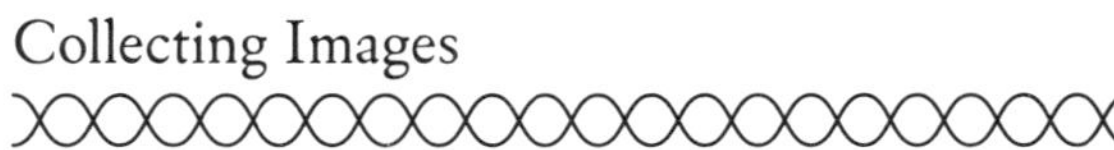

In the remainder of this introduction, I explain the research framework and methodology of collecting, reading, and writing with images. The study's starting point is investigating the contemporary practice of effigy protest as it has become visible in the news media in visual documents and written reports. As this information is most readily accessible online, data is collected through extensive internet searches. Most of the images and reports were found on established news media, digital news, open-access picture agency, stock photo

15 This research relies on images sourced from websites as follows: news (34 percent); picture and stock photo agencies (32 percent); institutional archives, libraries, and museums (12 percent); blogs (12 percent); other (10 percent). See for detailed source list: "Image References," p. 283.

16 I tried to use the Google function "search by image" for my query, but this led to few relevant results.

agency, and newspaper websites. Less used sources were government-funded institutional archives, university libraries, museum archives, personal blogs and photo-sharing sites.[15] The resulting data is very diverse. While predominantly photographic, there are also scans of historical prints and illustrations from secondary literature. The written accounts consist largely of contemporary news reports and a smaller number of descriptions from secondary literature.

Even though I searched for images, I used language as my excavation tool, finding the images of effigy protests via the tags attached to them or keywords in associated written reports.[16] I used various languages for the searches, but English, being the internet's main tongue, led to most results. In addition, from the languages I used – including German, Dutch, French, Spanish, Russian, and Farsi – English is the only one with a specific and widely used word for the practice (to burn/hang in effigy) and the doll (effigy) that I was searching for. German and French, for instance, use the Latin appendix "in/en effigie" for the practice, but it has not entered everyday use, and both languages lack a specific noun for the doll itself. The other languages do not have a specific word for "effigy" either, and use words that are translated as puppet, dummy, or doll.

The language and internet use certainly influenced my results, as my data originates to a large degree from Western news media sources, establishing a largely Western and Anglo-Saxon view of events that often happened in very different cultural and political contexts (58 percent of the events in the collection are from non-Western countries). Nevertheless, English provided the best access to non-Western sources as it is spoken in many non-Western countries and websites are often translated into English to reach larger international audiences.

I sourced freely accessible data so that I could see the images, and then think and talk about them. I own them as memories, mental images, but not as objects. I don't have the authority to archive them as they are not my property. I cannot exhibit them, but the copyright law allows me to cite them in my discourse. The data from these many different sources constitute a collection that is not fixed, but in motion, changing according to the direction of the research. This collection should not be considered an authoritative archive, but a research collection determined by the conditions I describe above and shaped by the ongoing development of the research.

In total I collected data of about 3,000 political demonstrations worldwide, in which effigies were used in some form. The oldest example from Europe dates back to 1328 in Italy, when the troops of Holy Roman Emperor Louis IV on their campaign to unseat Pope John XXII burned him in effigy.[17] My earliest example from the US is the hanging of a tax collector at the beginning of the American Revolution in 1765 and from Asia the parading and burning an effigy depicting the British Home Secretary Sir John Simon in 1930 in India's long struggle for independence. In most non-Western countries, my records start in the 1950s.

The collection is structured by nation-state grouped into continental regions; inside these categories, data are ordered chronologically. Overall, the distribution is uneven. In the process of collecting, it appeared that some countries and regions – the US, South Asia, and the Middle East – seemed more prevalent than others, because the practice was very visible in the news media and of current political relevance. Subsequently, I concentrated my efforts on those countries

17 Brückner, *Bildnis und Brauch*, 197–201.

17

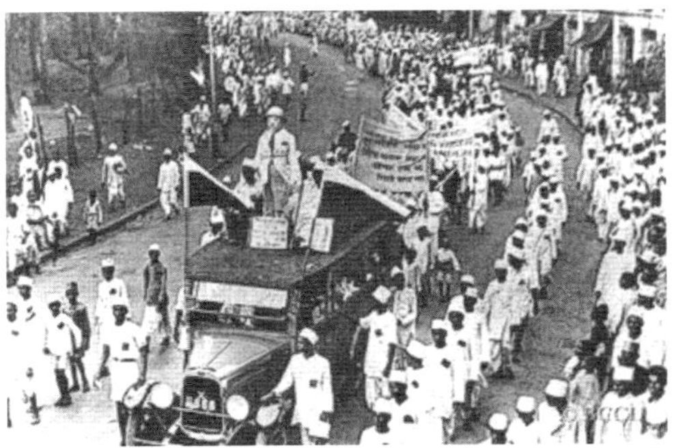

1930_06_25_India: British Home Secretary Simon

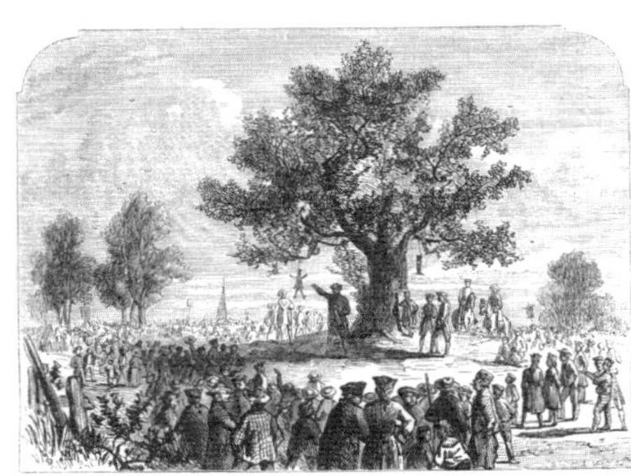

1765_08_14_USA-MA: stamp master Oliver

18 See also Index, page 311.

19 See Hito Steyerl, "In Defense of the Poor Image," *e-flux journal* 10 (2009).

and regions in order to arrive at a collection that would be substantial enough to garner conclusions about effigy practice.

The data shows significant differences in the number of effigy protests in different countries. The countries with the most effigy protests are Pakistan, Palestine, and Afghanistan, followed by Libya, the US, India, and Egypt.[18] The reasons for this frequency differ, however: in Pakistan, India, and the US the practice is a well-established form of protest used consistently over time and in a wide variety of political conflicts; in Palestine, the practice has been used regularly since the 1970s, but almost exclusively in the context of the conflict with Israel; in Afghanistan, the first effigy protest was reported in 1999, with frequency only increasing from 2005 onwards in relation to the US occupation and incidents perceived as insults to Islam by Western actors; and in Egypt and Libya, most protests have been staged in the context of a single politically tumultuous period, namely the Arab Spring in 2011 and its aftermath.

Although the initial source material is heterogenous, the internet homogenizes data and impoverishes images. Every image, be it a woodcut, an analog photograph from a negative, or a video still from a smartphone camera enters my collection as a digital image – disembodied, displayed on a screen at rather low resolution.[19] Yet a photograph's materiality, its mode of production and history of distribution, often remains traceable even in poor images.

This photograph from 1903, shows the hanging effigy of strike breaker Frank Curry in Chicago.○ It must have been a

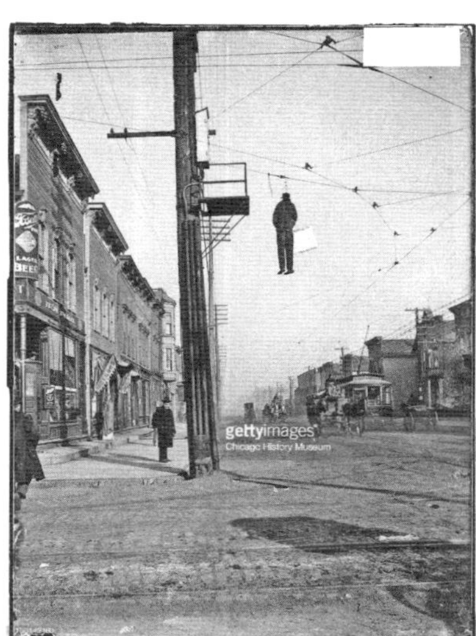

○ 1903_11_19_USA-IL: strike breaker Frank Curry

beautiful sunny day when this image was shot in November. Four horse-drawn carts drive through a rather empty street alongside an electrical tram, which links the photograph to a transitional moment in the ongoing industrialization of American society. Three pedestrians are visible, one man in hat and coat has stopped, turned, and looks straight into the lens of the camera, acknowledging the photographer, while the effigy hangs from the tram cables five meters above without anyone paying attention. It is a beautifully composed image: the utility pole almost violently bifurcates the image vertically, a bit left of center, while the man turned to the camera strikes a balance with the silhouette of the hanging figure in the sky – one wonders if the photographer staged the man's position. The emptiness of the street belies the charged context of the hanging effigy, the fierce and violent labor dispute of the railway strike in that time. But nothing of the turmoil that must have riveted the city and its inhabitants at the time is visible in this photograph. The image shows edges that identify the "original" as a 4×5 inch glass negative, which hints at the considerable effort involved in producing a photograph then, due to the size of the equipment and the elaborate processing. It also points to the *Chicago Daily News*'s eagerness to serve its readers with photographic images and the technological possibilities of the time to reproduce photographs in print.[20] The watermark of Getty Images is embedded in the middle of the image and the reference number on the lower left corner, marking Getty's collaboration with the Chicago History Museum in the digitization of the *Chicago Daily News* photo archive. If we zoom in closer, we can see that the effigy is made from workers' pants and jacket and bears a sign that we see only from the back. A second photograph from the Chicago Daily News Collection in the Getty Images archive shows another effigy of a strike

20   I don't know if this particular image was ever published.

21   The *Chicago Daily News Negatives Collection* in the Getty Images archive consists of 179 digitized images of glass negatives dating from 1900 until 1916.

breaker hanged in a similar manner during a strike in 1904, indicating that the practice was not uncommon.[21]

Reading Images

22   Richard V. Ericson, "How Journalists Visualize Fact," *Annals of the American Academy of Political and Social Science* 560 (1998): 85.

Hanging or burning effigies as political protest is a layered image practice that not only includes the production of effigies and performances staged with them, but also the mediation of the event of which my data is comprised. The recorded events are performances of protest, *tableaux vivants,* scenes staged to become living images visible to those present as well as those reached through photographs published in the media. There are therefore four layers to my data: media image, photographic image, performed image of communal punishment, and sculpted image or effigy. Each of these four layers comes with its own theoretical framework and set of questions. Because I am most interested in how these layers relate and together communicate protester's message to varied audiences, I focus more on performances and effigies visible in the photographs, while keeping in mind that these become visible to me and most spectators only as photographs or as descriptions through the media.

The first two layers – the media image and photographic image – are closely linked, since the photojournalists who record events are part of a media apparatus. Mediation entails a number of operational manipulations. Photojournalists determine the camera position and the moment at which actors, action, and surroundings turn into the pictorial elements that together represent the protest.[22] Photographers frame the performance according to their aesthetics and the conventions and expectations of the news outlet. On top of that, picture editors at the news outlet add their own frame by selecting, editing, cropping, and adding captions. These procedures embed the photographs within the discourse of the specific media outlet and its audience.

Nevertheless, it is impossible to reduce a photograph to only one perspective, and photographs are characterized by "fragmentation, ambiguity, dislocation and uncertainty."[23] Photography theorist Ariella Azoulay characterizes a photograph as both partial and singular, neither icon nor purely document.[24] It exhibits a "specific pattern of excess and lack" that points to the conditions of its production and dissemination.[25] For Azoulay, a photograph is the "product of an event shared by several participants,"[26] a complex cultural construct that involves multiple actors, and that unfolds as an event in a series of encounters. The first is the "encounter – even a violent one – between a photographer, a photographed subject and a camera."[27] The second encounter is between photograph and spectator who takes part in the production of the image's meaning. Both encounters shape the meaning of a photograph. None of the actors are able to fully determine the meaning of the photograph and "their attempt to determine and shape what will be seen in the frame and the power relations between those participants within it leaves traces that enable one to reconstruct the complexity of the event of photography."[28] By interrogating the space between the photographs' fragmentary character and their singularity, with careful consideration of their "practical, social, cultural, and medial environments,"[29] it is possible – and necessary – to read them in ways beyond and counter to the first obvious meaning.

Emphasizing the social and political implications of news photography, Azoulay conceives photography as a civil contract, which not only establishes a reciprocal relationship between the people photographed and the viewer, but also a

23 Elizabeth Edwards, *Raw Histories: Photographs, Anthropology and Museums* (Oxford: Berg, 2001), 192.

24 Ariella Azoulay, "Archive," *Political Concepts: A Critical Lexicon* 1 (2011): 10, political-concepts.org/issue1/archive/.

25 Azoulay, "Archive," 9.

26 Azoulay, "Archive," 9.

27 Ariella Azoulay, *The Civil Contract of Photography* (New York: Zone Books, 2008), 13.

28 Ariella Azoulay, "Potential History: Thinking through Violence," *Critical Inquiry* 39, no. 3 (2013): 556.

29 Eder and Klonk, "Introduction," 17.

30 Azoulay, *The Civil Contract*, 20.

31 See chapter 2, "Performing Protest."

certain responsibility.[30] The spectators' responsibility is to prevent the foreclosure of the photograph's meaning by any dominant narrative. Especially if it concerns news photographs in situations of crisis, one cannot conceive the photographer as the sole author of the image and the media outlet as the one who determines its meaning. Instead, as Azoulay points out, one has to consider the specific interests of the photographed subjects in the production and dissemination of the images and attempt to recover their suppressed side of the story. In the case of most of the photographs I investigate, protesters performing effigies actively take part in the photograph's production. They seek out the camera and stage the scene to be photographed in order to address wider audiences.[31] The agency of the subjects in these photographs is evident, inviting a reading into the intentions and attitudes of protesters as they try to pierce the obfuscating screen of the media while they communicate through it.

Writing with Images

32 W. J. T. Mitchell, "Method, Madness, Montage: Aby Warburg to John Nash," lecture at the Warburg Institute, London, November 4, 2016, youtube.com/user/ WarburgInstitute/videos.

33 Elizabeth Edwards, "Introduction," in *Anthropology and Photography, 1860–1920*, ed. Elizabeth Edwards (New Haven: Yale University Press, 1992), 4.

Ordering the data rationally, following geographical and chronological criteria, is one way to work with it. This order situates events in their historical geographical context and allows for inquiry with respect to genealogies, cultural specificity, and development over time. Another approach is to take the images themselves as entry points into the study of the living cultural practice whose remnants are these violent and grotesque images. I read the images closely for clues as to how to think about the practice as a whole.[32] I analyze their visual content for gestures, expressions, and constellations, as well as their different layers in relation to each other.[33] The images activate each other and resonate with one another;

patterns in the different layers of the photographs and events they depict become visible.

I follow the clues hidden in single images as well as their accumulation within a large number of images, seeking resemblances, associations, and affinities. Moving between close and distant reading, connections between the images across time and origin are established, revealing semantic traces and patterns that further direct my research. With the collection set in motion, new configurations appear that ask for different trans-disciplinary perspectives.

In reading the practice through images, some photographs become especially significant. These belong to a class of images that the visual culture scholar W. J. T. Mitchell describes as "meta-pictures," which reflect "on the practices of pictorial representation."[34] They can embody, or rather picture, an argument, lead the investigation in a specific direction, or cause it to branch out in several directions. This image from India is an example of such a meta-picture at the intersection of several lines of thinking that I follow in my research: the relaxed attitude of the group of protesters hints at the relatively common use of effigies in political conflicts in India and calls for research into the genealogy of the practice. A sense of animation of the effigy underscores the skill of its maker as well as an uncanny interaction between it and the protesters, steering the research toward anthropology and

34   W. J. T. Mitchell, *Picture Theory: Essays on Verbal and Visual Representation* (Chicago: University of Chicago Press, 1994), 9, 35.

23

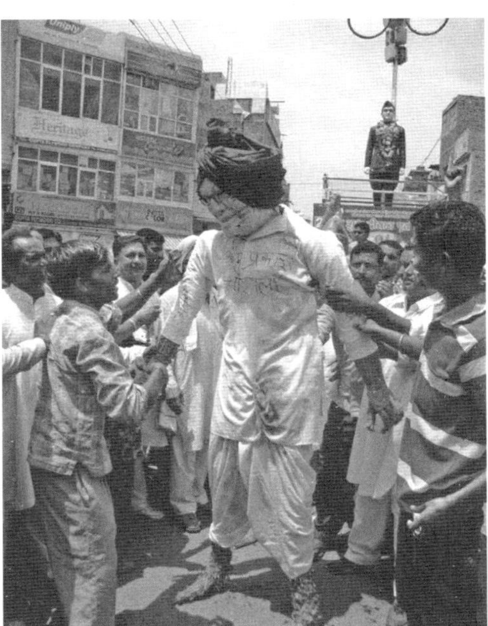

○ 2011_08_01_India: Om Parkash Chautala

35 Walter Benjamin, *The Arcades Project* (Cambridge, MA: Belknap Press, 2002), 473.

36 Benjamin, *The Arcades Project*, 475.

37 Susan Buck-Morss, *The Dialectics of Seeing: Walter Benjamin and the Arcades Project* (Cambridge, MA: MIT Press, 1989), 6.

38 Giorgio Agamben, *Potentialities: Collected Essays in Philosophy* (Stanford: Stanford University Press, 1999), 95.

39 Aby Warburg, *The Renewal of Pagan Antiquity: Contributions to the Cultural History of the European Renaissance*, trans. David Britt (Los Angeles: Getty Research Center for the History of Art and the Humanities, 1999), 585.

40 Agamben, *Potentialities*, 100.

41 Philippe-Alain Michaud, *Aby Warburg and the Image in Motion* (New York: Zone Books, 2007), 252.

psychology. The similar iconography of the garlanded statue in the background suggests an engagement with iconology.

Other images provide sudden, lucid insights without detailed analysis. Philosopher Walter Benjamin terms these images "dialectical"; they emerge "suddenly, in a flash" in the "now of [their] recognizability."[35] Elaborating on the relationship between images and knowledge he writes: "To thinking belongs the movement as well as the arrest of thoughts. Where thinking comes to a standstill in a constellation saturated with tensions – there the dialectical image appears."[36] Political philosopher Susan Buck-Morss specifies that Benjamin's "dialectics of seeing" relies "on the interpretive power of images that make conceptual points concretely, with reference to the world outside the text."[37] These images embody a certain memory or knowledge. For instance, the photograph of a hanged effigy of an African American voter from 1939 concretely makes the link to lynching as a practice of racial subjugation, so that this monstrous image, as the trace of an event in time, evokes an earlier specific social and political environment.

In the same sense, art historian Aby Warburg, whose work has gained attention far beyond his own field and has become an inspiration for artists in the last twenty years, regarded, in philosopher Giorgio Agamben's words, "the image as the organ of social memory."[38] By tracing the reappearance of image motifs over time and their migration across cultures, Warburg aimed to study the "historical psychology of human expression."[39] Focusing on the relation between images, he pursued "an 'iconology of the interval,' a study of the *Zwischenraum* in which the incessant symbolic work of social memory is carried out."[40] The iconology of the interval studies the "interrelationships between the figures in their complex, autonomous arrangement."[41] Because these cannot be reduced to discourse, Warburg created montages of heterogenous images – the "maps" of his *Mnemosyne Atlas* – to make the connections between images with distant origins in time and location visible.[42] On large plates covered with black canvas, Warburg pinned reproductions of artworks and cultural artefacts from antiquity to the Renaissance, as well as contemporary images found in advertisements and newspapers. Through their arrangement, Warburg traced the lineage and survival of gestures and other visual tropes, which he called *Pathosformeln* (pathos formulas). The montages were his research tools, and the atlas a laboratory in continuous motion, expanding over time, with a growing collection of images in changing constellations. It remains unfinished, and only photographs of its different stages are preserved.

Art historian Georges Didi-Huberman points out the affinities between Warburg, Benjamin, and French intellectual Georges Bataille in their attention to images: "Warburg's practice pursues the kind of knowledge obtainable through montage – the nonstandard kind recommended, practiced, and theorized in the same period by Benjamin in his *Arcades* and Georges Bataille in his journal *Documents*."[43] Referring to literary theorist Maurice Blanchot, Didi-Huberman characterizes montage as a way of writing with images. He stresses, though, that this kind of writing does not aim to reduce the "problems of the image" to speech, but to "unfold the image as the environment of appearance and disappearance."[44] In "a dynamic montage of heterogeneities," knowledge is created in the dialectical movement between the singularity of photographic images and the constellations into which they are brought.[45] The image montage creates a *Denkraum* (thinking space) that enables the dialectical movement between imagination and reason.

25

42 Warburg also used the maps as a presentation device during lectures. Colleen Becker, "Aby Warburg's *Pathosformel* as Methodological Paradigm," *Journal of Art Historiography* 9 (2013): 4.

43 Georges Didi-Huberman, "Warburg's Haunted House," *Common Knowledge* 18, no. 1 (2012): 51.

44 Georges Didi-Huberman, *Remontagen der erlittenen Zeit* (Paderborn: Wilhelm Fink, 2014), 78.

45 Georges Didi-Huberman, *Atlas: How to Carry the World on One's Back* (Madrid: Museo Reina Sofia, 2011), 109–10.

46 James Elkins, "Writing with Images: 3/1 Georges Rodenbach," *Writing with Images* (website), 2014, writingwithimages.com.

I take Warburg's *Mnemosyne Atlas* as the model to guide my study of burning effigies: I arrange the images into spatial montages, some kind of maps to use as research tools, according to resemblances, patterns, and associations that create semantic connections. From this an argument forms that is not linear but courses through the maps from key images to clusters of images to others, meandering, branching out, and occasionally returning to earlier associative lines of seeing and thinking. In a dialectical movement, the image maps inform my thinking that in turn shapes the arrangement of images. From the associative relations laid out in the maps, I identify relevant, productive lines of inquiry, relating the image practice to theory from different fields: history, art history, anthropology, performance studies, photography theory, iconology, visual studies, and political philosophy. Based on the associative arrangements of the material, the text is not strictly linear either. Each chapter moves in different directions to intersect at certain points in the dissertation.

For publication as a book, I arrange the image maps in a semi-linear narrative that runs parallel to the text. The narratives of image and text meet intermittently. The text connects directly to key images in the development of this argument and engages with theoretical aspects of image practice. The images ground the argument, tying it to specific events and contexts, while keeping the text on edge. Because of their polysemic nature, they resist finite conclusions and instead open up alternative readings, complicating the argument. The reader should spend at least as much time with the images as with the text – moving from image to text and back again, as visual studies scholar James Elkins suggests in *Writing with Images,* in a slow reading of the argument in the interaction between these media.[46]

Structure of the Book

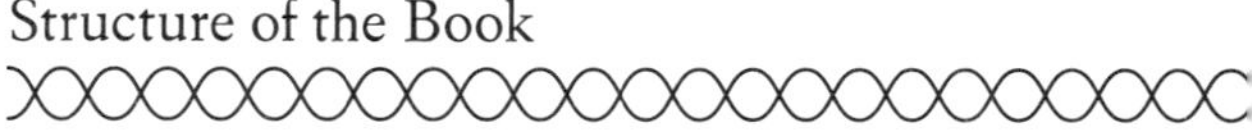

During the process of close reading and ordering the images, certain characteristics central to the effigy protest practice became evident. These characteristics determined the structure of the various image montages, or maps, and the approaches of my research in each chapter. Some montages follow a "rational" diachronic and geographical order, situating effigy practice in specific political and historical contexts. Other montages are ordered synchronically, guided by association, resemblance, affinities, or motifs. Chronological and spatial order presupposes causal connections and development over time, revealing genealogies and ways of transfer, and shedding light on the politics of the practice in specific political constellations. Establishing connections through resemblances and motifs, illuminates general characteristics of effigy protests: aspects of performance, aesthetics, attitudes, imaginaries of the social, and the relation to the political. The diversity of approaches reflected in the succession of chapters, captures the phenomenon of effigy protests in all its facets, a trans-disciplinary approach that is, I argue, necessary to comprehensively assess the practice of hanging or burning effigies.

Chapters 1 and 2 introduce the basic parameters of the practice. Chapter 1, "Double Bodies," offers a definition of the term "effigy" through a genealogy of effigy practices. Based in ancient Roman image culture, effigies were used as substitute bodies in political rituals, formal justice, popular justice, and calendrical rituals throughout the course of European history. Effigies do not represent physical private bodies, but rather their public extensions: the social and political aspects of a person, the political office and the sovereign power invested in it.

Chapter 2, "Performing Protest," takes insights from performance and ritual studies to understand how an effigy protest unfolds as a performance of punishment of a perpetrator by a community and to what effect. I describe the stages of the performance: the making and parading of effigies, setting, execution, and mediation of the performance. Staging and embodiment have strong effects on the memory and identity of participants and create alternative imaginaries for the political sphere, while news images and reports emerge as integral and intended parts of the live performances and extend their reach. As compressed descriptions of the conflicts, the media images are pathos formulas of protest, to use Aby Warburg's terminology, recognizable formulaic images, which enable the communication between diverse audiences across temporal and cultural distances. Moving between embodied performance and mediated report, the practice is activated from and re-inscribed into the social memory to become part of the political protest repertoire.

I then present three diachronic chapters, focusing on countries in which effigy protests have appeared most prominently in news media over the last twenty years. Chapter 3, "Effigy Protests in the History of the United States," shows the development of effigy protests in one specific country, the United States, over an extended period of time, from the American Revolution in 1765 until the present day. Rooted in two traditional effigy practices, effigy protest has come to address a large variety of political conflicts. It is used to positively affirm the existing order, to suppress resistance through violent threat, or to challenge that order and demand change. Some effigy protests, staged for instance in the struggle for and against civil rights in the 1950s and '60s, pointedly articulate the conflict that lies at the heart of modern liberal democracy, between the principles of popular sovereignty and universal human rights.

Chapter 4, "Effigy Protests in Egypt, Iran, Afghanistan and Across the Middle East," traces the genealogies of effigy protests in Egypt, Iran, and Afghanistan and the wider region, from the perspective of Western news media. Most political effigy protests in these countries were staged in protest against Western cultural, economic, and military domination. These protests hint at the apparent lack of justice and channels for redress in international conflicts. I concentrate in this chapter on different modes of transfer: with migrating people, by appropriation, and through the news media. Lastly, I elaborate on the role and limitations of the media in cross-cultural communication contributing to emerging transnational and cross-cultural public spheres.

Chapter 5, "Dialogic Communication: Effigy Protests in Iraq," zooms in on a period in one country, Iraq, to inquire into a series of effigy protests staged against US military occupation in Baghdad between 2005 and 2009. From a Western perspective, I explore the communication between different populations through symbolic visual signs and how image practices from Islamic and Western cultural contexts interrelate. The communication via news media leads to a shared symbolic language developed dialogically across national and cultural borders, as described in chapter 5.

The last two chapters return to general characteristics of effigy protests. Chapter 6, "Resemblance and the Grotesque," focuses on operational aspects of images and their aesthetics. I read effigy practice in relation to different notions of resemblance, in which resemblance is an operation that not only recognizes but also constructs relationships between actors and objects. I then introduce the grotesque as an image operation equally relevant to effigy protests, but which disrupts the ordering principle of resemblance. The grotesque distorts the object and exposes it to mockery and debasement. While based on the same mechanisms as resemblance, the grotesque exerts a form of exclusionary violence that ridicules and insults the political opponent and aims to influence the political sphere.

Chapter 7, "Violence and Laughter," explores violence and laughter, which paradoxically permeate the performance of protest effigies in regard to their effect on the social and political sphere. Yet neither violence nor laughter is reducible to one form, nor do they neatly align. With that in mind, I consider the relation between effigy protest, conflicting notions of justice and the law, and the configuration of the political. I investigate how laughter figures in these different constellations as either subjugating or liberating. Relating to current discourse in political philosophy, I differentiate between effigy protests that exert extreme subjugating violence, which destroys the possibilities of politics, and violence that is unavoidable as an aspect of resistance against an oppressive political status quo.

In the conclusion, I bring together the different strands developed in this study. I evaluate the findings in relation to each other, and indicate trajectories for further productive inquiry. Finally, I evaluate the role effigy practice can play in relation to the political as an indicator of injustice and violence and as a symptom of fundamental conflicts at the internal and external limits of contemporary liberal democracy.

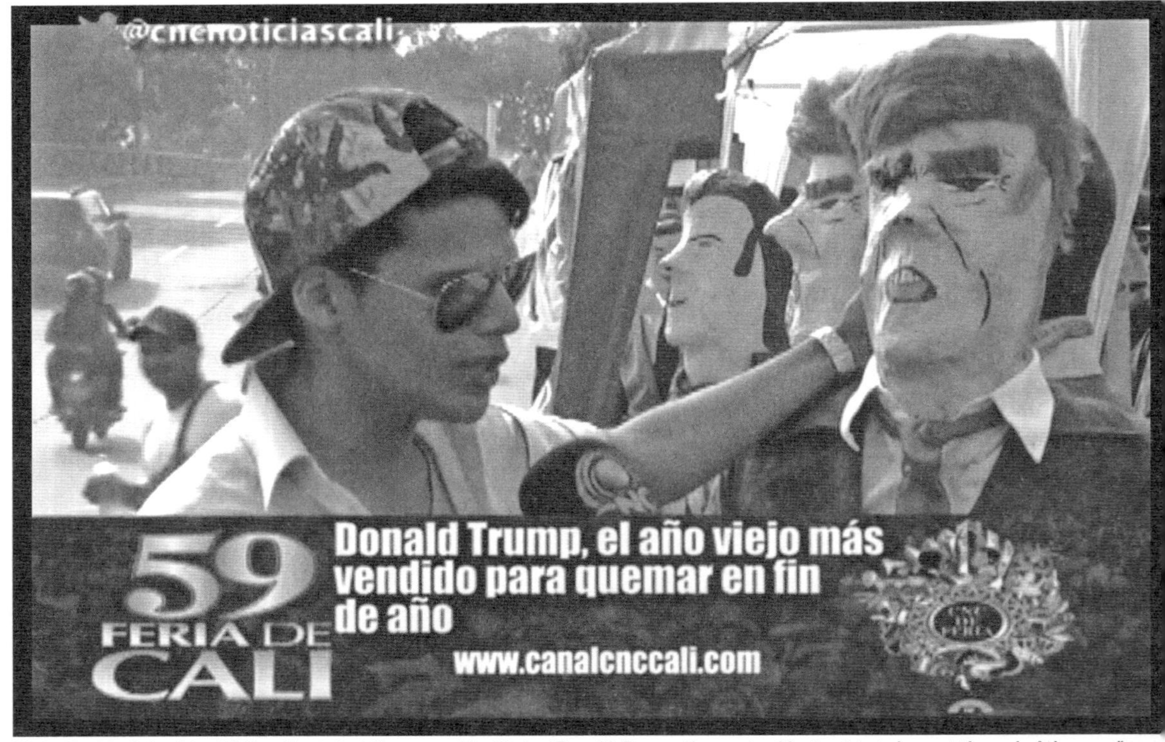

2016_12_28_Columbia: US President elect Trump as Año Viejo; "Donald Trump, the most-sold *año viejo* to burn at the end of the year."

Double Bodies

Double Bodies

In an effigy protest, a political conflict and its resolution are staged through the theatrical and symbolic punishment of an individual by a community. This symbolic punishment obviously does not affect the physical body of the targeted person. Instead, it ridicules, insults, and humiliates. An attack on an effigy attacks someone's reputation and social standing. Therefore, a protest effigy seems to embody an individual's social or political status, and highlights the division between private body and public body recurrent in Western political thought.

Philosopher Judith Butler, who contests precisely this division – for instance, in relation to philosopher Hannah Arendt's notion of the political – terms these two aspects the "private body… preoccupied with the repetitive labor of reproducing the material conditions of life," and the "public body," which appears "to speak and act."[1] Butler makes clear that this bifurcation of the body is an operation of power, "the effect of a certain regulation of bodily appearance" in

1 See Judith Butler, "Bodies in Alliance and the Politics of the Street," *transversal* (website) (2011), eipcp.net/transversal/1011/butler/en.

2   Hans Belting, *Bild-Anthropologie: Entwürfe für eine Bildwissenschaft* (Munich: Wilhelm Fink Verlag, 2001), 115–42.

Western political thought and practice. The notion of the public body is further subdivided into various social, political, and judicial aspects. The conditions of the social body, determined by social relations and codes of conduct, infer an individual's good name, honor, reputation, the face that needs to be saved, the public persona or image. The political aspects attached or superimposed onto the private body include the legal person, citizenship, and political office, or categories like nobility and sovereignty. These social and political aspects of the public body are made visible in various ways, with official insignia, like heraldic signs, or clothing linked to status and class.[2] They are also made visible figuratively in honorary paintings, reliefs, busts, and public sculptures. These figurative representations of the social and political body are closely associated with the term "effigy."

Social and Political Effigy Traditions in Europe

3   The entry "effigy" in the *Oxford English Dictionary* reads: "1. A likeness, portrait, or image. Now chiefly applied to a sculptured representation, or to a habited image, as in 2.; also to a portrait on a coin; in a wider sense somewhat arch. 2. Phrases. in effigy: under the form, or by means of, a portrait or image; also *fig.* to execute in effigy, to hang in effigy, to burn in effigy: to inflict upon an image the semblance of the punishment which the original is considered to have deserved; formerly done by way of carrying out a judicial sentence on a criminal who had escaped; now only as an expression of popular indignation or hatred." *Oxford English Dictionary*, s.v. "effigy," oed.com.

4   In archeology, the terms "effigy mound" and "effigy vessel" are used for burial mounds and containers in the shape of humans or animals in pre-Columbian cultures. Since this more general meaning is not relevant to my study, I don't address it here.

5   Julius von Schlosser, "History of Portraiture in Wax," in *Ephemeral Bodies: Wax Sculpture and the Human Figure*, ed. Roberta Panzanelli (Los Angeles: Getty Publications, 2008), 183–90; and Susan Buck-Morss "Visual Empire," *Diacritics* 37, no. 2/3 (2007): 177.

In the past, the term effigy has been used quite broadly to mean an image or a representation of a person in visual art, literature, and theater.[3] Currently, the term more narrowly denotes makeshift figurative representations of individuals made for, ridiculed and executed in political protests. Additionally, effigy is one half of compound nouns, born of genealogical and semantic relations to certain figurative sculptures: tomb effigy, funeral effigy, and coin effigy.[4] While each is a pictorial representation of someone's physical appearance, more importantly, they represent the social and political status of the individual depicted.

The roots of these European image traditions are found in ancient Roman image culture,[5] where public spaces, temples, as well as private houses were crowded with sculptural

34

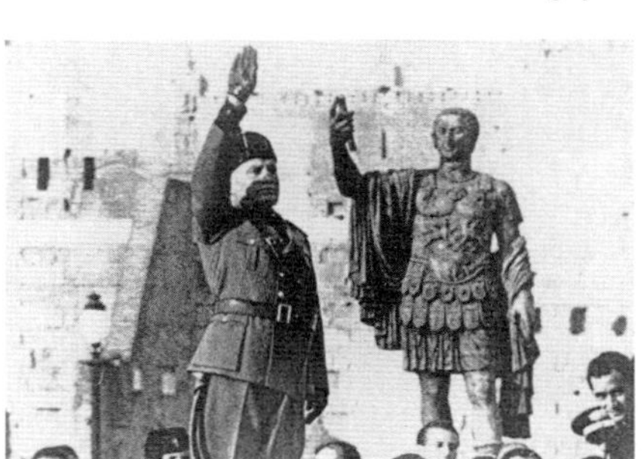

1935_Rome, Italy: Mussolini in front of a statue of Julius Caesar

representations of individuals. Statues of ancestors, gods, emperors, senators, and other important personages were part of Roman ritual life. The images of ancestors, exhibited inside the family home, facilitated the transfer of status from the family to the individual. Statues in public space represented the social and political position of those depicted within the hierarchy of Roman society, codified by location, size, material, pose, and attire.[6] Images designated for lasting veneration were made from durable material like marble, bronze, or wood, while images used in ephemeral funerary rites were made of wood, cloth, and wax.[7] During the Roman Empire (between 27 BCE and 395 CE), minting golden coins was the exclusive right of the emperor.[8] Their portraits on coins, a signs of imperial sovereignty, was also called effigy.[9] The image of the legitimate ruler was the basis for economic interactions. As a ubiquitous, travelling medium, coins spread the ruler's presence throughout the empire and manifested their claim to the throne. Statues, funeral, and coin effigies were just some of the media used in Rome to manifest power. These same media could also be used to delegitimize power in the political ritual of *damnatio memoriae*, during which images of a disgraced person were condemned to destruction to erase their memory.[10] All three types of Roman effigies – coin, statues, and ritual – continued to be used in varying degrees throughout European history.

This employment was not always without conflict, since the image prohibition of Abrahamic religions was a counter-force against abundant use of images. Developed in mono-theistic Judaism in the millennium before the Common Era, the prohibition was established to avert the dangers of idolatry: mistaking the image for what it represents, and containing and reducing the omnipotent God in the image. Instead, in Judaism, the word and other non-iconic signs were given

35

6   Peter Stewart, *Statues in Roman Society: Representation and Response* (Oxford: Oxford University Press, 2003), 80.

7   Harald Keller, "Effigie," in *Reallexikon zur Deutschen Kunstgeschichte* vol. 4 (1956): 743–49, *RDK Labor* (website), rdklabor.de/w/?oldid=89345.

8   In numismatics, the portrait on the coin is still called an effigy.

9   Alexander Del Mar, *The Middle Ages Revisited* (New York: Cambridge Encyclopedia Co., 1900), 276.

10   Effigies were only the figurative forms of images of power, next to non-figurative images like emblems and heraldic signs, or built structures like palaces and temples.

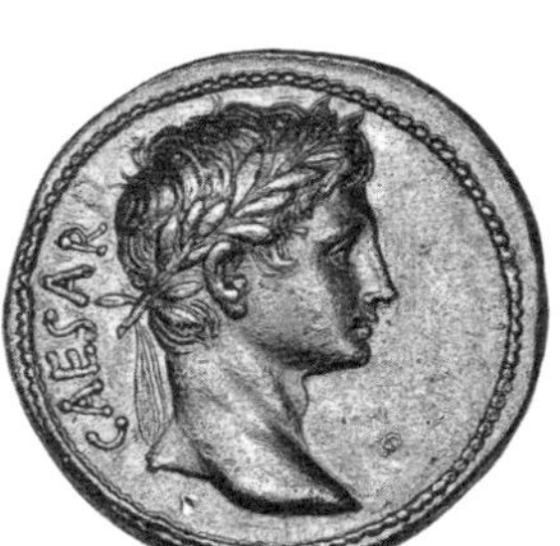

gold aureus: 20 BC_Rome (Emperor Augustus)

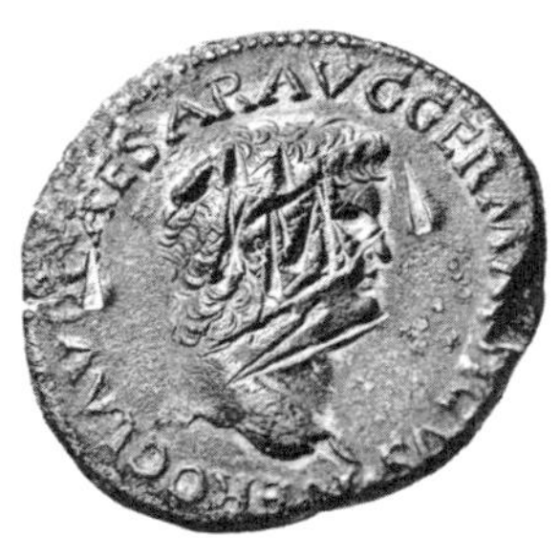

damnatio memoriae on a coin: 64_Rome (Emperor Nero)

11   Marie-José Mondzain, *Image, Icon, Economy: The Byzantine Origins of the Contemporary Imaginary* (Stanford: Stanford University Press, 2005), 21.

12   *New American Standard Bible*, Col. 1:15, biblegateway.com/versions/New-American-Standard-Bible-NASB/.

13   *New American Standard Bible*, Col. 1:16.

14   Marie-José Mondzain, "Iconic Space and the Rule of Lands," *Hypatia* 15, no. 4 (2000): 74.

15   Mondzain, *Image, Icon, Economy*, 22–23.

primacy in regulating the relationship between God and His Chosen People. This an-iconic impulse was adopted by the newer monotheistic religions, Christianity developing from the first century onwards, and Islam founded by Muhammad early in the sixth century.

In the burgeoning Christian religion, though, the idea of the incarnation of Christ made it possible to think of images as representations of divine power. Christ, the incarnation of the invisible God, was conceived as the image of God, his historical manifestation.[11] "He is the image of the invisible God, the firstborn of all creation,"[12] asserts apostle Paul in his letter to the Colossians, establishing in the next line Christ as the source of all earthly power: "For by Him all things were created, both in the heavens and on earth, visible and invisible, whether thrones or dominions or rulers or authorities – all things have been created through Him and for Him."[13] Christ, as the incarnation of God, connected the temporal power of the earthly ruler with the eternal power of God and introduced a paradoxical relationship between the visible and invisible, between image and truth.[14]

This paradox could not be solved dogmatically, as art historian and philosopher Marie-José Mondzain describes in her book *Image, Icon, Economy: The Byzantine Origins of the Contemporary Imaginary* (1996), and the Church Fathers developed sophisticated arguments around the status of the image in relation to power in order to philosophically manage the enigmatic relationship between image, truth, and power.[15] Christ was thought to be fully human as well as fully divine. His two natures – the divine and the human – were understood as separate but coexistent within one body, which was thought of as an image. Through analogy, this enigmatic double nature and its containment in an image was transferred to the Byzantine emperors. Eternal power was folded into temporal power, as the emperor derived his legitimacy and authority from the metaphorical as well as the iconic analogy with Christ. Christ and the emperor were presented as two aspects of the same power. They appeared as two sides of the same coin — literally — when at the beginning of the eighth century, Emperor Justinian II of Byzantium had coins minted with an image of Christ on one side and an effigy of himself on the other.[16]

Compatible with Roman traditions, the overlapping of divine and earthly power also became the template for the medieval European doctrine of divine kingship, in which questions about representation and the image remained central. While in Byzantium the paradoxical relationship between image and truth led to the two periods of Byzantine Iconoclasm in the eighth and early ninth centuries, in the Roman Church, the role of images in worship was not challenged until the Reformation in the sixteenth century. Despite cleansing church spaces and religious practices of images in parts of Europe, the representation of power with images of the ruler in the form of statues and coin effigies remained ubiquitous, and was adopted in other sociopolitical contexts including funeral rites and judicial procedures.

In the Middle Ages, tomb effigies appeared in France and England and were in use up until the nineteenth century. Tomb effigies are sculptures of stone or bronze on top of a tomb that depict the deceased lying in eternal sleep. The effigies represent the public body of the deceased, reflected in

16 Mondzain, *Image, Icon, Economy*, 157.

37

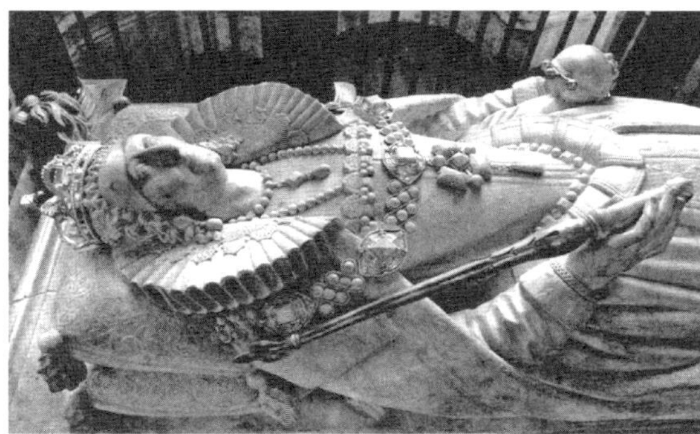

tomb effigy: 1603_UK (Elizabeth I)

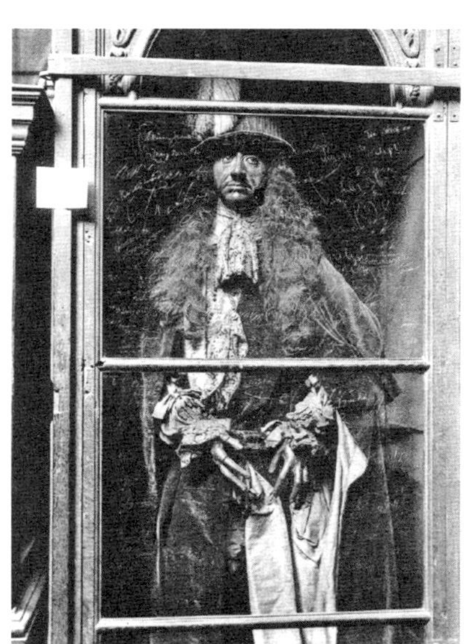

funeral effigy: 1685_UK (King Charles II)

17 Hans Belting devotes one chapter of his book *Bild-Anthropologie* to the heraldic sign, which he understands as a non-mimetic medium of the social body. Belting, *Bild-Anthropologie*, 115–42.

18 Transi-tombs became customary in the fifteenth and sixteenth century.

19 Ernst H. Kantorowicz, *The King's Two Bodies: A Study in Mediaeval Political Theology* (Princeton: Princeton University Press, 1957), 382–84.

20 Kantorowicz, *The King's Two Bodies*, 419–37.

21 Horst Bredekamp, *Thomas Hobbes: Der Leviathan* (Berlin: Akademie Verlag, 2012), 103–7; and Thomas Hobbes, *Leviathan*, ed. G. C. A. Gaskin (New York: Oxford University Press, [1651] 1996), 7.

their clothes, attributes, and heraldic signs.[17] As a variation on tomb effigies, *transi* tombs show an additional, second effigy of the decomposing corpse.[18] This sculptural doubling makes the conceptual doubling of the body into private and public – mortal and eternal – even more explicit.

A similar doubling of the body occurred in the lifelike effigies in the funerary rituals of kings in early modern France and England. Deriving from divine kingship, the king and queen – analogous to Christ, being both human and divine – had a mortal human body and an immortal body, their body politic.[19] Upon death, the immortal body was embodied by a life-size and lifelike effigy made of wood, cloth, and wax, which was used during the funeral ceremony.[20] The effigy was dressed in the royal regalia and waited upon as if alive, while the monarch's physical remains remained hidden in the coffin.

In the seventeenth century, the figure of the sovereign reemerged in philosopher Thomas Hobbes's book *Leviathan* (1651). Written at a time when the English monarchy was in crisis, this reconfigured figure of sovereign power was a visualization of his social contract theory. Art historian Horst Bredekamp suggests Hobbes was inspired by English funeral effigies to imagine the sovereign as an "artificial man."[21] The *Leviathan*, and especially the image on its frontispiece, was an iconic emblem for a series of displacements that transferred the power of the collective to an individual, be it the king or any other chosen or elected representative. Political philosopher Susan Buck-Morss writes:

> the sovereign figure as personification of the collective demonstrates the power of the visible image to close the circle between constituting and constituted power, explaining why even when the illegalities of an

38

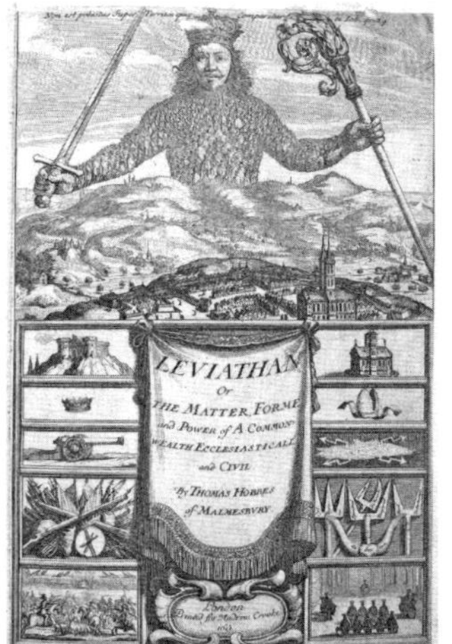

Leviathan (frontispice), Thomas Hobbes, 1651

individual sovereign are exposed, the faith of the believer is still not shaken.[22]

The figure of the sovereign still has strong global resonance in political thought today, demonstrating the capacity of images to make absence present, and abstract concepts comprehensible.[23]

In the same period that funeral effigies emerged, the punishment of effigies became customary in formal justice throughout Europe and was practiced until the nineteenth century for crimes like desertion, treason, heresy, or counter-feiting.[24] If a perpetrator could not be apprehended, their effigy was tried and punished instead. In February 1667, an effigy of banker Louys Bais was hanged in Paris on order of the court for gambling away the king's tax money.[25] In 1673, Johan Baron de Montbas's effigy was hanged by martial court for cowardice and treason for failure to defend the Rhine at Lobith against the French.[26] In 1689, Capiteyn Rambac's effigy met the same fate in Liège, Belgium for desertion.[27] In 1732, the effigies of eight counterfeiters were executed in Brussels.[28] Some effigies were accorded the full pomp of real executions, like that of Kai Lykke in Denmark in 1661,[29] while others were executed rather summarily. During the Spanish Inquisition, about two-fifths of the condemned, having fled the country, were burned in effigy instead of in person.[30]

22   Buck-Morss, "Visual Empire," 172.

23   Hans Belting, "Image, Medium, Body: A New Approach to Iconology," *Critical Inquiry* 31, no. 2 (2005): 312–13.

24   Wolfgang Brückner, *Bildnis und Brauch: Studien zur Bildfunktion der Effigies* (Berlin: Erich Schmidt Verlag, 1966), 311.

25   *Ordinaris dingsdaeghse courante*, March 1, 1667.

26   "De la Haye le 26 Juillet," *La gazette d'Amsterdam*, July 27, 1673.

27   "Duytslant en d'aengrensende Rijcken," *Oprechte Haerlemsche courant*, December 27, 1689.

28   "Hoe men vroeger strafte," *Bataviaasch Nieuwsblad*, March 27, 1920.

29   See chapter 7, "Violence and Laughter."

30   *De Curaçaosche Courant*, June 16, 1820; and Wikipedia, s.v. "Spanish Inquisition."

39

Wenen: Eergisteren heeft de teregtstelling van den leider der October-omwenteling, Kuchenbäcker, die ter dood veroordeeld is, in effigie plaats gehad. Deze strafoefen-ing had eene groote menigte volks getrok-ken. [Vienna: The day before yesterday, Kuchenbäcker, the leader of the October Uprising was executed in effigy. The punishment attracted a large crowd.] —*Groninger Courant*, Netherlands, 18 Dec 1849

formal effigy punishment: 1849_12_16_ Austria (revolutionary leader Kuchenbäcker)

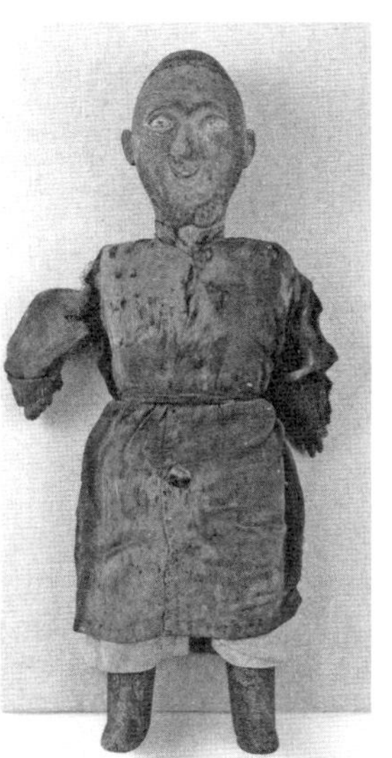

Inquisition effigy: 1544_ Majorca, Spain

formal effigy punishment: 1789_ Belgium (Pensionary of Brabant De Cock)

31 Michel Foucault, *Discipline and Punish: The Birth of the Prison* (New York: Vintage Books, 1977), 47–48.

32 Karl Härter, "Images of Dishonoured Rebels and Infamous Revolts: Political Crime, Shaming Punishments and Defamation in the Early Modern Pictorial Media," in *Images of Shame*, ed. Carolin Behrmann (Berlin: De Gruyter, 2016), 115–16; Shaming punishments that mark a person with a degraded identity still exist today in formal justice. Martha C. Nussbaum, *Hiding from Humanity: Disgust, Shame, and the Law* (Princeton: Princeton University Press, 2006), 230.

33 Brückner, *Bildnis und Brauch*, 196.

34 Michael J. Pfeifer, *The Roots of Rough Justice: Origins of American Lynching* (Chicago: University of Illinois, 2011), 3; Isaac Taylor describes two instances of public shaming with an effigy called "riding the stang" in Welburn, UK. Isaac Taylor, "Riding the Stang at Welburn," *The Folk-Lore Journal* 1, no. 9 (1883): 298–99; Gerard Rooijakkers, *Eer en schande: Volksgebruiken van het oude Brabant* (Nijmegen: SUN, 1995), 185–87; Violet Alford, "Rough Music or Charivari," *Folklore* 70, no. 4 (1959): 505–18; and Edward Muir, *Ritual in Early Modern Europe* (Cambridge: Cambridge University Press, 2005), 109–12.

35 E. P. Thompson, "Rough Music Reconsidered," *Folklore* 103, no. 1 (1992): 11.

While this symbolic punishment did not have the same legal status as real executions – the trial was repeated if the accused was caught – they had a number of important functions. They made the crimes and sentences public, and brought the procedures of the law to a satisfying end by repairing the crime's damage to the body politic.[31] What is more important is that these effigy punishments had actual consequences for the delinquent. As art historian Karl Härter points out, the public punishment of the effigy blemished the honor and reputation of the perpetrator, with lasting consequences for himself and his family.[32]

Similar to effigy punishment in formal justice, and possibly its precursor, is effigy punishment as a custom of popular justice.[33] This technique of social shaming, exclusion, and punishment by a community is subsumed under the terms "rough music," *Katzenmusik* (cats music) in German, *Ketelmuziek* (kettle music) in Dutch, and *charivari* (tumultuous noise) in French.[34] Widespread throughout Europe at least since the Middle Ages and still in use in the twentieth century, it was brought over to some colonies such as New England and the West Indies. Traditionally, rough music was employed in response to violations of sexual norms and marital customs of a community, like marrying below status, adultery, wife-beating, or husband-beating.[35]

40

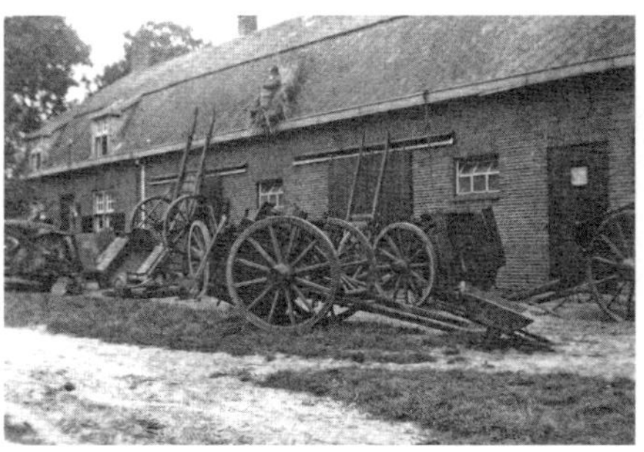

rough music: 1727_UK ("The skimmington: rough music that mocked cuckolds, hen-pecked husbands and shrewish wives")

○ rough music: 1952_Netherlands (unfaithful suitor)

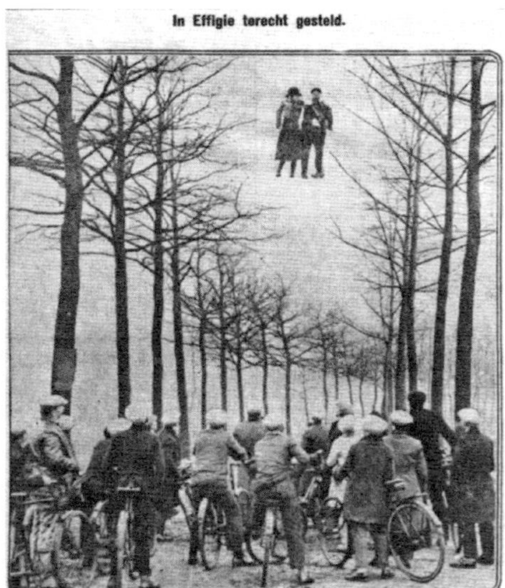

rough music: 1930_Netherlands (wedding couple)

The most common practice was the performance of a mock concert in front of the perpetrator's house: beating on pots and pans for three consecutive nights. But the punishment could also include the parading, trial, and punishment of an effigy depicting the perpetrator or the abuse of the perpetrator themselves.[36] In one example of rough music from Brabant in the Netherlands in 1952, the property of a farmer was barricaded with disabled carts and an effigy on a bed frame was put on the roof of the barn to humiliate him for breaking his marriage promise.[○, 37] Sometimes an effigy execution was preceded by a community trial or a mock trial, and concluded with a mock burial. These ritual performances ridiculed, humiliated, and ostracized the perpetrators and could affect their social standing for a long time.[38]

These punishing effigy practices are often popularly associated with magical practices performed with images referred to as "voodoo."[39] What is meant by "magic," though, remains unclear, frequently alluding to the belief that a ritual enacted on a doll can affect the physical body of the target by, for instance, inflicting physical pain. In his seminal study on punishment of effigies in formal justice in early modern Europe, ethnologist and art historian Wolfgang Brückner insists that there is no magic in these punishments and states that contemporary opinion did not see these as magical either.[40] Recent scholarship also appears to have little interest in magic and focuses instead on the social, political, and judicial aspects of effigy punishing practice.[41] Even though a strict binary distinction between social, political, and magical practices fails to take into account the social aspects of magic, the most important aspect in the burning or hanging of effigies, especially in political protests, is their relation to the social and political realm, which determines my focus.

36   Muir, *Ritual in Early Modern Europe*, 110.

37   Rooïjakkers, *Eer en schande*, 7–11.

38   Thompson, "Rough Music Reconsidered," 9.

39   An article from 1898 describes the political practice along witchcraft, public shaming, and formal punishing customs, dismissing the possibility of magic. "Custom of Burning Effigies," *Wichita Daily Eagle*, October 25, 1898.

40   Brückner, *Bildnis und Brauch*, 202.

41   Carolin Behrmann, "Figura Infamante Schandbilder und die Ethik der *oeconomia*," in *Images of Shame*, ed. Carolin Behrmann (Berlin: De Gruyter, 2016), Apple Books edition.

Carnival Effigies

Apart from effigy practices in social, political, and judicial contexts, burning effigies played and still plays a role in traditional holidays related to carnival. These traditions celebrate annual cycles – death and rebirth, the return of spring after winter – with the expulsion of the exhausted forces of the previous year. The adverse forces of decline and death are personalized in general figures and embodied with effigies representing *Año Viejo* (the Old Year), Winter, Carnival, Maslenitsa, or the Witch among many others. The effigies are burned in festivals on New Year's Eve, at the end of carnival proper, or around Easter, to mark and foster the rejuvenation of nature and the purification of the community. These festivals exist in a large variety of locally specific forms all over Europe.

In some places, these traditions have been adapted to fit changing belief systems. In Greece, Spain, and Poland, the pagan carnival figures have been replaced by effigies of "Judas" and burned before Easter. The British Guy Fawkes Day was introduced to celebrate the deliverance of King James I from a Catholic conspiracy in 1605, but acquired many carnivalesque elements like bonfires, the burning of

42

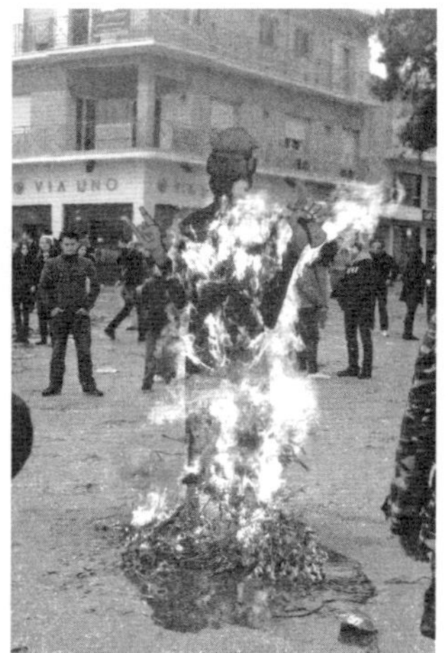

Carnival: 2010_Keratea, Greece

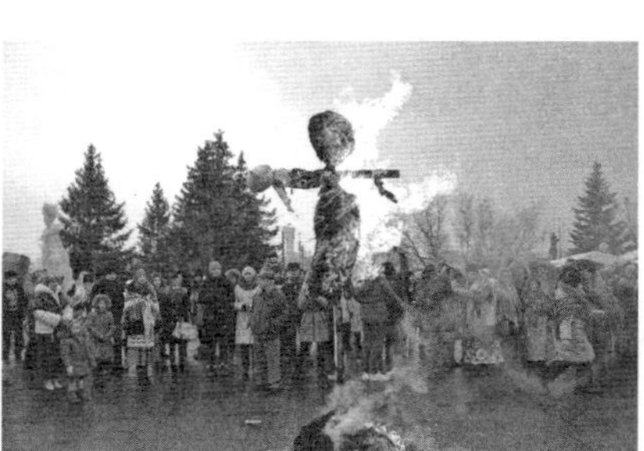

Maslenitsa: 2015_Russia

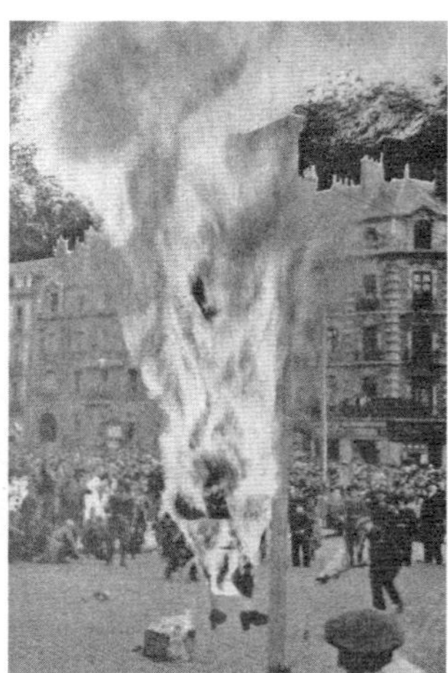

Mere-Folle: 1935_ Dijon, France

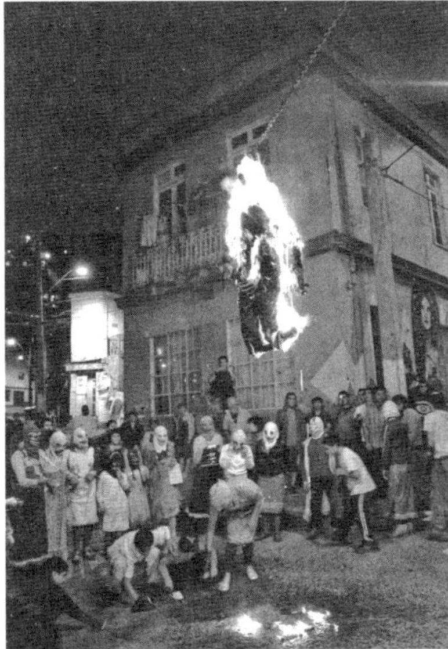

Judas: 2010_Valparaiso, Chile

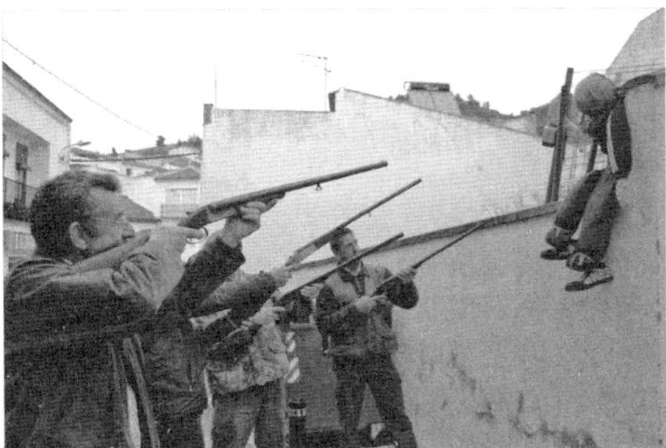

Judas: 2016_Cordoba, Spain

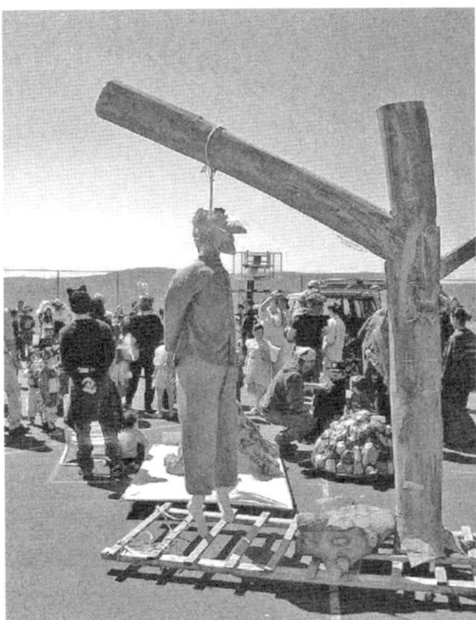

Haman: 2011_Israel

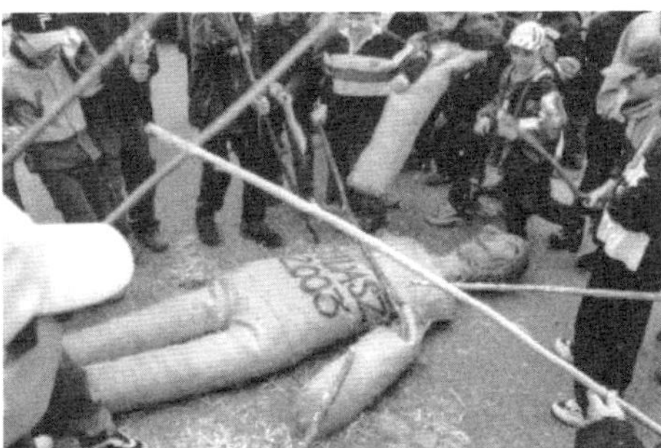

Judas: 2003_Pruchnik, Poland

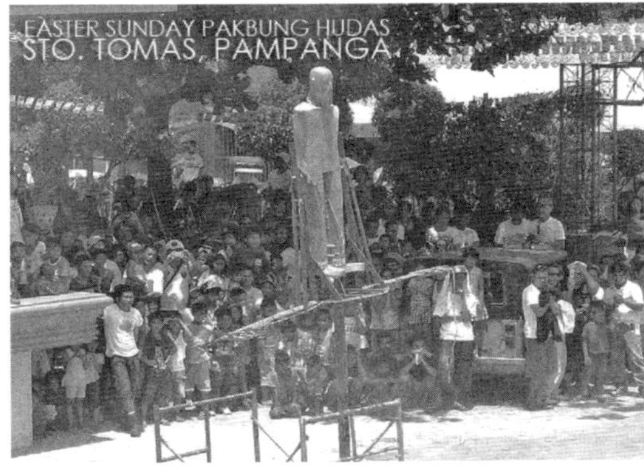

Judas: 2010_Pampange, Philippines

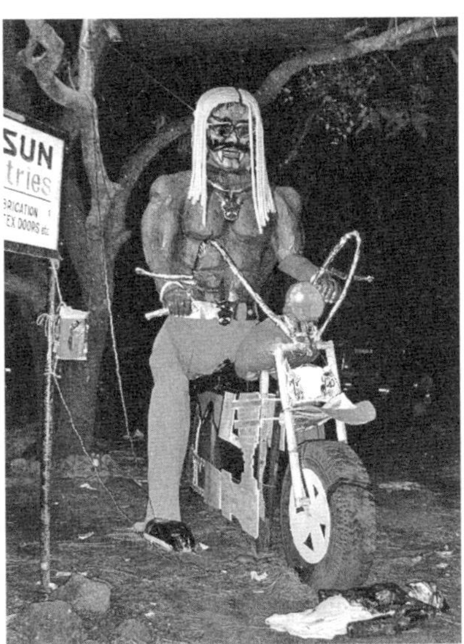

demon Narkasur: 2014_Panjim, India

42 C. Elliott Horowitz, "The Rite to Be Reckless: On the Perpetration and Interpretation of Purim Violence," *Poetics Today* 15, no. 1 (1994): 9–54.

effigies, and the sense of exuberance and festive disorder from the older celtic festival Samhain. Similar ritual festivals, which deal with the struggle between adverse and beneficial forces and that include effigy burning exist in Hindu cultures in India (Ravana, Holika, Narkasur), Pakistan (Ravana), Nepal (Ghantakarna), and Bali (Ogoh-ogoh). During the Jewish "carnival" Purim, effigies of Haman, the antagonist in the Book of Esther, are hanged and burned.[42] Many of these traditional practices have been taken to other countries and continents by migrating populations. European traditions, spread globally during colonial times, are still part of vibrant local cultures in the Americas and elsewhere. Guy Fawkes Day, for instance, spread to New England, Canada, South Africa,

44

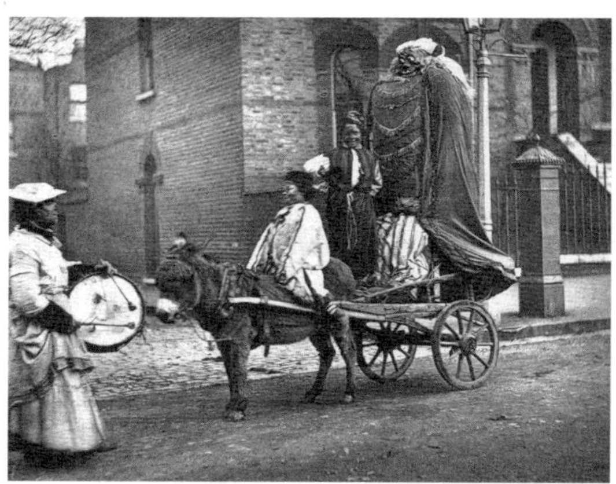

Guy Fawkes: 1877_London, UK

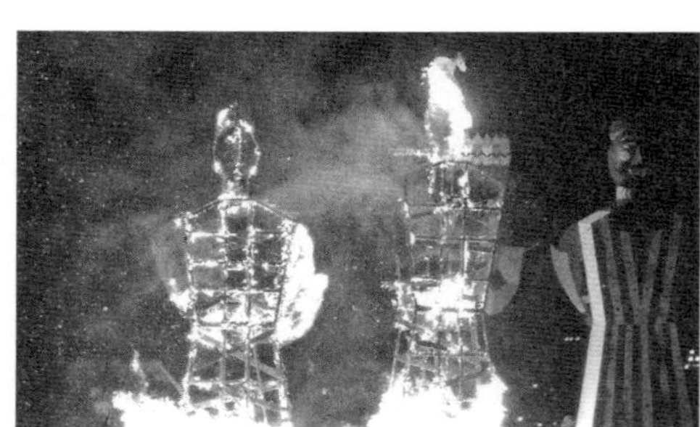

Ravana: 2010_Edinburgh, UK

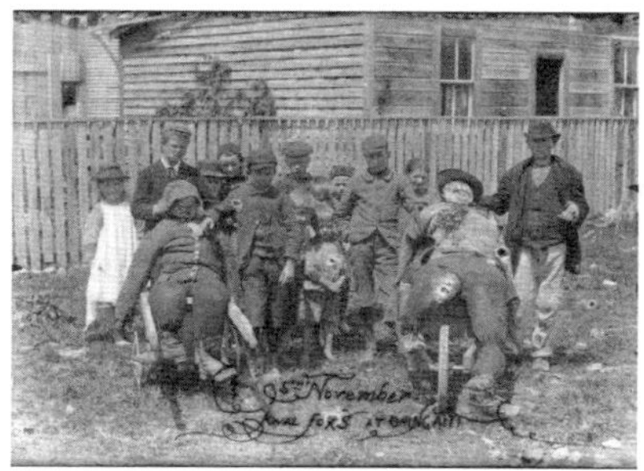

Guy Fawkes: 1900_New Zealand

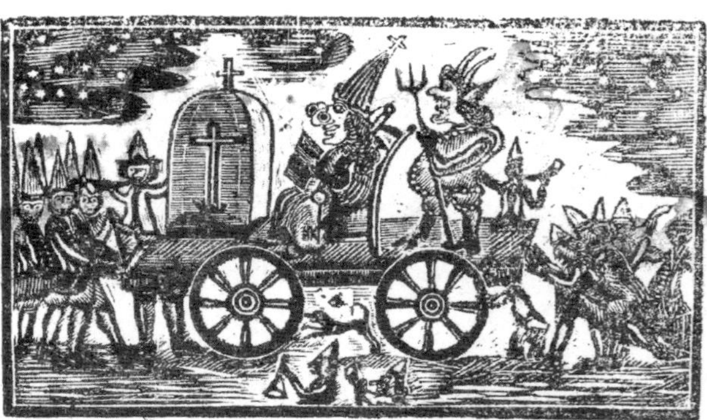

Pope Day: 1768_Boston, USA-MA (from British Guy Fawkes Day)

Botswana, and New Zealand. The Spanish traditions of burning *Año Viejo* and Judas are celebrated all over Latin America as well as in the Philippines.[43] The Indian festivals in which Ravana and Holika are burned in effigy also take place in, for instance, Trinidad and the United Kingdom. The spread of effigy traditions across so many different cultures and their enormous variance indicates that the practice is very adaptable and migrates easily.

These traditional practices often acquire political layers. While the form and time of traditional festivals remain constant, traditional figures are replaced by contemporary politicians. In the effigy traditions of *Año Viejo* and Judas in Latin America and Guy Fawkes Day in the UK, this political turn has become an established part of celebrations with effigies of contemporary politicians burned each year.

In a farther-reaching appropriation, traditional forms are often removed from the ritual context and used in explicitly political protests. This shift becomes visible in the form of protest effigies, when, for instance in India, the ten-headed demon king Ravana has come to represent the ministers of the government in a protest unrelated to the original festival.[44] The personification of an abstract adversary like Winter or Ravana is replaced with the figurative image of a political

43 Rosario Cruz-Lucero. "Judas and his Phallus: The Carnivalesque Narratives of Holy Week in Catholic Philippines," *History and Anthropology* 17, no. 1 (2006): 39–56.

44 Over all, India and Pakistan seem to be the countries in which the practice of burning effigies in protests is most prevalent. A search in the digital archive of *The Hinau* resulted in 221 hits over a five-month period in 2006. A similar search in the *New York Times* archive over the same period yielded only 4 hits. No Pakistani newspaper archive is available online. Göttke, *Burning Images: Performing Effigies as Political Protest*, 315.

45

Giant effigies of Hitler and the Emperor of Japan were burned with ignominy in place of the customary figures of Judas in the Holy Saturday celebrations in Rio de Janeiro yesterday.
—*Palestine Post*, Jerusalem, 5 Apr 1942

1942_04_04_Brazil: Hitler + Japanese Emperor Hirohito as Judas

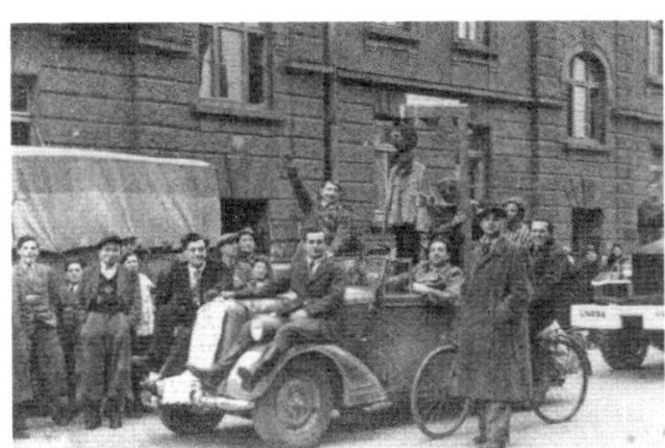

1946_03_00_Germany: Hitler as Haman

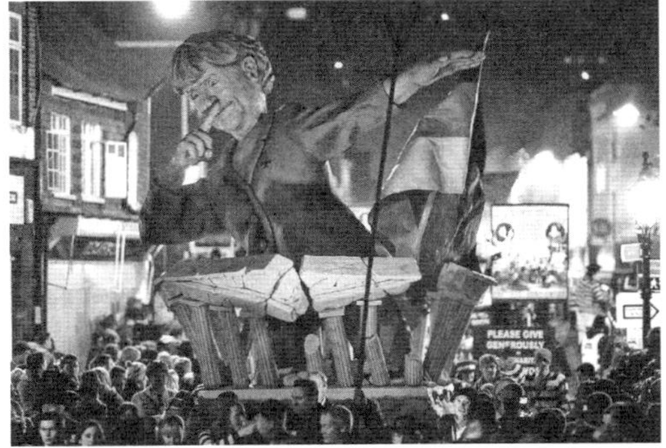

2012_11_05_Lewes, UK: German Chanc Merkel as Guy Fawkes

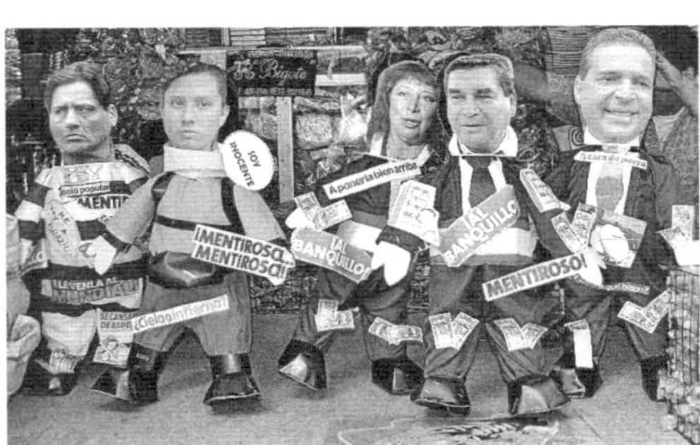

2012_12_30_Peru: various politicians as Año Viejo

representative deemed responsible for an adverse situation. The notions of evil and adversity associated with the traditional figures are activated in political effigy protests: the conspirator Guy Fawkes, the traitor Judas, the evil archenemy Haman, the scapegoat Nubbel – in the Cologne carnival a kind of mascot for revelers, who later blame him for their carnival transgressions and excesses. The semantic proximity between notions of purification in advancing renewal and punishment to demand change allows for the cross-over between traditional and political practices.

The archetypal figures of exclusion, the scapegoat, the traitor, the evil archenemy are affectively used in political protest. Protesters substitute the living private body of their enemy with the animated material body of the effigy. Through resemblance, the material body is superimposed with the abstract public body of the depicted and associated with evil and abject. These bodies are entangled in varying degrees of separation and dependence, and manipulation of either can affect the other. A punch in the physical face, even the face of the substitute effigy, humiliates, and the humiliating loss of the symbolic face can affect physical well-being. In the hands of the protesters, the effigy becomes a humble but devious medium to manipulate the entanglement of bodies: the material substitute, the private, and the public body.

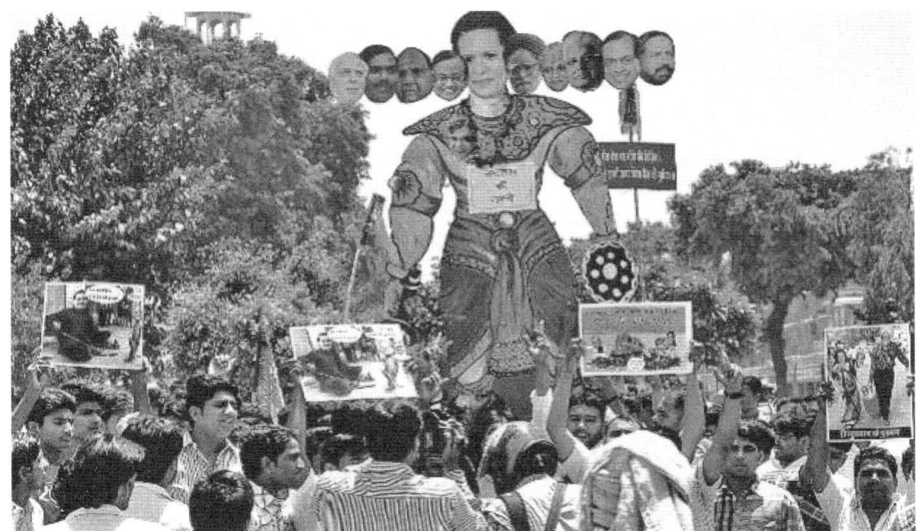

2013_05_09_India: UPA government as Ravana

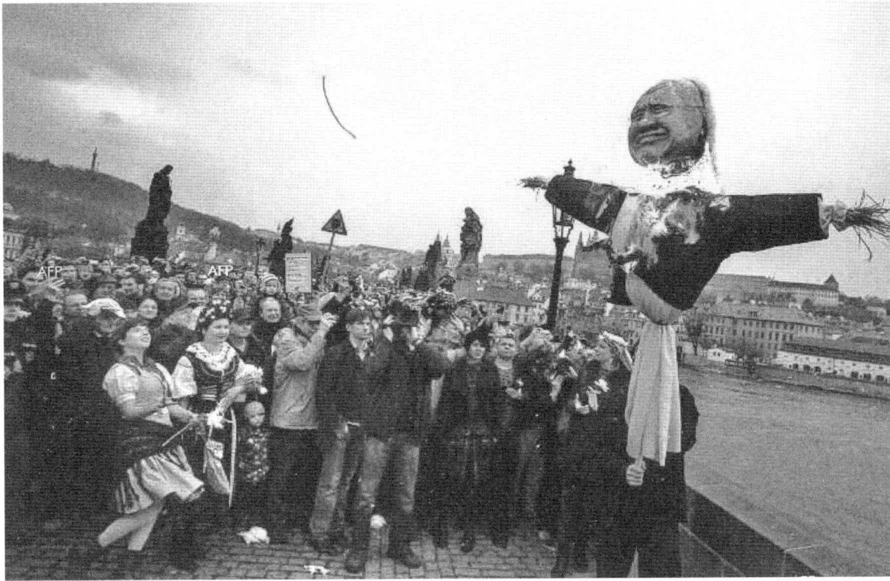

2013_03_07_Czech Republic: President Klaus as Morena

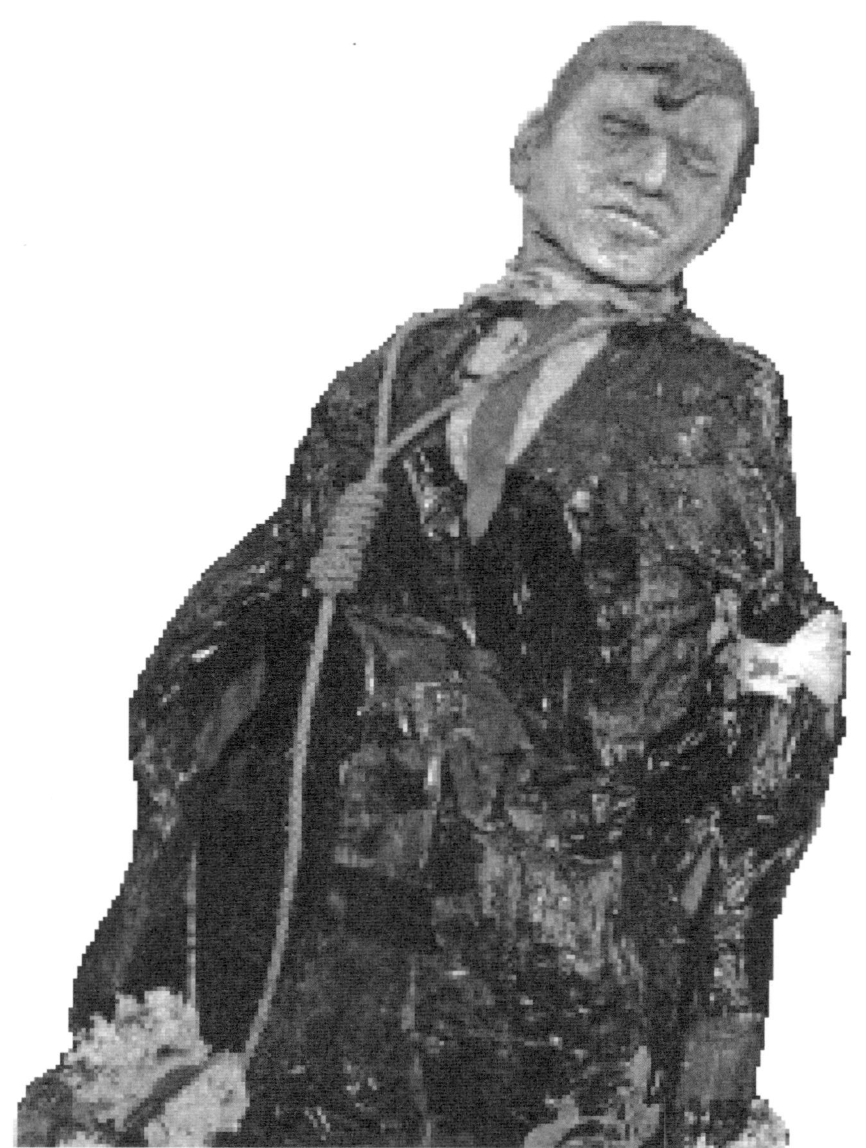

2010_05_01_UK: Premier Brown

Performing Protest

Performance

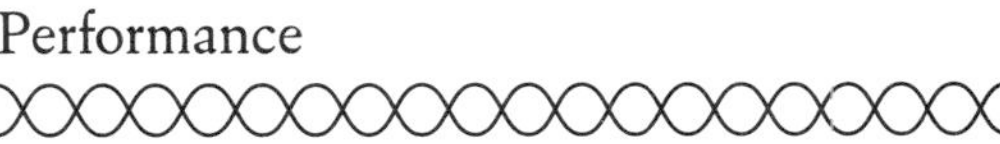

Performance and ritual scholars have often observed that their areas of study are central to politics.[1] These areas are also important to understanding the effigy practice as a political practice, its theatricality and ritual quality evident in the reports and images replete with actors and props, theatrical exaggeration and pathos. Staging such a public performance also implies the presence of an audience, of which both immediate spectators and news consumers are part. Following performance theorist and practitioner Diana Taylor, in this chapter I use the concept "performance" as the methodological lens through which I investigate political performances constituted by effigy protests.[2] This perspective highlights effigy hangings or burnings as cultural and embodied practices that performatively shape social reality.[3]

Through enactment and re-enactment, performances create social reality and form social memory, they make the symbolic order of society visible and at the same time performatively construct and enforce that order.[4] Performance

1   Catherine Bell, *Ritual: Perspectives and Dimensions* (Oxford: Oxford University Press, 1997), 129–36; Victor Turner, *The Ritual Process* (Ithaca, NY: Cornell University Press, 1969); David I. Kertzer, *Ritual, Politics & Power* (New Haven: Yale University Press, 1988); Richard Schechner, *Performance Studies: An Introduction*, 3rd edition (London: Routledge, 2006), 29; Diana Taylor, "Performance and Politics," *Identities* 21, no. 4 (2014): 337–43; and Jeffrey C. Alexander, "Introduction," *Performance and Power* (Cambridge: Polity Press, 2011), eBook.

2   Diana Taylor, *The Archive and the Repertoire: Performing Cultural Memory in the Americas* (Durham, NC: Duke University Press, 2003), 2.

3   Sruti Bala, "The Entangled Vocabulary of Performance," *Rupkatha, Journal on Interdisciplinary Studies in Humanities* 5, no. 2 (2013): 19.

4   Schechner, *Performance Studies*, 42–43.

5   Judith Butler, "Bodies in Alliance and the Politics of the Street," *transversal* (website), (2011), eipcp.net/transversal/1011/butler/en.

6   See chapter 3, "Effigy Protests in the History of the United States."

and ritual, however, also play a role in contesting existing political orders and creating alternative memories and imaginaries. The performance of protest provides the embodied presence on which, as political philosopher Judith Butler stresses, the political subject depends especially in resistance to marginalization.[5]

Within the framework of performance, this chapter addresses fundamental questions posed by the practice of effigy protests: how does it bring actors and audiences into being? How does it create alternative imaginaries of society and influence social relations through its symbolic staging? How does its embodiment in performance relate to the way in which it is mediated? How do these performances produce and transfer social knowledge, memory, and identity? Finally, how is the practice itself transferred between different communities over time?

The following text describes the elaborate performance of protest against British taxation in Lebanon, Connecticut in 1765. Partly adapted from the Pope Day celebrations and also traditional effigy practices related to popular justice,[6] the performance followed the general script of public punishment, filled in with improvised details and parodic elements.

The mob at Lebanon undertook to send Ingersol *to his own place*. They made three effigies: one to represent Mr. Grenville [prime minister of Great Britain]; another Ingersol; and a third, the Devil. The last was dressed with a wig, hat and black coat, given by parson Solomon Williams, of Lebanon. Mr. Grenville was honoured with a hat, wig, and coat, a present from Mr. Jonathan Trumbull, who was afterwards chosen Governor. Mr. Ingersol was dressed in red, with a lawyer's wig, a wooden sword, and his hat under his left arm, by the

generosity of Joseph Trumbull. Thus equipped, the effigies were put into a cart with ropes about their necks,
and drawn towards the gallows. A dialogue ensued
between the criminals. Some friendship seemed to sub-
sist between Mr. Grenville and the Devil, while nothing
but sueers and frowns passed from the Devil to Ingersol;
and the fawning reverence of the latter gave his infernal
highness such offence, that he turned up his breech and
discharged fire, brimstone, and tar, in Ingersol's face,
setting him all in a blaze; which, however, Mr. Grenville
generously extinguished with a squint. This was many
times repeated. As the procession advanced, the mob
exclaimed, "Behold the just reward of our *agent, who
sold himself to Grenville, like Judas, at a price!*" In this
manner the farce was continued till midnight, at which
time they arrived at the gallows; where a person in a long
shirt, in derision of the surplice of a church clergyman,
addressed the criminals with republican atticisms, raller-
ies, &c. concluding thus: "May your deaths be tedious
and intolerable, and may your *souls sink quick down to
hell,* the residence of tyrants, traitors, and devils!" The
effigies were then turned off, and after hanging some
time, were hoisted upon the top of a huge pile of wood,
and burnt, that their bodies might share a similar fate
with their souls. This pious transaction exalted the character of Mr. Trumbull, and facilitated his election to the
office of Governor: and what was of further advantage to
him, his mob judged that the bones of Ingersol's effigy
merited Christian burial according to the rites of the
church of England, though he had been brought up a
Sober Dissenter; and resolved, therefore, to bury his
bones in Hebron. Accordingly thither they repaired;
and, having made a coffin, dug a grave in a cross street,

and made every other preparation for the interment, they sent for the Episcopal clergyman there to attend the funeral of the bones of Ingersol the traitor. The clergyman told the messengers that neither his office nor person were to be sported with, nor was it his business to bury *Sober Dissenteri,* who abuse the church while living. The mob, enraged at this answer, ordered a party to bring the clergyman by force, or send him to hell after Ingersol. This alarmed the people of the town, who instantly loaded their muskets in defence of the clergyman. Thus checked in their mad career, the mob contented themselves with a solemn funeral procession, drums beating, and horns blowing, and buried the coffin in the cross street, one of the pantomimes bawling out, *We commit* this traitor's bones *to the earth, ashes to dust and dust to ashes, in sure and certain hope* that his soul is in hell with all tories and enemies of Zion. Then, having driven a stake through the coffin, and each cast a stone upon the grave, they broke a few windows, cursed such clergymen as rode in chaifes and were above the controul of God's people, and went off with a witless saying, viz. "It is better to live with the church militant than with the church triumphant."[7]

The protesters staged a mock execution and mock funeral of the tax collector Jared Ingersoll with much attention to detail, each of which are crucial to the protest narrative. The gentleman's outfit and lawyer's wig signified the social standing of a British loyalist, the reference to Judas and the monetary reward signified treason. Before the mob performed the execution of stamp master Ingersoll in effigy, they had abducted the actual tax collector who was forced to resign after being brought before the "special Assembly" of Connecticut notables opposing the tax.[8] The effigy burning theatrically restaged this forced resignation. Characteristic of performance, the burning made visible the protest against taxation and ritualized the enactment and threat of punishment. Furthermore, it entertained the assembled crowd and acted as a publicity tool for revolt against British colonial rule.[9]

Performance theorist Richard Schechner describes performances as "marked, framed, or heightened behavior separated out from just 'living life.'"[10] They are enactments of rehearsed behavior that conform to the social roles. With respect to politics, Schechner claims "the politician, activist, lawyer, or terrorist all use techniques of performance… to present, demonstrate, protest, or support specific social actions – actions designed to maintain, modify, or overturn the existing social order."[11]

In an effigy performance, the social or political conflict is dramatized, staged, and played out. Protesters experience the staged conflict and its resolution immersed in the performance, with the adversary made bodily present through the effigy for ritualized punishment.[12] Rituals are certain kinds of performance. They are "collective memories encoded into actions,"[13] and have an increased potential to shape the social structure of a community.[14] Rituals create a specific time/ space outside the normal state of being, which ritual scholar Victor Turner calls their "liminality," a state that brings about transition and transformation.[15] In the liminality of a ritual, participants can form interpersonal bonds, in Turner's terminology a *communitas*, that allows for an experience of

53

8   *A General History of Connecticut*, 342–43.

9   Schechner, *Performance Studies*, 46.

10   Schechner, *Performance Studies*, 35.

11   Schechner, *Performance Studies*, 76.

12   Hans Belting, *Bild-Anthropologie: Entwürfe für eine Bildwissenschaft* (Munich: Wilhelm Fink Verlag, 2001), 147.

13   Schechner, *Performance Studies*, 52.

14   Schechner, *Performance Studies*, 79.

15   Turner, *The Ritual Process*, 128.

16   Schechner, *Performance Studies*, 46.

Richard Schechner proposes that there are seven functions of performance:

1. to entertain;
2. to make something that is beautiful;
3. to mark or change identity;
4. to make or foster community;
5. to heal;
6. to teach, persuade, or convince;
7. to deal with the sacred and/or the demonic.[16]

Applying Schechner's categories to the performances of effigies, their main functions are: 4. fostering community; 3. marking the identity of the protesting group; 6. persuading and convincing the adversaries of neccessary change; and 5. healing the crisis in society. Two other functions play a role as well, since the performance for sure is: 1. entertaining for the participants; as well as 7. dealing with the sacred and the demonic, in addressing the division between good and evil, between justice and injustice. The only function that the effigy performances decidedly not do is: 2. to make something beautiful. On the contrary: staging conflict and violence, they create the ugly, the vile, the demonic, and the deformed. That does not mean that there are no moments of beauty and wonder in the many images I have collected. But these moments seem to appear rather accidentally and unintended in the course of a performance.

17   Turner, *The Ritual Process*, 128.

18   Louis Marin, *On Representation* (Stanford: Stanford University Press, 2001), 52.

19   See Butler, "Bodies in Alliance."

20   Bell, *Ritual*, p. xi.

21   See Butler, "Bodies in Alliance."

22   Carl Death, "Counter-Conducts: A Foucauldian Analytics of Protest," *Social Movement Studies: Journal of Social, Cultural and Political Protest* 9, no. 3 (2010): 245.

23   Schechner, *Performance Studies*, 91–94; and Diana Taylor, *Performance* (Durham, NC: Duke University Press, 2016), 133.

24   Schechner, *Performance Studies*, 42.

25   Taylor, *The Archive and the Repertoire*, 4–5.

community beyond normative social constraints.[17] These experiences can be formative for the creation of new identities. And while a ritual usually affirms existing social structures, its liminal time/space also has the potential to transform social structures and identities.

As a form of ritual, political protest creates a similar liminality. It affords the creation of communitas and opens up the possibility for social change.[18] When a person decides to join a protest, they step out of their ordinary life and assume the role of protester engaging in ritualized actions and forms of speech: marching, chanting, gesturing, or burning effigies. Butler calls this liminal time of the protest a "time of the interval," an anarchist passage with the potential to install a new order.[19] Similar to participating in a ritual, protesters gain experiential knowledge by embodying revised "assumptions about their place in a larger order of things."[20] Being present, speaking, and acting in public space, protesters formulate shared grievances and objectives. Acting together, protesters perform the potential for an alternative order of relationships in the space they contest.[21] "Through the acts of protesting and demonstrating, new identities and subjectivities are performatively constituted."[22]

Performance theorists stress that the hypothetical and conditional – the "as if" and the "what if" – are the fundamental qualities of performance.[23] In their make-believe – imagining and acting out a protest – participants "make beliefs," that is, they construct a belief system for the participant community.[24] The performance of protest proposes alternative political imaginaries and social relations, staging them as though real. The experience of communal action creates social identities and memories, which can form the basis for future action.[25] In that way, these performances can have a lasting effect on the communities involved.

54

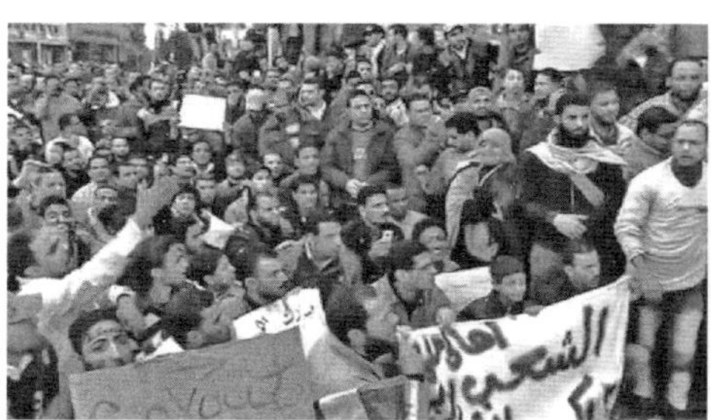

○ 2011_02_01_ Egypt: President Mubarak and government members

(a)

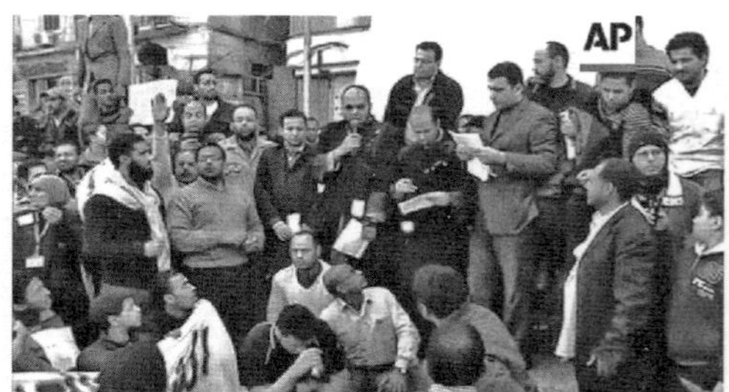

(b)

During the 2011 uprising in Egypt, activists in Tahrir Square, Cairo staged a mock trial, mock execution, and mock funeral with three effigies of President Hosni Mubarak and two other members of the government.○ The effigies were made from stuffed fabric, with painted faces, suits, and ties, and covered with slogans and signs considered to be defamatory in that context: the Star of David and dollar notes stuck out of one of the figure's pockets. In an Associated Press video, an activist can be seen reading the indictment of the president and a "judge" writing a note, with the public intently watching proceedings. Later, two of the effigies were hanged from the crossbeams of the traffic lights high above the crowd – one bearing a sign reading: "The people want a trial for the murderous president." These hung there for at least a week and were featured in many press photographs. The third effigy was carried around the square in a mock funeral and eventually torn to pieces. Similar mock trials were repeated either with effigies or actors.

The staging of the trials raised a fascinating question: what if Egypt had an independent judicial system and the president was subject to the rule of law? Employing the discourse of formal justice, the protesters drew on the legitimacy of the rule of law and the letter of the constitution as a strategy of resistance against the extra-legal state of emergency that characterized Mubarak's regime.[26] By reconfiguring the ritualized scenario of the trial, protesters accessed the normative qualities of official political ritual and gave the protesters' demand to unseat the president a socially and politically acceptable form. Mubarak faced the people he was accountable to in a substitute body, his crimes were announced and the protesters' objectives formulated.[27] The mock trial projected the image of the authoritarian ruler as subject to the rule of law, and educated the audience about the limits of

[26] Legal anthropologist Sally Engle Merry describes other examples of resistance by appropriating forms and symbols of the law. Sally Engle Merry, "Resistance and the Cultural Power of Law," *Law & Society Review* 29, no. 1 (1995): 21.

[27] Hanan Sabea, "I Dreamed of Being a People," *Political Aesthetics of Global Protest: The Arab Spring and Beyond*, ed. Pnina Werbner, Martin Webb, and Kathryn Spellman-Poots (Edinburgh: Edinburgh University Press, 2014), 71.

55

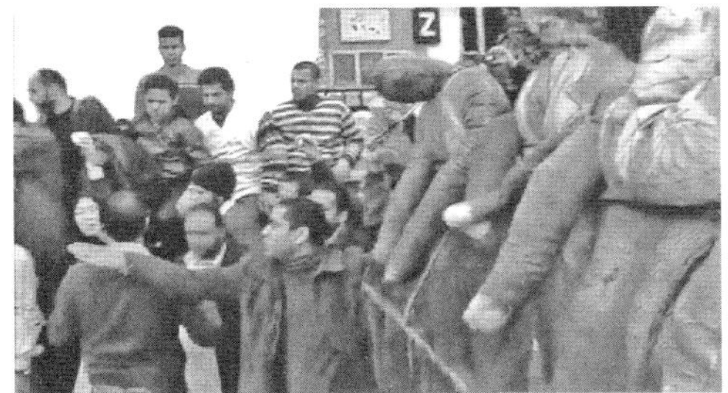

(c)

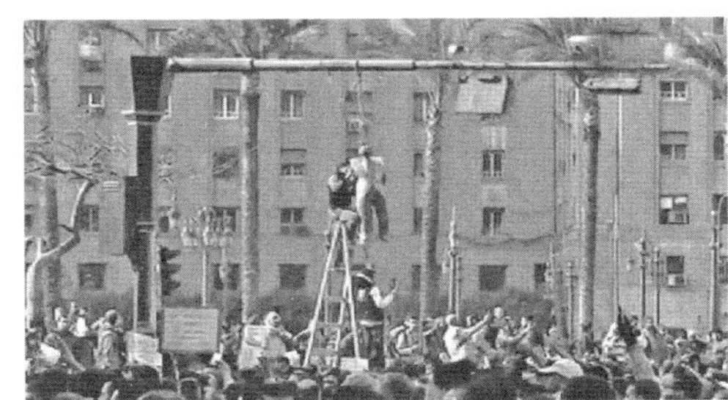

(d)

28 Schechner, *Performance Studies*, 124.

29 In 2012, Mubarak was sentenced to life imprisonment for his responsibility in the death of peaceful protesters during the 2011 revolution. After several appeals and retrials, his conviction was overturned in 2017 and he was released from detention.

30 Taylor, *Performance*, 140.

31 Iris Marion Young, *Justice and the Politics of Difference* (Princeton: Princeton University Press, 2011), 6.

32 Bell, *Ritual*, 79; and Taylor, *Performance*, 208.

government. The audience in the square became the audience at the president's trial, both delivering justice and participating in legal procedure. Together with the larger protest, the performance staged an alternative reality demanded by the protesters, making it visible and imaginable.[28] Repeatedly staging Mubarak's trial created an imaginary, a memory, which projected its force into the future and seemed to influence reality: six months after the first mock trial in the square, Mubarak stood trial before a real judge.[29]

While the scenario of the performance is not predictive of the future – and it often fails to become realized – it can open up, in Taylor's words, a "framework within which thinking takes place."[30] As such it creates the space where alternative orders can be imagined.[31] The rituals of official political manifestations (military parades, a coronation, a trial) present and perform the political order as the legitimate one and as if it was the only one possible. They close off the space of possibility. The performances of protest on the other hand, open up this space and create alternative imaginaries in the social memory. They contest existing power relations, present alternative orders, and negotiate for change.[32]

Scenario

33 Taylor, *The Archive and the Repertoire*, 54.

To understand how effigy protests are structured, communicated, and remembered, it is useful to look at their scenario as a condensed description of the protest performance. Taylor describes the scenario as "a paradigm that is formulaic, portable, repeatable, and often banal because it leaves out complexity, reduces conflict to its stock elements, and encourages fantasies of participation."[33] A scenario is a compact narrative and semantic structure that describes all constituent elements of a performance: the social setting, plot, attitudes, and affective reactions.[34] In the social arena, scenarios offer social actors a framework by which to guide their action through familiar and recognizable structures. Taylor suggests analyzing the scenario of social dramas to understand the underlying behaviors and social structures, since it is not based on only verbal expressions "but demands that we also pay attention to milieux and corporeal behaviors such as gestures, attitudes, and tones not reducible to language."[35] By investigating the scenario, three aspects of performance come into focus: the narrative within a specific social setting; the plot as a structure for the action; and the range of corporeal and emotional engagement prescribed for the actors in the "gestures, attitudes, and tones" transmitted with the scenario.

In terms of social relations, the narrative of an effigy protest can be described as the symbolic punishment of a perpetrator by the community in order to establish or reestablish the just order of society. The perpetrators are often individuals, but in the political sphere they can also be the representative of a group, like a party; or they are presented as an abstract entity like the government. The scenario suggests a specific social setting: an antagonistic conflict between two opposing groups and the lack of alternative means to address the grievances. It suggests a community in crisis, in a state of injustice, and in need of change that the ritual-like performance can help to bring about.

The emotional and affective charges prescribed by the scenario of protest can include anger over perceived injustice, righteousness or jeering sense of superiority, exhilaration from participation in the performance, unifying sense of community, outrage over hurtful performance, relief in playing out redressing injustice, or ironic resignation over the performance's lack of effect. Depending on place in conflict and

34 Taylor, *The Archive and the Repertoire*, 31.

35 Taylor, *The Archive and the Repertoire*, 28.

disposition, the emotional charge differs for actors and audience members in each case. Nevertheless, the narrative of capital punishment invariably produces violent images and elicits strong emotional response.

The scenario of an effigy protest develops in six more or less pronounced stages that are practically and/or semantically fundamental: (1) making; (2) dedication to the figure it represents through inscribing the name and/or attaching a picture and other identifying traits and symbols; (3) presentation to an audience; (4) animation through interaction, suggesting a degree of agency; (5) debasement through defaming inscriptions, attributes, or symbolic actions; and (6) execution.

These stages (except the fourth) are clearly visible in the series of photographs from a demonstration in Jalalabad, Afghanistan, in 2012$^\bigcirc$, where hundreds of students protested against the massacre of sixteen civilians by a US Army sergeant two days before in Kandahar province: (1) the body is made from grey pants and a green shirt sewn together wrapped in a warm brown coat and stuffed with straw, with a head of white cloth covered with a green cap; (2) no markings appear during the march, as the effigy's representation is revealed as US President Barack Obama only at the final point of assembly, visible in a photograph of a protester inscribing the green shirt and a piece of paper with the name; (3) a protester carries the effigy at shoulder height with a stick stuck through the crotch, presenting it to marchers and onlookers; (4) the protesters in this case don't interact with the effigy as if it was alive; (5) its mouth has devilish pointy teeth, tears flow down from his eyes, and the text on the paper reads: "OBAMA Son of the Bitch"; and (6) the protesters have arranged themselves in a circle around the burning effigy on the ground, raising their fists and shouting slogans, presenting themselves and their performance to the photographers.

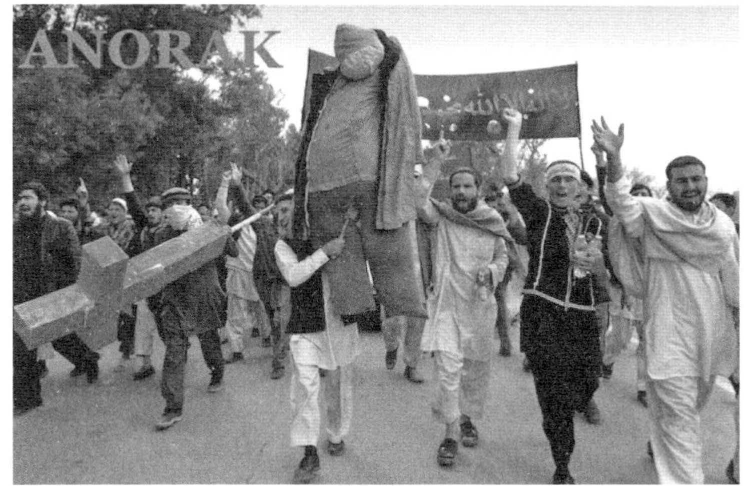

○ 2012_03_13_Afghanistan: US President Obama

(a)

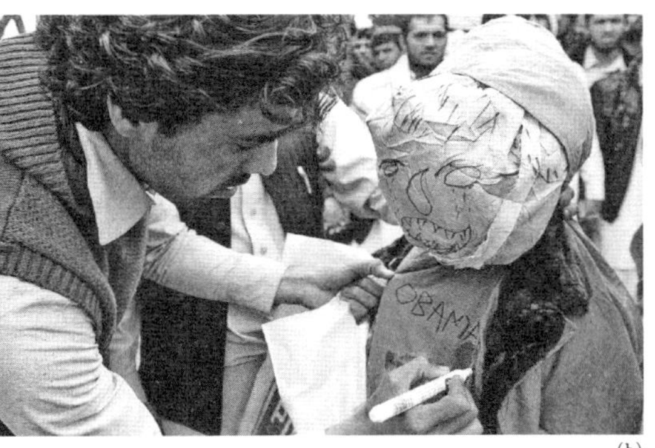

(b)

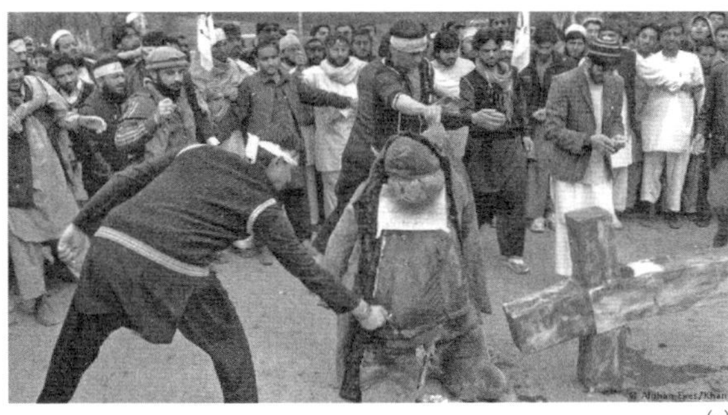

(c)

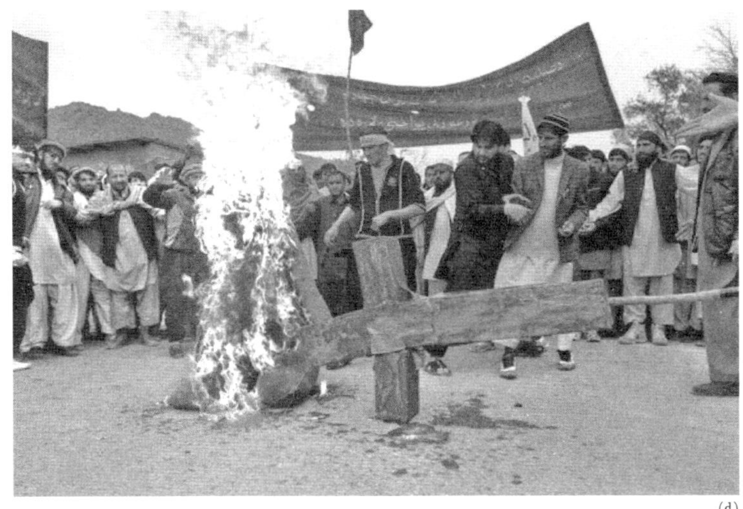

(d)

Making

36 Hans Belting, "Image, Medium, Body: A New Approach to Iconology," *Critical Inquiry* 31, no. 2 (2005): 305.

Although there is no prescription for how to produce an effigy, its intended purpose sets up a framework: it needs to be light so that it can be carried in marches; it must be big enough to be visible to an audience; and it should catch fire quickly and thoroughly if meant to burn so no remnant of the despised figure remains lest it spoil the purification. Making begins with the physical carrier of the depiction: a body. It is often made of old clothes – pants and a shirt sewn together or overalls – stuffed with light, flammable material like straw, paper, or plastic foil. Sometimes the whole body is sewn from cloth, making it even more of a medium, like an empty canvas upon which the image is painted.[36] The head can be many things: a pillow, ball, a stuffed plastic bag, a watering can, carved from Styrofoam. Sometimes it is carefully sculpted from papier-mâché.

60

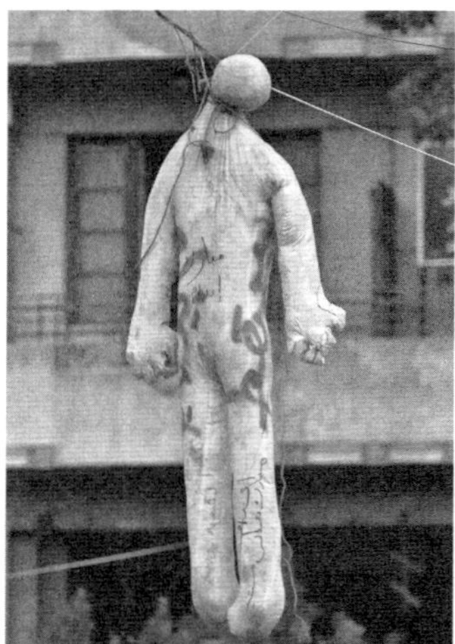

2012_02_02_Egypt: Field Marshall Tantawi

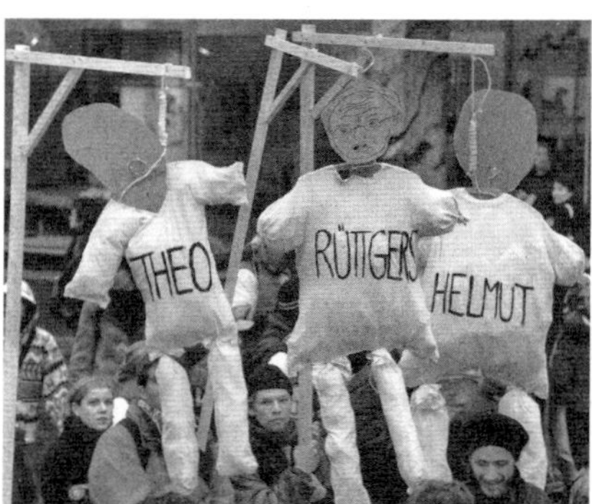

1997_12_04_Germany: Minister Waigel + Minister Rüttgers + Chancellor Kohl

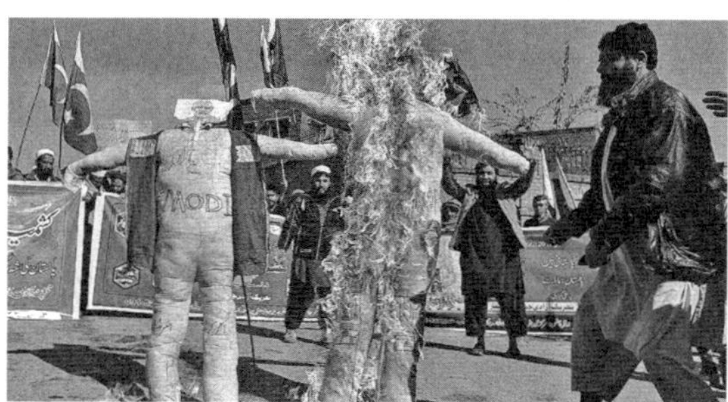

2017_08_30_Pakistan: Indian Premier Modi + US President Trump

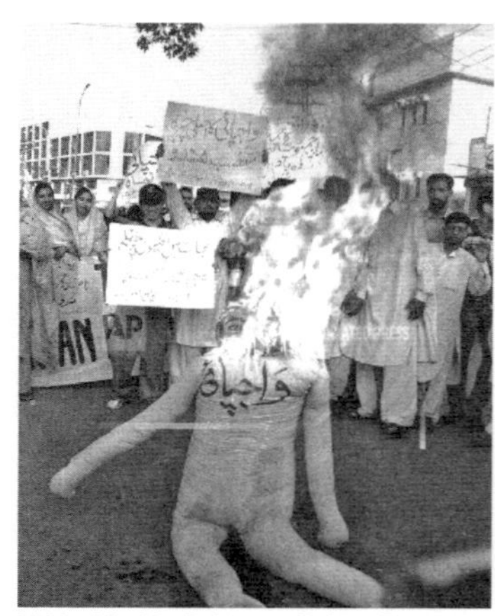

2000_06_22_Pakistan: Indian Premier Vajpayee

Currently, as printers are readily available, photographs of the depicted are regularly added. A sheet of paper with a portrait is attached, usually to the head, sometimes multiple images are used. In some cases, the creator makes an effort to shape the two-dimensional photograph into a three-dimensional head. With their realistic expressions, photographs evoke a vivid but strangely distorted liveliness. The figures seem present and engaged, but somehow complacent and unperturbed by the excitement going on around them.

Most protest effigies look like scarecrows improvised by amateurs, but some show real craftsmanship. In many Latin American countries, papier-mâché effigies for traditional celebrations at New Year and Easter are widely available in local markets. In northern India, specialized craftspeople use bamboo and paper to fabricate immense effigies of Ravana for the festival of Dussehra; in eastern India, straw and clay are used to make beautifully crafted Durga effigies. The quality craftsmanship and style of some protest effigies makes evident their professional manufacture.

61

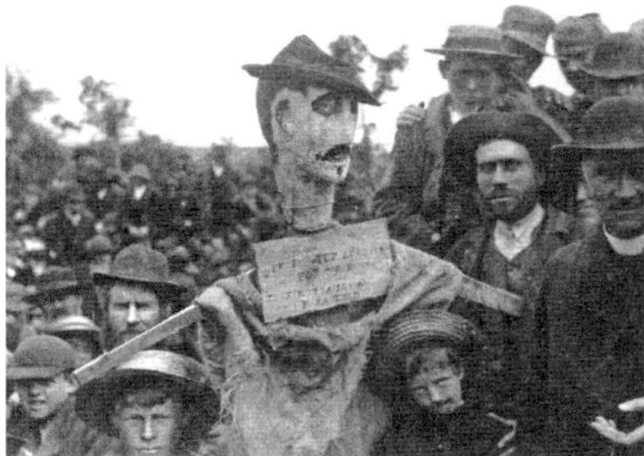

1887_06_03_Ireland: Sheriff McMahon

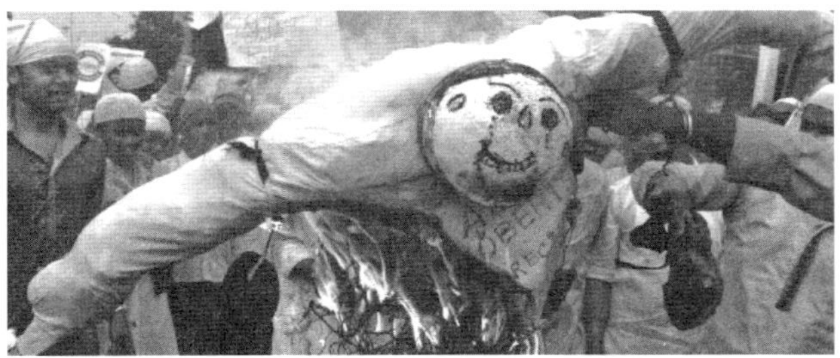

2012_10_05_India: film producer Roberts

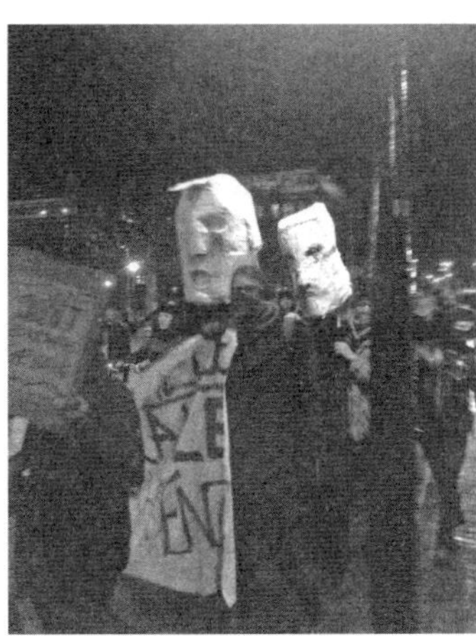

2017_01_20_Netherlands: US President Trump + Geert Wilders

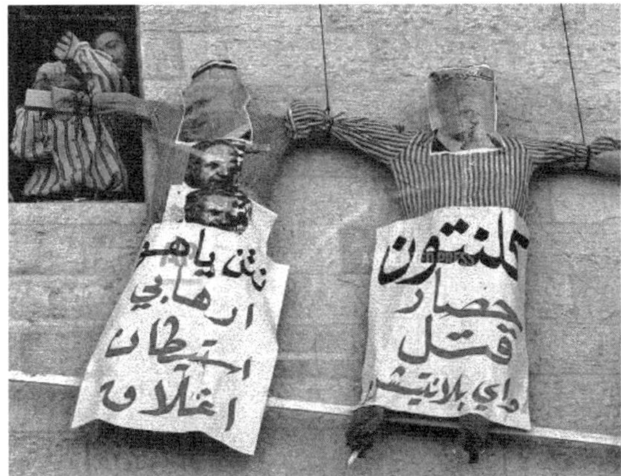

1998_11_09_Palestine: Premier Netanyahu + US President Clinton

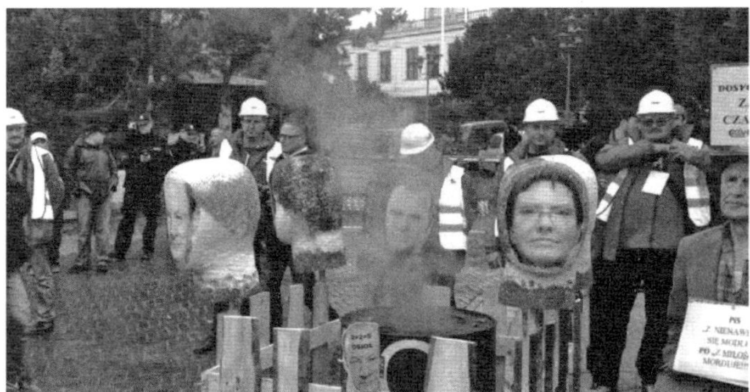

2013_09_11_Poland: government of Premier Tusk

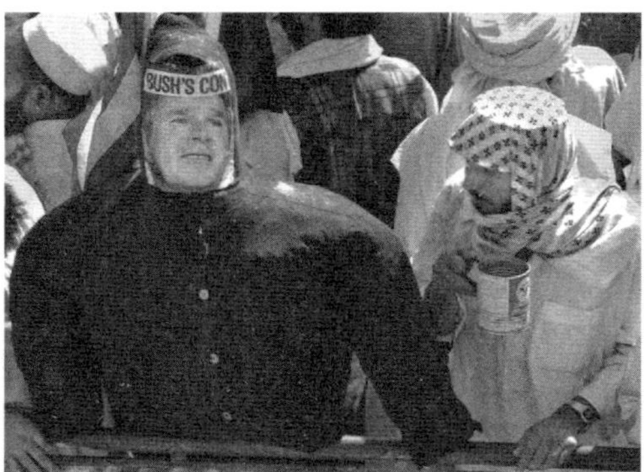

2001_10_12_Pakistan: US President Bush

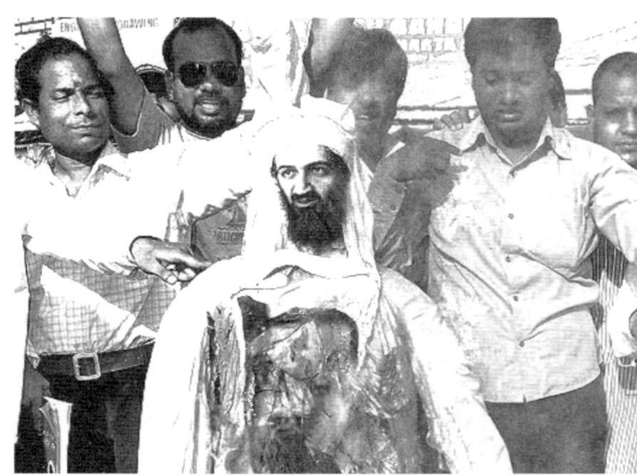

2010_08_24_India: Osama bin Laden

The making is often collaborative. In some of the relatively few photographs I was able to source that show the process, people work together and the conviviality between them is palpable. Indeed, the making is the first stage of the communal action constituting an effigy protest. Most effigies are life-size, evoking bodily presence in opposition to the protesters, making the performance that much more effective. The smaller they are the less possible to call them effigies, but rather dolls as their destruction lacks the corporeal quality of an effigy. Effigies can, depending on the makers' ambition, be very large. Conducive to gigantification is that effigy protests tend to become communal traditions fueling the competition with earlier iterations or competing protest groups. This can be observed, for instance, in the Philippines, where artist collectives, like UGATLahi, have produced gigantic effigies on

63

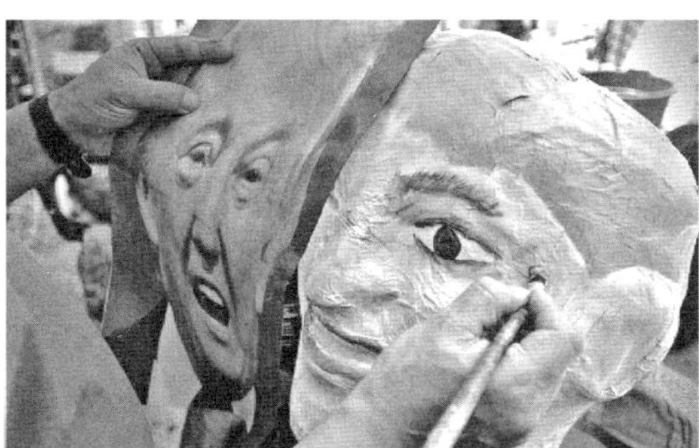

2016_03_27_Mexico: US presidential candidate Trump as Año Viejo

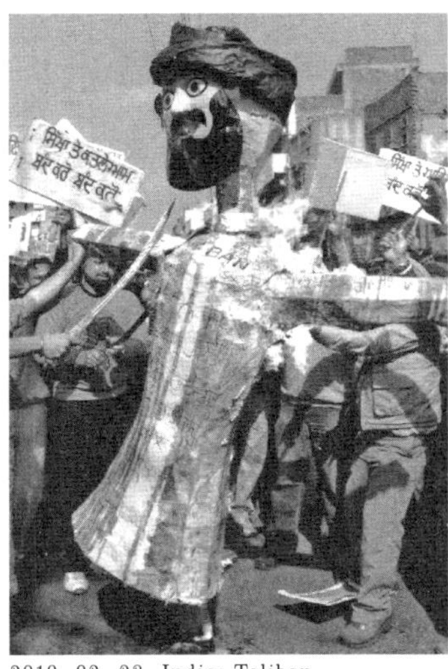

2010_02_23_India: Taliban

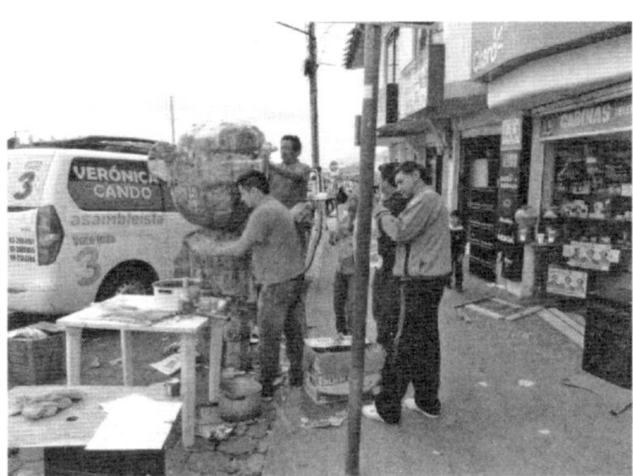

2012_12_30_Ecuador: Central Bank gov Delgado as Año Viejo

37 Lisa Cariño Ito, "Dissident Puppets: The Effigy in Philippine Radical Politics" (bachelor's thesis, University of the Philippines Diliman, 2005), 92, 37.

elaborate floats for their protests against successive presidents since the 1980s.[37]

It is fascinating to study the photographs in detail and imagine the creative process that goes into making effigies. This alone is deserving of a book-length study on techniques and materials, as well as the mindset, effort and dedication, and richness or lack of imagination of these artists. One could then reflect on the decision to represent the head of an American pastor with a plastic watering can, or admire effigies as canvases covered in drawings and calligraphy. One striking image shows a dark hooded figure made from tar paper or the like, attached to it a photo of Bashar al-Assad; how else could you depict a president who sacrificed his

64

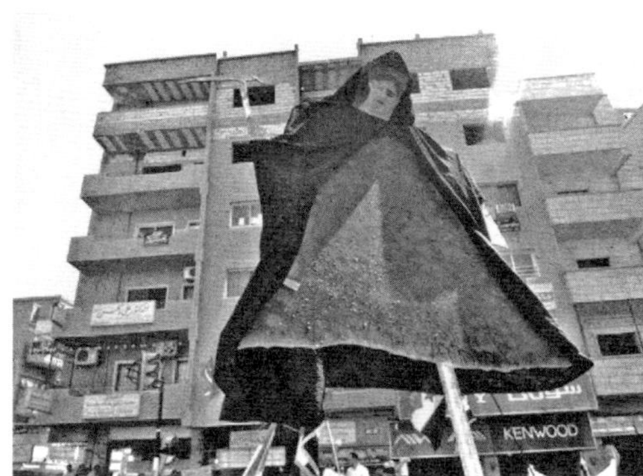

2011_07_22_Syria: President Assad

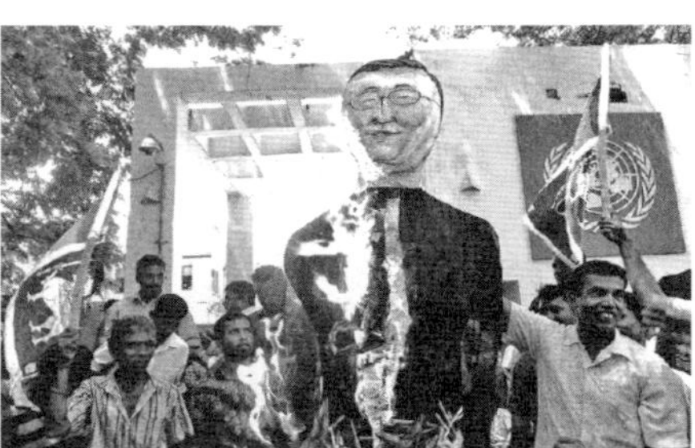

2010_07_06_Sri Lanka: UN Secretary General Ban Ki-moon

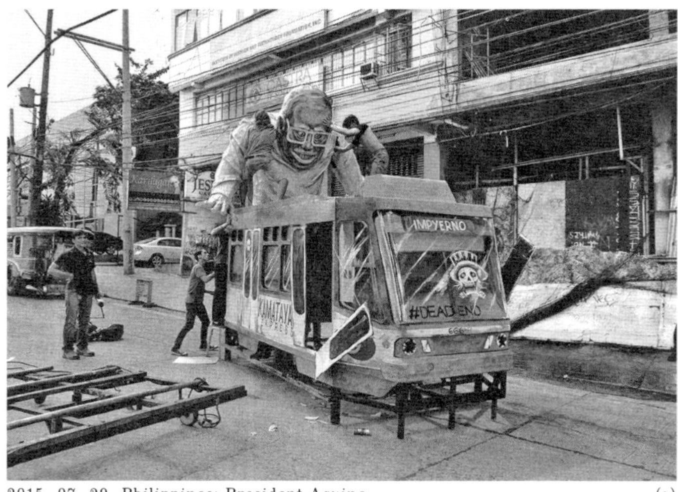

2015_07_29_Philippines: President Aquino

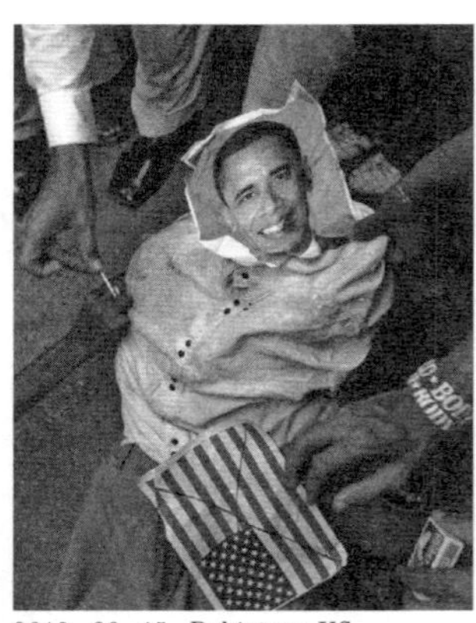

2012_09_15_Pakistan: US President Obama

(a)

people to stay in power? Another shows Ban Ki Moon's over-size head carved from Styrofoam, an enigmatic but friendly smile on his face while being burned. Many feature Obama, whether smiling out from a picture stuck onto his effigy that lies crumpled at protesters' feet, or as an effigy with a crudely drawn, expressive face, photographed as if shouting out slogans with his companion protester. Zoomed in, one digital photograph of British Prime Minister Gordon Brown shows him as an abstract ecce homo, the grotesque character of the effigy is echoed in the way the images falls apart into disjointed pixels as we get closer to it.○

65

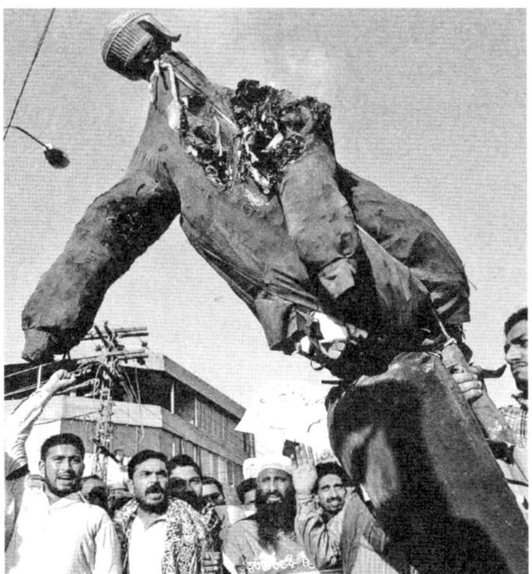

2012_09_11_Pakistan: US pastor Jones

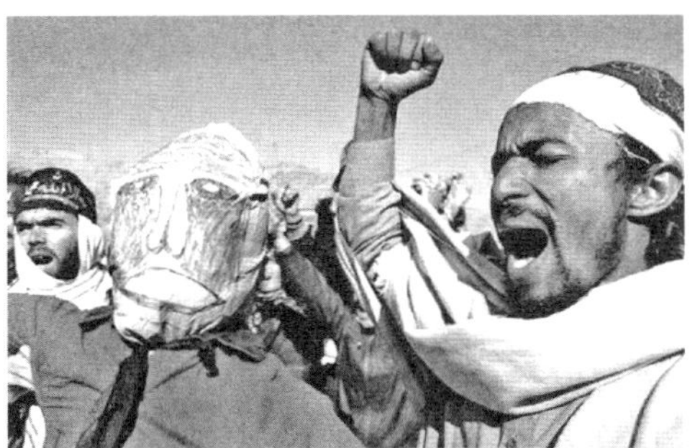

2012_02_2ᴇ_Afghanistan: US President Obama

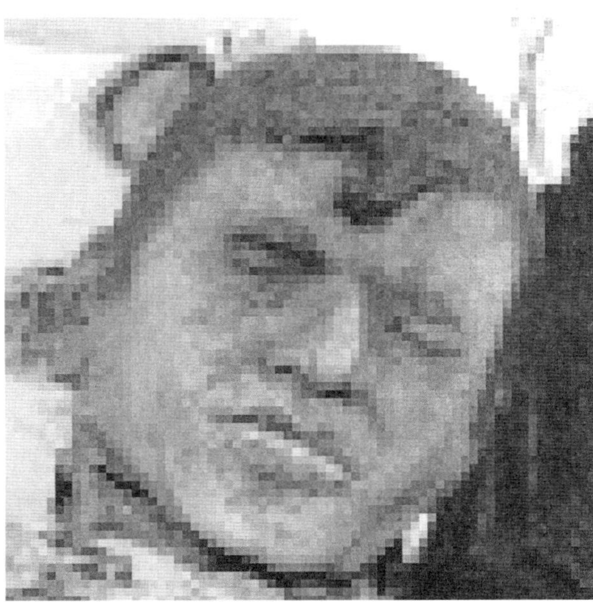

○ 2010_05_01_UK: Premier Brown

Dedication

For the performance to make sense, the effigy needs to be associated with the specific figure being targeted. In many cases, the identity of the effigy might be clear from the context of the performance, but most often significant efforts are made to ensure this. The image is grafted onto the dummy through drawing, painting, or attaching a photograph. But to unambiguously connect the dummy to the depicted personality, most often their name is inscribed on the body of the effigy. Other symbols and attributes help with identification, like flags, organizational acronyms, briefcases, or specific items of clothing.

66

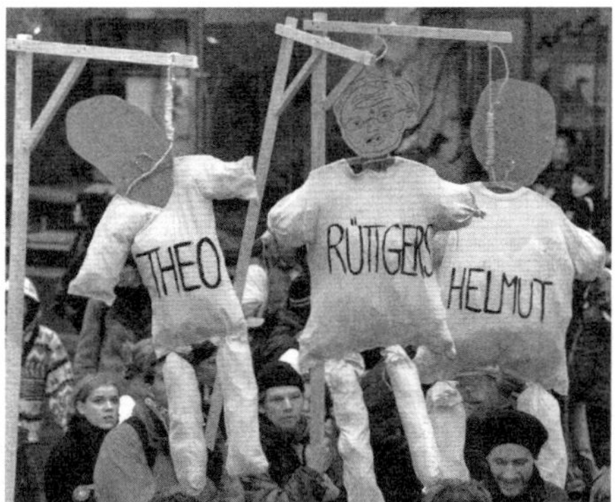

1997_12_04_Germany: Minister Waigel + Minister Rüttgers + Chancellor Kohl

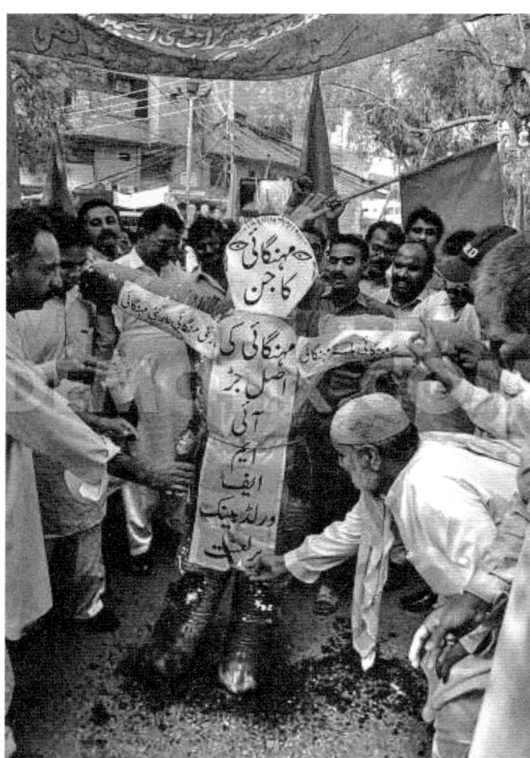

2012_05_01_Pakistan: World Bank

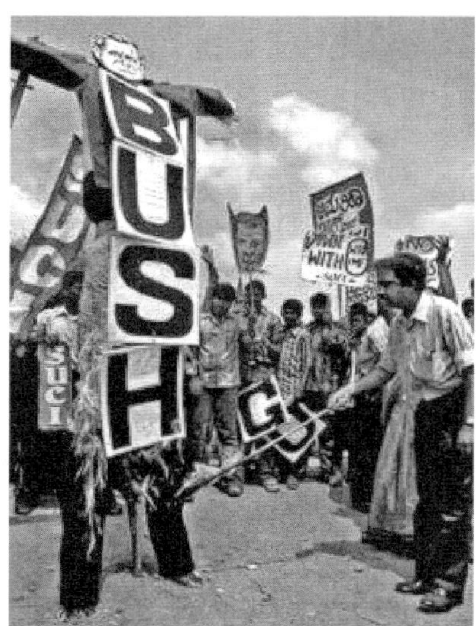

2006_03_01_India: US President Bush

Presentation

With the beginning of the performance, the effigy is presented to participants and spectators, itself a participant of sorts joining in the parade, carried by a protester, or riding along on a stick like a banner. Alternatively, the effigy can be installed on a pedestal, or hanged from a rope. The depicted is made present in the effigy in anticipation of the ritual of reversal, debasement, and punishment.[38] This presentation paradoxically confirms the depicted figure's position of power, unavoidably affirming status since the ritual demands their presence.

38 Belting, "Image, Medium, Body," 308–9.

67

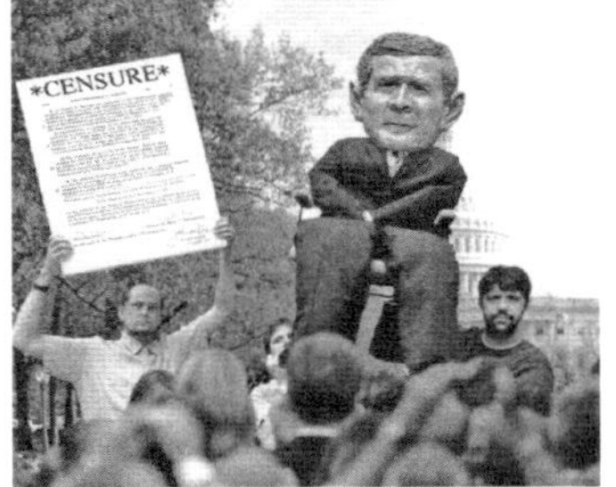

2007_08_24_USA-DC: President Bush

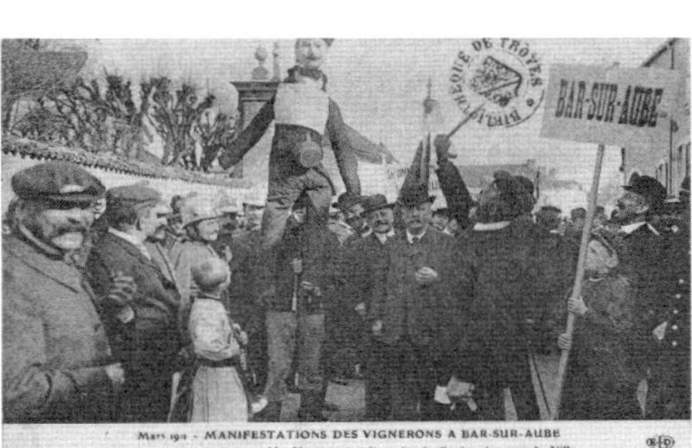

1911_03_19_France: Council President Monis (a)

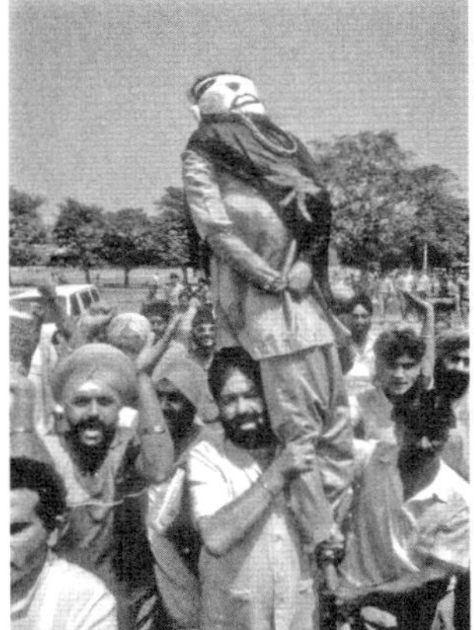

1990_04_19_India: Pakistani Premier Bhutto (a)

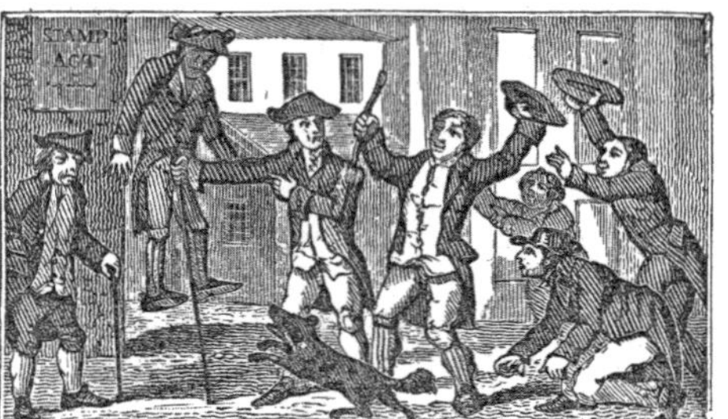

1765_08_14_USA-MA_Tory

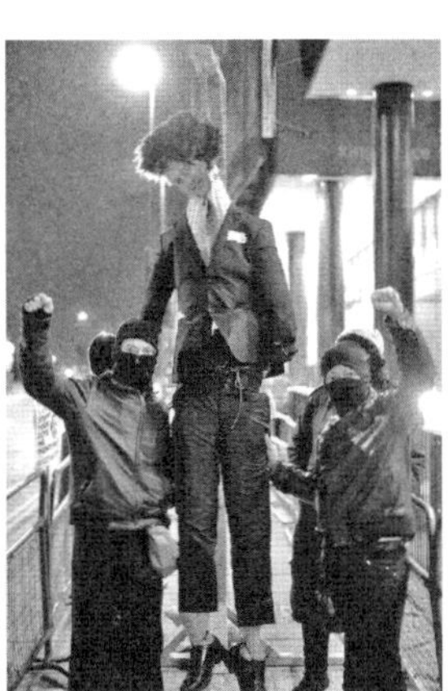

2011_04_08_UK: Nick Clegg

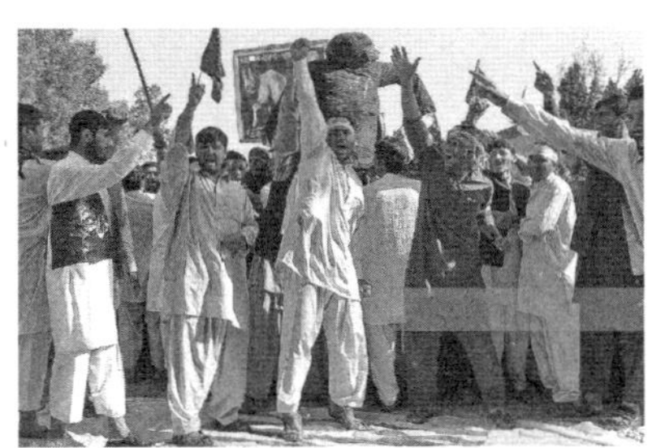

2012_09_19_Afghanistan: US President Obama

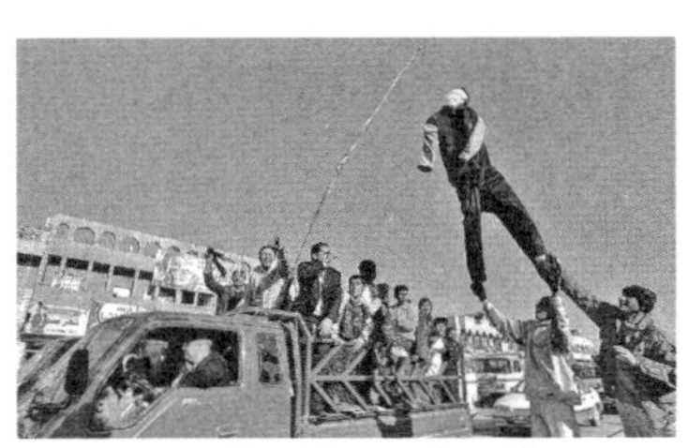

2006_12_30_Iraq: former President Saddam Hussein (a)

Animation

39 Schechner, *Performance Studies*, 203.

40 Horst Bredekamp describes this form of animation through first-person inscriptions for antique sculptures and artifacts. Horst Bredekamp, *Theorie des Bildakts* (Berlin: Suhrkamp Verlag, 2010), 59–69.

At some moment during the process of dedication, the effigy is animated, it comes to life. It is a form of consecration not only instigated by the makers, but even more through the actions and perceptions of the performer-participants and observers who interact with the puppets as if they had a life of their own.[39] While most inscriptions refer to the effigies, state the names of the depicted and add insulting descriptors like "dog" or "monster," some inscriptions address the effigy and through it the one it depicts: "Hassan Rot Op!" (Hassan, get lost!), or "Go Back to Africa Where You Belong." In some cases, effigies are given a voice and speak in the first person through inscriptions: "Soy Ruben Costas, Vende Patria" (I am Ruben Costas, Traitor), "I am Shetan Rushdie," "The World is Mine," or "I'm Bush, Kill Me." The effigies acquire a form of agency, the ability to speak and interact with the protesters as animated, physical semi-beings with the possibility to influence their human companions, aiding in the lifelike characteristic that makes this form of protest so engaging.[40]

68

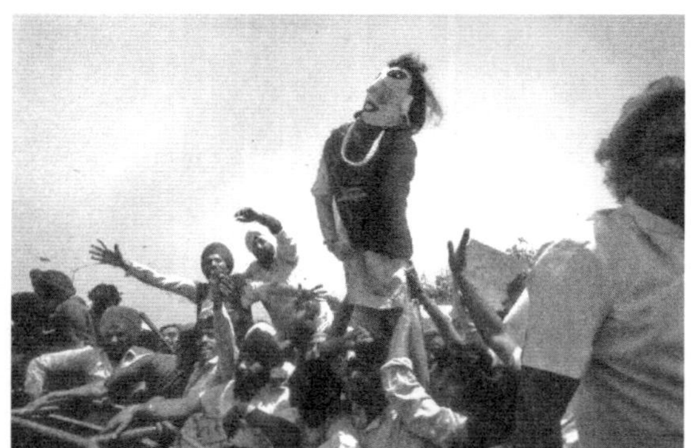

1990_04_19_India: Pakistani Premier Bhutto

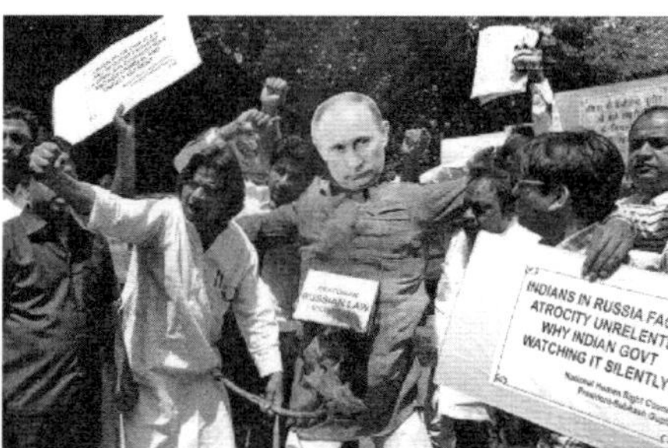

2013_04_10_India: Russian President Putin

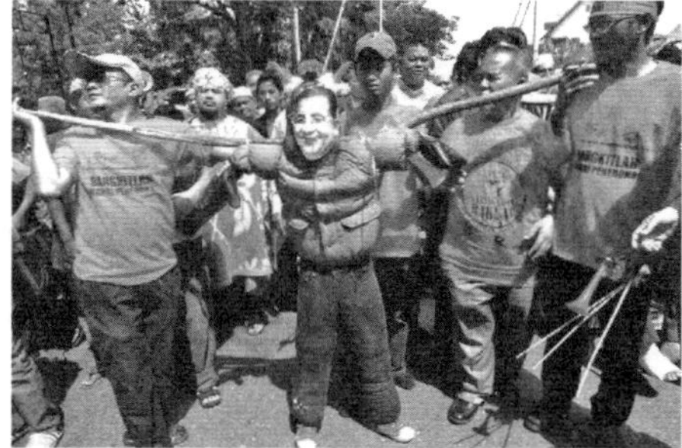

2012_12_28_Malaysia: FELDA chairman Samad

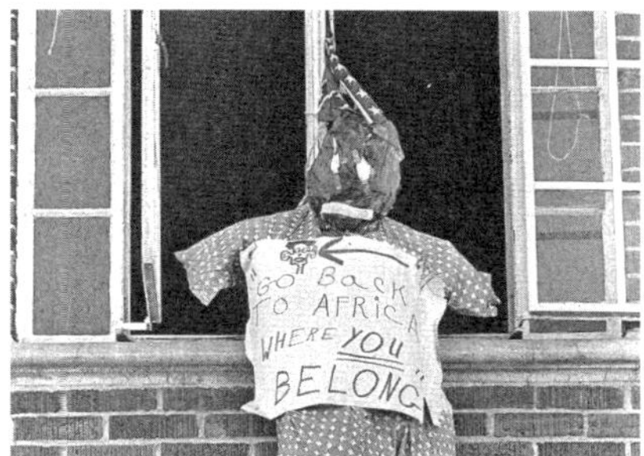

1962_10_03_USA-MA: African-American student

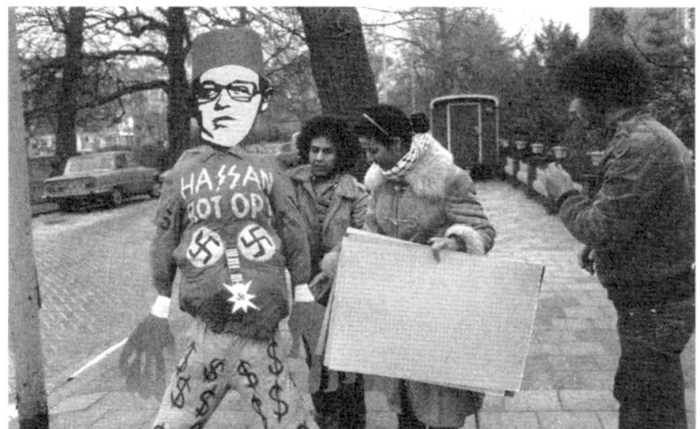

1981_03_05_Netherlands: Moroccan King Hassan II

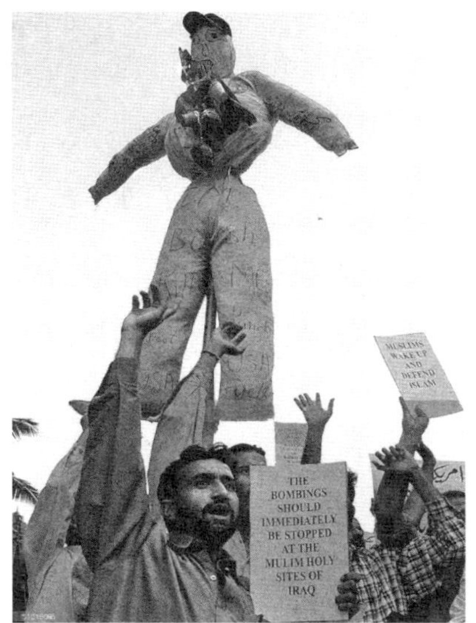

2004_08_25_Pakistan: US President Bush

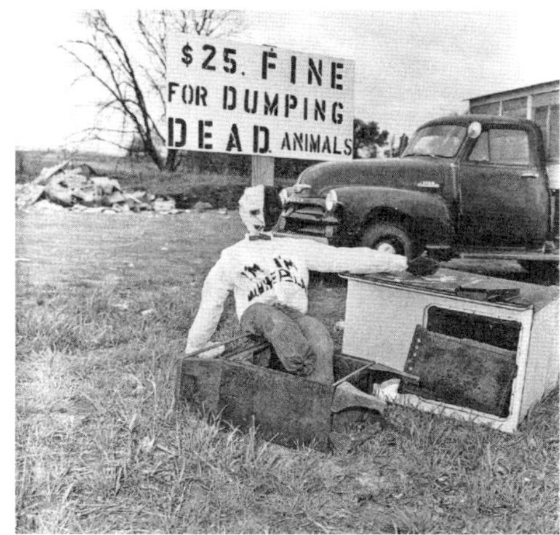

1960_04_02_USA-TX: author John Howard Griffin

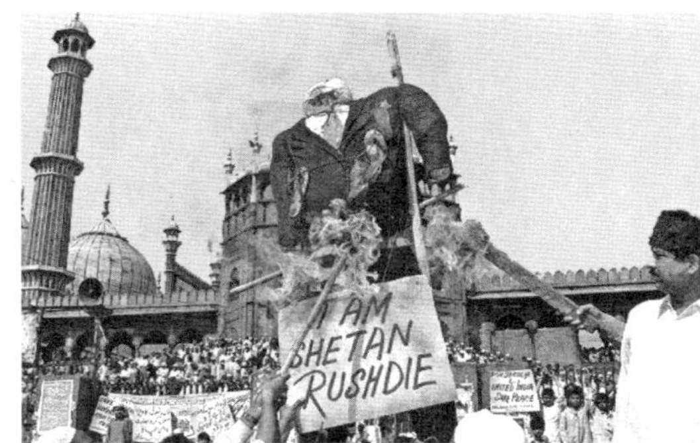

1989_02_19_India: author Salman Rushdie

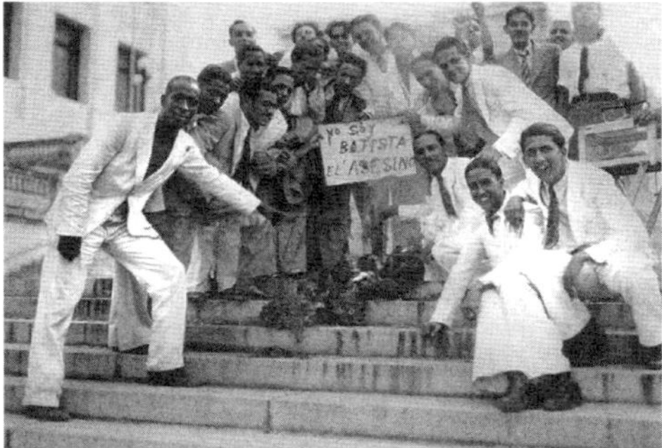

1953_05_00_Cuba: President Batista

Debasement

In presenting the effigy to a public, it is often demeaned: spectators are invited to participate and contribute to its punishment by kicking, punching, hitting, defiling with paint, throwing things at it, and other threatening gestures like raised fists or guns pointed its way. Signs of the reversal of status are often added to it: devil's horns or teeth, nooses, or shackles.[41] In Muslim countries hitting and decorating the effigies with shoes is popular. This debasement recalls the practice of humiliating a convict at the pillory, during which spectators' participation contributes to the punishment.

70

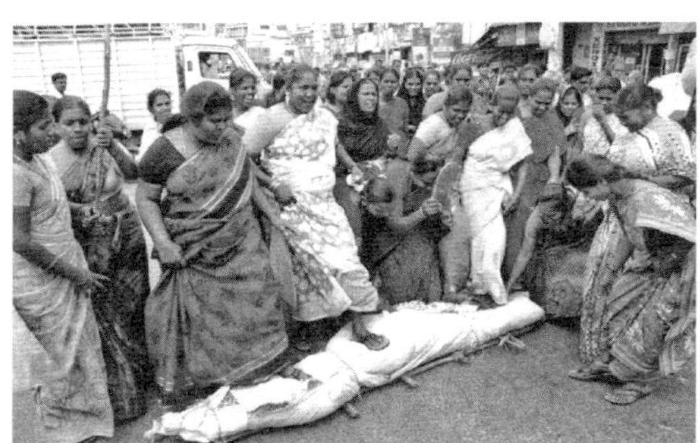

2013_08_01_India: INC president Sonia Gandhi

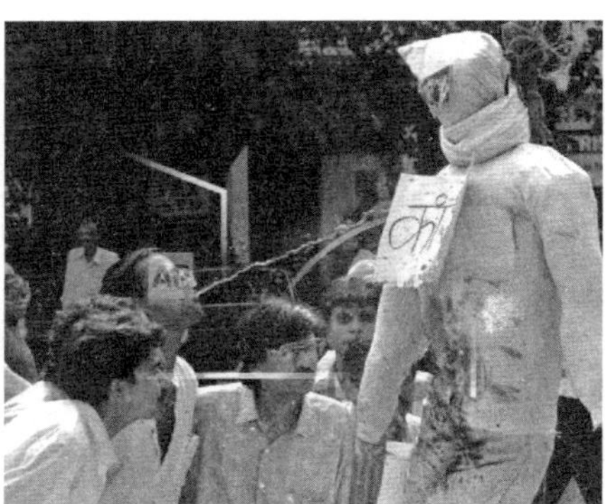

1996_10_28_India: BSP chief Ram

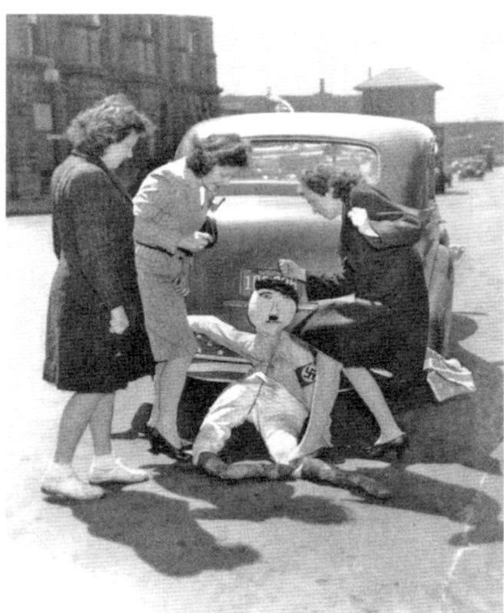

1945_05_08_USA-IN: Hitler

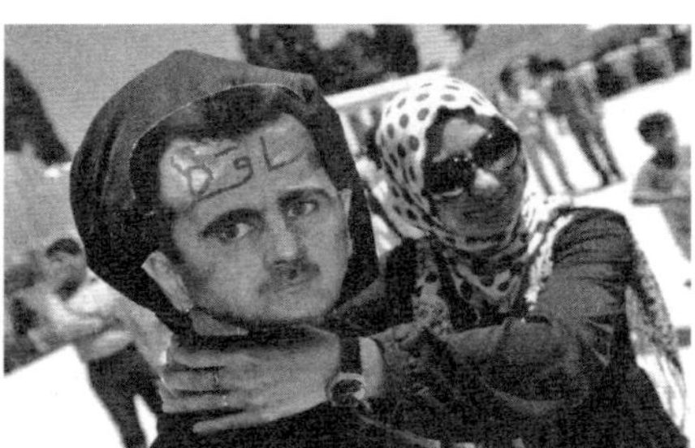

2011_06_24_Turkey: Syrian President Assad

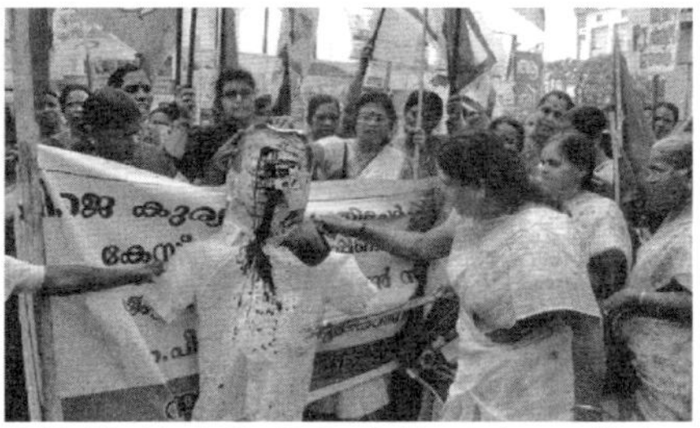

2013_02_08_India: Rajya Sabha chairman Kurien

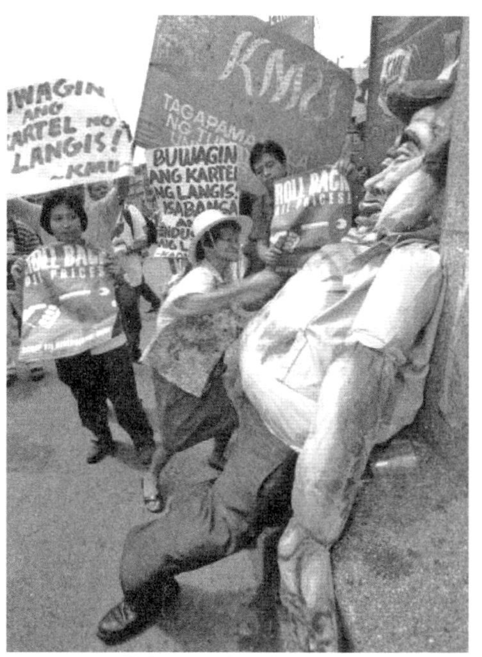

2000_03_16_Philippines: President Estrada

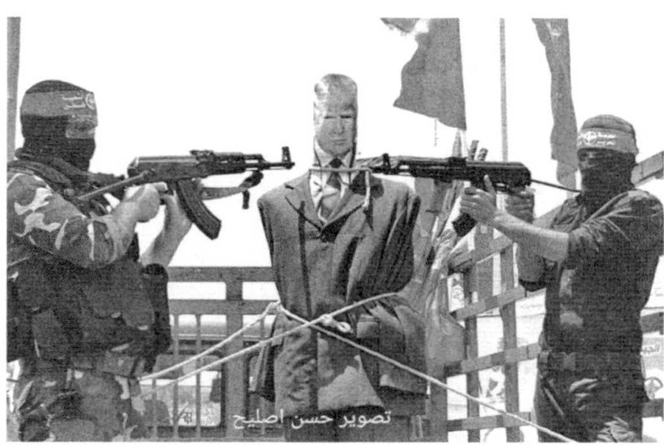

2017_05_23_Palestine: US President Trump

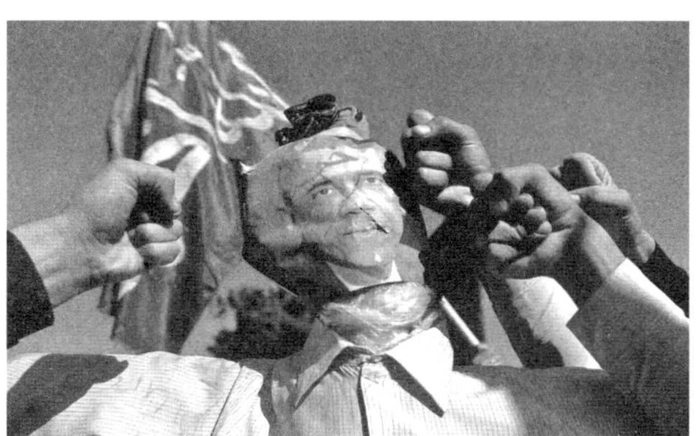

2013_11_19_Afghanistan: US President Obama

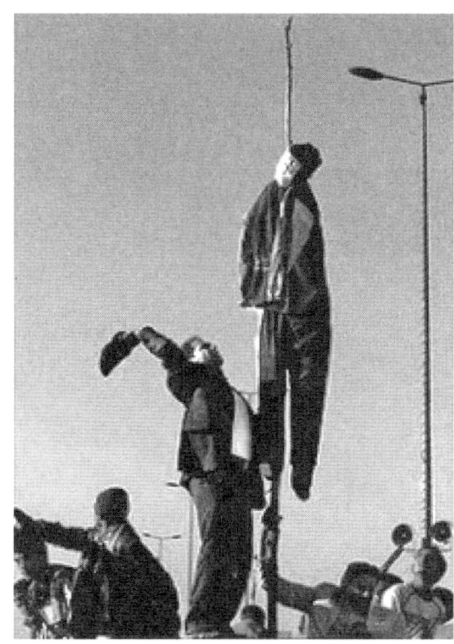

2006_12_30_Iraq: former President Saddam Hussein

(b)

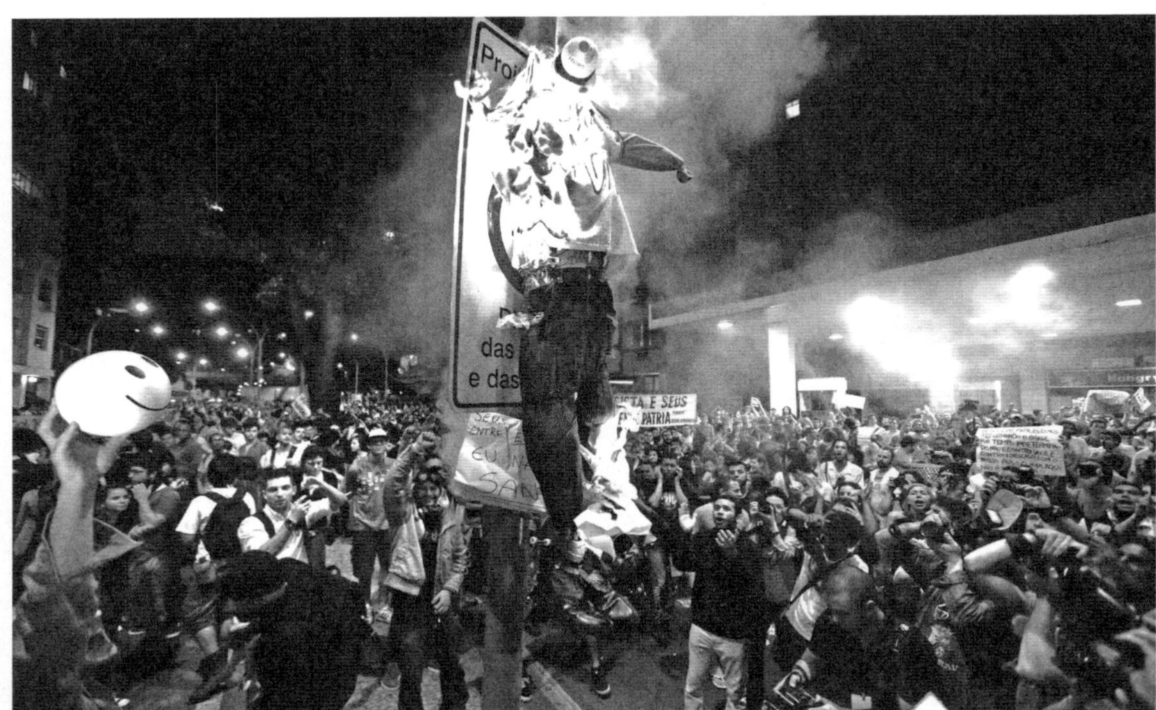

2013_07_22_Brazil: Governor Cabral

Execution

As the climax of the performance, the effigy is executed. Most often, it is doused with a flammable liquid, set on fire, and burned down to a heap of smoldering ashes. Alternatively, it is hanged on improvised gallows or from trees, bridges, and cranes. Sometimes it is burned after hanging, and at others left as a lasting sign of humiliation.[42] Other forms of execution also occur: decapitation, stabbing, and beatings, even being dragged by cars or torn to pieces.

42 See also chapter 3, "Effigy Protests in the History of the United States."

73

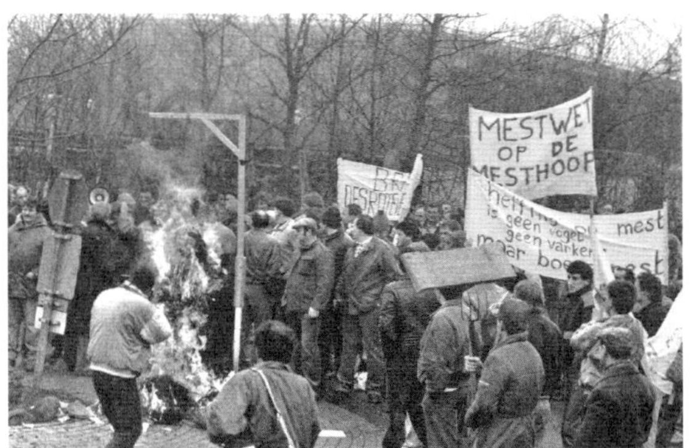

1988_03_03_Netherlands: Minister Braks

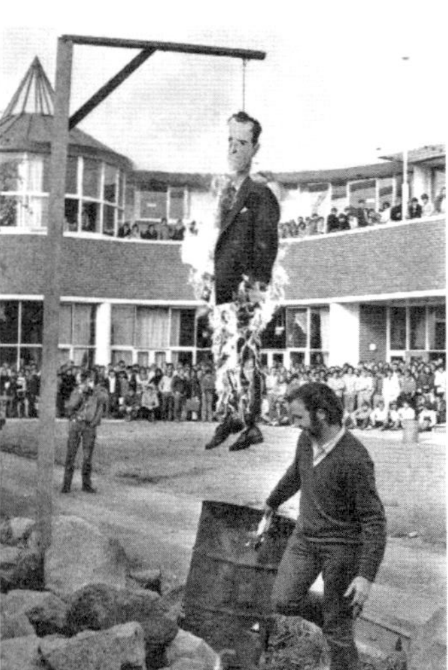

1970_05_00_New Zealand: US President Nixon

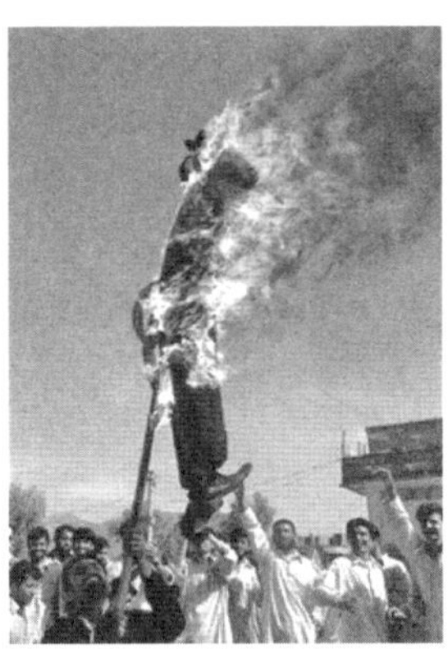

2007_05_01_Afghanistan: US President Bush

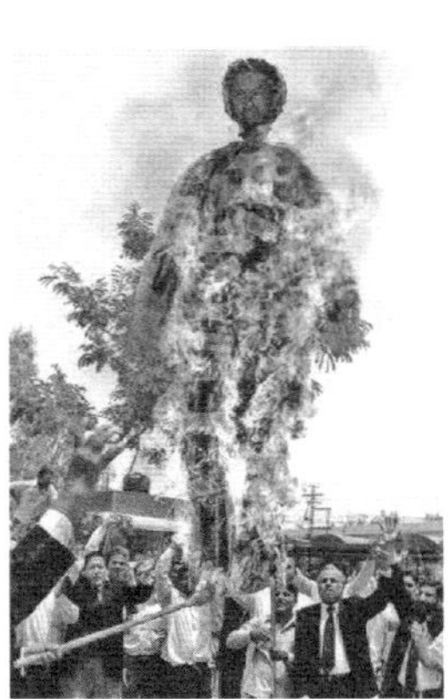

2008_06_09_Pakistan: President Musharraf

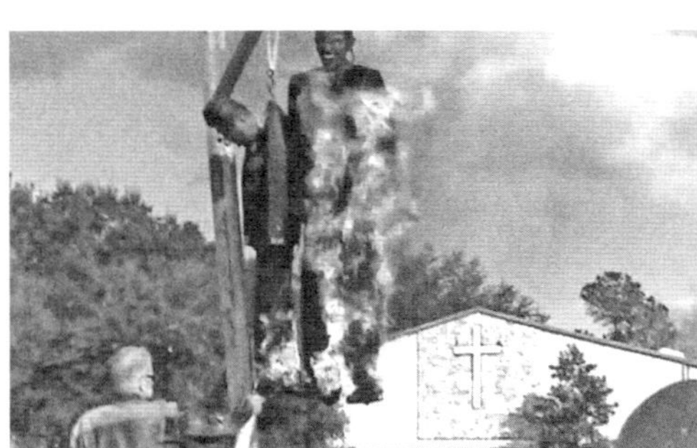

2013_01_28_USA-FL: Presidents Obama + Clinton

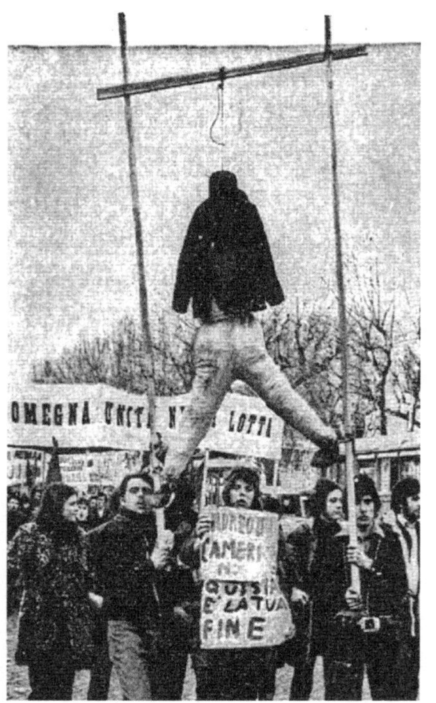

1973_06_17_Italy: Premier Andreotti

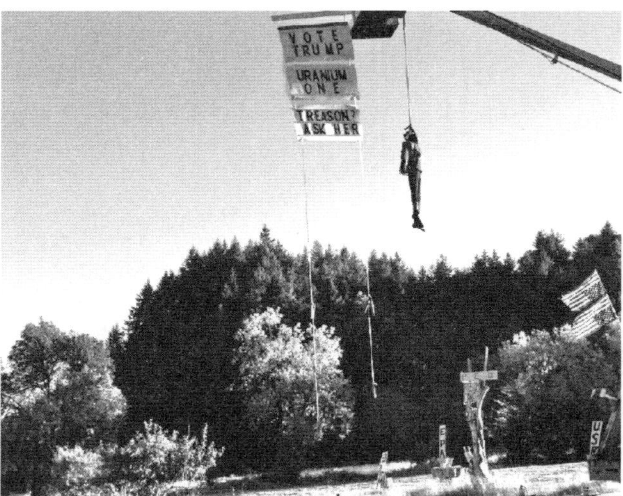

2016_09_15_USA-OH: presidential candidate Hillary Clinton

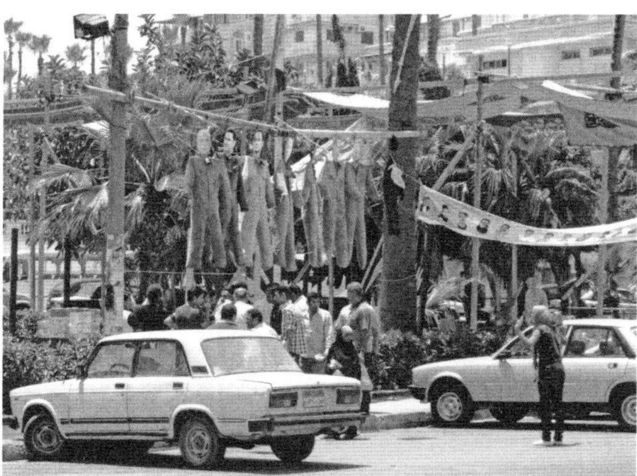

2012_06_07_Egypt: former President Mubarak and government members

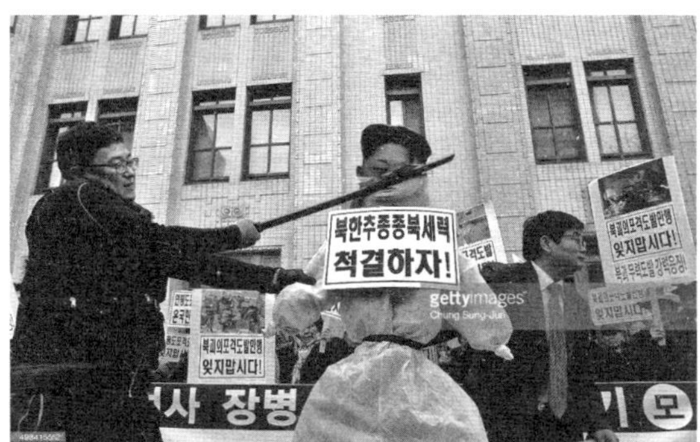

2015_11_23_South Korea: North Korean leader Kim Jong-un

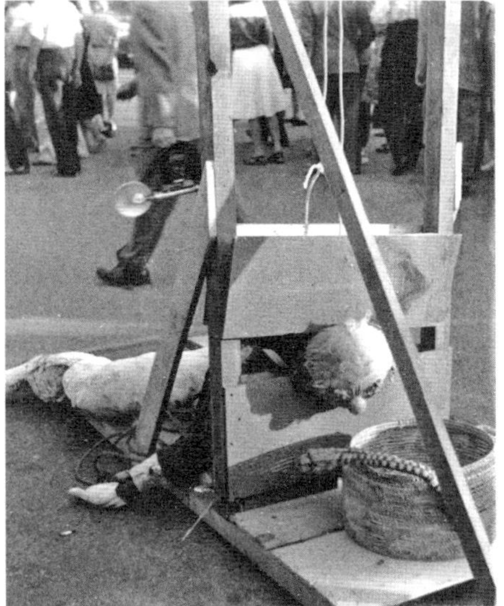

1941_07_00_USA-CA: Walt Disney   (b)

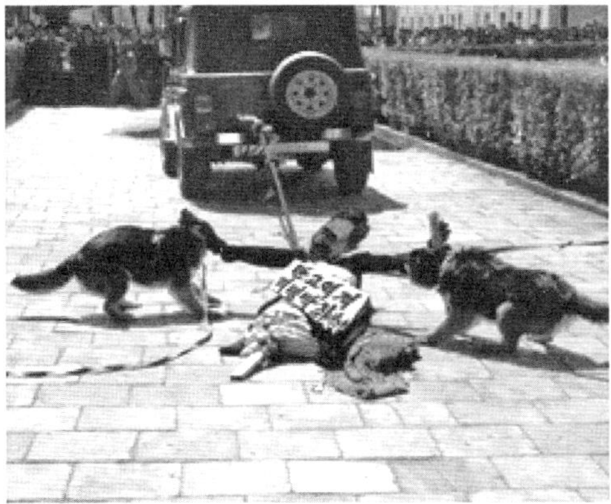

2012_04_26_North Korea: South Korean President Lee

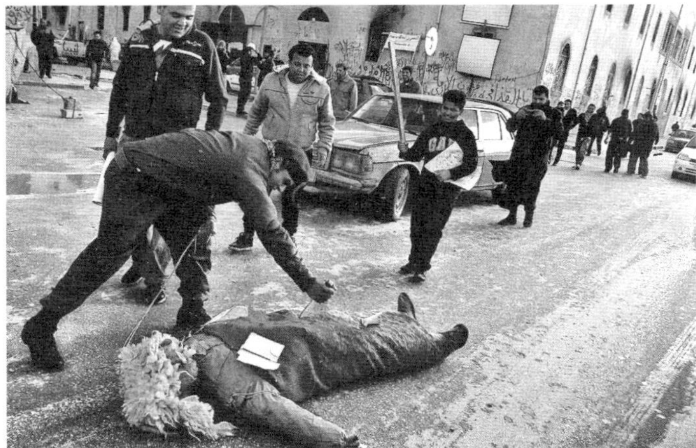

2011_06_28_Libya: Colonel Gaddafi

The Stage

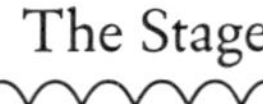

43 Taylor, *The Archive and the Repertoire*, 32.

When the dramatic part of the performance is about to begin, protesters turn their attention toward the effigy. An open circular space forms around it: a stage. Participants are divided into roles: stage managers encouraging actors and communicating with the audience; protagonists engaging actively with the effigy, beating, hitting, and setting it on fire; and observers. Antagonistic participants might be present – counter-protesters and policemen guarding or policing the protest. Since members of these groups usually remain on the periphery, they are not often visible in photographs of effigy protests. Nevertheless, even if they are not physically present, antagonistic actors and the general public are also addressed. As Taylor points out: "the scenario places spectators within its frame, implicating us in its ethics and politics."[43] As the demand that the general public take sides is inscribed in the scenario of a political protest, it implicates sympathetic, antagonistic, and neutral audiences. The ritual-like performance of a political protest binds the whole social and political community. It stages the social constellation of involved groups, the conflict, and its emotional effects, and publicly proposes a possible solution to the community.

76

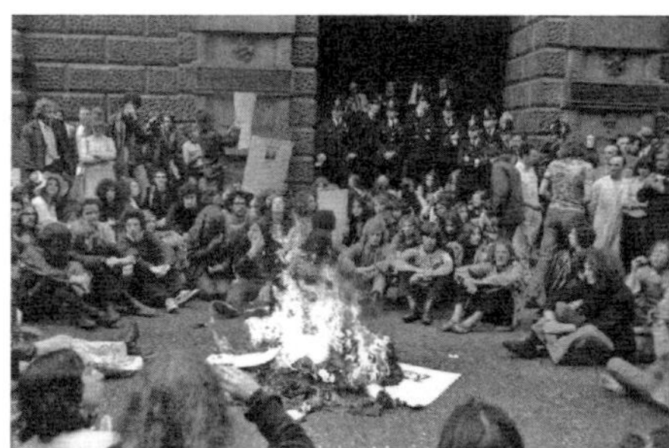

1971_08_05_UK: Judge Argyle

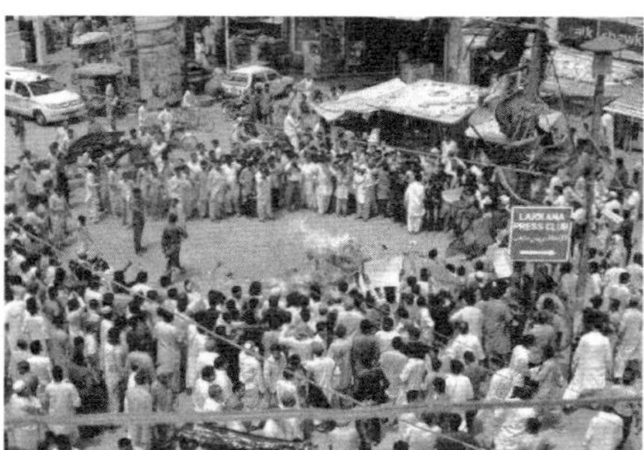

2012_06_12_Pakistan: electricity company

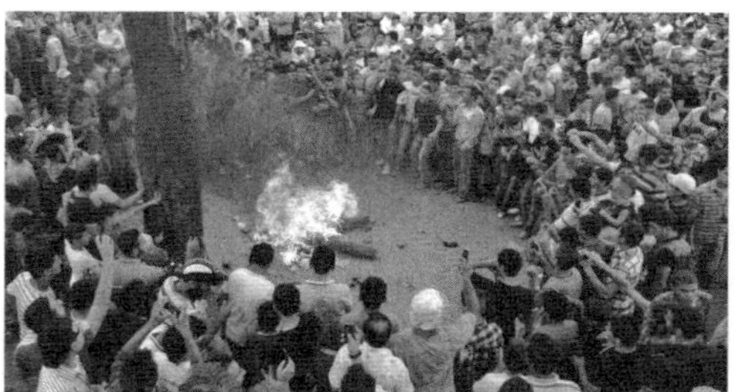

2011_10_07_Lebanon: Syrian President Assad

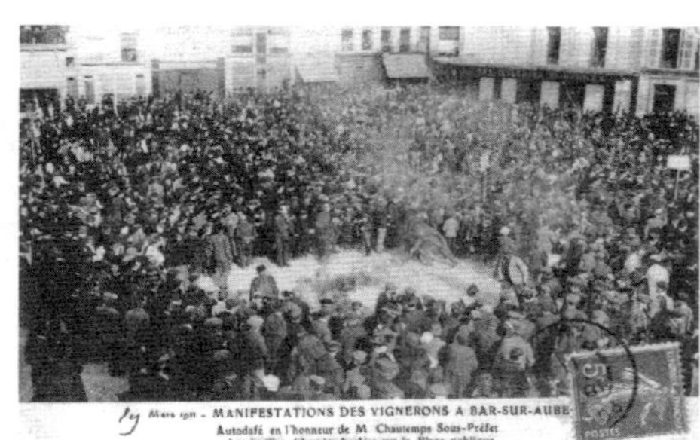

1911_03_19_France: Council President Monis   (b)

Communication of a political protest is vital for it to become visible and lay claims in a public sphere and mediation is the only way to communicate with a wider audience. As an archaic and low-tech genre of protest that produces spectacular symbolic images, burning effigies is successful in attracting the attention of the news media. This is true not only of the visual mass media of the twentieth and twenty-first century – print media have been vital to the success of political protest and in forming a public sphere for centuries.[44] The first protest against British colonial policies in Boston, at the onset of the American Revolution on August 14, 1765, featured an elaborate effigy performance. It was reported in detail in the *Boston Gazette* and reprinted in newspapers across the colonies.[45] The newspaper reports served as the blueprint for further protests in New England and effigy performance became a favorite revolutionary protest practice.

A report or a photograph of an effigy protest is already evidence that the news media were present. It is important to keep in mind that the very presence of the photographer and camera influences the course of the event.[46] In many effigy protests, the camera's presence makes the space's division into a stage and audience area even more distinct. Initiators and active participants often assemble behind the burning effigy

44   Vikki Bell, "Introduction: The Potential of an 'Unfolding Constellation': Imagining Fraser's Transnational Public Sphere," *Theory, Culture & Society* 24, no. 4 (2007): 1.

45   *Boston Gazette*, August 19, 1765.

46   Ariella Azoulay, *Civil Imagination* (London: Verso, 2012), 19.

77

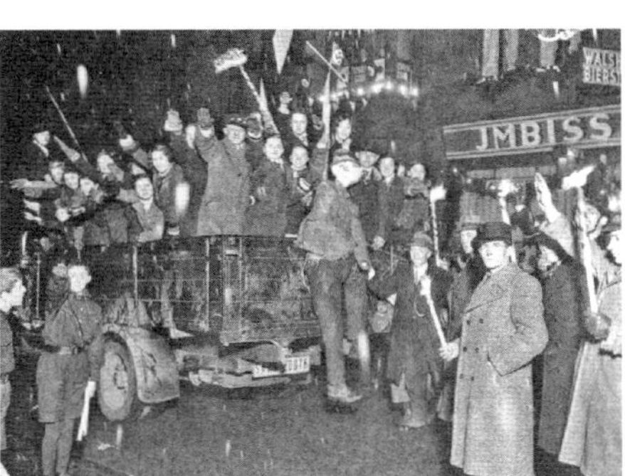

1935_01_22_Germany: editor Max Braun

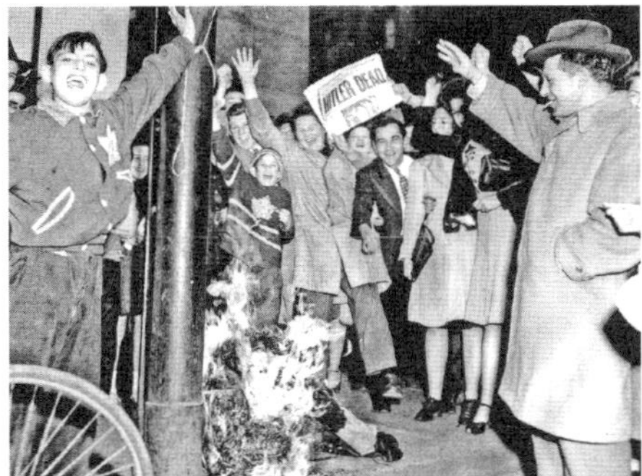

1945_05_02_Canada: Hitler

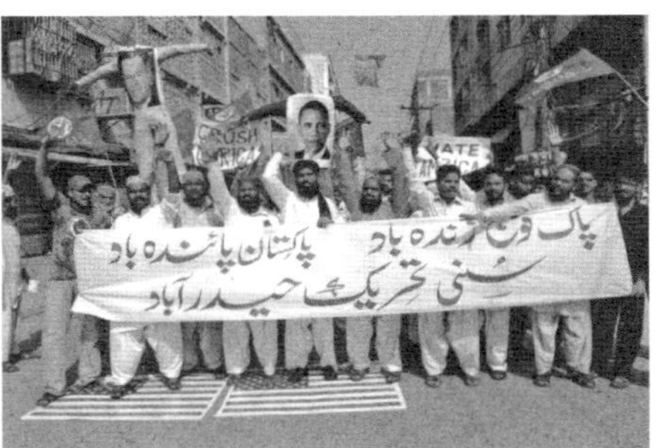

2011_09_27_Pakistan: US President Obama + US Vice President Biden   (a)

47 Butler, "Bodies in Alliance," and Florian Göttke, "A Protester in Homs, Syria," *open! Platform for Art, Culture and the Public Domain* (2013), onlineopen.org/a-protester-in-homs-syria.

with placards and flags, presenting themselves to the camera, forming themselves into an image of protest.[47] Their demands address not just the immediate audience, but to an equal degree the representatives of the news media.

The staging and framing of photographs suggest different kinds of recipients. Some photographs employ a first-person shooter perspective, making the viewer a participant in the action. Other photographs take a distant point of view, constructing the viewer as a disinterested observer. Many, however, show the effigy burning, as though staged for the camera, making the viewer the addressee, the antagonistic recipient provoked by the effigy. Similarly, the framing caters to media outlets' different audiences. Since specific outlets are situated in the contested social and political sphere, they are positioned on one or the other side of the protest and often frame the report accordingly, participating in creating antagonistic and sympathetic recipients.

In some cases, a photograph makes obvious that the division between the stage and media audience was planned. During a protest rally organized by followers of Shia cleric Muqtada al-Sadr in Baghdad in 2008, effigies of US President George W. Bush and Secretary of State Condoleezza Rice were burned.○ In the background of this photograph, cordoned off by a fence, is what reports describe as thousands of participants attending the rally. The effigy burning itself would have hardly been visible to protesters, appearing to be staged for the cameras and a few dignitaries. The main addressee is not the audience present in the square, but those reached by news media.

Even in small and seemingly less organized protests, the main addressee can be mediated audiences. In this

78

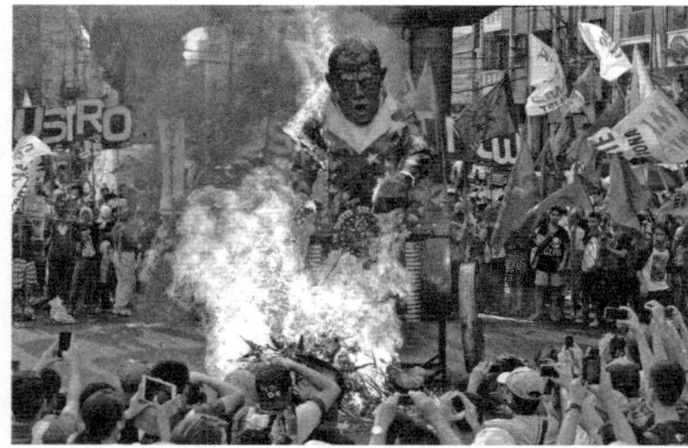

2014_04_28_Philippines: US President Obama   (b)

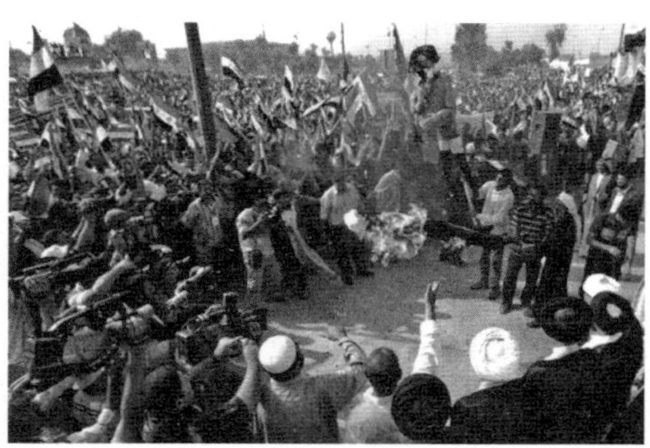

○ 2008_10_18_Iraq: US President Bush + US Secretary of State Rice   (f)

photograph, we see a small protest in Bangladesh, staged apparently in the semi-public space of a madrassa with participants dressed alike, possibly all students at the school.⓪ Nevertheless, the presence of a large number of cameras in the upper left corner of the crowd suggests that the production of images was the main aim of the performance, attesting to the organizers' intention to reach their audience through media.

Another example in which organizers were well aware of the media's importance involve the protests against successive governments in the Philippines. Over the last two decades, National Democratic Front of the Philippines (NDFP) activists have developed the burning of effigies into a carnival-like spectacle. Large numbers of artists, artisans, and volunteers work collectively. They choose a theme and create large effigy floats with an elaborate pictorial program, visually narrating the political issues they protest against. In well-organized theatrical processions, they move the effigies along a route. In a moving performance, groups of actors engage with the effigies in different ways, of which burning is only the last cathartic act. Over the years, organizers have more and more refined the choreography of the performances with the media in mind, to provide spectacular images and insure the most broad coverage possible.[48]

Embodied protest and its mediation have become tightly entangled. Today, more than ever, it is impossible to imagine a protest without its mediation. Even though the physical dimensions of political protest in public space are considered paramount to making political claims, the mediated protest becomes an extension of the space of the protest. As Butler puts it: "the media *is* the scene or the space in its extended

48 Ito, *Dissident Puppets*, 148–55.

79

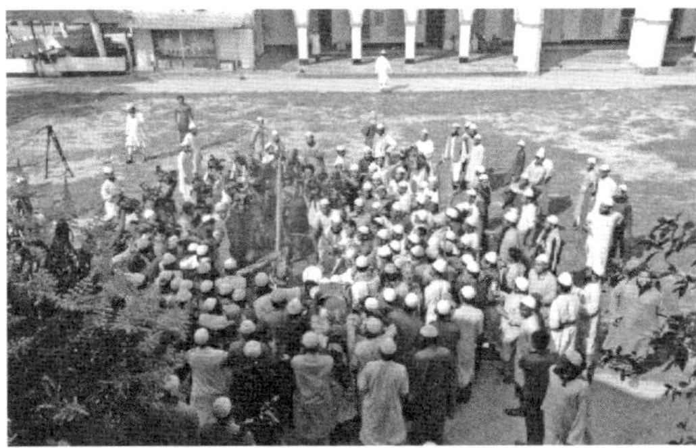

⓪ 2013_02_24_Bangladesh: "atheist blogger"

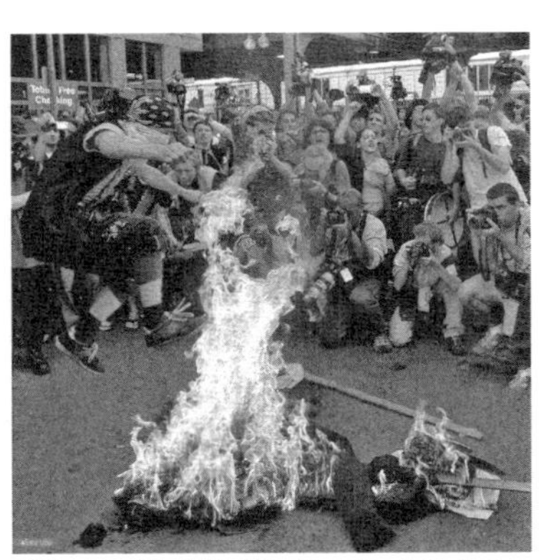

2004_07_29_USA-MA: President Bush + Senator Kerry

49 Butler, "Bodies in Alliance."

50 Schechner, *Performance Studies*, 124.

51 Nancy Fraser, "Transnationalizing the Public Sphere: On the Legitimacy and Efficacy of Public Opinion in a Post-Westphalian World," *Theory, Culture & Society* 24, no. 4 (2007): 19.

52 Butler, "Bodies in Alliance."

and replicable visual and audible dimensions."[49] That does not mean that the experiences of protest on the street and through media are the same. Even though both immediate and mediated audiences are addressed, their experience and involvement differs. The potential of the mediated protest to implicate the audience is diminished: it becomes more of a choice whether to engage, even though contemporary social media affords a degree of involvement and supportive action. Some mediated audiences sympathetic to protesters can spread reports of the events and influence public opinion through sharing and commenting. Antagonistic audiences are also emotionally affected, and possibly activated to engage further. But to audiences unaffected by the protest, the reports and images might be just more in a row of spectacles, emptied of urgency and disconnected from the conflict at hand and the social context.[50] Additionally, since the different news media have their own agenda, the protesters' message is easily reframed or distorted.

While the news media have been identified as part of the public sphere in the framework of the nation-state in the past, political philosopher Nancy Fraser points out that the recent rapid expansion of the media allowed for new, if uneven and weak, transnational public spheres to emerge.[51] In these transnational public spheres, identities and imaginaries can be negotiated, and, to a degree, the existing order can be challenged beyond the limits of the nation-state. To cite Butler again: "The media requires those bodies on the street to have an event, even as the street requires the media to exist in a global arena."[52]

Memory

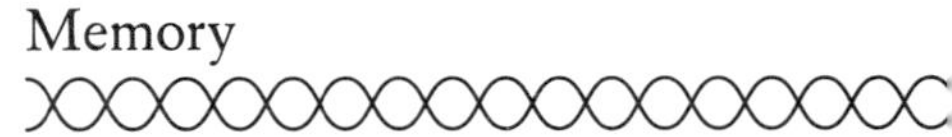

Reports on political protests in the media extend the embodied performances on the street. In addition, reports form an entry point to the stabilized memory of the "archive": the vast collection of supposedly unchangeable records including texts, pictures, buildings, and artefacts. Taylor, though, stresses that cultural memory is constituted not just by the institutionalized knowledge of the archive, but also the embodied knowledge of the "repertoire," comprised of reiterative practices, acts, rituals, and performances.[53] Both the repertoire and the archive are "in a constant state of interaction" and subject to change.[54] What enables the movement of embodied social knowledge from repertoire to the archive and back again is in her view, the scenario. Its compact form makes it suitable for transfer and adaptation to new situations.

The embodied performance of an effigy protest enters the media in the form of reports and photographs, condensed descriptions of the performance that are forms of the scenario. Reading, listening, and watching a report becomes the experience and memory for distant audiences. The protest is relayed to their memory through the scenario. On the one hand, the media are the extended space of embodied protest and the reports are one form in which the protest is experienced. On the other hand, mediation transposes the event into a stable medium: a text or an image. In that sense, the media are part of the archive, albeit less stable than institutionalized forms of the archive, like the library, the museum, or the canon of political ritual. The news media might be characterized as intermediary storage spaces continually in flux, containing reports that are being written, re-written, partly discarded, and partly solidified as social memory. In the creation of social memory, mediating scenarios is crucial

53   Taylor, *The Archive and the Repertoire*, 19–20.

54   Taylor, *The Archive and the Repertoire*, 21.

55 Taylor, *Performance*, 139.

56 Taylor, *The Archive and the Repertoire*, 28–29.

57 Caroline van Eck, *Art, Agency and Living Presence* (Leiden: Leiden University Press, 2015), 32–35.

58 Rosalind Krauss, "... and then Turn Away? An Essay on James Coleman," *October* 81 (1997): 10.

59 Gotthold Ephraim Lessing writes on the need for the artist to depict the decisive moment of a dramatic occurrence. Gotthold Ephraim Lessing, *Laokoon oder Über die Grenzen der Malerei und Poesie* (Urbana, IL: Project Gutenberg, 2004), 21.

to moving from embodiment to archive.

The scenario of protest is retrieved from embodied memory, re-enacted in the performance of protest, mediated by the media, and rewritten into the archive not as a copy, but as a reinterpretation.[55] A given scenario is always adapted for a specific occasion. Due to its generality, the scenario allows for considerable improvisation and elaboration, in response to context, actors, conflict, etc. While the scenario remains the same, each effigy performance varies in form, mood, social and political configuration, meaning, and effect.[56] Even though the media report on specific events, their descriptions point back to the general scenario and inscribe it into the archive.

The form in which the scenario is inscribed is often just a photograph or short sentence about the protest in a news report: a snapshot in an ongoing conflict even more compressed than a scenario. An effigy protest conjures up the image of a burning figure surrounded by agitated protesters demanding justice. This image is not necessarily based on the memory of an actual single photograph, but is rather a vivid mental image distilled from multiple reports and/or photographs.[57] Art historian Caroline van Eck describes the close relation and interaction between metaphor, ekphrasis (description of images), mental images and memory based on texts from ancient Greek rhetoric and philosophy. And also Rosalind Krauss evokes the link between photographic image and collective memory by citing photographer Gisèle Freund: "It's always the still image and not the one in motion that stays etched in our minds, becoming ever after part of our collective memory."[58]

I would argue that the whole practice of burning effigies as the expression of political protest can be compressed into a single iconic and formulaic image.[59] Like the scenario, this

---

President Harrison was burned by the Union League at Jeffersonville on account of a post office appointment.
—*The Columbus Journal*, NE, 27 Nov 1889

1889_11_13_USA: President Harrison

In East Beirut, Christians hanged Syrian President Hafez al-Assad in effigy, pinning a sign on the dummy reading: "Death to Syria."
—*New Strait Times*, Malaysia, 27 Mar 1989

1989_03_26_Lebanon: Syrian President Assad

mental image includes the basic structure and narrative, social setting, and emotional charge. For instance, the 19th century engraving showing an effigy of New Hampshire's stamp master Meserve on a pole, a few stones in the air, and a group of revolutionaries cheering on the performance.○ Many news photographers would probably be inclined to take a picture of that moment, when all elements combine to match the mental image: an assembled crowd in a public space, acting together, expressing their shared emotions in a symbolic gesture of punishment.

This formulaic image compressed in the scenario falls under art historian Aby Warburg's *pathos formula,* which philosopher Giorgio Agamben defines as the "indissoluble intertwining of emotional charge and an iconographic formula in which it is impossible to distinguish between form and content."[60] Warburg searched for shared expressions of heightened emotions in Renaissance art and Renaissance *Festwesen* (culture of celebrations), finding them in the formulaic images of bodily gestures that Renaissance artists recuperated from art from antiquity. In Warburg's view pathos formulas are the vehicles of our collective memory.[61] Visual culture theorist W. J. T. Mitchell describes them as film stills, "snapshots of emotional life, that have left the image behind as a clue."[62] The images of effigy protests, pathos formulas of protest, transmit the scenario of the performance and a complex interplay of emotions related to the outrage over injustice. They show a perpetrator being punished as a communal action and the relief following the cathartic resolution. Even if few photographs of these protests precisely match this iconic image, most conjure it.

A characteristic of pathos formulas is the ability to travel. Even more compressed than scenarios, they can survive multiple moves across cultural spheres,[63] and can adapt to various

83

60 Giorgio Agamben, *Potentialities: Collected Essays in Philosophy,* trans. Daniel Heller-Roazen (Stanford: Stanford University Press, 1999), 90.

61 Kurt W. Forster, "Introduction," in Aby Warburg, *The Renewal of Pagan Antiquity: Contributions to the Cultural History of the European Renaissance* (Los Angeles: Getty Research Institute, 1999), 36.

62 W. J. T. Mitchell, "Method, Madness, Montage: Aby Warburg to John Nash," lecture at the Warburg Institute, London, November 4, 2016, www.youtube.com/user/WarburgInstitute/videos.

63 Gertrude Bing, "Vorwort," in Aby Warburg, *Gesammelte Schriften,* ed. Gertrude Bing (Berlin: G. B. Teubner, 1932), xii.

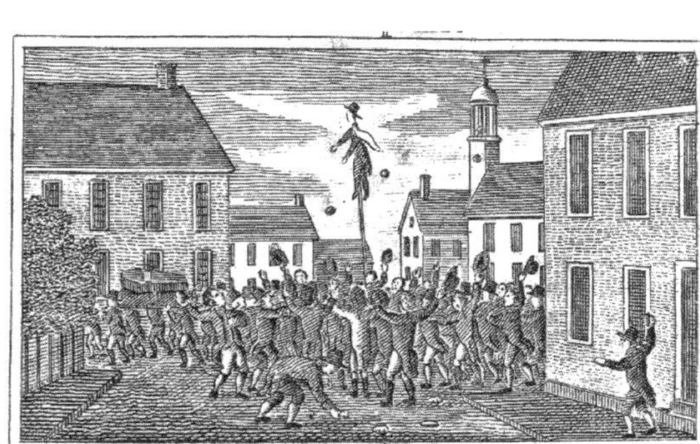

○ 1765_09_12_USA-NH: stamp master Meserve

64 Bredekamp, *Theorie des Bildakts*, 298.

65 Taylor, *The Archive and the Repertoire*, 20–26.

66 Georges Didi-Huberman, *Uprisings*, (Paris: Jeu de Paume, 2016), 304.

contexts.[64] The practice of hanging or burning effigies as a theatrical form of political protest, transmitted through its images, has crossed over from traditional ritual practices to contemporary politics. As shown in the following chapters, it has traversed cultural borders, from European ritual to Philippine politics, British political ritual to Middle-Eastern counter-protests, Shia mourning rituals to international politics. Each time, the practice is reactivated, reinvented, and re-inscribed with a new context-specific meaning. Nevertheless, its basic structure and emotional effect remains intact, surviving manifold iterations in local communities as well as globally mediated conflicts. The scenario of a ritual-like performance that expresses communal outrage is part of a repertoire shared across time and cultures, that can be activated, as Taylor suggests, to imagine and embody alternatives to the existing order.[65]

Warburg collected examples of pathos formulas in the *Mnemosyne Atlas*, described in the introduction. In the *Atlas*, the contours of the pathos formulas of triumph, of destruction, of suffering, and of grief, become visible. While other pathos formulas also appear, though less clearly, a pathos formula of protest, as art historian Georges Didi-Huberman remarks, appears to be surprisingly absent.[66] In 2016, Didi-Huberman attempted to capture the pathos formulas of protest in the exhibition *Uprisings* at the Jeu de Paume in Paris, where he assembled hundreds of images that show gestures of uprising. Designed as a research tool, the images are arranged in a vast montage in the spirit of Warburg's *Atlas*. In the catalog, Didi-Huberman asks:

> How do images draw so often from our memories in order to give shape to our desires for emancipation? And how does a poetic dimension manage to be created in the

very heart of our gestures of uprising and *as a gesture of uprising?*[67]

Effigy protest belongs, I believe, to these gestures of uprising. But, as it will become clear in the following chapters, it is too simple to associate them only with resistance. As a symbolic visual form, it is too ambiguous in its semantics to claim it as a gesture of a specific progressive political form. In chapters 7 and 8, I investigate how desires and imaginaries are articulated in the gestures and images of effigy performances, and how their specific grotesque appearance relates both to violence and laughter. First, however, I trace the genealogies of effigy protests in a number of countries to detail how effigy protests are situated in specific political constellations and how they affect them.

67 Georges Didi-Huberman, "Introduction," *Uprisings* (Paris: Jeu de Paume, 2016), 17–20 (italics in the original).

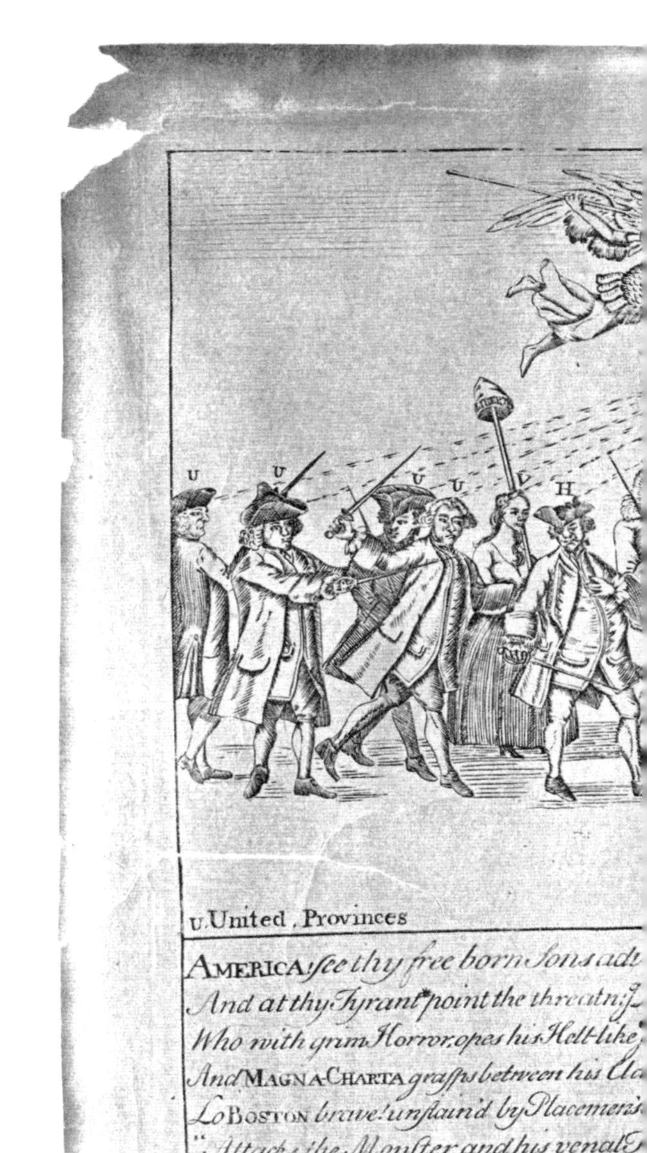

u. United, Provinces

AMERICA see thy free born Sons adt
And at thy Tyrant point the threatn'
Who with grim Horror opes his Hell-like
And MAGNA CHARTA grasps between his Cla
Lo BOSTON brave! unstain'd by Placemens
"Attacks the Monster and his venal
See loyal HAMPDEN to his Country true.
Presents his Weapon to the odious Cren
* Stamp Act

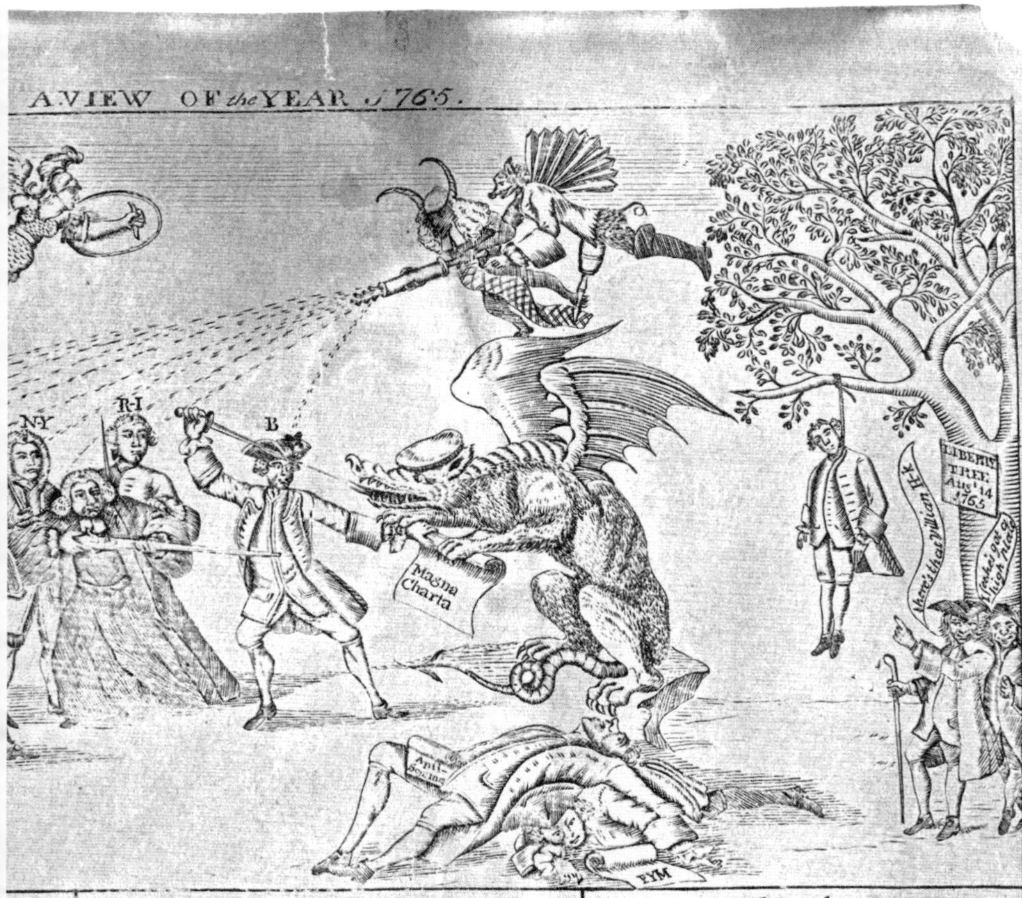
A VIEW OF the YEAR 1765.
NY
R-I
B
Magna Charta
Anti Sejanus
PYM
LIBERTY TREE Aug.t 14 1765
Here's that Villian H-k
Vengeance on Hugh Piece
See 'fore him prostrate treacherous PYM doth fall
And A-Sejanus loud for Mercy call!
Whilst brave RHODE-ISLAND, & NEW YORK support,
HAMPDEN and FREEDOM, in their brave Effort:
Front to VIRGINIA, bold NEW-HAMPSHIRE stands,
All firmly sworn to shake off slavish Bands
And each united Province faithful joins
Against this Monster and his curst Designs
Mounted aloft perfidious H—k you see,
Scorn'd by his Country, fits the Rope & Tree;
This be the real Fate! a fittest Place
For Freedoms Foes a selfish scornful Race:
"Above behold where Spite & Envy squirt,
Their Venom on the Heads they cannot hurt,"
But lo Minerva with her Spear and shield
Appears with Hopes to make the Harpies yield
Engrav'd Printed & Sold by P. Revere. BOSTON

Effigy Protests in the History of the United States

In the United States, the practice of hanging and burning effigies to express political positions dates back to before the American Revolution to the protests against the 1765 Stamp Act. The Stamp Act levied a tax on printed documents of all kinds, legal documents, newspapers, pamphlets, even playing cards. It had to be paid by purchasing stamps that had to be affixed to these products – hence the Stamp Act. Some people saw a lucrative job for themselves as newly appointed stamp master, but most colonists didn't approve. Besides being a burden on the cash-strapped economy, they feared that it would just be the first of many other taxes to come and give the British government a tighter grip on internal affairs of the colonies. Furthermore, they hadn't been consulted about it, and considered it a dangerous overreach of the British parliament, a denial of their rights as Englishmen under the Bill of Rights 1689. "No taxation without consultation" became one of the slogans of the growing resistance.

The New England colonies had started to develop a shared identity. British colonial policies and other matters of common concern, were widely discussed in person – on

1 "News in the Age of Revolution," American Antiquarian Society (website), accessed Aug 8, 2020, americanantiquarian.org/earlyamericannewsmedia/exhibits/show/age-of-revolution.

street corners, in coffee houses, and church gatherings — and were disseminated through dispatches and letters, as well as in printed form in broadsides and the growing number of newspapers.[1] The Stamp Act for the first time introduced a direct tax on the colonies, and the colonists had to say a lot about it.

Most newspapers, which were directly affected by the new tax on printed matter, supported the revolution, rapidly spreading news of protests against the Stamp Act and the effigy performances featured within them. As a result, the hanging and burning of effigies became an important imaginative trope in the narrative of the revolution, and, subsequently, an accepted form of protest in partisan politics up to the present day, evidenced by frequent sightings of effigies of George W. Bush, Barack Obama, and Donald Trump over the past two decades. With this long continuous history of public political expression, the US provides a unique case study with which to examine how this ephemeral political practice developed; this chapter looks into the traditions underlying effigy protests, how they change over time, and how they are used in political conflicts, within the laboratory of one country over an extended period.

In the US, this form of protest can be traced back to two traditional effigy practices appropriated and adapted by the American revolutionaries: common practices of popular justice (rough music) and the carnivalesque festivities of Pope Day celebrations imported by colonists from Great Britain. From the early revolutionary events, effigy protests continued to be enacted and re-enacted, and acquired their own iconography in the political culture of the US. In reviewing this form of protest's establishment within different conflicts and power matrices, it becomes clear that it has been adapted to competing causes when it comes to partisan politics, labor issues, court cases, conflicts with foreign countries, and civil rights issues. Reconstructing the practice's articulations over time, shows its function with respect to power and competing notions of justice. Carefully considering the politics of each event and analyzing the effects on the communities reveals how effigy protests exemplify a core conflict in liberal democracies: popular sovereignty vs. individual civil rights.

Revolutionary Rough Music

On August 14, 1765, an effigy of newly appointed Massachusetts stamp master Andrew Oliver was found hanging from a tree in the center of Boston.○ Over the course of the day, a crowd assembled around the tree and grew to about 3,000. Agitators against the Stamp Act, who called themselves "Sons of Liberty," entertained the crowd with speeches and theatrical acts preventing the sheriff from cutting the Oliver effigy down, until the end of the day when they did so

91

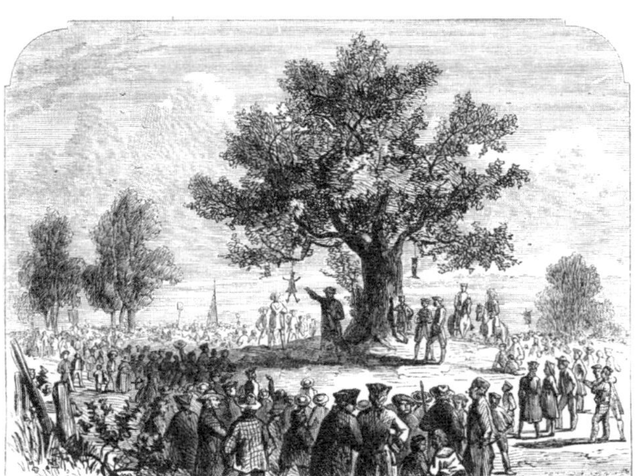

○ 1765_08_14_USA-MA: stamp master Oliver

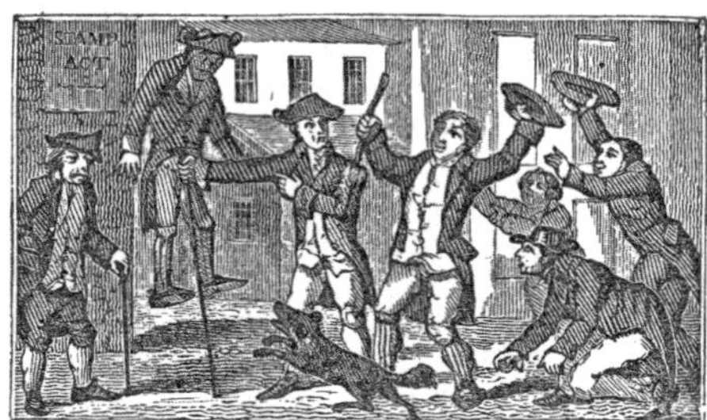

1765_08_00_USA-MA: Tory

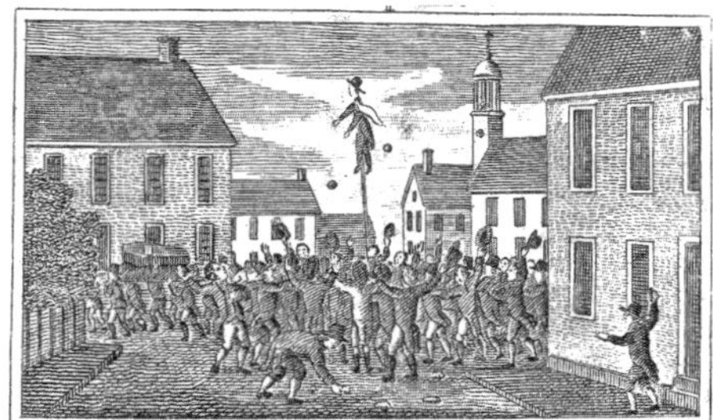

1765_09_12_USA-NH: stamp master Meserve

2 R. S. Longley, "Mob Activities in Revolutionary Massachusetts," *The New England Quarterly* 6, no. 1 (1933): 109.

3 A couple of years later, during a brief British occupation of Boston during the war, the British army cut the tree down and sold it as firewood.

4 *Boston Gazette*, August 19, 1765; *Boston Evening-Post*, August 19, 1765.

5 See chapter 1, "Double Bodies."

6 "Tarring and feathering" was considered an American invention, "a modern method of punishment." "Mob Activities," 112.

7 Longley, "Mob Activities," 114–15.

themselves. They nailed the effigy to a plank and marched the effigy to the newly built Stamp Office in the harbor. The mob leveled the office in thirty minutes, took the timber, and went to Oliver's house where they sawed off the effigy's head. They continued to an open area at Fort Hill, built a bonfire with office timber and set the effigy ablaze. Afterwards, they went back to ransack Oliver's house and tear down his fences.[2] The mob kept looking for Oliver until around midnight, when they quieted down and dispersed. The next day Oliver resigned as stamp master. This was the first open protest against the Stamp Act that ultimately led to the American Revolution. The tree came to be known as the liberty tree.[3] The protest was reported in detail by the *Boston Gazette* and the *Boston Evening-Post*,[4] which were widely read also in other colonies, rapidly spreading the fire of burning effigies.

The 1765 effigy burning in Boston – and the many that followed – was not invented during the anti-Stamp Act protests. The form was appropriated for political purposes from practices of popular justice, called "rough music."[5] In the US, rough music was rather violent as its variations could also include the demolition of property, carrying the victim on a pole, tarring and feathering, and other physical abuse.[6] While

92

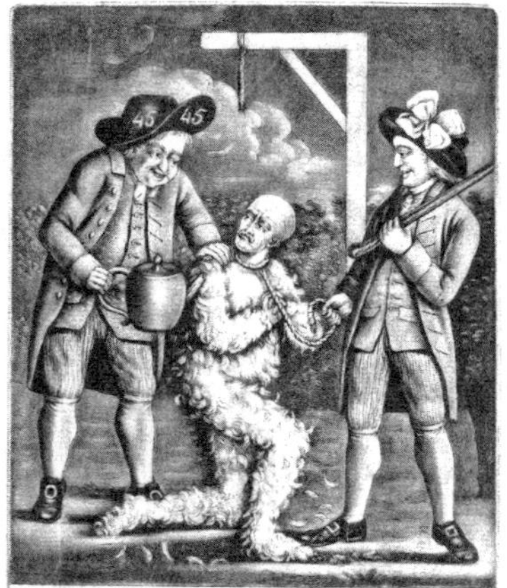

revolutionary mob practices: tar and feather

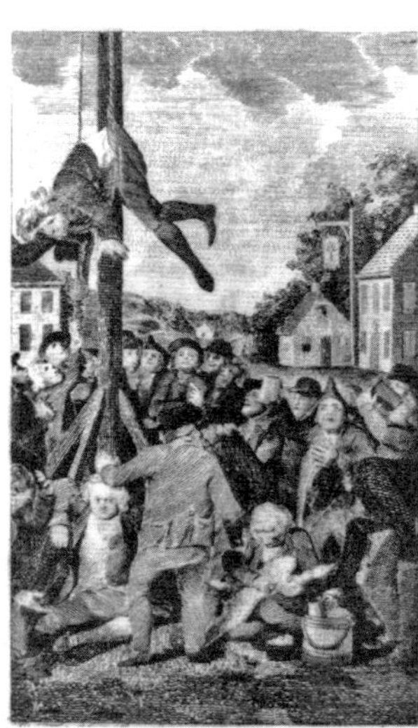

revolutionary mob practices: "The Tory's Day of Judgement"

After the tar and feathers had been administered, the victim was usually carted about the town. This provided an evening's entertainment for the mob, and never failed to draw a large audience.... Another favorite punishment for tories was the swing at the Liberty Pole. One end of a rope was fastened around the victim, the other thrown over the top of the Pole.

Then upwards, all hands hoisting sail
They swung him, like a keg of ale,
'Till to the pinnacle so fair
He rose like meteor in the air.[7]

revolutionary mob practices

parading, ridiculing, and executing a perpetrator's effigy is a symbolic form of punishment, it nevertheless includes a threat of further violence. Beyond punishing and shaming the targeted individual, these practices affect the larger community, coercing all members to abide by the rules. Rough music as the assertion of common law and upholding of communal values is usually driven by a populist, conservative position, which holds the established order and the interests of the dominant group in the community above the interests or rights of an individual, any other group, or system of law. It is usually employed to enforce traditional values and prevent change in the social order. In the protests against the Stamp Act, activists appropriated these conservative practices in order to change the political status quo.

Some cases of political effigy performances in the US still include the musical element that gave rough music its name. An article from September 14, 1861 in the New York newspaper *The Weekly Sun* reads: "Hon. Nathan Bristol, ex-Senator, …, well known for his secession proclivities, was waited on last night and treated with a serenade. The music consisted of a horse fiddle, tin pans etc. He was burned in effigy, and afterwards buried in the graveyard."[8]

93

8 "Another Candidate for Fort Lafayette," *Weekly Sun*, September 14, 1861.

9 Longley, "Mob Activities," 119.

10 Longley, "Mob Activities," 116.

11 Longley, "Mob Activities," 121.

The attack was first made upon the Marlborough merchant, Henry Barnes. On June 10, the mob, led by a youth who had been trained in the Boston affairs, destroying his carriage, and threw the cushions into a brook. Later they robbed his wagons for goods, tarred and feathered his horse, and turned it loose on the streets carrying on its back an effigy of its owner made from his wagon cover.[9]

1771_06_10_USA-MA: merchant Barnes

While the mob persecuted the informers, the radical leaders turned their attention to the importing merchants. Their names were posted in the newspapers, and prospective customers were warned away from their stores by effigies placed in front of the doorways. But before further persecution could be carried out, the ire of the mob was again aroused by the customs officials, and through them against the soldiers.[10]

1769_00_00_USA-MA: merchants

The most famous of all Boston's pre-war mobs was, of course, the Boston Tea Party. But it was not, as is sometimes assumed, an isolated or unusual phenomenon. It was but the greatest of many such expressions of mob violence, and was organised by the same radicals who had resisted the Stamp Act... . The Tea mob was carefully disguised. Some were dressed as Narragansett Indians with copper-coloured countenances and clothed in blankets. Others merely covered their faces with smut, and looked more like devils from the bottomless pit than men.[11]

revolutionary mob practices: 1773_12_16_Boston, USA

Less explicitly referencing the traditions of rough music – of shaming an individual – was a more recent event in the 2008 US elections. In reaction to the display of a Sarah Palin effigy as a Halloween decoration on a house in California, Palin sympathizers picketed in front of the house and unfurled big banners to obstruct the view. They set up an effigy of the effigy-maker with the inscription "Chad, how does it feel?" on a truck outside the property to shame him, giving him the uncomfortable experience of being hanged in effigy.

94

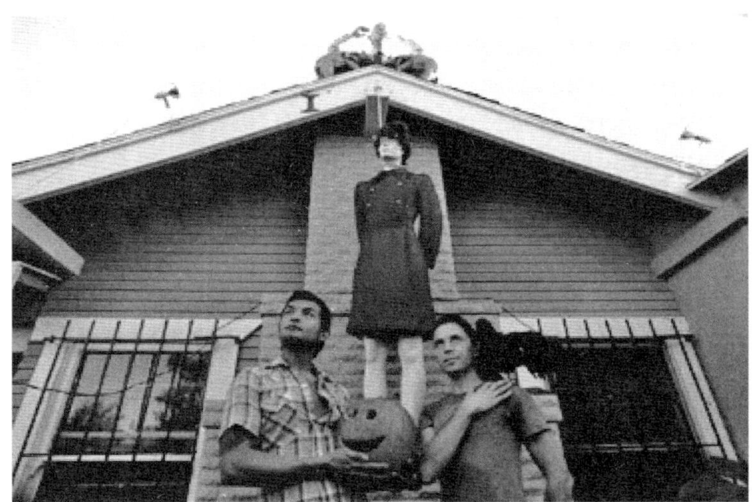
2008_10_29_USA-CA: Sarah Palin

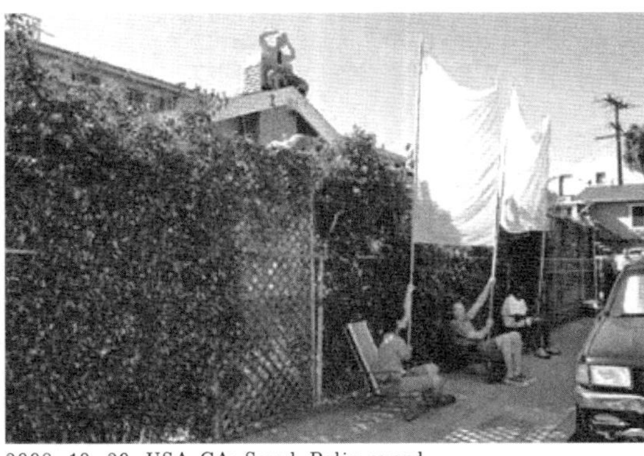
2008_10_29_USA-CA: Sarah Palin guard

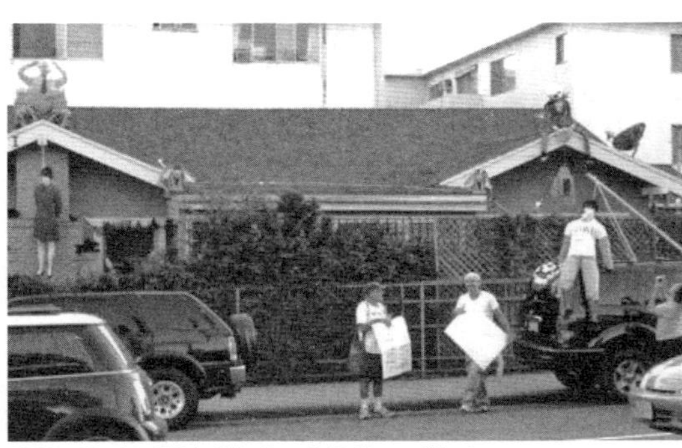
2008_10_31_USA-CA: Sarah Palin + Chad

Pope Day Appropriation

Some 1760's Stamp Act protests were complex theatrical performances that resembled the traditional British holiday involving bonfires and the burning of effigies known as Guy Fawkes Day celebrated on the 5th of November. The practice dates back to 1605, when a group of Catholic conspirators tried to blow up the parliament in London and kill King James I. Key conspirator Guy Fawkes was captured next to the gunpowder barrels smuggled into the cellars under the building, and was executed together with his co-conspirators. One year later, Parliament declared a national holiday to celebrate the King's miraculous rescue with parades and bonfires, an event still celebrated today in the United Kingdom and some of its former colonies. In New England, it was known under the name Pope Day and celebrated with processions featuring floats with elaborate pictorial programs and animated effigies of the pope, the devil, and other enemies of the crown, which were burned at the end of the procession.[12]

These raucous celebrations were full of grotesque imagery, carnivalesque reversal of order, and mocking performances,[13] regularly used to foment anti-Catholic sentiments in times of social and political conflicts. Mostly attended by the lower classes, they often turned riotous and violent, providing an opportunity to express discontent toward the

95

12   The first Pope Day celebration in Boston was in 1685. Jack Tager, *Boston Riots: Three Centuries of Social Violence* (Boston: Northeastern University Press, 2001), 45.

13   I discuss effigy protests in relation to Mikhail Bakhtin's concept of the carnivalesque in chapter 7, "Violence and Laughter."

14   Samuel Drake, The history and antiquities of Boston: from its settlement in 1630 to the year 1770 (Boston: Luther Stevens, 1856), 662.

An imposing pageant was carried along with the procession. It consisted of a figure, or figures, upon a platform, or stage, mounted upon wheels, and drawn by horses. On the front part of the stage a lantern was elevated some six or eight feet, constructed with transparent paper, upon which were inscriptions, suited to the occasion; usually significant of some obnoxious political characters of the day. The Pretender, on a gibbet, stood next the lantern, and in the centre of the platform stood the Pope, grotesquely attired, exhibiting a corresponding corpulency. In the rear stood a devil, with a superabundance of tail, with a trident in one hand, and a dark lantern in the other. Under the platform were placed boys, or persons of small size, who, with rods which extended up through the figures, caused them to perform certain motions with their heads, — as making them face to the right or left, according to circumstances, or rise up as though to look into chamber windows.[14]

Pope Day: 1762_Boston, USA-MA

15   Tager, *Boston Riots*, 41.

16   Longley, "Mob Activities," 102.

17   Tager, *Boston Riots*, 50.

18   Longley, "Mob Activities," 109.

19   Sherwood Collins, "Boston's Political Street Theatre: The Eighteenth-Century Pope Day Pageants," *Educational Theatre Journal* 25, no. 4 (1973): 408.

20   Tager, *Boston Riots*, 50.

21   Longley, "Mob Activities," 116–17.

elites.[15] Boston's Pope Day was especially tumultuous, with the North End and South End developing an intense rivalry in the 1740s.[16] Each neighborhood formed their own festival society, constructed an elaborate float with effigies of the pope and devil, and marched it from opposite sides to the bonfire site. Meeting in the middle, the groups engaged in a fierce battle to capture the rivals' float and thereby gain the right to burn the effigies. By the early 1760s, Pope Day had morphed into an annual ritual of violence. The holiday elicited the scorn of the local elites, but the authorities, fearing the backlash, were unable to prohibit it.

After the introduction of the Stamp Act in 1764, Pope Day was appropriated as an anti-British protest.[17] In Boston, the leaders of the North and South End mobs were recruited to lead the protests against the Stamp Act.[18] In years that followed, a row of perceived traitors to the patriot cause were burned alongside effigies of the pope and devil.[19] After independence, though, it seemed thoroughly inappropriate to celebrate the survival of a British monarch and in 1774 the last Pope Day in Boston was celebrated as Union Pope Day.[20] Nevertheless, the theatrical style and set-up of the Pope Day performance continued to be used in political demonstrations, as we see in 1780 on the occasion of the burning in effigy of traitor Benedict Arnold, a general in the Continental American Army who defected to the British.

96

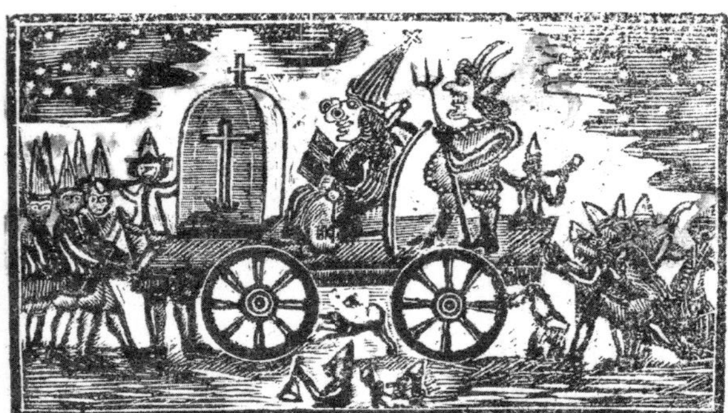

Pope Day: 1768_Boston, USA-MA

As the procession passed one of the shops, John Mein, who had rendered himself obnoxious to the radicals by his publications, and who had become involved in an altercation with some of them, fired a pistol into the crowd and wounded a soldier of the 47th regiment. A warrant was issued for Mein's arrest, but he could not be found. The following week, Pope Day was turned into a persecution of Mein, in an effort to drive him from the province. His effigy replaced that of the Pope in the usual parade. A label of the effigy announced, "Mean is the man, M—n is his name."[21]

1769_11_05_USA-MA: John Mein

The burning of Benedict Arnold's effigy followed the scenario of Pope Day pageants, with effigies of Arnold and the devil paraded on a horse-cart.○ The float presented a detailed visual narrative: Arnold's effigy holds a mask and reveals his double face beneath, the devil carries a purse with money offered to Arnold in one hand and raises his pitchfork, ready to take Arnold to hell. The pictorial program emphasizes the crime of treason and Arnold's duplicity. The dishonorable crime of treason was punished with an equally dishonorable display of his effigy. The performance combined entertainment, political statement, and ritual. Anthropologist Catherine Bell explains that political rituals construct power by "depict[ing] a group of people as a coherent and ordered community based on shared values and goals" and demonstrating the legitimacy of that order through the participation in the ritual.[22] The revolutionaries appropriated the established ritual of Pope Day pageants as well as rituals of formal justice to demonstrate the newly established power relations; that is, the burning of Arnold's effigy was a display of the emerging political order.

22 Catherine Bell, *Ritual: Perspectives and Dimensions* (Oxford: Oxford University Press, 1997), 129.

23 Samuel Hazard, ed., The *Register of Pennsylvania* (Philadelphia: W.F. Geddes, 1828), 286.

97

A Stage raised on the body of a cart, on which was an effigy of General Arnold sitting: this was dressed in regimentals, had two faces, emblematical of his traitorous conduct, a mask in his left hand, and a letter in his right from Belzebub, telling him that he had done all the mischief he could do, and now must hang himself.

At the back of the General was the figure of the Devil, dressed in black robes, shaking a purse of money at the General's left ear, and in his right hand a pitch-fork ready to drive him into hell as the reward due for the many crimes which his thirst of gold had made him commit.

In the front of the stage and before General Arnold, was placed a large lantern of transparent paper, with the consequences of his crimes thus delineated. (i.e.) on one part General Arnold on his knees before the Devil, who is pulling him into the flames — a label from the General's mouth with these words — "My dear sir, I have served you faithfully;" to which the Devil replies; "And I'll reward you."
...
"The effigy of this ingrate is therefore hanged, (for want of his body) as a Traitor to his native country, and a Betrayer of the laws of honour." ...

The procession was attended with a numerous concourse of people, who after expressing their abhorrence of the Treason and the Traitor, committed him to the flames, and left both the effigy and the original to sink into ashes and oblivion.[23]

1780_09_30_USA-PA: General Arnold

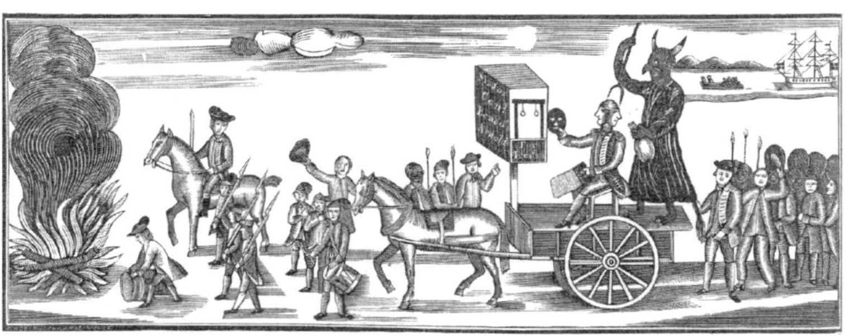

○ 1780_09_30_USA-PA: General Arnold

Between Affirmation and Contestation

Traditional effigy practices from popular justice and Pope Day celebrations were appropriated for political protests. The performance of popular justice was a semi-staged outburst of communal disapproval – improvised, fluid and prone to violent excesses, and used to coerce individuals or minority groups in the community by the threat of violence. The effigy performances of Pope Day were elaborate entertainments for the attending public geared toward celebrating communal values and identity. While these practices differed in style and formations of power, their scenarios were similar. This allowed for the mixing of both forms, combining threatening political opponents with celebrating community in various degrees. But even in some much later examples, their distinctive semantic emphases – on either coercion or community celebration – are clearly expressed, as I will show later in this chapter.

Stamp Act protest victims included stamp masters, officials in the colonial administration, merchants who refused to boycott the Stamp Act, and British Loyalists. The mob paraded their effigies, often congregating in front of the targeted's house. The effigies were ridiculed, beaten, hanged, and eventually burned, but the violence was often not limited to the representations. The targets of the mob's wrath were threatened and assaulted. Some victims were paraded through the streets in person, carried on poles, and dumped at the edge of town.[24] Some were tarred and feathered, maltreated, their property demolished, and their houses burnt

---

Whereas the infamous Nathanial Rogers, one of the Boston IMPORTERS, took a Journey to New York, and being arrived there, the Sons of Liberty had Intelligence of it, and assembling together carried his Effigy through the principal Streets of that City. Therefore he thinking it is unsafe to abide there any longer, speedily made his Escape and came to the East End of Long Island, and being on Shelter-Island, the Sons of Liberty there having Intelligence by a son of Liberty from New York, who he was, and the Reason of his precipitate Flight from thence – made his Effigy, which stood exposed to the Derision and Contempt of a Number of Spectators; then they fixed it upon a Pole, and carted it around by the principal Houses, (having this label on it's Breast, in Capitals, NATHANIEL ROGERS, one of the infamous Boston Importers).
—*Boston Gazette*, 11 Jun 1770

1770_06_01_USA-NY: merchant Rogers

down.[25] On the Bahaman island New Providence a mob forced the local stamp distributer into a coffin and proceeded to bury him alive until he signed his resignation.[26] In the early years of the American Revolution, numerous effigies were hanged and burned, causing loyalists to flee or accept change.[27]

With the start of the Revolutionary War for independence in 1776, as the political struggle was moved to the battlefield and corpses started piling up, the effigy burnings seem to have decreased.[28] After the war, the practice was revived in political disputes, as in 1794, when Chief Justice John Jay was hanged and burned in effigy as a traitor all over New England for negotiating an unfavorable treaty over trade and shipping rights with Great Britain.[29] During the revolution, the mob was instrumental in challenging British rule, and in the long century afterwards, groups from all corners of society mobilized their supporters to display their political clout.[30]

Collective action and manifestations in the streets continued to shape public life in the young US. Parades and demonstrations were important communication tools in the public sphere. From the revolutionary beginnings in anti-loyalist riots and rough music folk practices, parades developed in a number of styles that reflected the social, economic, and political position of the social groups that participated. In

25 Longley, "Mob Activities," 114–30.

26 *Boston Evening-Post*, October 21, 1765, The Annotated Newspapers of Harbottle Dorr, Massachusetts Historical Society, www.massh-ist.org/dorr/volume/1/sequence/247.

27 Longley, "Mob Activities," 128.

28 Longley, "Mob Activities," 128–29.

29 Albrecht Koschnik, "Political Conflict and Public Contest: Rituals of National Celebration in Philadelphia 1788–1815," *Pennsylvania Magazine of History and Biography* 118, no. 3 (1994): 230–33.

30 Longley, "Mob Activities," 104–5.

99

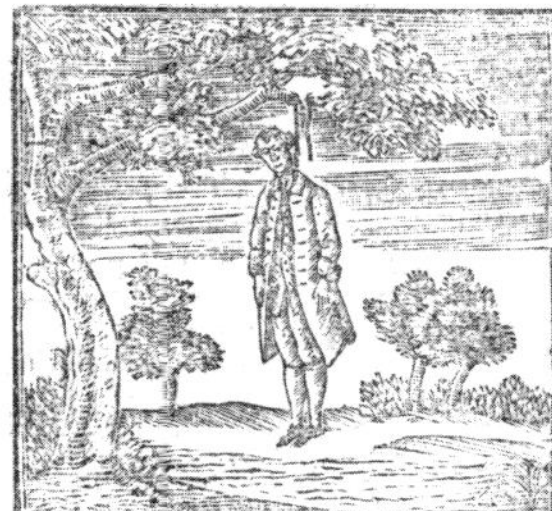
1775_04_00_USA-NY: publisher Rivingtor.

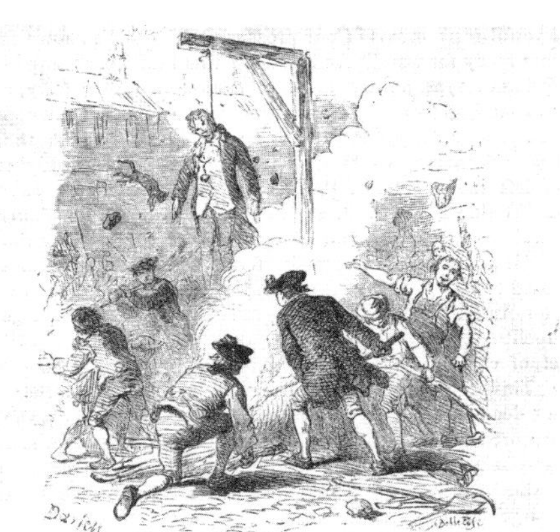

1795_08_00_USA: Chief Justice Jay

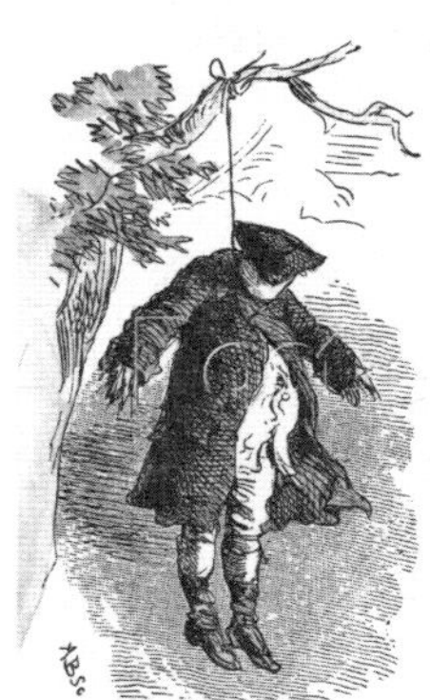
1774_00_00_USA-MA: Governor Hutchinson

31 Susan G. Davis, *Parades and Power, Street Theatre in Nineteenth-Century Philadelphia* (Philadelphia: Temple University Press, 1986), 19.

32 Koschnik, "Political Conflict," 212.

33 See the analysis of the *New York Times* archive in Göttke, *Burning Images: Performing Effigies as Political Protest*, 313–4.

post-revolution Philadelphia, between 1790 and 1860, the elaborate and well-funded parades of the official militias, which were recruited from the wealthy section of society, were countered and mocked by burlesque marches of the working class. "Respectability" of the powerful establishment set the standard of conduct against which the "rowdiness" of the growing group of disenfranchised workers was contrasted, those who tried to gain influence by organizing collective action.[31] Historian Albrecht Koschnik confirms that "crowd action – with its associated tactics and ritual, such as effigy processions and bonfires – was a legitimate institution."[32] The burning of effigies as a theatrical performance to publicly press on political issues had become an established form in US politics.

An analysis of the *New York Times* online archive shows that many different kinds of conflict took to the streets, and the use of effigy protests were not tied to one side of the political spectrum.[33] Political issues on all levels – local, state, and national – were disputed with effigy protests throughout US history. Sometimes demonstrations were organized by one or another party to denounce opponents. At other times constituents would hang and burn their representatives as traitors for supporting the "wrong" cause. While these performances often led to outbursts in the press affiliated with the targeted party, they usually did not hurt the career of the depicted. They had become an accepted form of expressing political positions. Some conflicts addressed with effigy protests stand out: labor issues, since the mid-nineteenth century; military conflicts with foreign countries; controversial rulings in criminal trials; and the abolition of slavery, later desegregation and civil rights. All were especially relevant to the societal development and the political identity in the US as described in the following paragraphs.

Outrage! We are informed that a party of Whigs, on Sunday morning last, hung Mr. Montgomery, the Democratic Republican Candidate elect from this District, in effigy, at Chapel Hill. Commentary is unnecessary.
—*North-Carolina Standard*, Raleigh, 16 Aug 1837

1837_08_13_USA-NC: Mr. Montgomery

John P. St. John was burned in effigy here tonight, and such wild scenes were enacted as never before were witnessed in Topeka. Fully 3000 men and boys watched the image of St. John go up in flames from a telegraph pole in front of the Western Union telegraph office. Capt. P. H. Conrey made a short speech, declaring St. John had violated every trust and confidence of the people of Kansas, and that the State should be cleared of his name.
—*Memphis Daily Appeal*, TN, 7 Nov 1884

1884_11_06_USA-KA: John St.John

At Rockwood, Tenn., State Senator D. R. Nelson and Representative I. A. Dail were burned in effigy by the citizens, who were angry at some vote of the legislators. Images were fastened to a mule and a parade was made, after which a hanging and burning took place.
—*New York Times*, 7 Apr 1889

1889_04_06_USA-TN: Sen Nelson + Rep Dale

The Buffalo Courier very truly says: "Our political history discloses the curious fact, that no individual has been burnt in effigy in this country for any act he may have committed as a public man, who's popularity has not been materially increased by the operation." The Courier continues: "Burning in effigy has been a common affair since the organisation of the government. In 1776, George Washington, Patrick Henry, and John Hancock were burnt in effigy in the streets of our cities. In 1800, thomas Jefferson was burnt in effigy, because he advocated the rights of the people and opposed the property qualification of voters. In 1812. James Madison was burned in effigy, because he advocated the war with England, which secured to American seamen their rights. In 1836, Andrew Jackson was burnt in effigy, because he crushed the famous swindling called the "United States Bank," and beat the British at New Orleans in 1814. In 1846, George M. Dallas was burned in effigy, because he voted for the people's tariff, which is now in operation, and which did not make the grass grow in the middle of the streets of our cities, as many of the croakers predicted it would."
—*Nashville Union and American*, TN, 28 Apr 1854

effects of effigy burning

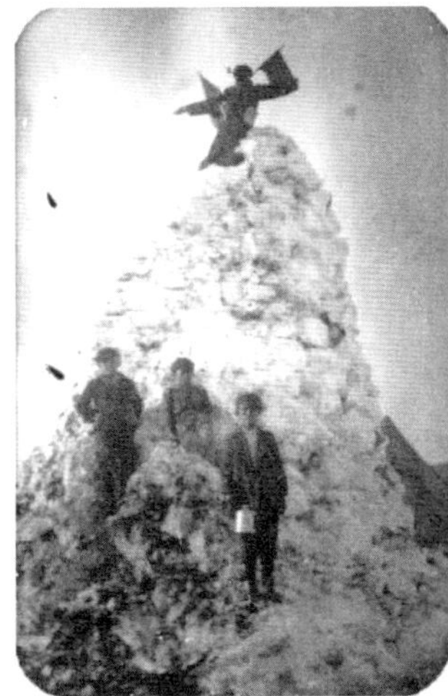

1914_00_00_USA-CO: mine owner

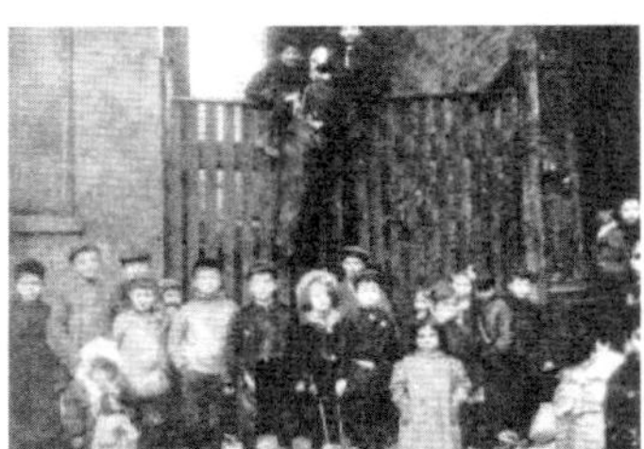

1907_12_27_USA-NY: landlord (rent-strike)

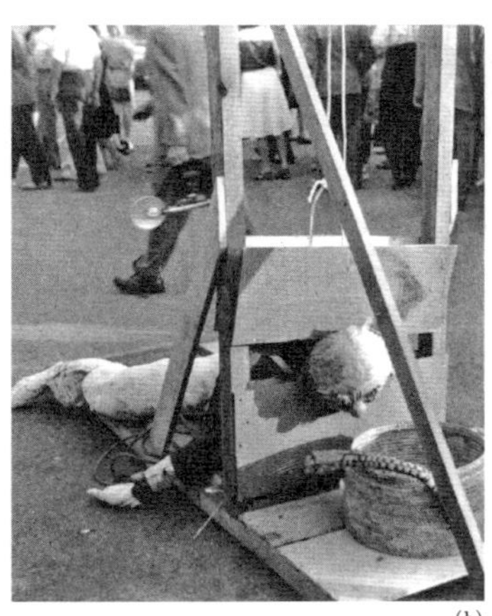

(b)

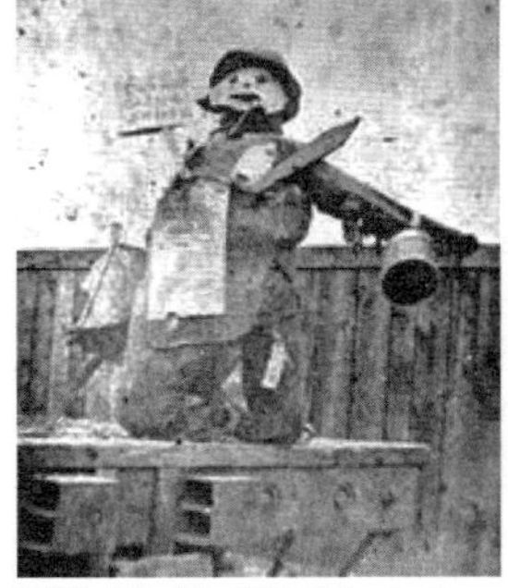

1892_00_00_USA-PA: steel factory manager

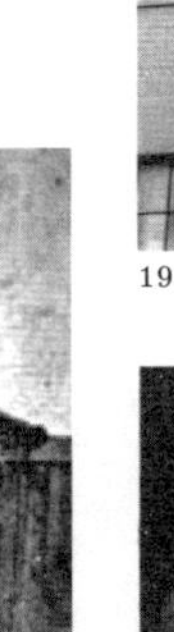

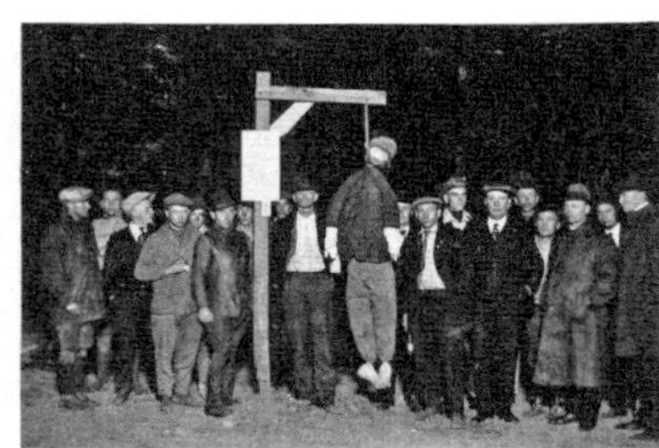

1937_01_00_USA-MI: strike breakers

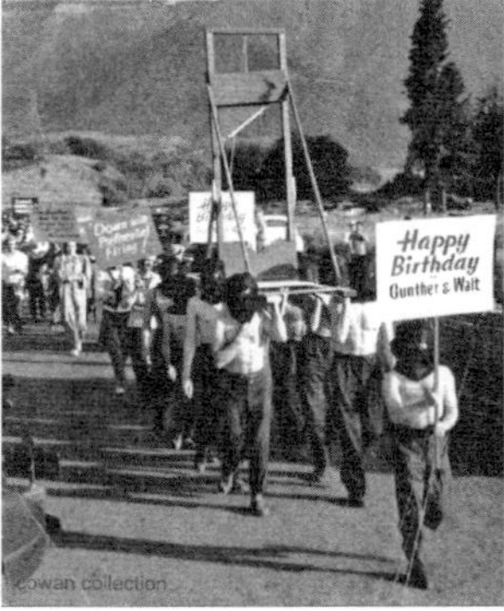

1941_07_00_USA-CA: Walt Disney (b)

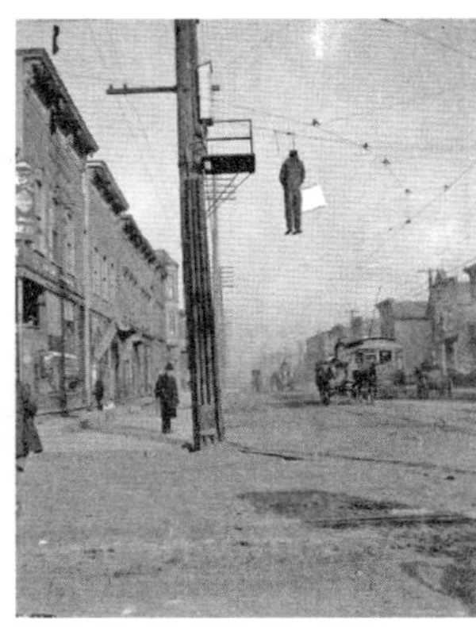

1919_00_00_USA-CA: member of anarchist union

1903_11_19_USA-IL: strike breaker Frank Curry

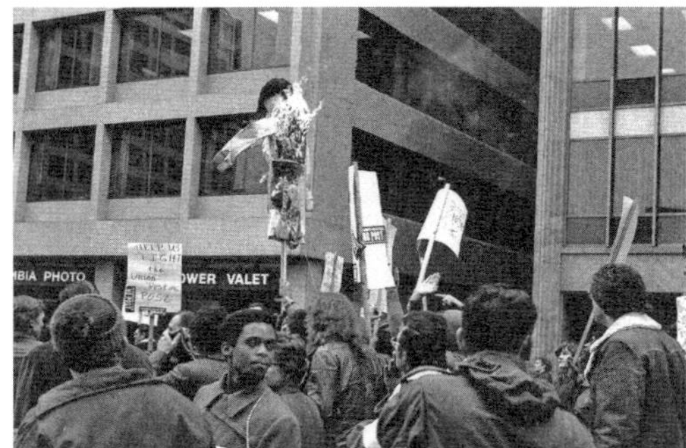

1976_10_02_USA-DC: publisher Graham

From the 1860s until the 1980s, striking workers hanged effigies in their desperate struggle for basic rights, a living wage, and better working conditions. Effigies appeared, for instance, during the coal miners' strike of 1867 in Illinois, the longshoremen strike of 1887 in New Jersey, the iron workers' strike of 1892 in Pennsylvania, the railway strike of 1903 in Chicago, the strike at General Motors in Chicago in 1936, and the strike at an auto parts factory in Elwood, Indiana in 1977. Sometimes these effigies depicted company presidents and managers, but more often, strikebreakers that the bosses brought in to break the workers' bargaining power. These effigy performances functioned in the tradition of popular justice, shaming, threatening, and ostracizing the individuals who did not support the workers' collective action.

The hanging and burning of foreign leaders in effigy took off during World War I with effigies of German Kaiser Wilhelm II.[34] A photograph and description of his effigy burning on an October Sunday in 1917 in Rhinelander, WI was printed in the *Milwaukee Journal*.○ The photograph is barely legible: a big pile of something and a figure resembling an astronaut bearing a sign reading: "Der Kaiser." The description in the article on the other hand is very vivid,

103

34 During the Spanish-American War in 1898, effigies of the Spanish king, prime minister, and the governor of Cuba were burned in effigy. "Boy King in Effigy," *Chicago Tribune*, April 16, 1898; "Sagasta Hanged in Effigy," *New York Times*, April 12, 1898; and *New York Times*, April 22, 1898.

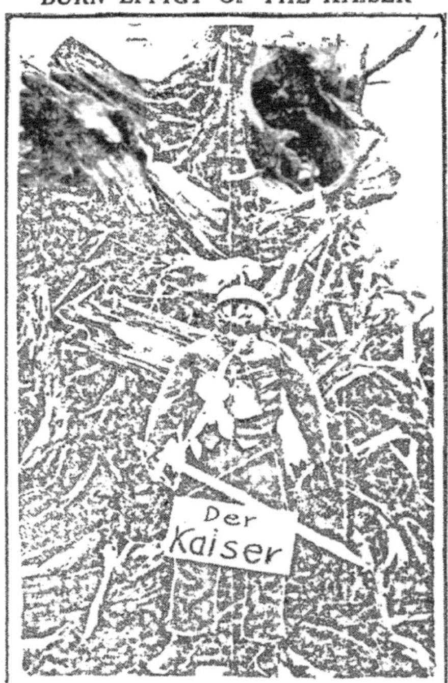

○ 1917_10_17_USA-WI: German Kaiser Wilhelm II

At the land clearing demonstration recently, after stumps had been pulled, blasted and piled in one huge pile, the effigy of the kaiser was burned. His head consisted of a pumpkin his helmet a tin pan, the spike of his helmet a nail covered with tinfoil, his mustache, a frayed piece of rope: the iron cross, two railroad spikes fastened together, his badges, numerous pieces of tin; and his sword a piece of lath, was designed and constructed by Lawrence Livingston. The effigy was elevated to the top of the pile and fastened there, with the sword pointing directly upwards. In a very few minutes the roaring flames reached the kaiser. The most spectacular feature was when the right arm, holding the sword, dropped in a most lifelike manner, the sword falling into the flames.

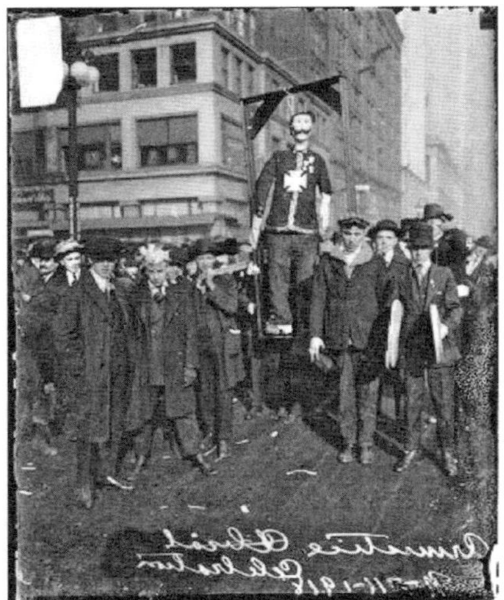

1918_11_11_USA-IL: German Kaiser Wilhelm II

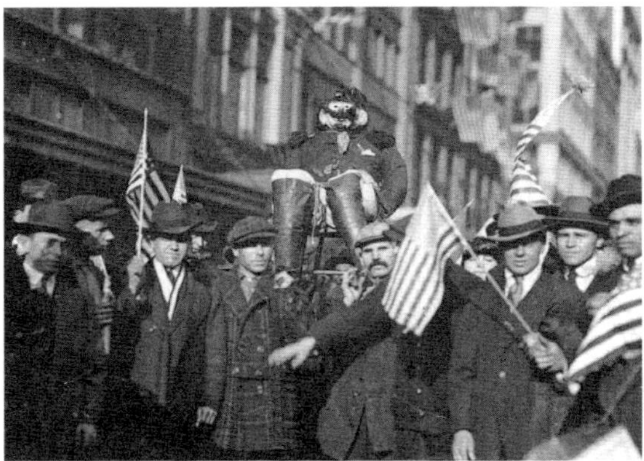

1918_11_11_USA-MI: German Kaiser Wilhelm II

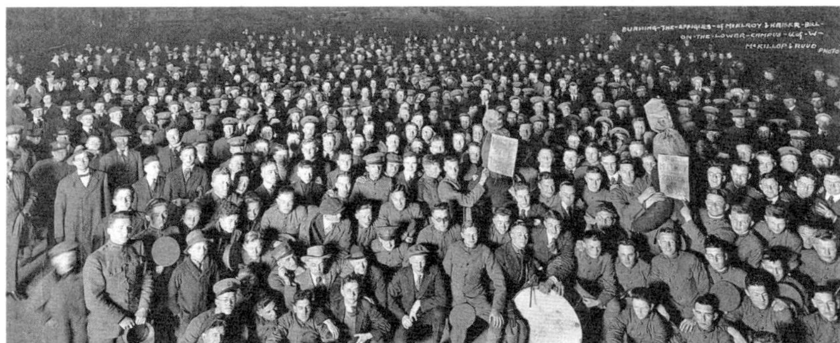

1918_04_16_USA-WI: German Kaiser Wilhelm II + McElroy (a)

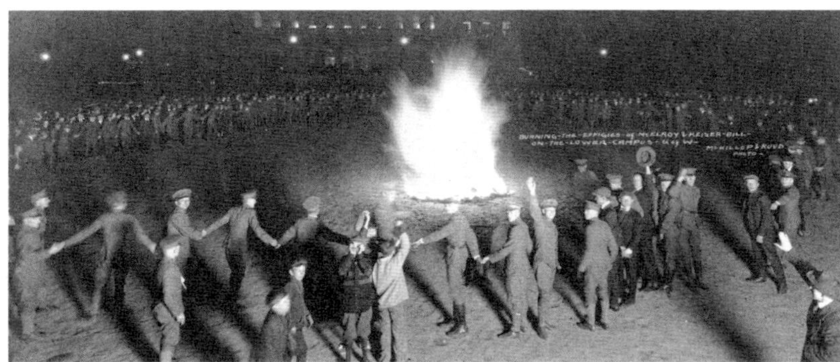

(b)

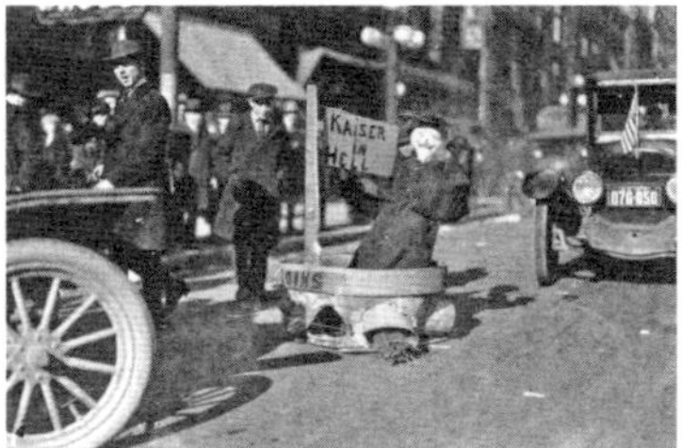

1918_11_12_USA-NY: German Kaiser
Wilhelm II

naming the effigy's designer and describing it and its demise in great detail.

The event is rather festive, taking the communal clearing of a piece of land and the availability of a huge pile of wood that needed to be burned as an occasion to burn an effigy. The care and dedication with which the effigy is made and the lifelike gesture at the end of its burning make it a satisfying and successful performance. Notwithstanding the festive spirit, the German name of the town hints at underlying dilemmas in German-American communities. Far from unified in their political positions, they were under pressure to demonstrate their loyalty to their fellow citizens in the US, and burning the effigy was one way to do so.

Wilhelm II was hanged, beaten, and burned in effigy throughout the US during WWI, but most often at the end of the war, on Armistice Day in November 1918. This pattern repeated itself during WWII with the effigies of German Chancellor Adolf Hitler and Japanese Emperor Hirohito. The first events at which Hitler was paraded in effigy were the Labor Day parades of 1933 and 1935 in New York, organized by the Communist Party and the workers' unions. The effigies appeared as props on floats in a bid to mobilize the people and create awareness of the threatening emergence of an enemy, when most in the US deemed the rise of the National Socialist German Workers' Party a European issue.

Some Hitler effigies were employed to promote paper and scrap metal collection, additional material resources needed to take on the enemy.○ The parody of the

105

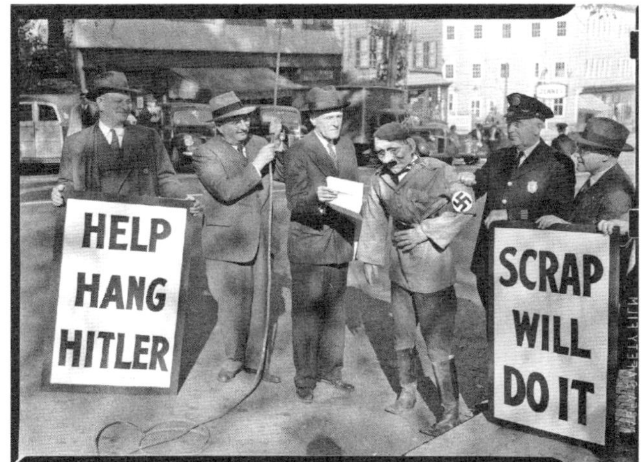

○ 1940_00_00_USA-MA: Hitler

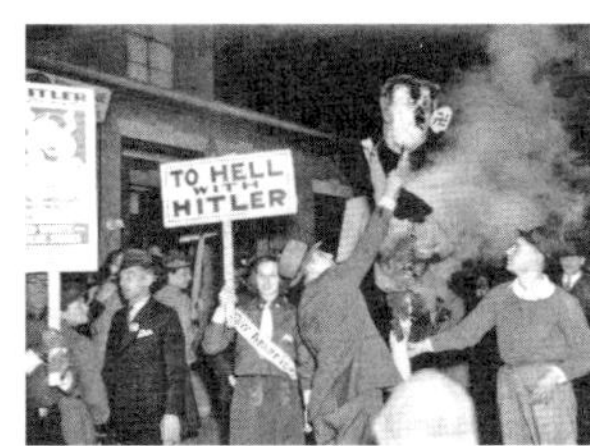

1938_10_02_USA-NJ: Hitler

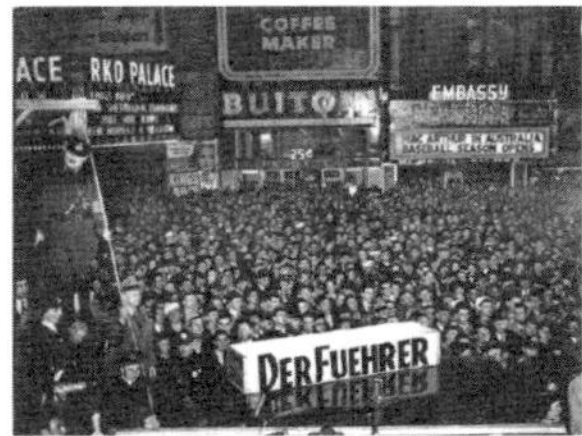

1942_04_20_USA-NY: Hitler

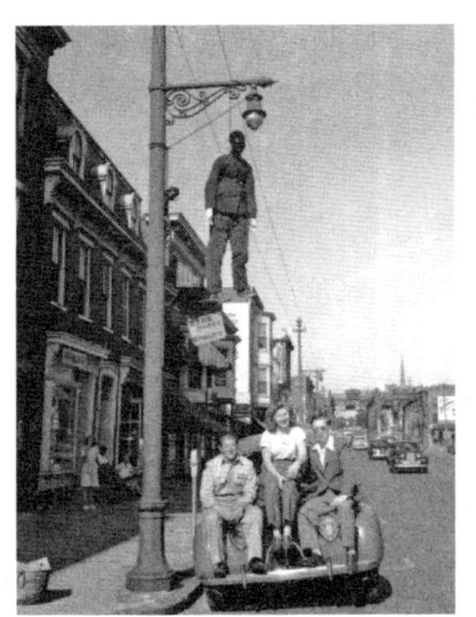

1942_00_00_USA: Japanese Emperor Hirohito

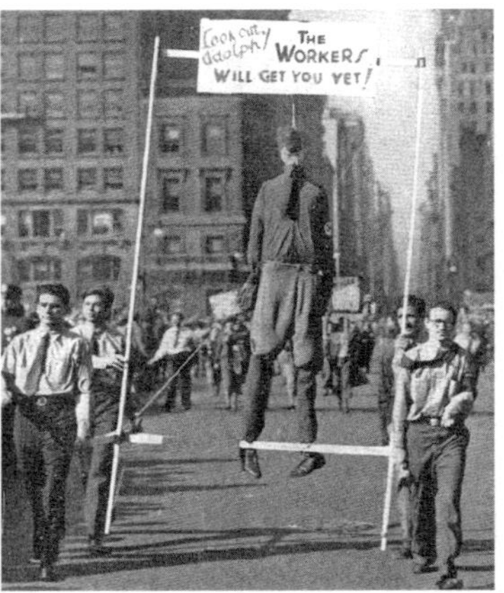

1934_05_01_USA-NY: Hitler

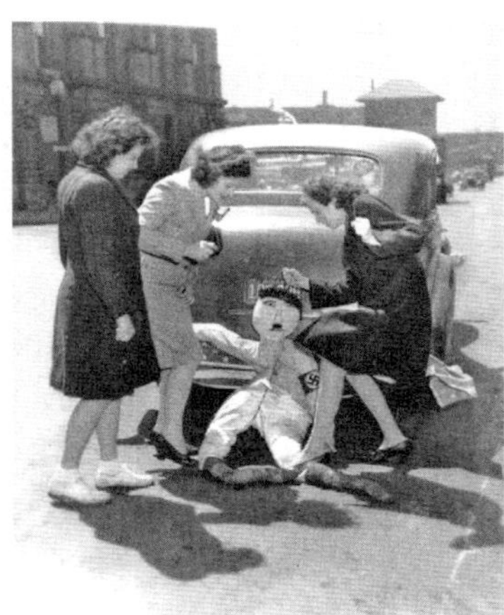

1945_05_08_USA-IN: Hitler

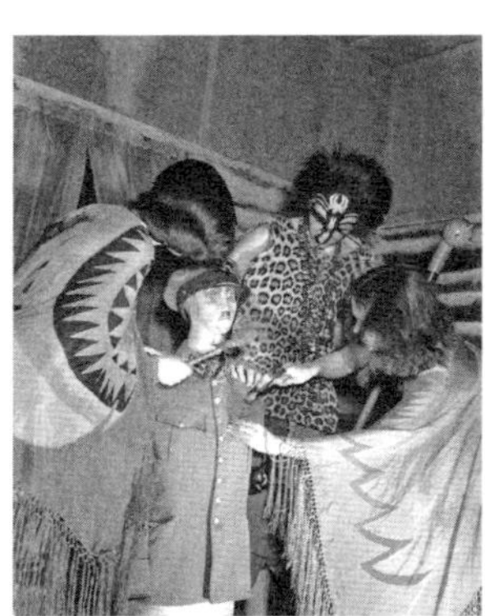

○ 1941_01_22_USA-MD: Hitler

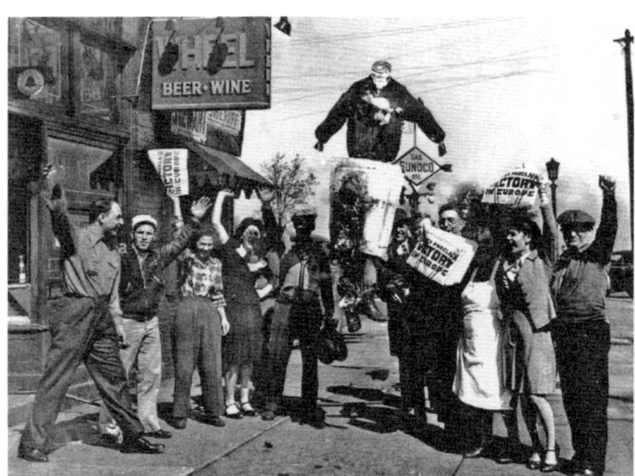

1945_05_08_USA-OH: Hitler

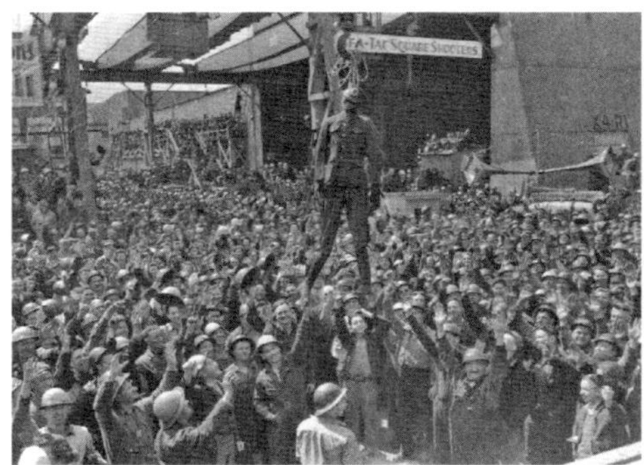

1943_05_10_USA-WA: Japanese Emperor Hirohito

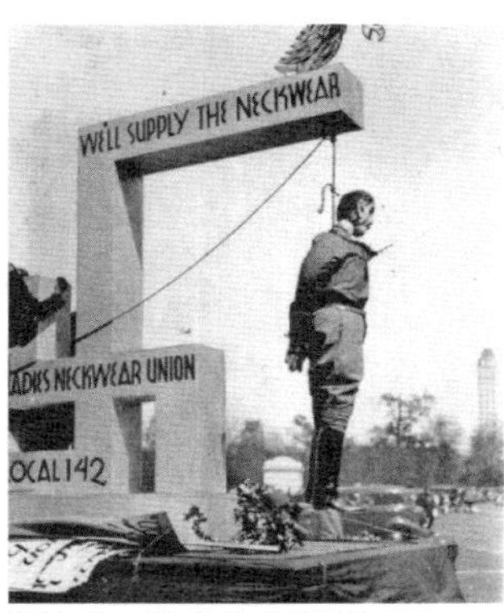

1935_05_01_USA-NY: Hitler

voodoo-like "hexing party" on a January night in 1941 seemed aimed rather at mobilizing the mental forces necessary to stand up to the enemy.○ Most Hitler effigies, though, appeared only after the capitulation of Nazi Germany and the suicide of its leader in 1945. On May 8 at Victory Day parties all over the US, communities celebrated the end of the war by hanging effigies of Hitler and in August, Hirohito. These performances were not staged to protest against the existing order at home, nor was the communication with the enemy of importance. The participants denounced, ridiculed, and degraded the distant enemy, but never posed an actual threat to the foreign leaders. As quasi-ritual political demonstrations, they were not a direct claim to power. Staged at a distance in relation to an outside other, they were not divisive but rather unifying and affirmative. The participants were in celebratory and carnivalesque mood, using caricature and parody to deal with the existential threat of the war with liberating laughter. The demonstrations mentioned here function as cathartic performances acknowledging sacrifice, while celebrating renewal after the end of the war. They again share affinity with traditional calendrical rituals that mark and advance the cycle of death and rebirth of nature and society.

Effigy protests against foreign leaders were staged throughout the twentieth century in the US. In 1960, Cuban exiles displaced by revolution at home, beat an effigy of Fidel Castro in Miami. That same year, US citizens hanged an effigy of Soviet Union leader Nikita Khrushchev on the occasion of his visit to the United Nations in New York, related to

107

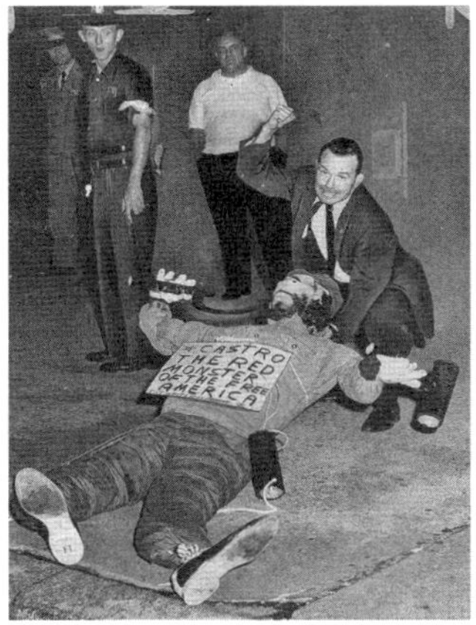

1960_07_26_USA-FL: Cuban President Castro   (a)

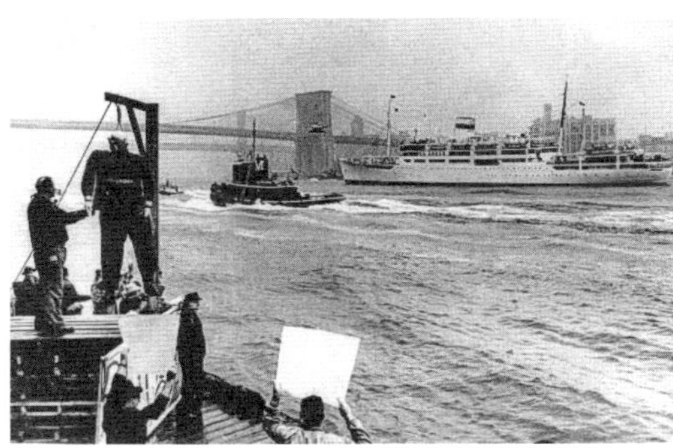

1960_09_19_USA-NY: USSR leader Khrushchev

the antagonism of the two world powers during the Cold War. But in 1980, it was Afghan expatriats who burned the effigy of Khrushchev's successor Leonid Brezhnev in protest against the Soviet invasion of Afghanistan. In 1967, high school students in Massachusetts hanged an effigy of Vietnam's leader Hồ Chí Minh in protest against anti-Vietnam-War protests. In 1979, when revolutionaries occupied the US embassy in Tehran and took its personnel hostage, American students burned effigies of Iranian leader Ayatollah Khomeini in response to Iranian students burning effigies of the Iranian Shah and US President Jimmy Carter. Three years later, it was Iranian students in exile who burned the effigy of Khomeini in protest against his policies at home. In 1995, Cuban exiles were photographed dragging an effigy of Castro through the streets of Miami, this time in protest of Clinton's policy changes that restricted Cuban immigration. Other foreign leaders hanged or burned in effigy were King Hussein of Jordan, Soviet leader Yuri Andropov, UK Prime Minister Margaret Thatcher, President of the Philippines Ferdinand Marcos, Chinese leader Deng Xiaoping, President of Iraq Saddam Hussein, and Osama bin Laden.

108

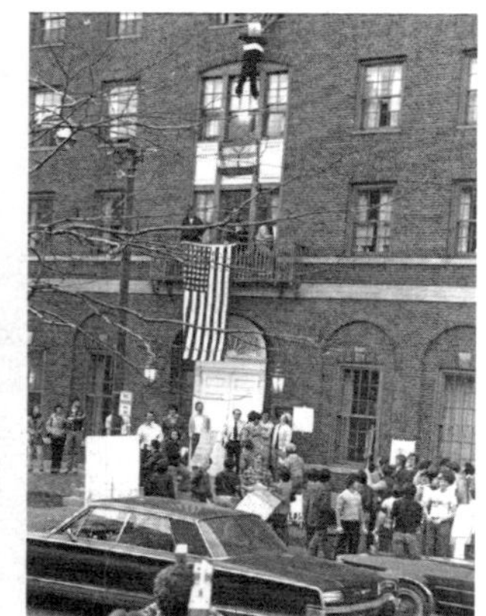

1979_11_00_USA-PA: Iranian leader Ayatollah Khomeini

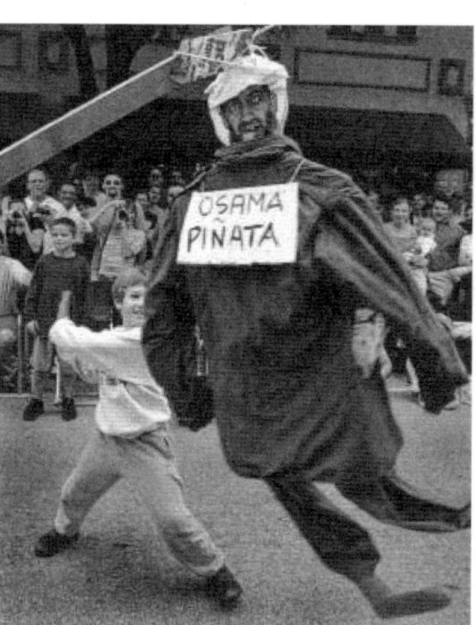

2001_12_30_USA-FL: Osama bin Laden

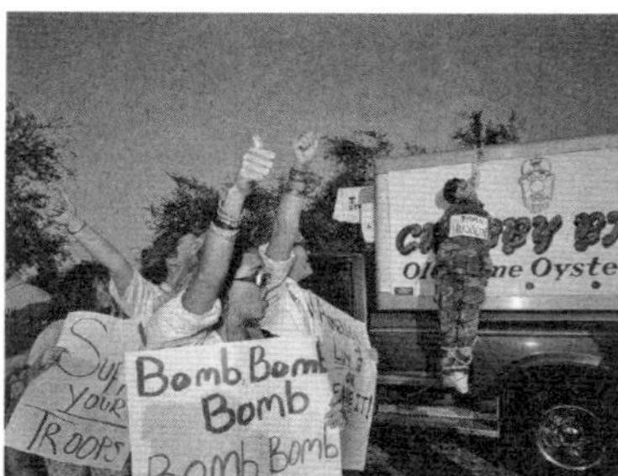

1990_00_00_USA-FL: Iraqi President Saddam Hussein

These protests were not necessarily staged to change policies of the foreign country, but rather – often organized by US based immigrant groups – to influence US American foreign policy. In 1979, for instance, demonstrators burned an effigy of Castro in protest of his visit to the UN, while another group supported his visit. Similarly, the demonstrators hanging Hussein in August 1990 supported the government's war in Iraq, while other demonstrators, like those in January 1991, opposed it. These protests not only reflect international conflicts, but also the complexity of US domestic politics influenced by partisan politics and layered alliances of communities from varying backgrounds.

Effigy Protests and the Imagination of Justice

As a performance of punishment, the practice of hanging or burning effigies is closely tied to both formal and informal justice.[35] Especially in common law legal systems, which are based on precedent, a common sense of justice bears large influence on the legislative process and the application of law. In the US, people often expect the courts to reflect the community's sense of justice more than the letter of the law. Popular justice and lynching has often been experienced as a legitimate continuation of formal law, especially when its enforcement was lacking or appeared too slow.[36] It is unsurprising that throughout US history effigies of judges and juries were hanged in response to formal trials, when the community did not agree with the verdict delivered.

In 1896, residents of the small North Dakota town of Medora were enraged over an acquittal in a murder case and hanged the members of the jury in effigy.[○, 37] In the banner visible in the photograph, the foreman is identified and the

35 See the introduction.

36 Michael J. Pfeifer, *The Roots of Rough Justice: Origins of American Lynching* (Chicago: University of Illinois, 2011), 5.

37 "Education > Lesson Plans > Visual Evidence," *State Historical Society of North Dakota* (website), http://history.nd.gov/historicsites/chateau/chateauLesson/visual_photographs.html.

Last evening Judge Canonge was burnt in effigy in Lafayette. This outbreak of popular indignation was caused, we learn, by the course of the Judge in relation to Mr. Speakman and others concerned in a late suit before Criminal Court.
—*True American*, New Orleans, LA, 27 May 1839

1839_05_26_USA-LA: Judge Canonge

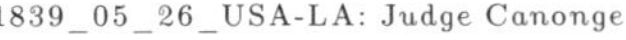

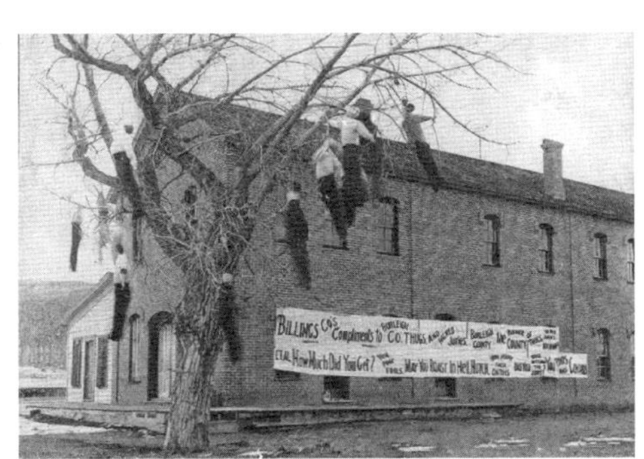

○ 1896_01_09_USA-ND: members of a jury

38 "Three De Autremonts are Hanged in Effigy," *New York Times*, June 25, 1927.

39 Carrie Sharlow, "Michigan Lawyers in History: Stephen J. Roth," *Michigan Bar Journal* (2012): 44–45.

40 Larry Ryckman, "Peaceful but noisy crowds protest release of Dan White from prison," *Evening Independent*, January 7, 1984.

41 "Flags burned at protests of abortion ruling," *Toledo Blade*, July 5, 1989.

42 Kevin Reece, "Effigy of Obama is not a Houston-area protest," *KHOU 11 News*, November 5, 2012.

whole jury is accused of accepting bribes. In 1903, a similar case resulted in the hanging of four effigies representing the governor, district attorney, and district judge of Bowie County, Texas. In 1927, citizens of Ashland, Oregon hanged the three De Autremont brothers in effigy for robbing a train and killing four people, furious they escaped the gallows and were only sentenced to life.[38] In 1972, a mock trial against Judge Stephen John Roth was staged and his effigy burned in Wyandotte, Michigan for his verdict forcing Detroit schools to integrate.[39] In 1984, San Francisco residents protested the early release of San Francisco Mayor George Moscone and City Supervisor Harvey Milk's murderer Dan White having served only five years. The protesters performed fifteen minutes of noise in the middle of the night in the tradition of rough music, and burned the murderer in effigy.[40] In 1989, protesters burned the effigy of a Supreme Court judge during a demonstration against the court decision to uphold a Missouri law that restricts abortion.[41] And in 2012, an effigy of President Barack Obama was hanged from a trailer between effigies of local enforcement officers and state officials of North Carolina who, according to the creator, failed to properly investigate the shooting death of a family member.○, [42]

In all of these cases, the mock trials and effigy executions comment disapprovingly on the enactment of law in specific cases and the overall state of justice in the country. Protesters appropriate ritualistic legal procedures when confronting political issues with mock trials, mock judges, mock persecutors, mock juries, mock executions, and mock burials. During the Stamp Act protests in September 1765, the effigy of stamp master Meserve was brought to a trial in a special court in Portsmouth, New Hampshire. The *New Hampshire Gazette* reports that Meserve appeared before the jury in the form of his "virtual representative" – his effigy:

The verdict gave much dissatisfaction in Waynesburgh, and a procession numbering about 200 persons, marched through the town the night following the conclusion of the trial, with music, banners &c., and concluded proceedings of a rather boisterous character, by burning the jury in effigy in front of the jail.
—*Democrat and Sentinel*, Ebensburg, PA, 11 Jan 1860

1860_01_11_USA-PA: jury

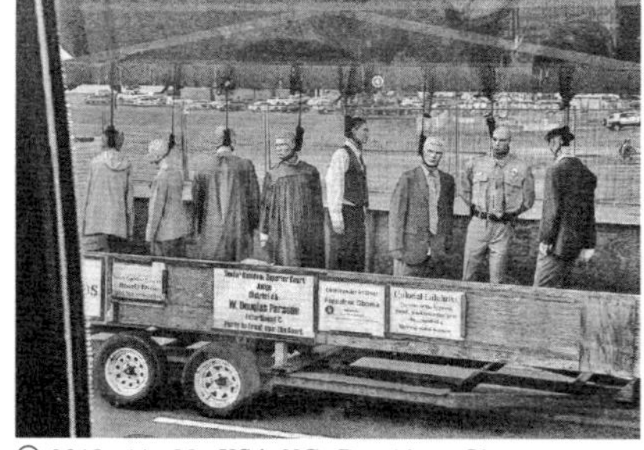

○ 2012_11_00_USA-NC: President Obama

Several Arguments were used on behalf of the Respondent, but the Evidence being so full, the Jury brought him in Guilty, without going off the Stand. The Judges then sentenced the Prisoner to be carried from hence to the Place of Execution, and there to hang by the Neck till Dead; then his Remains to be taken down and burnt to Ashes.[43]

In 1934, City College of New York students staged a mock trial of College President Frederick B. Robinson, protesting the visit of a delegation of Italian Fascist students, burning him and Mussolini in effigy.[44] In 1941, members of the American fascist party "Friends of Progress" staged a mock trial to impeach President Franklin D. Roosevelt with a life-size effigy standing in at the trial.[45] In 1972, University of Virginia students staged a mock trial of President Richard Nixon during a demonstration against the Vietnam War. They convicted him of war crimes and hanged his effigy from a traffic light.[46] In 1979, protesters convicted and burned an effigy of Jane Fonda in front of her house in Santa Monica, California for "dishonoring the American military" with her visit to North Vietnam.[47]

These effigy protests express the close connection between politics and the notion of justice, and the fraught relationship between popular and formal justice. During the American Revolution, hanging and burning effigies were claims to sovereignty and independence. Legal historian Steven Wilf states: "the power to judge and to impose capital sentences – even mock capital sentences – was a fundamental act of sovereignty."[48] That the US was born from a popular uprising against colonial rule strengthened the idea of "the people" as the source of legitimacy and that a common sense of justice should be the basis for formal law. The 1790s saw

43 J. L. Bell, "Portsmouth's Anti-Stamp Protest," *Boston 1775: History, Analysis, and Unabashed Gossip about the Start of the American Revolution in Massachusetts* (blog), September 12, 2015, boston1775.blogspot.com/2015/09/portsmouths-anti-stamp-protest.html.

44 David F. Burg, "'Oust Robinson Week,'" *Encyclopedia of Student and Youth Movements* (New York: Facts On File, Inc., 1998).

45 People v. Noble. Crim. No. 1816. Third Dist. (April 24, 1945). *Justitia, US Law*, law.justia.com/cases/california/calapp2d/68/853.html.

46 "Nixon burned in effigy at Virginia University," *Kingsport Times-News*, May 14, 1972.

47 "Youths Stage Mocktrial, Hang Jane Fonda in Effigy," *Lakeland Ledger*, October 9, 1979.

48 Steven Wilf, *Law's Imagined Republic: Popular Politics and Criminal Justice in Revolutionary America* (Cambridge: Cambridge University Press, 2010), 94.

III

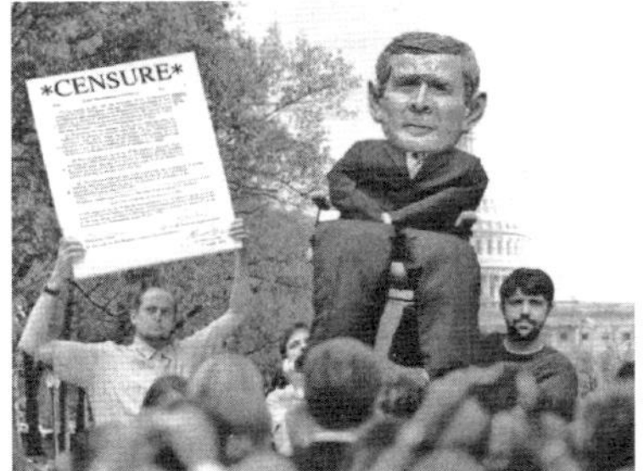

Washington, DC – In an emblematic move intended to stand in for the official symbolic reprimand of the President, a vehemently well-mannered mob of demonstrators censured an effigy of George W. Bush Tuesday, making known its displeasure over such actions as illegal wiretapping and the politically motivated firing of federal lawyers.
—*The Onion*, Madison, WI, 24 Aug 2007

2007_08_24_USA-DC: President Bush

49 Wilf, *Law's Imagined Republic*, 146.

50 Wilf, *Law's Imagined Republic*, 193.

51 Pfeifer, *The Roots of Rough Justice*, 94.

profound statutory reforms of American criminal law, moving away from the British penal code toward a more rational legal system "representative of a more virtuous republic."[49] The reforms reduced sanguinary punishments, established sentences proportional to crimes, formalized court procedures, and aimed to create a "legal language and symbolism accessible to the common people."[50] Nevertheless, the understanding of the law as constituted by the will of the people often came into conflict with the liberal understanding of law and due process. Working-class people and in rural communities especially were skeptical about how formal justice would serve their interests, and resorted to taking the law into their own hands in various forms of rough justice.[51] The staging of effigy executions in these divisive political and social conflicts brings into focus the subjugating effects of the performances, which I examine in the following section.

Un-Civil Rights Effigies

52 W. E. B. Du Bois, *Black Reconstruction in America* (Philadelphia: Albert Saifer, 1935), 3.

53 "When the Abolitionists began their attacks on the South's system of slavery, Southerners in their resentment and regional patriotism, ... began not just to defend but to glorify their way of life, and the idealization of the plantation, which employed most of the slaves, was their basic method." Earl F. Bargainnier, "The Plantation: Southern Icon," in *Icons of America*, ed. Ray B. Brown and Marshall Fishwick (Bowling Green, OH: Popular Press, 1978), 272.

Since the founding days of the US, the question of slavery and the civil rights of Americans of African descent has been a divisive topic. Slavery stood in stark contrast to the revolution's ideals of the equality of men expressed in the Declaration of Independence.[52] These civil rights only applied to white men, a limitation soon challenged by abolitionists.

In the North, abolition had much support, and by 1804, all northern states of the Union had gradually introduced laws to abolish slavery. The South, though, widely perceived abolition as a threat to the economic system and Southern identity.[53] Their economy relied on enslaved people as the workforce for the large plantations that produced raw materials like cotton and sugar, tobacco and hemp. Enslaved people represented capital: they were exchanged for money, used as collateral, and given as inheritance. The number of enslaved people in the US was huge: the census of 1800 counted 900,000, which amounted to 17 percent of the population. In 1860, the percentage had decreased to 13 percent, but the number of enslaved people increased to almost 4 million and the percentage of enslaved people in the South was above 30 percent. In South Carolina and Mississippi, their number amounted to over than 50 percent of the population and in some counties over 80 percent.[54] The white population in the South – plantation owners and working class alike – feared the effects that the abolition of slavery would have on the economy, the labor market, and the social organization of their communities. The plantation owners in the South were for the most part not content to retain the status quo, since the extension of slavery into new territories in the West was deemed crucial for the continued growth of the Southern economic system. This was a development that the federal government dominated by Northern Republicans, wanted to prevent by all means.

Between 1830 and 1860, the abolition of slavery was driven by activists from the North as well as by acts of rebellion in the South – even though the latter part of this history is less recognized. Many northern activists were white religiously inspired humanists who regarded slavery as bad for society, while many others were African Americans, still enslaved people, or former enslaved people such as Frederick Douglass and Sojourner Truth. They toured the South, gave speeches, and helped set up the "Underground Railway," a clandestine network of routes and safe houses to help enslaved people escape to the North. Northern activists started a massive mail campaign to distribute abolitionist literature, like the journal *Human Rights*, newspapers *The*

54   E. Hergesheimer, *Map Showing the Distribution of the Slave Population of the Southern States of the United States Compiled from the Census of 1860*, The United States Coast Survey, commons.wikimedia.org/wiki/File:SlavePopulationUS1860.jpg.

Liberator and the *North Star* and children's magazine *Slave's Friend*.

Southern communities reacted viciously to the supposed threat to their economic system, identity, and way of life.[55] Fugitive slaves were hunted, punished, and sometimes abducted from the North. Participants in slave revolts were executed.[56] Abolition activists were intimidated, hanged and burned in effigy, and subjected to other forms of popular justice. Slavery was the major issue in the conflict that lead to the secession of eleven southern states from the Union in 1860, forming the Confederate States of America.[57] A news report from Charleston, South Carolina, describes the celebration of secession. The demonstration was festive, a statement of political positions and identities that included the execution in effigy of their opponent Abraham Lincoln.○

Abolitionists and Union defenders staged similar effigy protests: the 23rd Pennsylvania Volunteer Infantry hanged an effigy of President of the Confederacy Jefferson Davis while they played football and chased a greased pig for entertainment⊚: an effigy of pro-secession New York State Senator Nathan Bristol was burned in the small town Waverly, NY, while a mock concert was played.

The federal government did not recognize the secession and offered negotiation. When Confederate militias attacked Fort Sumpter in South Carolina, the American Civil War broke out, lasting until 1865. After the Union victory, slavery

114

55 "We regard every man in our midst an enemy to the institutions of the South, who does not boldly declare that he believes African slavery to be a social, moral, and political blessing," *Atlanta Confederacy*, 1860, cited in *The Anti-Slavery History of the John-Brown-Year* (New York: American Anti-Slavery Society, 1861), 167, hdl.handle.net/2027/nyp.33433081995288.

56 Herbert Aptheker, "American Negro Slave Revolts," *Science & Society* 1, no. 4 (1937): 512–38.

57 These states were South Carolina, Mississippi, Florida, Alabama, Georgia, Louisiana, Texas, Virginia, Arkansas, North Carolina, and Tennessee.

58 Lloyd Garrison, "Letters of William Lloyd Garrison I–VI, July 5, 1836," in "Anti-Garrison Effigy," Reading Garrison's Letters (blog), http://www.readinggarrisonsletters.com.

... some unknown but patriotic artist, (rejoicing in his liberty,) with considerable labor, but not much skill, made an effigy of straw, and suspended it upon a post in Main Street, to which was fastened a label containing these condemnatory words – "Garrison, the abolitionist; fit subject for the gallows."[58]

1836_07_05_USA: W L Garrison

Last night our citizens turned out en masse to celebrate the event by a torchlight procession; the torches being of native pine, made a handsome appearance. All the residences along the line were filled with the fair sex, who sanctioned the proceedings by the waving of handkerchiefs, &c. Midway in the procession, between the two lines, was the effigy of Abe Lincoln, with the following placard suspended in the right hand: "Abe Lincoln, First President Northern Confederacy." The effigy was ridden on a rail, and carried by two negroes. After marching through the principal streets, the effigy was taken to a scaffold and hung by the negroes in charge of the same; the fire being applied, it was speedily consumed amid the cheers of the multitude.
—*Richmond Daily Dispatch*, VA, 14 Nov 1860

○ 1860_11_09_USA-SC: President Lincoln

was formally abolished. Nevertheless, discrimination of African Americans continued, especially in the South. From everyday discrimination and disenfranchisement, segregation in the Southern states was slowly formalized with the so-called Jim Crow laws enacted by white-dominated state legislatures. Severe forms of popular justice enforced social and political hierarchies, with lynching the most extreme. While lynching was not solely directed against African Americans, the number of black victims was three times higher than white and Hispanic victims combined.

Lynching in the nineteenth century was a mass spectacle, a display of white supremacy, sometimes attended by hundreds. It included torture, hanging, subsequent mutilation, and sometimes burning of the corpses. Despite many attempts, lynching was never made a federal crime, due to resistance by Southern members of the US Senate — a fact for which the senate issued an official apology in 2005.[59] And although lynching could have been prosecuted under state murder statutes, most cases were never even brought to court. Trials were considered futile, since the juries would consist of people from the same ethnic background and political conviction as the killers. Furthermore, popular justice was often considered a legitimate extension of formal justice — an expedited form of the same system, when the regular procedures of the law seemed too slow or just too cumbersome. The pretext often given to justify lynching was the need to protect

59 "June 13th, 2005, United States Senate Formally Apologizes for Failure to Pass Anti-Lynching Bills," *Equal Justice Initiative*, racialinjustice.eji.org/timeline/2000s/.

115

Hon. Nathan Bristol, Ex-State Senator, ... , well known for his secession proclivities, was waited on last night and treated with a serenade. The music consisted of a horse-fiddle, tin pans, &c. He was burned in effigy, and afterwards buried in effigy in the graveyard. There was considerable excitement.
—*New York Times*, 9 Sep 1861

1862_09_09_USNY: Senator Bristol

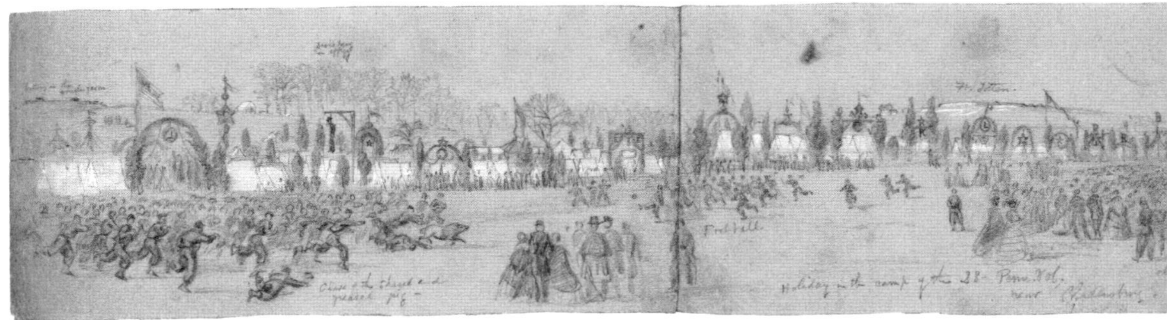

1861_12_25_USA-MD: Confederacy President Davis

60 See Ida B. Wells, *Lynch Law in Georgia* (Chicago: Chicago Colored Citizens, 1899).

61 "April 18th, 1946: Davis Knight Marries Junie Lee Spradley in Mississippi," Equal Justice Initiative (Montgomery, AL), https://racialinjustice.eji.org/timeline/1940s/.

white women from rape by African-Americans – a myth spread by Southern apologists already soundly debunked by civil rights activist Ida B. Wells in 1899.[60] Lynchings peaked in the last two decades of the nineteenth century and had mostly subsided by the end of wwii – corresponding exactly to the period when hanging effigies in the context of racial discrimination increases in frequency in my records.

In Florida, in 1939, conjoined with Ku Klux Klan demonstrations, effigies of African Americans bearing the sign "This n..... voted" were hanged in Miami. The effigies were unmistakably used by the kkk to threaten any African American who dared exercise their constitutional right to vote. By then, the National Association for the Advancement of Colored People (naacp) had begun organizing the African American vote more proactively and defied kkk threats. In the following decades, the desegregation of the military, public institutions, public transport, public school system, and housing laws became focal points for civil rights activists who encountered fierce resistance from the white

116

In an effort to intimidate the Negroes of this city and prevent the appearance of Congressman Oscar DePriest of Illinois ..., the Ku Klux Klan burned the Congressman in effigy here. ... They fired pistols and machine guns and otherwise intimidated the colored folks. They paraded every section where Negroes live. [On the same page, the newspaper reports the lynching of an African-American man in South Carolina by a white posse of 600.]
—*The Afro American*, Baltimore, MD, 28 Jun 1930

1930_06_23_USA-MD: De Priest

City election officials predicted today a record negro vote despite a warning by paraders in Ku Klux Klan regalia ... An effigy bearing the legend "this nigger voted" hung from a pole opposite a precinct polling place today as a city primary election opened. White-robed and capped men paraded in 75 automobiles through the negro section last night, burned 25 crosses and threw out red-lettered cards with "K.K.K." on them, warning negroes to stay away from the polls. A hangman's noose dangled from one of the cars.
—*The Evening Independent*, Miami, FL, 2 May 1939

1939_05_01_USA-FL: African-American voter (b)

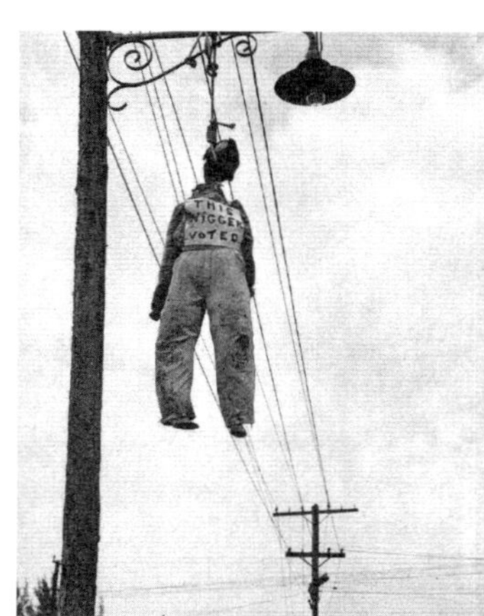

1939_05_01_USA-FL: African-American voter (a)

In 1946, a court in Mississippi convicted Davis Knight of being black and guilty of marrying outside of his race. The Supreme Court of Mississippi reversed the decision citing that the State had failed to prove that Knight was at least one-eighth black. White Mississippian's hanged members of the Court in effigy.[61]

1946_00_00_USA-MS: members of Mississippi Supreme Court Justices

population. Only a persistent campaign by a large number of activists with considerable courage in the face of threatening violence, in combination with federal legislation support and enforcement dismantled the overt politics of disenfranchisement.

In the 1950s and 1960s many effigies were hanged in the context of the resistance to African American integration. Effigies often represented vulnerable individuals and marginalized groups who had to face the threat of physical violence: African American voters, NAACP activists, white activists, African American students, supportive politicians or judges who ruled in favor of integration. In this struggle, local administrations and state governments often colluded against the implementation of federal laws, such as the desegregation of public schools following the Supreme Court decision from 1954 in Brown v Board of Education. In Arkansas, Governor Faubus announced in September 1957 that he would employ the National Guard to prevent the nine registered African American students from entering Little Rock High School.

117

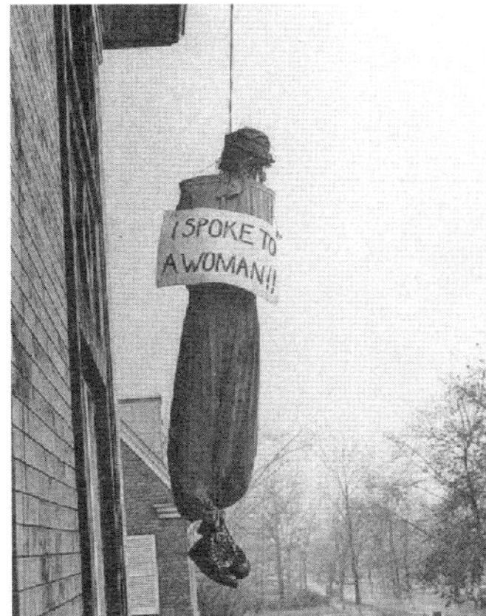

1945_00_00_USA-OH: African-American man

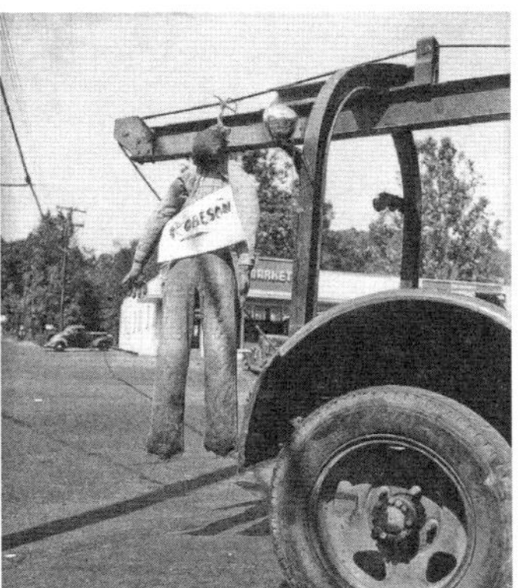

1949_04_09_USA-NY: actor and activist Paul Robeson

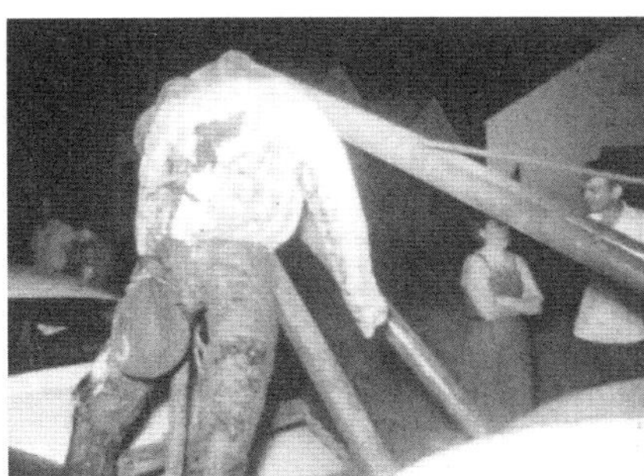

1956_09_03_USA-TX: African-American home-owner

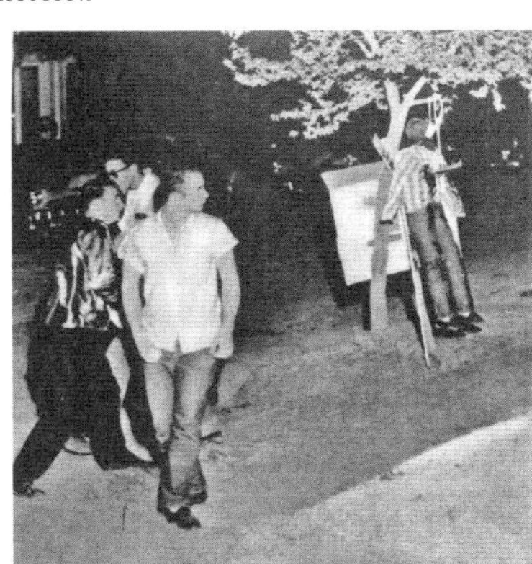

1956_09_15_USA-TX: African-American home-owner

62 In a demonstration of support, progressive students in Los Angeles and Toronto, Canada, hanged Governor Faubus in effigy in retaliation. "History of School Integration in the U.S.," *History*, A+E Television Networks (website), hwww.history.com/topics/black-history/central-high-school-integration.

63 See Carolyn Kleiner Butler, "Down in Mississippi," *Smithsonian Magazine*, February 2005, www.smithsonianmag.com/history/down-in-mississippi-85827990/.

Local police had been tasked by a federal court to escort the students to school but not before President Dwight Eisenhower sent 1,200 members of the US Army's 101st Airborne Division that the "Little Rock nine" could spend their first day at school. During the entire year, the army remained posted at the school to protect the students. The students were insulted and harassed and on one occasion, white students hanged, kicked, and burned an effigy of an African American student outside the school.○, 62

In 1961, James Meredith was denied admittance and sued the University of Mississippi for racial discrimination. The United States Court of Appeals and the US Supreme Court found in his favor, but the governor of Mississippi continued to block his admission. Only after US Attorney General Robert F. Kennedy sent federal marshals and the Mississippi National Guard to enforce the court order, could Meredith enroll in October 1962. When he entered the university accompanied by US marshals, he was greeted with an effigy hanging on his residence hall.⊙⊙ He endured extreme harassment and isolation, yet successfully graduated a year later. In 1966, Meredith organized the "March Against Fear" from Memphis, Tennessee to Jackson, Mississippi. On the second day, he was shot and wounded by an unemployed white man from Memphis.63

118

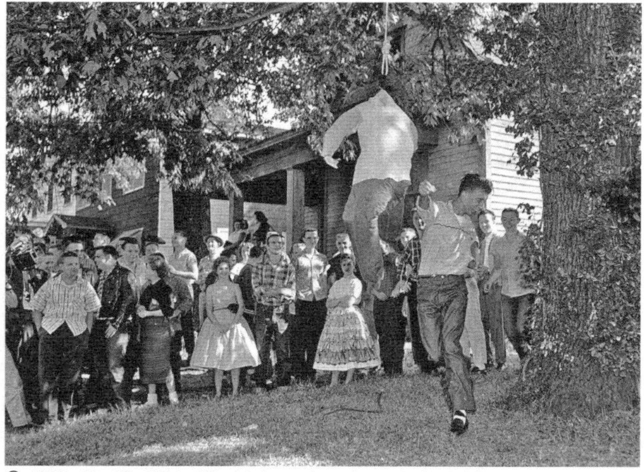

○ 1957_10_03_USA-AR: African-American student (a)

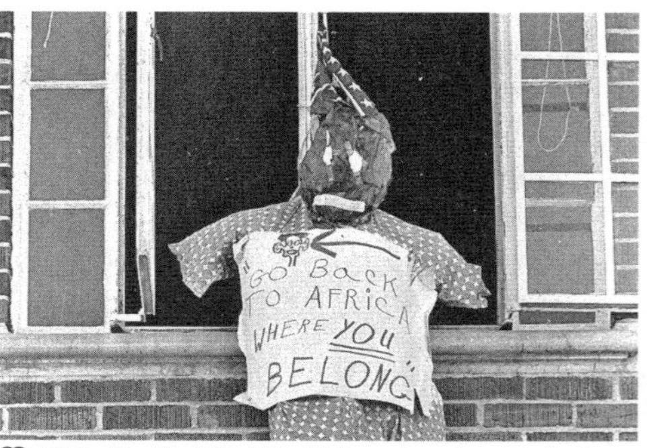

⊙⊙ 1962_10_03_USA-MS: African-American student

In Montgomery, Alabama, two effigies were installed in the town square in broad daylight on an August morning in 1956 in the wake of the boycott against segregated buses. A sign identified the makers of the display as Union members, supposedly respectable town folk who enjoyed the support of their community. The threat that these effigies constituted was serious as shown by the murder of three civil rights activists – one black and two white – who went missing while investigating the arson of a black church used as a "Freedom School" in Neshoba County, Mississippi in June 1964. Six weeks later, their bodies were found buried in a partially constructed dam.

In 1960, John Howard Griffin published *Black Like Me* detailing his experiences of discrimination while traveling disguised as a black man in the South. The famous bestseller remained controversial. In his hometown Mansfield, Texas, his effigy was hanged on Main Street, a cross was burned in front of the local still-segregated school for African Americans, and a local bar put up a sign reading "No albinos allowed." His effigy eventually ended up in the local garbage dump, where a photographer for the local newspaper took a picture of it under a sign announcing a fine for dumping dead animals.

In 1963, members of the National States Rights Party hanged an effigy of Dr. Martin Luther King, Jr. in front of the

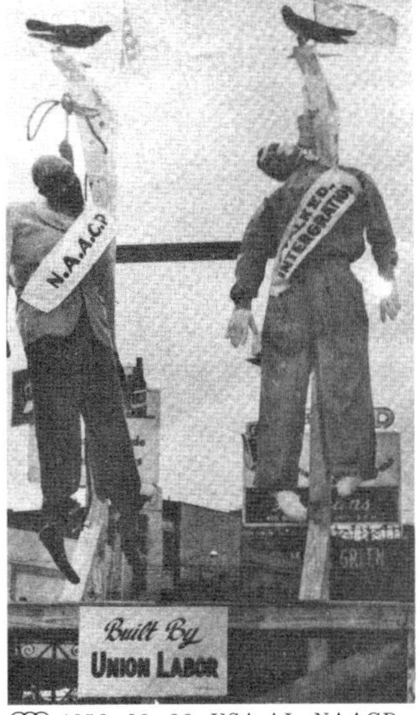

1956_08_06_USA-AL: NAACP activists

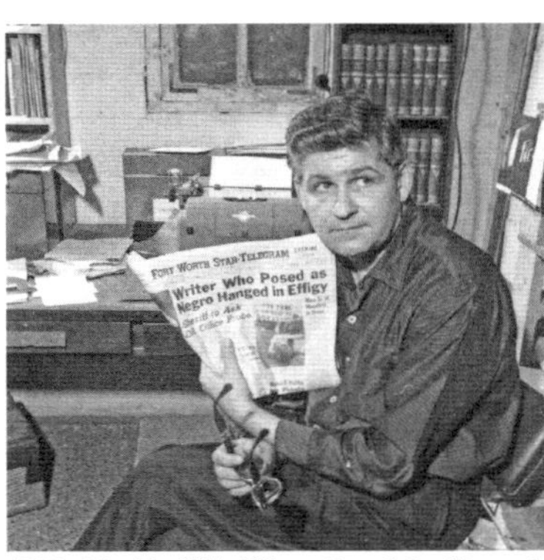

1960_04_02_USA-TX: author John Howard Griffin posing with a newspaper showing his effigy

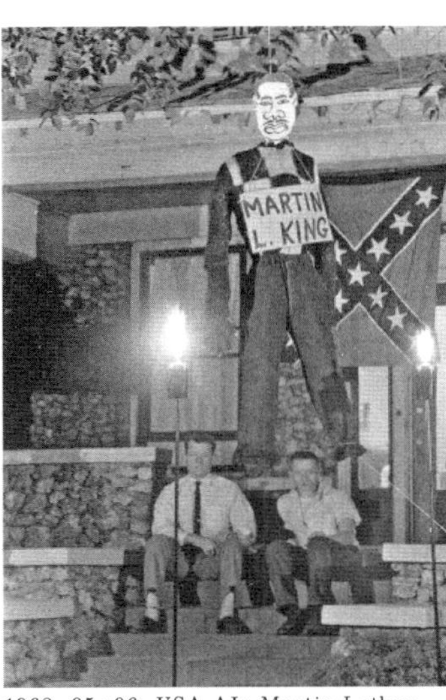

1963_05_06_USA-AL: Martin Luther King

64   Peter Kuryla, "Parties Down at the Square Amid Courtroom Melodramas: A Reconsideration of the Modern Civil Rights Movement demonstration," *Patterns of Prejudice* 43, no. 1 (2009): 22–23.

party headquarters in Birmingham, Alabama, where King campaigned with the Southern Christian Leadership Conference (SCLC) to end racial segregation. In March 1968, King was shot by James Earl Ray, a volunteer for the George Wallace's presidential campaign, Wallace being the former Governor of Alabama and champion of segregation.

As the struggle for desegregation and civil rights flowed from the struggle for abolition of slavery from a century before, so do the effigy hangings continue the practice of lynching in a less extreme form.[64] These performances were not benign forms of symbolic expression. Many effigies show an anonymous body, an African American voter, student, neighbor, or activist. They present the private body publicly exhibited, degraded, and violated, devoid of political status. They performatively affirm and enact the statues of African Americans as second-class citizens. As part of a continuous set of practices, from insidious forms of discrimination to open physical violence, they comprise a form of violent subjugation.

Civil Rights Effigies

65   Before the advent of the student movement in the 1960s, effigy protests similarly situated in challenging existing power structures are relatively rare.

With the students' movement at the end of the 1960s, effigy performances became more numerous in protests favoring progressive politics.[65] These demonstrations were staged for a variety of causes, to advance racial integration, for First Nations' rights, and against the Vietnam War. Publicness and visibility were paramount as they required the creation of a

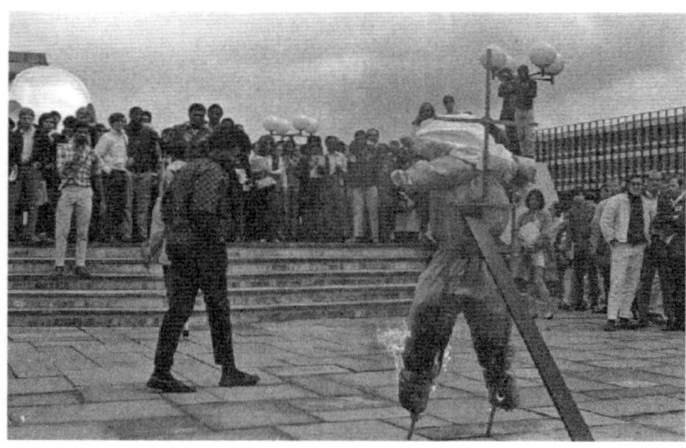

1969_00_00_USA-NY: college administrator

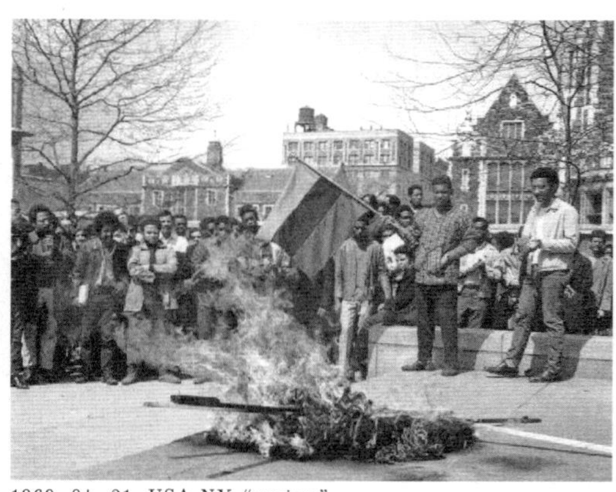

1969_04_21_USA-NY: "racism"

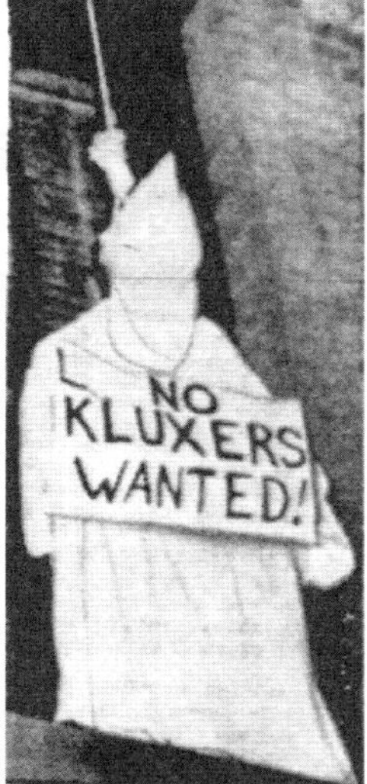

1948_12_00_USA-GA:
member of the KKK

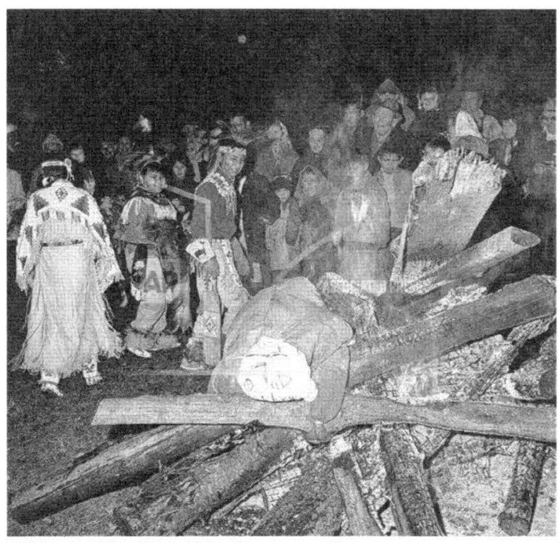

1966_01_30_USA-WA: Governor Evans

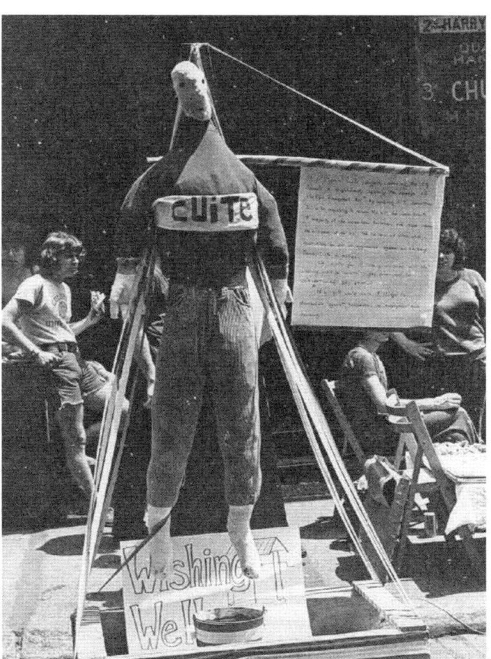

1971_06_26_USA-NY: Thomas Cuite (gay rights protest)

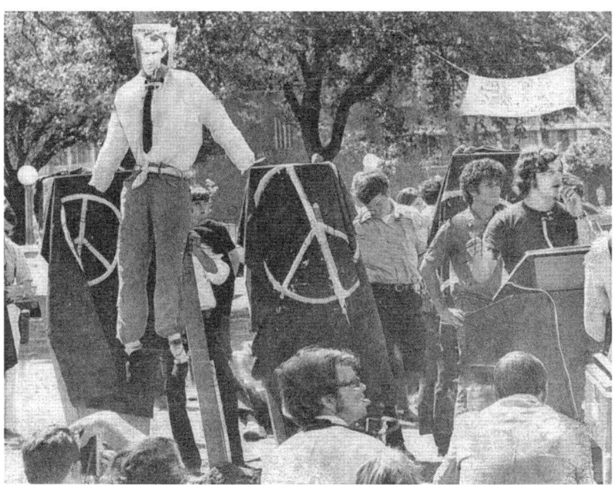

1970_05_05_USA-LA: President Nixon

presence in public space and public consciousness to become a political force. The need for visibility influenced the way effigies are performed. Civil rights protesters usually paraded and burned their effigies openly, providing for spectacular moments. They paraded, ridiculed, and burned figures of power like elected officials, or abstract entities like "racism" in a reversal of existing power relations.

In the photographs of protests, this difference is not always clearly visible. For instance, the pictures of the hanging and burning of an effigy of Nixon during a protest against the Vietnam War at Southern Illinois University○, and the hanging and burning effigy of an African American student in a protest against the desegregation of Little Rock High School⓪, look quite similar. In both photo-series, several individuals are seen actively engaging with the effigy, hitting, punching, and finally setting it on fire, while most others surrounding the performances retain the role of sceptical, sometimes bemused spectator. The crowd in Little Rock seems diverse, with people of different age and appearance, while the spectators at Southern Illinois University seem to be university students. The important difference is that in the first set of images the protesters were in close proximity to the African American students who entered the high school, who were threatened with actual physical violence. In the second series, the protesters were nowhere near the target of their

122

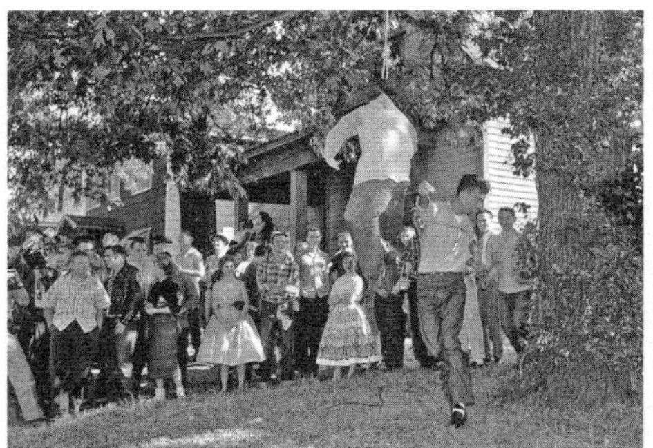

⓪ 1957_10_03_USA-AR: African-American student (a)

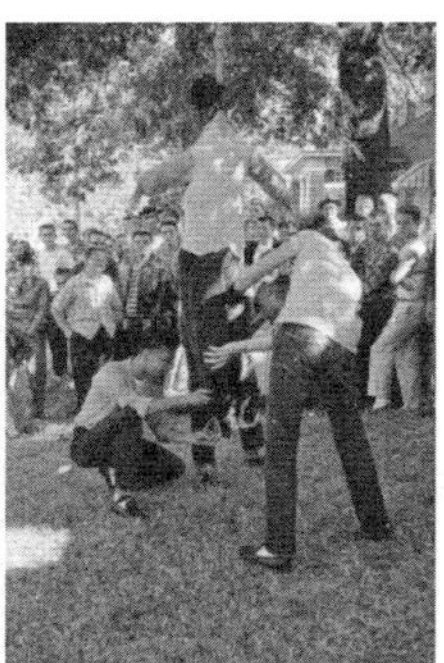

1957_10_03_USA-AR: African-American student (b)

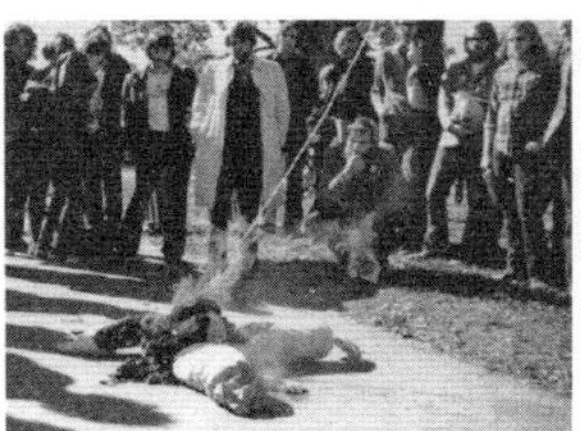

○ 1972_00_00_USA-IL: President Nixon (a)

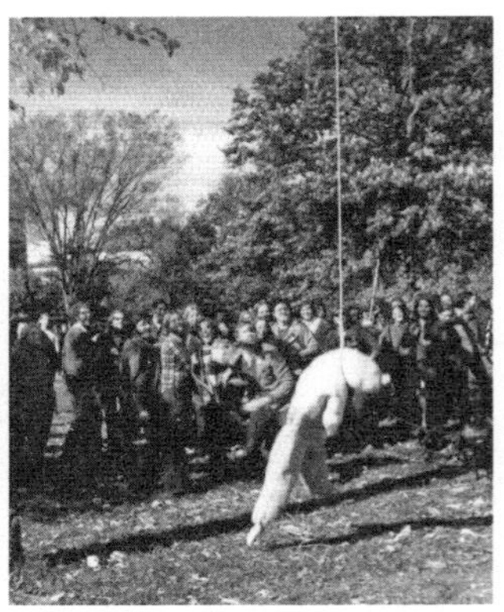

1972_00_00_USA-IL: President Nixon (b)

anger, President Nixon and didn't pose a threat. Even though the photographs may appear equally violent, the violence experienced by the African American students was clearly of a different order. This apparent visual similarity and difference in effect points to the necessity to further investigate the kind of violence these protests exert and to judge in each case whether an effigy protest constitutes an actual threat or a symbolic expression. I will further elaborate on this distinction in chapter 7, "Violence and Laughter."

Hanging and Burning Presidents

Almost all US presidents have been hanged in effigy, but few of them as often as the last three: George W. Bush, Barack Obama, and Donald Trump. In the '80s and '90s the use of effigies in protests in the US had diminished,[66] but from 2001 onwards effigy hanging and burning made a comeback – this time along party lines. Bush effigies were paraded at demonstrations against the Iraq War in San Francisco, Chicago, New York, Los Angeles, Denver, and Washington DC. Most of them were hanged, some were burned, some were worn in the form of big masks and used to stage a kind of protest theater. After 2003, the toppling of Bush papier-mâché statues became popular in anti-war protests – appropriated from

66 See the analysis of newspaper reports in the *New York Times* archive. Göttke, *Burning Images: Performing Effigies as Political Protest*, 313–4.

123

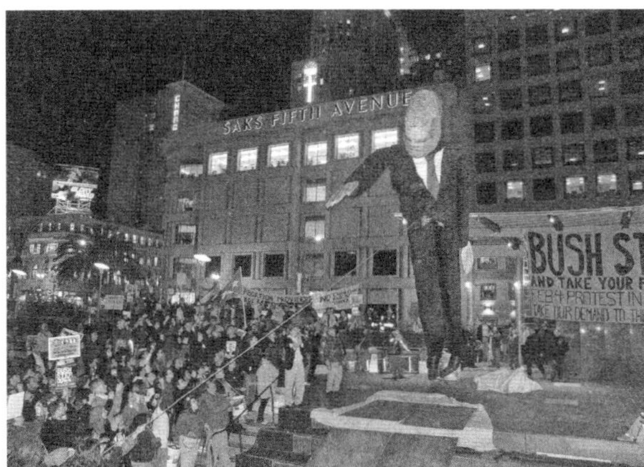

2006_00_00_USA-CA: President Bush

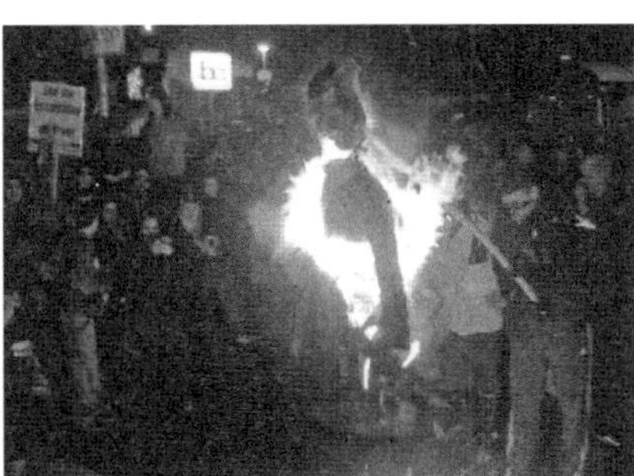

2004_11_02_USA-CA: President Bush

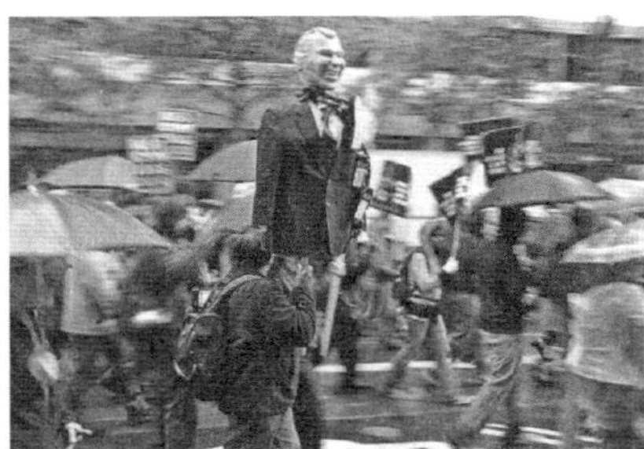

2006_10_05_USA-CA: President Bush

67 Florian Göttke, *Toppled* (Rotterdam: Post Editions, 2010), 120–22.

68 I include these chair hangings, because they form an interesting sub-section of effigies that allows avoiding the crass image of a hanging body, while still communicating the contempt that people foster toward Barack Obama that permeated discussions in republican circles during the re-election campaign.

69 The watermelon is a derogatory term used by racists whites in the South to signify the "ignorant" African American.

70 Nick Wing, "Secret Service Visits Man Who Hung Obama Effigy From Tree As 'Spooky' Halloween Decoration," *Huffington Post*, October 25, 2012.

the toppling of Saddam's statue in Baghdad.[67] Imitating the Iraqi journalist who threw a shoe at Bush during a news conference in 2008, shoe-throwing became a favorite expression of contempt. I found a total of 27 Bush effigy protests that were staged in the 8 years Bush was in office, predominantly in reaction to political developments and the president's politics, especially the war in Iraq.

Obama was hanged in effigy even more often. I found records of 32 Obama effigies in the US. The effigies appeared mainly before his election in 2008 and re-election in 2012, roughly coinciding with Halloween, and most of them in the South. None were paraded during demonstrations, but instead hanged in rural (22) and suburban (5) areas, from trees (13), or from makeshift gallows (3), in front yards (22), from bridges and billboards (3). Only four were burned. An interesting twist in the use of Obama effigies happened after the Republican Convention in 2012, where Clint Eastwood performed a sketch on stage talking to a chair as if it was Obama, after which chairs appeared strung up in nooses.[68] Even though just a few showed overtly racist symbols like the watermelon, these invariably incited discussions about racism and lynch justice.[69] The images and scenes they evoked were too directly linked to the discriminatory practices of the not-so-distant past. Some of the people who had hanged Obama's effigies, expressed surprise by this reading, bent to the public pressure and took the effigies down.[70] Others refused to engage in the discussion and hid behind their right to freedom of speech. It is clear, that the effects of an effigy performance depend not only on the way it is performed, but also its context. In the light of the resistance to his presidency and delegitimization efforts by, for instance, the "birther movement," Obama's effigies were regularly seen in the context of racial discrimination and the continuing denial of civil rights.

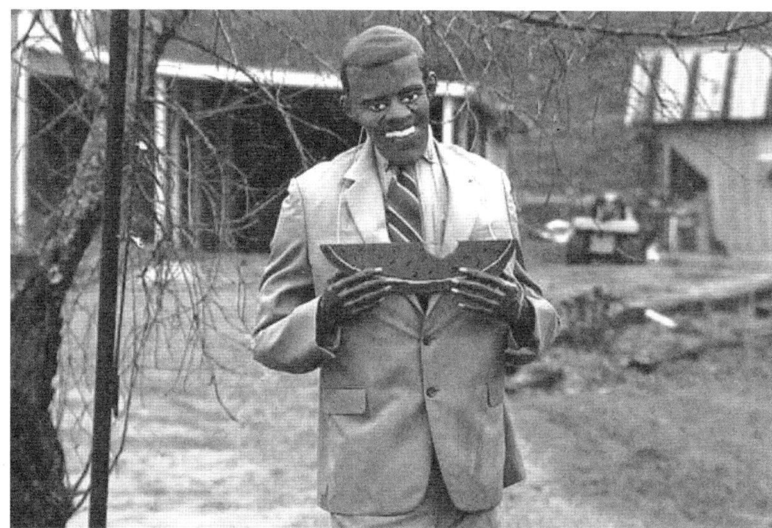

2012_12_28_USA-KT: President Obama

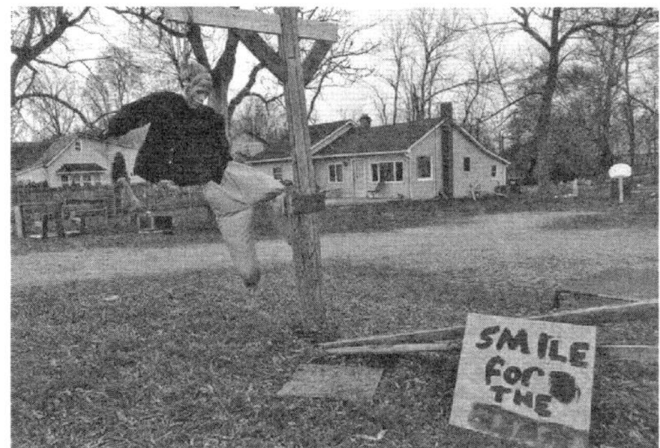

2012_10_31_USA-IN: President Obama

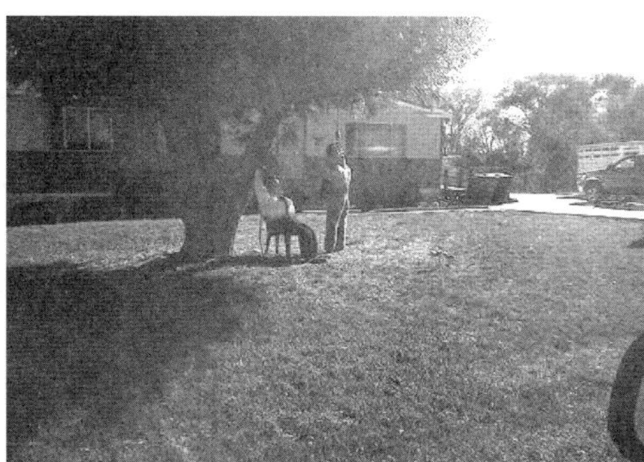

2012_10_29_USA-UT: President Obama + Mitt Romney

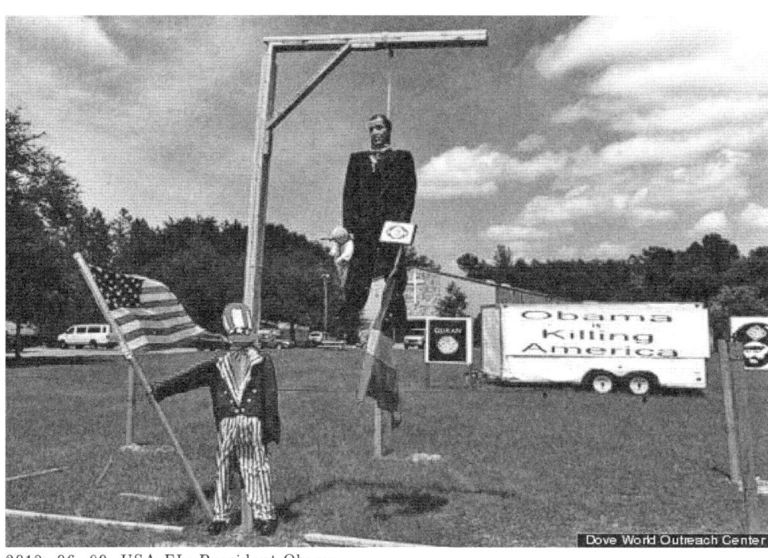

2012_06_09_USA-FL: President Obama

Effigies of Trump began to appear just after he announced his candidacy in 2015 with derogatory remarks about Mexican immigrants. After his election in November 2016, protesters in large demonstrations in Los Angeles, Oakland, New Orleans, and New York burned his effigies chanting: "Not my president!" and effigy protests have been repeated since. Trump's effigies are often made in the form of *piñatas* and are beaten to a pulp by protesters, or resemble traditional Mexican effigy practices of burning *Año Viejo* or Judas. With these cultural references, protesters assert the identity of immigrant communities in the US and denounce the politics of exclusion that are so characteristic of Trump's administration.

In these examples, the division between effigy protests derived from popular justice on the one hand and from communal celebrations of change becomes visible again in form. While Obama's effigies were predominantly hanged as

126

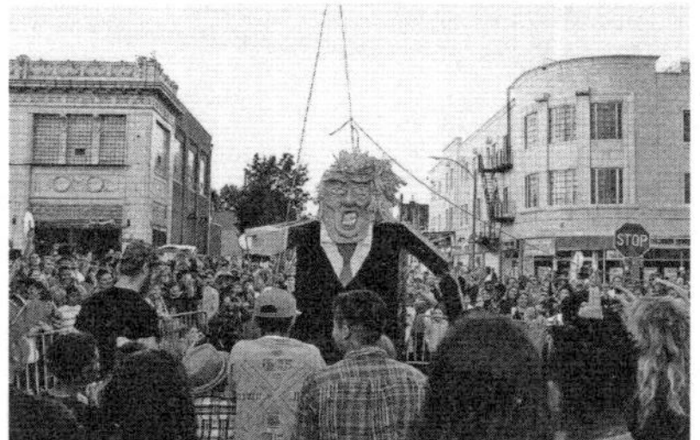

2015_09_13_USA-LA: presidential candidate Trump

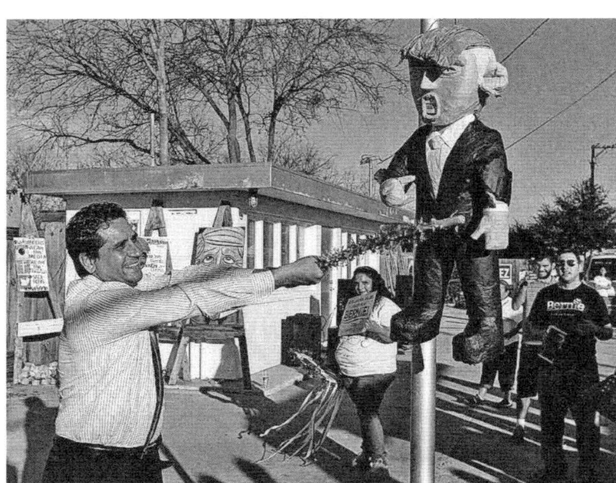

2016_01_30_USA-TX: presidential candidate Trump

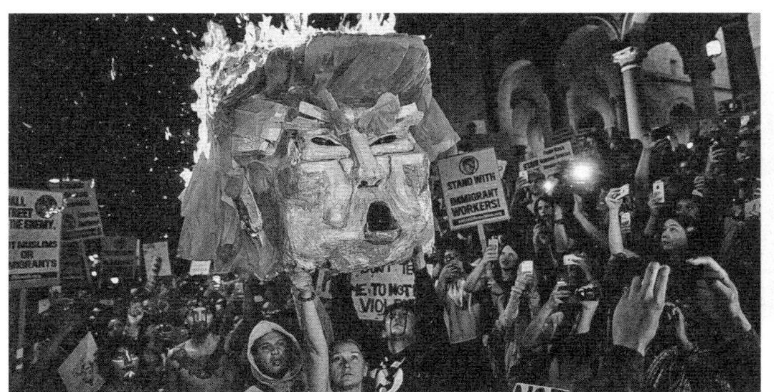

2016_11_09_USA-CA: President elect Trump

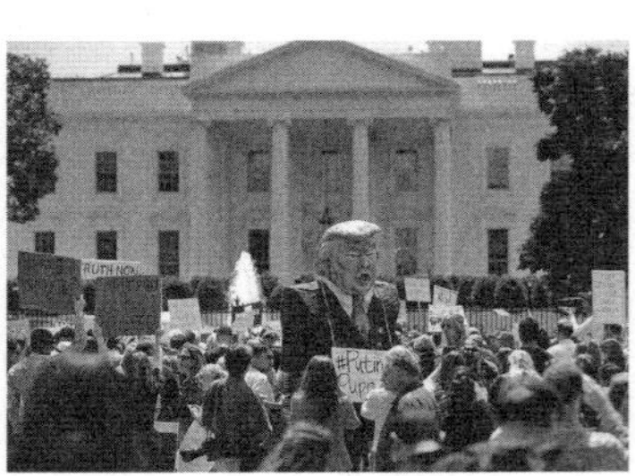

2017_05_10_USA-DC: President Trump

threatening signs similar to the un-civil rights effigies described earlier, Trump's effigies were beaten or burned in ephemeral performances during communal demonstrations. While the protesters who hanged Obama in effigy propose a return to previous oppressive race-relations, the protesters who burned Trump in effigy promote a more inclusive society.

Effigy Protests and the Democratic Paradox

In the effigy demonstrations between un-civil rights and civil rights protest, the conflict between the popular sovereign determining politics and the principles of individual rights and the rule of law comes into focus. It is a conflict that lies at the foundation of liberal democracy, "between the sovereign subject that founds the law and the law that delimits a space for politics within which the sovereign will can be expressed."[71] In political philosophy, this conflict has been identified as the "democratic paradox" that "emerges in the circular relation between the constituent power and the constituted power."[72]

The American Revolution broke with established British imperial rule under King George III legitimized by the transcendental authority of God. Revolutionaries used secret gatherings, mass rallies, and the press to publicize their cause and garner support. Through threats, physical violence, and popular justice like effigy protests, they intimidated their opponents and upended the old regime. In that revolutionary moment, outside of the law, the people claimed the right to govern themselves. Political theorist Chantal Mouffe asserts that at that moment "the old democratic principle that 'power should be exercised by the people' emerge[d] again" and modern democracy came into being.[73]

71 Andrew Schaap, "Aboriginal Sovereignty and the Democratic Paradox," in *The Politics of Radical Democracy*, ed. Adrian Little and Mona Lloyd (Edinburgh: Edinburgh University Press, 2009), 52.

72 Schaap, "Aboriginal Sovereignty," 52.

73 Chantal Mouffe, *The Democratic Paradox* (London: Verso, 2000), 2.

74 Mouffe, *The Democratic Paradox*, 2.

75 Mouffe, *The Democratic Paradox*, 2.

76 The Oxford English Dictionary defines "demos" as "the populace of a democratic state, regarded as the source of political power or legitimacy." *Oxford English Dictionary*, s.v. "demos," www.oed.com.

77 Heiner Bielefeldt, "Carl Schmitt's Critique of Liberalism: Systematic Reconstruction and Countercriticism," *Canadian Journal of Law & Jurisprudence* 10, no.1 (1997): 68–69; Chantal Mouffe, "Carl Schmitt and the Paradox of Liberal Democracy," *Canadian Journal of Law & Jurisprudence* 10, no. 1 (1997): 25.

78 Schaap, "Aboriginal Sovereignty," 53.

After the revolution, new political institutions and a new political order were established. Through the constitutional assembly of delegates from the thirteen states, the people of the colonies as the constituent power gave themselves a symbolic framework expressed in two of the most progressive documents of the time: the Declaration of Independence, and the Constitution. This framework was informed "by the liberal discourse, with its strong emphasis on the value of individual liberty and on human rights."[74] These documents set the standard against which individual rights in relation to a community came to be measured. In the US, modern liberal democracy was established as a form of rule, combining the principle of popular sovereignty with a "symbolic framework within which this democratic rule is exercised."[75] Mouffe made clear the paradoxical relationship between these two founding principles. While democracy establishes an exclusionary boundary in determining the demos and the majority of citizens decides on the rules of the community,[76] the framework of individual rights enshrined in the Constitution limits the exercise of the people's sovereignty. The democratic paradox was inscribed into the US political system at its founding moment.

There are different theories on how to deal with this paradoxical conflict between two principles. Political theorist Carl Schmitt, for instance, rejects outright the restrictions that liberal individual rights pose to the democratic process and emphasizes the primacy of the popular sovereign.[77] Sociologist Jürgen Habermas on the other hand conceives the two principles of popular sovereignty and the rule of law to be co-constituent in modern liberal democracy and stresses the need for public deliberation and consensus to reconcile the paradox.[78] In contrast to Habermas, Mouffe argues that there is only a contingent articulation of both principles in modern liberal democracies and no conceptual connection between popular sovereignty and the rule of law.[79] Nevertheless, she acknowledges the productive role that liberal discourse on rights plays to keep democracy alive, and states the need for "conflictual consensus" between adversaries who recognize each other as legitimate participants in democratic discourse.[80] This recognition of the opponent as part of the agonistic democratic discourse, though, is exactly what is often lacking.

Since the founding of the US, the disenfranchisement of African Americans brought the principles of democracy and representative government into crisis.[81] In colonial times, free African American men who met property requirements had the right to vote in many states, even in the South. After independence, however, many states excluded African Americans from the right to vote. While in the northern states African Americans gained enfranchisement when property requirements were abolished, they were completely disenfranchised in the South under the consolidation of the plantation system.[82] After the abolition of slavery in 1865, racial segregation continued, especially in the South, formalized by the Jim Crow laws that ensured that the African American population could not exercise their full civil rights. The Voting Rights act of 1965 intended to eliminate restrictions, but to date, state governments still devise measures like gerrymandering or strict voter registration laws to curtail the political weight of African Americans.[83]

The challenge of the status quo by the civil rights struggle was seen as a threat to existing economic structures and white Southern identity, leading to fears of disempowerment. The white population felt entitled to continue their way of life, built on the exclusion and subjugation of African Americans.[84] In the 1950s and '60s, demonstrators in the

79 Schaap, "Aboriginal Sovereignty," 58.

80 Chantal Mouffe, *On the Political* (London: Routledge, 2005), 63.

81 Manisha Sinha, "The Caning of Charles Sumner: Slavery, Race, and Ideology in the Age of the Civil War," *Journal of the Early Republic* 23, no. 2 (2003): 235–36.

82 Du Bois, *Black Reconstruction*, 22–23.

83 Another such measure is felony disenfranchisement, which disproportionately affects the African American population. Martha Nussbaum, *Hiding from Humanity* (Princeton: Princeton University Press, 2004), 249.

84 Robyn Duff Ladino, *Desegregating Texas Schools: Eisenhower, Shivers and the Crisis at Mansfield High* (Austin: University of Texas Press, 1996), xiii, 96.

85 The Universal Declaration of Human Rights was adopted in 1948 by the United Nations General Assembly. In 1951, the Civil Rights Congress attempted to charge the United States with complicity in the genocide of African Americans at the United Nations. Wikipedia, s.v. "We_Charge_Genocide."

un-civil rights protests against school integration insisted on the right of the popular sovereign to determine who to exclude from the demos against the individual rights of African Americans for equal access to government services. They hanged effigies of African American students who tried to enroll in public schools and universities to intimidate them in attempts to maintain the dominant white supremacist order.

In contrast, civil rights protesters claimed equal rights for all citizens granted by the Declaration of Independence, Constitution, and Universal Declaration of Human Rights.[85] In the long history of struggle, US activists used the discourse of universal human rights and the rule of law to counter the exclusionary force of the constituent power. By hanging or burning governors and state officials in effigy, they demanded change. The civil rights protests also claimed the right of the popular sovereign to elect or discharge their representatives, but proposed expanding the demos to include those formerly excluded.

Effigy Protests and the Imagination of Democracy

It might seem paradoxical that un-civil rights and civil rights protests could use the same form, the hanging and burning of effigies for opposite purposes: the people against the margin-alized Other and the Other people against the existing order. The performance of an effigy as political protest is not fixed in meaning but open to adaptation and inversion, and can be used strategically to generate, stabilize, and contest power relations.

Already during the revolution, the politics of this practice were ambiguous. The driving force behind the revolution was not the working class, but the well-off merchants and craftspeople who aspired to self-determination and economic independence from Britain.[86] The small group from Boston that secretly organized the resistance against the Stamp Act grew rapidly and came to be known as "Sons of Liberty." This upcoming elite sought an alliance with the lower classes against the British colonial administration and the loyalist upper class, and instrumentalized the mob for their own interests. To achieve their goals, the revolutionaries enacted considerable pressure and outright violence against their opponents. The practice of burning effigies during the revolution was liberating on the one hand and oppressive on the other.

An analysis of the *New York Times* archive confirms that in US history effigy demonstrations were most often staged either in partisan conflicts, where both sides vied for an increase in influence but didn't challenge the general structures of power, or in demonstrations that affirmed existing power relations.[87] Effigy demonstrations that aimed to dislodge established power structures and promote a more equitable and inclusive order were rather scarce. Protests organized by the labor movement from the 1880s until 1910, the 1920s, and '30s used effigies and continued to do so with reduced frequency from the 1950s until the early 1980s. One 1910 demonstration saw a group of suffragists burning an effigy of President Woodrow Wilson. Only in the student and counterculture movement from 1966 until 1975, in protests for civil rights, for the freedom of speech, and against the Vietnam War, did protesters more consistently challenge the dominant order in the US by burning the president and state representatives in effigy.

Examining the use of effigies in political conflicts in the US over 250 years, it is surprising how little the practice has

86 Longley, "Mob Activities," 109–12.

87 The *New York Times* published reports of effigy protests consistently between 1852 and 2017. Twenty percent of effigy performances were in protests that attempted to change power relations in favor of underprivileged groups.

changed since it derived from two different traditions, popular justice and Pope Day celebrations. From their original context and later adaptations during the American Revolution emerge imaginaries that remain recognizable in effigy protests to this day. The activation of these imaginaries in different formations of power results in different outcomes: the struggle for political influence between competing parties; the affirmative celebration of community in times of war; the subjugation and exclusion of minority groups from political participation; and – in a reversal of the subjugating practice – the demand for change and an inclusive reordering of society. Effigy performances that embody competing principles of exclusive popular sovereignty and inclusive liberal civil rights highlight the conflict at the heart of contemporary liberal democracy. They embody competing US political imaginaries, made visible again in the effigies of Obama and Trump.

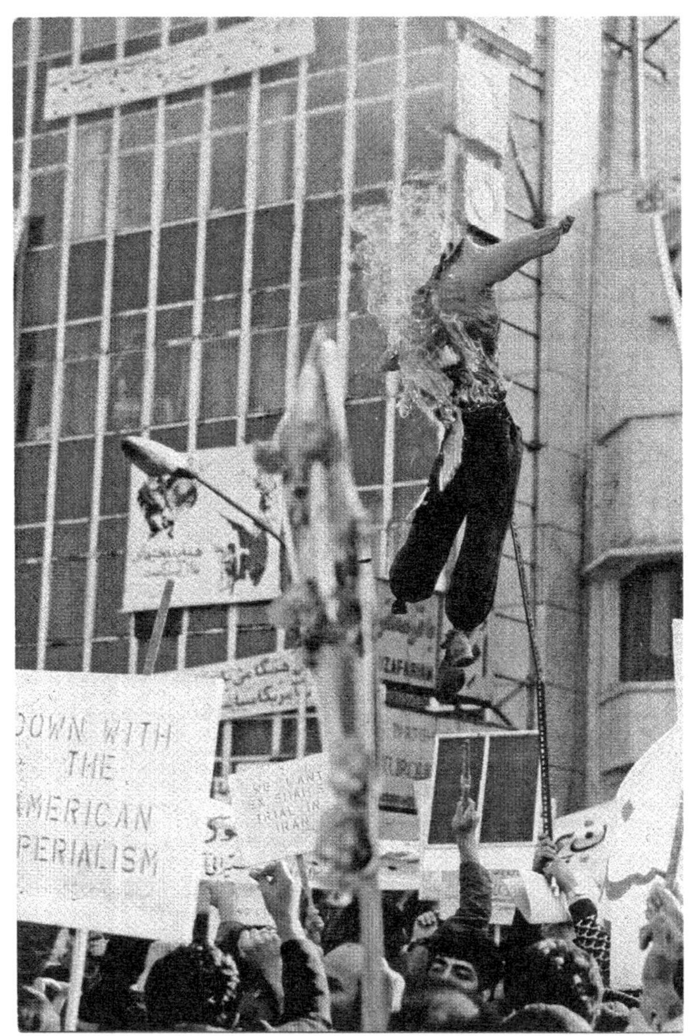

1979_12_00_Iran: US President Carter   (a)

Effigy Protests in Egypt, Iran, Afghanistan, and Across the Middle East

Exercising Protest

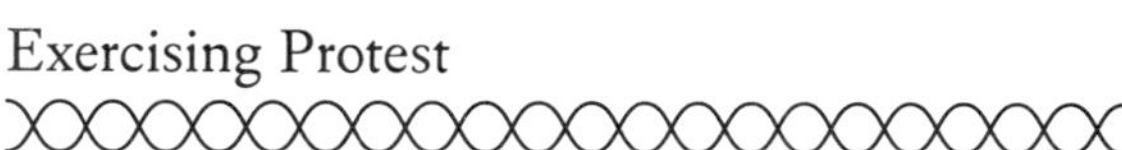

Over the past two decades, effigy protests from Afghanistan, Pakistan, Iraq, Lebanon, Palestine, and Egypt – have featured prominently in the Western news media. They have provided vivid symbolic images to highlight some of the most volatile international conflicts of these years. Most protests addressed the contentious military engagement of the United States and its allies in Afghanistan and Iraq, while some were staged as objections to a range of incidents initiated by Western groups or individuals and experienced as insults to Islam, like the Muhammad cartoons or a number of Quran burnings. Yet another cluster of effigy protests were staged in Egypt, Libya, Yemen, and Syria during the Arab Spring between 2011 and 2014, where demonstrators punished effigies depicting their own dictatorial rulers to demand change of their countries' political systems.

The protests I address in this lengthy chapter occurred in countries with different cultures and histories. While they share Islam as the majority religion, they may even be more

1   Edward Said, *Covering Islam: How the Media and the Experts Determine How We See the World*, revised edition (New York: Vintage Books: 1997).

united through their relationships with the "West," through shared experiences of colonialism and contemporary experiences of Western cultural, economic, and military hegemony. Then again, this shared experience might be perceived as a united phenomenon solely from a Western media perspective, often shaped by an essentializing discourse on the "Muslim world." From this perspective, effigy protests tend to be framed as the expressions of "Muslim anger" toward "the West." Since the image collection I work with is gathered mainly from English-language media, this study examines these events through the framework of that media. While I cannot disengage from this perspective, it does not completely determine the meaning of the images either. As I discuss in the introduction, a photograph is a complex cultural construct involving multiple actors whose contribution cannot be entirely erased. Reading the images for the traces of the photographed subjects' agency in relation to the historical and political context of the event, I attempt to counter the Western media framing. I then show how actors in these countries use the Western media to communicate with audiences in the West and express their resistance to the West's hegemonic influence. Being aware that the practice of burning effigies is no more than a symptom of geopolitical developments, I attempt to delineate the genealogical lines of effigy protests in a number of Muslim-majority countries in the Middle East and South Asia. I investigate why they have recently become increasingly visible and how they function in the contemporary global media environment.

In his 1981 book *Covering Islam: How the Media and the Experts Determine How We See the World*, postcolonial studies scholar Edward Said had already concluded that Western media discourse about Islam is severely biased.[1] Said analyzes the relationship between the world of Islam and the West through Western media discourse on "Islam," especially US media coverage of the 1979 Iran hostage crisis when revolutionary students occupied the US embassy in Tehran and took the embassy personnel hostage. He accuses the Western media of gross simplification and vilification when using the signifier "Islam." Lumping together billions of people, "dozens of countries, societies, traditions, languages, and, of course, all infinite number of different experiences,"[2] "reduces them all to a special malevolent and unthinking essence."[3]

Thirty years later, after 9/11 and a rising tide of "Islamist terrorist attacks," postcolonial studies scholars Peter Morey and Amina Yaqin suggest in their book *Framing Muslims: Stereotyping and Representation After 9/11* (2011) that the media discourse has not changed much.[4] The stereotype of the backward, irrational, and violent Muslim is still prevalent in Western mainstream media. Historian of the Middle East Cemil Aydin points out that the dialogic nature of the discourse of the "Muslim world," fueled by both Western Islamophobia built on the "legacy of imperial racialization of Muslim-ness" and by various forms of pan-Islamism, developed from the "intellectual and political strategies of Muslim resistance to this racialized identity."[5] While most protests I describe express, first and foremost, a resistance to specific policies of Western countries, they also react to the continuous malicious stereotyping in the Western media – calling for the recognition of diverse Muslim communities and their concerns.[6] This trend would signal the emergence, or rather, the existence of an Islamic transnational public sphere – a public sphere not bound by a nation-state but one including communities in Muslim-majority countries as well as diasporic communities in the West. Scholar of comparative religion Armando Salvatore notes that this transnational

2 Said, *Covering Islam*, xv.

3 Said, *Covering Islam*, 8.

4 Peter Morey and Amina Yaqin, *Framing Muslims* (Cambridge, MA: Harvard University Press, 2011), 1, 5.

5 Cemil Aydin, *The Idea of the Muslim World: A Global Intellectual History* (Cambridge, MA: Harvard University Press, 2017), 6.

6 Said, *Covering Islam*, vi; Morey and Yaqin, *Framing Muslims*, 179.

7   Armando Salvatore, "The Exit from a Westphalian Framing of Political Space and the Emergence of a Transnational Islamic Public," *Theory, Culture & Society* 24, no. 4 (2007): 49–50.

8   Nancy Fraser, "Transnationalizing the Public Sphere: On the Legitimacy and Efficacy of Public Opinion in a Post-Westphalian World," *Theory, Culture & Society* 24, no. 4 (2007): 7–8.

9   Nancy Fraser, "Rethinking the Public Sphere: A Contribution to the Critique of Actually Existing Democracy," *Social Text* 25/26 (1990): 75–76.

10   Nancy Fraser, "Rethinking the Public Sphere," 67.

11   Morey and Yaqin, *Framing Muslims*, 30–31.

Islamic public sphere actually precedes the globalization spreading from the West and builds on older networks based on traditional imaginaries of justice and the common good, and the idea of a global Islamic community or *Ummah*. With that, he suggests, it indeed fulfils the ideas of social connectivity and the public use of reason on which sociologist Jürgen Habermas's theory of the public sphere relies.[7]

Political theorist Nancy Fraser, however, has pointed out that transnational public spheres lack the normative legitimacy and political efficacy, which the public sphere in Habermas's political theory possesses.[8] In her view, they have to be seen as weak public spheres, which are not empowered by institutional integration, but are merely sites of opinion and will formation.[9] They are formed by, in Fraser's words, "subaltern counterpublics" who express their identities, interests, and needs in contestation with the dominant discourse.[10] Her analysis resonates with Said, Aydin as well as Morey and Yaqin who observe that the essentializing discourse of both Western Islamophobia and pan-Islamism have developed in reaction to each other.[11]

It has to be pointed out that the protests seem to confirm the Western media stereotype, which for a large part frames Muslims as irrational, anti-democratic, and violent. This is particularly true of effigy protests as they stage images of violent death, even though they are in themselves non-violent, symbolic expressions. This reflects the viciousness of the stereotype and the circularity of the media dynamic: to become visible and heard in the Western media, protesters have to perform the stereotype of the angry Muslim. It could be seen also as an affirmative re-appropriation of the stereotype, and a sign that there is indeed reason to be angry. Having to operate under the terms of the news media, protesters from these very diverse countries successfully use effigy protest as a strategy to gain access to the dominant Western discourse and have their voices be heard. At least to some degree, with the photographs of effigy protests in the news, they are able to regain agency and express their opinion in the public arena of Western media.

This Associated Press photograph of a motley group of protesters burning an effigy in an urban environment is very puzzling.○ At first glance, it seems to be just another protest in a Muslim country, of which we have seen so many in the last fifteen years. A closer examination reveals a number of discrepancies. The clothes worn by protesters vaguely resemble a variety of Muslim attire worn over jeans. But why would a Western-looking man – just visible at the right edge of the photograph – be talking on his telephone in the middle of a volatile protest? Furthermore, the group is strangely uncoordinated and unfocused, the performance has no center, there is no audience to address, and the place is completely nondescript. The caption of the photograph reveals that this "protest" was held outside a fake US consulate in a mock town named Erehwon. It was staged as an exercise to train security personnel for US embassies on a rural Virginia military base. The initial reason for the exercise, as stated in the caption, was the 2012 storming of the US diplomatic compound in Benghazi, Libya in which US Ambassador to Libya John Christopher Stevens and three security personnel were killed.

139

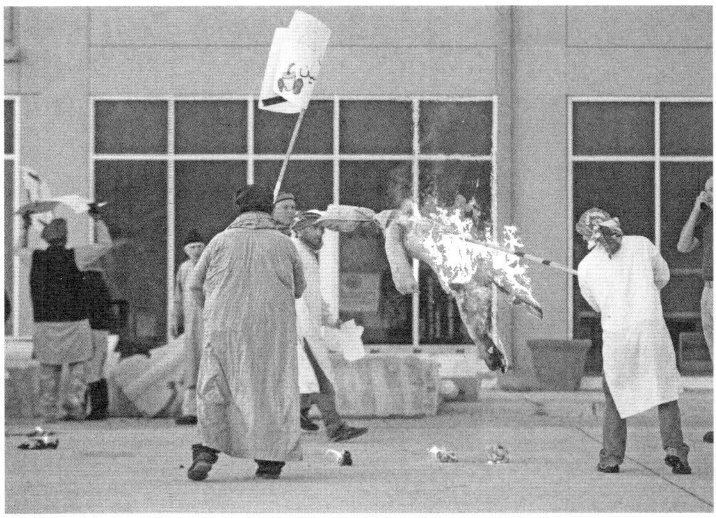

Virginia, US — Participants playing the roles of anti-American demonstrators burn a effigy outside a fake US Consulate during a US Diplomatic Security Service High Threat training program held at a mock town named Erehwon, "nowhere" spelled backwards, on a rural Virginia military base, Thursday. Two years after the deadly attack on a U.S. facility in Benghazi, Libya, the Diplomatic Security Service that is responsible for protecting some 100,000 Americans around the world has dramatically expanded training.

○ 2014_10_09_USA-VA: pretend effigy protest in US army exercise

12 Effigies of President Obama, the film producer, and Pastor Jones were burned in Pakistan (24), India (7), Afghanistan (5), Bangladesh (3), Sri Lanka (2) Palestine (2), and Lebanon (1).

13 I found reports featuring images of the hanging effigy and a cheering crowd beneath in several North American newspapers. The Associated Press distributed images and film reels of the event in the *Milwaukee Sentinel* (WI), December 19, 1956; *Quebec Chronicle Telegraph*, December 21, 1956; and *Montreal Gazette*, December 21, 1956.

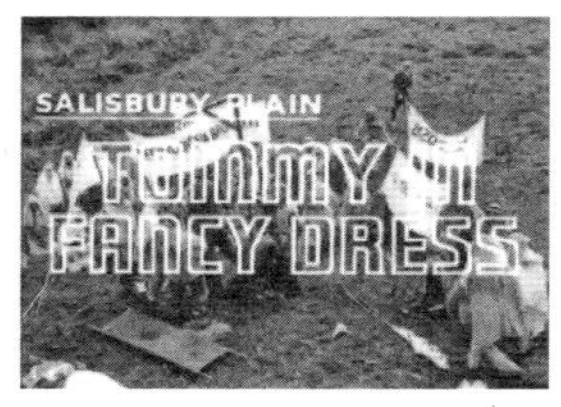

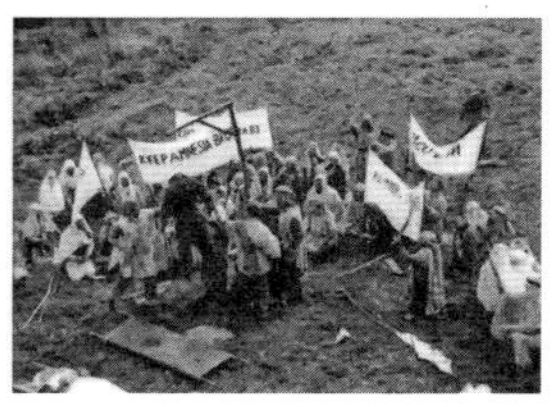

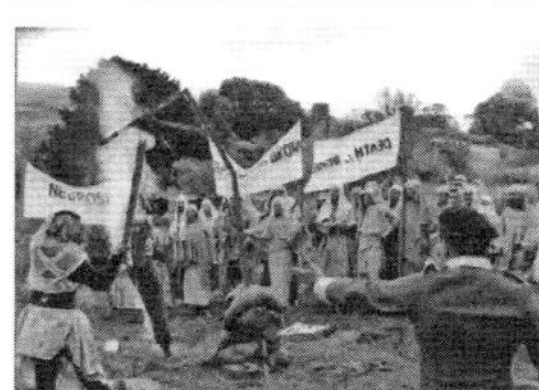

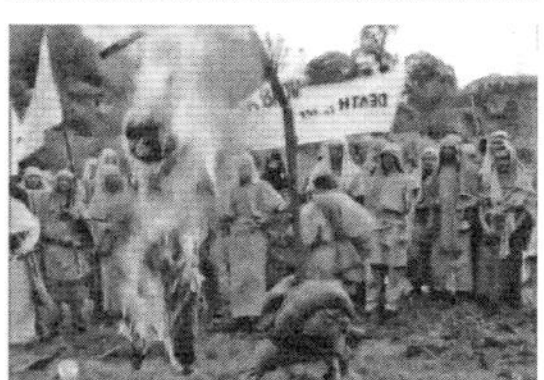

○ 1961_09_18_UK: pretend effigy protest in army exercise

Libyan militias had attacked the compound under the guise of region-wide protests against the inflammatory movie trailer "Innocence of Muslims" – many of which indeed featured burning effigies of President Barack Obama.[12]

A similar exercise was staged in 1961 in Salisbury, England as a British Pathé newsreel reports.○ In the British Army training scenario, the ruler of an unspecified Middle Eastern country appeals to the British for help against an unfriendly neighbor. As part of the scenario, the troops encounter a group of "Arab" protesters who burn an effigy, shout slogans, and confront the British troops. There is a lot of joking and irony in the voice-over and performance of soldiers playing Arab protesters. Nevertheless, the exercise acutely reveals the United Kingdom's myth of its relevance in the Middle East. This training scenario was likely devised in reaction to certain events during the Suez Crisis five years earlier, when the UK, France, and Israel briefly occupied the Suez Canal Zone. When the British withdrew its troops, people in Port Said celebrated by hanging effigies of British soldiers and the British prime minister. These images appeared widely in the international news media at the time,[13] and I assume reached a wide audience in Egypt and other countries in the region. The effigy performance in the 1961 exercise in Salisbury appears then as an echo of the 1956 effigy performance in Egypt. Just as the 2014 exercise in Virginia, it seems to have been a way to digest the protesters' actions and psychologically process the humiliation that the retreat from Egypt constituted. The exercises tacitly acknowledge the effigy performances' effectiveness in delivering a message while also mockingly incorporating it into the UK's own repertoire.

Spring Festival in Egypt

The 1956 effigy burning in Egypt might have been especially humiliating for its resemblance to the British "Guy Fawkes Day" customs in which effigies are burned each 5th of November. The similarity to the British holiday was no coincidence, since Port Said at the Mediterranean entry point to the Suez Canal has a similar festival called *Harq al-Limby* (Burning al-Limby) during which effigies of the British Lord Allenby are burned.[14] This festival dates back to the period after World War I, when Egypt was a British protectorate, and the Suez Canal was under British administration. During the war, a large contingent of British troops were stationed in Egypt, soldiers and supplies from India, Australia, and New Zealand were shipped through the Suez Canal, and the costs to the Egyptian economy and population were high.[15] Given their war contributions, Egyptian nationalists expected complete independence after the war. On November 12, 1918, one day after Armistice Day, a delegation of the Egyptian Nationalist movement under its leader Saad Zaghloul approached the High Commissioner in Egypt, Sir Reginald Wingate. The delegation demanded discussion of Egyptian independence but was dismissed. Instead, the commissioner ordered a crackdown on the Egyptian independence movement and had Zaghloul arrested in March 1919. The country erupted in demonstrations and strikes, sparking the first Egyptian Revolution. Lord Allenby, the much-hated Field Marshal of the Egyptian Expeditionary Forces, was dispatched to suppress the unrest, and remained High Commissioner until 1925.[16] At some point during his tenure, Port Said residents burned his effigy in protest of his draconian rule, thereafter becoming an established custom.[17]

14   Al-Limby is a spoonerism of Allenby.

15   For instance, the United Kingdom conscripted over 1.5 million Egyptians into the Labour Corps to support the British troops. Wikipedia, s.v. "Egyptian revolution of 1919."

16   Jan Romein, *The Asian Century: A History of Modern Nationalism in Asia* (Berkeley: University of California Press, 1962), 191.

17   Newspaper reports mentioning the roots of *Harq al-Limby*, connect the burning of Lord Allenby's effigy not to a specific event, but to his presence in Egypt, citing the years of his arrival and departure 1917 or 1925. All reports were written after the year 2000 and none of them cite a specific source. Shaden Shehab, "Effigy Burning Ban," *Al-Ahram Weekly* 585, May 9–15, 2002, weekly. ahram.org.eg/2002/585/eg7. htm; Osama Kamal, "A City Like," *Al-Ahram Weekly*, June 9, 2011, www.masress.com/en/ ahramweekly/26841; Madame Sosostris, "Pack of Cards," *Al-Ahram Weekly* 480, May 4–10, 2000, weekly.ahram.org.eg/ Archive/2000/480/people.htm; and "A Unique Story in the Public Spaces of Port Said," *RHET201-Research* (blog), May 21, 2010. abougendy.wordpress. com/2010/05/21/a-unique-story-in-the-public-spaces-of-port-said/.

18   See Mériam N. Belli, *An Incurable Past: Nasser's Egypt Then and Now* (Gainesville: University Press of Florida, 2013).

19   On October 28, 1969, an article in the *Ottawa Citizen* on Guy Fawkes Day noted "many English youngsters have already made their 'guy' – the effigy to be burned in the bonfire."

20   Still in 1951, the Navy, Army and Air Force Institute (NAAFI), which runs shops on British Military bases, shipped fireworks to Egypt for Guy Fawkes Day celebrations. *Times*, November 5, 1951.

21   "The 'Waiheathens' at Gallipoli: Diary and letters of a Waihi soldier Gerald (Tad) Morpeth, one of the six Morpeth brothers from Waihi who served in WW1," *Tauranga Memories: Remembering War* (website), http://tauranga.kete.net.nz/ remembering_war/documents/ show/426-the-waihea- thens-at-gallipoli.

22   Luci Gosling, "'Guy-ser' Bill—Remember, remember, the Fifth of November," *Picturing the Great War: The First World War Blog from Mary Evans Picture Library* (blog), November 5, 2013, http://blog. maryevans.com/2013/11/guy- ser-bill-remember-remember- the-fifth-of-november-.html.

Anthropologist Mériam N. Belli describes in her book *An Incurable Past: Nasser's Egypt Then and Now* (2013) the *Harq al-Limby*, the annual festive burning of al-Limby, based on interviews with Port Said residents conducted in the early 2000s.[18] Some of her sources contend that the burning of Allenby's effigy was invented by the people of Port Said, while others refer to unspecified customs from the country-side. Belli follows the latter argument and suggests that the burning of Allenby might have been an adaptation of calen-drical rituals involving bonfires practiced in the Upper Egyptian countryside – without being able to point to any concrete local tradition. As an alternative, I suggest that the Port Said residents appropriated the British custom of burn-ing Guy Fawkes. Though I also have no concrete evidence, I present a number of clues to support my hypothesis.

The celebration of Guy Fawkes Day was at that time still widely practiced in the UK and the British Empire.[19] Port Said had a sizable European population, consisting of work-ers and administrators of the Suez Canal. It is very likely that the British expat workers in Port Said celebrated their beloved custom, where their Egyptian co-workers and neigh-bors would witness the effigy burnings.[20] In the UK, the holi-day involved groups of neighborhood children constructing their own Fawkes effigy from old clothes stuffed with straw,

142

From the diary of Lt/Corporal Gerald Morpeth from New Zea-land: 5th November 1914: Guy Fawkes Day but no celebration and expect that the Kaiser is burnt in effigy in a good many places in the British Empire. We are still sailing north so the rumour is we may stop off at Colombo and then to Suez.[21]

1914_11_05_British Empire: German Kaiser Wilhelm II as Guy Fawkes

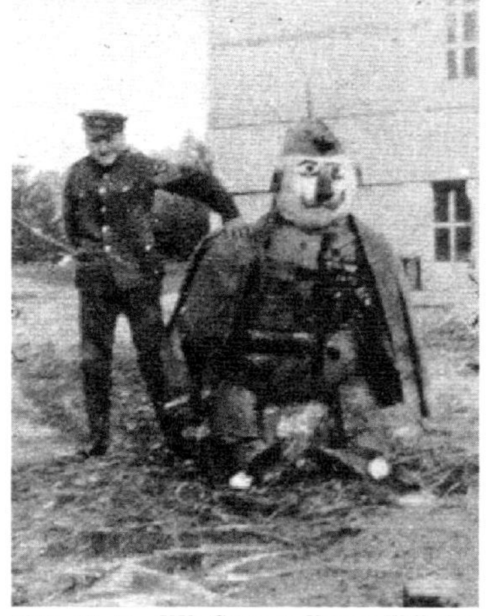

1915_11_05_UK: German Kaiser Wilhelm II as Guy Fawkes

With Guy Fawkes Night upon us, we thought it would be fun to share some Great War variations on a simple form of caricature associated with this British November tradition. Instead of a stuffed effigy of that wicked trai-tor, Guido Fawkes, to be burned, ceremoniously, atop a bonfire. The flames of First World War bonfires … were more likely to consume a likeness of the Kaiser – or Guy-ser – Fawkes.[22]

Guy Fawkes Night during WWI_UK

and begging for "a penny for the Guy" by displaying their dummies. Neighborhoods and even entire towns would sometimes compete for the most spectacular bonfire. The descriptions of the Port Said Allenby effigy burning by some of Belli's informants closely corresponds to this tradition.[23] Remembering the festival from the 1940s, they describe fabricating the dolls from old cloth stuffed with straw, collecting money for the celebration, and competing between neighborhoods for the most spectacular burning. That these elements were part of both Guy Fawkes Day and the al-Limby festival, supports the hypothesis that the latter was appropriated from the first.

During WWI, the likelihood that effigies were burned in Port Said even increased. More than 100,000 soldiers were stationed in the Canal Zone and even more soldiers passed through on troop transports from and to India, Australia, New Zealand, and other parts of the British Empire, where Guy Fawkes Day was also celebrated.[24] It is again likely that the soldiers celebrated this holiday as a welcome diversion from their military duties. It might be even more likely that the soldiers burned effigies of Kaiser Wilhelm on Armistice Day on November 11, 1918 – six days after Guy Fawkes Day – to celebrate the end of the war, like many of their comrades all over the English-speaking world. These celebratory

143

23 Belli, *An Incurable Past*, 77–79.

24 Guy Fawkes Day is to this day celebrated in Australia, New Zealand, Canada, and Bermuda.

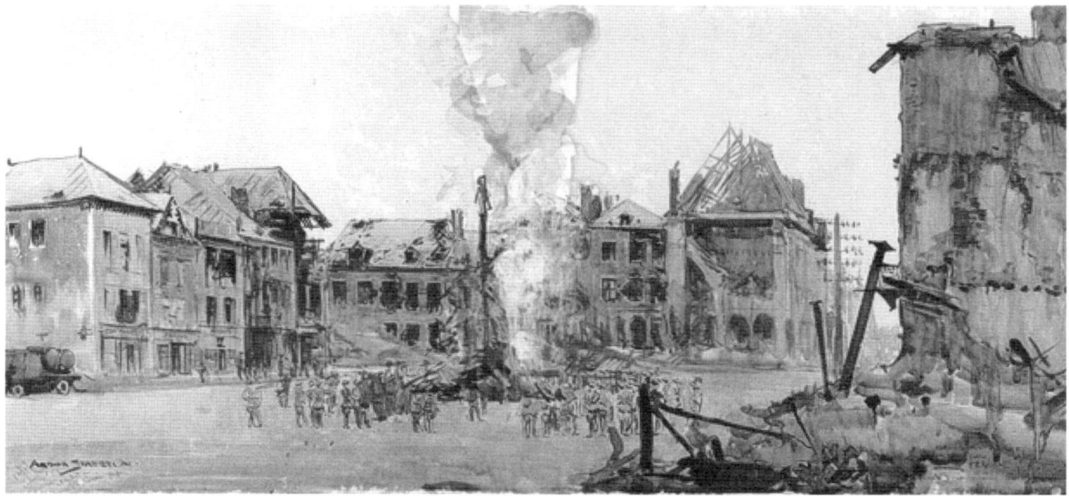

1918_11_12_France: German Kaiser Wilhelm II burned in effigy by Australian soldiers

burnings of Wilhelm occurred, for instance, in England,
Northern Ireland, France, Australia, New Zealand, the US,
and Canada. I suggest, therefore, that Egyptian nationalists
in Port Said appropriated the burning of Guy Fawkes and/or
of the German Kaiser to demand the end of the British occupation. From this first protest onwards it was associated with
the resistance against British colonial rule and repeatedly
used until after independence when it became part of the
annual spring festival *Sham el-Nessim* in Port Said.

Great Britain granted Egypt independence in 1922, but
continued to exert large influence on Egyptian politics and
retained control of the Suez Canal. In 1952, the second Egyptian revolution was fought to win complete independence
from Britain and brought renewed relevance to the *Harq al-
Limby* tradition as a sign of resistance. In January of that year,
the effigy of a British soldier was hanged in a Cairo street.

In 1956, Great Britain, France, and Israel invaded Egypt
and occupied the Suez Canal area and Sinai, but had to
retreat under pressure from the US and Soviet Union. In Port
Said, effigies of British Prime Minister Anthony Eden were

144

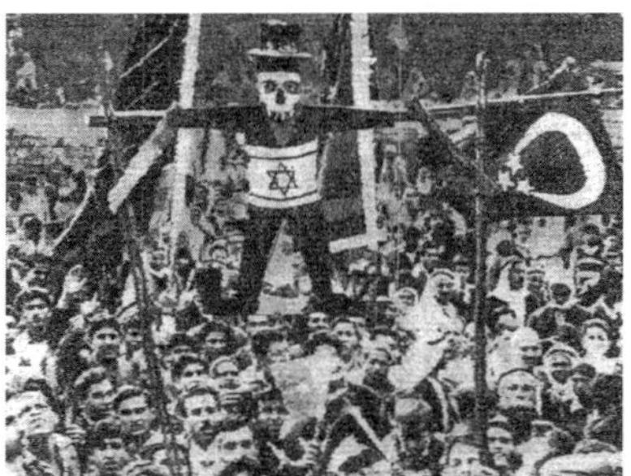

1957_03_14_Gaza: Israeli Premier
Ben-Gurion

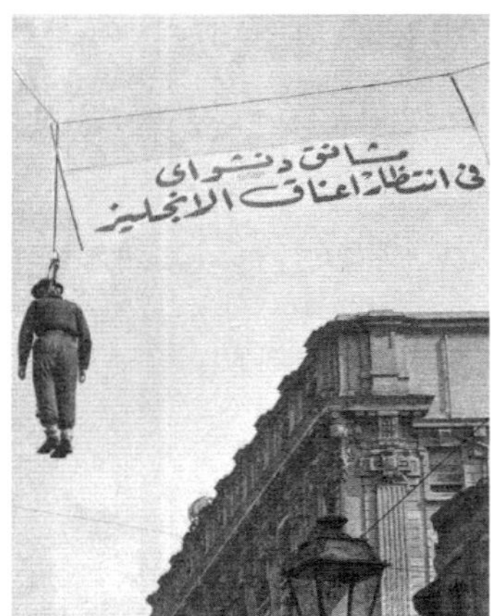

1952_01_03_Egypt: British soldier

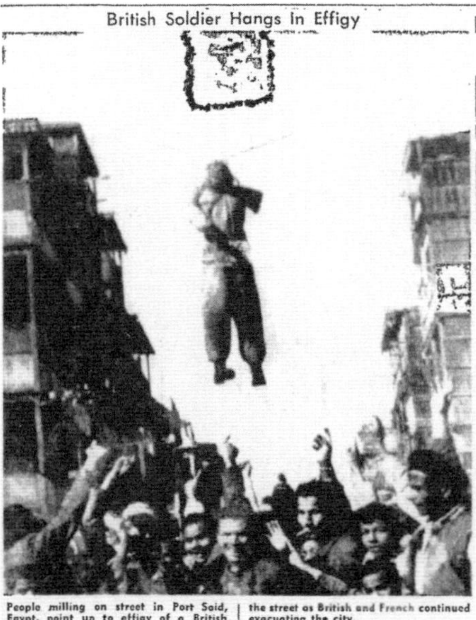

People milling on street in Port Said, Egypt, point up to effigy of a British soldier hanging from a wire strung across the street as British and French continued evacuating the city. (AP Photo)

○1956_12_21_Port Said, Egypt: UK Premier Eden

paraded in December 1956. One effigy strung from wire across the street under a portrait of Egyptian President Gamal Abdel Nasser attracted a lot of media attention as it marked the end of British occupation.○ A film clip from the British Pathé archives shows a second effigy being beaten by Egyptian protesters. Three weeks later, Israeli Prime Minister David Ben-Gurion was burned in effigy in Arish on the Sinai Peninsula, when Israel completed the withdrawal from the peninsula, and again in March 1957, celebrating Gaza's anticipated return to Egyptian administration.

Photographs from December 1957 show President Nasser during the anniversary celebrations of Victory Day in Port Said.⑩ Surrounded by a jubilant crowd, he is seen passing under an effigy hanging above: a sign of protest turned rally decoration. The hanging effigy had again become part of the memorialization of the Egyptian struggle for independence, a symbol of victory over the despised Western powers: Britain, France, and Israel. With the success of the revolution and the renewed national pride that resulted from it, the ritual of hanging and burning effigies of Allenby became a fixed

145

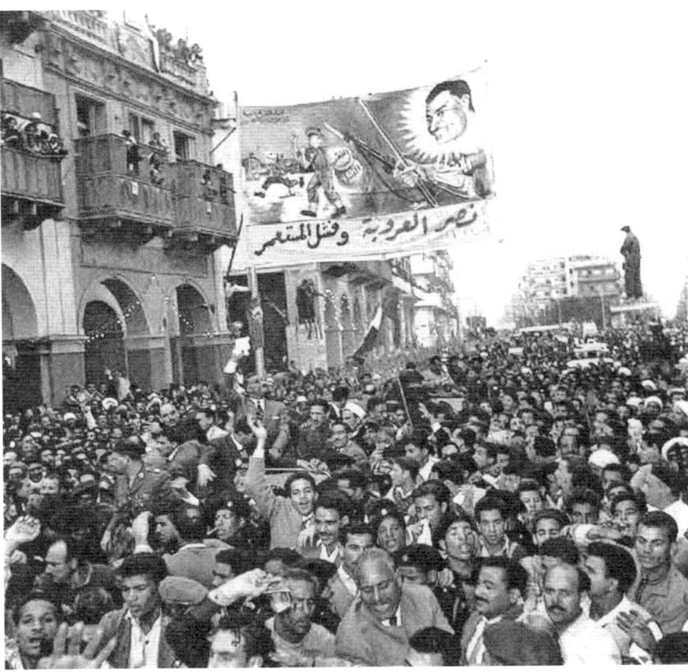

⑩ 1957_12_23_Port Said, Egypt: UK Premier Eden

25 Belli, *An Incurable Past*, 78–79.

26 M. F. Kalfat, "Port Said in the Evening, Port Said in the Morning," *Jadaliyya*, June 2, 2014.

part of the memory culture in Port Said. As part of the spring festival, the *Harq al-Limby* was celebrated in the streets of the town, where the neighborhoods would compete in creating the best Allenby effigy and the biggest bonfire.[25] The hanging and burning of effigies became an effective symbolic performance to protest foreign occupation and celebrate the restoration of sovereignty.

Over time, the effigy of the actual personage Lord Allenby transformed into "the Allenby" or "al-Limby," a general figure representing evil foreign influence. As the memory of Allenby's role in Egypt faded, his figure was often replaced by dummies representing the contemporary enemies of Egypt. In the 1970s, these were Israeli Prime Minister Golda Meir and Minister of Defense Moshe Dayan, in 1991 Saddam Hussein, and at the end of the 1990s Israeli Prime Minister Benjamin Netanyahu. Sometimes sports personalities, football referees, and abstract evils like "corruption" figured as the al-Limby, but it seems that the effigies never represented Egyptian politicians.[26] A few photographs give an insight into how the effigies were used as decorations for the spring festival. Before they were burned, the al-Limby effigies were displayed for a number of days suspended above the street, on a stage filled with characters with placards indicating their

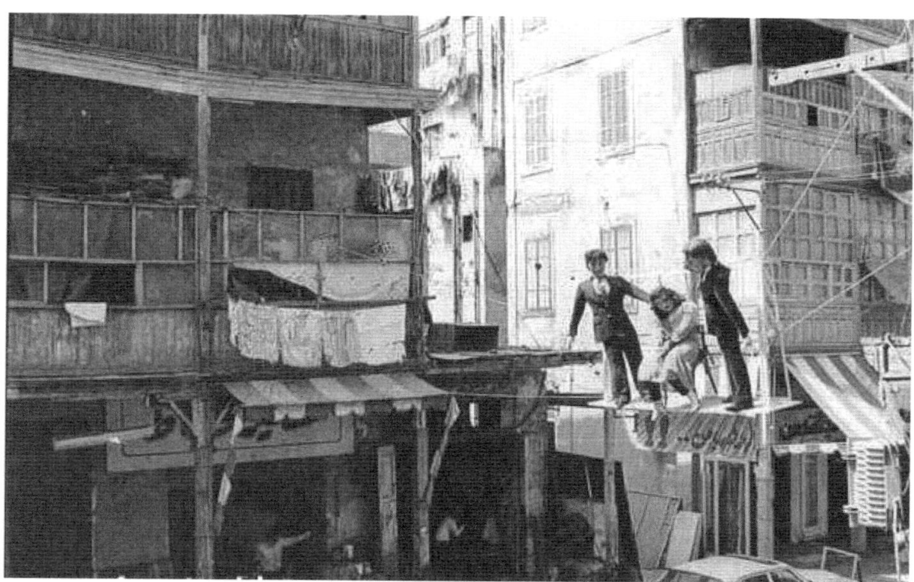

al-Limby: 1990s_Port Said, Egypt

names, or carried through the streets in a procession. In 2000, the Egyptian government outlawed the burning of effigies during *Harq al-Limby* out of fire and pollution concerns, which is why the effigies of Israeli Prime Minister Ariel Sharon in 2001 and US President George W. Bush in 2003 were not burned but paraded and ridiculed.

From Egypt to Palestine

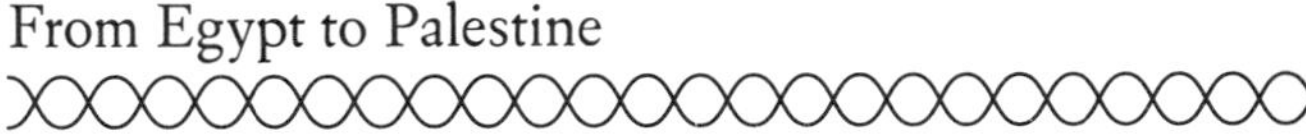

In addition to the effigy protests commemorating the Egyptian struggle for independence in Port Said, there are reports of a few more effigies being burned in the process of consolidating the Egyptian sovereign nation-state. In 1959, an effigy of Nasser was hanged in Baghdad for his support of the pro-Arab revolt in Mosul, Iraq. In retaliation, and because of his stance against joining the United Arab Republic under Nasser, an effigy of Iraqi Prime Minister Qāsim was hanged in effigy in Cairo. After the Six-Day War with Israel, in 1967, when most Egyptian Jews were expelled from the country, effigies of Jews were hanged in the streets of Cairo and others representing Israel and the US; US President Lyndon Johnson and British Prime Minister Harold Wilson were burned in Port Said for their countries' lack of support against Israel.

It is during the Egyptian conflict with Israel that the practice of burning effigies seems to have been adopted by

147

A crowd of 300.000 saw the premier of Iraq hanged in effigy Monday. The Cairo demonstrators hanged effigies of Premier Abdul Karim Kassem alongside the bodies of dogs, cats and rats. Men and women screamed, "We shall bottle your blood, Kassem."
—*Chicago Tribune*, 17 Mar 1959

1959_03_16_Egypt: Iraqi Premier Kassem

Iraqi demonstrators hanged President Nasser in effigy today in Rashid Street, Baghdad's main thoroughfare. The United Arab Republic leader, a hero of the masses here just eight months ago, was a target of crowds calling for vengeance as a result of the Mosul rebellion against the regime of Premier Kassim.
—*New York Times*, 12 Mar 1959

1959_03_11_Iraq: Egyptian President Nasser

The crowds clamored for death to Egypt's President Nasser. A throng of ragged youth holding Mr. Nasser's effigy over their heads snake-danced on fashionable Avenue Mohammed V.
—*Toledo Blade*, OH, 27 Apr 1965

1965_04_27_Tunisia: Egyptian President Nasser

27 "Who's Behind Egypt's Rampage Against Palestinians?" Executive Intelligence Review 5, no. 8 (1978): 6.

protesters in other countries of the region. In Tunis in 1965, an effigy of Nasser was paraded because he criticized Tunisia for not joining the Arab boycott of West Germany over its plan to recognize the state of Israel. I was not able to find photographs of the effigy parade in Tunisia, but the way the Queen Elizabeth's effigy is hanged in Lebanon, just after the Six-Day War in 1967, on wires above the street○, closely resembles photographs from instances in Egypt in 1952 and 1956 featuring effigies of British occupiers. This resemblance in form makes it seem plausible that Lebanese protesters saw the Egyptian protests in the news and replicated them.

In 1969, an effigy of Dayan was burned by a group of children in Nablus (part of Jordan but then occupied by

148

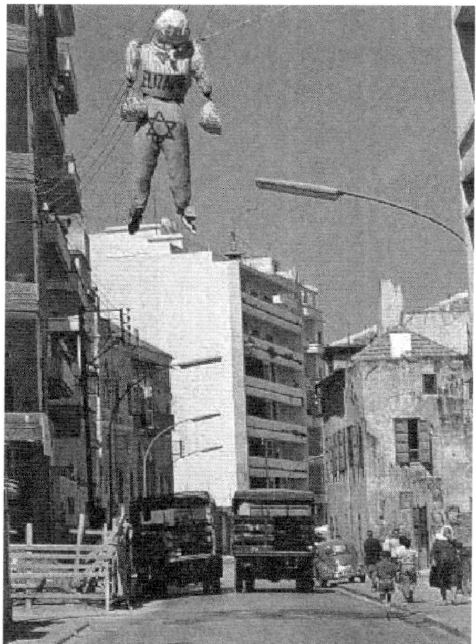

○ 1967_06_00_Lebanon: British Queen Elizabeth

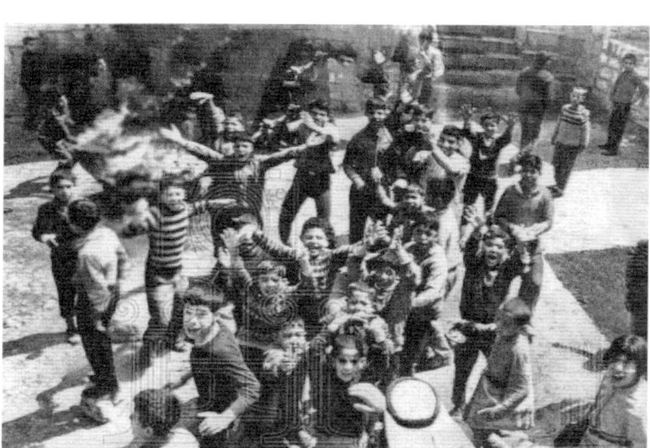

1969_04_09_Palestine: Israeli defense minster Dayan

Student demonstrators burned Golda Meir in effigy today less than three blocks from where the Israeli premier was attending a meeting of international Socialist leaders. Students shouted "Golda murderer" as they marched down the Boulevard St. Germain carrying aloft Palestinian flags and the portrait of a Palestinian leader who died here Tuesday.
—*Kentucky New Era*, Hopkinsville, 13 Jan 1973

1973_01_13_France: Israeli Premier Meir

Simultaneously, the right wing press ran cartoons of PLO chief Yasser Arafat with his hands dripping blood while uncontrolled mobs roamed the streets of Cairo burning Arafat in effigy.[27]

1978_02_28_Egypt: PLO Chief Arafat

Yasir Arafat, chairman of the Palestine Liberation Organisation, vowed to chase Americans out of the Middle East and to "chop off the hands" of President Carter, President Anwar el-Sadat of Egypt and Prime Minister Menachem Begin of Israel. He spoke to a group of guerrilla recruits at a the Sabra Palestinian camp here as effigies of the three signers were burned.
—*New York Times*, 27 Mar 1979

1979_03_26_Palestine: US President Carter, Egyptian President Sadat, Israeli Premier Begin

Israel) and in 1970 in the U K "hundreds of pro-Arab demonstrators paraded with an effigy of Israeli Defense Minister Moshe Dayan hanging from a makeshift gallows" over ongoing hostilities during the slow-boiling War of Attrition.[28] In Lebanon, U S envoys were paraded and burned in effigy by Palestinian refugees in April 1970 and May 1971, when they met with Lebanon's leaders to discuss the situation in the Middle East. Palestinian expats also burned effigies of their enemies like King Hussein of Jordan in 1971 in New York and in France of Meir, following the Israeli prime minister's attendance at a meeting of the Socialist International in 1973. The Israeli-Egyptian peace process from 1977 to 1979 led to fierce protests in the region. Sadat effigies were burned in Lebanon (two in 1977 and 1978 and one in 1979 accompanied by effigies of U S President Jimmy Carter and Israeli Prime Minister Menachem Begin), in Palestine in 1978, and twice in Iraq in 1979. In 1978, Yasser Arafat, leader of the Palestinian Liberation Organization (PLO), was hanged in effigy for the PLO's resistance against the peace process

28 "Israeli, Arab Guns in 2 Duels," *Evening News* (Newburgh, NY), May 19, 1970.

149

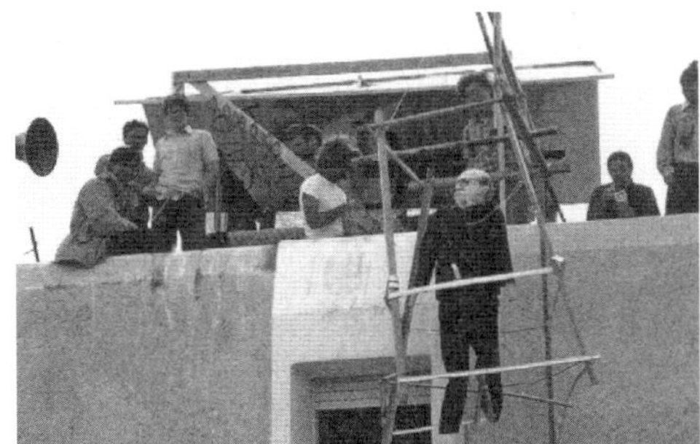

1982_03_11_Israel: Premier Begin

Almost 10,000 people carrying Palestinian and Lebanese flags marched in Moslem west Beirut on Wednesday to protest an Israeli's killing of seven Palestinians near Tel Aviv this weekend. … The protesters also burned effigies of President Bush and Israel's Prime Ministers Yitzhak Shamir in front fo the five-story U.N. office.
—*Sun-Journal*, Lewiston, ME, 24 May 1990

1990_05_23_Lebanon: US President Bush + Israeli Premier Shamir

Iraqi President Hassan Al Bakr and Vice President Saddam Hussein led a parade past tens of thousands of persons who lined Baghdad's streets. Later a huge effigy of Sadat was burned in the city's central square.
—*Observer Reporter*, Washington, PA, 2 May 1979

1979_05_01_Iraq: Egyptian President Sadat

Millions of Moslems in Asia, Africa, and the Middle East stopped work today in an unprecedented show of support for Palestinians in Israel-occupied lands after Sunday's shooting on the sacred Temple Mount in Jerusalem. Government offices, private firms, and banks closed from Mali in West Africa to Pakistan, where demonstrators burned effigies of Israeli Prime Minister Menachem Begin and President Reagan.
—*Glasgow Herald*, 15 Apr 1982

1982_04_14_Pakistan: Israeli Premier Begin + US President Reagan

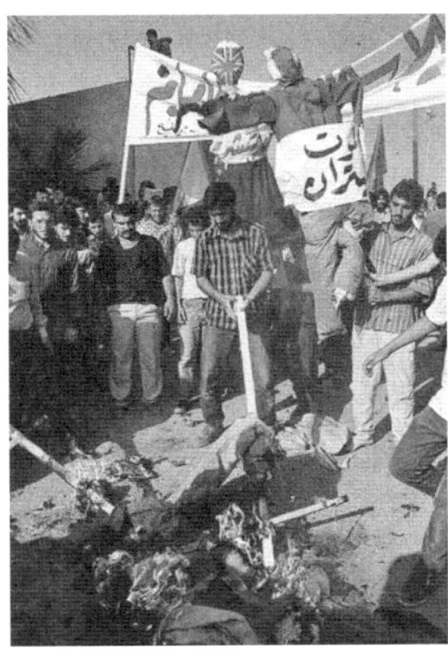

1987_07_24_Lebanon: USA + France

between Egypt and Israel and their alleged involvement in the assassination of a close associate of Egyptian President Anwar el-Sadat in Cyprus.

Protests in the Israeli-Palestine conflict that feature effigies continue, often sparked by inflammatory events like the shooting of Palestinians on the Temple Mount by a Jewish civilian in 1982, the Sabra and Shatila massacre in a Palestinian refugee camp in Lebanon in 1982, Israeli military offensives in Lebanon and Gaza, and the assassination of Palestinian leaders. Effigy protests accompany all stages in the ever-changing never-resolving conflict. Between 1980 and 2017, all Israeli Prime Ministers and all US Presidents were burned in effigy multiple times: Menachem Begin (6), Ronald Reagan (4), Yitzhak Shamir (3), George Bush (3), Yitzhak Rabin (6), Benjamin Netanyahu (13), Bill Clinton (2), Ehud Barak (3), Ariel Sharon (19), George W. Bush (19), Ehud Olmert (13), Barack Obama (10), and Donald Trump (2).

150

Yasser Arafat, Shimon Peres and Yitzhak Rabin received the Nobel Peace Prize on Saturday and pledged to pursue their mission of healing the anguished Middle East. ... But in a fresh reminder of continuing hatred and bitterness, Jewish extremists burned an effigy of Rabin outside city hall and scullfed with an Arab waving a Palestinian flag.
—*Item*, Sumter, SC, 10 Dec 1994

1994_12_10_Norway: Israeli Premier Rabin

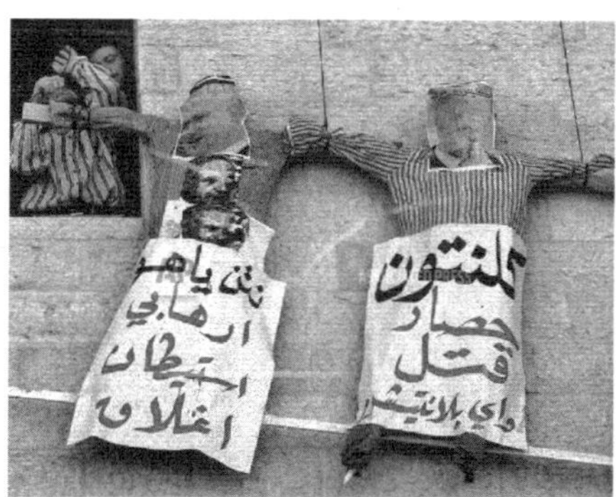

1998_11_09_Palestine: Israeli Premier Netanyahu + US President Clinton

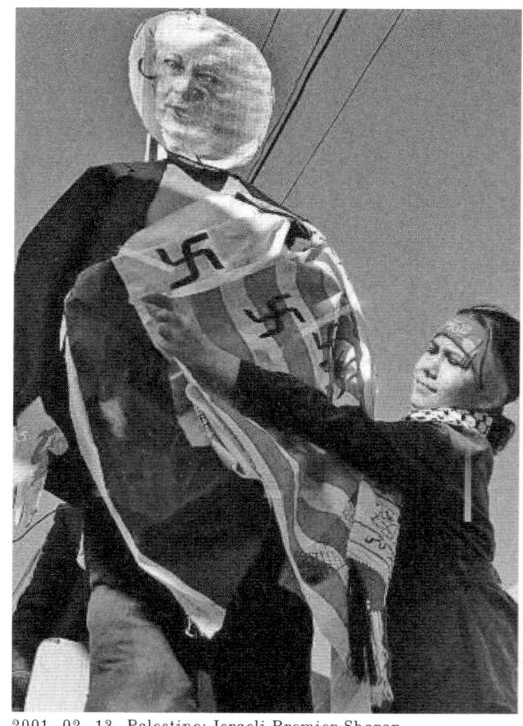

2001_02_13_Palestine: Israeli Premier Sharon

Most protests were staged in Palestine and Lebanon, which had accepted large numbers of Palestinian refugees. Additionally, groups in other countries often felt the urge to express their position in the conflict and pressure their governments to take action. I list a few incidents in the Israel-Palestine conflict that show the breadth of Muslim communities' responses in many countries. In 2006, in protest against Israel's offensive in South Lebanon, protesters burnt effigies of US President George W. Bush and Israeli Prime Minister Ehud Olmert in Palestine (1), Pakistan (5), India (4), Turkey (3), Syria (1), Iraq (1), and Malaysia (1). In protest of the 2008–2009 Gaza War, effigies of Olmert, Bush, Obama, Egyptian President Hosni Mubarak, and Israeli Foreign Minister Tzipi Livni are burned in Palestine (3), Lebanon (2), Pakistan (3) Afghanistan (1), India (1), Indonesia (1), Syria (1), and Azerbaijan (1).

In this partial genealogy, I chart the use of effigies in protests in Egypt and the countries of the Levant and from

151

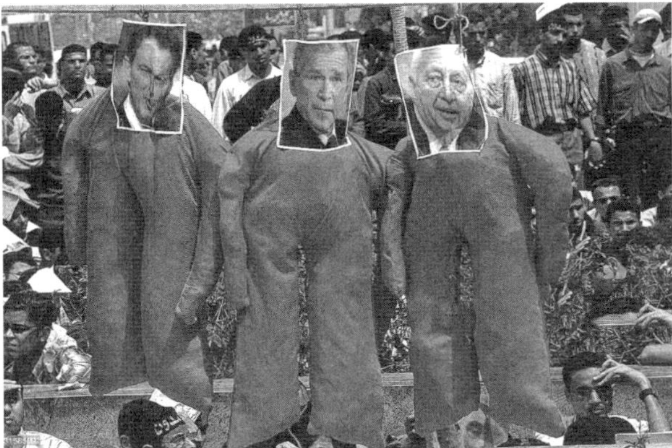

2004_03_30_Egypt: US President Bush + British Premier Blair + Israeli Premier Sharon

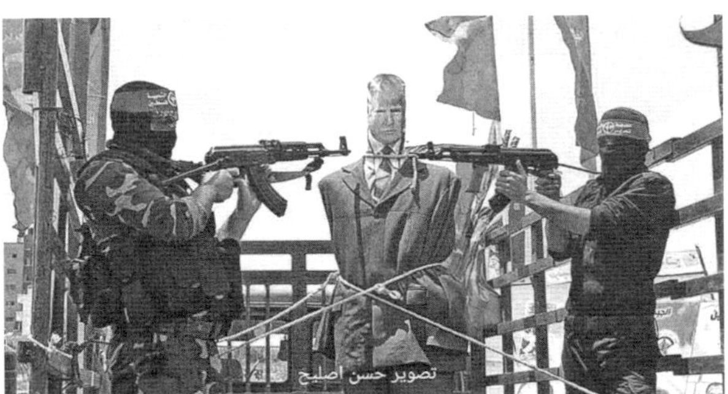

2017_05_23_Gaza: US President Trump

Protesters in Gaza City burned Abbas' effigy, denouncing him as puppet of the United States, which lifted an aid embargo against the West Bank this week while maintaining it in Gaza.
—*Eugene Register-Guard*, OR, 22 Jun 2007

2007_06_22_Gaza: Palestinian President Abbas

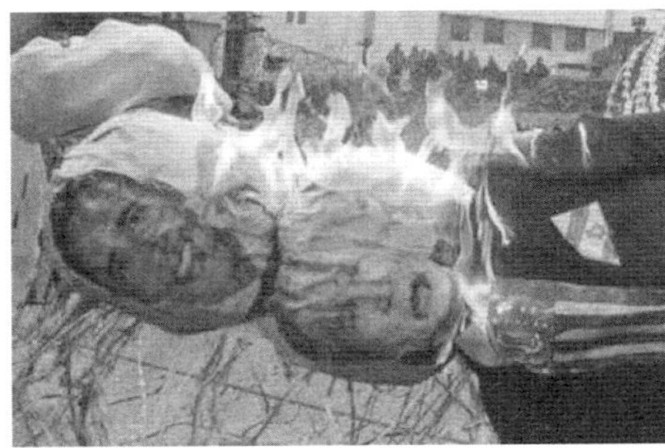

2009_01_18_Lebanon: US Presidents Bush + Obama

the first mentioned appearance in Egypt around 1919, when they appear to have been appropriated from a British celebration to protest against colonial rule. Since then, effigies recur in the continuing struggle against Western influence in Egypt and the conflict between Israel and Palestine. They have become an established form to protest foreign influence in the region.

Hostage Crisis in Tehran

On November 4, 1979, an angry mob of young Islamic revolutionary students overran the US Embassy in Tehran, taking more than sixty Americans hostage. The occupiers demanded the extradition of Shah Reza Pahlavi who stayed in the US after traveling there for medical treatment. For weeks, demonstrations were staged for the international news in front of the embassy, and almost daily an effigy of the Shah, President Carter or Uncle Sam was paraded and burned.[29] The hostage crisis was accompanied by intense media coverage in the US, which the Iranian protesters and state officials exploited handily to demonstrate their defiance of the world power.

29   James Yuenger, "U.S. Embassy: Where It All Started," *Chicago Tribune*, January 21, 1981.

152

Hamid Zarakani, aged 28, of Hither Green Lane, Lewisham, was fined £60 for assault by magistrates at Horseferry Road court yesterday after admitting hitting a policeman in the groin with a wooden effigy of the Shah of Iran.
—*Times*, 13 Sep 1978

1978_09_12_UK: Iranian Shah Reza Pahlavi

San Francisco — Thousands of Iranians and their supporters marched Saturday from the city's waterfront, down busy Market Street and through the city's financial district to the Iranian Consulate, where they burned an effigy of Shah Mohammed Reza Pahlevi.
—*Herald-Journal*, Spartanburg, SC 31 Dec 1978

1978_12_31_USA-CA: Shah Reza Pahlavi

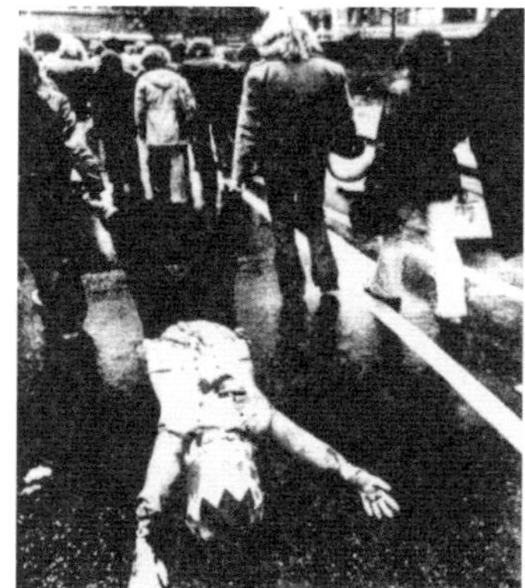

1978_11_24_Germany: Iranian Shah Reza Pahlavi

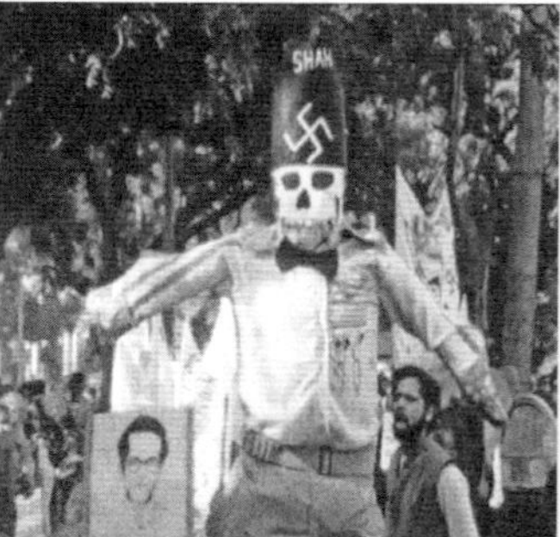

1978_12_18_India: Iranian Shah Reza Pahlavi

The 52 hostages were held for 444 days and only released the day after President Ronald Reagan was sworn into office.

The US was closely associated with the authoritarian regime of the Shah. They had engineered the Shah's return to power in 1953, and supported his suppression of dissent from leftists and the religious conservatives. From 1963 to 1978 the Shah introduced far-reaching reforms to modernize the country, which profoundly changed social and political structures. The disenchantment with the Shah's policies became the driving force of a sustained campaign that lead to the revolution in 1979. It was supported by a wide coalition of religious and nationalist groups, secular and religious students, merchants, and intellectuals. "The intensely egalitarian, anti-establishment and communitarian aspects of Shia Islam [were] marshalled against the tyrannical, agnostic, frivolous and iniquitous features of the rule of the elite."[30] After months of demonstrations and strikes that paralyzed the country, Pahlavi abdicated and left Iran on January 16, 1979. On January 30, Ayatollah Ruhollah Khomeini returned from exile in Paris, where he had posed as moderate while working for the Islamic revolution. In April 1979, the Islamic Republic of Iran was installed by national referendum and Ayatollah

30   R. K. Ramazani, "Iran's Revolution: Patterns, Problems and Prospects," *International Affairs* 56, no. 3 (1980): 446.

153

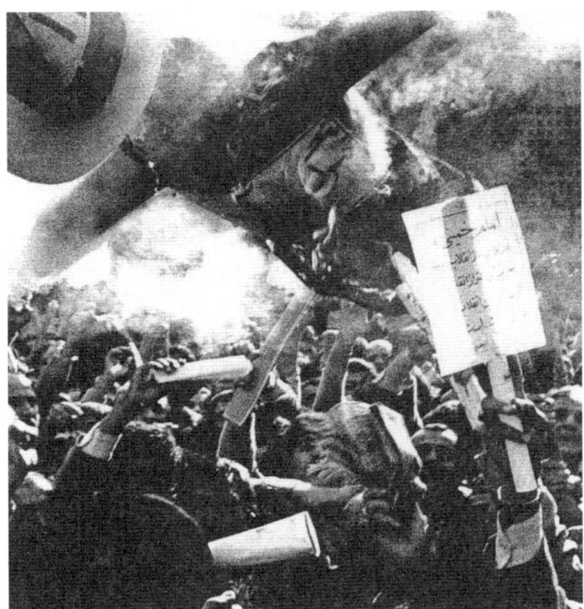
1979_02_18_Iran: Uncle Sam

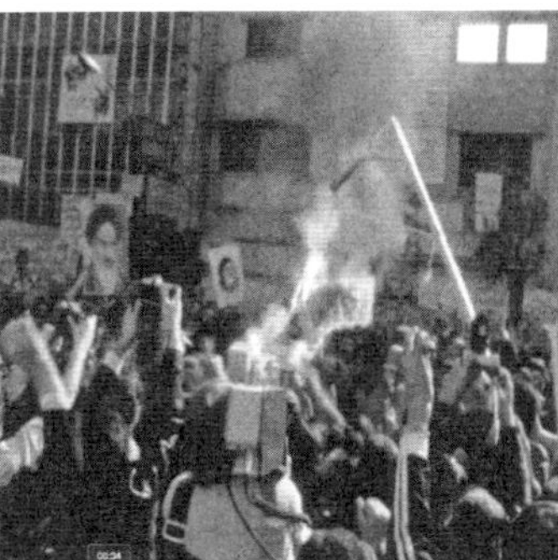
1979_11_09_Iran: US President Carter

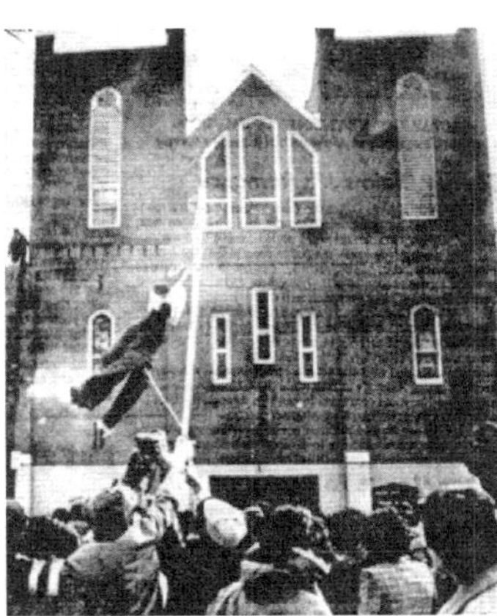
1979_01_14_USA-GA: President Carter

31   Police prevented them from burning the effigy.

32   Yuenger, "U.S. Embassy," 4.

33   T. Fahd and A. Rippin, "Shayṭān," in *Encyclopaedia of Islam, Second Edition*, ed. P. Bearman et al., referenceworks. brillonline.com/browse/ encyclopaedia-of-islam-2.

34   Peter Chelkowski, review of "Warring Souls, Youth, Media and Martyrdom in Post-revolution Iran" by Roxanne Varzi, *Comparative Studies of South Asia, Africa and the Middle East* 29, no. 2 (2009): 344.

Khomeini became Supreme Leader, a supervising position above all legislative, executive, and judicial institutions in Iran.

Early on, the struggle against the Shah had been taken to the streets outside of Iran. Already in 1972, Iranian students in the UK had protested against his visit by trying to burn his effigy.[31] These protests intensified in 1976 and his effigies were burned in the US, the UK, Italy, Germany, and India. After his abdication, Iranian protesters focused their anger on the US, which favored a moderate secular government and tried to sideline the Islamic activist movement. In February, the first effigy of Uncle Sam was burned, followed by effigies of Carter and Begin in May. In November 1979, radical students stormed the US embassy and took its personnel hostage. In the first weeks of the hostage crisis, the daily burning of Carter and Uncle Sam effigies firmly established it as a means to protest US interference in Iranian politics.[32] The first effigies were three-dimensional caricatures, often cut-out shapes with drawings of Carter or the Shah, with ridiculing and demonizing features: pointy ears, horns, and protruding teeth – the typical attributes of Satan.[33] The politicians' names were attached to the effigies, complemented by defamatory signs: the Star of David, the Swastika, dollar signs, the American Flag, the acronym CIA, or the Israeli flag.

Already since 1963, Ayatollah Khomeini had framed the Shia rituals of *Ashura*, which commemorates the death of Muhammad's grandson Imam Husayn ibn Ali during the Battle of Karbala, in political terms to further his goal of establishing an Islamic Republic. The religious processions of Ashura were transformed into mass protests against the Shah.[34] Part of the Persian tradition of Ashura is *Ta'ziyeh*, the passion play narrating the martyrdom of Imam Hussayn. Exemplifying Shia Islam's position of resistance in relation to

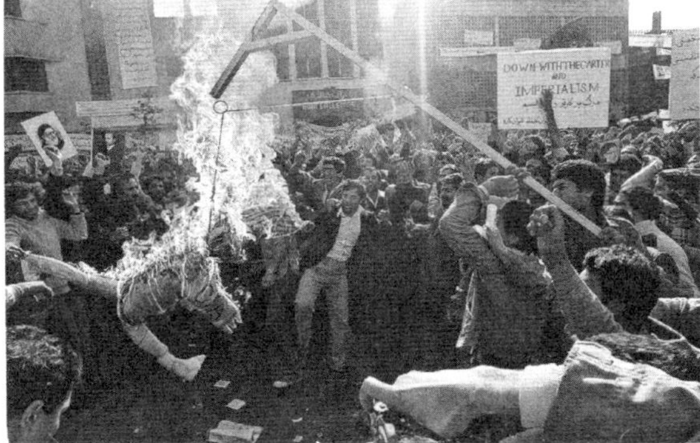

1979_11_13_Iran: Uncle Sam

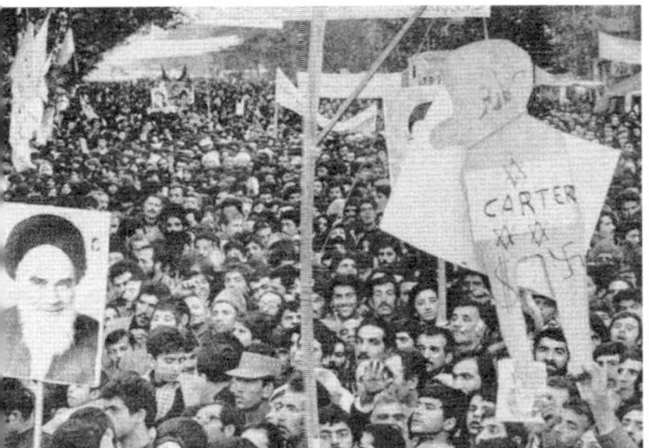

79_11_25_Iran: US President Carter

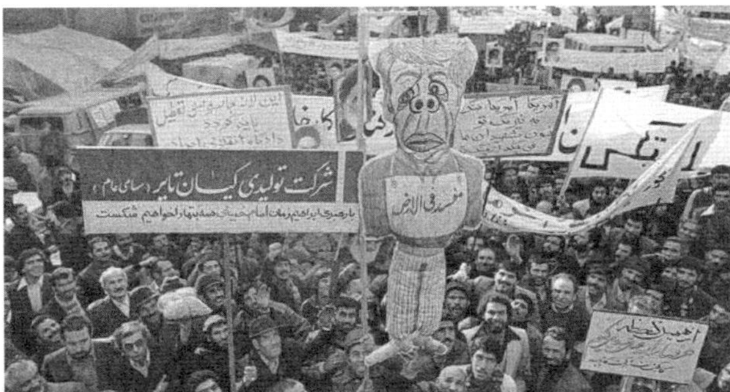

1979_12_23_Iran: US President Carter

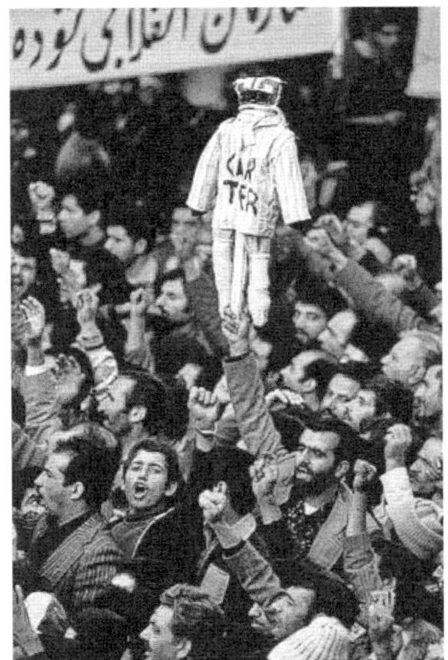

1979_11_00_Iran: US President Carter

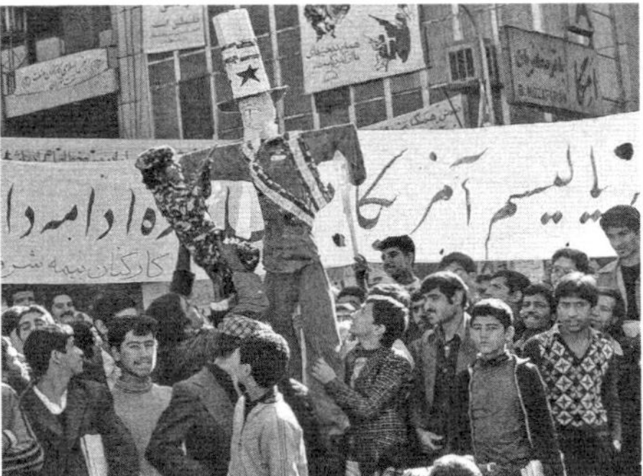

1979_11_18_Iran: Uncle Sam

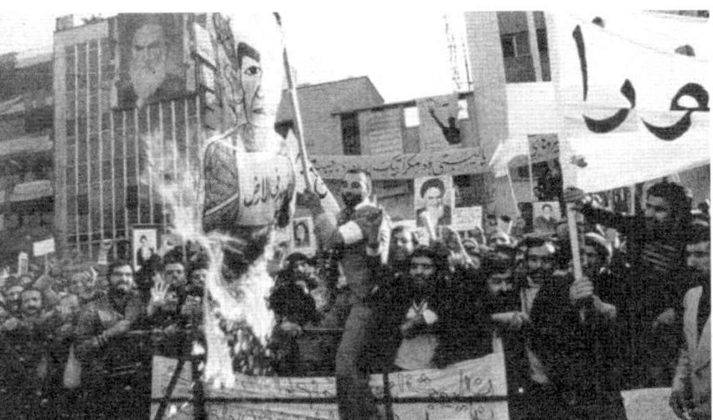

1979_12_15_Iran: Shah Reza Pahlevi

35   Hamid Dabashi, "Ta'ziyeh as Theatre of Protest," *TDR* 49, no. 4 (2005): 92–94.

36   In popular perception, the figure merged with Umar ibn Kattab, the second caliph in Sunni tradition. After the Iranian Revolution, the practice was discouraged, to avoid negative impact on the relations with Sunni communities. Nevertheless, Umar kushan is still practiced by Shia communities in parts of Iran, Azerbaijan and India. Azam Torab, *Performing Islam: Gender and Ritual in Islam* (Leiden: Brill, 2007), 196; R. Tapper, "Azerbaijan: Population and its Occupations and Culture," in *Encyclopaedia Iranica Online* (1996), iranicaonline.org/articles/azerbaijan-v.

37   Michael M. J. Fischer, *Iran: From Religious Dispute to Revolution* (Cambridge, MA: Harvard University Press, 1980), 177; Babak Rahimi mentions a description of the ritual from 1624 in Isfahan. Babak Rahimi, "A History of (Safavid) Muharram Rituals," in *Theater State and the Formation of Early Modern Public Sphere in Iran*, (Brill Online, 2011): 228.

38   Peter Chelkowski, "Popular Entertainment, Media and Social Change in Twentieth-Century Iran," in *The Cambridge History of Iran*, ed. Peter Avery et al. (Cambridge: Cambridge University Press, 1991), 7:766.

39   Rebecca Ansary Pettys, "The Ta'ziyeh: Ritual Enactment of Persian Renewal," *Theatre Journal* 33, no. 3 (1981): 354.

power, Ta'ziyeh is also a social and political drama, a theatre of protest.[35] It provides many moments for the people to actively participate in the drama, and identify with the narrative of struggle and sacrifice. Extending the symbolism of Karbala, Ta'ziyeh lends itself as a framework to recast contemporary conflicts in the universal framework of the fight of good versus evil.

A minor event in the Persian Ta'ziyeh used to be *Umar kushan* (the killing of Umar).[36] In that ritual, effigies of the military commander of caliph Yazid I'st army Umar ibn Sa'd, were made from wood, cloth, and straw, and filled with firecrackers and donkey turds.[37] The effigies were paraded, mocked, and eventually burned in a carnivalesque spectacle. In an essay in the *Cambridge History of Iran*, cultural historian Peter Chelkowski explains that "during the 1978–9 revolution, the effigy of Umar was replaced by those of President Carter and/or the late Shah."[38] Even though the protesters might have been aware of earlier effigy protests in the region, the burning of effigies in the protests of the Iranian Revolution were thus at least partly appropriated from the *Umar Kushan* tradition. The protesters blended the Shia ritual of suffering and resistance with contemporary political activism for religious and national renewal.[39] The U S was symbolically tied to the first injustice, the assassination of

156

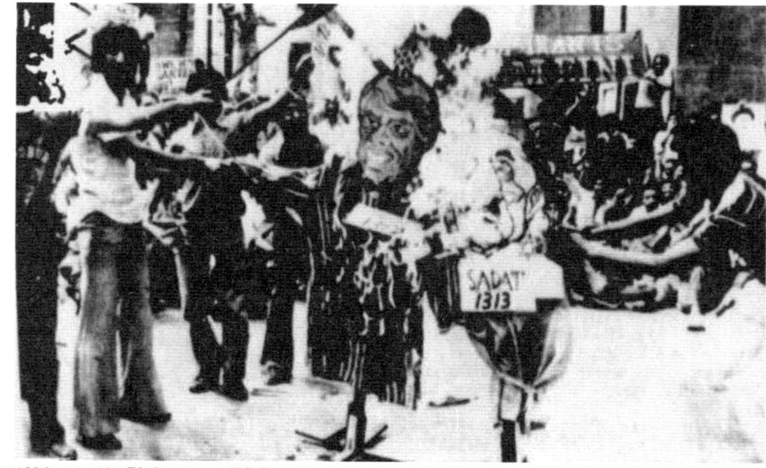

1979_11_13_Philippines: US President Carter

Imam Hussayn ibn Ali from Shia Islam's founding myth. The US was recast as the Great Satan, the eternal force of evil that lies at the base of all conflicts and injustices.[40] Symbolically, the exorcism of the Western Satan performed by protesters served to purify Iranian society.

Protests by Iranian students in support of the Iranian Revolution had continued in the UK, US, Germany, Iran, India, Libya, the Philippines, and Panama (where the Shah went to recover from his medical treatment). But with the hostage taking at the US embassy in Tehran, the atmosphere for Iranian students in the West and especially in the US became grim. The few Iranians who continued to demonstrate in favor of the Iranian Revolution were intimidated. Demands were made to deport Iranian students, and effigies of Ayatollah Khomeini instead of Carter were burned in counter demonstrations on university campuses and elsewhere.

Just as the driving force of the revolution in Iran and abroad were Iranian students, the counter-demonstrations in the US were also led by students. A high school student from Maine was cited in a newspaper article: "Iran burned our flag and we were insulted. So we burned one of their flags in return."[41] Student populations from different continents communicated with each other by mirroring each other's protest

157

40 William O. Beeman, "Images of the Great Satan," in *Religion and Politics in Iran* (New Haven: Yale University Press, 1983), 217; US President George W. Bush later reciprocated by framing Iran as part of the "Axis of Evil" in his State of the Union Address, Washington, DC, January 29, 2002. George W. Bush, "Address Before a Joint Session of the Congress on the State of the Union," January 29, 2002. *The American Presidency Project* (website), presidency.ucsb.edu/node/211864.

41 "American Anger Over Iran Grows," *Evening Independent*, December 1, 1979.

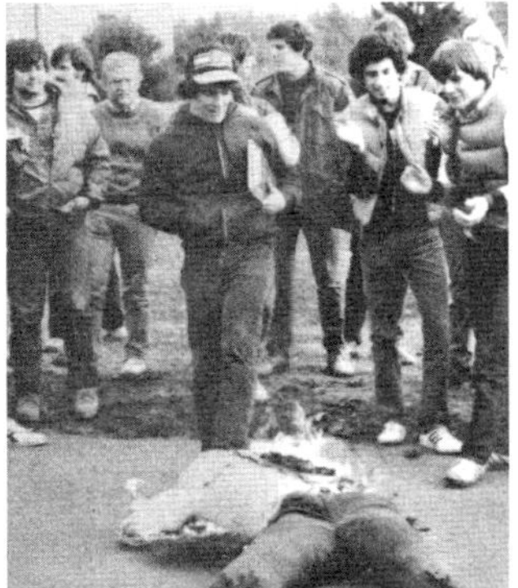

1979_11_15_USA-MA: Iranian leader Khomeini

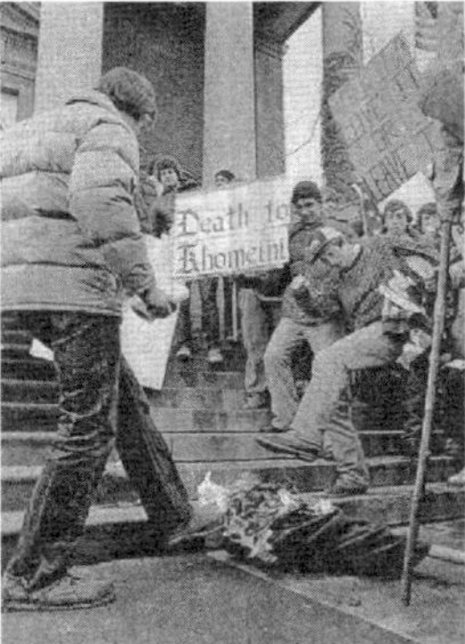

1979_11_16_USA-NY: Iranian leader Khomeini

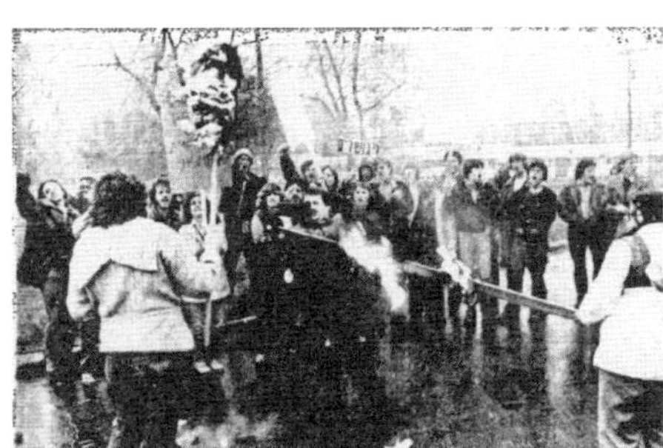

1979_11_15_USA-ME: Iranian leader Khomeini

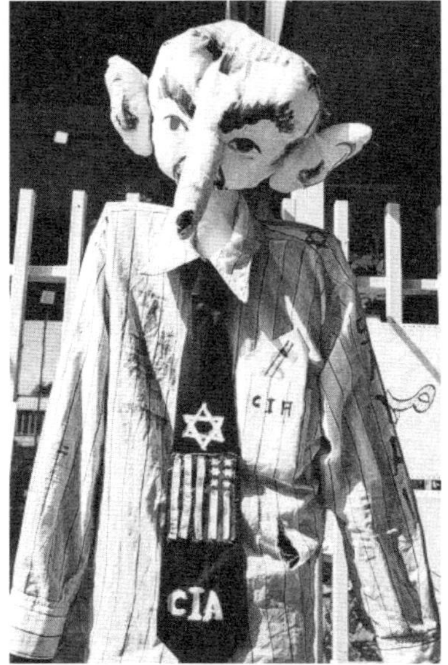

1981_01_01_Iran: Uncle Sam

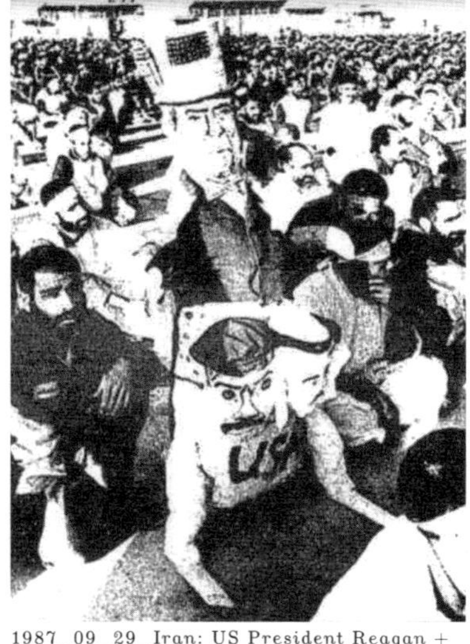

1987_09_29_Iran: US President Reagan +
Iraqi President Saddam Hussein

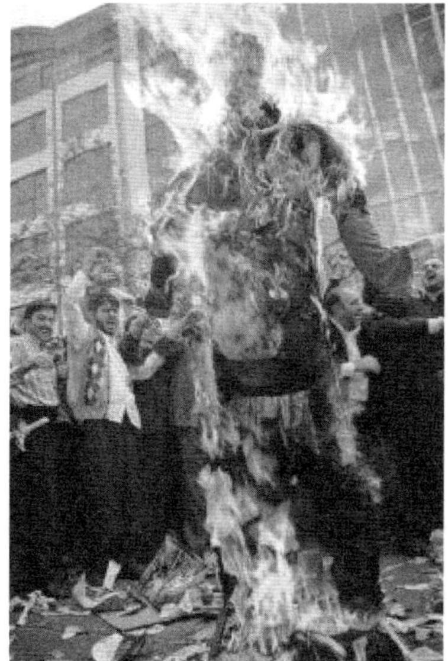

2001_11_04_Iran: Uncle Sam

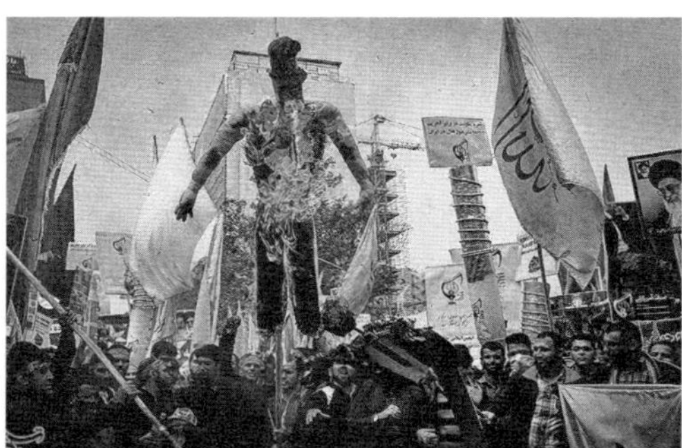

2013_11_07_Iran: US Pres Obama + US Sec of State
Kerry + Israeli Premier Netanyahu

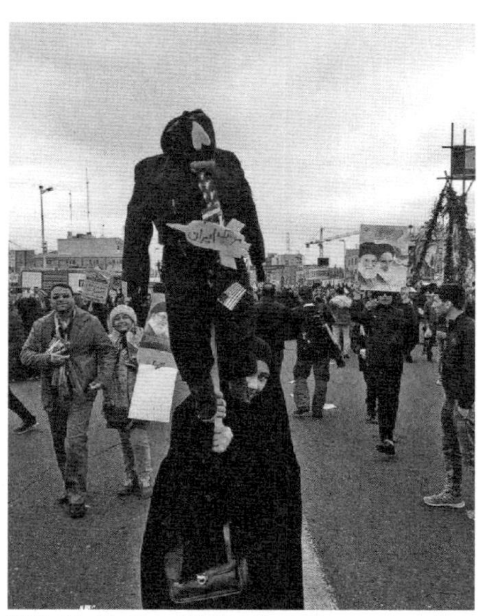

2016_02_10_Iran: US President Obama

vocabulary, a shared symbolic language of protest facilitated by the news media. The burning effigy became an iconic visual reference in the conflict.

Even after hostages were released on January 20, 1981, the protests continued on both sides, fueled by Khomeini's and other hardliner politicians' grandstanding as well as by the US's counter-measures that were not successful in reigning the country in. Other conflicts merged into this growing animosity. On November 25, 1981, the *Herald Journal* reported from the Philippines:

> One hundred Iranian students screamed "down with Reagan", burned effigies of President Reagan, Saudi Arabian King Khaled and Israeli Prime Minister Menachem Begin in a demonstration Wednesday to protest the Saudi's Middle East plan which implicitly recognizes Israel, police said. The demonstration took place behind the Iranian Embassy.[42]

Multiple issues come together here: the hostage crisis in Tehran from two years earlier, the rivalry between Iran and Saudi Arabia, the Sunni/Shia divide, and the Israel-Palestine conflict – and all this happening in the Philippines, which had its own experience with US military presence and the US's unwavering support for Filipino autocratic ruler Ferdinand Marcos. The report shows a complicated constellation of groups and interests, connected in dynamic transnational alliances.

42 *Herald Journal*, November 25, 1981.

159

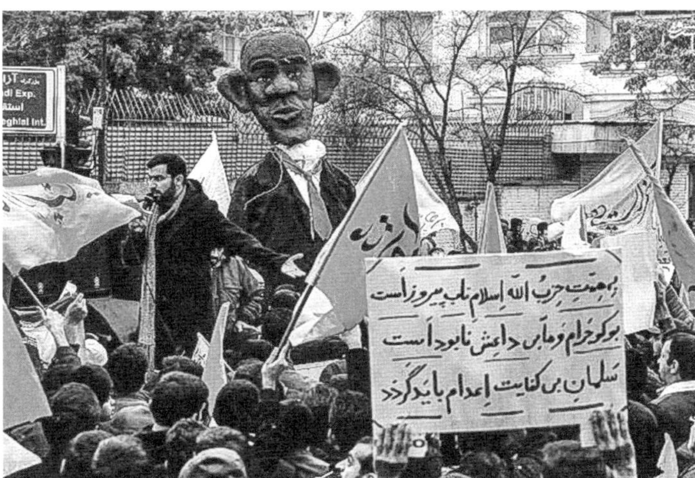

2016_01_14_Iran: US President Obama

43 Catherine Bell, *Ritual: Perspectives and Dimensions* (Oxford: Oxford University Press, 1997), 129.

44 Ann Rigney, "Plenitude, scarcity and the circulation of cultural memory," *Journal of European Studies* 35, no. 1 (2005/2006): 18. Pierre Nora first coined the concept *lieux de memoire* as places or objects that have acquired significance for the collective memory.

45 An article in the *New York Times* describes that the demonstration celebrating the 23rd anniversary of the revolution "felt more like a carnival, complete with a gold coin on offer for the best Uncle Sam effigy." Neil MacFarquhar, "Millions in Iran Rally Against U.S.," *New York Times*, February 12, 2002.

Soon after the hostage crisis was resolved, the process of memorializing the revolution began. During mass demonstrations celebrating the revolution in February and the takeover of the US embassy in November, effigies of Uncle Sam and the sitting US president are paraded and burned. The demonstrations against US imperialism have become a ritual in themselves, integrating the conflict with the US into Islamic Republic political-religious ritual.[43] The parading, hanging, and burning of effigies was reinvented as a tradition in service of creating the imagined political community of the republic. The annual performance became a *lieu de memoire,* a site of memory, which scholar of memory culture Ann Rigney describes as a "self-perpetuating vortex of symbolic investment … providing [a] common framework for appropriating the past."[44] Just as the burning in effigy of Umar in the tradition of Ta'ziyeh, burning Uncle Sam in effigy became a ritualized practice to create and foster the shared imaginaries of struggle, resistance, and overcoming.[45]

On the other side of the conflict, in the US, effigy burnings in Tehran also became a *lieu de memoire* evidenced by a postcard◯ printed in the US in 1981 with a burning effigy of Carter in Tehran. As a medium meant to communicate with and be shared, the image of Carter's effigy came to symbolize the communal trauma of the hostage crisis.

160

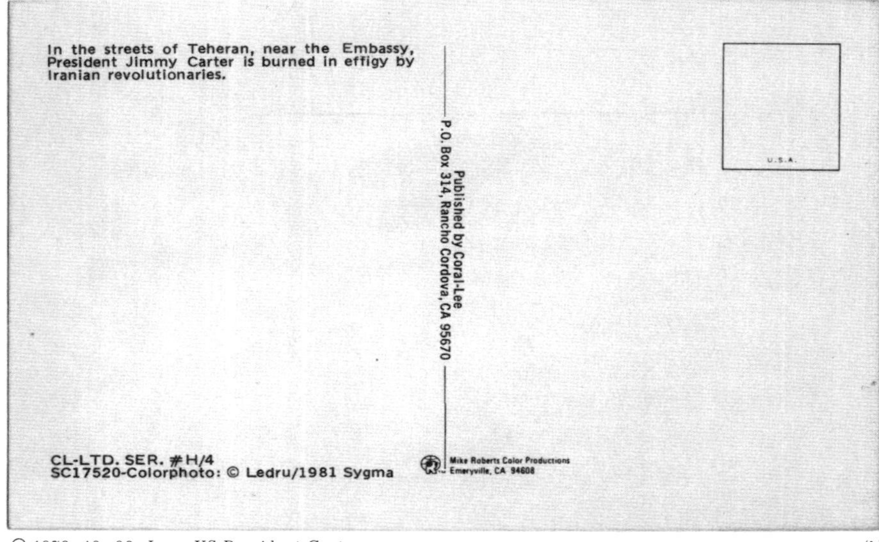

◯ 1979_12_00_Iran: US President Carter

(b)

Another *lieu de memoire* in the Iranian calendar, *Quds Day* (International Jerusalem Day) was initiated by Ayatollah Khomeini with a fatwa early in the Iranian Revolution in October 1979. The marches and effigy burning in support of the Palestinian cause and against the state of Israel and its control of the holy city of Jerusalem emphasize an imaginary "Muslim world" to unify diverse Muslim communities around the world. Before 2002, Quds Day was mainly celebrated in Iran and by allied Shia groups close to its politics in Iraq and Lebanon. Since 2002, it has become more widespread and demonstrations now occur in Pakistan, Azerbaijan, and Nigeria as well as minority-Muslim countries like the US and Canada, and some countries in Europe and South Africa.[46] While Quds Day is largely organized by Shia groups,[47] it nonetheless resonates across Muslim communities, recalling the conflict with Israel and the principled position of Iran in it. Under the guise of liberating Jerusalem, Khomeini and his successors tie the conflict between Iran and the US to the conflict between Israel and Palestine, embedded within a larger narrative of the struggle between the "Muslim World" and "the West."

Effigy protests in Iran, according to this genealogy, were adapted from a traditional practice that mockingly denounces the evil enemy during commemorations of Ashura. Similar to that in Port Said in Egypt, the practice became part of Iranian memory culture, an invented tradition in support of the official version of Iranian identity. While in Egypt commemoration was established by local communities, in Iran the protest practice and re-enactments were promoted and framed by state actors. In both countries, the original effigy protests effectively use international media to communicate transnationally with diverse publics.

46   Ayla Schbley and Clark McCauley, "Political, Religious, and Psychological Characteristics of Muslim Protest Marchers in Eight European Cities: Jerusalem Day 2002," *Terrorism and Political Violence* 17, no. 4 (2005): 554.

47   Matthias Küntzel, "Tehran's Efforts to Mobilize Antisemitism: The Global Impact," in *Deciphering the New Antisemitism*, ed. Alvin H. Rosenfeld (Indiana: Indiana University Press, 2015), 521.

48   "General Information on Azerbaijani Jewish Organizations," Jews of Eurasia (website), http://jewseurasia.org/page423.

In early September 2010, Islamists held an anti-Israeli rally in Baku, Azerbaijan, dedicated to the so-called El-Quds day (El-Quds is the name Islamists use for Jerusalem). An effigy of Israeli Prime Minister B. Netanyahu and the flags of Armenia, Israel, the U.S., and the United Kingdom were burned at the rally.[48]

2010_09_00_Azerbaijan: Israeli Premier Netanyahu

The Rushdie Affair

In 1989, a controversy around the book *The Satanic Verses* by British Indian author Salman Rushdie led to a major international crisis that shook the West's confidence in its relationships with Muslim communities in their midst and abroad. The book was published in September 1988 in the UK and drew immediate criticism from British Muslims as insulting Islam, demanding it be banned under British blasphemy laws.[49] Because both the publisher and government officials failed to respond to their complaints, UK activists organized national and international publicity campaigns. After two large demonstrations in Bolton and Bradford, where the book and an effigy of the author were burned, the protests succeeding in winning media attention. The anger spread to the protesters' countries of origin, inciting protests in Pakistan, India, and Bangladesh that became increasingly violent.

On February 14, Ayatollah Khomeini of Iran weighed in on the side of the protesters and issued a fatwa, condemning Rushdie and his publishers to death and calling on Muslims worldwide to execute his verdict.[50] The fatwa raised the stakes in the controversy enormously. The conflict about respecting Muslim values in British society was elevated to a

162

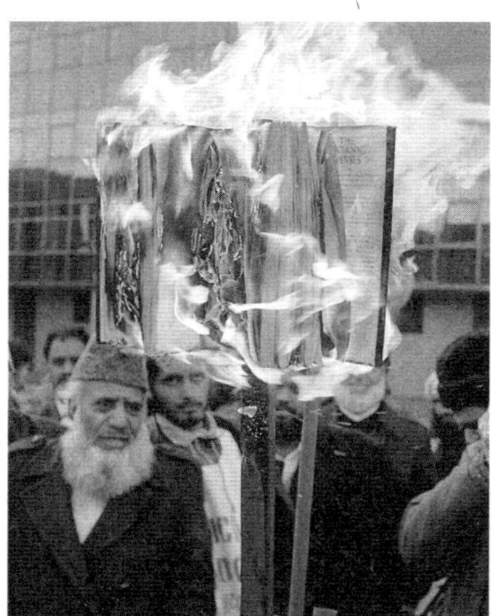

1989_01_14_UK: The Satanic Verses

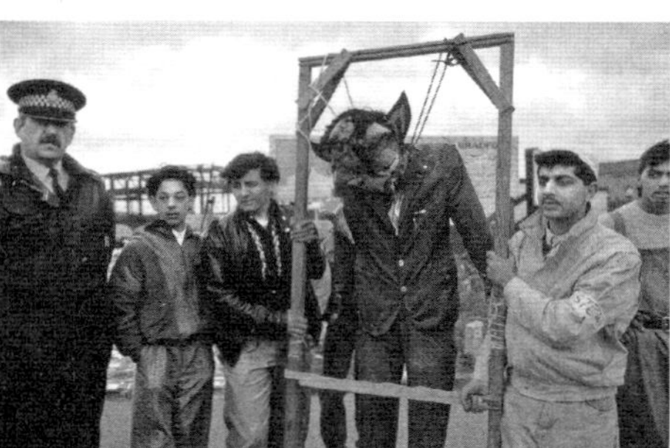

1989_01_14_UK: author Salman Rushdie

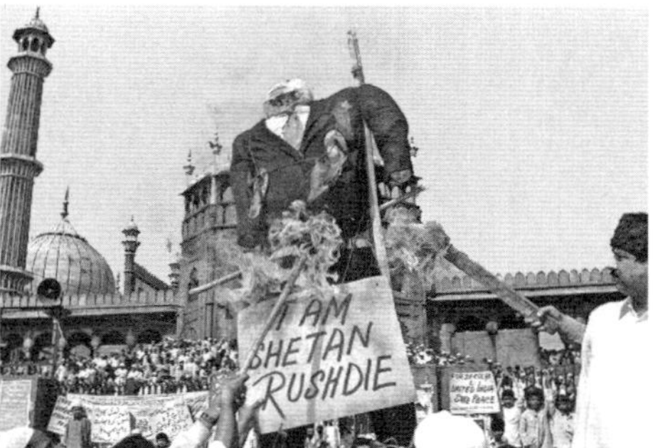

1989_02_19_India: author Salman Rushdie

mortal struggle between the honor and sanctity of the Islamic religion and Western democratic values like freedom of speech.[51] The fatwa changed the character of effigy burnings from largely symbolic expressions to violently charged threats on Rushdie's life. Concerned that someone would act on the fatwa, Rushdie went into hiding.

In the months following the fatwa, effigy protests were staged in India, Pakistan, Iran, Lebanon, and Thailand. In the West, Muslim communities protested against further translations and distribution. Large demonstrations took place in the UK, France, the Netherlands, Canada, and the US. Protesters employed threatening and violent rhetoric, bookshops were firebombed, and effigies burned. Even in Beijing, Muslim students protested against the book and its author and the book was banned in Iran, India, Pakistan, Egypt, Bangladesh, Sudan, South Africa, Sri Lanka, Kenya, Thailand, Tanzania, Indonesia, and Singapore.[52] In 1999 and 2000, demonstrations against Rushdie erupted again in India when the government granted him a visa to visit the country. When Queen Elizabeth knighted Rushdie in 2007, it was seen as an affront and protests were staged in a number of countries, which in India and Pakistan featured effigies of the author.

163

51 Werbner, "Divided Loyalties," 310 and Aydin, *The Idea of the Muslim World*, 220.

52 Robin Lustig, Martin Bailey, Simon de Bruxelles, and Ian Mather, "War of the Word," *Guardian*, February 19, 1989.

Thousands of American Moslems prayed and burned effigies of Salman Rushdie in front of his publisher's office Saturday to demand that his book "Satanic Verses" be banned in the United States.
—*Sunday Telegraph*, NH, 26 Feb 1989

1989_02_25_USA-NY: author Salman Rushdie

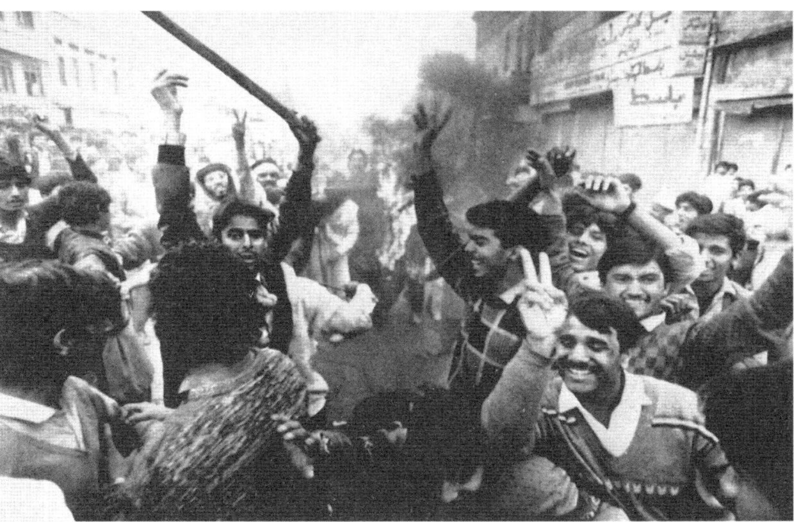

1989_02_26_Pakistan: author Salman Rushdie

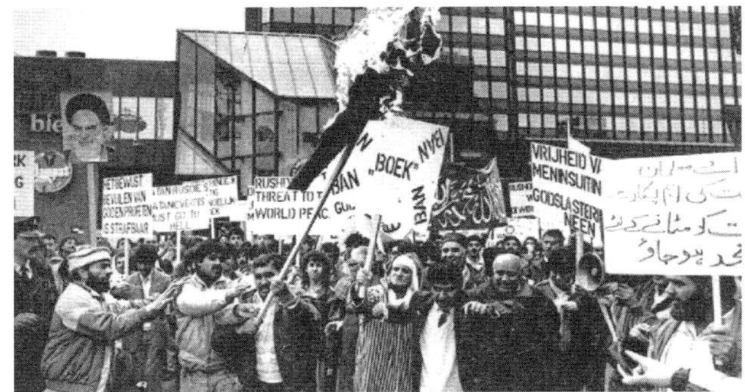

1989_03_05_Netherlands: author Salman Rushdie

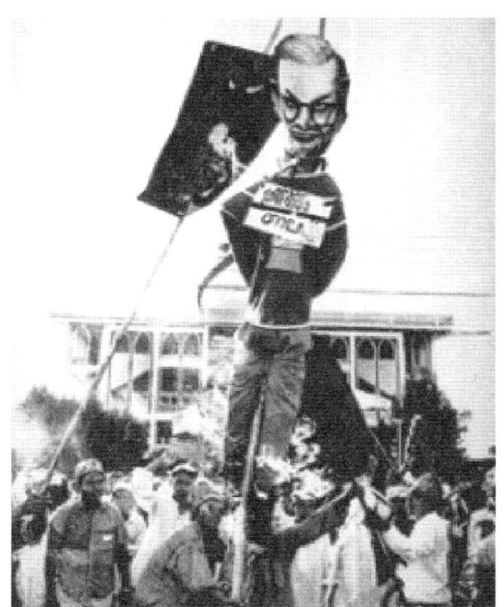

1989_03_07_Thailand: author Salman Rushdie

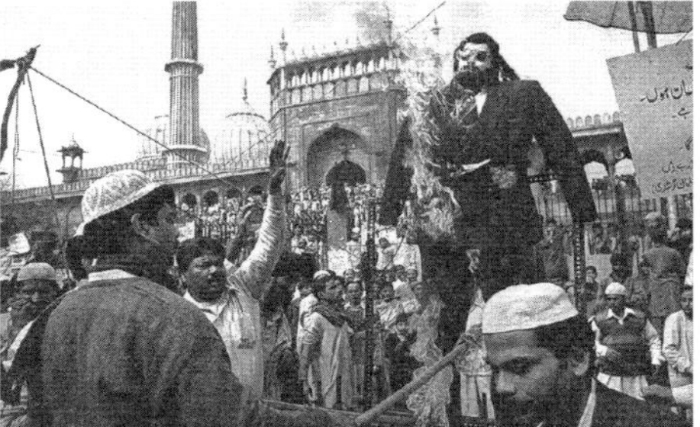

1999_02_09_India: author Salman Rushdie

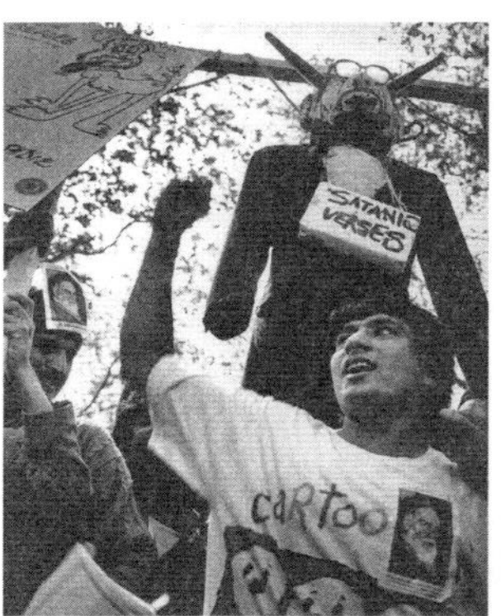

1989_05_27_UK: author Salman Rushdie

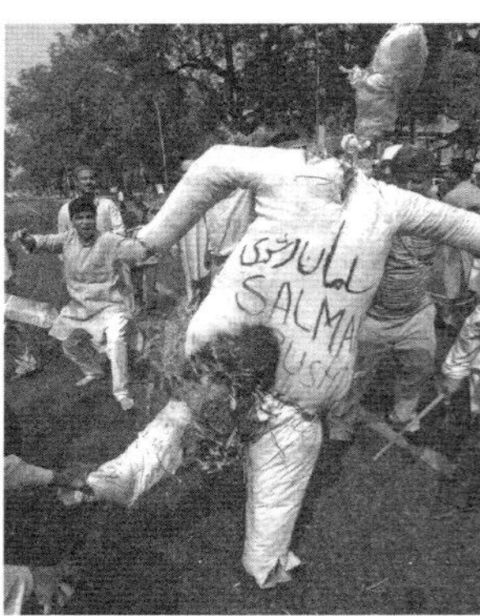

2000_04_14_India: author Salman Rushdie

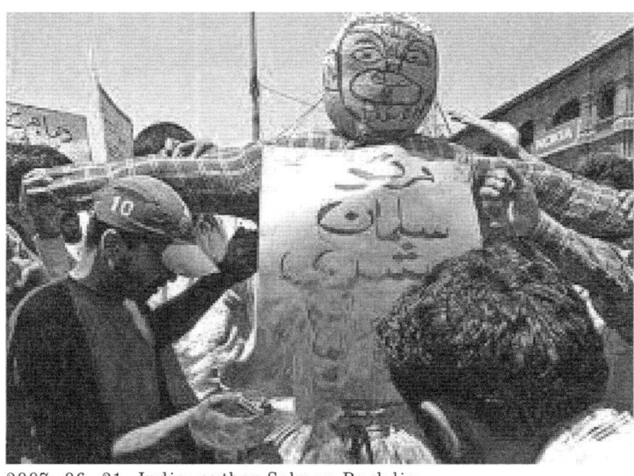

2007_06_21_India: author Salman Rushdie

"I am Shetan Rushdie" reads the sign around the neck of the effigy burned in front of the largest mosque in New Delhi in 1989. Like many effigies in Iran, effigies paraded and burned in the U K had Satanic features: horns, pointy ears, and protruding teeth – not surprising since the title of Rushdie's book references Satan. Rushdie came to embody a specter of Muslim anxiety, the emigrant apostate who succumbed to Western secularism and relativism, a traitor to his own culture.[53] In the West, the affair stirred up anxieties about a supposedly threatening rise of Islam in Europe and the incompatibility of Islam with Western liberal democracy. It was an early example of a conflict framed in cultural terms, rather than colonial or military ones. Since the year 2000, this has become increasingly common, as the genealogy of effigy protests in Afghanistan detailed in the following section reveal.

Occupations of Afghanistan

Between 2005 and 2015, effigy protests in Afghanistan against Western policies successfully caught the attention of the Western news media. The practice, though, appears to have been adopted there rather recently. At least a survey of the English-language Afghani newspaper the *Kabul Times* from February 1962 to September 1983 revealed no effigy demonstration in Afghanistan itself, while eighteen articles report on burning effigies in protests in other countries.[54] Seventeen of these took place outside Afghanistan, in Asia (7), Europe (6), and the Americas (4). These contain reporting on a motley of international conflicts, such as Malaysian students protesting against Indonesia over border disputes in 1963, Filippino students protesting against Malaysia in 1968

53 Werbner, "Divided Loyalties," 311.

54 *Kabul Times*, March 20, 1982; March 19, 1983; March 20, 1983. *The University of Arizona Digital Libraries Collection*, content.library.arizona.edu/cdm/landingpage/collection/p16127coll6; and *Digital Commons at University of Nebraska*, digitalcommons.unl.edu/afghanenglish/index.html.

over claims to Malaysian Sabah on northern Borneo, or Irish-Americans in New York protesting the death of Bobby Sands, member of the Provisional Irish Republican Army in 1981, during a hunger strike while in British detention. While the *Kabul Times* only served an English-speaking audience in Afghanistan, it does indicate that burning effigies was probably not a domestic protest practice. Just one report, from March 24, 1983, mentions effigy burnings in Afghanistan. This protest was a state-sanctioned mass demonstration organized by the communist People's Democratic Party of Afghanistan (PDPA). This celebratory "grand march" in socialist fashion, displayed "the will of the people" in commemorating the fifth anniversary of the socialist Saur Revolution and coincided with the *Nauruz* new year celebration. The pictures accompanying the article, however, reveal that demonstrators did not burn effigies of Reagan and Bush, but instead burned a large placard with a cartoon denouncing the American interference in the civil war.

The trace to actual effigies being burned leads to Iran, when Afghans living in Tehran took up the practice in response to the Soviet Army invading Afghanistan in

166

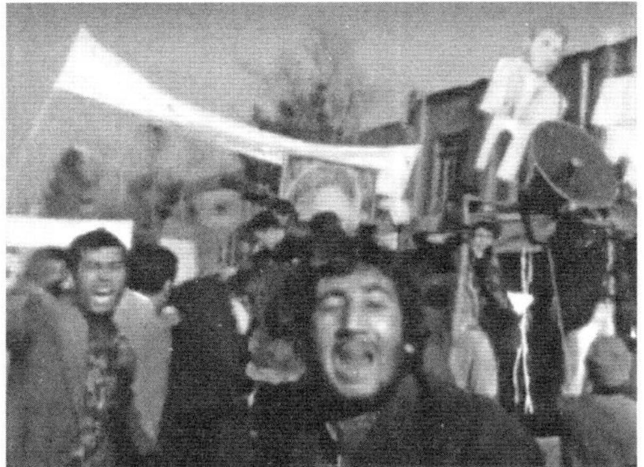

○ 1979_12_31_Iran: USSR leader Brezhnev + Afghan President Karmal

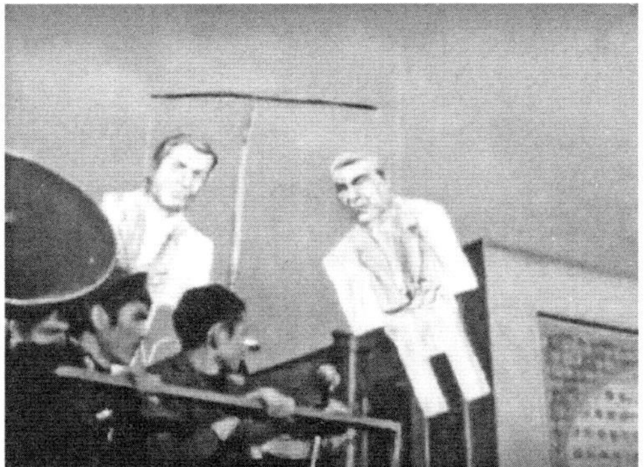

1979_12_31_Iran: USSR leader Brezhnev + Afghan President Karmal

In Dacca, Bangladesh, police fired tear gas into a crowd of angry demonstrators Friday at the Soviet cultural centre, where effigies of Russian leaders were burned to protest Moscow's military intervention in Afghanistan.
—*Sarasota Herald Tribune*, FL, 5 Jan 1980

1980_01_05_Bangladesh: Soviet leaders

In Frankfurt, West Germany, some 300 Afghans marched through the city chanting "Soviets out of Afghanistan." A march in Bonn drew another 600 Afghan students. An Afghan was detained briefly in Frankfurt for burning an effigy of Soviet President Leonid Brezhnev.
—*Sarasota Herald Tribune*, FL, 27 Dec 1980

1980_12_27_DE: USSR leader Brezhnev

December 1979. The Saur Revolution in April 1978 against Afghan President Mohammed Daoud Khan had been followed by an uprising in the east of the country, supported by Pakistan and the US, which lead to the government losing control over large territories outside the larger cities. Because of the increasing rivalry inside the leading socialist party PDPA the Soviet Union decided to intervene and invade the country on 27 December 1979 to support Deputy Secretary of the PDPA Babrak Karmal against his rival Hafizullah Amin, General Secretary of the PDPA. Less than a week later, in the midst of the ongoing hostage ciris and demonstrations against the US in front of its Tehran embassy, Afghan expats staged a protest against the Soviet invasion, carrying effigies of Karmal and Soviet Union leader Leonid Brezhnev.○ I presume Afghan protesters witnessed the nearly daily effigy burning of the Shah and Carter either live or through the media. Seeing the Iranian student protests gain global media attention, they probably realized the performance's potential to publicize and support their cause.

167

55 Richard S. Ehrlich, "The fourth anniversary of the Soviet takeover in Afghanistan," UPI (website) http://www.upi.com/Archives/1983/12/27/The-fourth-anniversary-of-the-Soviet-takeover-in-Afghanistan/3157441349200/.

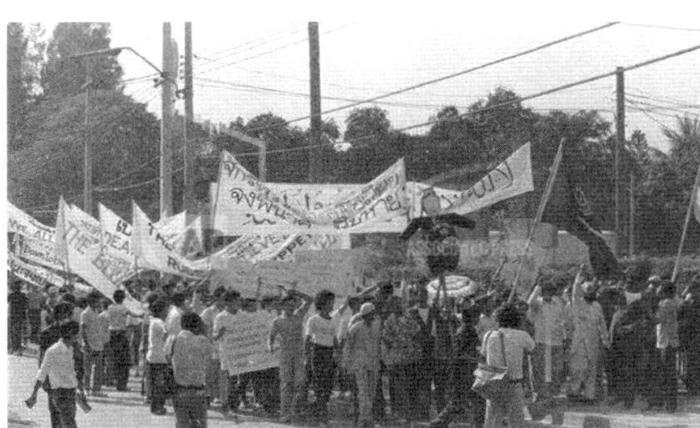

1980_01_11_Thailand: USSR leader Brezhnev

Outside the U.N. building, about 200 young men demonstrating against Soviet intervention in Afghanistan burned a Soviet flag and hanged a four-foot effigy of Soviet President Leonid Brezhnev. About two dozen demonstrators staged a brief sit-down in the street, blocking traffic until police hauled one demonstrator away and the crowd broke up.
—*Ledger*, Lakeland, FL, 2 Oct 1982

1982_10_02_USA-NY: USSR leader Brezhnev

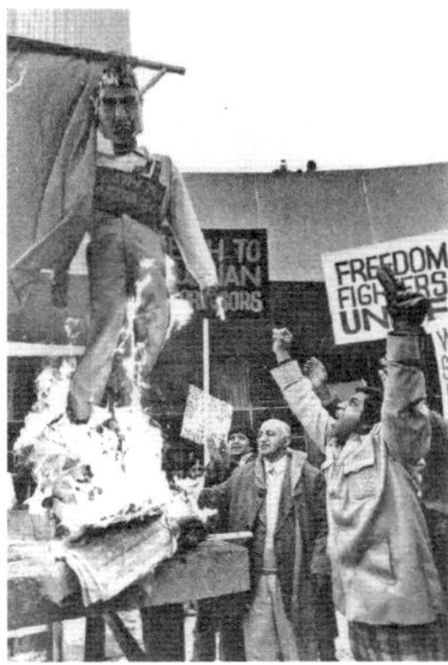

1980_01_06_Canada: USSR leader Brezhnev

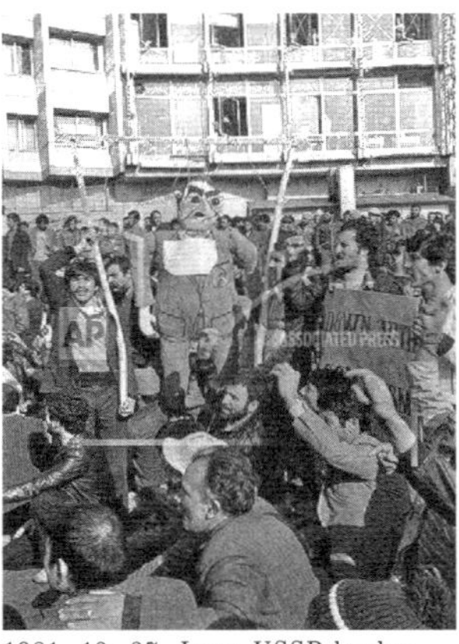

1981_12_27_Iran: USSR leader Brezhnev

The fourth anniversary of the Soviet takeover in Afghanistan was marked Tuesday by refugees chanting 'Death to the Russians' in India, anti-Soviet demonstrations in Thailand and West Germany and a sharp rebuke by the European Common Market. ... In Iran, Afghan Moslems set Soviet flags afire and burned Karmal in effigy in Tehran, the Iranian national news agency reported.[55]

1983_12_27_Iran: Afghan President Karmal

56 "Moslems Condemn Soviet Invasion of Afghanistan," *Pittsburg Post-Gazette*, January 29, 1980.

In January, similar protests against Soviet invasion were staged in New York in front of the United Nations, in Bangladesh, Canada, and Thailand with effigies of Brezhnev. Additional protests were held in Turkey and Paris. Also in January 1980, the foreign ministers from thirty-four nations at a conference of the Organization of Islamic Cooperation adopted a resolution demanding "the immediate, urgent and unconditional withdrawal of Soviet troops" from Afghanistan.[56] While protesters in Bangladesh and Thailand were local Muslims, those in New York and Canada were Afghan expatriates protesting by burning Brezhnev in effigy.

Until the Soviet Union withdrew its troops from Afghanistan in 1989, Afghans living abroad held rallies in many countries to commemorate the invasion and remind the international public of the ongoing war and Soviet occupation of Afghanistan. Demonstrations that featured the burning of effigies of Soviet leaders Brezhnev, Yuri Andropov, Konstantin Chernenko, and Mikhail Gorbachev, were held in Germany (1980), the US (1982), Iran (1981, 1983, 1984) India

168

New Delhi — More than 2,000 stone throwing Afghan refugees burned effigies of Russian President Constantine Chernenko in front of the Soviet embassy today to mark the fifth anniversary of Moscow's invasion of Afghanistan.
—*New Straits Times*, Kuala Lumpur, Malaysia, 27 Dec 1984

1984_12_26_India: USSR leader Chernenko

In Karachi, about 500 Afghan refugees burned effigies of Karmal and Soviet leader Mikhail Gorbachev to chants to "Death to the Soviet Union."
—*Montreal Gazette*, 28 Dec 1985

1985_12_27_Pakistan: Afghan President Karmal + USSR leader Gorbachev

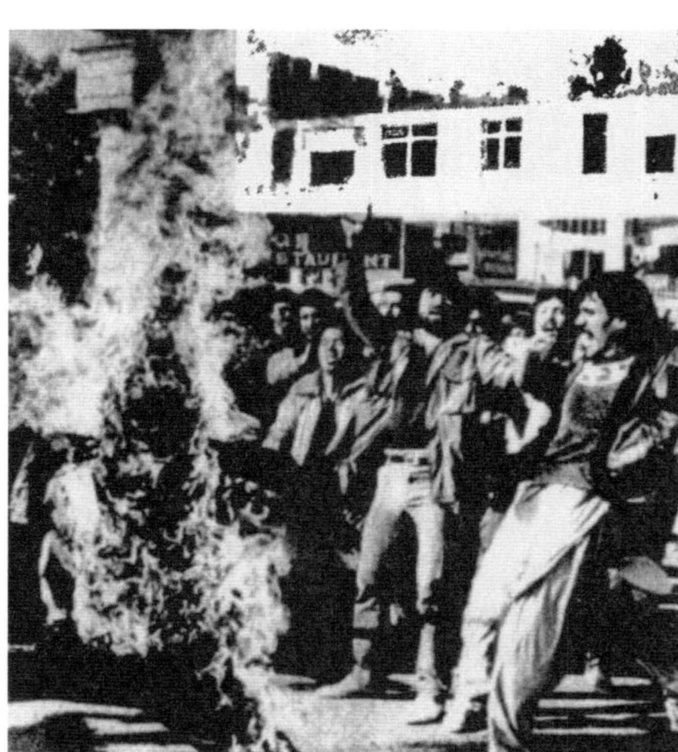

1986_12_28_Pakistan: USSR leader Gorbachev

(1980, 1984, 1987, 1988) Pakistan (1985, 1986, 1987, 1988), and the Netherlands (1987), many in front of Soviet embassies.[57]

It was only ten years after the end of the Soviet occupation that effigies first began to appear in protests taking place within Afghanistan. In 1999, when the US pressured the Taliban government to extradite Osama bin Laden, protesters in Afghanistan burned President Bill Clinton in effigy. Two years later, after 9/11, President George W. Bush issued an ultimatum to the Taliban government once again to extradite Bin Laden, the suspected mastermind behind the attacks. When the Taliban did not comply, Bush ordered the invasion of Afghanistan and the ouster of its government. Demonstrators in Afghanistan again responded to US pressure by burning effigies of Bush (3), and many more were burned by sympathetic protesters in neighboring Pakistan (20), where the practice is very common. The US military engagement in Iraq in 2003 had even wider global resonance. Before the actual invasion in March, effigy burnings of Bush and UK Prime Minister Tony Blair already took place in Thailand, Indonesia, Bangladesh, India, Pakistan, Syria, Egypt, Australia, the UK, the US, Canada, and Peru.

From 2005 on, effigy protests became more common in Afghanistan. Between 2005 and 2015, effigies were burned on sixty-one occasions. Only three of those burned represented Afghan politicians, while the others predominantly were Western heads of state. Obama was burned thirty-one times in effigy and Bush on seven occasions. Nine effigies represented politicians from neighboring countries Pakistan and Iran. Twenty-three protests were held against US military

[57] Iran, Pakistan, and India, where most effigy burnings occurred – had absorbed large numbers of expats and refugees from Afghanistan.

169

The Hague – About 1,000 protesters marched on the Soviet embassy in the Hague on Sunday and burned an effigy of Soviet leader Mikhail Gorbachev to mark the eighth anniversary of Moscow's military intervention in Afghanistan. The protesters, many of them Afghans, also burned Soviet flags at the demonstration.
—*Manila Standard*, Philippines, 29 Dec 1987

1987_12_27_NL: USSR leader Gorbachev

In New Delhi, about 300 chanting Afghan refugees burned an effigy of Soviet leader Mikhail Gorbachev during protests marking the anniversary of the Soviet intervention.
—*New Straits Times*, Kuala Lumpur, Malaysia, 29 Dec 1988

1988_12_28_India: USSR leader Gorbachev

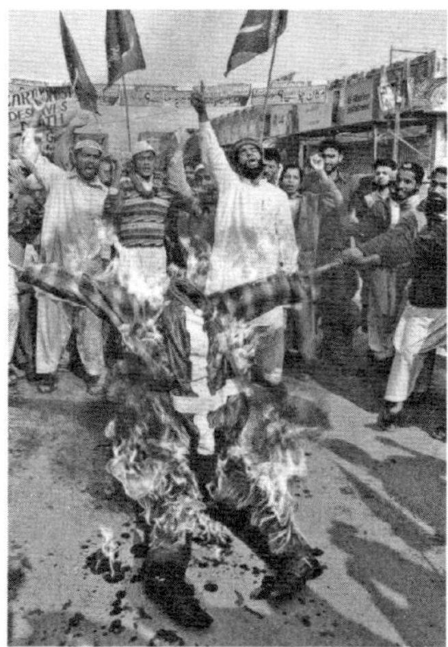

2008_02_15_Pakistan: Danish PM
Rasmussen

Thousands of demonstrators in Kabul,
the Afghan capital, sacked the long-
abandoned U.S. Embassy yesterday, setting five cars ablaze, ripping down the
U.S. seal above the front entrance and
burning American flags and an effigy of
President Bush while chanting "Long
Live Osama!" the Associated Press
reported from the city.
—*Pittsburgh Post-Gazette*, PE, 27 Sep
2001

2001_09_26_Afghanistan: US President Bush

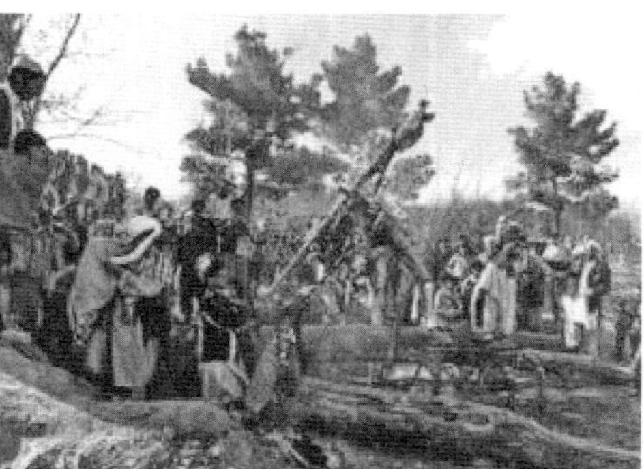

2008_03_21_Afghanistan: Dutch politician Wilders

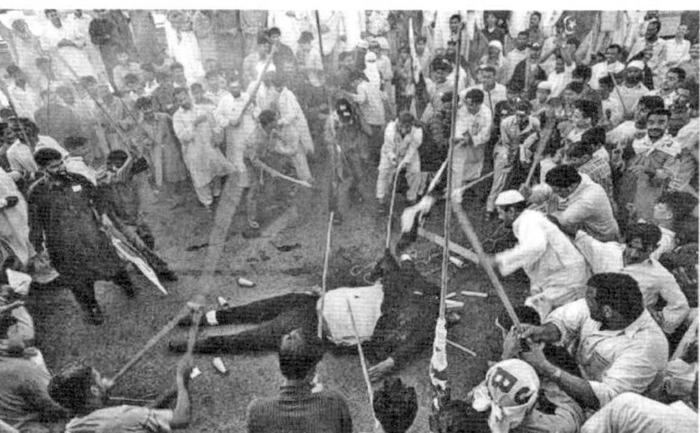

2006_02_24_Pakistan: Danish cartoonist

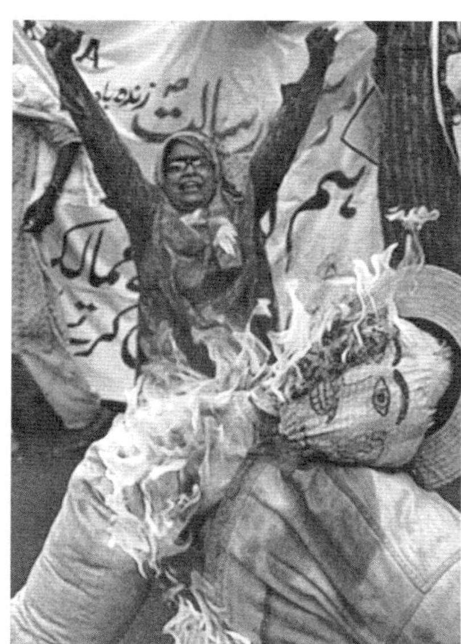

2008_03_30_Pakistan: Dutch politician
Wilders

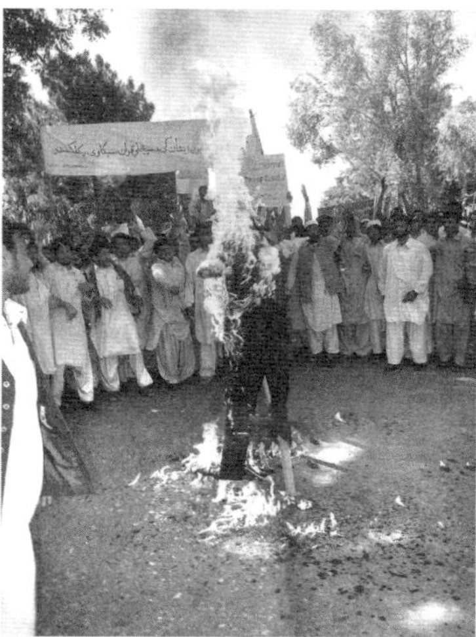

2005_05_11_Afghanistan: US President
Bush

operations resulting in civilian casualties, but even more demonstrations – twenty-six – protested intended or perceived insults to Islam.

The roots of effigy practice in Afghanistan apparently lie in its appropriation by Afghan migrants, students, and refugees in Tehran and other countries outside Afghanistan. These expatriates most likely introduced it to the country after the Soviet Army withdrawal, becoming a well-established practice by 2015. Less than half of the protests addressed US military operations in Afghanistan, focusing instead on insults to Islam. This hints at the unifying effect of conflicts that turn on cultural issues between Islam and the West.

Insults to Islam

The unifying effect of cultural conflicts extended to Muslim communities around the globe. To a Western public seemingly small incidents could cause international crises in the relationship between the "West" and the "Muslim world." In 2005, reports of a Quran desecration in US detention camp at Guantanamo Bay sparked protests that featured effigies of President Bush in Pakistan (9), Afghanistan (1), and Indonesia (1). Even wider resonance had the publication of cartoons depicting the Prophet Muhammad in the Danish newspaper *Jyllands-Posten* in September 2005.[58] In the Western media the cartoons were described as the exercise of free of speech; from a pious Muslim perspective, these were denounced as blasphemous insults to Islam.[59] After a judicial complaint against the newspaper was dismissed, Danish imams campaigned to spread the knowledge about the cartoons. Protests by Muslim communities across the globe

58 These protests might seem a recent phenomenon, but already in 1966, Muslim students in Srinagar, India burned an effigy of UK Prime Minister Harold Wilson to protest a cartoon published in the *Times*. The *New York Times* reported: "The cartoon depicted Mr. Wilson as Mohammed and President de Gaulle as a Common Market mountain, an allusion to the proverb: 'If the mountain doesn't come to Mohammed, Mohammed must go to the mountain.'" "Indian Moslems Burn Effigy of Wilson to Assail Cartoon," *New York Times*, November 12, 1966.

59 Göran Larsson, *Muslims and the New Media: Historical and Contemporary Debates* (Farnham, UK: Ashgate, 2011), 47–48, 69.

171

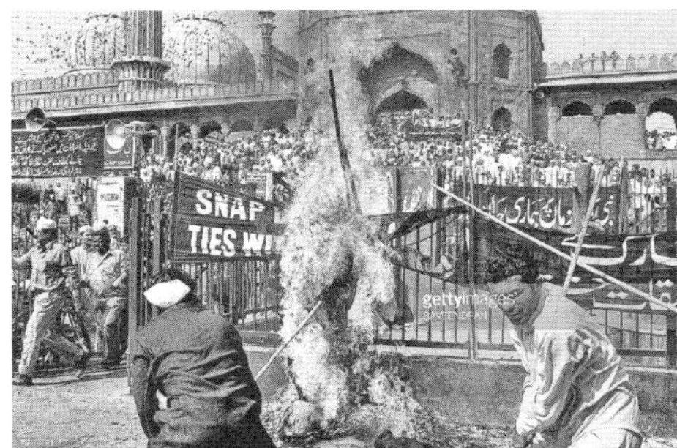

2006_02_10_India: Danish government

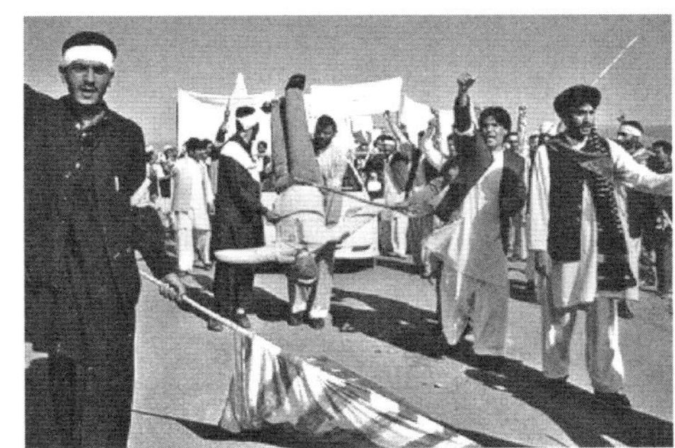

2009_10_22_Afghanistan: US President Obama

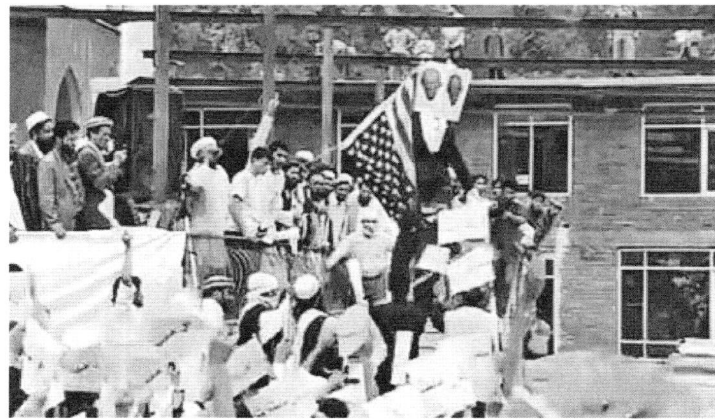

2010_09_06_Afghanistan: US pastor Jones

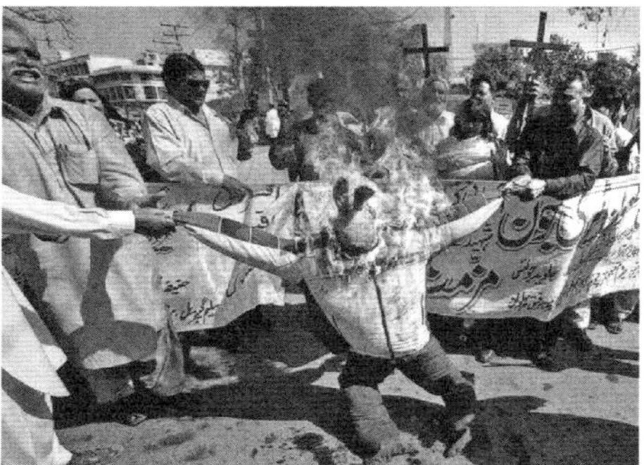

2011_05_23_Pakistan: US pastor Jones

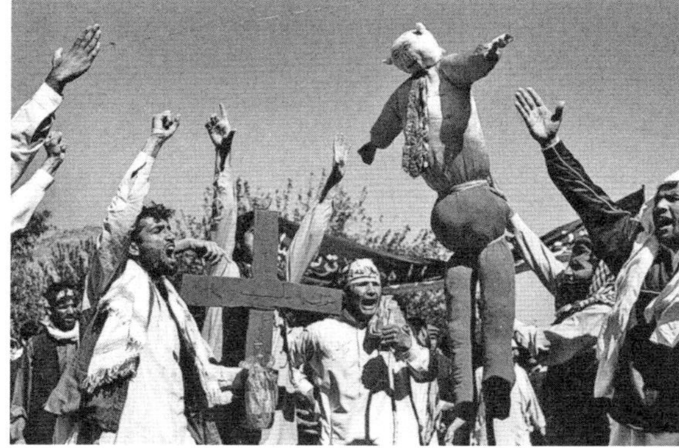

2011_04_03_Afghanistan: US President Obama   (a)

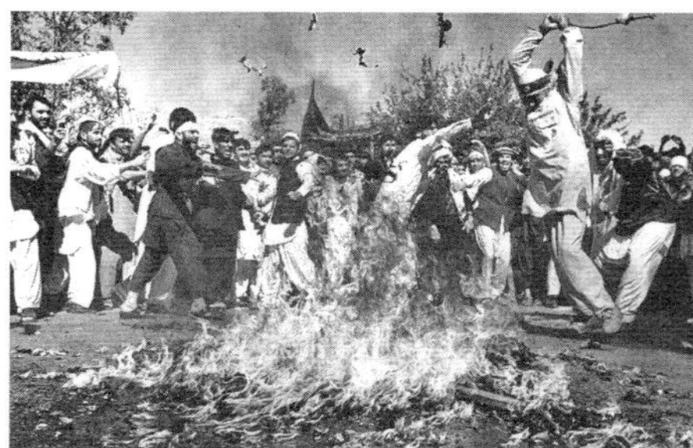

2011_04_03_Afghanistan: US President Obama   (b)

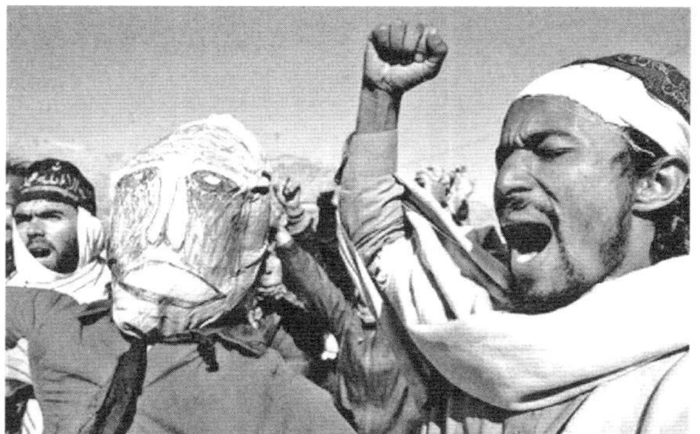

2012_02_23_Afghanistan: US President Obama

erupted in February 2006. Effigies of the cartoonist, the editor of the newspaper, Danish Prime Minister Anders Fogh Rasmussen, and Bush were burned in Pakistan (18), Turkey (1), Afghanistan (1), India (1), and Palestine (1). Some protests became violent and more than 200 people were killed. Saddam Hussein's death sentence in November 2006, and his undignified execution in December, led to protests featuring effigies of Bush in Pakistan (3), Nepal (1), Bangladesh (1), Jordan (1), and India (8).[60] In March 2008, the release of the film *Fitna* (Arabic for trial, affliction, or distress) by Dutch right-wing populist politician Geert Wilders led to effigy protests in Pakistan (4) and Afghanistan (2). In October 2009 and February 2012, soldiers from the International Security Assistance Force (ISAF) in Afghanistan inadvertently burned copies of the Quran, which sparked effigy protests in Afghanistan (11) and Pakistan (4).

Even more widely protested was the Quran burning by small Florida fringe church Pastor Terry Jones in 2010 on the anniversary of 9/11 to draw attention to – in his view – Islam's violent and evil nature. His publicity stunt received wide notice in the US and beyond, as US politicians of the highest rank tried to persuade him not to go through with it. In the end he agreed, but the harm was already done. Protests erupted across the globe; effigies of Obama and Jones were burned in Pakistan (2), Afghanistan (1), India (1), and Iran (1). More than twenty protesters were killed in clashes with the police in Afghanistan, Pakistan, and Indian Kashmir. In April 2011, the pastor reiterated his intent and burned a copy of the Quran in spite of renewed rebuke,

60 The protests in India were organized not by Muslim groups but by communists who had close ties with Iraq under Saddam Hussein.

173

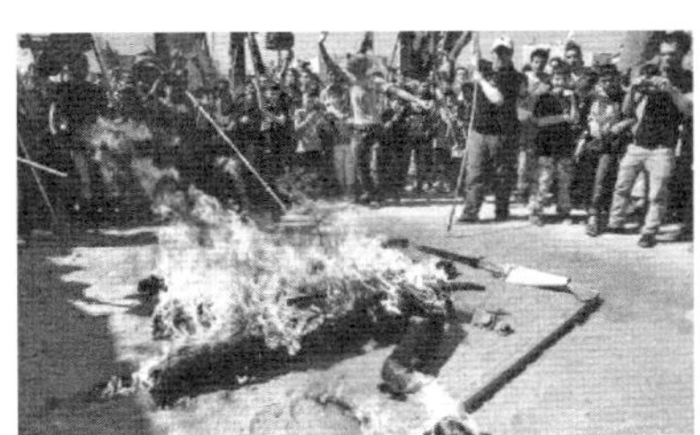

2012_09_14_Lebanon: US President Obama

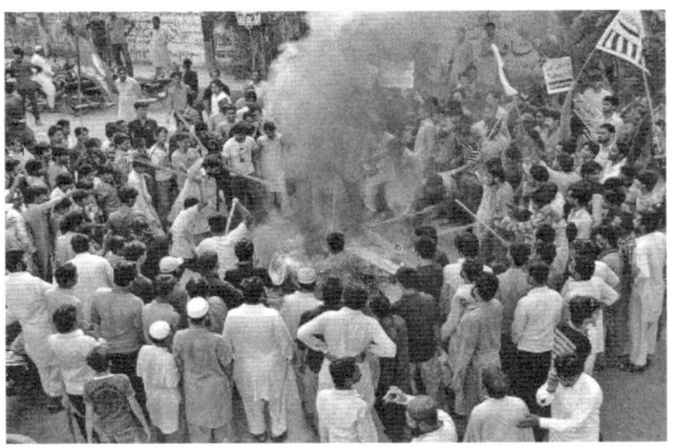

2012_09_16_Pakistan: effigy

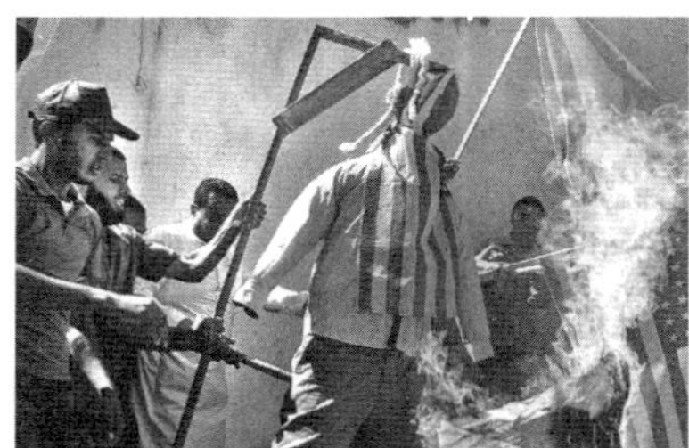

2012_09_14_Palestine: US President Obama

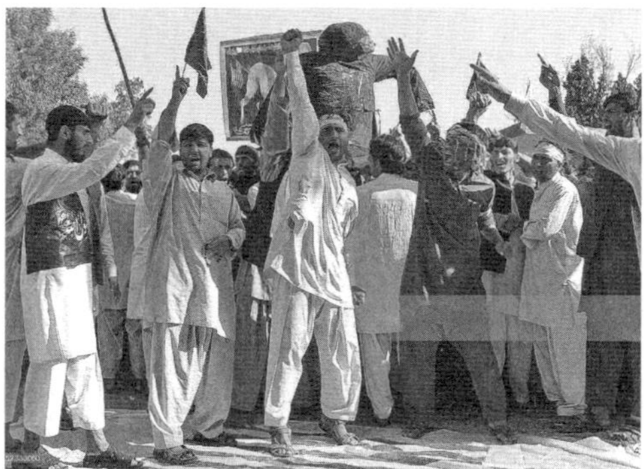

2012_09_19_Afghanistan: US President Obama

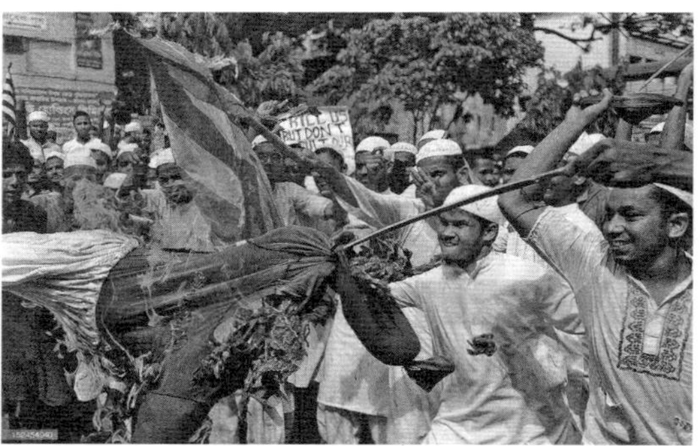

2012_09_21_Bangladesh: US President Obama

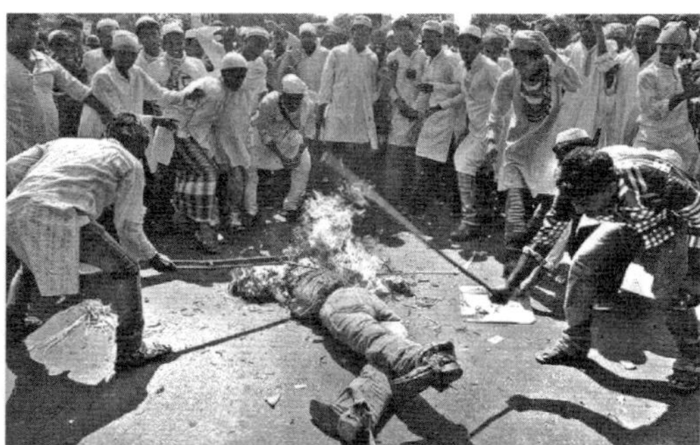

2012_09_27_India: US President Obama

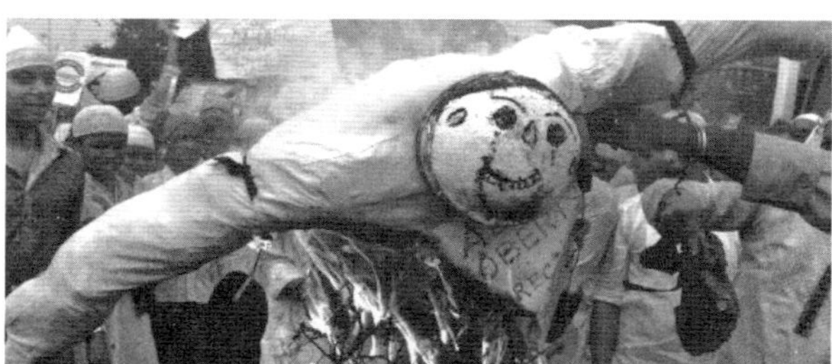

2012_10_05_India: filmproducer Roberts

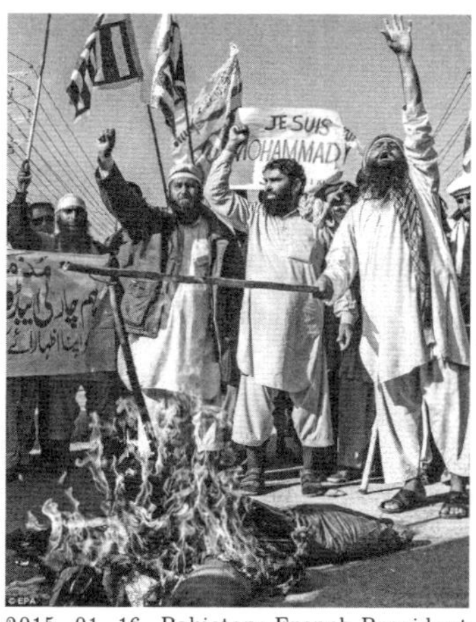

2015_01_16_Pakistan: French President Hollande

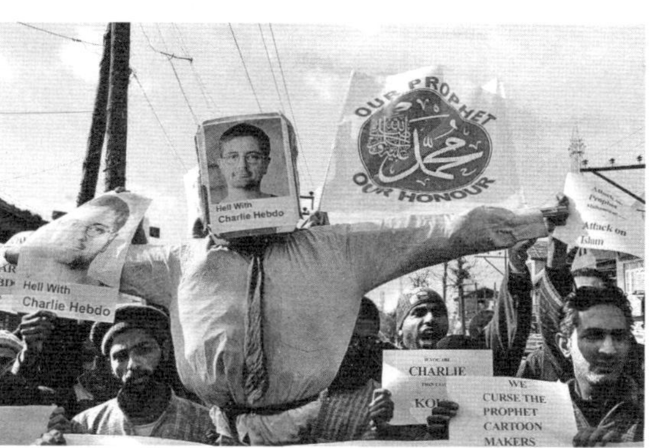

2015_01_23_India: Charlie Hebdo director Charb

resulting again in protests and more than twenty deaths in Afghanistan and Pakistan. Again, effigies of Obama and Jones were burned in Afghanistan (4) and Pakistan (4).[61]

In September 2012, a California man produced a "trailer" to a movie called *Innocence of Muslims*, denigrating Muslim beliefs, and posted it online. After a period of promotion by among others, Jones, awareness of the film spread. Protests erupted in countries with large Muslim populations, often staged in front of US embassies. Protesters were killed in Tunisia, Yemen, Sudan, and Pakistan. In Benghazi, US ambassador John Christopher Stevens and three security personnel were killed in an attack on the compound of the American diplomatic mission. Effigies of Obama as well as the film's producer and, again, Jones were burned in Pakistan (24), India (7), Afghanistan (5), Bangladesh (3), Sri Lanka (2), Palestine (2), and Lebanon (1).

In January 2015, two members of Al Qaeda in Yemen attacked the offices of the satirical magazine *Charlie Hebdo* in Paris, killing twelve and injuring eleven, over the publication of cartoons critical of Islam. France and much of the world was in utter shock. A mass demonstration was staged in Paris, drawing millions. The marchers expressed solidarity with the victims through the slogan "Je suis Charlie." Reacting to the Paris marchers, Muslim counter-demonstrators in some countries reacting to this dismissal of Muslim concerns, carried the slogan: "Je suis Mohammed," "Je suis Muslim," or "If you are Charlie, then I am Kouchi," referring to one of the attackers. Effigies of *Charlie Hebdo* and French

61   In the domestic sphere, pastor Jones also targeted President Obama and other leaders of the Democratic leaders for their policies. In 2012, he exhibited an effigy of Obama hanging from a gallows in front of his church. In January 2013 he announced the "National Burn Effigies of Obama Day" and torched effigies of Obama and President Bill Clinton.

175

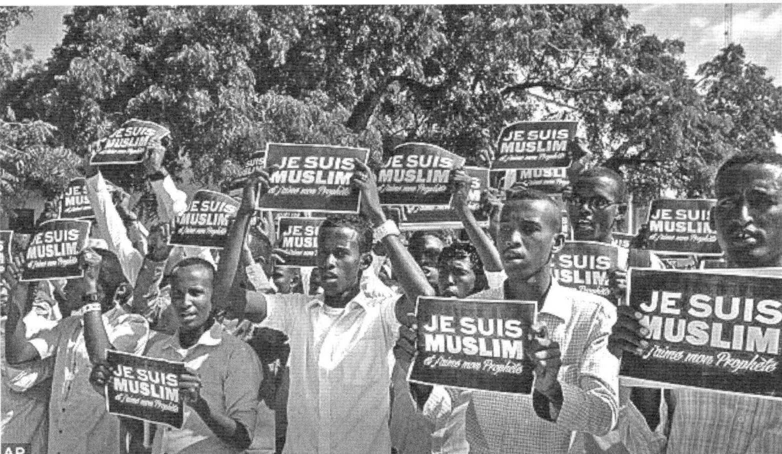

2015_01_17_Somalia: Charlie Hebdo protest

President François Hollande were burned in Pakistan (7), India (2), and Afghanistan (1). While the incidents interpreted as insults to Islam led to condemnations in many Muslim-majority countries, larger protests often took place in countries that were already embroiled in military conflicts with the US and its Western allies. Therefore, it is impossible to see the conflicts about cultural dominance as isolated from other issues. Rather they should be seen as occasions on which the anger about systemic disadvantages and the experience of cultural, military, and economic domination are expressed to transnational Muslim and Western audiences.

As I argue in chapter 2, "Performing Protest," media images are extensions of the performances, and constitute a relatively direct form of communication between protesters and audiences. As visual forms of communication, they function across language and cultural barriers. Even though they are framed and mediated, images of protests are less filtered than, for instance, newspaper reports written by foreign correspondents. In addition to the symbolic visual expression, protest signs in English or French that are legible in many photographs also transmit protesters' voices. Images of protests are traces of their speech, carrying their intent although fragmented and simplified. Using this and other spectacular visual forms of protest, even groups with a low level of organization are – to some degree – able to transmit their arguments. This makes burning or hanging of effigies a potent way by which to communicate through media.

These protests communicate anger tied to specific incidents, and denounce the injustices suffered. Recognizing protests by Muslim communities as legitimate, albeit antagonistic, expressions of discontent toward specific Western policies and attitudes, they should also be seen as attempts at cross-cultural communication through the news media, expressing Muslim values and sensitivities to Western publics. What Salvatore describes as the Islamic transnational public sphere overlaps with those in the West. The concerns voiced in the former are transmitted to the latter through various media channels, just as expressions of opinion in Western public spheres, as with the Muhammad cartoons, were received in public spheres in Muslim-majority countries. This process of contestation and exchange expands the discursive space of the news media, allowing for the inclusion of diverging voices and opening both publics' memories and identities for change.[62]

62 Michael Rothberg, "Multidirectional Memory in Migratory Settings: The Case of Post-Holocaust Germany," in *Transnational Memory: Circulation, Articulation, Scales*, ed. Chiara De Cesari and Ann Rigney (De Gruyter Online, 2014), 126.

Arab Uprisings

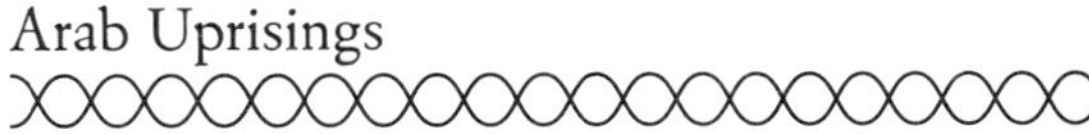

The Arab Spring of 2011 serves as a vivid example of the convergence of diverse public spheres and the emergence of transnational alliances. Demonstrators stood up to their governments and protested against the corruption, nepotism, social inequality, and structural poverty that marred many of the autocratic regimes in the region.[63] These protests led to enthousiastic rejoinders of solidarity from opposition groups in countries across the globe.

In Egypt, the growing discontent was first channeled by the grassroots labor movement that emerged in 2000. Activists organized a large number of strikes and demonstrations involving some effigy hangings and burnings.[64] Activist groups from the labor movement became the motors of the popular uprising in 2011.[65] From the start of these protests on January 25, effigies of President Hosni Mubarak appeared in Tahrir Square, the earliest rudimentary cardboard cut-outs, covered in slogans and drawings or photographs of Mubarak and hanged from traffic lights.

63 Arshin Adib-Moghhaddam, "The Arab Revolts, Islam and Postmodernity," *Middle East Journal of Culture and Communication* 5, no. 1 (2012): 4.

64 Dina Bishara, "Labor Movements in Tunisia and Egypt: Drivers vs. Objects of Change in Transition from Authoritarian Rule," *SWP Comments* 1 (2014): 2.

65 Atul Aneja, "Protest Movements in West Asia: Some Impressions," *Strategic Analysis* 35, no. 4 (2011): 549.

66 Jeremy Brecher, "In the Shadow of the Pyramids," Jeremy Brecher (blog), March 14, 2007, www.jeremybrecher. org/labor/in-the-shadow-of-the-pyramids/.

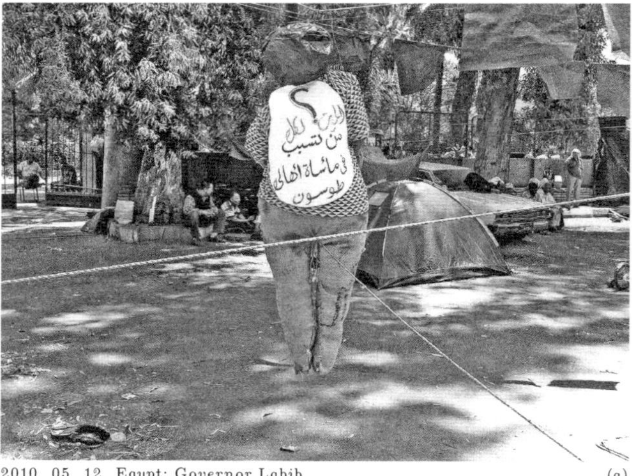
2010_05_12_Egypt: Governor Labib   (a)

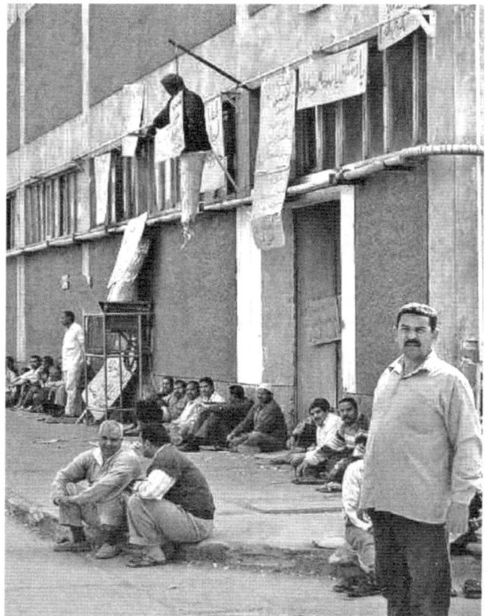
2009_03_10_Egypt: Company lawyer al-Dossuqy

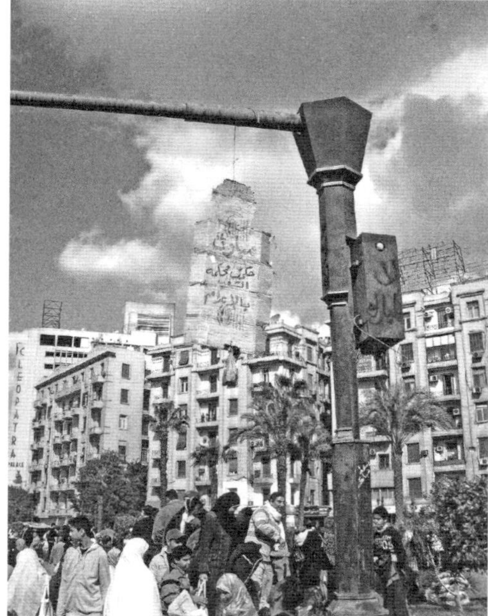
2011_01_31_Egypt: President Mubarak

At the very end of 2006 AD another group of Egyptian workers, angered at the denial of their year-end bonus and the corrup-tion of their managers, quit work and shut down their workplaces. The strike startled the Egyptian people, and apparently the government and the government-owned employer as well. ... Workers blamed the new chairman of the company, Mahmoud El-Gibaly, for squandering company assets in corrupt deals and appointing incompetent cronies to high positions. They carried coffins labeled "El-Gibaly is dead" and hung him in effigy. After five days, the government retreated and offered to restore the bonuses.[66]

2006_12_00_Egypt: company chairman El-Gibaly

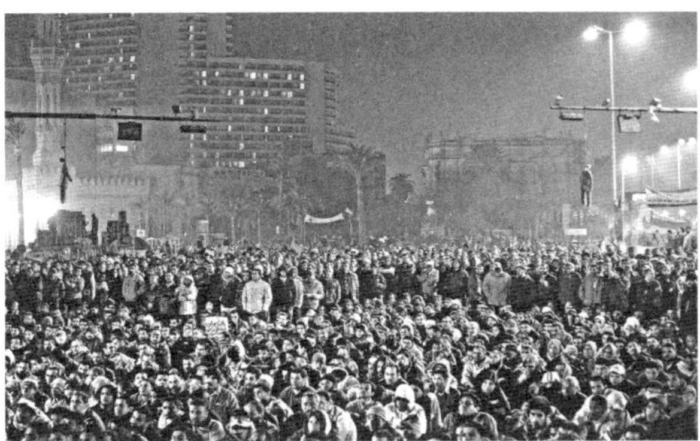

2011_02_02_Egypt: President Mubarak

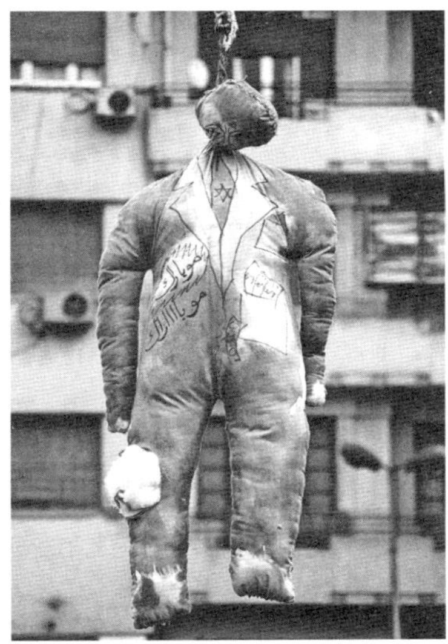

2011_02_03_Egypt: President Mubarak

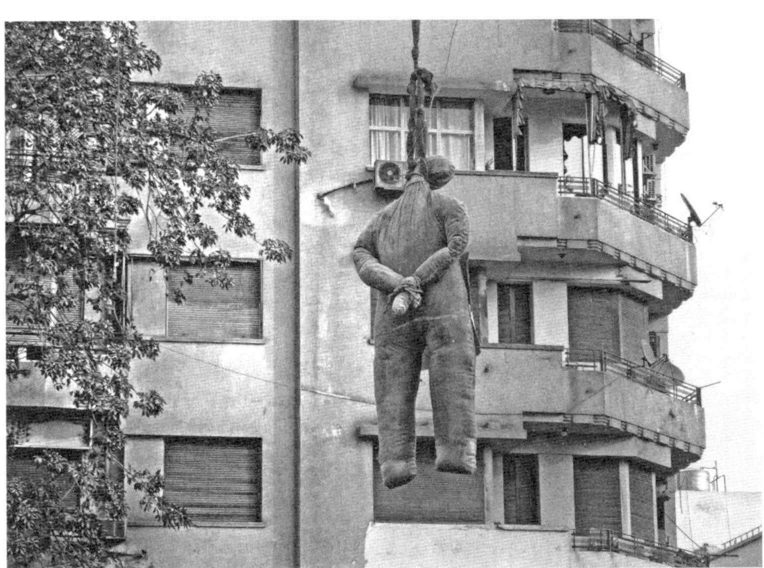

2011_02_04_Egypt: President Mubarak

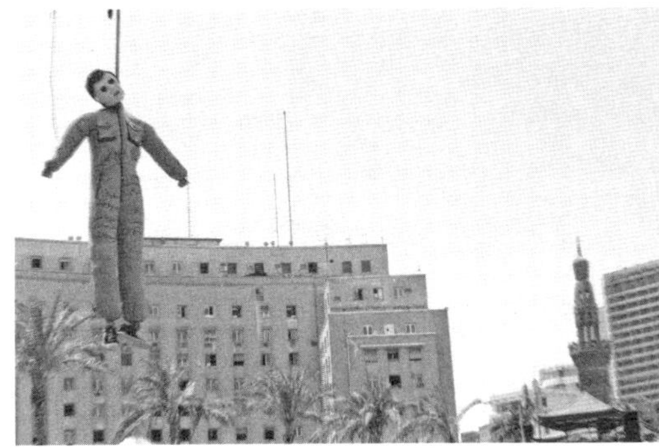

2012_04_26_Egypt: intelligence chief Suleiman

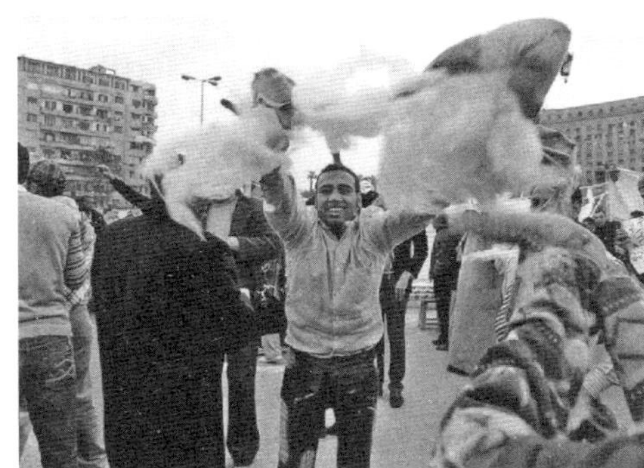

2011_02_07_Egypt: President Mubarak

As described in chapter 2, "Performing Protest," on February 1, activists in Tahrir Square staged a mock trial, mock execution, and mock funeral with three, now more elaborately produced, effigies of Mubarak and two other members of the government. Two of the effigies were hanged and the third was paraded on a stretcher through the crowd and torn to pieces.

The mock trial of Mubarak on Tahrir Square was repeated at least twice: April 8, 2011 and June 8, 2012, commenting on developments of his second official trial. These performances included a bench of judges, prosecutors, and the accused, who in these cases was represented by an actor wearing a Mubarak mask. One demonstration staged by a pro-Mubarak faction elsewhere in Cairo, featured an effigy of Mohammad El Baradei, a leading dissident and vocal critic of the government with the slogan: "Yes to Mubarak – No to traitors." All other effigies I found were displayed in protests against the ruling government. Most of them featured representations of Mubarak, but after he was ousted, protesters directed their anger toward his successors. An effigy of Omar Suleiman, Director of General Intelligence Directorate, who served briefly as vice-president (January 29–February 11), was hanged in April 2012. Field Marshal Mohamed Hussein Tantawi, Chairman of the Supreme Council of the Armed Forces (SCAF) of Egypt, who ruled the country immediately following Mubarak's ousting in February 2011 until June 2012, was hanged in effigy three times, in April and

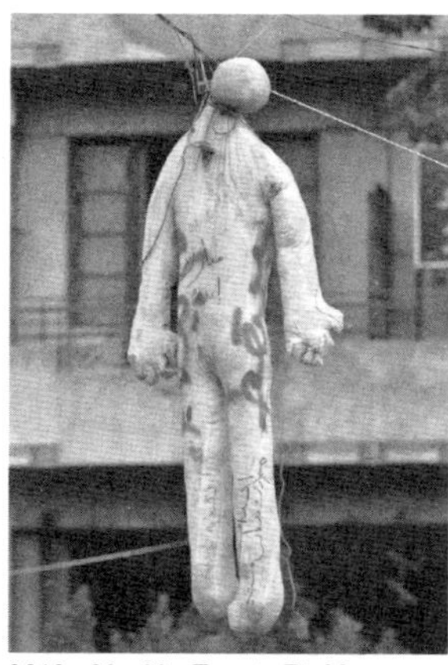

2012_02_02_Egypt: Field Marshal Tantawi

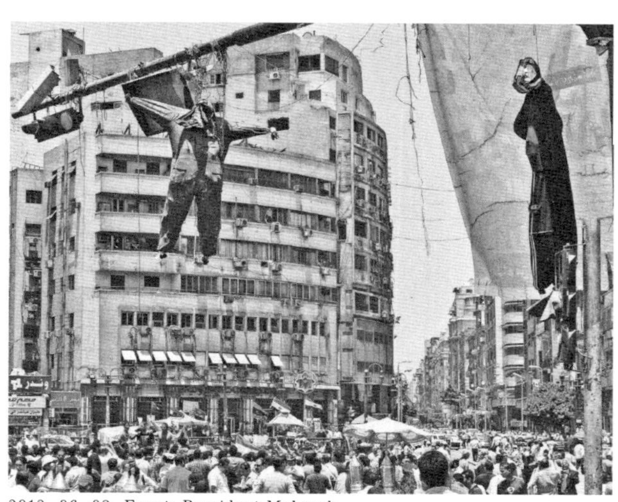

2012_06_03_Egypt: President Mubarak

November of 2011 and February 2012. In February 2013, President Mohamed Morsi was hanged in effigy, and in June and November of the same year his successor President Abdel Fattah al-Sisi.

On a few occasions, effigies of foreign adversaries were hanged in Tahrir Square. Some were the usual suspects: personifications of Israel and its secret service Mossad. In January 2012, an effigy of Syrian President Bashar al-Assad was hanged by Syrian emigrants and refugees in protest of his refusal to step down. I found evidence of thirty-six effigies created in Egypt between 2011 and 2014. Only one effigy, of former SCAF member Hassan al-Roweny, was burned. All others were hanged, from buildings, lampposts, and traffic lights, most of them (27) in Tahrir Square. On several occasions, effigies were presented as defendants in mock trials, underwent mock executions, and were buried in mock funerals.

During the trials against Mubarak, his sons, and fellow government officials, effigies were often clad in orange prison jumpsuits, immediately recognizable from their use at Guantanamo Bay detention camp and Abu Ghraib prison.

181

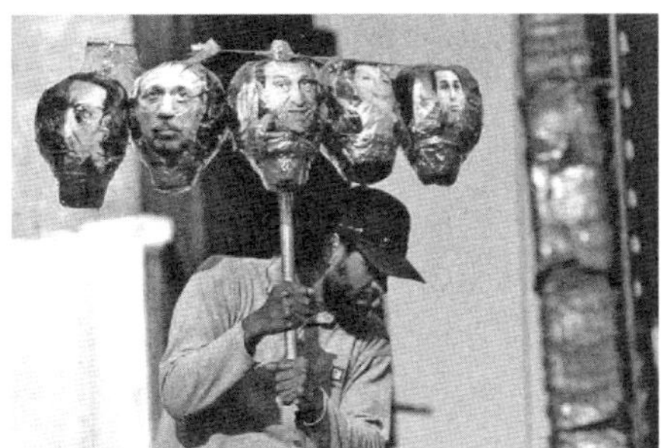

2012_06_07_Egypt: President Mubarak and government

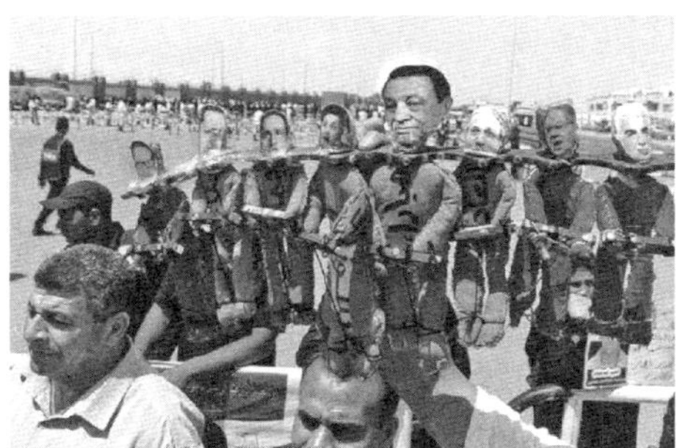

2013_05_11_Egypt: President Mubarak and government

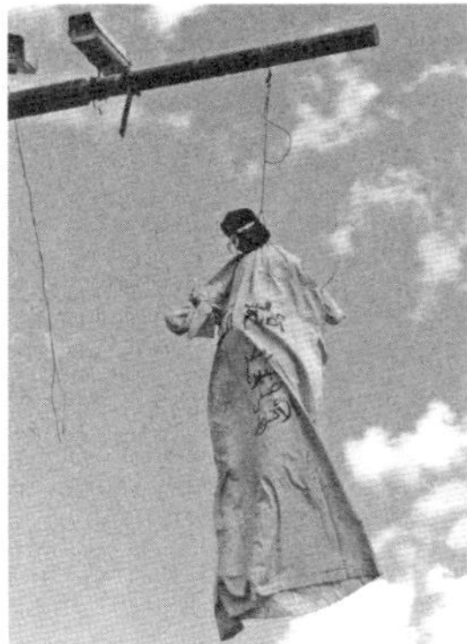

2013_02_03_Egypt: President Morsi

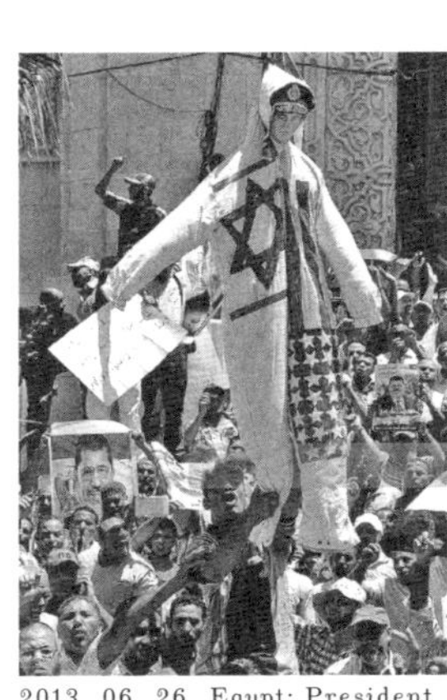

2013_06_26_Egypt: President al-Sisi

67 Jeremy Brecher, "In the
Shadow of the Pyramids,"
Jeremy Brecher (blog), March
14, 2007, www.jeremybrecher.
org/labor/in-the-shadow-of-
the-pyramids/.

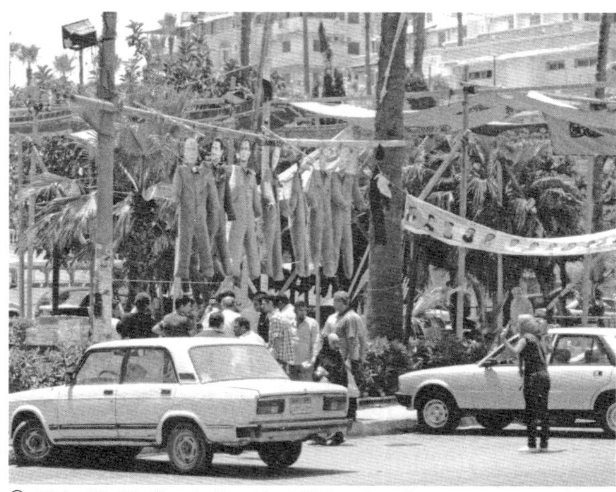

○ 2012_06_07_Egypt: President Mubarak and government members

They took me to a mini Madame Tussauds, on a raised
dais in a main street, of life-size effigies of a clownish
Mubarak and his family, above all his son and heir
Gamal, now in prison. It also included rows of members
of his coterie and a ghoulish Mu'ammar Qadhafi. Men,
women and children were gazing and taking photographs. The atmosphere was that of a fairground. "Next
week we will burn them in a public show of solidarity,"
one man said.[67]

al-Limby: 2011_04_00_Egypt: former President Mubarak + his
family + Gaddafi

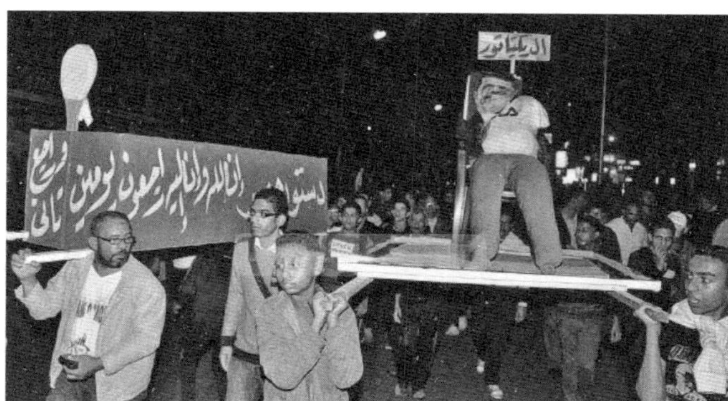

al-Limby: 2012_11_28_Egypt (President Morsi)

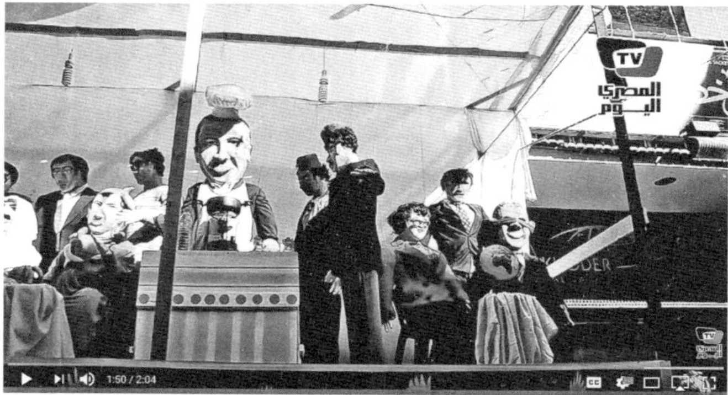

al-Limby: 2014_04_19_Egypt: Turkish President Erdoğan + US President
Obama + Qatari royal family + others

One photograph shows a row of eight effigies of Mubarak and co-defendants in the trial, hanging from a large wooden beam strung up between a lamppost and palm tree.○ On several occasions, protesters paraded or displayed smaller effigies of ousted government members outside the Egyptian police academy in Cairo where Mubarak's actual trial took place. Clad in orange and bound in shackles with nooses around their necks, they hung from miniature gallows – some of them had their heads cut off, bloody and dangling, with photographs of the accused pasted on (January 2012, February 2012, June 2012, May 2013).

In nearby Port Said, the April 2011 *Harq al-Limby* was also characterized by the revolutionary Tahrir spirit. The al-Limbys burned that year were Mubarak, his wife, their son Gamal, and a row of government officials. These domestic villains were joined in effigy by Libyan leader Muammar Gaddafi. In 2013, the al-Limby was Morsi, who had tried to ban the festival.[68] In 2014, local artist Mohsen Khodeir made effigies of then Turkish Prime Minister (now President) Recep Tayyip Erdoğan, the Qatari royal family, Obama, Netanyahu, and Egyptian satirist Bassem Youssef to be burned on *Harq al-Limby*.[69] In 2015, Khodeir modeled the hooded fighters of ISIS and their victims in a replica of gruesome media images.

The protest movement that came to be known as the Arab Uprising began in Tunisia and quickly spread to Egypt, Libya, Syria, Yemen, and Bahrain. In Tunisia, no effigy burning or hanging was reported, but the act that started the movement was a related symbolic act. In an act of self-sacrifice, street vendor Mohamed Bouazizi set himself on fire in response to the confiscation of his wares and humiliation suffered at the hands of municipal officials. Out of desperation, he turned himself and his suffering into a sign, making visible

68 "Port Said's Allenby effigies wear masks of Erdogan, Qatari Emir," *Cairo Post*, April 21, 2014.

69 "Effigies for Easter," *Al-Ahram Weekly* 1242, May 16, 2016.

with his body the injustice of the social system and the violence enacted by the government. The violent image of a burning body – registered as a mental image since no photographs of the incident exist – draws likeness to the burning of effigies, even though self-immolation is on a completely different scale of physical violence.

In Yemen, a day after an activist hanged an effigy of President Ali Abdullah Saleh in Zinjibar on February 28, 2010, the activist was killed by security forces who raided his home. A year later, in February, April, and October 2011, Saleh effigies were hanged in a few demonstrations against the government demanding democratic reforms drawing on the influence of the Tunisian and Egyptian uprisings. In November, Saleh resigned from his post and left for Saudi Arabia. In Syria between July 2011 and June 2012, effigies of Assad were hanged on five occasions in various cities under rebel control, and outside Syria in Turkey, Lebanon, and Yemen. In Libya, all the effigies that appeared in the rebel stronghold Benghazi and in other rebel-held cities, depicted Gaddafi. These hangings also connoted the desire for justice and punishment, even though formal legal procedures are not visibly referenced. Gaddafi's effigies were strung up, stabbed, or depicted with blood-stained faces prescient of the way he was later killed and his body exhibited in order to produce a final debasing image of the dictator.

184

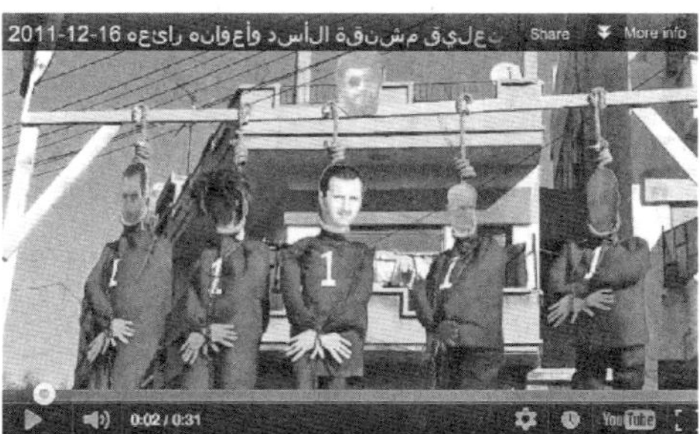

2011_12_16_Syria: President Assad and ministers

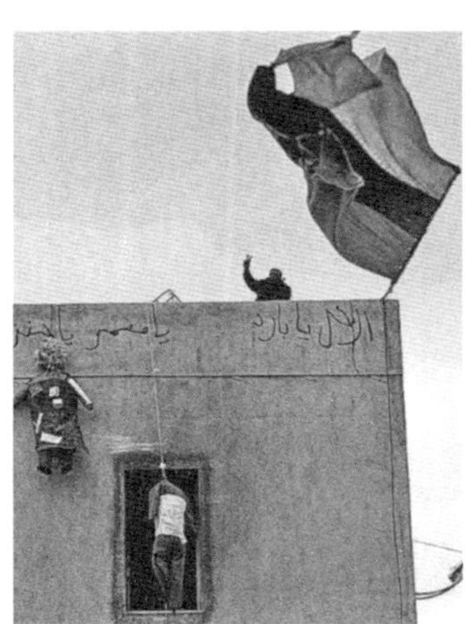

2011_02_24_Libya: Colonel Gaddafi

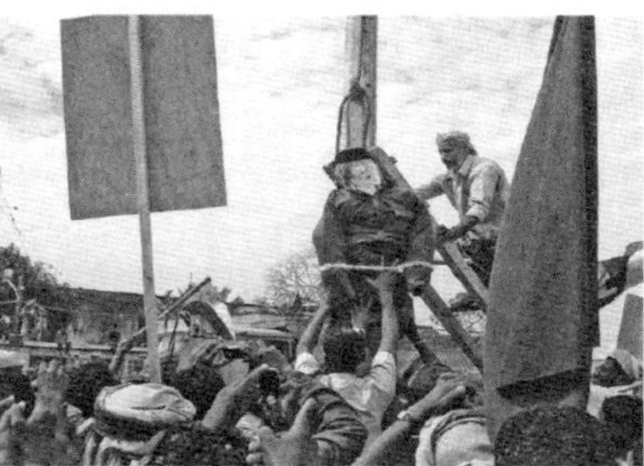

2010_03_02_Yemen: President Saleh

Neither in Libya, Syria, nor Yemen was it customary to hang or burn effigies before the Arab Spring. In a short span of time, the revolutionary movement became transnational, exemplifying how weak opposition movements can accumulate the strength to profoundly influence domestic politics and a region's imaginaries. Furthermore, it inspired activists in many other countries through sharing ideas, strategies, and practices.[70]

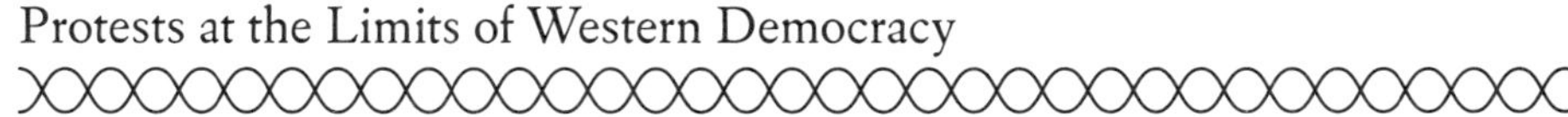

70 Pnina Werbner, Martin Webb and Kathryn Spellman-Poots, "Introduction," in Webner et al. (ed.), *The Political Aesthetics of Global Protest: The Arab Spring and Beyond* (Edinburgh: Edinburgh University Press 2014), 3.

Protests at the Limits of Western Democracy

The genealogical lines of effigy protest I describe in this chapter make clear that they did not occur throughout an amorphous "Muslim World." Instead, effigy protest emerged at specific historical moments of colonial conflict and military interventions. In these genealogies distinct ways of transfer appear: in Egypt, the British holiday tradition was appropriated as a tool against British rule and postcolonial influence; in Iran, a domestic Shia ritual was adapted for political use against US influence; in Afghanistan, Afghan emigrants in Iran and elsewhere adopted the practice and later took it back home. The first genealogical line can be drawn from Egypt's early twentieth century anti-colonial struggle against Britain to protests against Israel; the second from the 1979 Iranian revolution to protests against the Soviet Union's occupation in Afghanistan in 1979 and against Israel's denial of Palestinian's rights. In the beginning of the new millennium, these lines seem to blur as protests spread more widely across the region in demonstrations against US-led invasions in Afghanistan and Iraq, and in response to incidents experienced as insults to Islam.

Seen from the historical trajectory of Islam, the "West" is

71   Mohammed Arkoun, *The Unthought in Contemporary Islamic Thought* (London: Saqi Books, 2002), 16.

72   Chandra Muzaffar, "Islam, Justice and Politics," in *The New Voices of Islam: Reforming Politics and Modernity*, ed. Mehran Kamrava (London: I. B. Tauris, 2006), 224.

73   Judith Butler, *Precarious Life: The Powers of Mourning and Violence* (London: Verso Books, 2004), 34.

74   See chapter 1, "Double Bodies."

often considered a "hostile hegemonic geopolitical sphere," impossible to escape since the eighteenth and nineteenth centuries, and broadly responsible for a historic decline since the thirteenth century.[71] Emphasizing the central role of justice in Islam, Islamic reformist philosopher Chandra Muzaffar proposes that Muslim reactions to Western domination "may in fact be a cry for justice, a plea for a more equitable relationship with the West."[72]

After 9/11, the US embarked on the so-called War on Terror, pressuring the government in Afghanistan to extradite Osama bin Laden. The War on Terror metastasized with military operations in Afghanistan, Iraq, Libya, Syria, the Sahara, and the Philippines, with enormous consequences for countries and people, and still there seems to be no end in sight. Judith Butler writes that

> the infinite paranoia that imagines the war against terrorism as a war without end will be one that justifies itself endlessly in relation to the spectral infinity of its enemy, regardless of whether or not there are established grounds to suspect the continuing operation of terror cells with violent aims.[73]

The War on Terror created a state of exception outside of any legal framework, based on overwhelming military power, and one-sided sense of justice in which the US President assumed power over life and death. It could be argued that in the person of the US president, the absolute sovereign has reappeared, which in European history is closely tied to the use of effigies.[74] The frequent protests in Afghanistan, Pakistan, and Iraq between 2001 and 2013, thematize the figure of the sovereign with burning effigies of President Bush and his successor President Obama. They point to the limits of Western democracies, beyond which lies the state of emergency characterized by injustice and abuse of sovereign power.

The sense of injustice extended far beyond the military. Promoting Western liberal democracy self-servingly as the only and universally legitimate form of governance, as Bush did in a 2003 speech,[75] fails to "recognize that different life worlds produce their own cultures with their own horizons of intelligibility."[76] Theorists of radical democracy have challenged this Western-centric perspective, pointing to "liberal democracy's intertwined history with, legitimations of, and key complicities with, capitalist rule and expansion."[77] The economic and cultural dynamics tied to the globalization of Western capitalist modernity is making alternative forms of living increasingly impossible. These imposed "Western values" are then experienced as violence and injustice. As symbolic expression, effigy protest facilitates communication in an emerging transnational and cross-cultural public sphere, communicating the lack of accountability and means for redress in a globalizing world outside democratic control, and dominated by Western nations, economic systems, and political discourse.[78]

In October 2009, protesters in Kabul burned an effigy of Obama in protest against the burning of a Quran by ISAF troops. They carried a banner reading: "No Democracy – We want just Islam."  The second part can be read as: "We only want Islam" but also as "We want the Islam that is just." Rejecting Western domination, the sign expresses the wish for justice and self-determination – a truly democratic impulse.

187

75 George W. Bush, "President Bush Discusses Freedom in Iraq and Middle East: Remarks by President George W. Bush at the 20th Anniversary of the National Endowment for Democracy," *The White House* (website), November 6, 2003, georgewbush-whitehouse.archives.gov/news/releases/2003/11/20031106-2.html.

76 Janet Conway and Jakeet Singh, "Radical Democracy in Global Perspective: Notes from the Pluriverse," *Third World Quarterly* 32, no. 4 (2011): 703.

77 Conway and Singh, "Radical Democracy," 692.

78 Nancy Fraser, "Reframing Justice in a Globalizing World," *The New Left Review* 36 (2005): 78.

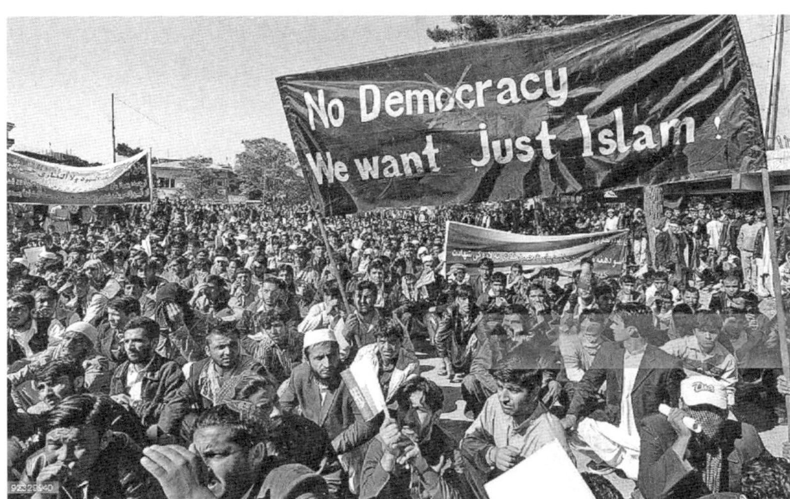

○ 2009_10_25_Afghanistan: US President Obama

Many posters and banners carried in effigy protests are written in English and seek dialogue with an international Western audience. Sometimes the messages are not very sophisticated: "Hate Amrica," and Crush Amrica" (Pakistan, 2011), "Black dog Obama" (Afghanistan, 2012), or "World's bigest terrist Bush" (India, 2006). Others are also very clear but more pronounced, like "JUSTICE NOW!" (India, 2013), "We want peace in Iraq" (Bangladesh, 2003), or "Stop Killing Innocent Libyans" (Sri Lanka, 2011). Some slogans try to communicate the Muslim values that were injured by the events, which sparked the protests: "Kill us but don't insult our Prophet" (Bangladesh, 2012) or "We are ready to Die for the Honour of our Holy Prophet – From: District Bar Association, RWP" (Pakistan, 2012).

Some address Western audiences, like the one announcing a boycott of Danish products after the publication of the Muhammad cartoons in a Danish newspaper: "Not sale Danemark products" (Pakistan, 2006). After the attack on the French satirical magazine Charlie Hebdo, protesters' communication with Western audiences is layered. Protesters in India, burning an effigy of ISIS, declared: "We stand with Paris," adding another voice to the discussion.

In 2011, the effigy protests of the Arab Spring movements opened another chapter: here the effigy protest was reimagined against oppression by domestic regimes. Protests were suddenly aligned with the Western self-image of free democratic expression, and proved inspirational for Western audiences. The movements corrected – at least to some degree and for some time – media discourse about Islam's incompatibility with democracy and led to new alignments and affiliations in the transnational, cross-cultural public sphere. Building on the findings in this chapter about the communicative aspects of protests, in the next I focus on a short period in one country, investigating a string of effigy protests in Baghdad between 2005 and 2009 against US military occupation. I follow the question regarding how Islamic and Western attitudes toward images influence each other and how this interplay is reflected in effigy protests.

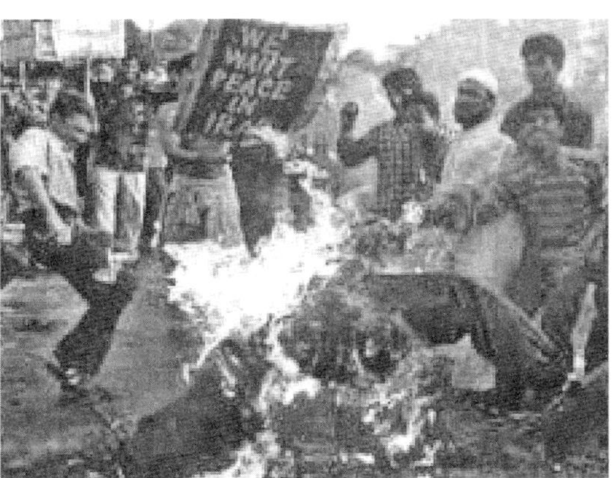

2003_04_11_Bangladesh: US President Bush

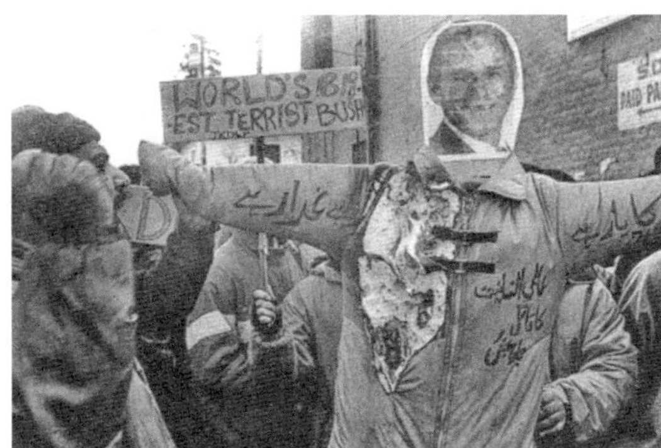

2006_12_30_India: US President Bush

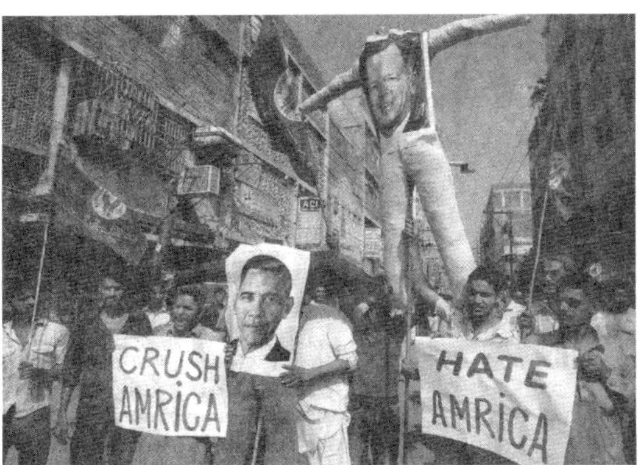

2011_09_27_Pakistan: US President Obama   (b)

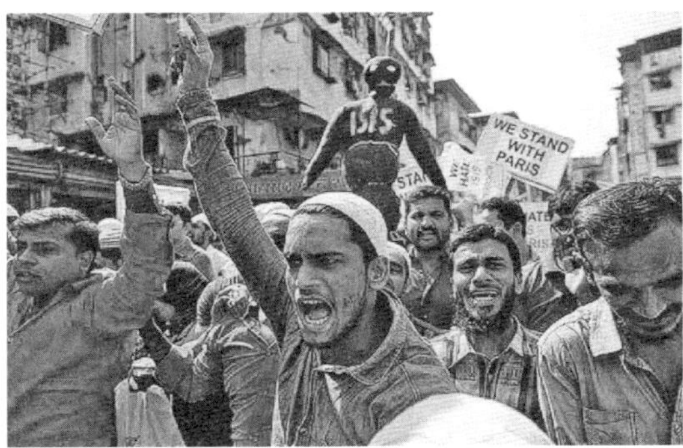

2015_11_17_India: ISIS

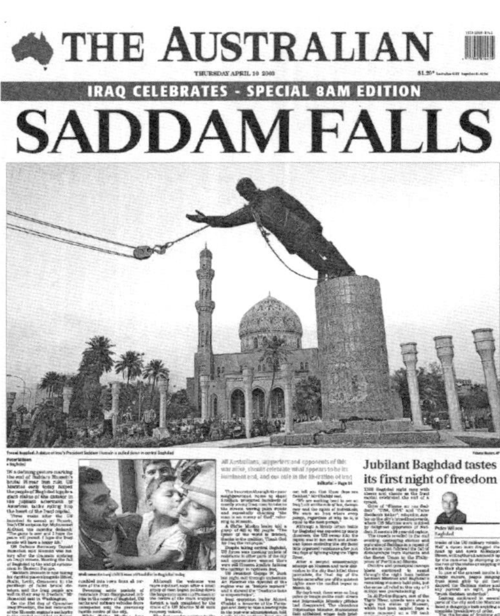
THE AUSTRALIAN
THURSDAY APRIL 10 2003
IRAQ CELEBRATES - SPECIAL 8AM EDITION
SADDAM FALLS
Jubilant Baghdad tastes its first night of freedom
Brisbane $79
one way
qantas.com

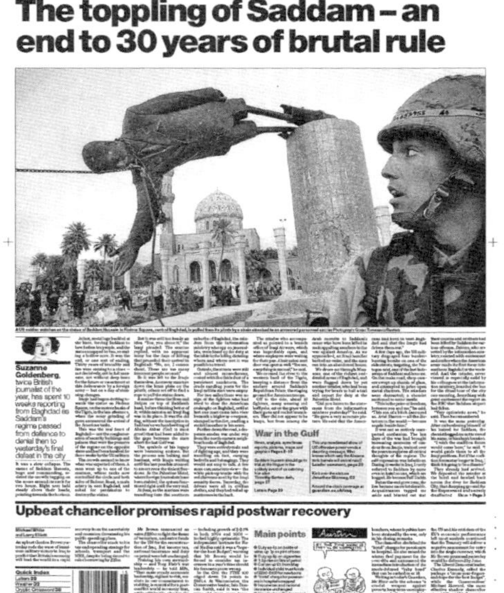
Budget 2003
Pull-out, pages 13-24
12 pages of news, comment and analysis
Life
A new section for science
Plus Online and jobs
The Guardian
The toppling of Saddam – an end to 30 years of brutal rule
Suzanne Goldenberg
War in the Gulf
Upbeat chancellor promises rapid postwar recovery
Main points

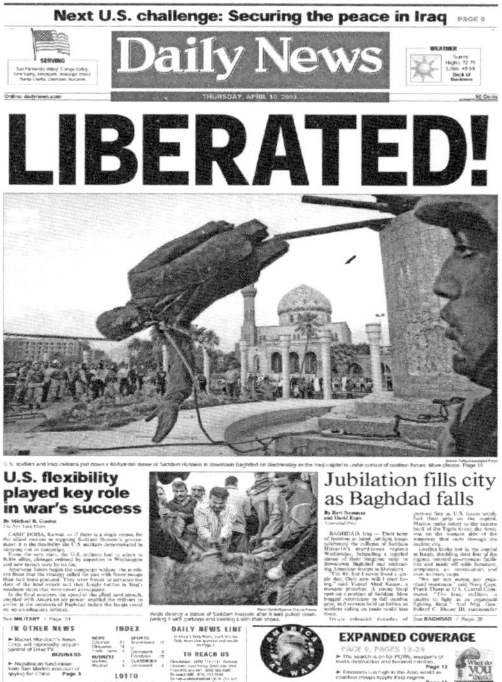
Next U.S. challenge: Securing the peace in Iraq
PAGE 8
SERVING
Daily News
THURSDAY, APRIL 10, 2003
WEATHER
LIBERATED!
U.S. flexibility played key role in war's success
By Michael R. Gordon
The New York Times
Jubilation fills city as Baghdad falls
By Ravi Nessman
Associated Press
IN OTHER NEWS
INDEX
DAILY NEWS LINE
TO REACH US
LOTTO
ONLINE
EXPANDED COVERAGE
PAGES 12-24
AMERICA AT WAR

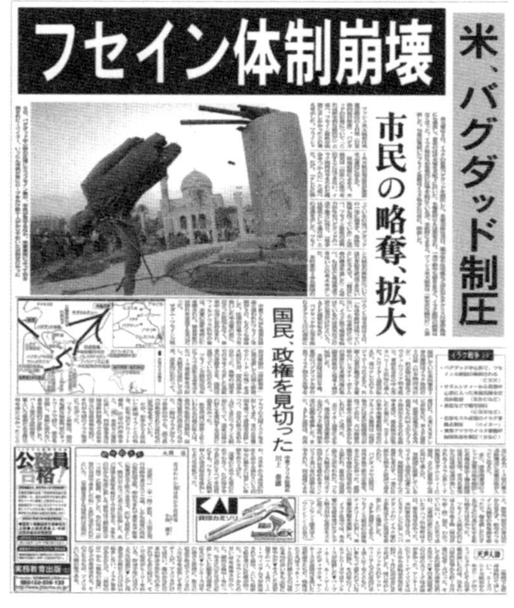
フセイン体制崩壊
米、バグダッド制圧
市民の略奪、拡大
国民、政権を見切った
KAI

Dialogic Communication

XXXXXXXXXXXXXXXXXXXXXXXXXXXXXXXXXXXXXXXXXXXXXXXXX

E f f i g y P r o t e s t s i n I r a q

The Plinth

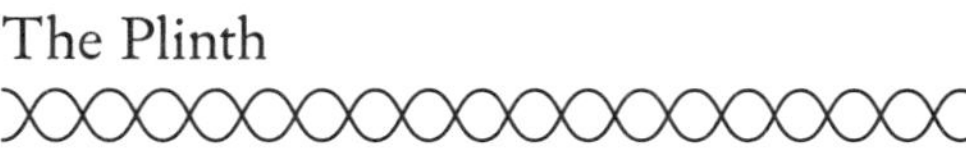

The iconoclastic act of toppling Saddam Hussein's statue on Baghdad's Firdos Square in April 2003, signaled the end of his regime. The intense media coverage of the event instantaneously elevated the square to a *lieu de mémoire,* a site memorializing this specific moment in the Iraq War.[1] But right from the start, the site was contested, as the event elicited divergent readings at home and abroad.[2]

In the decade that followed, Firdos Square remained in focus for the international news media as a vibrant public forum and site of protests against the United States's occupation. Followers of the Shia cleric Muqtada al-Sadr organized protests that restaged the event, replacing Saddam's statue with effigies of US President George W. Bush.[3] They used this form of symbolic theatrical protest to attract media attention and to communicate their position not just to a domestic audience but also to Western audiences.

I use Iraq under occupation as a case study to examine how different cultural traditions of mediating power influence

1 Pierre Nora, "Between Memory and History: Les Lieux de Mémoire," *Representations* 26 (1989): 12–14.

2 Florian Göttke, *Toppled* (Rotterdam: Post Editions, 2010), 48.

3 It is unclear if the protesters appropriated Iraqi cultural traditions, like the Ta'ziyeh in Iran, for the political effigy performances in Baghdad, or if they were inspired by, for instance, the Iranian effigy protests against the United States from 1979 onwards, which I describe in chapter 4, "Effigy Protests in Egypt, Iran, Afghanistan, and Across the Middle East."

4   Göttke, *Toppled*, 11–15.

5   In France, the need to make the identity of the French Republic visible in the urban environment led to a veritable "statuomania" between 1870 and 1945. Sergiusz Michalski, *Public Monuments: Art in Political Bondage 1870–1997* (London: Reaktion Books, 1998), 13–55.

6   Göttke, *Toppled*, 133.

each other. As before, I argue that communication through media builds on and further develops a shared symbolic language, leading to dialogue across cultural borders. More specifically, here I show how effigy protests, facilitated and complicated antagonistic communication between publics in the "West" and Iraq as seen through the news reports and images of predominantly Western media.

The statue in Firdos Square portrayed Saddam as a statesman in Western dress, a suit and tie. Erected just a year before the war in celebration of his sixty-fifth birthday, it was one of the many visual signs of his dictatorial power and cult of personality.[4] To bolster his regime's legitimacy, Saddam appropriated many narratives and discourses: he projected onto himself the myth of the old Babylonian kings and the historical figure Saladin as the liberator of Jerusalem; he instrumentalized traditional tribal power structures; he accumulated military positions and political offices of the nation-state; he maintained a constant presence in the news media and followed the European tradition of manifesting power visually with statues and monuments in urban public space,[5] and his portrait multiplied on coins, public buildings, offices and private homes. These images became icons of absolute sovereignty – demonstrating his omnipresence and omnipotence.

On the morning of April 9, 2003, Saddam appeared on TV for the last time as president of Iraq. That afternoon, when American soldiers and Iraqi citizens toppled his statue in front of assembled international news media, Saddam's regime ended. As the statue was a direct expression of his power, its fall became the visible manifestation of the regime's collapse.[6]

Afterwards, for a time, the square became a thriving public forum: a place to express political positions, voice

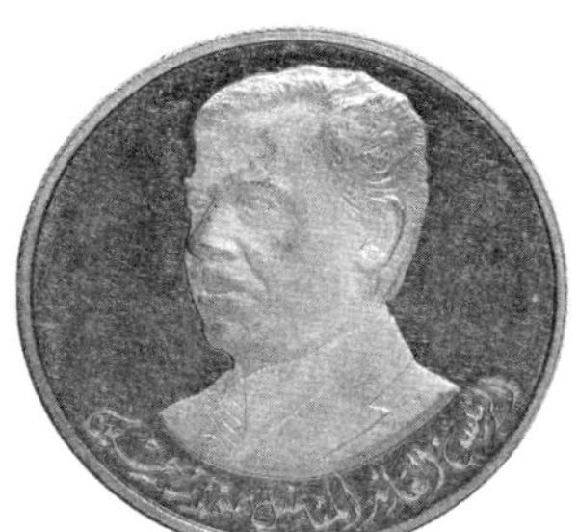

gold 50 dinars: 1980_Iraq (Saddam Hussein)

demands, and interact with journalists of the international news media. The plinth, a placeholder for the absent image of power, didn't remain empty for long; an artist's collective proposed a different vision of Iraqi identity and future by erecting a sculpture on top symbolizing freedom and the unity of Iraq.[7] The square also became the site for manifestations and demonstrations against the new powers in Iraq. In April 2005, on the second anniversary of the statue's fall, Bush, British Prime Minister Tony Blair, and Saddam were presented on a podium in front of the plinth as effigies, clad in red prison jumpsuits with neckties bearing their names. The effigies were shackled, nooses tied around their necks, and their faces transformed into those of werewolves. The three leaders, enemies in real life, became monsters of the same kind.[8]

Three years later, in October 2008, the effigies of Bush and US Secretary of State Condoleezza Rice were burned in protest of the planned security agreement between Iraq and the US during a rally organized by al-Sadr, the Iran-backed

7   The sculpture depicted a family of three, holding a crescent moon and a sun, and was erected in May 2003 on the initiative of the artist collective Najeen and created by Bassem Hamad al-Dawiri.

8   The protesters seem to build on the theme of King Nebuchadnezzar, to whom Saddam Hussein had often compared himself as the builder of Babylon. As a punishment from god, the king went mad, living like an animal – according to some, a werewolf – for seven years. Reading this story through Giorgio Agamben's "Homo Sacer," the monster also represents the other side of the sovereign. the homo sacer, the one that can be killed but not sacrificed. See Giorgio Agamben, *Homo Sacer: Sovereign Power and Bare Life* (Stanford: Stanford University Press, 1998).

193

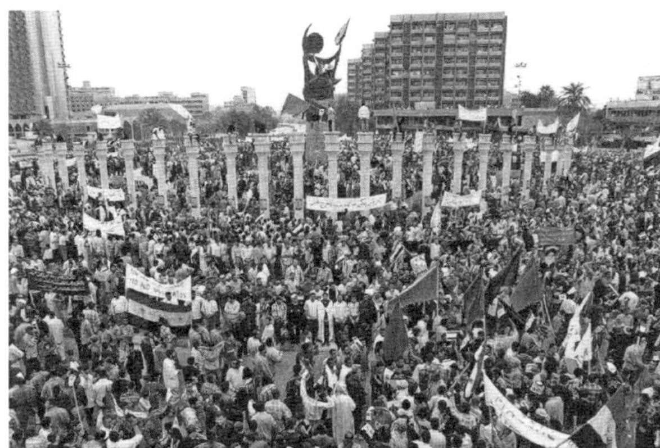

2005_04_09_Iraq: Saddam Hussein + US President Bush + British Premier Blair   (a)

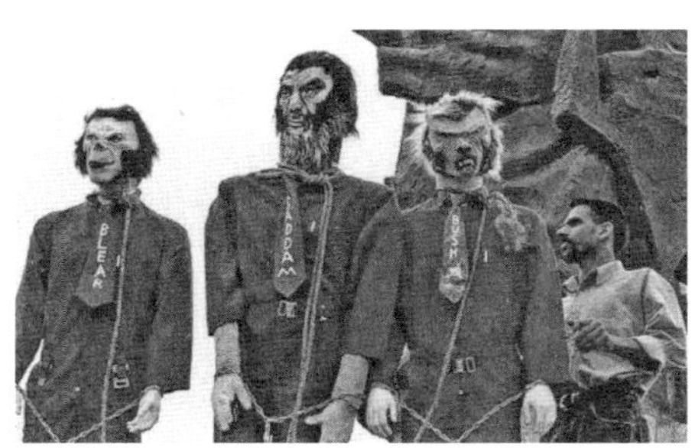

(c)

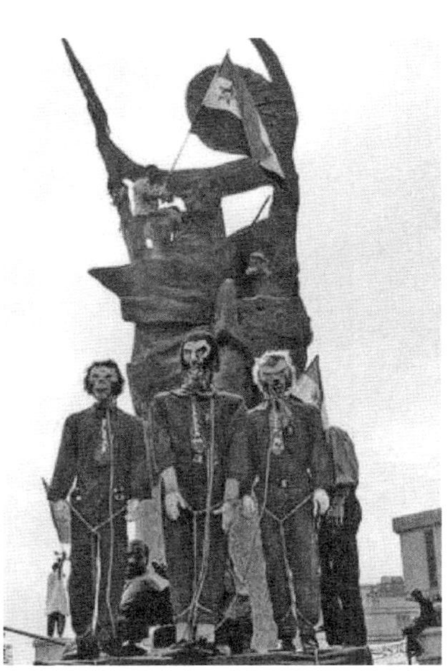

(b)

Shia cleric who was one of the most influential politicians in post-Saddam Iraq. Rice's effigy is dressed in black and grey, in an insulting array of clothing: a skimpy skirt, long stockings, and a handbag, with pink slippers for earrings with soles adorned by Stars of David (considered defamatory in an anti-Israel context). Bush's effigy wears a white shirt and red tie. Holding a popsicle, he seems mangled from the years of occupying Iraq, his head and right arm dressed in bandages. Most photographs from the effigy performance show two figures burning intensely, in front of a crowd. A wide-angle photograph of the scene shows people handling the burning effigies separated from the mass of protesters behind them.○ The left lower corner of the photograph shows the real public for whom the effigies are performed: a throng of photo- and video-journalists recording the event. The effigy burning could not have been highly visible to the assembled crowd, many barred from participating. Rather than a means to channel communal sentiment and aggression during protest, this performance appears to have been first and foremost a media spectacle, staged to spread images of the violated bodies of detested us American leaders.

194

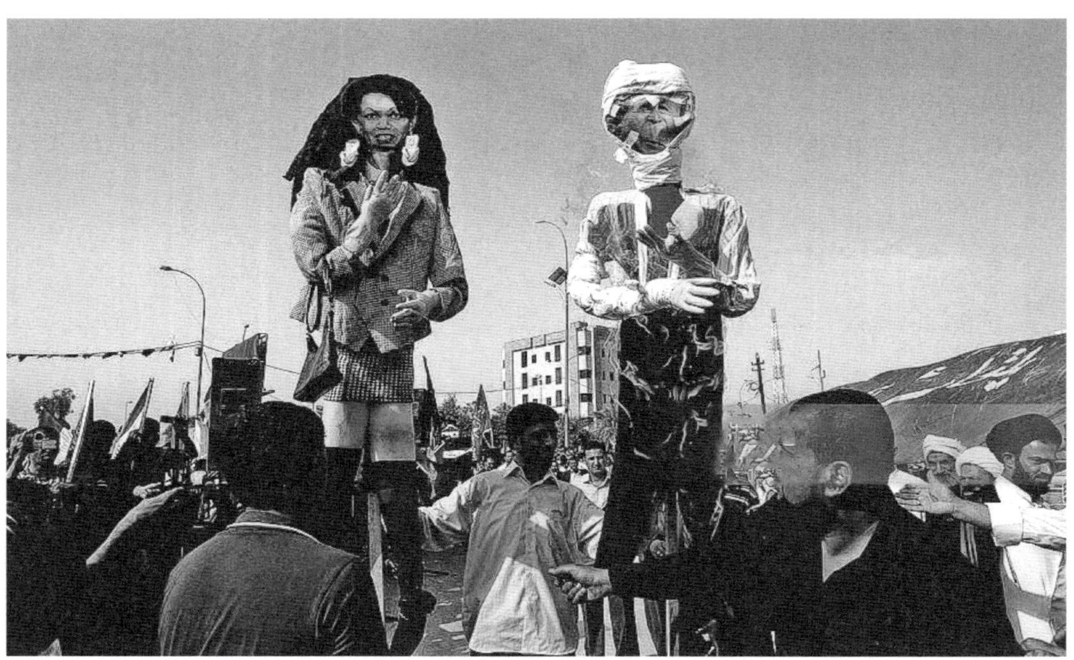

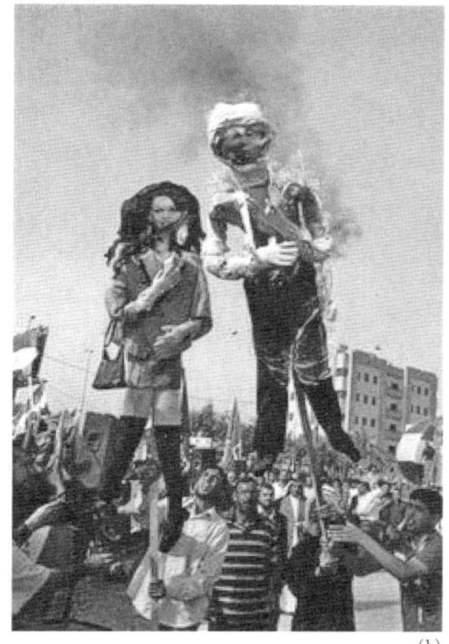

(b)

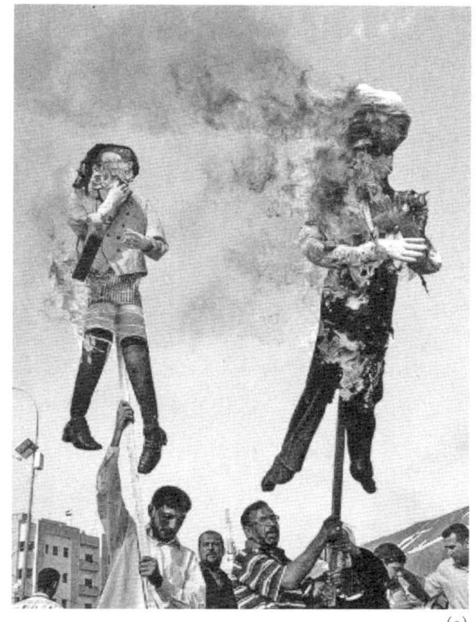

(c)

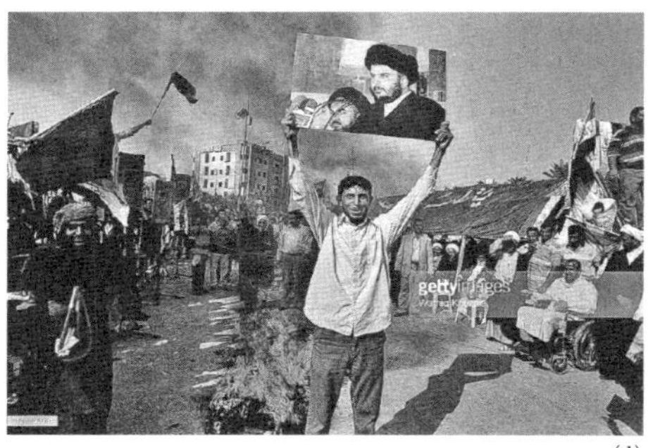

(d)

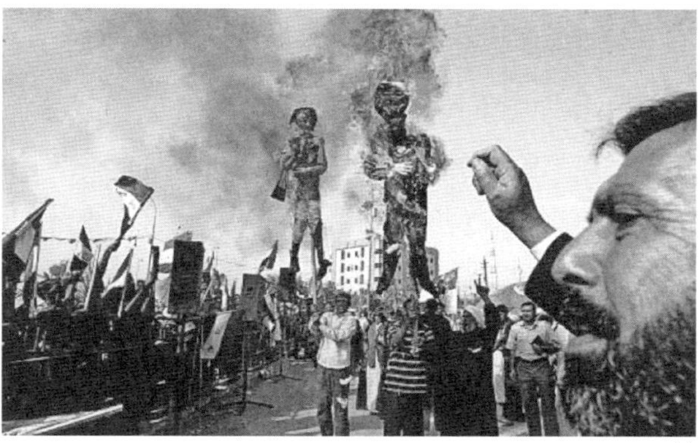

(e)

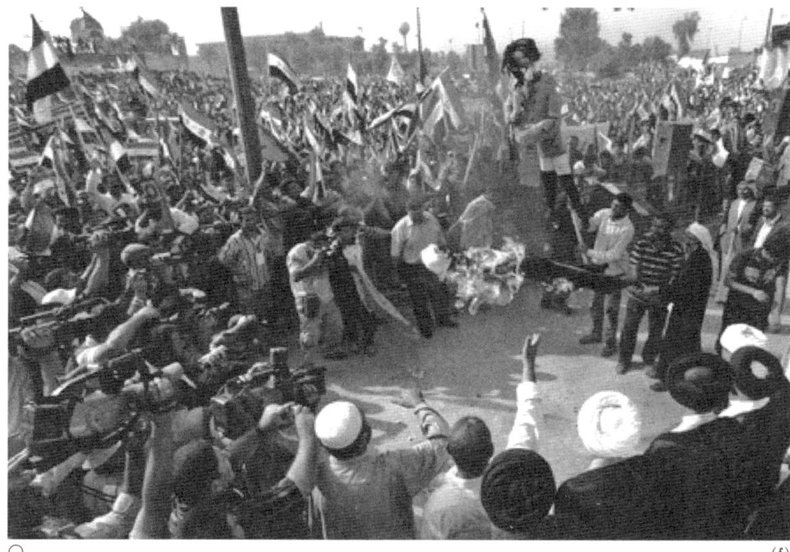

(f)

A month later, another Bush effigy was attached to Saddam's plinth on the square, this time doubled in size, increasing the spectacle's visibility for the assembled crowd. It is dressed in a Western suit and tie, just like Saddam's destroyed statue. The suit stands in marked contrast to the turban and cleric's robe al-Sadr usually wears. Bush's effigy holds a whip in its right hand and in its left a suitcase with the inscription reading: "US-Iraq security pact" in Arabic. The toppling of the former Iraqi sovereign was restaged with that of his successor now wielding power over Iraq.

Six months later, for the sixth anniversary of Saddam's fall, yet another Bush effigy was prepared: a towering figure, at least three times the size of the former president was burned on the same plinth. This time the maker did not bother to fabricate a jacket – Bush was retired after all – but the light-blue shirt and red tie clearly identify him as a Western official. The sheer size of the effigy, as well as the attention to detail including neat tailoring reveals considerable effort. The photograph of a grumpy Bush is molded around the effigy's head. A strange doubling of the collar and the tailored shirt occurs, but instead of disturbing the overall image, this detail somehow confirms the veracity of the effigy.

196

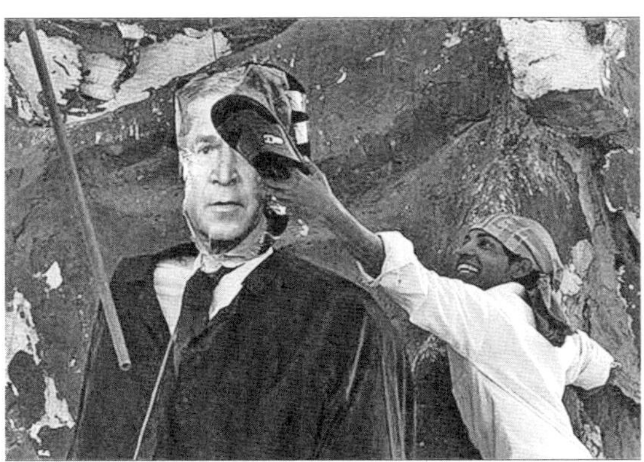

2008_11_21_Iraq: US President Bush (a)

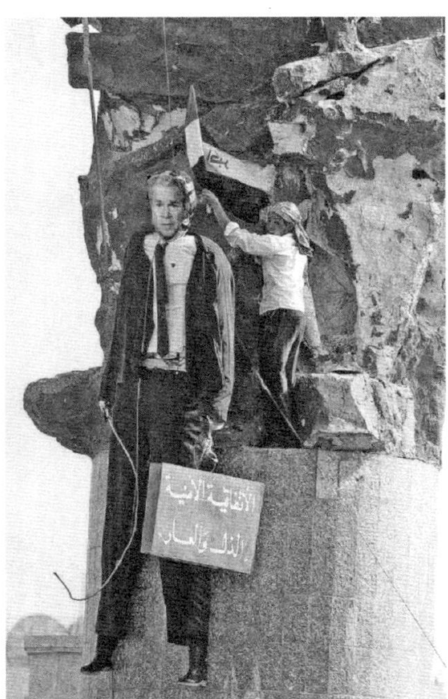

(b)

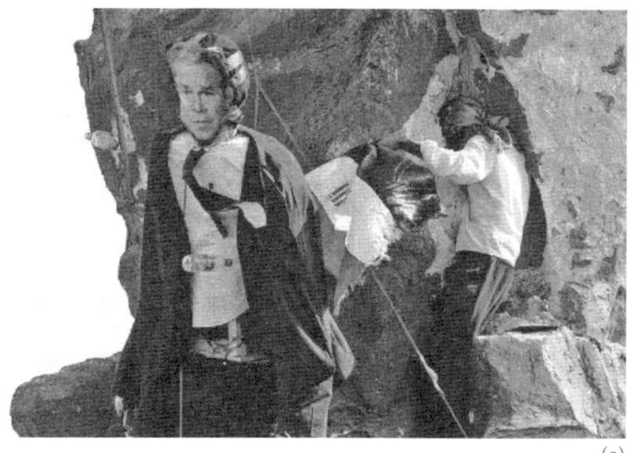

(c)

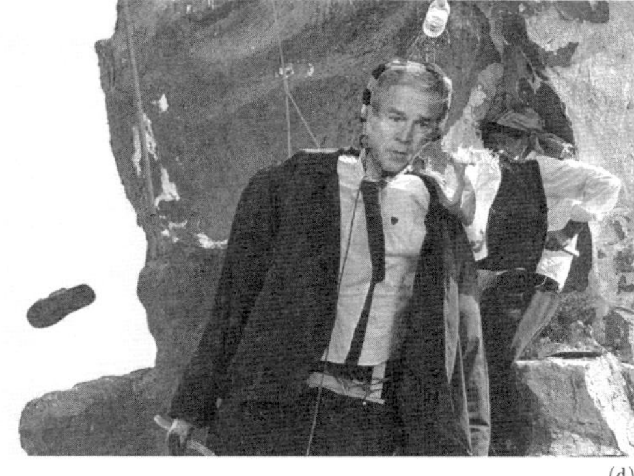

(d)

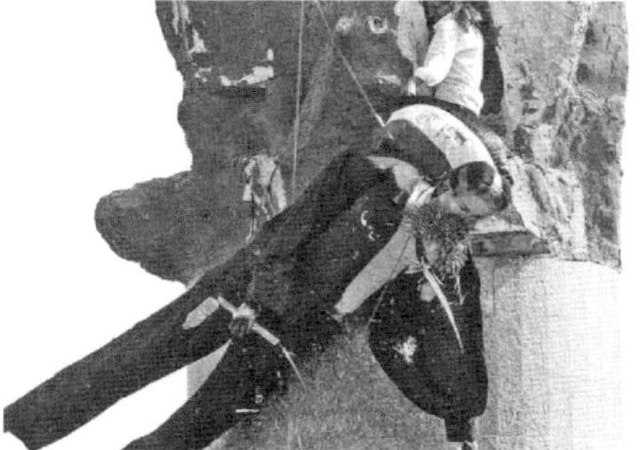

(e)

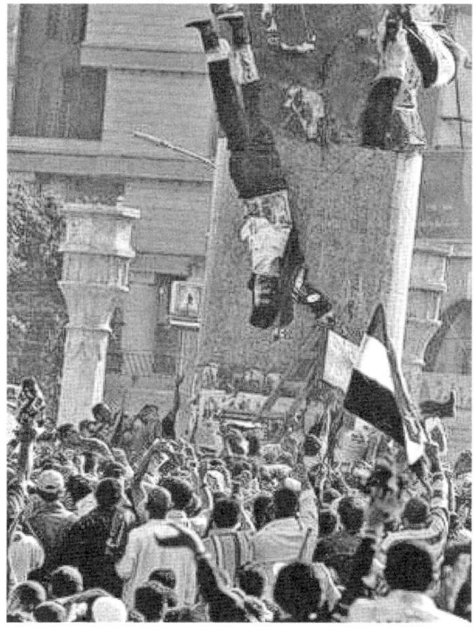

(f)

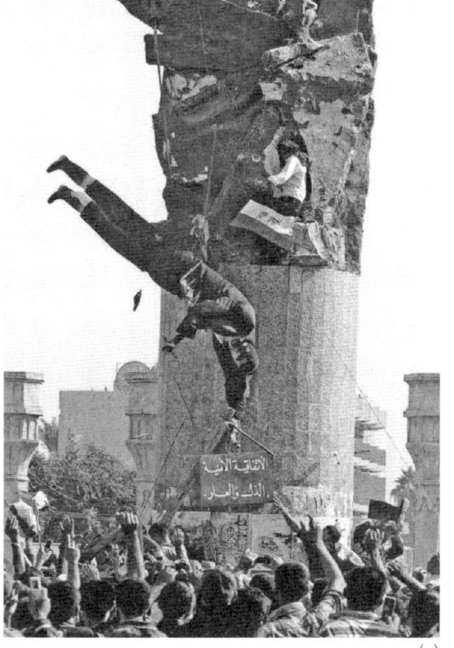

(g)

In one photograph, the maker adds what appears to be an unraveled piece of a woven plastic bag to the head, apparently meant to depict Bush's hair.○ I interpret this as an attempt to hide the abrupt transition between the photograph and the formless rest of the head, and to breach the excessive smoothness of the silhouette and shiny surface of the stuffed plastic bag: an effort to increase the verisimilitude of the effigy by rendering the two-dimensional photographic face, which ensures recognizability, more functional as a sculpted part of

198

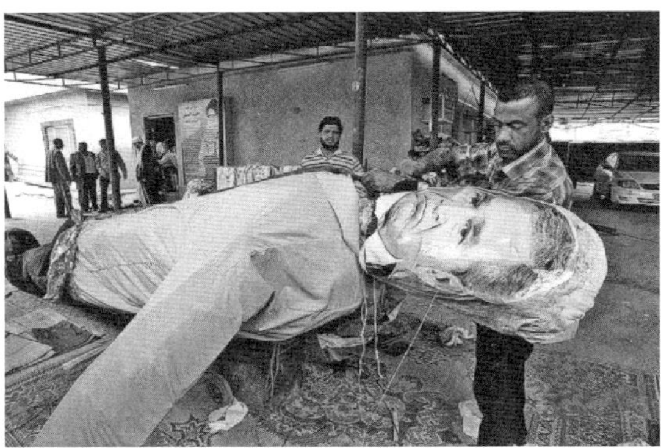

2009_04_07_Iraq: former US President Bush (a)

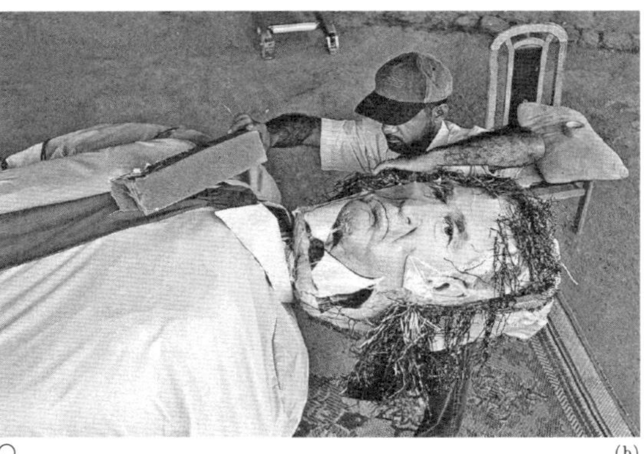

○ (b)

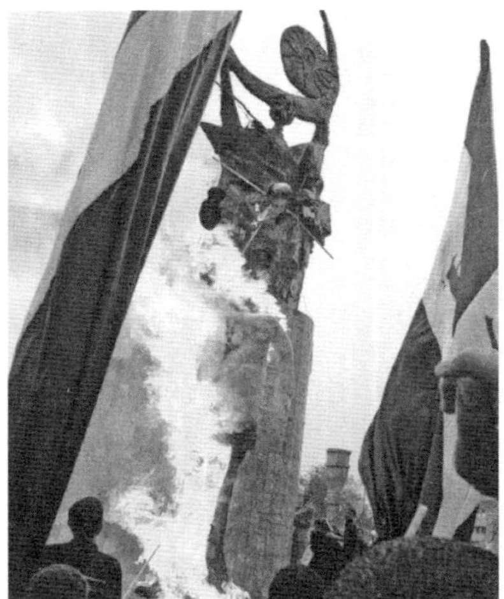

2009_04_09_Iraq: former US President Bush
(a)

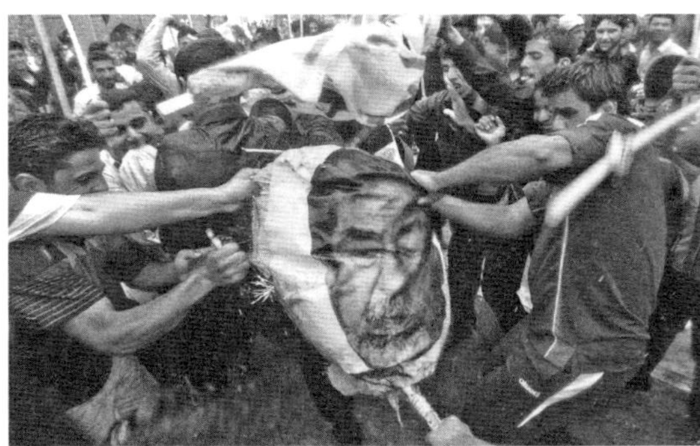

2009_04_09_Iraq: Saddam Hussein

the body. The effigy was attached to the plinth and set alight during a demonstration against the occupation by the US-led coalition with around 10,000 participants organized by al-Sadr followers. In the photographs, a large crowd in the oval square carry a sea of Iraqi flags. In addition to Bush, a similarly sculpted head of Saddam is carried around and eventually torn to pieces.

Mediated Presence

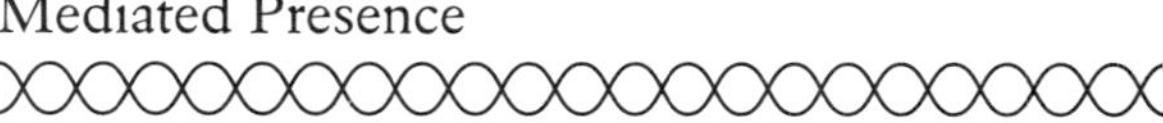

As I elaborate in chapter 1, "Double Bodies," Christianity's early awareness of the power of visual representation led to a complex, contested, and highly theorized understanding of images in relation to truth and power. In due course, Western image and media culture formed the basis on which contemporary global media developed. In Islam, the insistence on an-iconicity of the sacred led to a different configuration of the image in relation to truth and power. God's intentions were revealed through the Quran, and the body that hears, memorizes, and recites the text becomes the medium that transmits the word of God.[9] Authority is transferred not through the visual, but through the unadulterated word.[10] Privileging the word, Islamic culture developed non-representational media, like the Friday sermon and calligraphy,[11] and employed media like the cassette tape, used extensively to spread the sermons of Ayatollah Ruhollah Khomeini in the 1970s.[12] The cultural difference in attitudes and traditions regarding the mediation of power can be traced in photographs from the protests in Baghdad staged by al-Sadr's followers.

Al-Sadr is the scion of one of the most important Shia houses and the son of the widely respected Iraqi Shia cleric Grand Ayatollah Mohammad Sadeq al-Sadr. From the

9   Mohammed Arkoun, *The Unthought in Contemporary Islamic Thought* (London: Saqi Books, 2002), 208.

10   For instance, while Muslim rulers initially adopted Byzantine iconography on their coins, the images were later replaced by text from the Quran. Oleg Grabar, "From the Icon to Aniconism: Islam and the Image," *Museum International* 55, no. 2 (2003): 49.

11   Grabar, "From the Icon to Aniconism," 51–52.

12   Annabelle Sreberny and Ali Mohammadi, *Small Media, Big Revolution: Communication, Culture, and the Iranian Revolution* (Minneapolis: University of Minnesota Press, 1994), 120.

13 Nicholas Pelham, *A New Muslim Order: The Shia and the Middle East Sectarian Crisis* (London: I. B. Tauris, 2008), 143–50.

beginning of the Iraq War he positioned himself against the US-led war and occupation as well as the conservative Shia establishment around Ayatollah Ali al-Sistani. Al-Sadr positions himself not in sectarian but in Arab nationalist terms against the US occupation as well as against Iranian influence. Initially excluded from the political establishment, he organized his followers into a powerful political movement and has robust support among Iraq's impoverished Shia population. In the areas under his control, he established a police force, local courts following Sharia law, and a militia, the Mahdi Army, with some 60,000 members. In 2003 and 2004, his militia engaged in operations against coalition forces, at one time effectively controlling the seven southern provinces of Iraq. After a US military backlash, he negotiated acceptance into the political establishment. In December 2005, his coalition won 35 percent of votes for parliament, becoming a pivotal force in Iraqi politics.[13]

Al-Sadr cultivates his image as an eminent figure, using the pulpit as his stage and the Friday sermon as his moment of enunciation. In his role as a Shia cleric, he is obliged to stay out of the fray of daily politics, but his ambition to play a role in Iraqi politics is evident. Maneuvering between the two, he limits his appearances in order to increase his impact in the moments he does present himself to his public. Although absent from the rally, he is its guiding spirit: his photographic images, carried by the protesters are omnipresent.

200

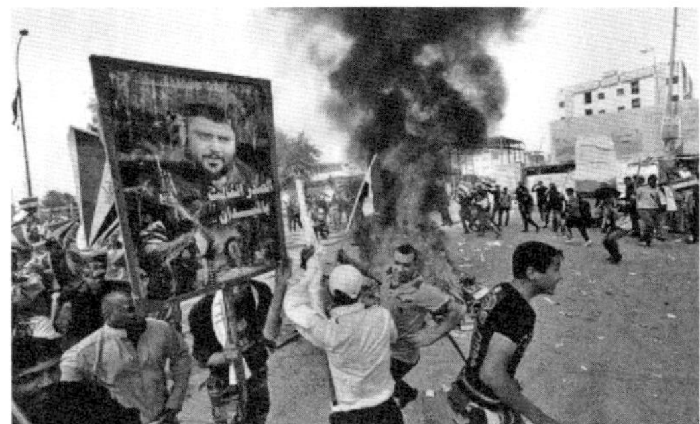

2011_04_09_Iraq: former US President Bush

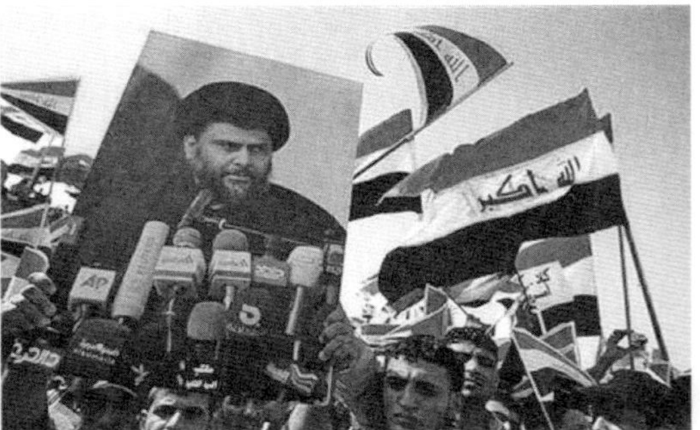

2013_01_02_Iraq

Very often in these photographs, Al-Sadr is depicted preaching, voicing, and transmitting the word of God, the source of his theocratic authority.[14] He has become an image that speaks in front of microphones wielded by the media. Assuming the voice of the protesters, the effigy burning becomes al-Sadr's speech, made explicit by a protester presenting a portrait of a speaking al-Sadr in front of the burning effigy. The image extends the reach of his voice through his doubly mediated presence.

Al-Sadr skillfully manages the economy of presence in the triangle of power, image, and media. He couples his theological authority – which in Islam relies on the word of the Quran and its interpretation – with the legitimizing authority of visual media. While he is usually absent, emphasizing speech, he uses visual media to manifest and spread presence,[15] positioning himself at the nexus of political authority of the state, theocratic authority of religion, and iconic authority, which political philosopher Susan Buck-Morss ascribes to the global news media.[16] His influence is made apparent by the large following he is able to mobilize. The protestors in the street stand in for al-Sadr's body; they represent a partial Iraqi Shia body politic.

201

14 Arkoun, *The Unthought*, 208.

15 Marie-José Mondzain, *Image, Icon, Economy: The Byzantine Origins of the Contemporary Imaginary* (Stanford: Stanford University Press, 2005), 223.

16 Susan Buck-Morss, "Visual Empire," *Diacritics* 37, no. 2/3 (2007): 182–83.

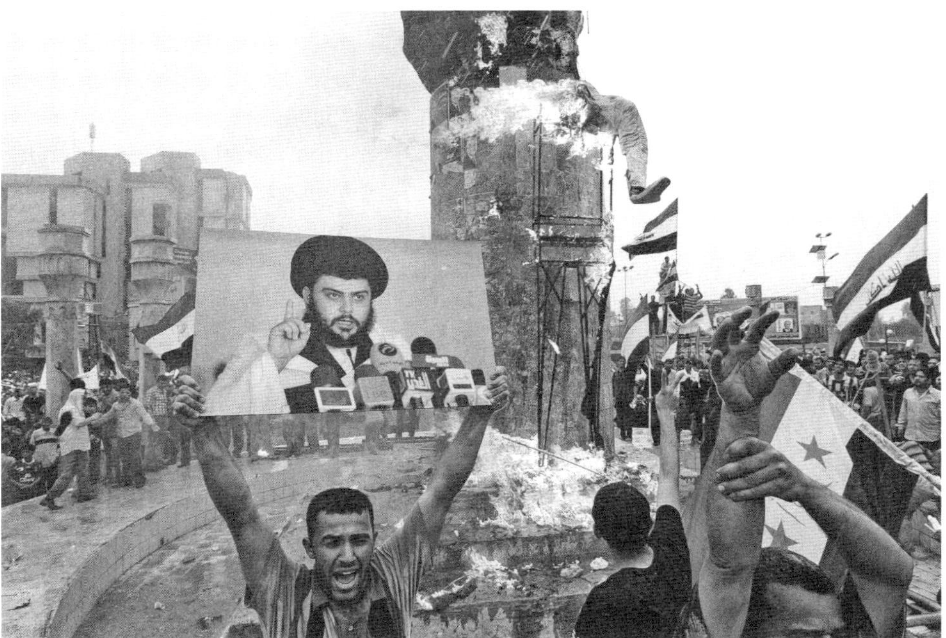

○ 2009_04_09_Iraq: former US President Bush

17 See chapter 1, "Double Bodies."

18 Hans Belting, *Bild-Anthropologie: Entwürfe für eine Bildwissenschaft* (Munich: Wilhelm Fink Verlag, 2001), 143.

19 Belting, *Bild-Anthropologie*, 25, 147.

The image of al-Sadr, which in the strict sense is not that of a sovereign, meets another image of sovereign power: the effigy of Bush, by then no longer president. In the US, he was only the representative of the sovereign, "the people," but in the state of exception established through war and occupation, as noted earlier, it can be argued that in Iraq he had wielded actual sovereign power over life and death.

In the Christian European tradition, effigies in the political sphere developed, based on the earlier Roman image culture, a close relationship to the figure of the sovereign, and the idea of the incarnation of Christ.[17] They depict not so much the private body, but the public body of the depicted. In the square in Baghdad, attached to the plinth that once displayed the statue of former sovereign Saddam, effigies seem to act in a similar way: in the maker's workshop, the effigy of Bush is first a material carrier of an image, onto which the likeness is attached. In front of the protesters, the image is made present in a physical medium resembling a body. Animated as it interacts with the acting bodies of protesters in the street,[18] the effigy substitutes Bush's absent body, so that the ritual of reversal, debasement, and punishment can be carried out.[19]

There are three bodies that are combined in the effigy: the physical carrier made of stuffed cloth, a likeness of Bush standing in for his private body, and a public political body, the US president. These distinctions appear in the photographs from Baghdad. The attitudes and acts of the people engaging with the effigy signal slight semantic shifts in how they address one body or another: protesters experience the physical resistance of the effigy's material body when they beat it; the sense of physical punishment, by bombarding the effigy with plastic bottles and shoes emphasizes the vulnerability of the private body; when the effigy is attacked with denigrating signs and actions and finally set alight, protesters target the president's political body as US sovereign, dethroned and destroyed in a ritual of carnivalesque reversal. Through these acts, the status of the image is continuously transformed, kept unstable, shifting backwards and forwards – from manufactured doll, to representative of a sovereign country, to embodiment of an individual, until in a last transformation the image and its carrier is destroyed and Bush's substitute material body is turned into a heap of ashes.

Dialogic Communication

In each event, the site of the protest is constant, a dual site: the physical space of Firdos Square, where the symbolic toppling of Saddam's statue occurred; and the virtual space of the news media, which communicates the event globally. This interlinking created the outsized effect of the event. In the years following, protesters and the media converged time and again at this site to stage re-enactments of the toppling. These enactments were inflections and modulations of the original event, adapting the form and message to the specific moment in time and its political requirements – reflecting and commenting on the past to influence the present.

The destruction of Saddam's statues – in Firdos Square among many others – executed by Iraqi citizens and US soldiers, did not stem from an image prohibition in the religious sense. Instead, it was aimed at images representing the power of the despised ruler.[20] This image destruction in turn led to the production of new images of destroyed statues and empty plinths. Punishing Bush's effigies created another round of images, and gave the protesters a presence in the media. With this image practice, they collectively contested US domination

20 While it is widely believed that the toppling of Saddam's statue was staged by the US Military, Iraqi citizens at least participated, and on that same day, Iraqi protesters elsewhere in Baghdad and Iraq made sure none of the many statues of Saddam survived. Göttke, *Toppled*, 57–68.

21 Buck-Morss, "Visual Empire," 183–85.

22 Mikhail Bakhtin, *The Dialogic Imagination: Four Essays* (Austin: University of Texas Press, 1981), 291.

in the global news media, the sphere termed by Buck-Morss as the "visual empire."[21]

I do not claim that protesters in Baghdad actively had these layered image concepts in mind, but rather that they freely associated with the images present: the plinth, the statue, toppling, suit, werewolf, microphone, their leader, their adversary. Recombining these in various ways, the actors in the square were in active dialogue with these varied image concepts through referencing, appropriating, and adapting the symbolic expressions of earlier actors from their own and "Western" culture. Through repetition, the practice of burning effigies became what literary critic Mikhail Bakhtin has called "dialogic": a shared symbolic language that dynamically develops in communication across national and cultural borders and incorporates multiple connotations.[22]

In this last photograph, al-Sadr appears as Saddam's successor on the plinth: an assemblage of what's left of the legs of Saddam's bronze statue, the protester's living body substituting al-Sadr's torso, and his photographic portrait as the head.○ The hybrid assemblage of disparate image elements is staged for the media. The image symbolically expressed al-Sadr's rise in stature on the ruins of the old regime, supported by a popular movement. It was only made possible through the symbiotic "collaboration" of the protester on the plinth with the Iraqi photojournalist on the square. Both seized the potential of the event to create a complex, expressive, and dialogic image.

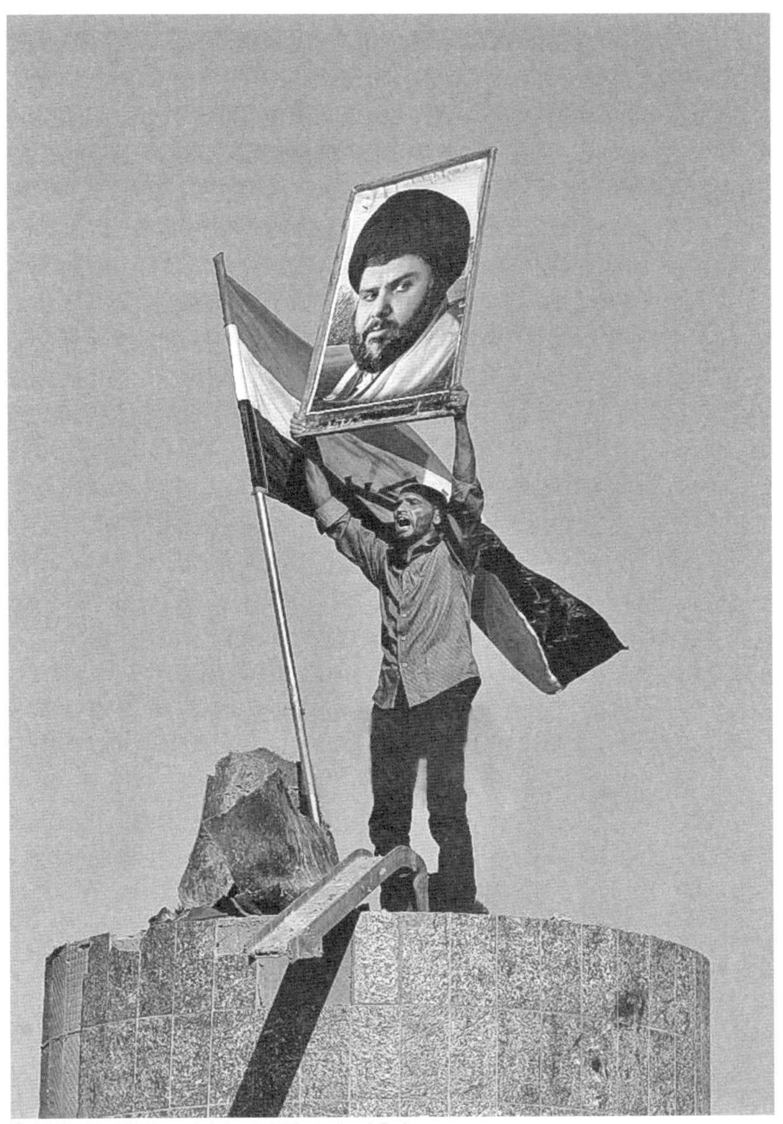

In 2011, the sculpture by
Bassem Hamad al-Dawiri
was removed from the plinth
and the remnant feet of
Saddam's statue reemerged.

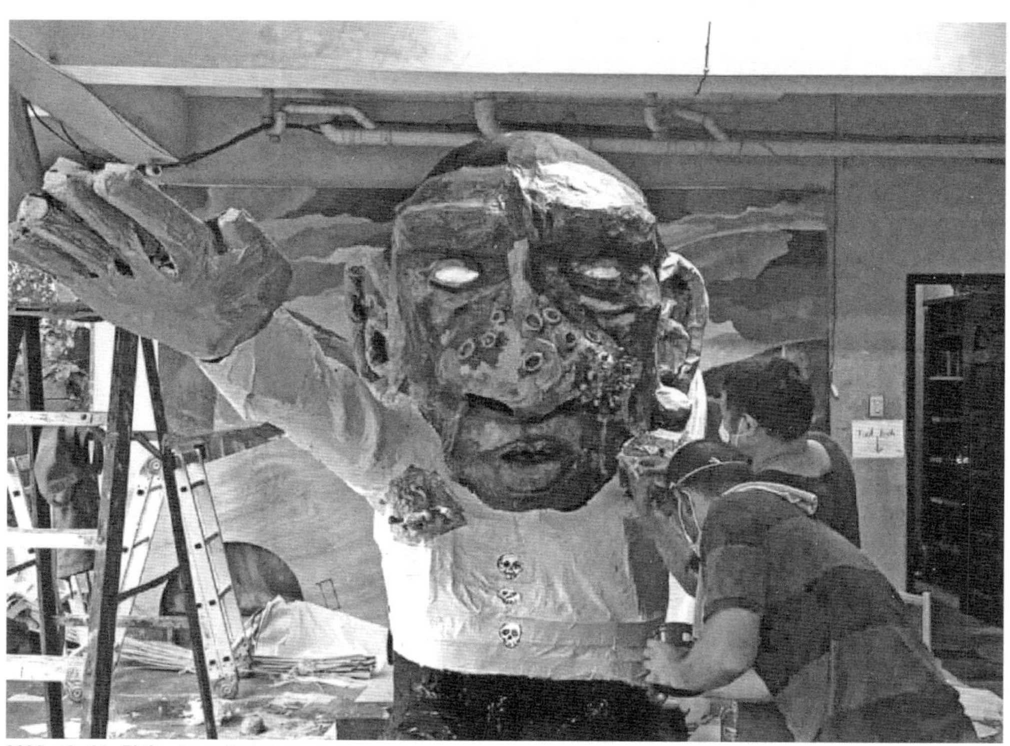

2020_12_09_Philippines: Duterte

Resemblance and the Grotesque

Resemblance

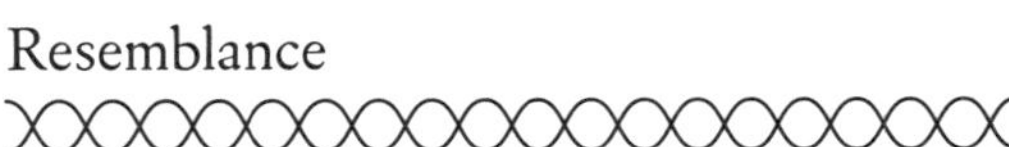

In the last three chapters I described effigy protests as they were staged in various specific countries, in specific contexts, which revealed certain genealogies of effigy protest, their location in certain power constellations, and their potential to communicate across cultural boundaries. In this chapter, I turn back to the practice's general characteristics and investigate the operational aspects of images active in effigy protests, concerning the effigies themselves and the media images they produce, focusing on their function in political constellations and how their aesthetics affectively shape social relations.

Protesters visible in photographs relate to effigies in different ways, using them as props in the performance or interacting with them as animated puppets with a life of their own. The images acquire a degree of agency and operate independently and out of control of any one actor – protester, spectator, photographer, editor, or news consumer. How the actors relate to the images is directed in part by the effigy's role in the protest scenario and by identifying the dummy

1   Michel Foucault, *The Order of Things: An Archeology of the Human Sciences* (London: Routledge: 2005), 20–28.

2   Johannes Endres, "Unähnliche Ähnlichkeit: Zu Analogie, Metapher und Verwandtschaft," in *Similitudo: Konzepte der Ähnlichkeit in Mittelalter und Früher Neuzeit*, ed. Jeanette Kohl, Martin Gaier, and Alberto Saviello (Munich: Wilhelm Fink Verlag, 2012), 33–34.

with the person it depicts through some form of resemblance. The recognition of resemblance also conditions the audience's emotional response to the photographs produced from these performances.

In *The Order of Things* (1966), philosopher Michel Foucault describes the central role of resemblance in the production of knowledge in Western culture until the end of the sixteenth century.[1] The detection of resemblance between distinct objects or phenomena indicated a similarity in function, mechanism, and purpose. Resemblance could also be employed rhetorically to construct relationships between objects. In this way, the knowledge of one phenomenon could be successfully transferred to another. Establishing resemblance integrated the unknown into the categories of the known, potentially creating ordering relationships between objects. Resemblance itself was, as Foucault writes, structured into intricately varied rhetorical forms. These ranged from convenience (spatial proximity), emulation through copying or mimicking, analogy (the inference of similarity from one aspect to another), to sympathy (being affected in a similar way). Ultimately, almost everything could resemble almost everything else, if one could find the right rhetoric to argue it. Only the establishment of certain conventions in how to apply resemblance's forms and the pairing with an antinomy – for instance "sympathy" with "antipathy" – restricted how resemblance functioned.

With the invention of scientific inquiry as the primary method of knowledge production, resemblance was relegated to the margins of the sciences. A rather diffuse concept was left, which art historian Johannes Endres describes as subjective, relative, and variable, and dependent on the perspective and psychology of the judging subject.[2] In the arts, visual resemblance became the basic condition for the portrait from the late fifteenth-century until the beginning of the twentieth century.[3] Recognizability became crucial in regards to the latent claim that portraits possess living presence, authenticity, and authority.[4] One could assume, then, that a close visual resemblance would also be crucial to protest effigies – linking them to those they depict – and that the closer the visual likeness the more effective the effigy performance. It is indeed now the case that photos taken from media sources are regularly attached to effigies, but before computers and printers became widely available, visual resemblance was only occasionally emphasized – and even recent protest effigies often do not attempt to look like the person they depict.

More important than visual resemblance is that participants and audiences might correctly identify the depicted. This is most often achieved by inscribing their name onto the effigy, and by adding other identifiers like flags, symbols, and acronyms, as detailed in previous chapters. These work through the older figures of resemblance, association, and proximity, which enable the transfer of characteristics and qualities from one object to another, and which remain central to the function of effigies. In activating these resemblances, effigies are similar to the votive images (ex-voto), which art historian Georges Didi-Huberman analyzes.[5] Both appear as types of operational images that have remained outside the usual chronology of the evolution of style and aesthetics found in art history. Both the ex-voto and the effigy are examples of surviving representational forms, which drag with their archaic form older epistemological figures into contemporary practices. These residual forms of resemblance do not function in the systematic way Foucault describes, but operate much more pragmatically – or haphazardly. The different types of resemblance are operational in the ex-voto

3   Benjamin H. D. Buchloh, *Formalism and Historicity: Models and Methods in Twentieth-Century Art* (Cambridge, MA: MIT Press, 2015), 54.

4   Jeanette Kohl, Martin Gaier, and Alberto Saviello, "Ähnlichkeit als Kategorie der Porträtgeschichte," in *Similitudo*, 21.

5   Georges Didi-Huberman, "Ex-Voto: Image, Organ, Time," *L'Esprit Créateur* 47, no. 3 (2007): 7–16.

6 Didi-Huberman, "Ex-Voto," 13.

7 Endres, "Unähnliche Ähnlichkeit," 33.

8 Endres, "Unähnliche Ähnlichkeit," 47. Endres quotes the famous sentence by semiologist Charles Sanders Peirce: "The forms of the words similarity and dissimilarity suggest that one is the negative of the other, which is absurd, since everything is both similar and dissimilar to everything else."

9 Endres, "Unähnliche Ähnlichkeit," 34; Walter Benjamin, "Doctrine of the Similar" (1933), trans. Knut Tarnowski, *New German Critique*, 17 (1979): 66.

10 Incongruity theory is one of the main humor theories, analyzing it in cognitive processes. Carmen Popescu, "Sociological Perspectives on Humour: Conflict Theories and Ethnic Humour," *Word and Text, A Journal of Literary Studies and Linguistics* 1 (2010): 23–31.

11 Depicting President Bush as a dog would be an analogy, while hanging a shoe around the effigy of President Obama's neck would be the contagious transference by proximity.

– and in the effigy – in a contaminated way, in "a heuristic of resemblances."[6]

My investigation takes up three important functions of resemblance: first, the presupposition of an observer, a judging subject who perceives a resemblance between two objects[7]; second, that resemblance is only ever partial, an ordering principle that does not determine identity but similarity of a certain aspect, therefore at once establishing partial difference[8]; and third, the element of surprise in its recognition triggered by a sudden shift in perception that integrates the object into an ordering relation with another – a relation not previously perceived.[9] In the surprising simultaneous perception of similarity and difference we often find reason for laughter (conceptualized as "incongruity theory" in the study of humor[10]) and this points to another operation at work in certain images: the grotesque.

The grotesque emphasizes not the similar aspects of two objects, but the dissimilar, dissonant, unfitting. While resemblance creates ordering relations between objects, the grotesque creates dissonance and disorder. It alienates an object from what it should resemble. Nevertheless, the grotesque uses some of the very forms of resemblance, for instance analogy and proximity, to produce the contagious transference of alienating qualities.[11] I propose then the grotesque as resemblance's opposite, which counters the ordering operations of resemblance, without undoing the relations forged by resemblance altogether. I develop my argument synchronically with a series of images of effigy protests from different times and places across the globe showing the trans-historical and cross-cultural spread of resemblance and the grotesque.

Animation

The effigy of the senior Indian politician Om Prakash
Chautala stands in the center of a small knot of protesters in a
North Indian town. The effigy is two heads taller than the
protesters, supported almost tenderly by several outstretched
hands. It is beautifully made from straw and cloth, wearing
Chautala's signature green turban and spectacles; his name is
inscribed on its chest. Looking down benevolently, the effigy
seems to be involved in an intimate exchange with the protesters. In this photograph the effigy seems animated, almost
alive. The figure emanates warmth and dignified authority.
I would read the event as in honor of the effigy's prototype
– were it not for the flame licking at the bottom edge of his
shirt. I would like to draw attention to the second figure in
the photograph. On a pedestal behind the group stands a garlanded statue of Subhas Chandra Bose – a leading figure in
the Indian independence struggle.○ The two figures resemble one another in many aspects – their size, coloring, a certain kind of realism, both make present the absent personality

211

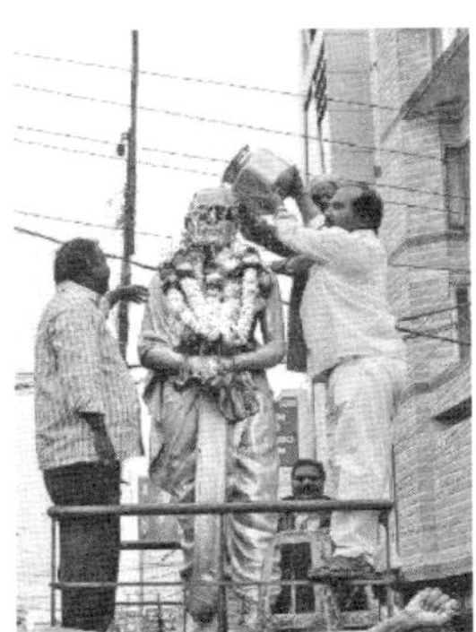

2013_08_01_India: Potti
Sriramulu (anointing the statue
by pouring milk)

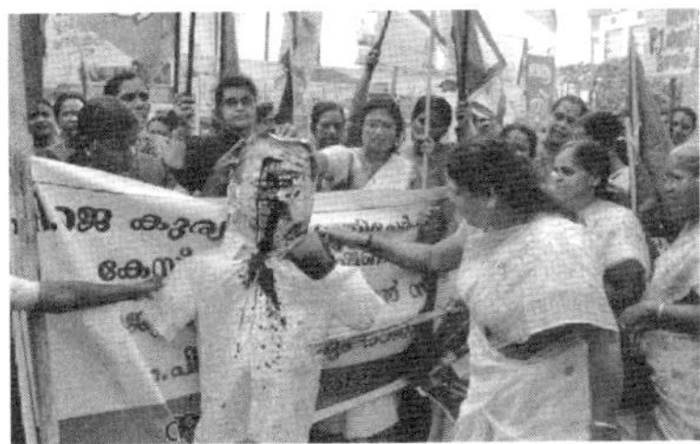

2013_02_08_India: Rajya Sabha chairman
Kurien

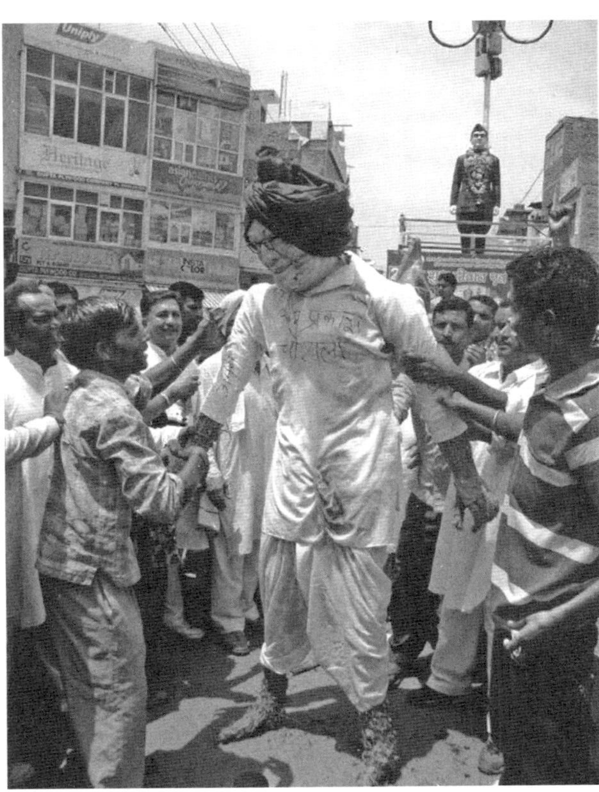

○ 2011_08_01_India: Om Parkash Chautala

12 Wolfgang Brückner, *Bildnis und Brauch: Studien zur Bildfunktion der Effigies* (Berlin: Erich Schmidt Verlag, 1966), 249.

– but their function in the social field is diametrically opposed. One is used to honor the depicted, the other to defame.

The use of two quite similar images for very different purposes confirms that a hypothesis attributed to seventeenth-century French penal scholar Pierre Ayrault still holds true today. In relation to effigy punishments (common practice in formal justice at that time, as introduced in chapter 2, "Performing Protest"), he claimed one can equally honor and dishonor someone with an image.[12] Images operate in the social sphere in both honorific and defamatory ways, depending on form, context and the conduct towards them. Great attention is given to pose, frame, plinth, and placement to make sure an image is honorable. Equally large effort is taken to avoid unflattering or disparaging images, like paparazzi photos, caricatures, or mugshots. A statue of durable material,

212

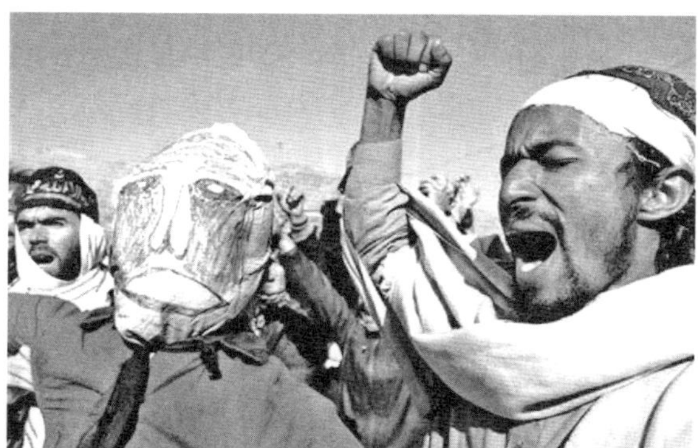
2012_02_23_Afghanistan: US President Obama

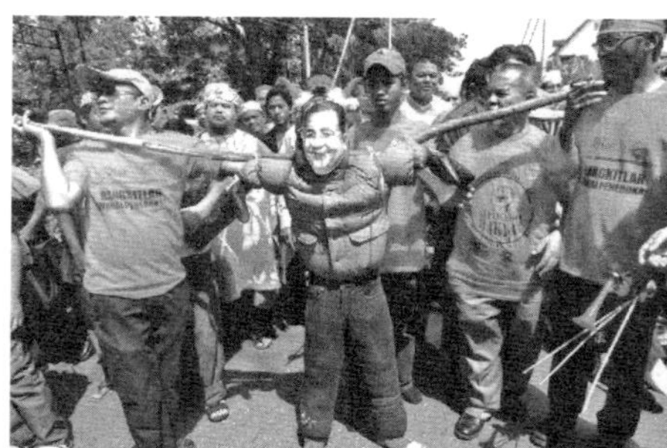
2012_12_28_Malaysia: FELDA chairman Samad

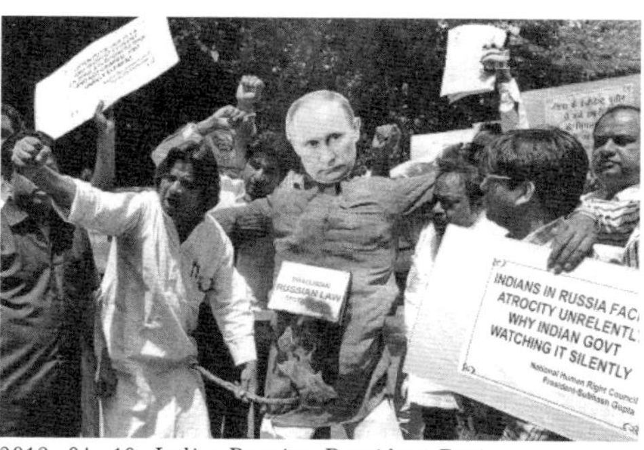

2013_04_10_India: Russian President Putin

elevated on a plinth as a framing device, ascribes status, until it is smeared or toppled. The ambiguous likeness of an effigy, created from malleable material, is especially unstable and susceptible to malicious manipulation.

Like other types of dolls and puppets, effigies often evoke the uncanny feeling that they are alive and dead at the same time – or neither dead nor alive, an ambiguity that makes them especially well-suited for their role in symbolic executions.[13] Through a lifelike posture or accidental movement of their limbs, they can give the impression of being animated in one moment and inanimate the next. Protesters' interactions with the unwieldy dolls tend to result in a sort of involuntary slapstick, wherein the roles of leader and follower sometimes seem reversed.[14] Looking at Prime Minister of Pakistan Benazir Bhutto's effigy in these two photographs. I find it hard to believe that her carriers could harbor any

213

13　Hans Belting, *Bild-Anthropologie: Entwürfe für eine Bildwissenschaft* (Munich: Wilhelm Fink Verlag, 2001), 146–49.

14　Richard Schechner, *Performance Studies: An Introduction*, 3rd edition (London: Routledge, 2004), 203–4.

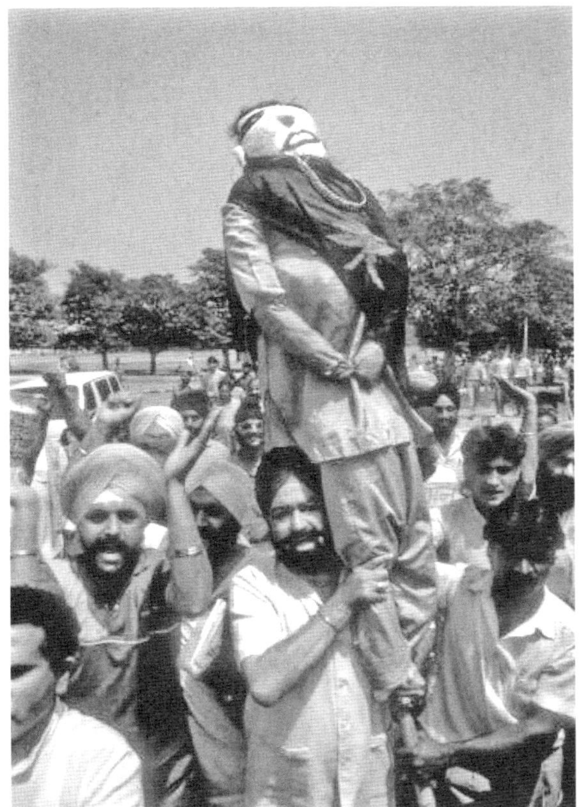

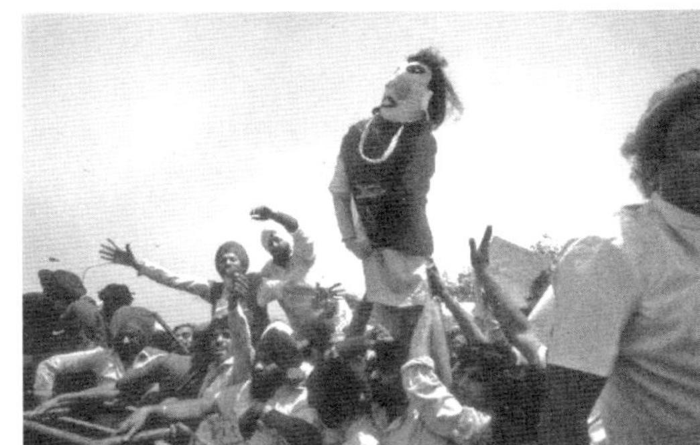

○ 1990_04_19_India: Pakistani Premier Benazir Bhutto　　　(a)　　　　　　　　　　　　　　　　　　(b)

15   Richard Schechner writes about animation of puppets: "Masks and puppets actually constitute second beings who interact with the human actors. These performing objects are suffused with a life force capable of transforming those who play with and through them." Schechner, *Performance Studies*, 203.

16   Paul Piris, "The Co-Presence and Ontological Ambiguity of the Puppet," in *Routledge Companion to Puppetry and Material Performance*, ed. Dassia N. Posner, Claudia Orenstein, and John Bell (New York: Routledge, 2014), 30–42 and here 35–37.

17   "Burn Effigy of the Kaiser," *Milwaukee Journal*, October 21, 1917.

hostile feelings toward her. In the way that her movement becomes one with those of the men carrying her, the photographs suggest she is in charge, leading the people in the demonstration, and that her animators are just the skillful puppeteers who enable the *grande dame* to rise to her role in the unfolding drama.[15] Many scenes recorded in such protests suggest the effigy as an autonomous subject present next to the protesters. A "co-presence" of puppet and actor is constructed through the bodily interaction between puppeteer and puppets.[16]

Another kind of lifelikeness speaks from a 1917 newspaper report in *The Milwaukee Journal*.○, [17] After the communal effort to clear a piece of land, villagers in Wisconsin staged a ritual of cleansing, burning uprooted trees and brushes and with them an effigy of the preeminent enemy at the time, German Emperor Wilhelm II. The image in the scan of the newspaper is almost illegible, but the reporter describes the scene vividly and draws special attention to the elements that signify a carnivalesque reversal of his high status: "His head consisted of a pumpkin, his helmet a tin pan, the spike of his helmet a nail covered with tinfoil, his mustache, a frayed piece of rope: the iron cross, two railroad spikes fastened together…" The article continues with a description of the effigy's burning, and ends with: "The most spectacular feature was when the right arm, holding the sword, dropped in a most lifelike manner, the sword falling into the flames." In this case, the moment of animation, the moment when the puppet comes alive, rests in the lifelikeness of a simple gesture. This gesture, the falling arm in the moment of the effigy's death, symbolically expresses the acceptance of defeat. It seems to have made the performance especially satisfying as this moment of animation aligned with the audience's imagination about the German Kaiser

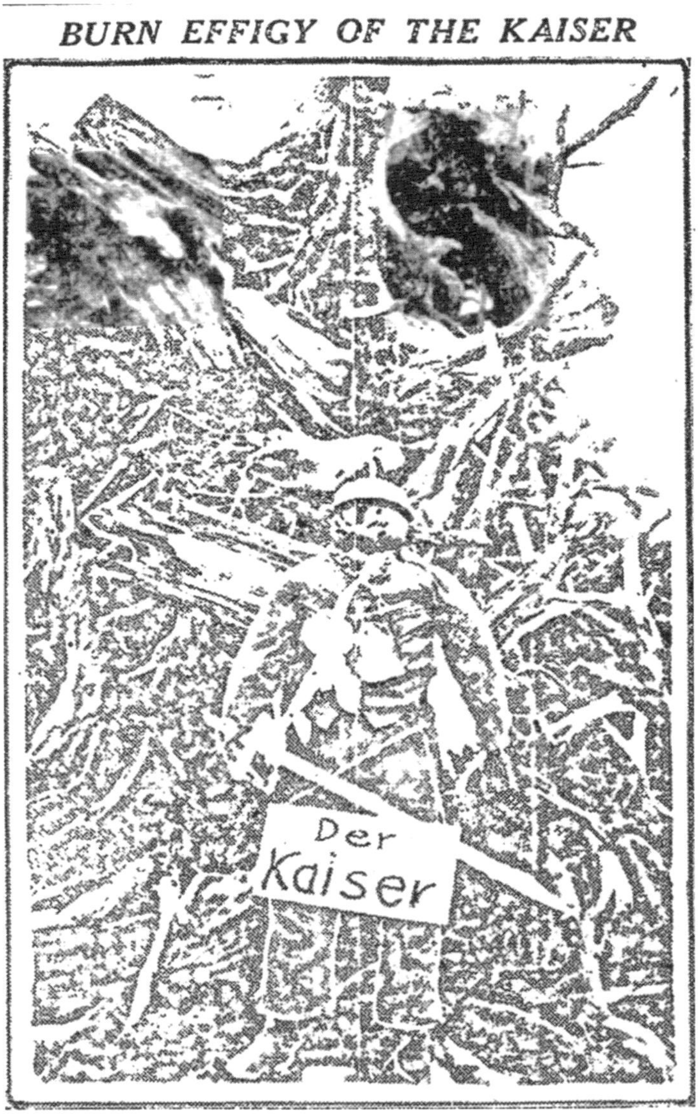

BURN EFFIGY OF THE KAISER

○ 1917_10_17_USA-WI: German Kaiser Wilhelm II

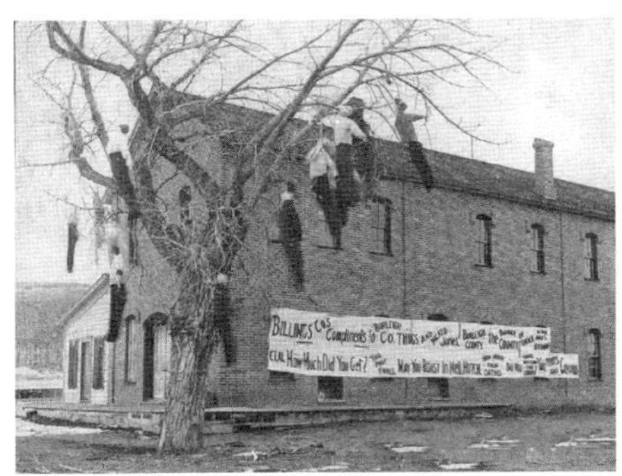

1896_01_06_USA-ND: members of a jury

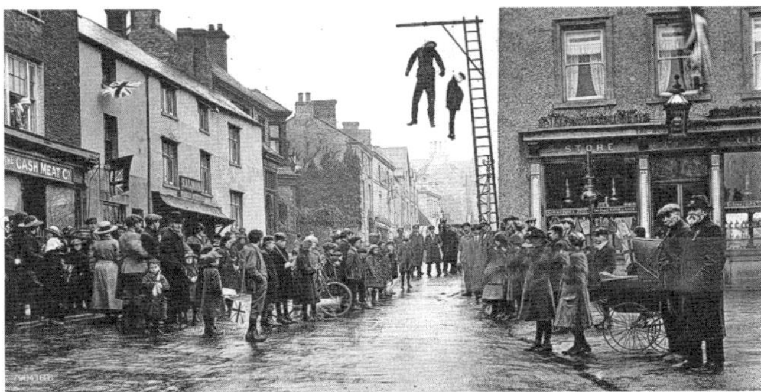

1918_11_11_UK: German Kaiser Wilhelm II + Little Willy

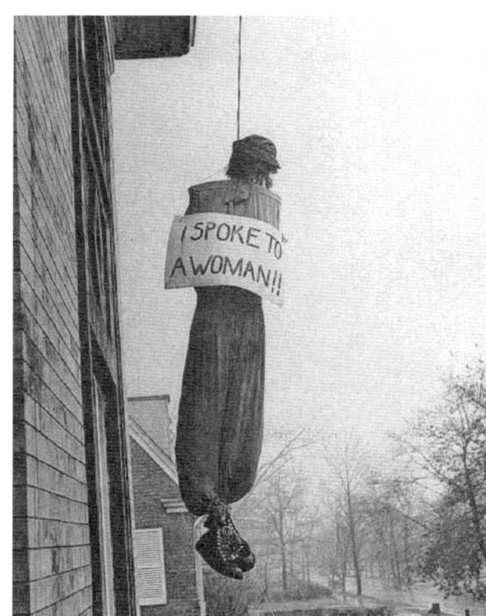

1945_00_00_USA-OH: African-American man

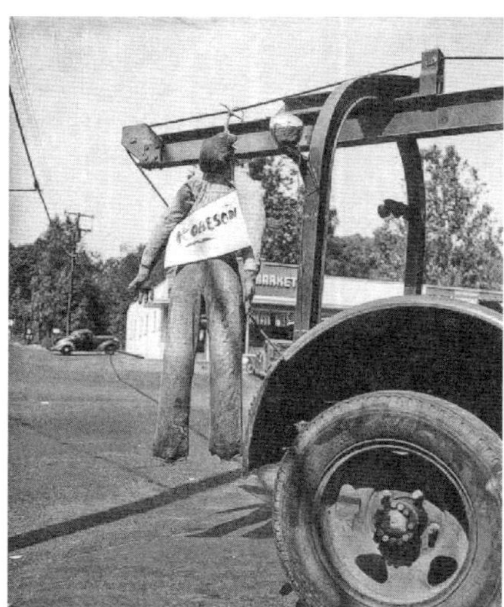

1949_04_09_USA-NY: actor and activist Paul Robeson

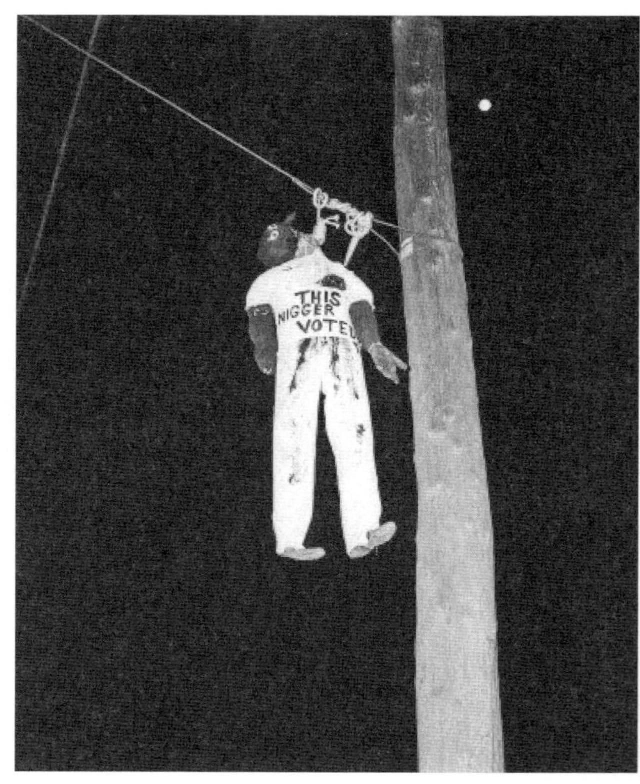

1939_05_03_USA-FL: African-American voter

meeting the end he so deserved. Nevertheless, it is a disturbing paradox that in the execution of the effigy, the notion of lifelikeness no longer relates to a living body, since the moment when lifelikeness increases the affective properties of the performance most, is also the moment of the effigy's torture and violent death.

The notion of lifelikeness is stretched to its limit when the effigy resembles not a living and dying body, but a dead human corpse mercilessly strung up from a tree or telephone pole. In fact, the resemblance here relates not so much to actual bodies as to other images that these effigy photographs evoke, namely the well-known photographs of lynchings from the late-nineteenth and early twentieth century. These horrific scenes of popular justice were distributed widely during the time in a variety of contexts:[18] in newspapers, as postcards, described in protest songs, or as evidence in the civil rights struggle. The images became *lieux de mémoire* of African American suffering and reference points in the cultural memory of the US and beyond.[19] It is exactly these images – still active the in the imagination of the South – that the effigy makers intended to evoke in order to tap into their potential for instilling fear in the African American community. The resemblance and similar function of effigy images to lynching images in this context reveals that the practices are not categorically different – the first a purely symbolic protest sign, the second a brutal act of vigilante justice. Enacted with the intention to activate the resemblance between the two, effigy hanging or burning is in fact part of a range of practices of violent oppression.[20]

Resemblance in the effigy executions comes in many forms. At times its close visual resemblance to the depicted is an intended aspect of the spectacle of punishment. These photographs show a tormented face and broken body

217

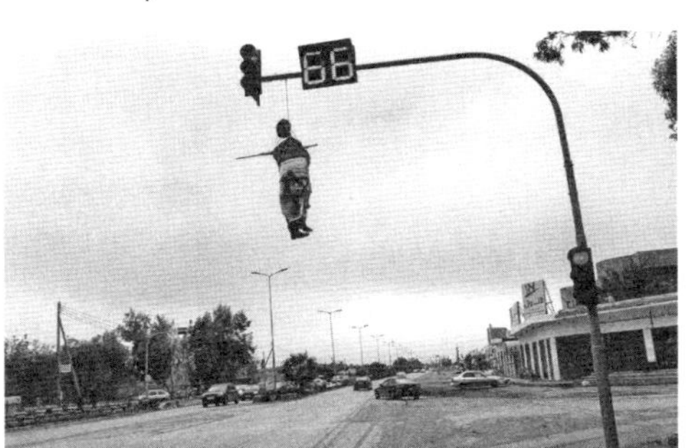

2011_05_08_Libya: effigy

18 Margit Rosen, "Shooting the Dead. Looking at Medusa's Face," *Iconoclash* (Karlsruhe/Cambridge, MA: ZKM/MIT Press, 2002), 248.

19 Udo J. Hebel, "Sites of Memory in U.S.-American Histories and Cultures," in *Cultural Memory Studies*, ed. Astrid Erll and Ansgar Nünning (Berlin: Walter de Gruyter, 2008), 52–53.

20 I will elaborate on the relation of effigy protest to violence in the following chapter.

21   Michel Foucault, *Discipline and Punish: The Birth of the Prison* (New York: Vintage Books, 1977), 48–49.

22   21 Brückner, *Bildnis und Brauch*, 303 (my translation).

The effigy Kai Lykke's imitated his person as closely as possible. It was fabricated in the style of the wax state portraits of the time,… life-size, mounted on a wooden core with movable limbs, dressed in a complete outfit including wig and white gloves. The effigy was dragged from the state prison, the so-called Blue Tower, to the place of execution, where 400 musketeers and 200 horsemen stood guard. The executioner's assistant arranged the figure to knee in the sand, loosened its collar, tied a piece of cloth over its eyes and tucked its hair in from the neck, all according to the rules. At first, the executioner cut off the effigy's oath hand, then with two strokes its head, while his assistant held up the delinquent's head at the hair in the usual way. The individual parts of the executed were dragged further and were presented to King Frederik and his court under a window of the palace, whereafter the hand and head were nailed to the pillory on the old market. For a few days, the effigy's torso was shown to the people in the executioners house for a fee and finally buried under the gallows.[22]

ⅠⅠ *formal justice:*
1661_Denmark: Kai Lykke

– shockingly realistic. The effigy of South Korean President Lee Myung-bak was attacked by a dog, run over by a tank, and stoned to death by a group of protesters, all before a disciplined and chanting public and the cameras of North Korean State Television.○ The excessive drama turns the figure's realism into an exaggerated, cinematic hyperrealism, in which one death is never enough, and the imagination must play out all possible scenarios. This symbolic excess corresponds to Foucault's interpretation of capital punishment in the seventeenth century:

> Its aim is not so much to re-establish a balance as to bring into play, as its extreme point, the dissymmetry between the subject who has dared to violate the law and the all-powerful sovereign who displays his strength…., the punishment is carried out in such a way as to give a spectacle not of measure, but of imbalance and excess; in this liturgy of punishment, there must be an emphatic affirmation of power and of its intrinsic superiority.[21]

This theatrical show of sovereign power that was integral to early modern executions was sometimes also performed on effigies. Kai Lykke, one of the richest men in Denmark, had been involved in intrigues at the Danish court and in 1661 was convicted of lèse-majesté.ⅠⅠ Since he had fled, the punishment was carried out on an effigy that was constructed to result in a very lifelike execution.

Equating lifelikeness with truth, the makers of both effigies — even though 360 years and continents apart — apparently strived for a similar spectacular realism to make the spectacle more effective. The effigy in North Korea was staged to counter and possibly exceed the irreverence exhibited by South Korean protesters towards North Korean leaders in earlier demonstrations.

218

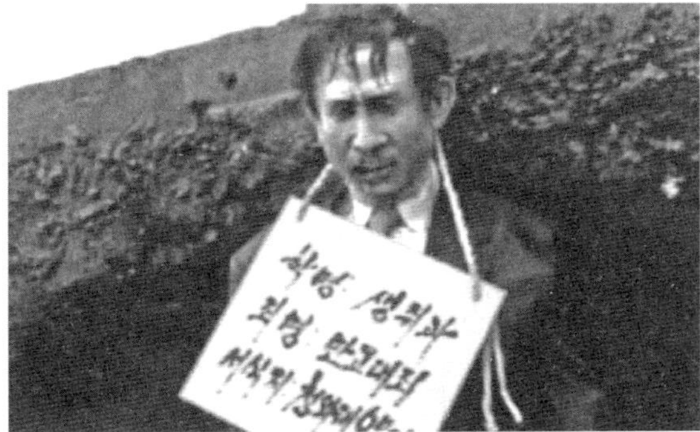

○ 2012_04_28_North Korea: South Korean President Lee   (a)

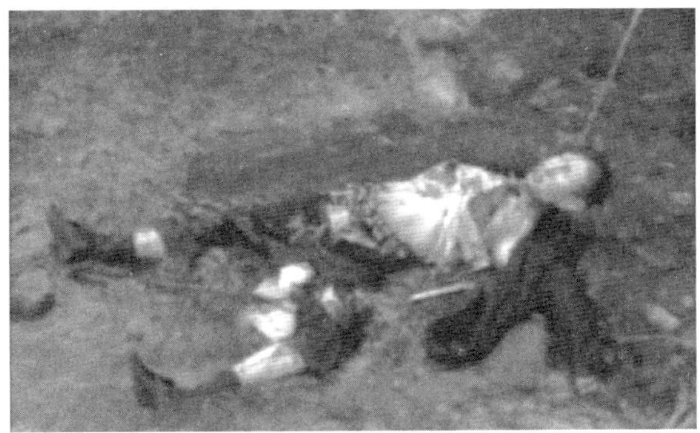

(b)

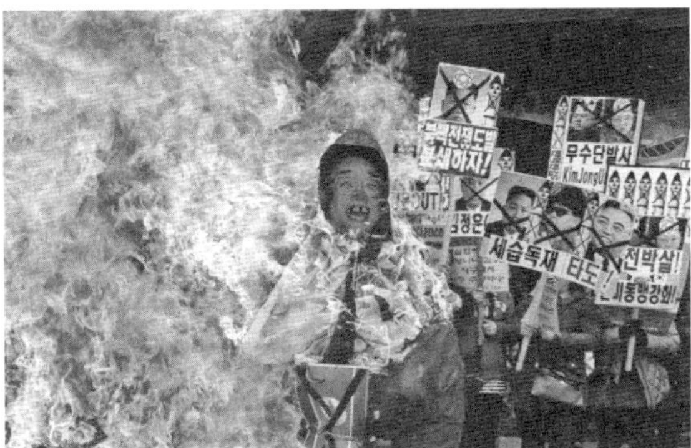

2013_04_16_South Korea: North Korean leader Kim Jong-il

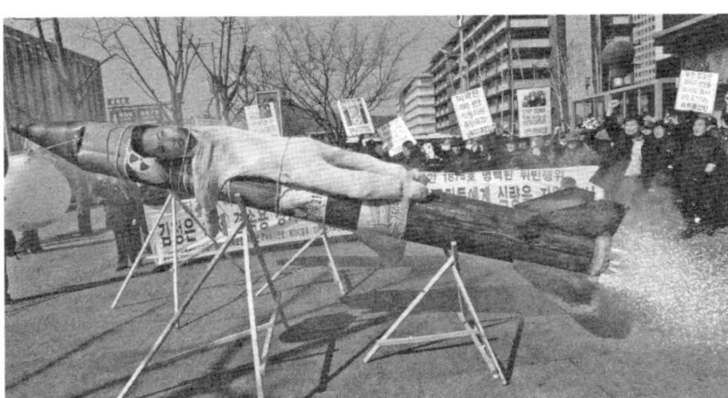

2012_03_20_South Korea: North Korean leader
Kim Jong-un

The Grotesque

The protesters in South Korea, who burned effigies of the North Korean president, however, seemed unconcerned with lifelikeness or any kind of realism. Their effigy performances were rather characterized by caricature and parody. They used photographic representations of their enemies to ensure correct identification, while their effigies had malformed anatomies, absurd bulges, dangling limbs, and distorted expressions – grotesque bodies that invited mockery and derision.

Most effigies look nothing like the depicted. Nonetheless, once identified in the pretend play as "the enemy," protesters interact with them as if they really are those they substitute. In assessing my collection of images, the aesthetic that characterizes most effigies across the globe is the grotesque. I argue that this is no accident and that the grotesque is unavoidable in the performance of protest that uses effigies to debase and insult an adversary.

Usually, effigies are made – like scarecrows – by amateurs in a do-it-yourself manner. Those who take up the task seem to find great pleasure in the making, visible in pictorial inventions and a creative use of materials. Nevertheless, the makers often lack the necessary skills to create life-size dolls, and the figures turn out grotesque, out of shape, indeed, out

220

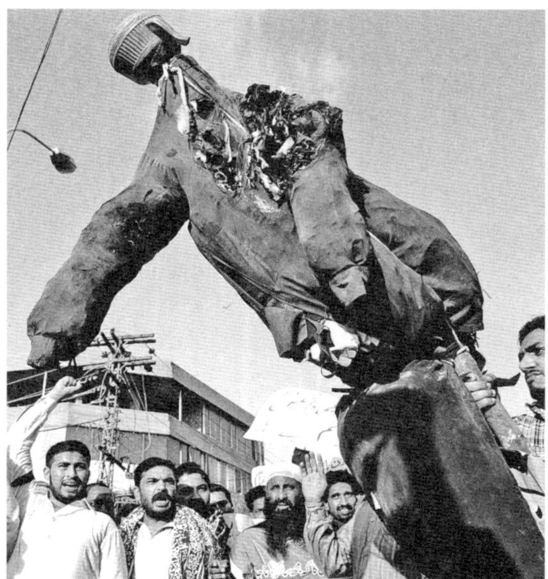

2012_09_11_Pakistan: US pastor Jones

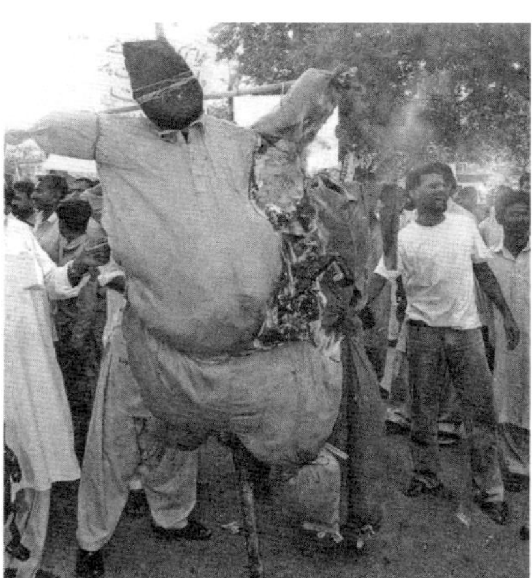

2011_10_10_Pakistan: PPP leader Mirza

of their makers' control. Their lack of defined form is not just due to the lack of skill since visual resemblance is often not even attempted. Instead, effigies are intentionally deformed. Exposed to mockery and derision, they become laughing-stocks. The lack of form expressed as excess, makes the fig-ures disturbing and unfitting; their deformation induces dis-gust. The unwieldy dolls, made from disjointed elements and too big to handle, are the monsters from our nightmares who engage with their makers in a performance of denigration, characterized by slapstick and laughter, cruelty and repulsion.

Effigies make the physical private body, which, accord-ing to political philosopher Judith Butler, conditions the pub-lic body, but never appears as such, open to public scrutiny and violation.[23] The effigies are associated with everything that is considered low: excrement, filth, the soles of shoes, bodily functions, fluids, and excess. Through contagious association, the depicted is defiled and debased. The effigies reduce the person to the material conditions of bare life.

In this photograph from 1945, the most powerful and most despised enemy of humankind, Adolf Hitler, who had dragged half of the world into a brutal six-year war, ended up a powerless empty shell, as in numerous effigy performances at the end of WWII.○ "Wanted dead or alive for millions of

23   Judith Butler, "Bodies in Alliance and the Politics of the Street," *transversal* (2011).

221

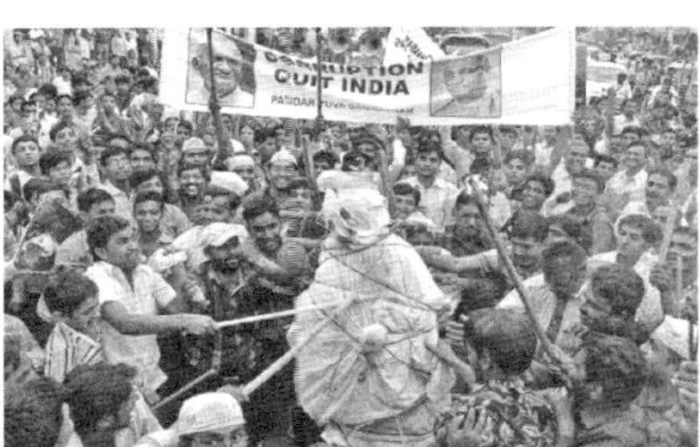

2011_08_24_India: "corruption"

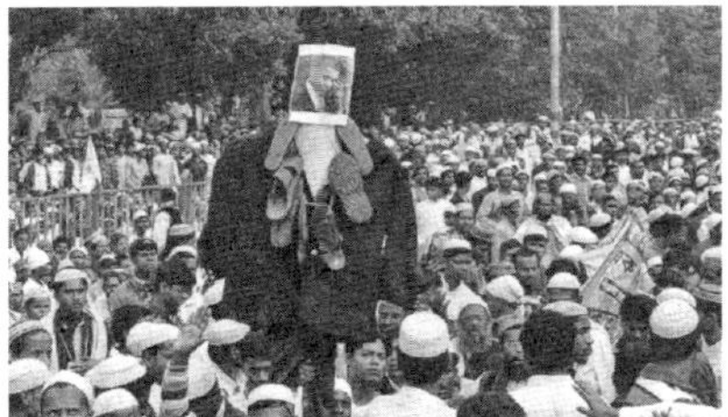

2013_01_16_India: US President Obama

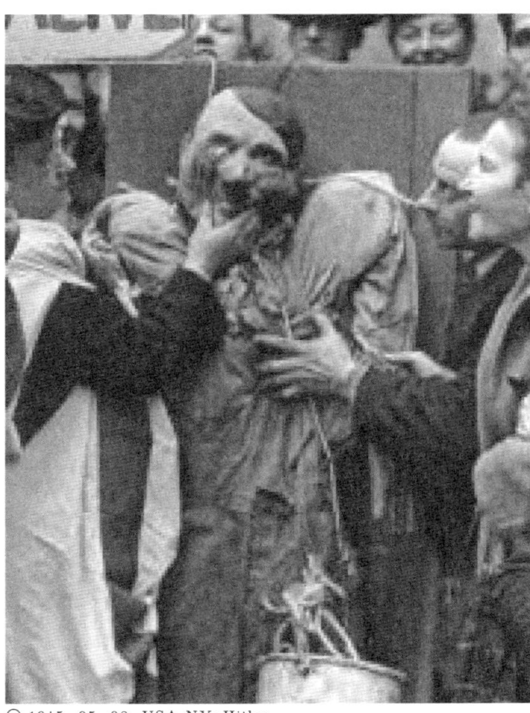

○ 1945_05_08_USA-NY: Hitler

murders," Hitler is a puppet in the hands of the people, who have overcome his rule. The people, now in charge, manhandle the effigy's body, beat it, tear at it, insult it, and distort its face. Through the bodily abuse of the effigy, through handling and deforming the effigy, Hitler is stripped of rank and honor, depersonalized, degraded to the level he had previously attributed to his enemies.

Another common strategy of debasement is association with animals. Politicians like us President George W. Bush, Russian President Putin, or French President Hollande are associated with dogs and donkeys; President Barack Obama is presented with a sign "Black Dog Obama" or depicted as monkey (both intended as racist insults). In Iraq, Bush, Saddam Hussein, and British Prime Minister Tony Blair are depicted as werewolves. In the Philippines, over the course of several years, protesters have developed a practice that includes a complex visual and theatrical language with which to debase their presidents as grotesque hybrid creatures: vultures, sharks, vampires, zombies, and pigs — even Godzilla. The presidents are dehumanized, expelled from the category of the human and made animal.

222

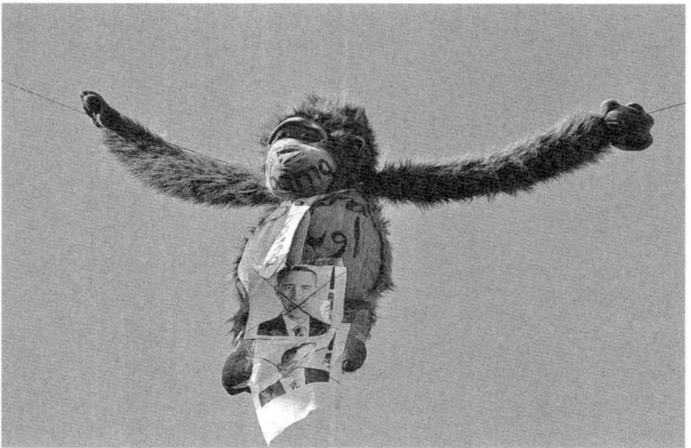

2012_09_21_Afghanistan: US Pres Obama and pastor Jones

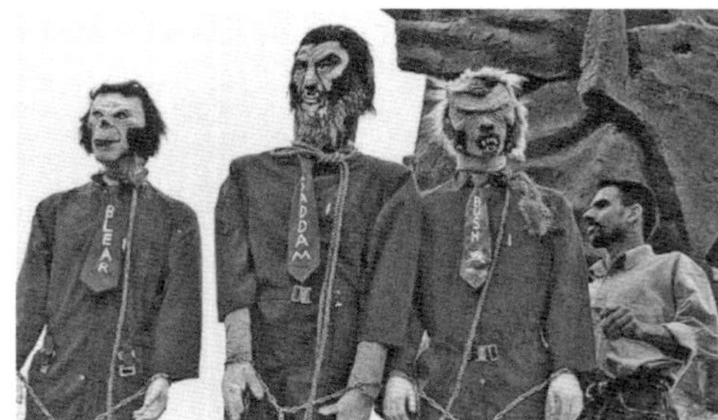

2005_04_09_Iraq: Saddam Hussein, US President Bush + British Premier Blair

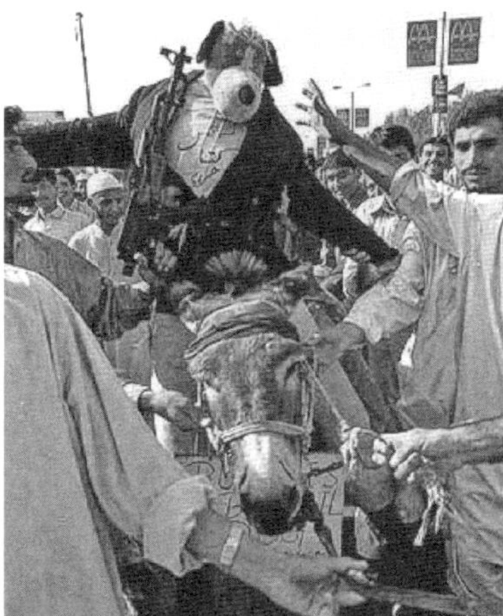

2001_11_09_Pakistan: US President Bush

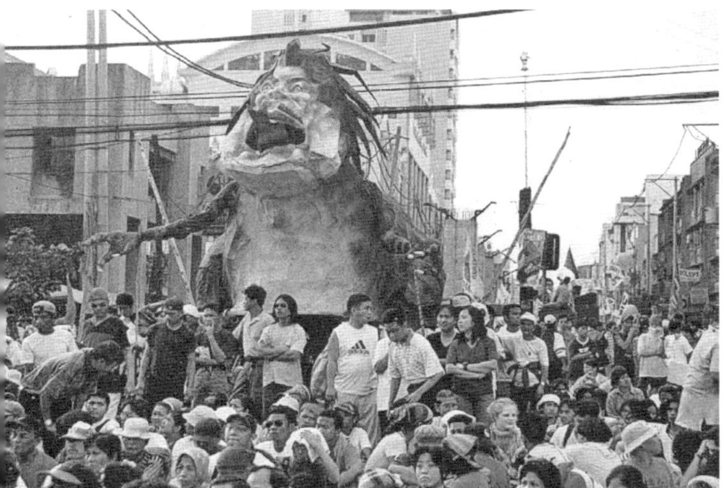

000_12_00_Philippines: President Estrada as Godzilla

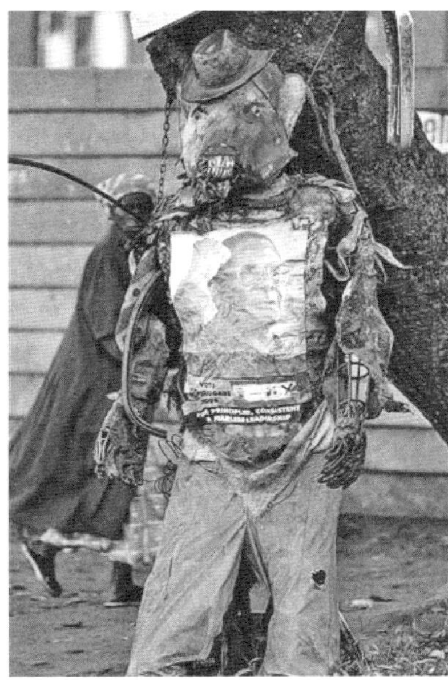

2008_04_03_Zimbabwe: President Mugabe

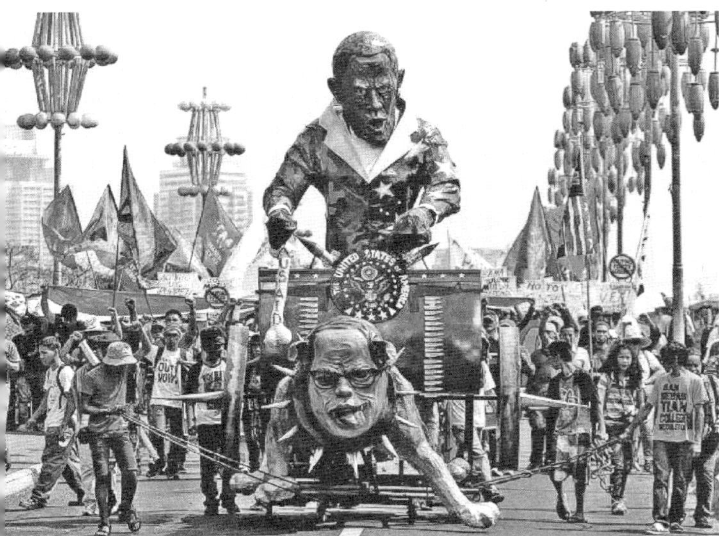

014_04_28_Philippines: President Aquino + US President Obama

A crowd of 300.000 saw the premier of Iraq hanged in effigy Monday. The Cairo demonstrators hanged effigies of Premier Abdul Karim Kassem alongside the bodies of dogs, cats and rats. Men and women screamed: "We shall bottle your blood, Kassem." —Chicago Tribune, 17 Mar 1959

1959_03_16_Egypt: Iraqi Premier Kassem

Yet another strategy is demonization. Imagine the demon haunting Pakistani society, the "Killer of Muslims" as a union of Bush and Obama with the face of a devil proudly presented to the camera by two young Pakistani men.○ Or consider the former Iranian President Mahmoud Ahmadinejad through the eyes of protesters in Afghanistan: a reptilian monster in one photograph and a blood-smeared butcher in another. Demonic signs are widely shared across cultures and consistent over time. The devil's horns appear

224

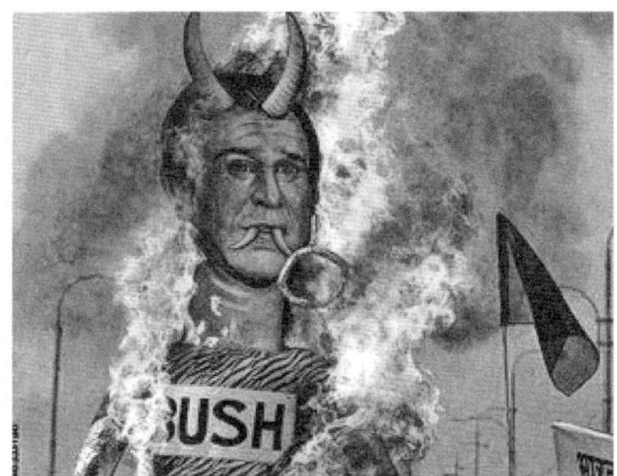
2007_01_04_India: US President Bush

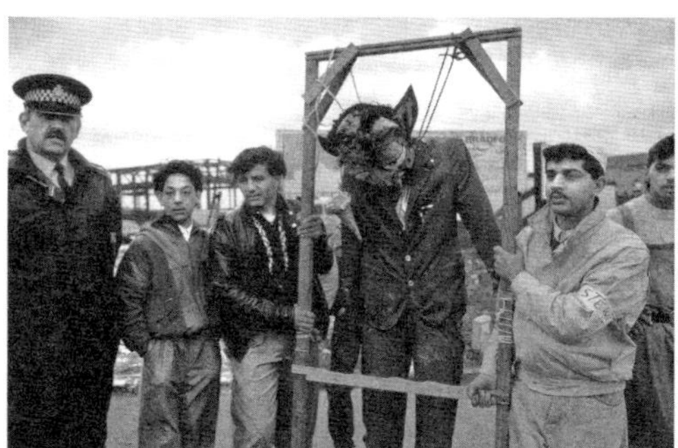
1989_01_14_UK_Salman Rushdie

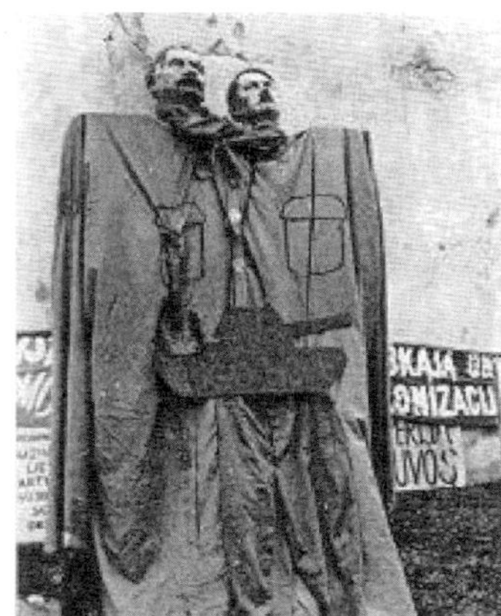
1939_00_00_Lithuania: Stalin and Hitler

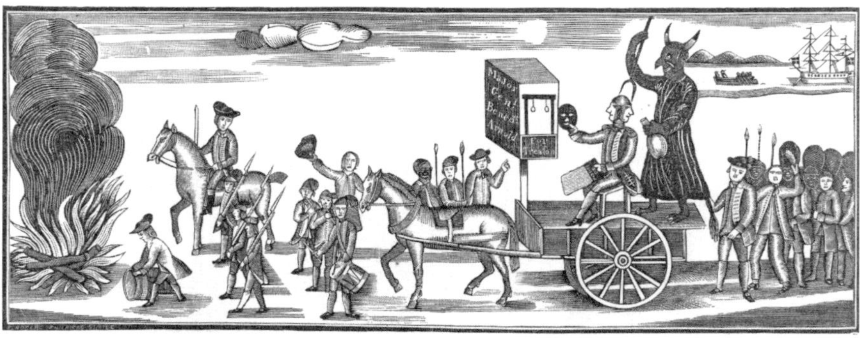
1780_09_30_USA-PA: General Arnold

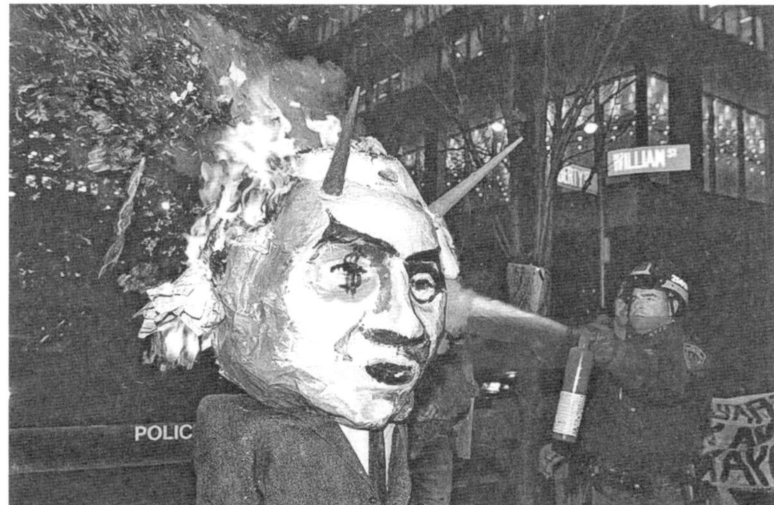

1995_02_17_USA-NY: US banks

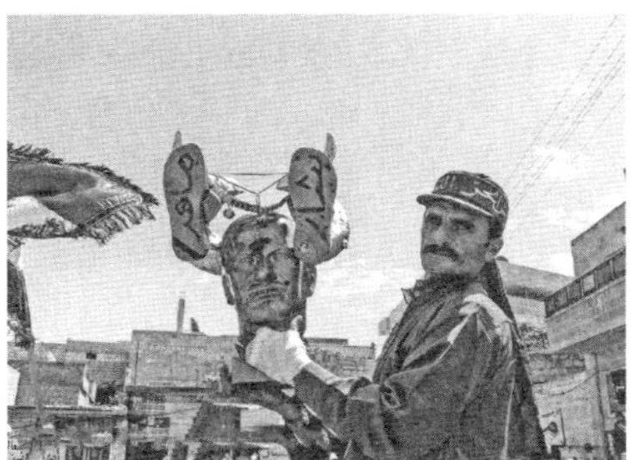

2012_05_00_Syria: President Assad

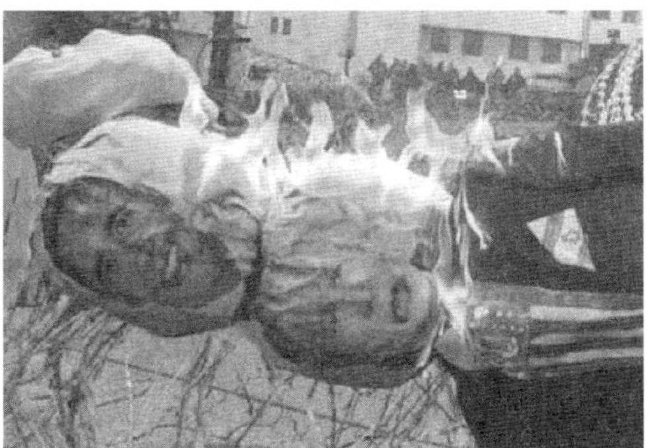

2009_01_18_Lebanon: US Presidents Bush + Obama

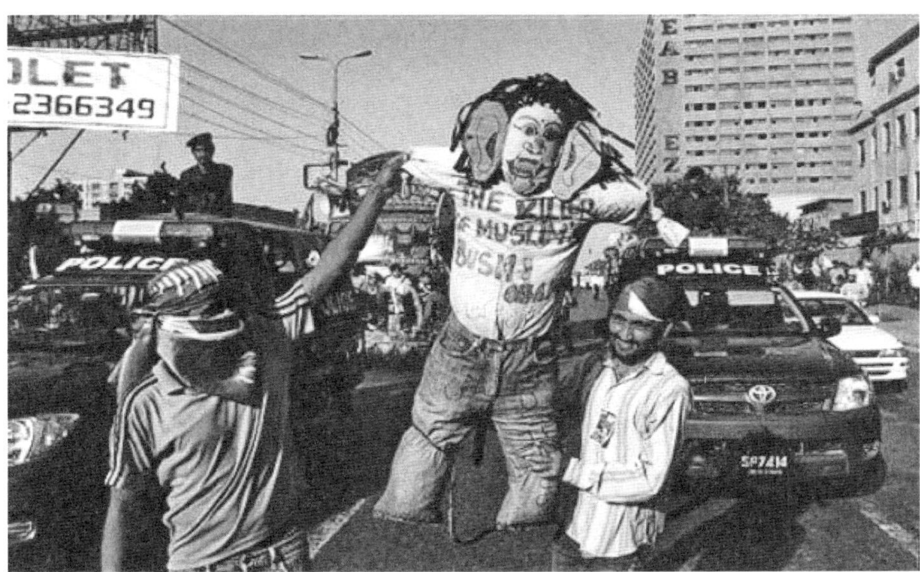

○ 2009_09_18_Pakistan: US Presidents Bush + Obama

on effigies of traitor General Benedict Arnold 1880 in the US, Salman Rushdie effigies in the UK and Lebanon in 1989, on Bush in India in 2011, and US banks in New York in 1995.

In 2013, the chemical company Union Carbide, responsible for the Bhopal chemical disaster twenty-nine years earlier, is depicted as a Western businessman, white-faced in a suit, red tie, and carrying a briefcase, his head adorned with devil's horns and pointed ears. His face is frozen in a demonic grin, eyes staring threateningly under his raised eyebrows. The body seems to have undergone a punishing ritual: pierced by nails with wounds that leak blood. Paraded through the streets and doused in a flammable liquid, it is set alight. Halfway through the burning, it transforms into an even more devilish image: completely black and framed by flickering flames. Behind the burning figure, a banner articulates the protesters' demands for justice. The aesthetic of the effigy and the multilayered ritual reveals the true nature of the chemical company and the incapacity of existing governmental structures to address the injustice inflicted on the people by the multinational corporation. Evil is presented not as an inherent quality, but as a sign of transgression and a category of social relations associated with injustice in the existing order that calls out for redress. This violation of justice is personified in the businessman or politician, made visible in the form of the effigy and the performance of its destruction.

Signs and attributes are often added to effigies, connoting evil and the abject in another form of resemblance: contagion through association. The Swastika, (derogatory treatment of) the Star of David, the dollar sign, and the CIA acronym, serve as signs of evil, greed, and duplicity. In the context of certain protests, these signs are considered offensive, often culturally specific, but through mediation in the contemporary global media environment these contagious

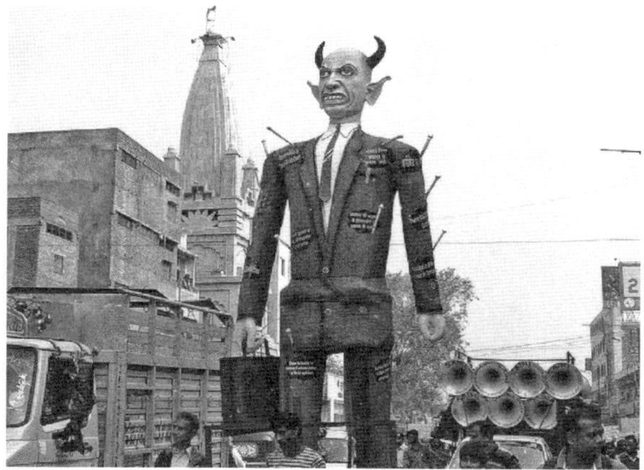

2013_12_03_India: Union Carbide CEO Anderson (a)

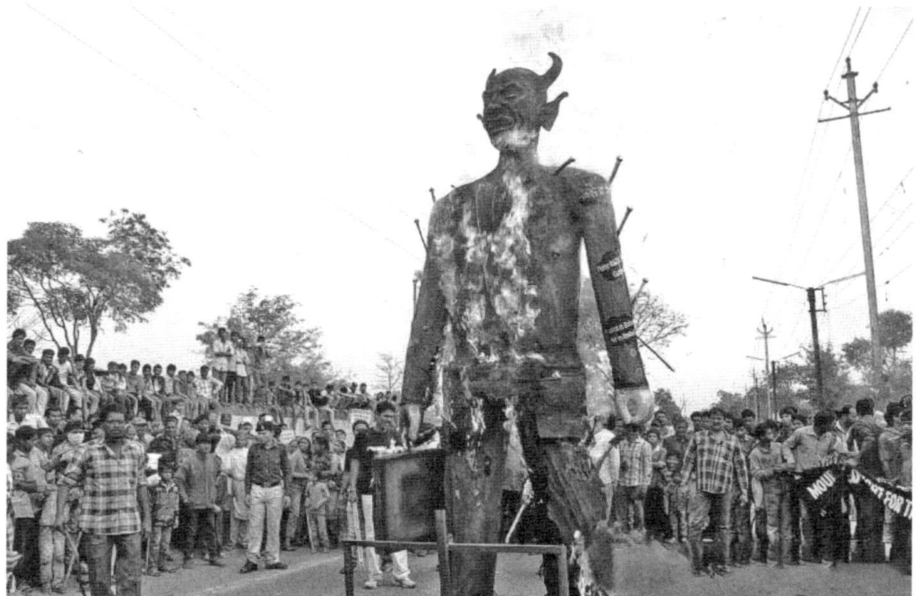

(b)

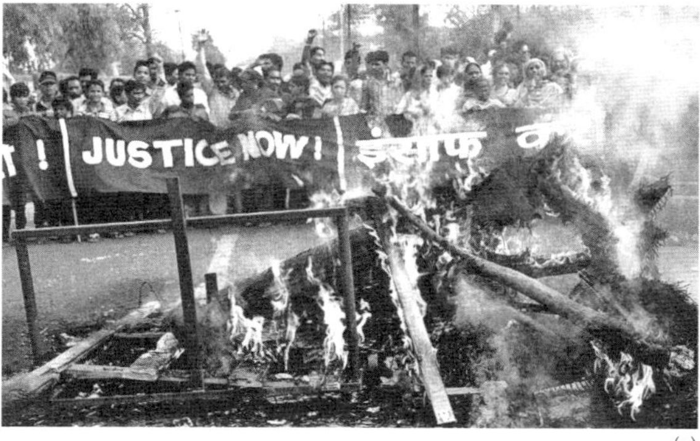

(c)

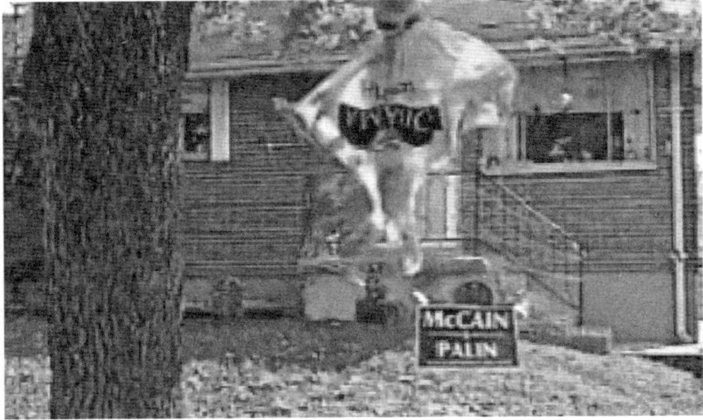

○ 2008_10_19_USA-OH: presidential candidate Obama   (a)

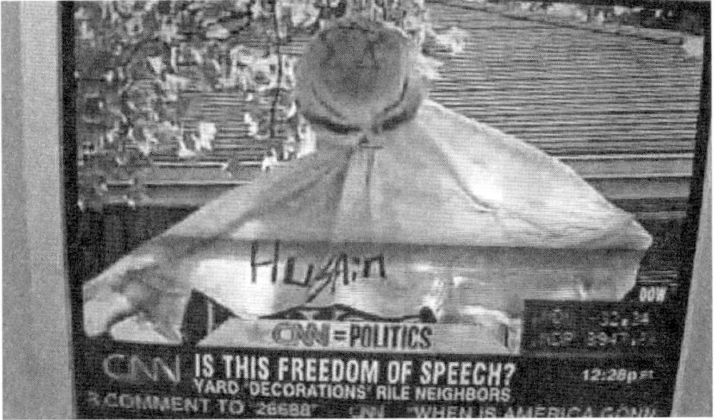

(b)

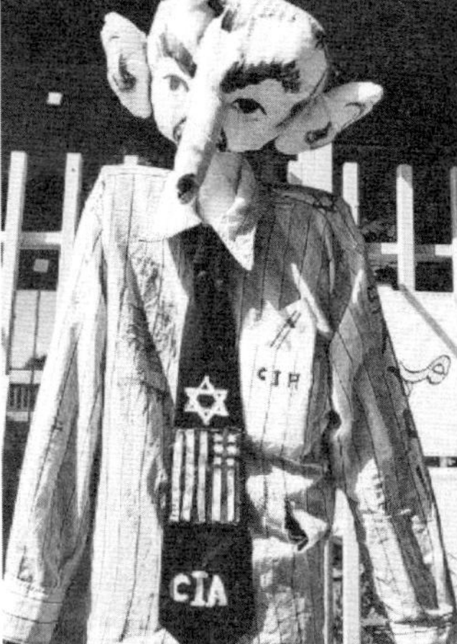

1981_01_01_Iran: Shah Reza Pahlavi

The ghostlike figure could be a reference to KKK robe and hood, and as such constitutes a threat of lynching, or a visualization of the racist term "spook"; displaying Obama's name (probably a campaign lawn sign) upside down, is a gesture of negation and defilement, similar to the practice of hanging a flag upside down; in this context the Star of David drawn on the figure's head has to be read as anti-Semitic, perhaps suggesting that then-presidential candidate Obama is "controlled" by Jewish interest groups, as per extreme right-wing conspiracy theories; the name "Hussain" written on the chest denounces his alleged Muslim faith. The use of Nazi SS-runes in the manner of writing the name, on the other hand, inscribe the effigy-maker's ideology onto the body of the effigy like a branding mark.

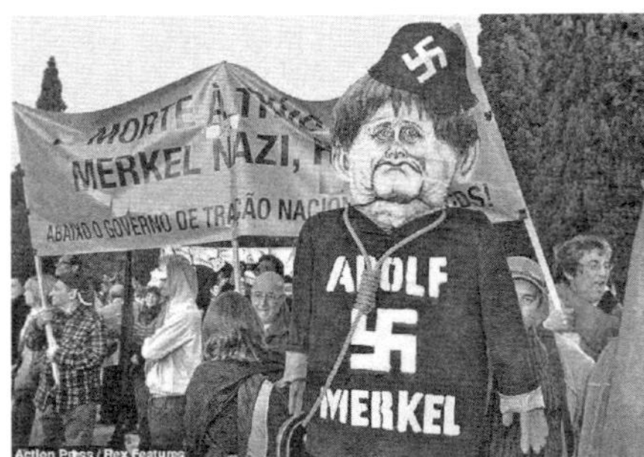

2012_11_15_Portugal: German chancellor Merkel

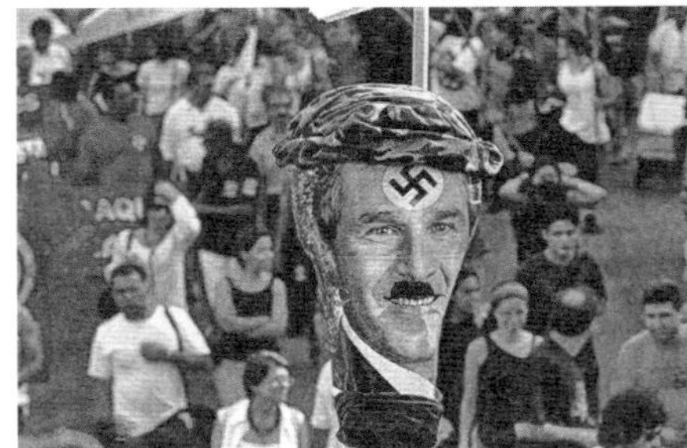

2005_03_19_Brazil: US President Bush

symbols have been widely shared across cultural borders, like the Swastika from European history or the shoe as a denigrating sign from Arab cultures. Denigrating signs are often convoluted when placed on the effigies. This ghostlike figure has Obama's name affixed on it upside down, the Star of David drawn on its head, his second (misspelled) name "Hussain," written on it as an indication of Muslim descent, *ss* written in the style of the *ss*-runes of Nazi Germany.○ Semantically, these signs do not necessarily go together, but that does not matter as long as the intent to denigrate is evident.

The operations I describe at work in the performances of effigies – deformation, debasement, dehumanization, and demonization – are all modes of the grotesque, the overarching aesthetics in effigy protests. A number of literary theorists, most notably Mikhail Bakhtin, Wolfgang Kayser, and Geoffrey Galt-Harpham, have investigated the grotesque from different perspectives in literature or art. More recently, literary critics Justin D. Edwards and Rune Graulund presented a critical guide to the term, its forms, uses, and appearance in theory. These scholars describe the grotesque in very similar terms, as monstrous, hybrid, anatomically indeterminate, ambivalent, exaggerated, transgressive, unfinished, or outgrowing. These terms fit the description of many effigies: a man morphing into an animal, a dog with the head of a president, the double-headed monster emerging from a man, or the figure of the sovereign in the process of disintegration.

The grotesque creates the incongruent body, the body out of bounds, the body out of control, the body outside of reason. The hybrid figures that demonization and dehumanization create oscillate between the human and the Other. These grotesque effigies exceed their own familiar species or are caught between species. Galt-Harpham writes that "our

229

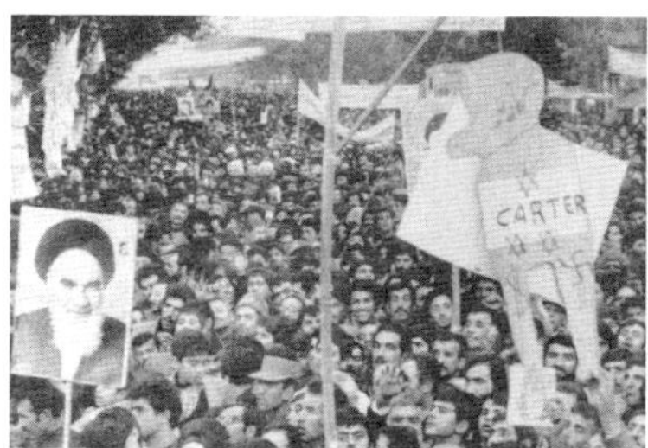

1979_11_25_Iran: US President Carter

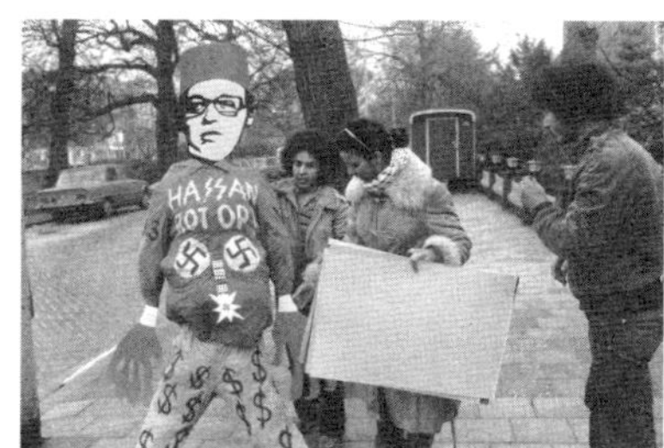

1981_03_05_Netherlands: Moroccan King Hassan II

24 Geoffrey Galt-Harpham, *On the Grotesque: Strategies of Contradiction in Art and Literature* (Princeton: Princeton University Press, 1982), 13.

25 Justin D. Edwards and Rune Graulund, *Grotesque* (London: Routledge, 2013), 78.

26 "Die Plötzlichkeit, die Überraschung gehört wesentlich zum Grotesken," Wolfgang Kayser, *Das Groteske, Seine Gestaltung in Malerei und Dichtung* (Oldenburg: Gerhard Stalling Verlag, 1961), 198–99.

27 Popescu, "Sociological Perspectives on Humour," 40–41.

28 Kayser, *Das Groteske*, 201.

29 Mikhail Bakhtin, *Rabelais and his World* (Indianapolis: University of Indiana Press, 1984), 24.

understanding is stranded in a 'liminal' phase, for the image appears to have an impossible split reference, and multiple forms inhabit a single image."[24] It is impossible to reconcile the debased, exaggerated, deformed bodies of the effigies with a human body. Just as the figures incorporate incompatible others, they elicit conflicting responses between laughter and terror, "fascination and repugnance, compassion and disgust, sympathy and confusion."[25] The realization of the impossibility to reasonably grasp the sense of these bodies can evoke a laughter that bursts out from the sudden realization of incomprehension.[26] This missing resemblance of the effigy with the figure depicted can be described as semantic incongruence, the recognition of which — according to the incongruity theory of humor — triggers laughter.[27] But the laughter of the grotesque is ambiguous: it might be light-hearted, cathartic, and liberating, but also hysterical, bitter, and derisive.[28]

As "a phenomenon in transformation, an as yet unfinished metamorphosis, of death and birth, growth and becoming," the grotesque is elusive.[29] Even though it is constant as a phenomenon, its form varies depending on the mode of thinking predominant at the time. Galt-Harpham claims that the grotesque "cannot be defined formally, thematically,

230

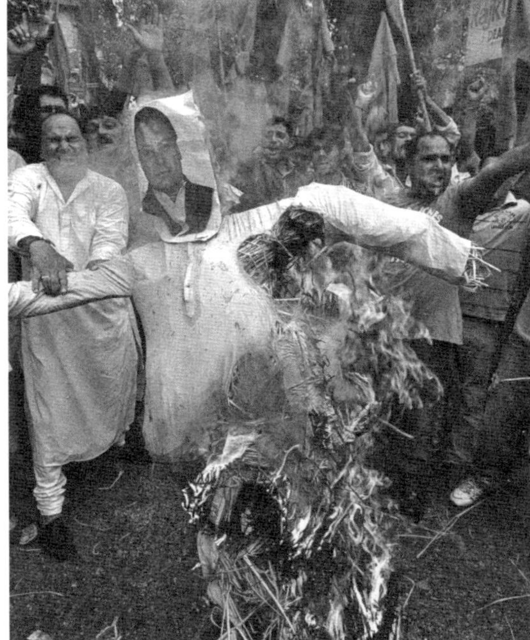

2013_09_27_India: Pakistani President Sharif

affectively, or even by relation to other concepts."[30] Edwards and Graulund conclude: "For if there is any one thing that defines 'the grotesque' it is precisely that it is hybrid, transgressive and always in motion."[31] What is more, as the grotesque stands "at a margin of consciousness between the known and the unknown, the perceived and the unperceived," it not only defies definition but even calls "into question the adequacy of our ways of organizing the world."[32] In Kayser's words, the grotesque figures constitute "a rebuke of any rationalism and all systematics of thought."[33] Consequently, the grotesque has an immense potential to challenge the existing order.

Although impossible to define conclusively, it is possible to differentiate the forms of the grotesque, as I have done earlier, according to their transgressive operations: debasement, demonization, dehumanization, and deformation. At the edge of deformation some figures embody the most radical form of the grotesque. Suspended in an unstable state of the human toward the unknown, they verge on the "formless" (*l'informe*), which French intellectual Georges Bataille introduced in the "Critical Dictionary," published in *Documents* in 1929.[34] In the entry "Formless" he does not attempt a definition, but recursively reflects on the dictionary in which the entry appears, fundamentally questioning the dictionary's capacity to construct an order of things.[35] While the hybridization resulting from demonization or dehumanization strains our capability to order the world, the formless denies any possibility of a stable order. As art historian Didi-Huberman writes in his book *Formlose Ähnlichkeit: oder die fröhliche Wissenschaft des Visuellen nach Georges Bataille*, Bataille's "formless" is "neither the simple negation of form nor the simple absence of form."[36] Instead it is "a certain capacity of forms to constantly deform themselves, to suddenly shift from

---

30 Galt-Harpham, *On the Grotesque*, xx.

31 Edwards and Graulund, *Grotesque*, 15.

32 Galt-Harpham, *On the Grotesque*, 3.

33 Kayser, *Das Groteske*, 203 (my translation).

34 Georges Bataille, "Critical Dictionary," in *Encyclopaedia Acephalica*, ed. Robert Lebel and Isabelle Waldberg (London: Atlas Press, 1995), 29–48.

35 Bataille's "Critical Dictionary" is in some sense similar to Jorge Luis Borges's "Chinese Encyclopedia," which Foucault writes about in the beginning of *The Order of Things* as an example to show the arbitrariness in any attempt to construct a coherent order of things. The formless would be the act of abstaining from the impulse to impose a classification onto the things in front of us. This abstinence would possibly open our minds to perceive things otherwise, outside of the usual framework, as singular entities, an outlook both exhilarating and terrifying. In the entry for "Formless," Bataille evokes the potential of the grotesque to derail our rationality, taking the universe as an example, saying that "the universe resembles nothing at all and is only formless, amounts to saying that the universe is something akin to a spider or a gob of spittle." In this little sentence, he forces together the most incomprehensible "object," the universe, which is before and beyond classification, with the most debased bodily fluid, spittle. In the same dictionary, spittle becomes the symbol of the formless. Michel Leiris, who writes the entry for "Spittle," describes it as inconsistent, undefined, imprecise, unverifiable, and non-hierarchical. Spittle is unclassifiable and with that impossible to comprehend in the system of rational thought. Bataille, "Critical Dictionary," 51–52; and Michel Leiris, "Spittle," in *Encyclopaedia Acepha-lica*, 79–80.

36 Georges Didi-Huberman, *Formlose Ähnlichkeit: oder die fröhliche Wissenschaft des Visuellen nach Georges Bataille* (Munich: Wilhelm Fink Verlag, 2010), 146 (my translation).

37 Didi-Huberman, *Formlose Ähnlichkeit*, 147 (my translation). I translate the German "Unähnlichkeit" as "dissemblance" in accordance with the English translation of Didi-Huberman's book *Fra Angelico*.

38 Georges Didi-Huberman, *Fra Angelico: Dissemblance and Figuration* (Chicago: Chicago University Press, 1995), 45–55.

resemblance to dissemblance."[37] In *Fra Angelico: Dissemblance and Figuration*, Didi-Huberman relates "dissemblance" to Adam's original sin and the subsequent loss of man's resemblance with God.[38] The grotesque, then, becomes a metaphor to describe the painful dissociation from man's true image. This aesthetics of loss is associated with the consciousness of our own death, but also with the embrace of death as a condition of life in the spirit of Bakhtin's liberating carnival.

Dissemblance

39 Didi-Huberman, *Formlose Ähnlichkeit*, 147 (my translation).

40 Yve-Alain Bois, "The Use Value of 'Formless,'" in *Formless: A User's Guide*, ed. Yve-Alain Bois and Rosalind Krauss (New York: Zone Books, 1997), 18.

While resemblance emerges as a surprise by a shift in perception that integrates the object into an ordering relation and in this way creates knowledge, the grotesque is forced upon the object. It defies, interrupts, or destroys the ordering principle of resemblance and distorts the object beyond recognizability. All the while, the grotesque uses some of the same mechanisms as resemblance, namely association, proximity, contact, and contagion. Didi-Huberman describes the "transgressive" or "excessive resemblances" as "constant contacts, which can force onto each and any form the potential of dissemblance."[39]

Because of its capacity to dislodge, art historian Yve-Alain Bois interprets the formless as "performative, like obscene words, the violence of which derives less from semantics than from the very *act* of their delivery" and concludes, that "the formless is an operation."[40] Bois's characterization of the formless as an operation also applies to the other forms of the grotesque. The grotesque employed in effigies is a performative aesthetics that effects the social and political

232

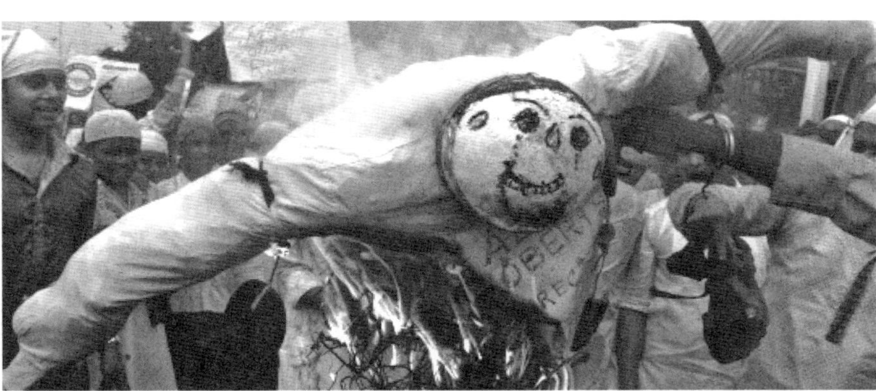

2012_10_05_India: film producer Roberts

relations of the depicted. The grotesque bodies perform a declassification – they cast the depicted out from the accepted norm and present them as categorically despicable.[41] In grotesque effigies, the unfitting, excessive, abject, unaesthetic, formless is forced onto the image of the depicted through the mechanisms of resemblance.

But resemblance is not a one-way street. Resemblance, as Foucault describes, constructs a reciprocal relationship. Consequently, we project the denigrating character traits of a grotesque effigy onto the person it depicts.[42] Like a contagious disease, the degrading aspects of effigies are transferred to the prototype: the person starts to resemble their caricature. Both operations, resemblance and the grotesque are integral to effigy protests and just like resemblance, the grotesque also produces knowledge. From Bakhtin's perspective, the grotesque and the laughter it produces reveal the truth about the world and power.[43] These debasing monsters that effigies depict, do not spring from their makers' fantasy by accident – they reveal the evil traits that were once hidden behind the mask of the human being and make them visible on the surface of their representation. While resemblance affirms the association of the effigy with the depicted, the grotesque reveals their "true" nature.

The effect of grotesque aesthetics becomes clear in the following example, the effigy of John Howard Griffin already mentioned in chapter 4, "Effigy Protests in Egypt, Iran, Afghanistan, and Across the Middle East". In 1960, Griffin published *Black Like Me* detailing his experience of racial discrimination while traveling disguised as a black man in the Deep South in the US. While his book became a bestseller, his effigy was hanged on Main Street in his hometown, a cross burned in front of the local black school, and a neighborhood bar put up a sign reading "No albinos allowed." The

41 Bois, "The Use Value of 'Formless'," 15–16.

42 Foucault, *The Order of Things*, 24.

43 Bakhtin, *Rabelais and His World*, 90–94.

effigy's head and face were divided into a white and a black half, the text on the shirt read: "I'M WHITE / I'M BLACK." ○ All of these signs connote the unacceptably ambiguous state the author had attained by transgressing the racial divide and mark his body as grotesque. The effigy characterizes him as half-black and half-white, the albino sign as black with an abnormally white appearance, while the photograph associates him with an animal rather than human. These visual and textual enunciations indicate the violation of rules of conduct and the transgression of boundaries. The makers of the effigy mark him as a traitor to his race, an abomination to be cast away into the garbage dump of his community. They not only announce the transgression but also perform the violent exclusion of the author from the dominant white community of his hometown.

The effigy performances that shame a transgressive individual, that symbolically punish a traitor, or that debase a powerful politician in order to change society, all aim to exclude the perpetrator from the community. They all employ similar forms of a grotesque aesthetics to ridicule, insult, and declassify the perpetrator. While the social and political constellations differ, effigy protests all exert a form of violence on those constellations in support of the established dominant order that segregates a community, or else as a demand that same community be more inclusive. In the next chapter I take up this duality further, inquiring into the laughter and violence that emerges from effigy protests in divergent political constellations.

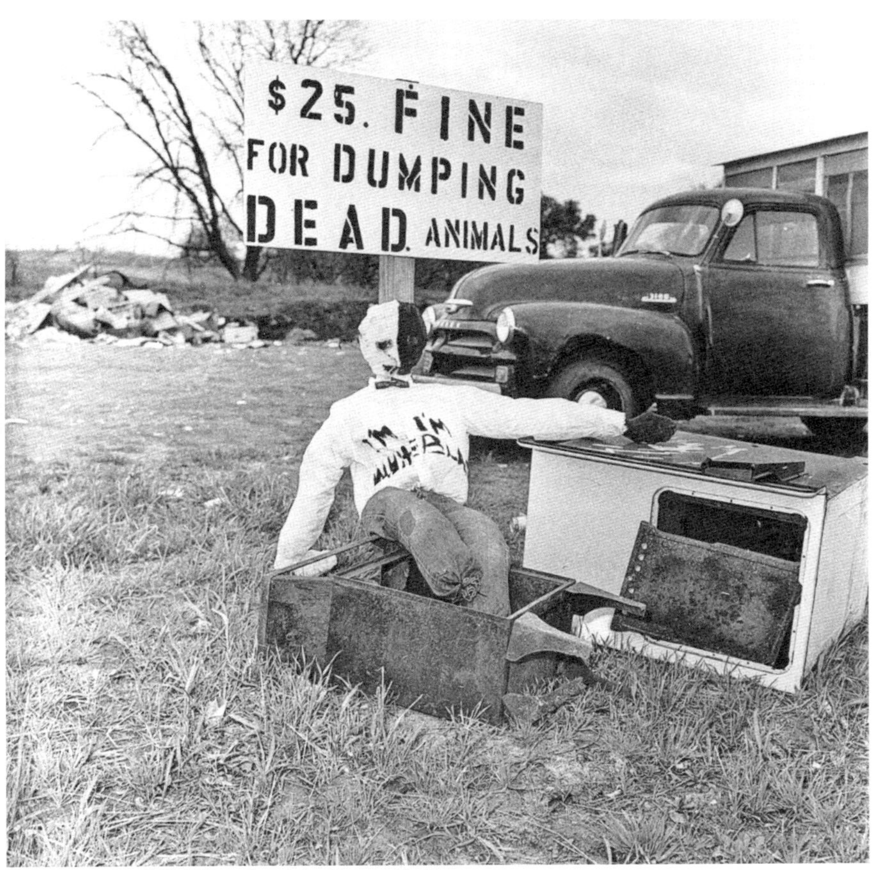

○ 1960_04_02_USA-TX: author John Howard Griffin

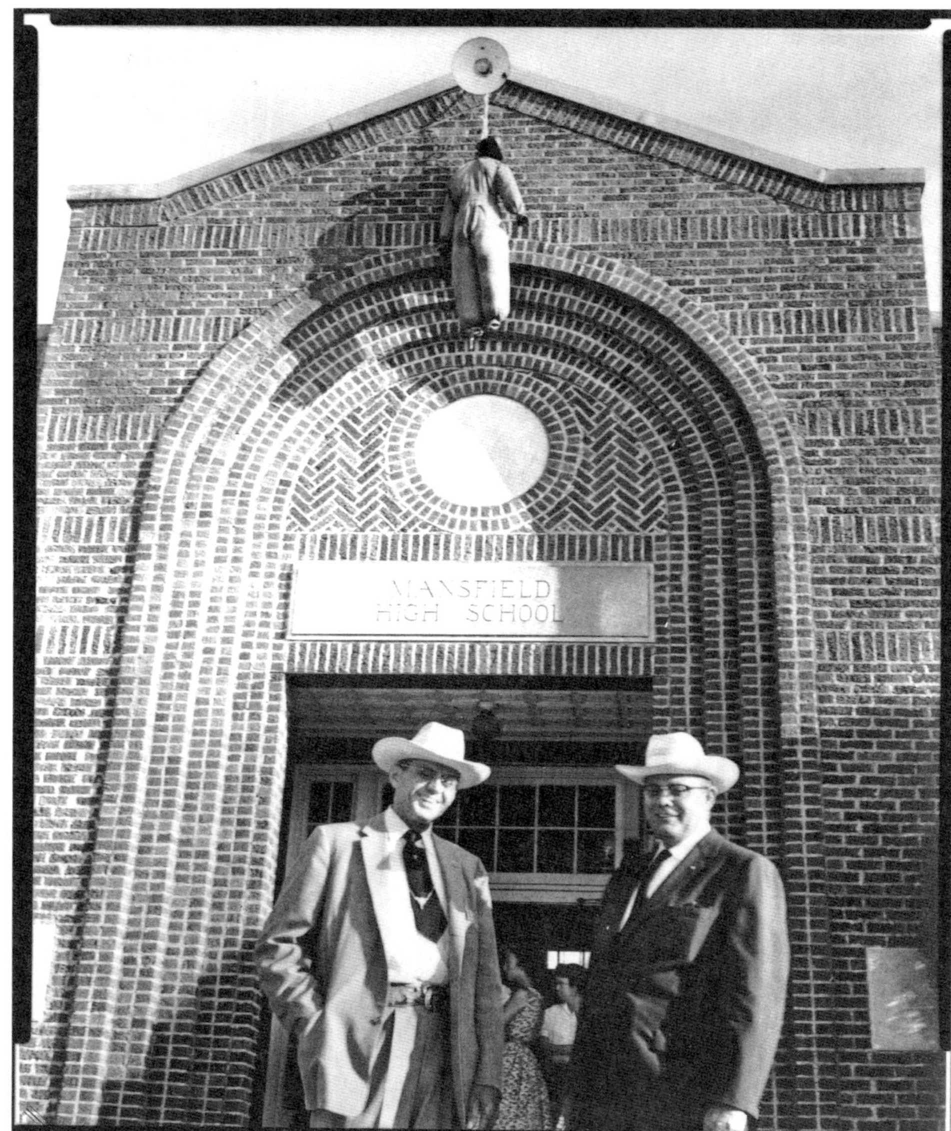

1956_08_30_USA-TX: African-American student (a)

Violence and Laughter

In the previous chapter, I examined how the grotesque aesthetics essential to effigy protests operate in the social and political sphere through insult and denigration. Grotesque performances not only produce violent images, but contribute to declassification, antagonism, and exclusion, and exert a form of violence. At the same time, the grotesque also produces communal laughter visible in many of the photographs, and the protesters often demand a more just and inclusive society.

The painful mix of violence and laughter is very characteristic of effigy protests and I want to look closer at this phenomenon and its effects in this chapter.

Both violence and laughter are notoriously difficult to define. Violence is found in all kinds of social relationships. Between subjective and objective, individual and collective, physical and symbolic, systemic and interpersonal, epistemic and normative forms, violence is "not reducible to a single medium of interpretation or a single academic discipline."[1]

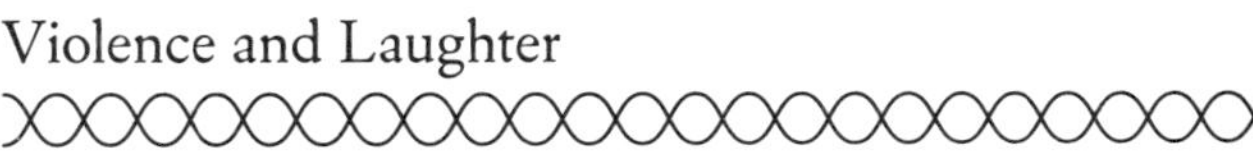

1 Christopher Yates, "Introduction," in *Philosophy and the Return of Violence Studies from this Widening Gyre*, ed. Nathan Eckstrand and Christopher Yates (New York: Continuum Books, 2011), 4.

2   Stefan Horlacher, "A Short Introduction to Theories of Humour, the Comic, and Laughter," *Amsterdamer Beiträge zur neueren Germanistik* 70, no. 1 (2009): 20.

3   Manfred Pfister, "Beckett's Tonic Laughter," *Samuel Beckett Today/Aujourd'hui*, 11 (2001): 50.

4   Hannah Arendt, *On Violence* (New York: Harvest Book, 1969), eBook, chapter II.

5   Mikhail Bakhtin, *Problems of Dostoevsky's Poetics* (Minneapolis: University of Minnesota Press, 1984), 127.

6   Mikhail Bakhtin, *Rabelais and His World* (Indianapolis: University of Indiana Press, 1984), 92.

7   Bakhtin, *Rabelais*, 90–91.

8   Pfister, "Beckett's Tonic Laughter," 49.

9   Bakhtin, *Rabelais and His World*, 12.

10   Horlacher, "A Short Introduction," 37.

11   Horlacher, "A Short Introduction," 26.

Since the study's topic is a form of political protest, I will look at effigy protests in relation to justice, resistance, and the law, and investigate what kind of violence and what kind of laughter emerges from effigy protests and how these react to and interact with violence in the configuration of the political.

Similarly to violence, no one theory "really manages to comprehensively explain the phenomenon of laughter," as literary studies scholar Stefan Horlacher observes: "THE laughter is an illusion since there are always only endlessly proliferating forms of laughter."[2] Laughter can be pure, the "laugh laughing at the laugh,"[3] or contaminated. Often laughter is associated with the affirmation of life, unifying effects, and the challenge to authority. Philosopher Hannah Arendt writes: "the greatest enemy of authority, therefore, is contempt, and the surest way to undermine it is laughter."[4] Literary theorist Mikhail Bakhtin describes carnival laughter as directed toward "a shift of authorities and truths, a shift of world orders."[5] It is "the social consciousness of all the people" and means "the defeat of power, of earthly kings, of the earthly upper classes, of all that oppresses and restricts."[6] He celebrates the "victory of laughter over fear… defeat of divine and human power, of authoritarian commandments and prohibitions, of death and punishment after death."[7] But other forms of laughter have also been characterized as aggressive, bitter,[8] derisive,[9] or satanic.[10] Laughter can express the superiority of the one who laughs, and be exclusionary.[11] Riddled with ambiguity and contradictions, it cannot be reduced to a single phenomenon.

There are many kinds of laughter that emerge in the performance of effigies. In some photographs, we see the makers posing with their creations. We can sense their pride in a well-executed effigy. They radiate a sense of achievement and satisfaction with the dolls they create and the messages of anger and ridicule that the grotesque figures communicate. In many other photographs of effigy protests we see cheering and laughter, and a playful engagement in the theatrical performances of the effigies' deaths. We can detect exhilaration in the crowd and triumphant laughter in seeing the enemy being unmasked, their true nature unveiled, and the long-deserved punishment finally meted out on their substitute body.

239

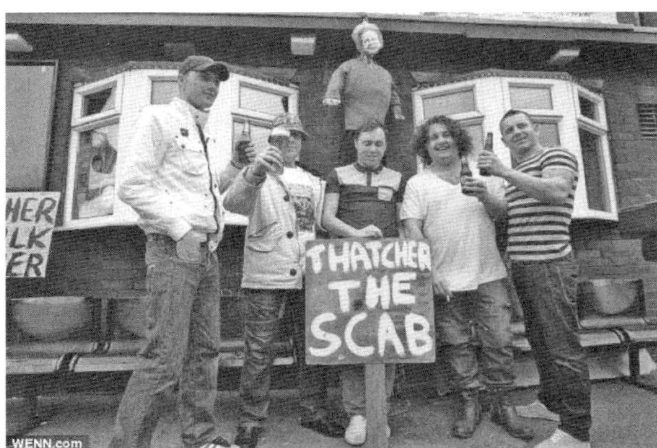

2013_04_17_UK: former Premier Thatcher

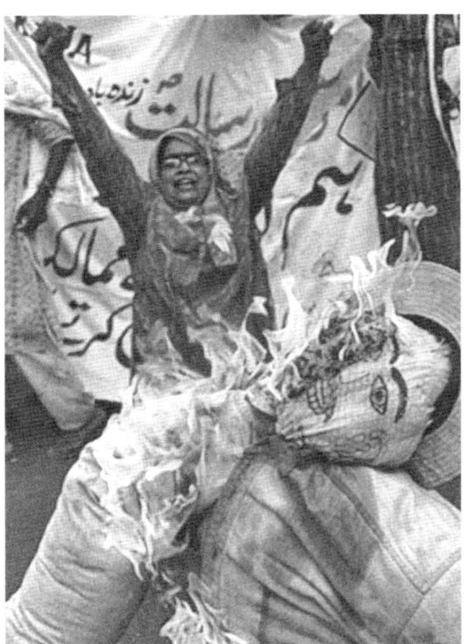
2008_03_30_Pakistan: Dutch politician Wilders

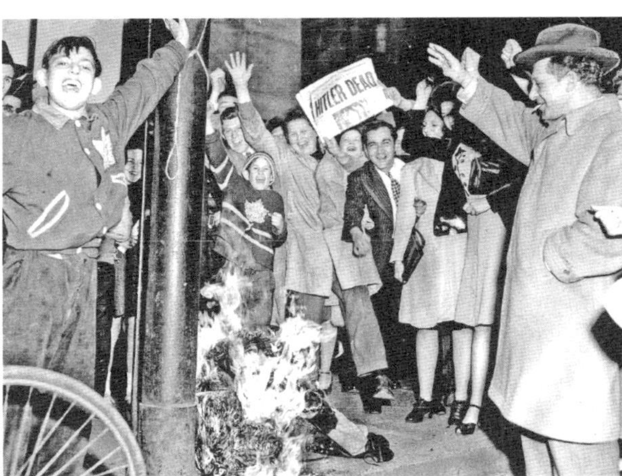

1945_05_02_Canada: Hitler

In some images one may notice a self-conscious, ironic laughter on the faces of some protesters. These participants seem to be aware of the absurdity of their actions and the ridiculousness of engaging in a perhaps completely inconsequential performance, which one can interpret as a stubborn belief in the prevalence of subversive laughter even in the face of likely defeat by an overwhelming state power. Knowing in advance that burning an effigy might fail to effect political change does not necessarily diminish the success or the urgency of the performance.

Looking at this photograph of a demonstration against the anti-Islam film trailer for *Innocence of Muslims* in Peshawar, we face what appears to be a large crowd of angry men, assembled around an effigy of US President Barack Obama stuck on a pole.○ The effigy is lowered to the ground to facilitate the beating with blows administered by seven or eight protesters. The effigy is made from stuffed jeans and an orange sweater. The head is missing, but a colorful cloth is

240

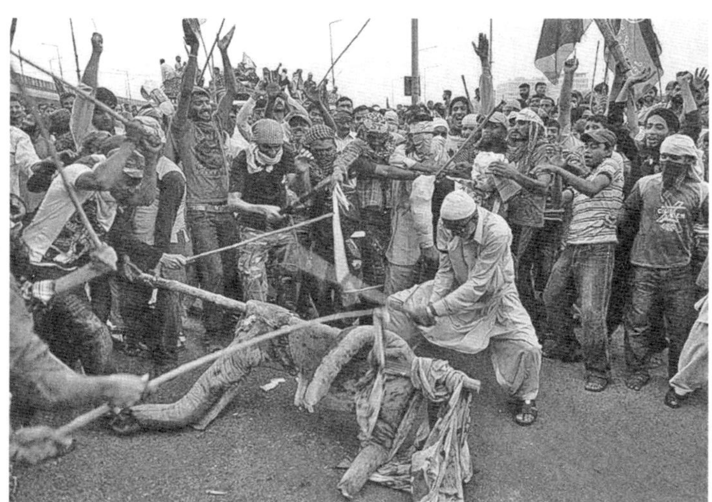

○ 2012_09_18_Pakistan: US President Obama

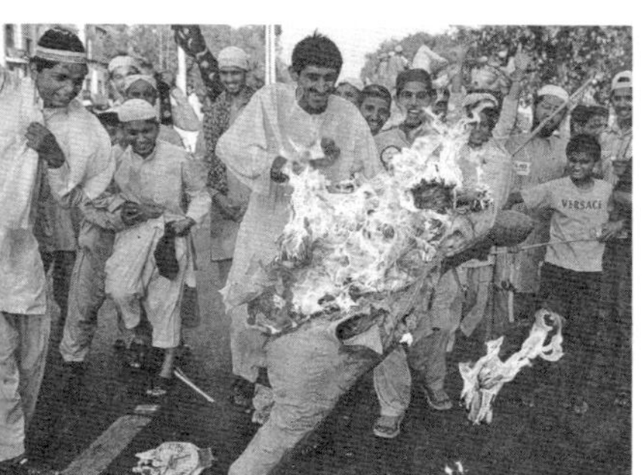

2010_05_00_Pakistan: US President Obama

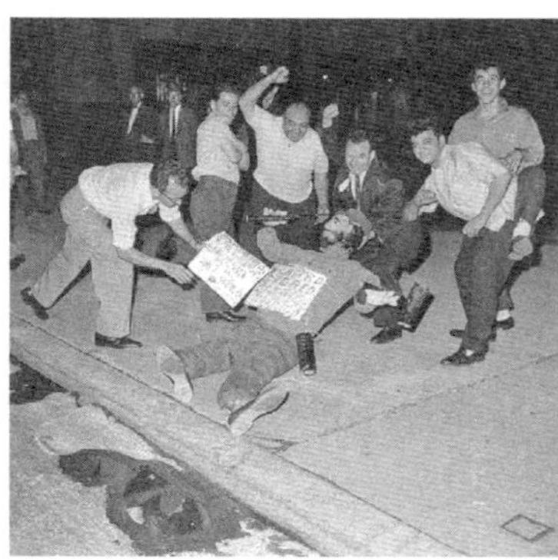

1960_07_26_USA-FL: Cuban President Castro

(b)

wrapped around the upper end of the pole. The protesters, mostly young men, carry green flags; many wear headbands with protest slogans and some have covered their faces. They are in a rambunctious mood, clapping, laughing, shouting, and cheering on the effigy's beating. The photograph gives the impression of a large crowd with an abundance of energy, more celebratory than angry, and keenly aware of their power as a group in that moment. Their sense of empowerment is gained through the staging of a fantasy: the imagined violent beating of their adversary as an act towards achieving justice.

Different motifs in the photographs of effigy protests create the impression of violence. These can deeply affect the viewer and contribute to the emotional charge of the pathos formulas of protest: (1) the burning human figure triggers the imagination of cruelty and suffering, expressing excessive symbolic violence and the power of the popular sovereign to punish the individual; (2) the hanging or battered effigy exhibits the violence enacted on it and represents the violent

241

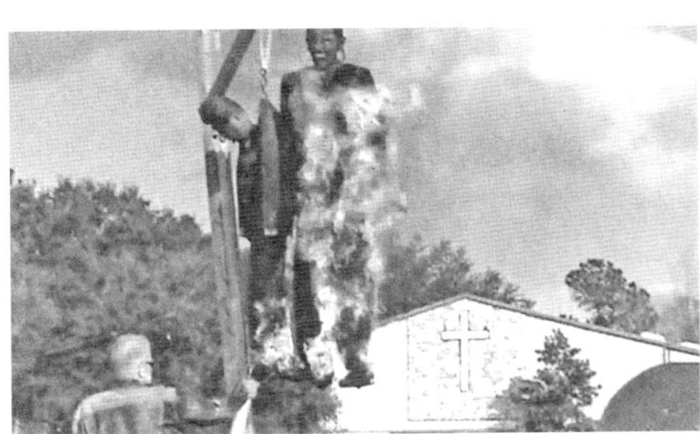
2013_01_28_USA-FL: Presidents Obama + Clinton

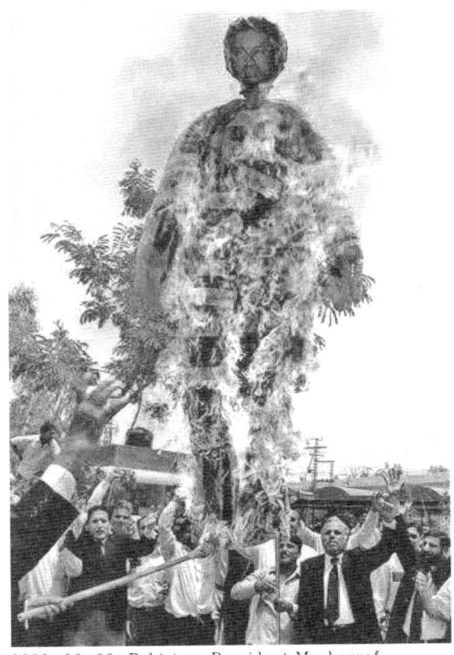
2008_06_09_Pakistan: President Musharraf

12 Aby Warburg, "Dürer und die italienische Antike," in Aby Warburg, *Gesammelte Schriften* (Leipzig: B. G. Teubner, 1932), 2:443–49.

transformation from animated being to thing – corpse – through objectification; and (3) the gestures of physical violence – punching, spitting, kicking, beating, hitting – the stick swung back, or suspended in its movement a fraction before impact on the body of the effigy evoke physical violence in action. This motif also appears in the images of the death of Orpheus around which art historian Aby Warburg built his famous text "Dürer und die Italienische Antike," where he used the term pathos formulas for the first time.○, 12

242

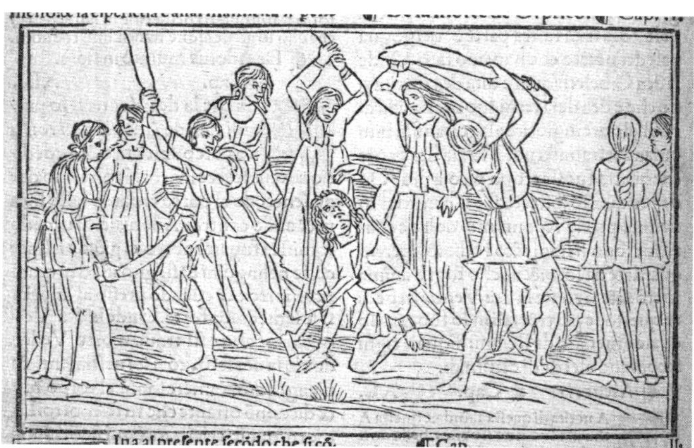

○ "The Death of Orpheus," Venice, 1501

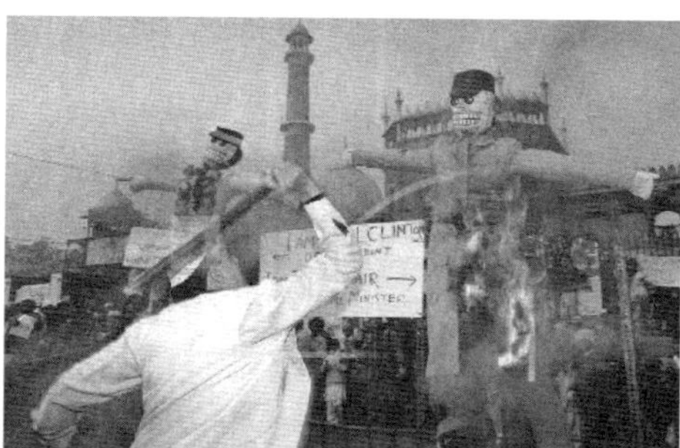

1998_12_18_India: US President Clinton

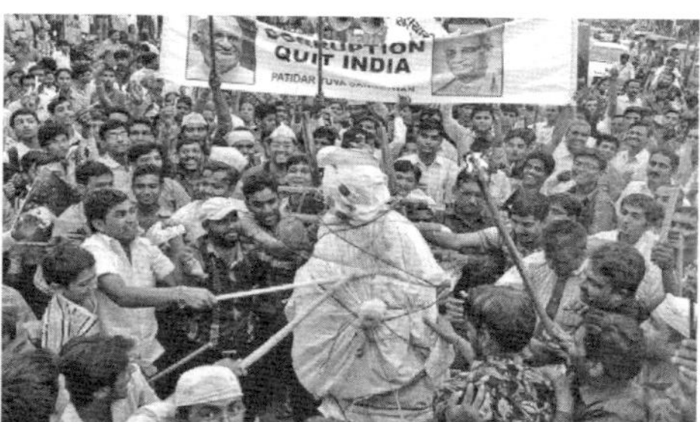

2011_08_24_India: "corruption"

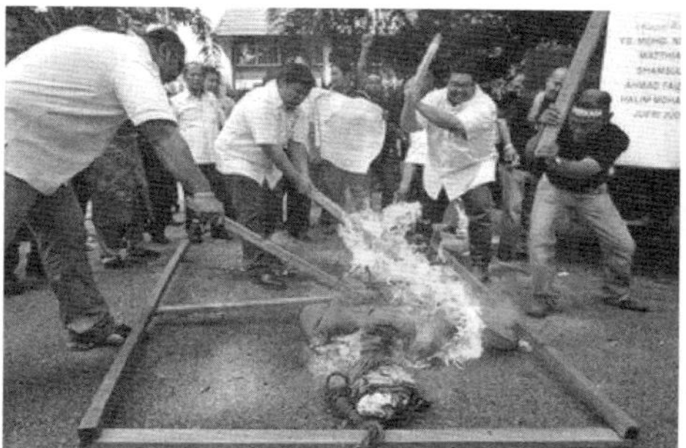

2010_06_07_Malaysia: Israeli Premier Netanyahu

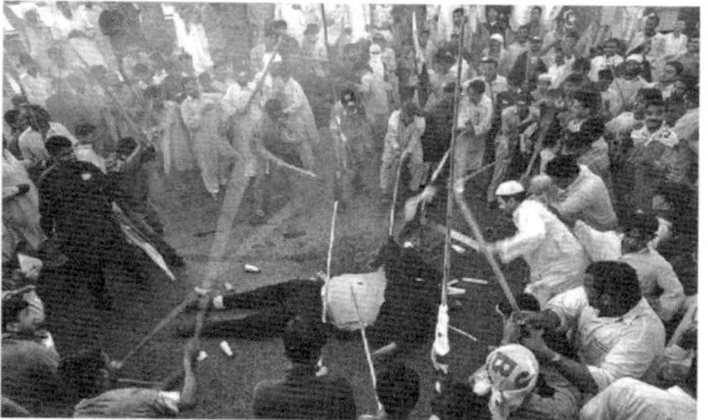

2006_02_24_Pakistan: Danish cartoonist

The people acting together, aroused by a common goal, emit the force of communal anger – and the violence that results from its release. This can be framed positively as the righteous and productive force against injustice and oppression, or negatively, as the oppressive and destructive violence of the mob punishing a transgression of communal order. In both versions, exclusion and violent punishment are staged as the resolution to the conflict and an appeal to justice is made, but the notions of justice are markedly different. In the first version, the appeal is directed toward justice as an imagined but possibly unachievable ideal; in the second, the appeal is directed toward justice as established by the existing order and current law.[13] Justice is revealed as a contested concept – framed by diverging discourses, contexts, and practices – that cannot be grasped outside its entanglement with power, violence, and the law.[14]

243

13 Étienne Balibar, "Introduction," in *The Borders of Justice*, ed. Étienne Balibar, Sandro Mezzadra, and Ranadir Samaddar (Philadelphia: Temple University Press, 2012), 5.

14 Étienne Balibar, "Justice and Equality: A Political Dilemma? Pascal, Plato, Marx," in *The Borders of Justice*, ed. Étienne Balibar, Sandro Mezzadra, and Ranadir Samaddar (Philadelphia: Temple University Press, 2012), 10.

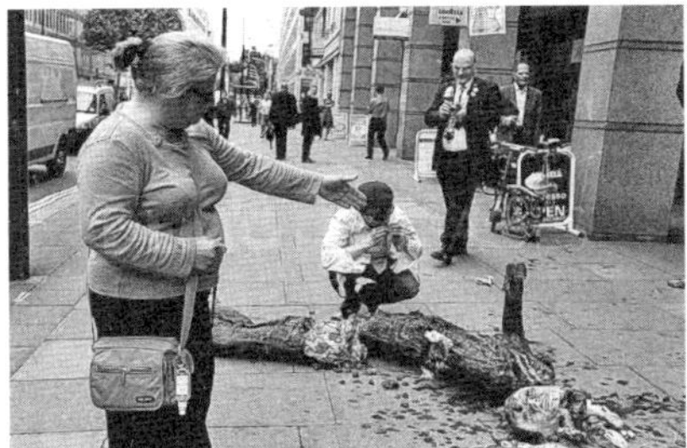

2009_06_00_UK: Premier Brown

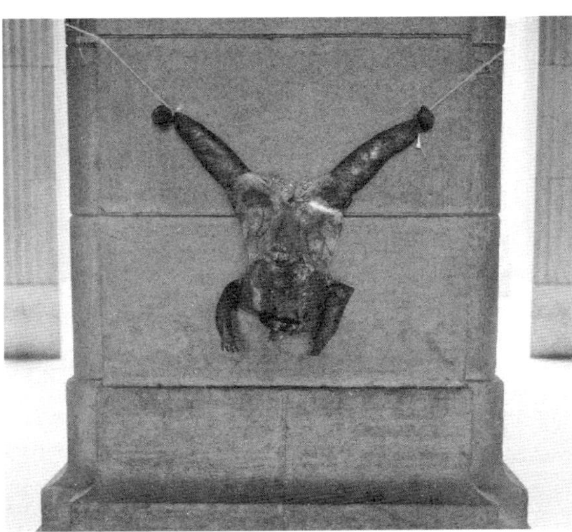

1959_01_00_Cuba: unkown effigy

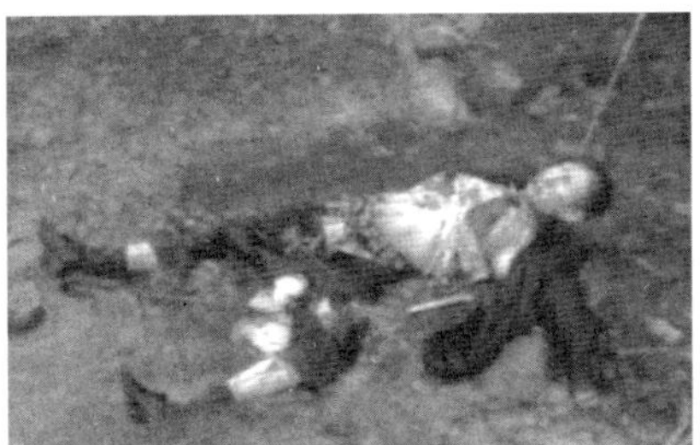

2012_04_28_North Korea: South Korean President Lee

(b)

15 Balibar, "Justice and Equality," 11.

16 Walter Benjamin "Critique of Violence," in *Selected Writings* (Cambridge, MA: Belknap Press, 1999), 1:284–86.

17 Balibar, "Justice and Equality," 14.

18 Balibar, "Justice and Equality," 28–29.

19 Étienne Balibar, "Some Questions on Politics and Violence," *Assemblage* 20 (1993): 12.

Political philosopher Étienne Balibar explores this entanglement in contemporary politics throughout his work. In the 2012 essay "Justice and Equality" he departs from a quote by philosopher Blaise Pascal, arguing that justice and power are necessarily linked.[15] On the one hand, any endeavor to establish a just order or to restore justice requires force. In the process, it will take on a form of organization and inevitably risks producing injustice itself. On the other hand, political power relies on the claim to justice for its legitimization. In that process, justice is institutionalized in the "rule of law," which creates its own contradictions.

Philosopher Walter Benjamin has argued in his 1921 essay "Zur Kritik der Gewalt" that instituting the law requires "law-making violence" and the existing order enacts "law-preserving violence" to ensure its perpetual existence.[16] Balibar agrees with Benjamin that there is no essential difference between law-preserving and law-making violence, and that any order of society, any system of law, is imbricated with violence. Yet, Balibar, thinking further in line with philosopher Jacques Derrida, observes that justice cannot be "expressed in legal terms and 'administered' as an object or a domain of conflictual interests in need of a mediation by the legal and especially the judiciary machine."[17] Justice is always in excess of the law. It can never be completely codified into law, and remains as a promise. Even though it can never be fully achieved, justice remains the lever that can be used to transform the system of law and make it more inclusive and just.[18]

Balibar argues that violence is associated with human experience and that some form and degree of it is unavoidable in the organization of the social. For him, "the question becomes, then: how to manage with violence under its different forms, how to choose among them and counter them."[19]

Balibar approaches the problem from the extremes to discover when violence becomes intolerable. He posits certain criteria to distinguish violence that is unavoidable in the practice of politics, from extreme un-civil and oppressive violence. Extreme, for instance, are forms of violence that make death more tolerable than life, but also insidious and relentless forms of violence of a lower degree, which make them "appear interminable, like a fate or an end in itself."[20] His ultimate criterion is that extreme violence aims toward the "annihilation of the possibilities of resistance."[21] The annihilation of resistance through a regime of violence also annihilates the space for politics. Therefore, resistance and revolt against oppressive regimes in pursuit of justice is necessary to safeguard the possibility of politics, even if revolt is always at risk of being turned into a new regime of violence.[22]

> In a world and a history irreparably marked by the existence of relationships of domination and violence, the possibility of politics is essentially bound up with practices of resistance, not only negatively, as the contestation of the established order, the demand for justice, and so on, but also positively, as a place where active subjectivities and collective solidarities are formed.[23]

Balibar argues for a politics of civility and the practice of "anti-violence," that is, the continuous work to reduce the violence of the existing order to achieve greater justice.[24] This politics of civility is set against the manifestations of violence exerted by the sovereign, state, or law. It is the work of civility to deconstruct the existing order and make its violence critically visible and further the conditions of the political.

All effigy protest performances announce violence with the punishment of the depicted. The question remains as to whether the theatrical executions of effigies are acts of

20　Étienne Balibar, "Violence and Civility: On the Limits of Political Anthropology," *differences: A Journal of Feminist Cultural Studies* 20, no. 2/3 (2009): 14.

21　Balibar, "Violence and Civility," 12.

22　Balibar, "Violence and Civility," 29.

23　Balibar, "Violence and Civility," 19.

24　Balibar, "Violence and Civility," 24–25.

25   J. L. Austin, *How To Do Things With Words* (Oxford: Clarendon Press, 1962), 5.

26   Judith Butler, *Excitable Speech: A Politics of the Performative* (London: Routledge, 1997), 51 (italics in the original).

resistance and necessary to make the political possible, or oppressive in and of themselves. In the chapter "Effigy Protests in the History of the United States" it became clear that effigy protests in the context of the demonstrations against integration in some United States's school systems contributed to the continued disenfranchisement and subjugation of African Americans. Other effigy protests did not pose an actual threat to the depicted powerful politicians, but were theatrical, non-violent expressions of discontent. This leads to the questions of when is the feigned violence visible in the staged executions merely symbolic, and under what conditions does it turn into actual oppressive violence? Or formulated differently: when do staged performances and images of burning effigies actually perform the violence they exhibit?

To make this distinction more clear, I turn to the notion of performativity, and consider effigy protests as speech acts. Speech is, as philosopher of language J. L. Austin shows, not just descriptive. It can, under certain conditions, become performative, meaning it can be an action and have real-life effects, like changing one's legal status from unmarried to married.[25] Philosopher Judith Butler further investigates the conditions of performativity in relation to hate speech in *Excitable Speech* (1997). She interrogates under which conditions speech becomes impermissible as actual violence. Butler reminds us here that not all performative acts are successful. She specifies that performative speech *"accumulates the force of authority through the repetition or citation of a prior and authoritative set of practices."*[26] That means that only if the speech act announcing violence is "authorized" by established practices, and believably invokes future injury, does it acquire performative force and becomes actual violence.

Oppressive Laughter

In 1956, a federal court ordered the desegregation of the only high school in Mansfield, a small Texas town near Fort Worth. The National Association for the Advancement of Colored People (NAACP) had initiated the lawsuit on behalf of African-American students as their daily commute to the nearest black high school in Fort Worth consisted of a long bus ride followed by a twenty block walk each way.[27] At the start of the school year, an angry mob of white residents gathered in front of the Mansfield High School and prevented the enrollment of black students. Three effigies depicting African-Americans were hanged, one on Mansfield High Street, one prominently on the flagpole of the school, and another over its main entrance. The Texas governor supported the protesters and dispatched a number of Texas

27 Robyn Duff Ladino, *Desegregating Texas Schools: Eisenhower, Shivers and the Crisis at Mansfield High* (Austin: University of Texas Press, 1996), 7.

247

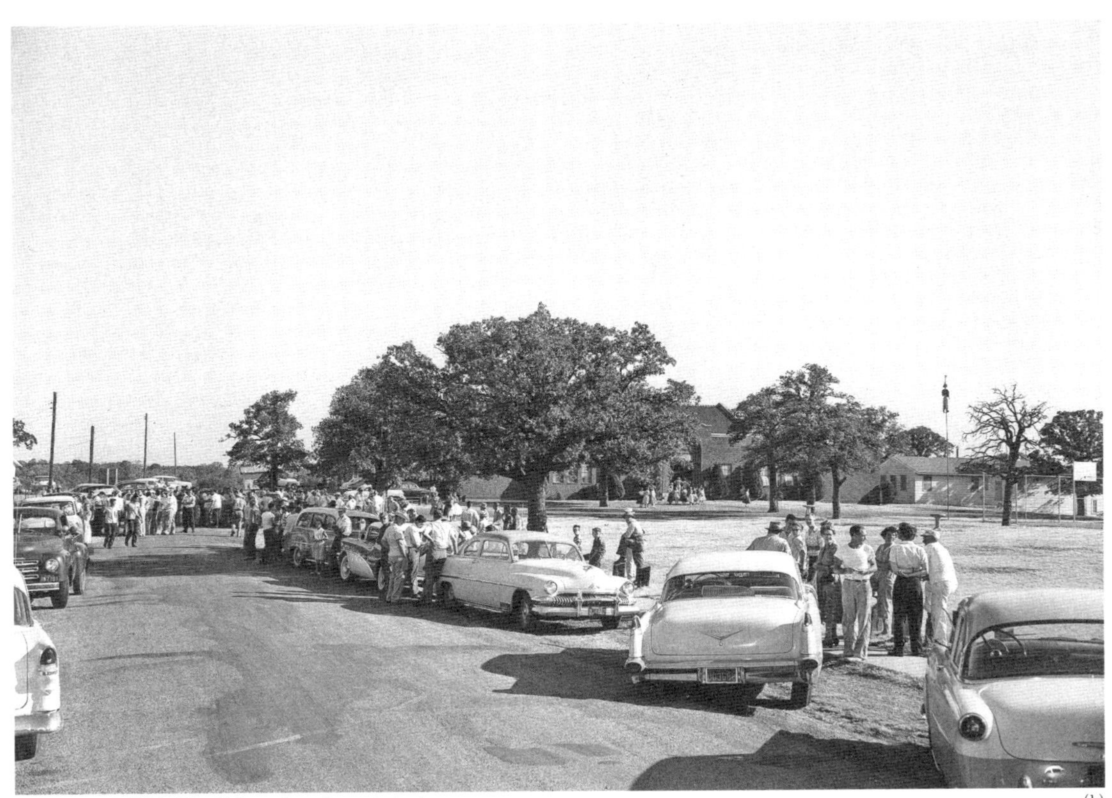

1956_08_30_USA-TX: African-American student

(b)

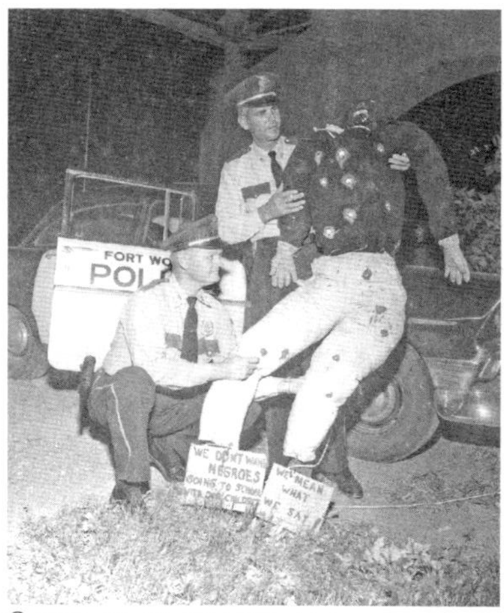
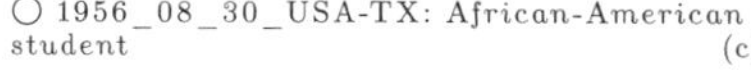

◯ 1956_08_30_USA-TX: African-American student (c)

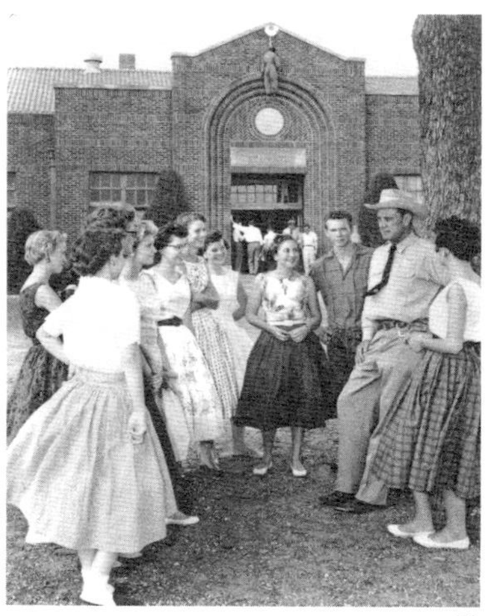

(d)

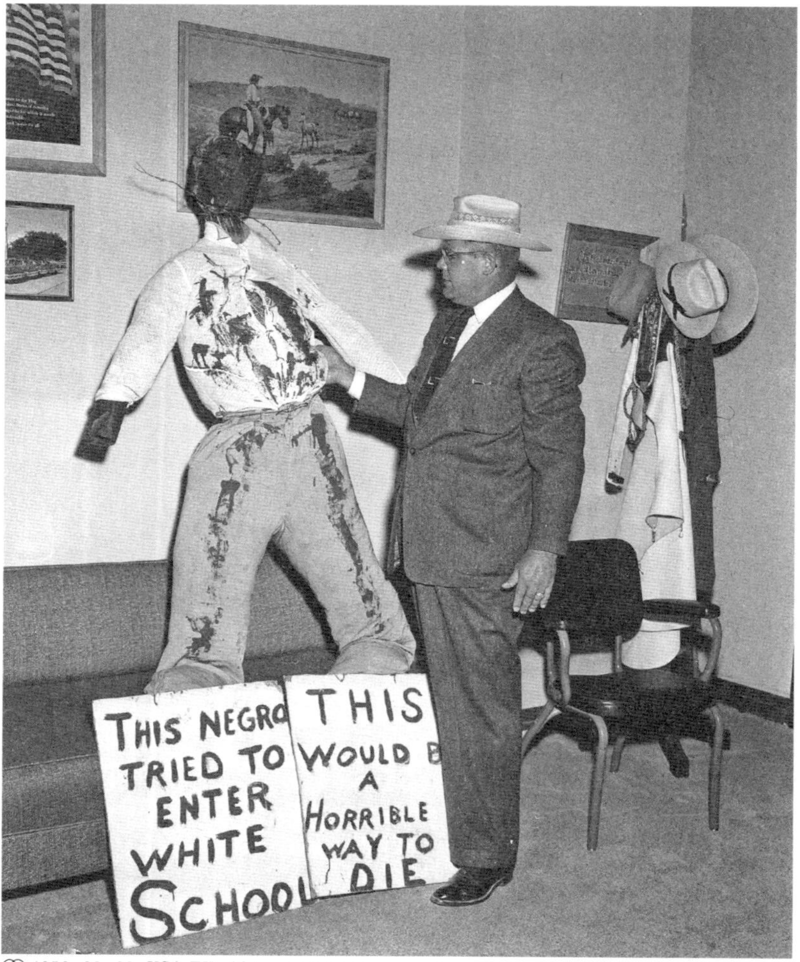

◯◯ 1956_08_30_USA-TX: African-American student (e)

Rangers to maintain order in front of the school. The protesters outside successfully prevented the African-American students from enrolling. The segregated status of the school was preserved for that year, and the federal court order was not enforced.

The collusion between town officials and the police force with the mob is visible in the photographs: the leisurely crowd in front of the school, unchallenged by the police; the local sheriff and a Texas Ranger posing for the camera under the hanging effigy, a smug smile on their faces indicative of their self-righteousness; the school girls and boy admiringly encircling a Texas Ranger; the sheriff and the two policemen posing with two effigies for the camera; the white school girls breezily entering the school building despite the effigy hanging above them. The scenes exude an air of normalcy, even a pleasant comfort with the actors paying little heed to a situation that is so charged with the violence of exclusion. The close-up photographs of two effigies show the mark of this systemic violence: one is riddled with round holes encircled with red paint, signifying bullet holes, the other with jagged tears and red paint to signify stab wounds and spattered blood.○, ○○ The signs at the effigies' feet carry threats that the white population will not tolerate the enrollment of black students and would resort to extreme physical violence to stop it.

These displays were not so much a political protest, but a forceful demonstration of existing race relations. The effigies in Mansfield and the many other "un-civil rights" effigies detailed in chapter "Effigy Protests in the History of the United States" were performed in continuity with the history of subjugation of the African-American population, from slavery to lynching, from the Jim Crow laws to the continued discrimination of African-Americans up to the present day. Authorized by these established oppressive practices, effigy

28 Martha C. Nussbaum, "Objectification," *Philosophy & Public Affairs* 24, no. 4 (1995): 257; Balibar, "Violence and Civility," 13.

29 "Belfast Situation Shorter Version Of Grave Riots In Belfast (1920)," *British Pathé*, 1920 (digitized film), british-pathe.com, film ID: 212.43; media urn: 21568.

performances in this political context were successfully performative in Butler's sense: they were not just symbolic expressions of violence, but violent acts themselves.

The hanging effigies displayed and enacted the exclusionary violence of US society, robbing African-American students of their status as political beings, denying their autonomy, and objectifying them – literally turning them into things to be violated.[28] The threats of violence were widely directed to include allied civil rights activists who challenged the unjust order. These displays represent Balibar's extreme violence, annihilating the possibility of resistance to a regime in which life is unlivable. This violence is coupled with denigrating laughter conveying the supremacy of the white population and subjugating the Other.

There are other examples of similarly violent and subjugating effigy protests from other countries. In 1920, amidst widespread sectarian violence during the Irish War of Independence, supporters of the Union with Britain hanged their Nationalist neighbors in effigy as warnings. An intertitle of the British Pathé newsreel reads: "Effigies dangling from windows are familiar sights in the streets of Belfast."[29] After the vote to reintegrate the Saarland into the German Reich in 1935, Nazis celebrated and dragged effigies of Max Braun, editor of social-democratic newspaper *Deutsche Freiheit*, through the streets. Braun had agitated against

250

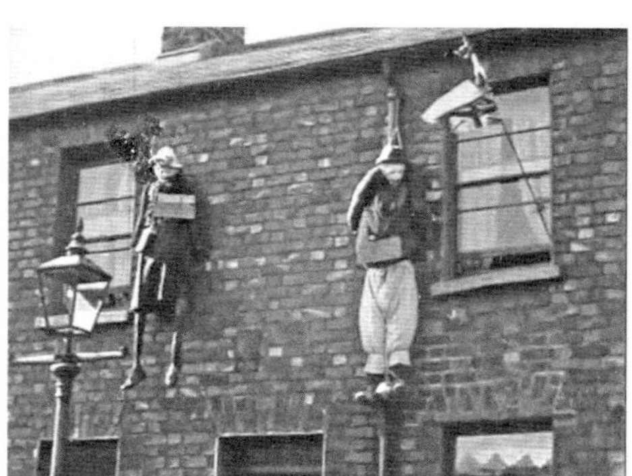

1920_09_06_Belfast, Northern Ireland: Nationalist residents

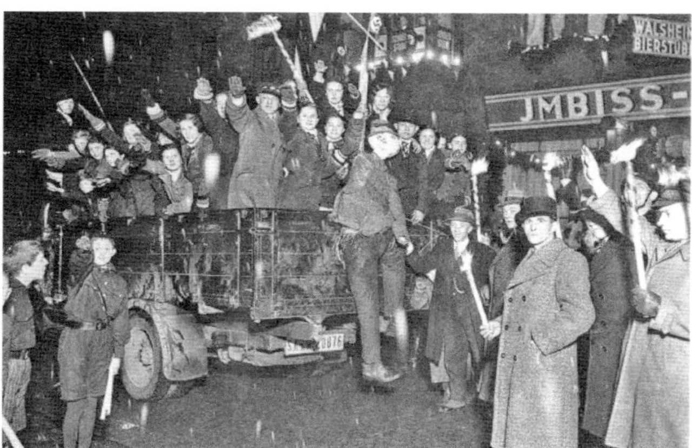

1935_01_22_Germany: editor Max Braun

reunification and evaded arrest and almost certain death in prison by escaping to France. In 2013, a group of students at a madrassa in Bangladesh beat and burned the effigy of an "atheist blogger." They reacted to demonstrations demanding tougher punishments for Islamic militia leaders responsible for war crimes committed during the Indo-Pakistani War of 1971. In 2015, a number of bloggers advocating for a secular Bangladesh were killed by Islamist activists. In all these cases, effigies were performed in the context of an established oppressive order and reiterating other authoritative practices. These manifestations have to be considered as successful speech acts, and constitute extreme violence. Their grotesque aesthetics, performance of violence, and denigrating laughter work in unison to subjugate the targeted group or individual.

251

30 Cade Johnson, "About 70 protest UC Berkeley professor Judith Butler's conference in Brazil," *Daily Californian* (Berkley), November 8, 2017, http://www.dailycal.org/2017/11/08/protesters-gather-at-conference-organized-by-campus-professor-judith-butler-in-brazil/.

31 Patty Loew and James Thannum, "After the Storm: Ojibwe Treaty Rights Twenty-Five Years after the Voigt Decision," *The American Indian Quarterly* 35, no. 2 (2011): 172–72.

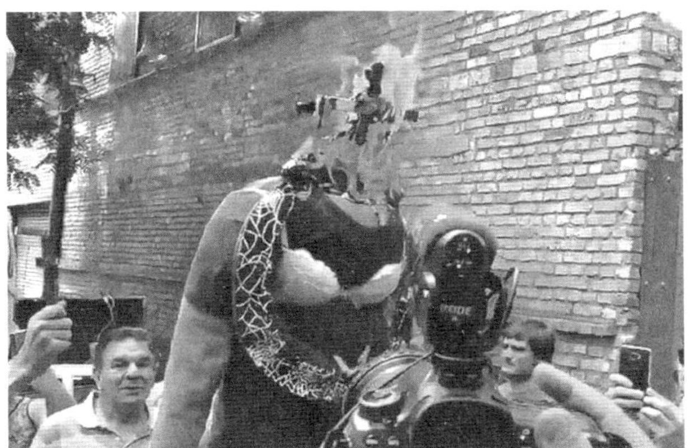

2017_11_08_Brazil: philosopher Judith Butler

A group of right-wing protesters brandished crucifixes, burned an effigy of Judith Butler and shouted: "Queimam a bruxa!" (Portuguese for "Burn the Witch!" in protest of Butler's gender theory. The protest took place in front of the venue for the conference "The End of Democracy" in Sao Paolo, Brazil, which Butler had organized. Butler called the burning of the effigy "injurious" and "upsetting."[30]

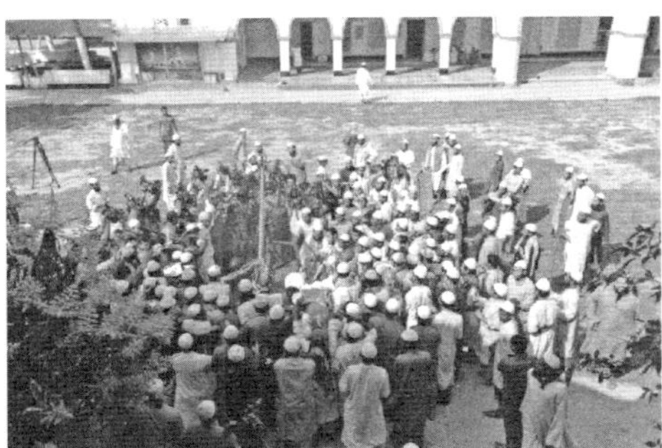

2013_02_24_Bangladesh: "atheist blogger"

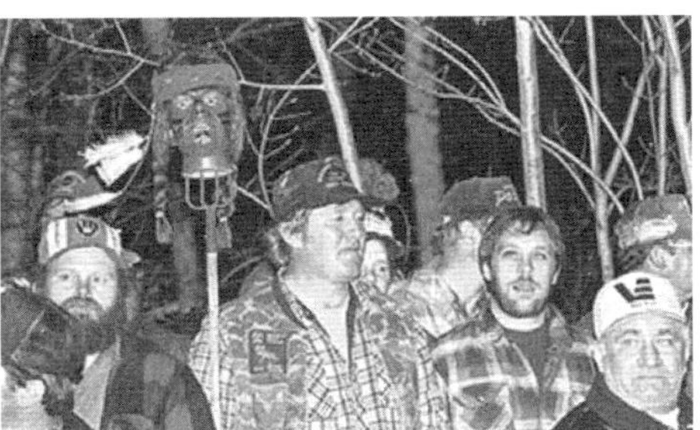

1989_05_00_USA-WI: Native American

Protesters displaying a speared head at a Wisconsin boat landing harass members of the Ojibwa tribe, who exercise their right to harvest fish in the Lac du Flambeau by spear fishing.[31]

The distinction between successful and unsuccessful speech acts, violent and symbolic effigy protests, is not always so clear, since it requires the evaluation of their "authorization." Furthermore, the character of effigy protests can change, as the previously cited examples of protests against Salman Rushdie's novel *The Satanic Verses* (1988) show. While effigy burnings of Rushdie were early on rather symbolic expressions demanding recognition of Muslim identity in British public life, Ayatollah Khomeini's fatwa calling on Muslims worldwide to kill the author changed their character dramatically. Since the fatwa was linked to the Ayatollah Khomeini's authority as an eminent Muslim cleric and the Supreme Leader of Iran, and incentivized by a US$ 1 million reward, the protests and effigy burnings became an imminent and believable threat against Rushdie's life – "authorized," they exerted oppressive violence. It is therefore necessary to carefully consider the constellation of actors in the network of power relations in each case to assess the kind of violence performed.

Liberating Laughter

In 1967, African-American students at Princeton University hanged an effigy of George Wallace, the former governor of Alabama and then a presidential candidate.○ With a protest sign reading: "Black Princeton in the Nation's Service" and T-shirts with "Black Dada" written across, they protested against a representative of state power who had fiercely opposed the desegregation of public schools in Alabama. In 1968, students of Johnson C. Smith University in Charlotte, North Carolina, burned an effigy of South Carolina Governor Robert Evander McNair in a demonstration protesting the

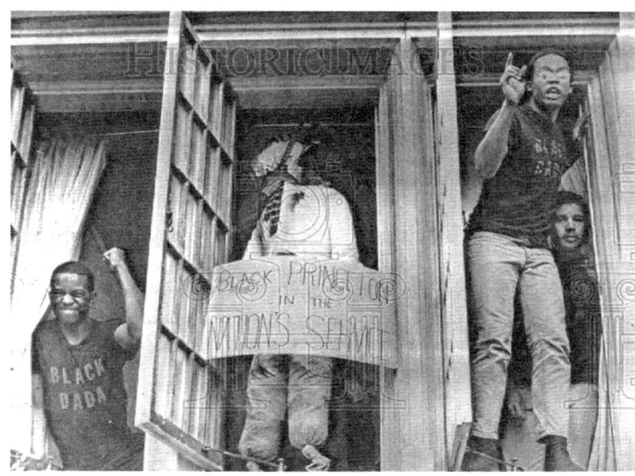
○ 1967_05_11_USA-NJ: former Alabama Governor Wallace

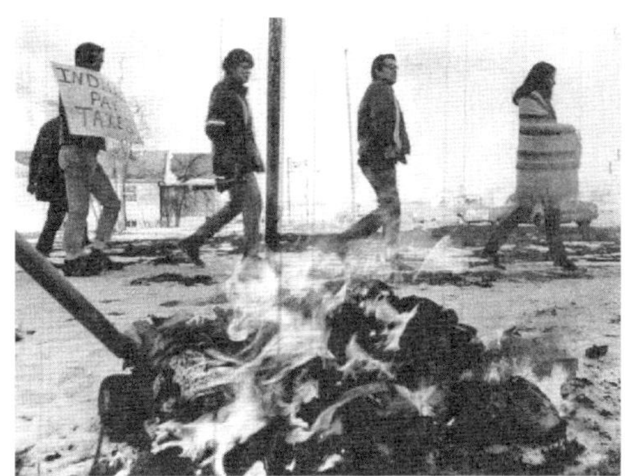
1970_03_21_USA-CO: Indian Affairs Commissioner

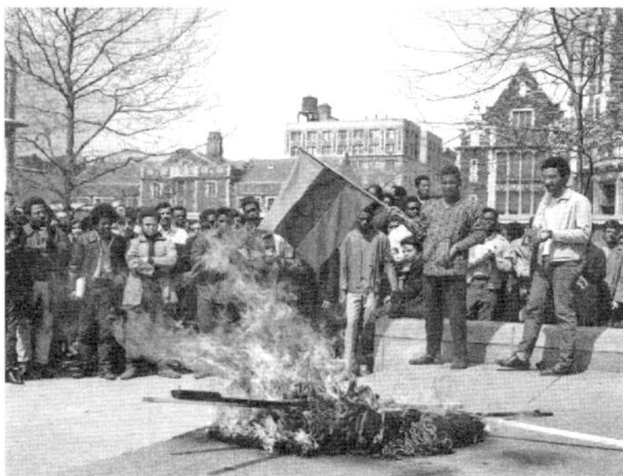
1969_04_21_USA-NY: "racism"

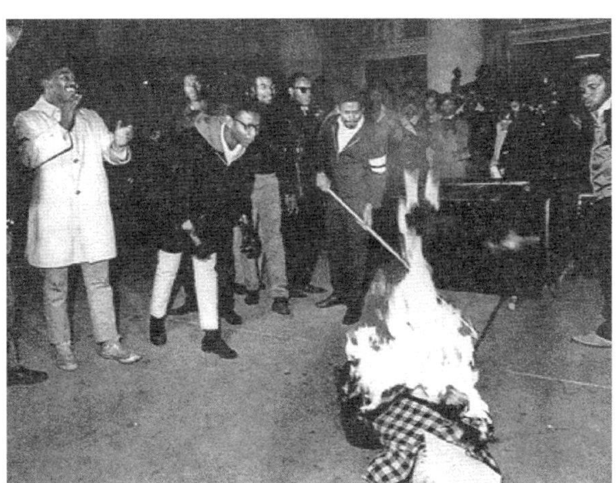
1968_02_16_USA-SC: Governor McNair

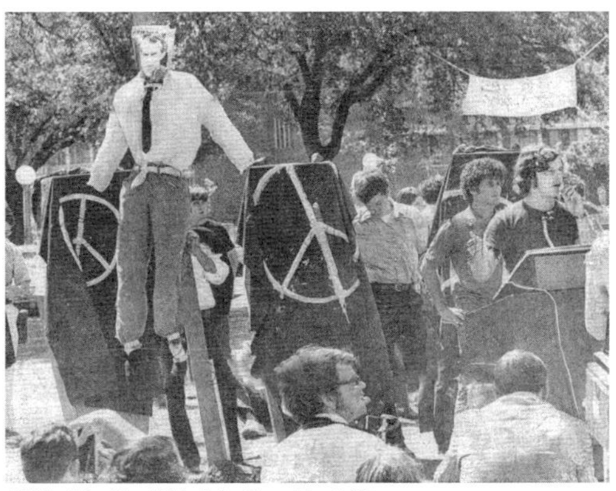
1970_05_05_USA-LA: President Nixon

deaths of three students in Orangeburg, South Carolina killed by law enforcement during a demonstration against racial discrimination. In 1969, African-American students at the City College of New York burned an effigy of "racism" as part of larger student movement demanding racial parity and more participation in college and university affairs. In 1970, indigenous peoples burned an effigy of the Commissioner for Indian Affairs in Littleton, Colorado to protest the discriminatory hiring and promotion practices of the Bureau of Indian Affairs. With these protests, civil rights activists appropriated earlier subjugating effigy protests and turned them upside down, contesting the existing relation of domination in order to demand change. In carnivalesque reversal, the violence inherent in the unjust order was turned back onto the figure of power and made visible on the body of the effigy. In that sense, both forms of effigy protest make the same violence visible, but in opposite constellations. Un-civil rights demonstrations affirm and exert exclusionary violence, a form of extreme violence that according to Balibar precludes the possibility of politics. Civil rights demonstrations on the other hand denounce and resist this exclusionary violence.

254

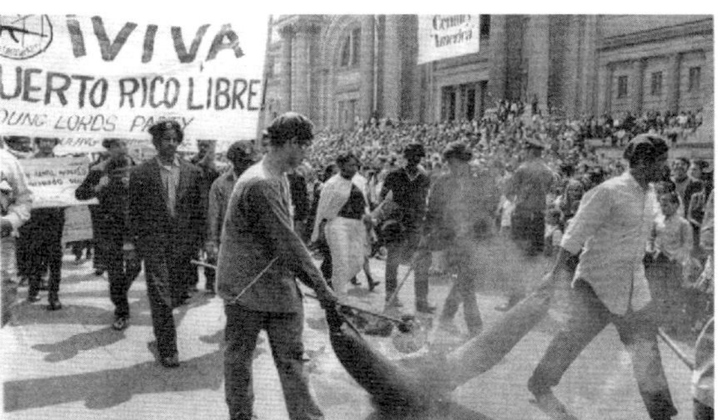

1970_06_07_USA-NY: mayor Lindsay

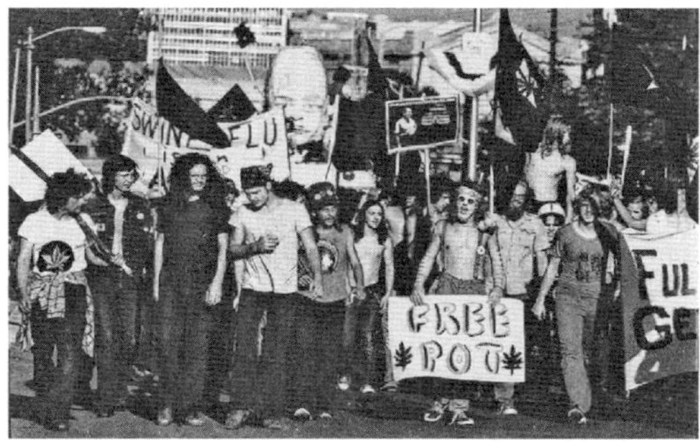

1976_00_00_USA-MS: President Ford

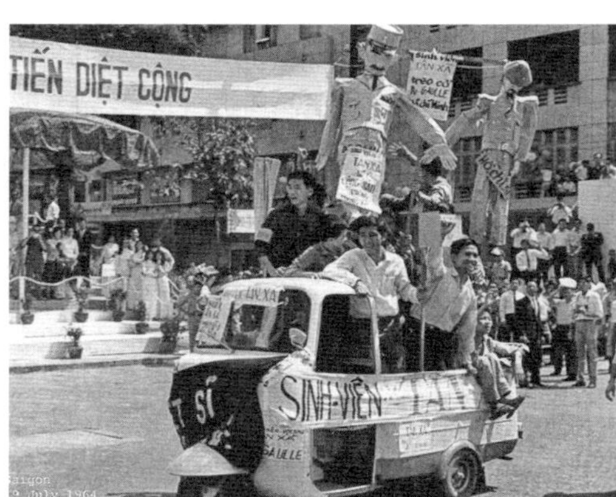

1964_07_19_Vietnam: CPV chairman Hồ Chí Minh + French President de Gaulle

While the two forms produce similar images of violence and both attempt the debasement of the depicted, they should not be considered as equally violent in form and degree. Since effigy performances in civil rights protests do not rely on any established authoritative practice, according to Butler's criteria, they are not successfully performative: they only exert symbolic violence. This also holds true for anti-Vietnam War effigy protests from 1965 until 1973 grounded in 1960s and '70s counterculture. These protests stage an imaginary alternative order with laughter as a weapon against the established power, forming subjectivities and collective solidarities. Following Balibar's arguments, they are forms of civic engagement that critically address the violence in society, legitimate forms of resistance necessary to make politics possible.

In traditional European carnival practices, the burning of effigies represents a symbolic punishment that serves as a means for ritual purification of the community. As part of the cycle of life, symbolic death becomes the prerequisite for rebirth and renewal. Literary theorist Mikhail Bakhtin, an influential thinker on carnival, which he does not situate in a specific place or time, proclaims that during carnival, the "unofficial" but "real life of the people" emerges and turns the world upside down.[32] Bakhtin embraced the literary violence of French Renaissance writer François Rabelais. In his novels, dirt and excrement, filth and excess, are all enveloped in roaring life-affirming laughter. It is an unruly laughter, characterized by bodily excess, disorder, and grotesque abundance. The laughter of carnival, expressed as bodily excess coupled with violence, becomes a resistant force against the existing order, any order. Many critics of Bakhtin point out that his analysis is based on Renaissance literature instead of existing carnival practices.[33] Indeed, he fails to take into account the temporality and liminality of carnival, the fact

255

32 Bakhtin, *Rabelais and His World*, 6–11.

33 For a detailed discussion of this dispute, see the introduction to Peter Stallybrass and Allon White, *The Politics and Poetics of Transgression* (New York: Cornell University Press, 1986), 1–26.

34 Veronika Zangl and Sruti Bala, "Editorial: Humour in Art and Activism," *European Journal of Humour Research* 3 (2016): 1–6.

35 Stallybrass and White, *The Politics and Poetics of Transgression*, 15.

36 Baz Kershaw, "Fighting in the Streets: Dramaturgies of Popular Protest 1968–1989," *New Theatre Quarterly* 13, no. 51 (1997): 261.

37 Kershaw, "Fighting in the Streets," 262.

38 Benjamin Shepard, *Queer Political Performance and Protest* (New York: Routledge, 2010), 2.

39 Claire Tancons, "Occupy Wall Street: Carnival Against Capital? Carnivalesque as Protest Sensibility," *e-flux journal* 30, no. 12 (2011).

40 Leila Nachwati, "Kafranbel: a paradigm of creative storytelling," *openDemocracy*, September 30, 2014, www.opendemocracy.net/north-africa-west-asia/leila-nachawati/kafranbel-paradigm-of-creative-storytelling-part-12.

41 Tancons, "Occupy Wall Street"; and Andrew Robinson, "In Theory Bakhtin: Carnival against Capital, Carnival against Power," *Ceasefire Magazine*, September 9, 2011, ceasefiremagazine.co.uk/in-theory-bakhtin-2/.

that carnival usually ends and order is re-established at the close of the cycle.

Nevertheless, carnival can be seen as a corrective imaginary that uniquely combines the strategies of reversal and debasement with the aesthetics of the grotesque. This imaginary can be activated against the oppressive order. Many scholars recognize the potential of theatrical, parodic, and carnivalesque strategies in protest movements of the twentieth and twenty-first century.[34] Literary theorists Peter Stallybrass and Allon White conceive Bakhtin's carnival as "a mobile set of symbolic practices, images and discourses," which can be employed in social revolts and conflicts.[35] There are many instances in which the carnivalesque has manifested itself in political protests: in 1968, when Parisian protesters dressed in costumes taken from a theatre wardrobe fought the police[36]; in 1970, during the occupation of the White House lawn in Washington in a Vietnam War protest[37]; in the 1990s exuberant Drag Marches for global social justice in New York[38]; and in the 2011 parodic performances during Occupy Wall Street in New York.[39] The carnivalesque is also present in the online cartoon protests that activists in Kafr Nabl, Syria staged from 2011 until 2017 in protest against President Bashar al-Assad's ruthless campaign against his own people.[40]

These protests, and most effigy performances, introduce elements of absurdity, play, and laughter in the face of state violence, which disrupts fixed divisions between protesters and police during protests and challenges the validity of the established political discourse.[41] It is also true that the un-civil-rights effigy protests I address before include elements of absurdity and laughter, but in their alignment with the existing dominant order, these demonstrations miss one crucial element of the carnivalesque: the reversal of order.

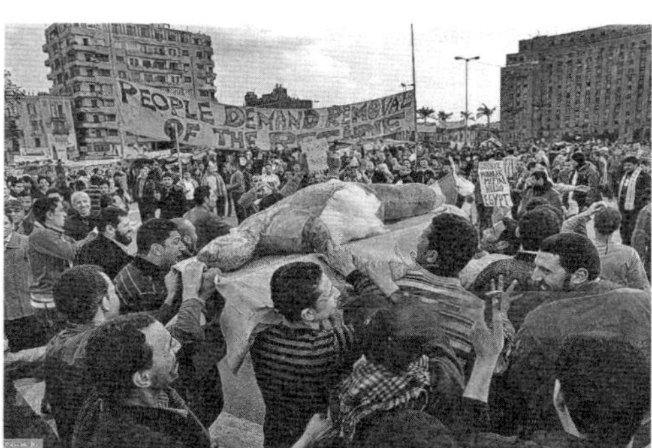

2011_02_07_Egypt: President Mubarak

The bodily aspects that carnivalesque violence and laughter emphasize are also important in Butler's reworking of philosopher Hannah Arendt's "space of appearance" during political protest. Butler stresses the importance of bodily presence in political protests as "political claims are made by bodies as they appear and act."[42] Critiquing Arendt, she points out that the space of appearance cannot be taken for granted for beings excluded from political recognition. It is the pre-political, private body with its material needs for food, defecation, sleep, and protection from violence that conditions the social and political body. It is the presence of the "bodies with needs, desires and requirements" that are able to create a new space of appearance. The unruly carnivalesque laughter at a protest accentuates the bodily presence of protesters, and it is especially these corporeal aspects that grant laughter its liberating potential. Performance theorist Allen S. Weiss writes that "laughter is one of the modes of sovereign conduct, a moment in which rationality is exceeded by a gratuitous affirmation of life, of contingency, of the body."[43] This corporeal laughter is mirrored in the corporeal violence enacted on the effigies whose power is contested. In the performative presence of bodies laughing and acting together, acting bodily with and on other bodies, a new space of appearance is created, constituted by inclusive alliances and a claim of equality.[44] This kind of laughter is indeed liberating — even if only for the short time-space of the protest. Butler emphasizes the transitory character of the time of protest when she writes: "Perhaps these are anarchist moments or anarchist passages, when the legitimacy of a regime is called into question, but when no new regime has yet come to take its place. This time of the interval is the time of the popular will, not a single will, not a unitary will, but one that is characterized by an alliance with the performative power to

257

42   Judith Butler, "Bodies in Alliance and the Politics of the Street," *transversal* (2011).

43   Allen S. Weiss, "Impossible Sovereignty: Between 'The Will to Power' and 'The Will to Chance'," *October* 36 (Cambridge, MA: MIT Press, 1986), 140.

44   Butler, "Bodies in Alliances."

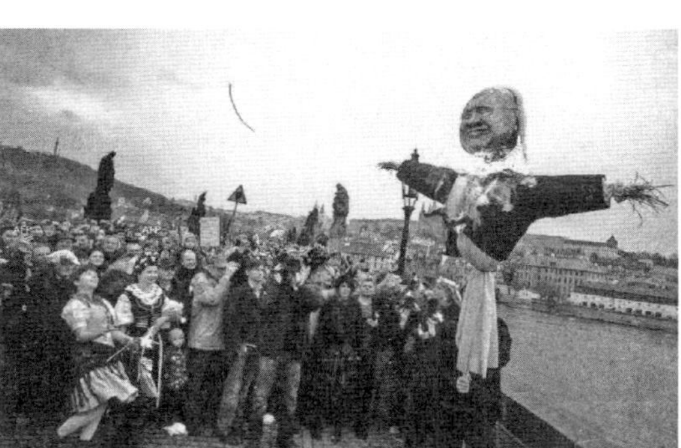

2013_03_07_Czech Rep: President Klaus as Morena

45 Butler, "Bodies in
Alliances."

lay claim to the public in a way that is not yet codified into law, and that can never be fully codified into law."[45] This liminal "time of the popular will" is in parallel to the liminal time of carnival. Both carry the revolutionary potential to challenge existing power constellations, time-spaces that have the potential to be transformative, even if never realized. Carnivalesque protests do not directly effect change; they can only show the possibility of a different order.

Not all effigy protests, however, divide neatly into subjugating demonstrations that enforce exclusionary order and liberating protest performances that aim to reconfigure social and political formation. Many effigy demonstrations don't operate in either side of this binary but work inside the accepted space of politics. On numerous occasions politicians are criticized and ridiculed with effigy protests in partisan politics. These performances do not propose a new constellation of the political formations, or a necessarily more just society, but only aim to shift dominance from one established group to another.

This is often true for effigy protests that denounce the leader of a foreign country. The demonstrations in Iraq against Bush were protests against the invasion of Iraqi politics and life by a foreign superpower, but the organizing political group of Muqtada al-Sadr was already a powerful faction in Iraqi politics, who staged demonstrations to

258

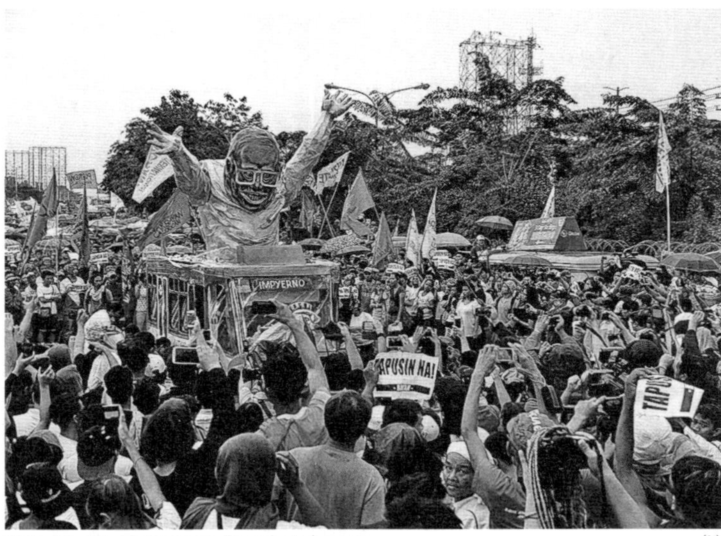

consolidate its position. Equally, effigy protests that target government officials in a country are not necessarily a form of protest that seeks to make society more just. Even though Obama effigies hanged in the US between 2008 and 2016 were not a believable threat to the President, they should be considered hate speech that performed actual violence toward African Americans. As these repeated earlier, subjugating practices and were connected to the "birther movement" aimed at delegitimizing the first African-American president, they exhibited and enacted pervasive discriminatory attitudes in US society.

In all cases the grotesque performance of an effigy is demeaning and insulting to whomever is depicted. The relation between laughter and violence is often an uneasy and unstable alliance, complicated and painful. In the best cases, effigy protest performances present the possibility for a different order and open up the space for change and greater justice. In the worst cases, they are tools for continued oppression. In between, they are distastefully crude or appropriately rude spectacles, ridiculing public figures who abuse their authority. It is therefore necessary to evaluate the social and political formation in which an effigy is performed in order to judge: how it affects social relations; the kind of violence; if the violence is permissible because necessary to ensure the conditions of the political or impermissible as an extreme form of subjugation; and if it is accompanied by the cruel laughter that assumes supremacy, or the liberating laughter of resistance that creates the very possibility of politics.

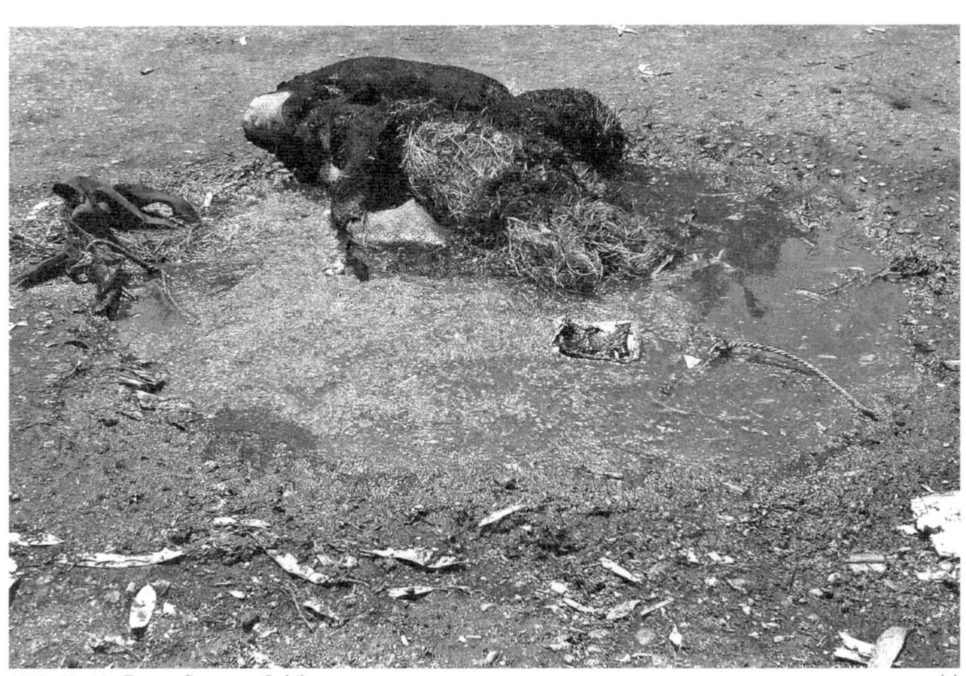

2010_05_12_ Egypt: Governor Labib

(a)

Conclusion

This study aimed to investigate a specific theatrical form of political protest: the execution of effigies by hanging, burning, or otherwise, and has brought together a vast number of records detailing effigy protests across time and geography. So many different conflicts, so many different iterations and variations of effigy protests, that it seems impossible to reduce effigy protests to merely one form. An archaic practice, rooted in different cultural and religious traditions, that also functions perfectly in the framework of contemporary news media for short-term political effect. A practice used in support of oppressive order by threatening violence or, contrastingly, in resistance to systemic violence.

Nonetheless, this study has shown that the hanging and burning of effigies remains recognizable across time and geography as one practice. It is consistent in that it communicates anger about what the protesters deem politically unjust. It is consistent in its scenario, the theatrical performance of punishment, which lends itself to appropriation and inversion. It is consistent in the shared grotesque aesthetic and in the uneasy combination of violence and laughter these performances exhibit.

The methodology for this study developed from my artistic practice focused on image practices in relation to the public sphere and is part of a growing range of practices of artistic research investigating existing material from archives, news media or social media. Ordering and arranging the images following themes derived from a close reading, led to diverse perspectives and inroads into the fields of anthropology, history, performance studies, iconology, art history, and political philosophy. Each perspective has been necessary to establish the framework of the study and each is crucial in understanding effigy protests – their histories and genealogies, form and aesthetics, affordances and effects.

Because the research is based on associatively organized image assemblages, it did not develop linearly in disciplinary frameworks. Instead the arguments in each chapter follows their own logic, intersect at different points of the text and complement each other. The composition of the image narrative, the size and arrangement of images in relation to each other and the text in the confines of the layout, is essential. Image narrative and text are like the two voices in a musical composition, each in turn taking the lead to introduce themes, structure the work, direct the reader, set tempo and rhythm, halt the attention or accelerate the flow.

The broad trans-disciplinary approach means some potentially relevant questions were left unanswered, and further research is warranted. It would be illuminating to study effigy protest even more closely in relation to Aby Warburg's concepts of *Bilderfahrzeug* (image vehicle) and *pathos formula*, as touched on in this text. Further in-depth case studies of single countries would more clearly show the practice's specificities. In India and Pakistan, for instance, effigy-burning is an incredibly vibrant political practice. In the Philippines, effigy protests against consecutive governments have developed into elaborate spectacles since the 1990s. In European countries, they have a very long and varied history, closely connected to formal and popular justice. A question guiding a comparative approach could be: what are the different imaginaries of justice that underlie effigy performance in different cultural contexts? Further theoretical work would also be fruitful in relation to affect theory, in order to investigate the effects of live performances and media reports on actors and audiences. Equally promising would be an investigation from the perspective of the agency of images, since the effigies function as semi-autonomous agents in the performance of protest.

Mobile Protest Practice

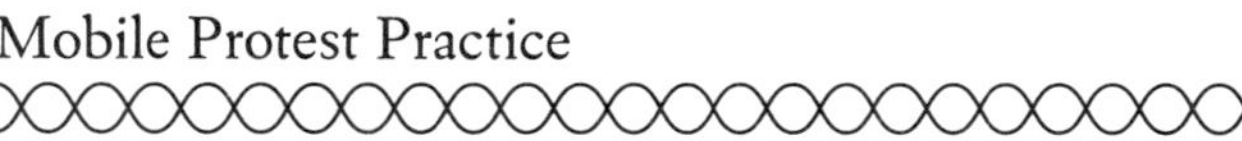

What this study has done is confirm that the burning and hanging of effigies as political protest is active, and alive in many regions: specific genealogies, practices, purposes, and means of dissemination emerged, enabling interpretations along various trajectories. In the case studies in chapters 3 and 4, I delineated different genealogies and modes of transfer. In the United States, the practice adapted traditional social or religious ritual to fit the purposes of political protest, and during the American Revolution embraced popular justice practices and the carnivalesque from colonial Pope Day celebrations. This also happened in Iran, where the carnivalesque Ashura tradition of *Umar Kushan*, which ridiculed a past enemy, was most likely appropriated in protests against the US during the Iranian Revolution in 1979. Cross-cultural appropriation occurred at the same time with Afghani students and refugees outside of Afghanistan protesting against the Soviet invasion of their country. Sixty years earlier, protesters in Port Said, Egypt likely copied British soldiers celebrating Guy Fawkes Day and the end of wwi by burning effigies of Kaiser Wilhelm II, appropriating it to protest British colonial rule during the Egyptian revolution from 1919.

The media's wide reporting on effigy protests during the American Revolution led to the form's spread across the colonies and establishment as a common practice in us politics. Similarly, us reporting on the hostage crisis in Tehran in 1979 of Iranian protesters burning effigies of us president Carter, sparked counter-protests in the us featuring effigies of Ayatollah Khomeini. Effigy demonstrations that triumphantly celebrated the end of the Suez crisis in Egypt in 1956, were widely shared by the media and most likely contributed to the dissemination of the practice in the Middle East in relation to the conflict with Israel. During the Arab Spring in 2011, reports of effigy executions in Cairo's Tahrir Square possibly inspired actors in Libya and Syria to do likewise with their leaders, or at least reactivated the memory of the genre from earlier iterations in the region.

While the practice is often adapted from traditional practices and celebrations, it also shows the tendency to develop back into commemorative traditions: in Iran, burning Uncle Sam and us presidents in effigy became a fixed feature of the commemorations of the Iranian Revolution; and in Egypt, the first recorded effigy protest that saw British Field Marshall Lord Allenby burned became an integral part of the spring festival in Port Said. Similarly, the effigy burning on Guy Fawkes Day in the United Kingdom changed its character over time. Initiated in 1606 as an anti-Catholic demonstration, it largely lost its political urgency and gradually transformed into a carnival tradition with political overtones. This study shows that performing an effigy as political protest is dynamically shaped by cultural and political parameters. The practice can be easily adapted to various needs in different cultural and political contexts. As a symbolic and visual practice, it affords image-based (non-language) cross-cultural communication and exchange.

The Performance of Resistance

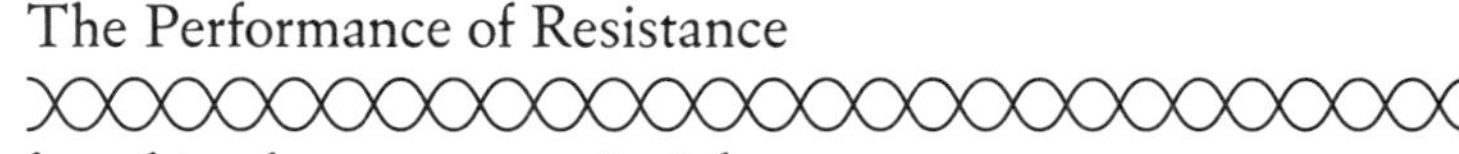

The lens of performance introduced in chapter 2 gave insight into the effects of the practice on those involved, and the relation between live protests and reporting in the news. Staging the conflict and its resolution as a performance of punishment makes the conflict concrete and tangible. The participants step out of everyday life and take up a role in the performance, which leads to a high degree of engagement with the protest and its goals. This engagement creates embodied memories, increases the participant's identification with the group, and strengthens group identity.

Yet the performances are staged to communicate. They are not only a form of collective action, but also one of collective speech, contributing to public discourse about matters of common concern in the public sphere, a contribution extended by the media images they generate. In 2011, images of hanging effigies from Tahrir Square were posted on Facebook and featured in mainstream media. In 1979, images of burning effigies on the streets of Tehran found their way to the front pages of us American newspapers, effectively reaching antagonistic publics who reacted to the demonstrations with counter-demonstrations, thus establishing a dialogue through the media and a common symbolic vocabulary (as with the early examples during the American Revolution), making clear the media's integral role in the practice.

The protesters stage the protest as a living image, a *tableau vivant* before the cameras with the explicit aim to produce photographic images for dissemination. The scenario of the protest, the social constellation, and emotional charge are inscribed in these formulaic images. In Warburg's terms pathos formulas of protest, spectacular and recognizable, they enable a direct form of communication between diverse publics, thereby contributing to emerging transnational and cross-cultural public spheres.

The Aesthetics of Resistance

In chapters 6 and 7, I show that the grotesque aesthetics of the effigies and the performance of punishment is essential for this protest practice. The grotesque operates in the social and political realm by activating different forms of resemblance, associating the effigy with the one it depicts, while at the same time violently distorting the image through deformation, debasement, dehumanization, or demonization. The grotesque makes the culprits' transgression visible and expels them from the rightful order.

While this exaggerated and antagonistic form of protest is often used in rather ordinary political conflicts that merely aim to shift influence from one group to the other, it is more pertinent when enacted in conflicts around the basic organization of the political. In conflicts that address questions of violence, exclusion and oppression, the scenario of the effigy protest as the resolution of injustice, matches the power constellation of the political conflict at hand. In demonstrations taking cues from popular justice, the minority group or individuals who violated community rules are sanctioned by the dominant group to stabilize the status quo.

The imaginary of justice is here aligned with the existing order. In protests against oppressive regimes, the existing order is identified as being in violation of the rights of the subjugated. Here, the protesters appeal to a higher form of justice and symbolically punish the political representative of the dominant order to demand change. In both forms, the experience of violence and injustice is made visible in the effigy performances, but in crucially different ways: In the first case, the insidious violence of oppression is made visible as a threat, and the violence of oppression is expressed in the grotesque body of the effigy and the violence enacted on it. In the second case, the insidious violence of oppression is turned back onto the figure of power and in carnivalesque reversal made visible in the mock-execution of the sovereign figure.

The grotesque becomes a sign of injustice, reflecting multiple forms of violence in society: the exclusionary force of popular sovereignty; the un-checked abuse of power; abstract oppressive phenomena like racism; the bureaucratic grotesque that produces violence through the blind application of rules; or the lawless violence of the state of exception established in contemporary wars and occupations. Accordingly, Michel Foucault describes grotesque sovereignty as "an inherent part of the mechanisms of power."[1] Making the grotesque visible, speaking truth in the face of power, is a vital step in the organization of resistance.

Even though effigy demonstrations are not always practiced as resistance against the established order, they nevertheless, at their heart, indicate violence in the formation of the political. When they align with the dominant power, effigy demonstrations make the violence in society visible while they enforce it. When performed against oppression, coupled with subversive laughter, and applied with the carnivalesque

1 Michel Foucault, *Abnormal: Lectures at the College de France 1974–1975* (London: Verso, 2003), 12.

strategy of reversal, they are acts of resistance against the violence of grotesque power.

Looking back to the beginning of my engagement with the topic, it seems no coincidence that the first report of an effigy protest to catch my eye took place shortly after September 11. The attack on the World Trade Center and the US's reaction brought a long-standing antagonism to the forefront of daily international politics once again and ushered in a period of intensely violent international conflicts that were mostly played out militarily in the Middle East. These conflicts were also reflected in increased numbers of effigy protests reacting to the experience of injustice, powerlessness and humiliation – experiences resulting not only from Western military dominance, but also from Western economic and cultural domination.

Effigy performances can effectively provide a mode of communication for subjugated voices in national and transnational public spheres and create alternative imaginaries in the constitution of the political. They do this not only in protests against the violence of international conflicts, but also address injustice at national levels as with the abuse of power by Egyptian President Hosni Mubarak, austerity politics imposed in several EU countries in the aftermath of the financial crisis of 2008, or the exclusionary politics of US President Donald Trump. In the painful combination of violence and laughter that they exhibit, these effigy performances point to societies' injustices and mechanisms of exclusion, while they also demonstrate the need for the continuous work of resistance to establish and maintain the space of the political.

Burning Images: A History of Effigy Protests

This publication investigates a specific theatrical form of political protest: the hanging and burning of effigies. It is a widely known form of protest, since the production of affective images for distribution in the news media is essential to the practice. Collecting these images and reports provided me with the material for my research. Beginning with a close reading, I ordered the images according to various criteria: geography, chronology, motifs, themes and associations and arranged them into assemblages that make the relations between images visible and legible.

As tools for the research, these image assemblages directed the inquiry into different disciplines (history, art history, anthropology, performance studies, photography theory, iconology, image studies, and political philosophy), bridging documentary and discursive modes of artistic research with academic research. The images assemblages are also integral part of my argumentation. This trans-disciplinary approach, I argue, made it possible to comprehensibly assess the effigy protest practice in a single study.

Effigy hanging and burning had become increasingly visible in the news media since 2001 particularly in protests against United States military operations in Afghanistan and Iraq, in US domestic politics and in the Arab Spring. Taking these recent events as points of departure, I investigated the conditions of this visual genre of protest, its roots and genealogies in a number of countries, its aesthetics and politics. Hanging and burning effigies is an archaic and ritualistic form of protest, yet is effectively communicated by global news media to access trans-national public spheres.

As a theatrical performance of punishment of a perpetrator by the community, effigy protests communicate communal outrage over experienced injustice. They speak viscerally through intensely affective images that emanate both violence and laughter. The grotesque inherent to effigy protests results in insult and mockery, in violence of degradation and declassification. Prone to appropriation and inversion, effigy protests can either align with and enforce the existing order or be a form of resistance. In both ways they make exclusionary violence in the constitution of the political visible.

In the introduction, I analyze the protest practice of hanging and burning effigies as a layered object of research including image production, performance, and mediation. I explain the framework and methodology of this study, which combines forms of artistic research — collecting, reading, and writing with images — with academic research from the fields of history, art history, anthropology, performance studies, photography theory, iconology, image studies, and political philosophy.

Chapter 1, "Double Bodies," offers a definition of the term "effigy" through a genealogy of effigy practices. Based in ancient Roman image culture, effigies were used as substitute bodies in political rituals, formal justice, popular justice, and calendrical rituals throughout the course of European history. Effigies do not represent physical private bodies, but rather their public extensions: the social and political aspects of a person, the political office and the sovereign power invested in it.

Chapter 2, "Performing Protest," takes insights from performance and ritual studies to understand how an effigy protest unfolds as a performance of punishment of a perpetrator by a community and to what effect. I describe the stages of the performance: the making and parading of effigies, setting, execution, and mediation of the performance. Staging and embodiment have strong effects on the memory and identity of participants and create alternative imaginaries for the political sphere, while news images and reports emerge as integral and intended parts of the live performances which extend their reach. As compressed descriptions of the conflicts, the media images are *pathos formulas* of protest, recognizable formulaic images, which enable the communication between diverse audiences across temporal and cultural distances. Moving between embodied performance and mediated report, the practice is activated from and re-inscribed into the social memory to become part of the political protest repertoire.

Chapter 3, "Effigy Protests in the History of the United States," shows the development of effigy protests in one specific country over an extended period of time, from the American Revolution in 1765 until the present day. Rooted in two traditional effigy practices, effigy protest has come to address a large variety of political conflicts with varying effects on society. It can positively affirm the existing order, it can suppress resistance through violent threat, or challenge that order and demand change. Some effigy protests, staged for instance in the struggle for and against civil rights in the

1950s and '60s, pointedly articulate the conflict that lies at the heart of modern liberal democracy, between the principles of popular sovereignty and universal human rights.

Chapter 4, "Effigy Protests in Egypt, Iran, Afghanistan and Across the Middle East," traces the genealogies of effigy protests in Egypt, Iran, and Afghanistan and the wider region, from the perspective of Western news media. Most political effigy protests in these countries were staged in protest against Western cultural, economic, and military domination. These protests hint at the apparent lack of justice and channels for redress in international conflicts. I concentrate in this chapter on different modes of transfer, with migrating people, by appropriation, and through the news media. Lastly, I elaborate on the role and limitations of the media in cross-cultural communication, contributing to emerging transnational and cross-cultural public spheres.

Chapter 5, "Dialogic Communication: Effigy Protests in Iraq," zooms in on a period in one country, Iraq, to inquire into a series of effigy protests staged against US military occupation in Baghdad between 2005 and 2009. From a Western perspective, I explore the communication between different populations through symbolic visual signs and how image practices from Islamic and Western cultural contexts interrelate. The communication via news media leads to a shared symbolic language developed dialogically across national and cultural borders, as described in chapter 5.

Chapter 6, "Resemblance and the Grotesque," fo-cuses on operational aspects of images and their aesthetics. I read effigy practice in relation to different notions of resemblance, in which resemblance is an operation that not only recognizes but also constructs relationships between actors and objects. I then introduce the grotesque as an image operation equally relevant to effigy protests, but which disrupts the ordering principle of resemblance. The grotesque distorts the object and exposes it to ridicule and debasement. While based on the same mechanisms as resemblance, the grotesque appears as a form of exclusionary violence that ridicules and insults the political opponent and aims to influence the political sphere.

Chapter 7, "Violence and Laughter," explores violence and laughter, which paradoxically permeate the performance of protest effigies in regard to their effect on the social and political sphere. Yet neither violence nor laughter is reducible to one form, nor do they neatly align. With that in mind, I consider the relation between effigy protest, conflicting notions of justice and the law, and the configuration of the political. I investigate how laughter figures in these different constellations as either subjugating or liberating. Relating to current discourse in political philosophy, I differentiate between effigy protests that exert extreme subjugating violence, which destroys the possibilities of politics, and violence that is unavoidable as an aspect of resistance against an oppressive political status quo.

In the conclusion, I bring together the different strands developed in this study. I evaluate the findings in relation to each other, and indicate trajectories for further productive inquiry. Finally, I evaluate the role effigy practice can play in relation to the political as an indicator of injustice and violence and as a symptom of fundamental conflicts at the internal and external limits of contemporary liberal democracy.

Adib-Moghhaddam, Arshin. "The Arab Revolts, Islam and Postmodernity." *Middle East Journal of Culture and Communication* 5, no. 1 (2012): 15–25. doi.org/10.1163/187398612X624337.

Agamben, Giorgio. *Potentialities: Collected Essays in Philosophy*. Translated by Daniel Heller-Roazen. Stanford: Stanford University Press, 1999.

———. *Homo Sacer: Sovereign Power and Bare Life*. Stanford: Stanford University Press, 1998.

Alexander, Jeffrey C. *Performance and Power*. Cambridge: Polity Press, 2011. eBook.

Alford, Violet. "Rough Music or Charivari." *Folklore* 70, no. 4 (1959): 505–18. jstor.org/stable/1258223.

"American Anger Over Iran Grows." *Evening Independent*, December 1, 1979. news.google.com/newspapers?id=zsJaAAAAIBAJ&sjid=JlkDAAAAIBAJ&pg=4667%2C15478.

Aneja, Atul. "Protest Movements in West Asia: Some Impressions." *Strategic Analysis* 35, no. 4 (2011): 547–51. doi.org/10.1080/09700161.2011.576090.

"The Annotated Newspapers by Harbottle Dorr, Jr." *Boston Gazette*, August 19, 1765. Massachusetts Historical Society (website). masshist.org/dorr/volume/1/sequence/172.

"The Annotated Newspapers by Harbottle Dorr, Jr." *Boston Evening-Post*, October 21, 1765. Massachusetts Historical Society (website). masshist.org/dorr/volume/1/sequence/247.

Anonymous. *A General History of Connecticut*. London, 1782.

"Another Candidate for Fort Lafayette." *Weekly Sun*, September 14, 1861. Chronicling America, Library of Congress. chroniclingamerica.loc.gov/lccn/sn99066040/1861-09-14/ed-1/seq-4/.

"Another Candidate for State Honors." *New York Times*, September 9, 1861. nyti.ms/2G6YgDD.

The Anti-Slavery History of the John-Brown-Year. New York: American Anti-Slavery Society, 1861. Hathi Trust Digital Library. hdl.handle.net/2027/nyp.33433081995288.

"April 18th, 1946: Davis Knight Marries Junie Lee Spradley in Mississippi." *Equal Justice Initiative* (Montgomery, AL). racialinjustice.eji.org/timeline/1940s/.

Aptheker, Herbert. "American Negro Slave Revolts." *Science & Society* 1, no. 4 (1937): 512–38. jstor.org/stable/40399115.

Arendt, Hannah. *On Violence*. New York: Harvest Book, 1969. ebook.

Arkoun, Mohammed. *The Unthought in Contemporary Islamic Thought*. London: Saqi Books, 2002.

Austin, J. L. *How To Do Things With Words*. Oxford: Clarendon Press, 1962.

Aydin, Cemil. *The Idea of the Muslim World: A Global Intellectual History*. Cambridge, MA: Harvard University Press, 2017.

Azoulay, Ariella. *The Civil Contract of Photography*. New York: Zone Books, 2008.

———. "Archive." *Political Concepts: A Critical Lexicon* 1 (2011): 1–14. political-concepts.org/issue1/archive/.

———. *Civil Imagination: A Political Ontology of Photography*. London: Verso, 2012.

———. *The Civil Contract of Photography*. New York: Zone Books, 2008.

———. "The Family of Man: A Visual Universal Declaration of Human Rights." In *The Human Snapshot*. Edited by Thomas Keenan and Tirdad Zolgahdr, 19–48. Berlin: Sternberg Press, 2013.

———. "Potential History: Thinking through Violence." *Critical Inquiry* 39, no. 3 (2013): 548–74. jstor.org/stable/10.1086/670045.

———. "Unlearning the Origins of Photography." Fotomuseum Winterthur (website), September 6, 2018. fotomuseum.ch/en/explore/still-searching/authors/10605_ariella_azoulay.

Bakhtin, Mikhail. *The Dialogic Imagination: Four Essays.* Austin: University of Texas Press, 1981.

———. *Rabelais and His World.* Indianapolis: University of Indiana Press, 1984 [1941].

———. *Problems of Dostoevsky's Poetics.* Minneapolis: University of Minnesota Press, 1984.

Bala, Sruti. "The Entangled Vocabulary of Performance." *Rupkatha Journal on Interdisciplinary Studies in Humanities* 5, no. 2 (2013): 12–21. hdl.handle.net/11245/2.129681.

Balibar, Étienne. "Some Questions on Politics and Violence." *Assemblage,* 20 (1993): 12–13. jstor.org/stable/3181676.

———. "Violence and Civility: On the Limits of Political Anthropology." *differences: A Journal of Feminist Cultural Studies* 20, no. 2/3 (2009): 9–35. doi.org/10.1215/10407391-2009-002.

———. "Introduction." *The Borders of Justice.* Edited by Étienne Balibar, Sandro Mezzadra, and Ranadir Samaddar, 1–8. Philadelphia: Temple University Press, 2012.

———. "Justice and Equality: A Political Dilemma? Pascal, Plato, Marx." *The Borders of Justice.* Edited by Étienne Balibar, Sandro Mezzadra, and Ranadir Samaddar, 9–31. Philadelphia: Temple University Press, 2012.

———. *Violence and Civility: On the Limits of Political Philosophy.* New York: Columbia University Press, 2015.

Bargainnier, Earl F. "The Plantation: Southern Icon." In *Icons of America.* Edited by Ray B. Brown and Marshall Fishwick. Bowling Green, OH: Popular Press, 1978.

Bataille, George, ed. "Critical Dictionary." In *Encyclopaedia Acephalica.* Edited by Robert Lebel and Isabelle Waldberg. 29–48. London: Atlas Press, 1995.

Becker, Colleen. "Aby Warburg's *Pathosformel* as Methodological Paradigm." *Journal of Art Historiography* 9, (2013): 1–25.

Beeman, William O. "Images of the Great Satan." *Religion and Politics in Iran.* New Haven: Yale University Press, 1983.

Behrmann, Carolin. "Figura Infamante: Schandbilder und die Ethik der *oeconomia.*" In *Images of Shame.* Edited by Carolin Behrmann. Berlin: De Gruyter, 2016. iBooks.

"Belfast Situation Shorter Version Of Grave Riots In Belfast (1920)." *British Pathé,* 1920 (digitized film). britishpathe.com, film ID: 212.43; media urn: 21568.

Bell, Catherine. *Ritual: Perspectives and Dimensions.* Oxford: Oxford University Press, 1997.

Bell, J. L. "Portsmouth's Anti-Stamp Protest." In *Boston 1775 - History, Analysis, and Unabashed Gossip about the Start of the American Revolution in Massachusetts* (blog). September 12, 2015. boston1775.blogspot.nl.

Bell, Vikki. "Introduction, The Potential of an 'Unfolding Constellation': Imagining Fraser's Transnational Public Sphere." *Theory, Culture & Society* 24, no. 4 (2007): 1–5. journals.sagepub.com.proxy.uba.uva.nl:2048/doi/pdf/10.1177/0263276407083018.

Belli, Mériam N. *An Incurable Past: Nasser's Egypt Then and Now.* Gainesville: University Press of Florida, 2013.

Belting, Hans. *Bild-Anthropologie: Entwürfe für eine Bildwissenschaft.* Munich: Wilhelm Fink Verlag, 2001.

———. "Image, Medium, Body: A New Approach to Iconology." *Critical Inquiry* 31, no. 2 (2005): 302–19. www-jstor-org.proxy.uba.uva.nl:2443/stable/10.1086/430962.

Benjamin, Walter. "Doctrine of the Similar." Translated by Knut Tarnowski. *New German Critique* 17 (1979) [1933]. www-jstor-org.proxy.uba.uva.nl:2443/stable/488010.

———. "Critique of Violence." In *Selected Writings,* vol. 1, 277–300. Cambridge, MA: Belknap Press, 1999.

———. *The Arcades Project.* Cambridge, MA: Belknap Press, 2002.

Bielefeldt, Heiner. "Carl Schmitt's Critique of Liberalism: Systematic Reconstruction and Countercriticism." *Canadian Journal of Law & Jurisprudence* 10, no. 1 (1997): 65–75. heinonline.org/HOL/P?h=hein.journals/caljp10&i=67&a=dXZhLm5s.

Bing, Gertrude. "Vorwort." In *Aby Warburg, Gesammelte Schriften.* Edited by Gertrude Bing. Berlin: G. B. Teubner, 1932.

Bishara, Dina. "Labor Movements in Tunisia and Egypt: Drivers vs. Objects of Change in Transition from Authoritarian Rule." *SWP Comments* 1, no. 1–8. Berlin: Stiftung Wissenschaft und Politik, 2014. swp-berlin.org/en/publication/labor-movements-in-tunisia-and-egypt/.

Du Bois, W. E. B. *Black Reconstruction in America.* Philadelphia: Albert Saifer, 1935.

Bois, Yve-Alain. "The Use Value of 'Formless'." In *Formless: A User's Guide.* Edited by Yve-Alain Bois and Rosalind Krauss. New York: Zone Books, 1997.

"Boy King in Effigy." *Chicago Tribune,* April 16, 1898. archives.chicagotribune.com/1898/04/16/page/9/article/say-they-made-bad-coin.

Brecher, Jeremy. "In the Shadow of the Pyramids." *Jeremy Brecher* (blog), March 14, 2007. jeremybrecher.org/labor/in-the-shadow-of-the-pyramids/.

Bredekamp, Horst. *Theorie des Bildakts.* Berlin: Suhrkamp Verlag, 2010.

———. *Thomas Hobbes, Der Leviathan: Das Urbild des modernen Staates und seine Gegenbilder, 1651-2001.* Berlin: Akademie Verlag, 2012.

"British Soldier Hangs in Effigy." *Milwaukee Sentinel,* December 19, 1956. news.google.com/newspapers?id=xl9QAAAAIBAJ&sjid=tg8EAAAAIBAJ&pg=5085%2

C4577148.

"British Soldier Hangs in Effigy." *Montreal Gazette*, December 21, 1956. news.google.com/newspapers?id=z7AtAAAAIBAJ&sjid=0ZgFAAAAIBAJ&pg=7360%2C4021640.

Brückner, Wolfgang. *Bildnis und Brauch: Studien zur Bildfunktion der Effigies*. Berlin: Erich Schmidt Verlag, 1966.

Buchloh, Benjamin H. D. *Formalism and Historicity: Models and Methods in Twentieth-Century Art*. Cambridge, MA: MIT Press, 2015.

Buck-Morss, Susan. *The Dialectics of Seeing: Walter Benjamin and the Arcades Project*. Cambridge, MA: MIT Press, 1989.

———. "Visual Empire." *Diacritics* 37, no. 2/3 (2007): 171–98. muse.jhu.edu/article/254740.

"Burn Effigy of the Kaiser." *Milwaukee Journal*, October 21, 1917. news.google.com/newspapers?id=4xAaAAAAIBAJ&sjid=FSEEAAAAIBAJ&pg=2535%2C65433 44.

Bush, George W. "Address Before a Joint Session of the Congress on the State of the Union." January 29, 2002. *The American Presidency Project* (website). presidency.ucsb.edu/node/211864.

———. "President Bush Discusses Freedom in Iraq and Middle East: Remarks by President George W. Bush at the 20th Anniversary of the National Endowment for Democracy." *The White House* (website), November 6, 2003. georgewbush-whitehouse.archives.gov/news/releases/2003/11/20031106-2.html.

Burg, David F. "'Oust Robinson Week'." *Encyclopedia of Student and Youth Movements*. New York: Facts On File, Inc., 1998. www.fofweb.com/History MainPrintPage.aspiPin=student00527&DataType=WorldHistory&WinType=Free.

Butler, Carolyn Kleiner. "Down in Mississippi." *Smithsonian Magazine*, February 2005, www.smithsonianmag.com/history/down-in-mississippi-85827990/.

Butler, Judith. *Excitable Speech: A Politics of the Performative*. London: Routledge, 1997.

———. *Precarious Life: The Powers of Mourning and Violence*. London: Verso Books, 2004.

———. "Bodies in Alliance and the Politics of the Street," *transversal* (website), September 2011. eipcp.net/transversal/1011/butler/en.

Chelkowski, Peter. "Popular Entertainment, Media and Social Change in Twentieth-Century Iran." In *The Cambridge History of Iran*, vol. 7, 765–814. Edited by P. Avery et al. Cambridge: Cambridge University Press, 1991. dx.doi.org/10.1017/CHOL9780521200950.022.

———. Review of "Warring Souls, Youth, Media and Martyrdom in Post-revolution Iran." By Roxanne Varzi. *Comparative Studies of South Asia, Africa and the Middle East* 29, no. 2 (2009): 343–45. muse.jhu.edu/article/315166.

Collins, Sherwood. "Boston's Political Street Theatre: The Eighteenth-Century Pope Day Pageants." *Educational Theatre Journal* 25, no. 4 (1973): 401–9. jstor.org/stable/3205593.

Conway, Janet, and Jakeet Singh. "Radical Democracy in Global Perspective: Notes from the Pluriverse." *Third World Quarterly* 32, no. 4 (2011): 689–706. dx.doi.org/10.1080/01436597.2011.570029

Cruz-Lucero, Rosario. "Judas and his Phallus: The Carnivalesque Narratives of Holy Week in Catholic Philippines." *History and Anthropology* 17, no. 1 (2006): 39–56. dx.doi.org/10.1080/02757200500395568.

"Custom of Burning Effigies." *Wichita Daily Eagle* (KA), October 25, 1898. Chronicling America, Library of Congress. chroniclingamerica.loc.gov/lccn/sn82014635/1898-10-25/ed-1/seq-4/.

Dabashi, Hamid. "Ta'ziyeh as Theatre of Protest." *TDR (1988–)* 49, no. 4 (2005): 91–99. jstor.org/stable/4488685.

Davis, Susan G. *Parades and Power, Street Theatre in Nineteenth-Century Philadelphia*. Philadelphia: Temple University Press, 1986.

"De la Haye le 26 Juillet." *La gazette d'Amsterdam*, July 27, 1673. resolver.kb.nl/resolve?urn=ddd:010965491:mpeg21:a0007.

Death, Carl, "Counter-Conducts: A Foucauldian Analytics of Protest", *Social Movement Studies: Journal of Social, Cultural and Political Protest* 9, no. 3 (2010): 234–51. dx.doi.org/10.1080/14742837.2010.493655.

Del Mar, Alexander. *The Middle Ages Revisited*. New York: Cambridge Encyclopedia Co., 1900.

Didi-Huberman, Georges. *Fra Angelico: Dissemblance and Figuration*. Chicago: Chicago University Press, 1995.

———. "Ex-Voto: Image, Organ, Time." *L'Esprit Créateur* 47, no. 3 (2007): 7–16. muse.jhu.edu/article/222858.

———. *Formlose Ähnlichkeit: oder die fröhliche Wissenschaft des Visuellen nach Georges Bataille*. Munich: Wilhelm Fink Verlag, 2010.

———. *Atlas: How to Carry the World on One's Back*. Madrid: Museo Reina Sofia, 2011.

———. *Remontagen der erlittenen Zeit*. Paderborn: Wilhelm Fink Verlag, 2014.

———. "Warburg's Haunted House." *Common Knowledge* 18, no. 1 (2012): 50–78. muse.jhu.edu/article/465061.

———. *Uprisings*. Paris: Jeu de Paume, 2016.

Drake, Samuel. *The History and Antiquities of Boston: From Its Settlement in 1630 to the Year 1770*. Boston: Luther Stevens, 1856.

"Duytslant en d'aengrensende Rijcken." *Oprechte Haerlemsche courant*, December 27, 1689. resolver.kb.nl/resolve?urn=ddd:011226125:mpeg21:a0004.

Eck, Caroline van. *Art, Agency and Living Presence*. Leiden: Leiden University Press, 2015.

Eder, Jens, and Charlotte Klonk. "Introduction." In: *Image Operations: Visual Media and Political Conflict*. Edited by Jens Eder and Charlotte Klonk. Manchester: Manchester University Press, 2017. Kindle edition.

Edwards, Elizabeth. "Introduction." In *Anthropology and Photography 1860–1920*. Edited by Elizabeth Edwards, 3–17. New Haven and London: Yale University Press, 1992.

————. *Raw Histories: Photographs, Anthropology and Museums*. Oxford: Berg, 2001.

Edwards, Justin D., and Rune Graulund. *Grotesque*. London: Routledge, 2013.

"Effigies for Easter." *Al Ahram Weekly* 1242, May 16, 2016. weekly.ahram.org.eg/News/11009/17/Effigies-for-Easter.aspx.

Ehrlich, Richard S. "The Fourth Anniversary of the Soviet Takeover in Afghanistan." United Press International. upi.com/Archives/1983/12/27/The-fourth-anniversary-of-the-Soviet-takeover-in-Afghanistan/3157441349200/.

Elkins, James. "Images as Arguments in Visual Studies." *Images – Journal for Visual Studies*, 2013. visual-studies.com/images/no1/elkins.html.

————. *Writing with Images* (website), 2014. writingwithimages.com.

————. "Afterword." In *Image Operations: Visual Media and Political Conflict*. Edited by Jens Eder and Charlotte Klonk. Manchester: Manchester University Press, 2017. Kindle edition.

Endres, Johannes. "Unähnliche Ähnlichkeit: Zu Analogie, Metapher und Verwandtschaft." In *Similitudo: Konzepte der Ähnlichkeit in Mittelalter und Früher Neuzeit*. Edited by Jeanette Kohl, Martin Gaier und Alberto Saviello, 29–58. Munich: Wilhelm Fink Verlag, 2012.

Ericson, Richard V. "How Journalists Visualize Fact." *Annals of the American Academy of Political and Social Science* 560 (1998): 83–95. jstor.org/stable/1048978.

Fahd, T., and A. Rippin, "S̲h̲ayṭān". In *Encyclopaedia of Islam*, Second Edition. Edited by P. Bearman et al. dx.doi.org/10.1163/1573-3912_islam_COM_1054.

Finke, Marcel. "Materialtäten und Praktiken." In *Bild: Ein Interdisziplinäres Handbuch*. Edited by Stephan Günzel and Dieter Mersch. Stuttgart: Verlag J. B. Metzler, 2014.

Fischer, Michael M. J. *Iran: From Religious Dispute to Revolution*. Cambridge, MA: Harvard University Press, 1980.

"Flags Burned at Protests of Abortion Ruling." *Toledo Blade*, July 5, 1989. news.google.com/newspapers?id=rENPAAAAIBAJ&sjid=_AIEAAAAIBAJ&pg=6281%2C1108259.

Forensic Architecture (website). www.forensic-architecture.org/project/.

Forster, Kurt W. "Introduction." In Aby Warburg. *The Renewal of Pagan Antiquity*. Los Angeles: Getty Research Institute, 1999.

Foucault, Michel. *Discipline and Punish: The Birth of the Prison*. New York: Vintage Books, 1977.

————. *The History of Sexuality*. 3 vols. New York: Vintage Books, 1990.

————. *Abnormal: Lectures at the College de France 1974–1975*. London: Verso, 2003.

————. *The Order of Things: An Archeology of the Human Sciences*. London: Routledge: 2005.

Fraser, Nancy. "Rethinking the Public Sphere: A Contribution to the Critique of Actually Existing Democracy." *Social Text* 25/26 (1990): 56–80. www.jstor.org/stable/466240.

————. "Reframing Justice in a Globalizing World," *The New Left Review* 36 (2005): 69–88.

————. "Transnationalizing the Public Sphere: On the Legitimacy and Efficacy of Public Opinion in a Post-Westphalian World." *Theory, Culture & Society* 24, no. 4 (2007): 7–30. do.org/10.1177/0263276407080090.

Galt-Harpham, Geoffrey. *On the Grotesque: Strategies of Contradiction in Art and Literature*. Princeton: Princeton University Press, 1982.

Gamboni, Dario. *The Destruction of Art: Iconoclasm and Vandalism Since the French Revolution*. London: Reaktion Books, 1997.

Garrison, Lloyd. *Letters of William Lloyd Garrison I–VI*, 5 July 1836. In "Anti-Garrison Effigy." *Reading Garrison's Letters* (blog). readinggarrisonsletters.com.

"General Information on Azerbaijani Jewish Organizations," *Jews of Eurasia* (website). jewseurasia.org/page423.

Göttke, Florian. *Toppled*. Rotterdam: Post Editions, 2010.

————. "A Protester in Homs, Syria." *open! Platform for Art, Culture and the Public Domain* (2013). onlineopen.org/a-protester-in-homs-syria.

————. "Burning Effigies with Bakhtinian Laughter." *European Journal of Humour Research* 3, no. 2/3 (2015): 129–144.

————. "Plaatsvervangende Lichamen: Het tragische lot van de effigie." *Metropolis M, tijdschrift over hedendaagse kunst* 2 (2017): 56–63.

————. "Of Falling Statues: Destabilizing a Media Icon." In Ted Hyunhak Yoon, *Decoding Dictatorial Statues*. Edited by Bernke Klein Zandvoort. Eindhoven: Onomatopee, 2019.

————. *Burning Images: Performing Effigies as Political Protest*, PhD Dissertation, University of Amsterdam, 2019.

Gosling, Luci. "'Guy-ser' Bill – Remember, Remember, the Fifth of November." *Picturing the Great War: The First World War Blog from Mary Evans Picture Library* (blog), November 5, 2013. blog.maryevans.com/2013/11/guy-ser-bill-remember-remember-the-fifth-of-november-.html.

Grabar, Oleg. "From the Icon to Aniconism: Islam and the Image." *Museum International* 55, no. 2 (2003): 46–53. doi-org.proxy.uba.uva.nl:2443/10.1046/j.1350-0775.2003.00425.

Härter, Karl. "Images of Dishonoured Rebels and Infamous Revolts: Political Crime, Shaming Punishments and Defamation in the Early Modern Pictorial Media." In *Images of Shame*. Edited by Caroline Behrmann. Berlin: De Gruyter, 2016. iBooks.

Hazard, Samuel, ed. *The Register of Pennsylvania*. Philadelphia: W. F. Geddes, 1828.

Hebel, Udo J. "Sites of Memory in U.S.-American Histories and Cultures." In *Cultural Memory Studies*. Edited by Astrid Erll and Ansgar Nünning, 47–60. Berlin: Walter de Gruyter, 2008.

Hergesheimer, E. *Map Showing the Distribution of the Slave Population of the Southern States of the United States Compiled from the Census of 1860*. The United States Coast Survey. 1861. commons.wikimedia.org/wiki/File:SlavePopulationUS1860.jpg.

"History of School Integration in the U.S." *History*, A+E Television Networks (website). history.com/topics/central-high-school-integration.

Hobbes, Thomas. *Leviathan*. Edited by G. C. A. Gaskin. New York: Oxford University Press, 1996.

"Hoe men vroeger strafte." *Bataviaasch Nieuwsblad*, March 27, 1920. resolver.kb.nl/resolve?urn=ddd:011038833:mpeg21:a0054.

Horlacher, Stefan. "A Short Introduction to Theories of Humour, the Comic, and Laughter," *Amsterdamer Beiträge zur neueren Germanistik* 70, no. 1 (2009): 17–47.

Horowitz, Elliott. "The Rite to Be Reckless: On the Perpetration and Interpretation of Purim Violence." *Poetics Today* 15, no. 1 (1994): 9–54. www-jstor-org.proxy.uba.uva.nl:2443/stable/1773202.

"Indian Moslems Burn Effigy of Wilson to Assail Cartoon." *New York Times*, November 12, 1966. nyti.ms/2zOeqMy

"Israeli, Arab Guns in 2 Duels." *Evening News*, May 19, 1970. news.google.com/newspapers?id=goJGAAAAIBAJ&sjid=JDANAAAAIBAJ&pg=720%2C3116829.

Ito, Lisa Cariño. "Dissident Puppets: The Effigy in Philippine Radical Politics." Bachelor's thesis, University of the Philippines Diliman, 2005.

Jay, Mike. "Bonfire Night in Lewes." In *Gunpowder Plots: A Celebration of 400 Years of British Carelessness with Explosives*, Antonia Fraser et al., 118–44. London: Penguin, 2005.

Johnson, Cade. "About 70 Protest UC Berkeley Professor Judith Butler's Conference in Brazil." *Daily Californian*, November 8, 2017. dailycal.org/2017/11/08/protesters-gather-at-conference-organized-by-campus-professor-judith-butler-in-brazil/.

"June 13th, 2005, United States Senate Formally Apologizes for Failure to Pass Anti-Lynching Bills." *Equal Justice Initiative* (website). racialinjustice.eji.org/timeline/2000s/.

Kabul Times (Afghanistan), March 20, 1982, March 19, 1983, March 20, 1983. *The University of Arizona Digital Libraries Collection*. http://content.library.arizona.edu/cdm/landingpage/collection/p16127coll6; and *Digital Commons at University of Nebraska*. digitalcommons.unl.edu/afghanenglish/index.html.

Kalfat, M. F. "Port Said in the Evening, Port Said in the Morning." *Jadaliyya*, June 2, 2014. jadaliyya.com/pages/index/17784/port-said-in-the-evening-port-said-in-the-morning/.

Kamal, Osama. "A City Like." *Al-Ahram Weekly*, June 9, 2011. masress.com/en/ahramweekly/26841.

Kantorowicz, Ernst H. *The King's Two Bodies: A Study in Mediaeval Political Theology*. Princeton: Princeton University Press, 1957.

Kayser, Wolfgang. *Das Groteske: Seine Gestaltung in Malerei und Dichtung*. Oldenburg: Gerhard Stalling Verlag, 1961.

Keller, Harald. "Effigie." In *Reallexikon zur Deutschen Kunstgeschichte*, vol. 4 (1956): 743–49. *RDK Labor* (website). rdklabor.de/w/?oldid=89345.

Kertzer, David I. *Ritual, Politics & Power*. New Haven and London: Yale University Press, 1988.

Kershaw, Baz. "Fighting in the Streets: Dramaturgies of Popular Protest, 1968–1989." *New Theatre Quarterly* 13, no. 51 (1997): 255–76. journals.cambridge.org/abstract_S0266464X0001126X.

Kohl, Jeanette, Martin Gaier, and Alberto Saviello. "Ähnlichkeit als Kategorie der Porträtgeschichte." In *Similitudo: Konzepte der Ähnlichkeit in Mittelalter und Früher Neuzeit*. Edited by Jeanette Kohl, Martin Gaier, and Alberto Saviello, 11–27. Munich: Wilhelm Fink Verlag, 2012.

Koschnik, Albrecht. "Political Conflict and Public Contest: Rituals of National Celebration in Philadelphia 1788–1815." In *The Pennsylvania Magazine of History and Biography* 118, no. 3 (1994): 209–48. jstor.org/stable/20092875.

Krauss, Rosalind. "… and then Turn Away? An Essay on James Coleman." *October* 81 (1997): 5–33. www-jstor-org.proxy.uba.uva.nl:2443/stable/779016.

Küntzel, Matthias. "Tehran's Efforts to Mobilize Antisemitism: the Global Impact." In *Deciphering the New Antisemitism*. Edited by Alvin H. Rosenfeld, 508–32. Indiana: Indiana University Press, 2015.

Kuryla, Peter. "Parties Down at the Square Amid Courtroom Melodramas: A Reconsideration of the Modern Civil Rights Movement Demonstration." *Patterns of Prejudice* 43, no. 1 (2009): 17–40. dx.doi.org/10.1080/00313220802636031.

Ladino, Robyn Duff. *Desegregating Texas Schools: Eisenhower, Shivers and the Crisis at Mansfield High*. Austin: University of Texas Press, 1996.

Larsson, Göran. *Muslims and the New Media: Historical and Contemporary*

Debates. Farnham, UK: Ashgate, 2011.

Latour, Bruno, and Peter Weibel. *Iconoclash*. Karlsruhe: ZKM/Cambridge, MA: MIT Press, 2002.

Leiris, Michel. "Spittle." In *Encyclopaedia Acephalica*. Edited by Robert Lebel and Isabelle Waldberg, 79–80. London: Atlas Press, 1995.

Lessing, Gotthold Ephraim. *Laokoon oder Über die Grenzen der Malerei und Poesie*. Project Gutenberg, 2004. eBook.

Loew, Patty, and James Thannum. "After the Storm: Ojibwe Treaty Rights Twenty-Five Years after the Voigt Decision." *The American Indian Quarterly* 35, no. 2 (2011).

Longley, R. S. "Mob Activities in Revolutionary Massachusetts." *The New England Quarterly* 6, no. 1 (1933): 98–130. www.jstor.org/stable/359364.

Lustig, Robin et al. "War of the Word." *The Guardian*, February 19, 1989. theguardian.com/uk/1989/feb/19/race.world.

MacFarquhar, Neil. "Millions in Iran Rally Against U.S." *New York Times*, February 12, 2002. nyti.ms/2G44SCp

Madame Sosostris. "Pack of Cards." *Al-Ahram Weekly* 480, May 4–10, 2000. weekly.ahram.org.eg/Archive/2000/480/people.htm.

Marin, Louis. *On Representation*. Stanford: Stanford University Press, 2001.

McGillivray, Don. "Gunpowder Plot: In Britain, They Still Search the Cellar as Parliament Opens." *Ottawa Citizen*. October 28, 1969. news.google.com/newspapers?id=Qq4yAAAAIBAJ&sjid=BeOFAAAAIBAJ&pg=5534%2C2855818

Merry, Sally Engle. "Resistance and the Cultural Power of Law." *Law & Society Review* 29, no. 1 (1995): 11–26. jstor.org/stable/3054052.

Michalski, Sergiusz. *Public Monuments: Art in Political Bondage 1870–1997*. London: Reaktion Books, 1998.

Michaud, Philippe-Alain. *Aby Warburg and the Image in Motion*. New York: Zone Books, 2007.

Millington, Peter. "Folklore and Customs." *The Nottinghamshire Heritage Gateway* (website). nottsheritagegateway.org.uk/themes/folklore/folkloregraphic.htm.

Mitchell, W. J. T. *Iconology: Image, Text, Ideology*. Chicago: University of Chicago Press, 1986.

———. *Picture Theory: Essays on Verbal and Visual Representation*. Chicago: University of Chicago Press, 1994.

———. "Method, Madness, Montage: Aby Warburg to John Nash." Lecture at the Warburg Institute, November 4, 2016. youtube.com/user/WarburgInstitute/videos.

Mondzain, Marie-José. "Iconic Space and the Rule of Lands." *Hypatia* 15, no. 4 (2000): 58–76. muse.jhu.edu/article/14142.

———. *Image, Icon, Economy: The Byzantine Origins of the Contemporary Imaginary*. Stanford: Stanford University Press, 2005.

Morey, Peter, and Amina Yaqin. *Framing Muslims*. Cambridge, MA: Harvard University Press, 2011. EBSCOhost eBook.

"Moslems Condemn Soviet Invasion of Afghanistan." *Pittsburg Post-Gazette* (PE), January 29, 1980. news.google.com/newspapers?id=Wp5RAAAAIBAJ&sjid=rG0DAAAAIBAJ&pg=6688%2C3799541.

Mostyn, Trevor. "Will Militant Islam Hijack Egypt's Beautiful Revolution?" *Planetary Movement* (blog), April 21, 2011. planetarymovement.org/index.php?option=com_content&task=view&id=536&Itemid=61.

Mouffe, Chantal. *The Democratic Paradox*. London: Verso, 2000.

———. *On the Political*. London: Routledge, 2005. eBook.

Mroué, Rabih. "Oppressive Regimes Wage War Against Cellphone Video – Rabih Mroué." Interview with Rabih Mroué. San Francisco Museum of Modern Art, July 9, 2018. youtube.com/watch?v=zRsNSmRpKmg.

Muir, Edward. *Ritual in Early Modern Europe*. Cambridge: Cambridge University Press, 1997.

Muzaffar, Chandra. "Islam, Justice and Politics." In *The New Voices of Islam: Reforming Politics and Modernity*. Edited by Mehran Kamrava, 213–30. London: I. B. Tauris, 2006.

Nachwati, Leila. "Kafranbel: A Paradigm of Creative Storytelling." *openDemocracy*. September 30, 2014. opendemocracy.net/north-africa-west-asia/leila-nachawati/kafranbel-paradigm-of-creative-storytelling-part-12.

New American Standard Bible, biblegateway.com/versions/New-American-Standard-Bible-NASB/.

"Nixon Burned in Effigy at Virginia University." *Kingsport Times-News*, May 14, 1972. newspapers.com/newspage/29426560/.

Nora, Pierre. "Between Memory and History: Les Lieux de Mémoire." *Representations* 26 (1989): 7–24. https://www-jstor-org.proxy.uba.uva.nl:2443/stable/2928520.

Norwood, Stephen H. *Strikebreaking and Intimidation: Mercenaries and Masculinity in Twentieth-Century America*. Chapel Hill, NC: University of North Carolina Press, 2002.

Nussbaum, Martha C. "Objectification." *Philosophy & Public Affairs* 24, no. 4 (1995): 249–91. www-jstor-org.proxy.uba.uva.nl:2443/stable/2961930.

———. *Hiding from Humanity: Disgust, Shame and the Law*. Princeton: Princeton University Press, 2006.

Orcutt, Kim. "'Matisse' Burns in Chicago." *The Armory Show at 100* (blog). March 26, 2013. http://armory.nyhistory.org/matisse-burns-in-chicago/.

Ordinaris dingsdaeghse courante (Amsterdam), May 1, 1667. resolver.kb.nl/resolve?urn=ddd:010758948:mpeg21:p002.

Oxford English Dictionary. www.oed.com.

Pelham, Nicholas. *A New Muslim Order: The Shia and the Middle East Sectarian Crisis.* London: I. B. Tauris, 2008.

People v. Noble. Crim. No. 1816. Third Dist. (April 24, 1945). *Justitia, US Law.* law.justia.com/cases/california/calapp2d/68/853.html.

Pettys, Rebecca Ansary. "The Ta'zieh: Ritual Enactment of Persian Renewal." *Theatre Journal* 33, no. 3 (1981): 341–54. http://proxy.uba.uva.nl:2048/docview/1290213470?accountid=14615.

Pfeifer, Michael J. *The Roots of Rough Justice: Origins of American Lynching.* Chicago: University of Illinois, 2011.

Pfister, Manfred. "Beckett's Tonic Laughter." *Samuel Beckett Today/Aujourd'hui* 11 (2001): 48–53. www.jstor.org/stable/25781354.

Piris, Paul. "The Co-Presence and Ontological Ambiguity of the Puppet." In *Routledge Companion to Puppetry and Material Performance*, edited by Dassia N. Posner, Claudia Orenstein, and John Bell, 30–42. New York: Routledge, 2014.

Popescu, Carmen. "Sociological Perspectives on Humour: Conflict Theories and Ethnic Humour." *Word and Text, A Journal of Literary Studies and Linguistics* 1 (2010): 37–44. ceeol.com.

"Port Said's Allenby Effigies Wear Masks of Erdogan, Qatari Emir." *Cairo Post*, April 21, 2014. www.thecairopost.com/news/107258/inside_egypt/port-saids-allenby-effigies-wear-masks-of-erdogan-qatari-emir.

Quebec Cronicle Telegraph, December 21, 1956. news.google.com/newspapers?id=NWVQAAAAIBAJ&sjid=CVcDAAAAIBAJ&pg=2841%2C6011774.

Rahimi, Babak. "A History of (Safavid) Muharram Rituals." In *Theater State and the Formation of Early Modern Public Sphere in Iran*. Brill Online, 2011. doi.org/10.1163/9789004207561_006.

Ramazani, R. K. "Iran's Revolution: Patterns, Problems and Prospects." *International Affairs* 56, no. 3 (1980): 443–57. jstor.org/stable/2617391.

"Reagan Burned in Effigy." *Herald Journal*, November 25, 1981. news.google.com/newspapers?id=iz4sAAAAIBAJ&sjid=xM0EAAAAIBAJ&pg=6737%2C5893408.

Reece, Kevin. "Effigy of Obama is not a Houston-area protest." *KHOU 11 News*, November 5, 2012. www.khou.com/news/Effigy-of-Obama-is-not-a-Houston-area-protest-177371201.html.

Rigney, Ann. "Plenitude, Scarcity and the Circulation of Cultural Memory." *Journal of European Studies* 35, no. 1 (2005/2006): 11–28. doi: 10.1177/0047244105051158.

Roach, Joseph. *Cities of the Dead: Circum-Atlantic Performance.* New York: Columbia University Press, 1996.

Robinson, Andrew. "In Theory Bakhtin: Carnival against Capital, Carnival against Power." Ceasefire. September 9, 2011. ceasefiremagazine.co.uk/in-theory-bakhtin-2/.

Romein, Jan. *The Asian Century: A History of Modern Nationalism in Asia.* Berkeley: University of California Press, 1962.

Rooijackers, Geraard. *Eer en schande: Volksgebruiken van het oude Brabant.* Nijmegen: SUN, 1995.

Rosen, Margit. "Shooting the Dead." In *Iconoclash*. Edited by Bruno Latour and Peter Weibel. Karlsruhe: ZKM/Cambridge, MA: MIT Press, 2002.

Rothberg, Michael. "Multidirectional Memory in Migratory Settings: The Case of Post-Holocaust Germany." *Transnational Memory: Circulation, Articulation, Scales.* Edited by Chiara De Cesari and Ann Rigney, 123–45. De Gruyter Online, 2014.

Ryckman, Larry. "Peaceful But Noisy Crowds Protest Release of Dan White from Prison." *Evening Independent*, January 7, 1984. news.google.com/newspapers?id=-7daAAAAIBAJ&sjid=ZVkDAAAAIBAJ&pg=2465%2C1430544.

Sabea, Hanan. "I Dreamed of Being a People." In *Political Aesthetics of Global Protest: The Arab Spring and Beyond*. Edited by Pnina Werbner, Martin Webb, K. Spellman-Poots, 66–82. Edinburgh: Edinburgh University Press, 2014.

"Sagasta Hanged in Effigy," *New York Times*, April 12, 1898. nyti.ms/2zNMxnB.

Said, Edward. *Covering Islam: How the Media and the Experts Determine How We See the World, Revised Edition.* New York: Vintage Books, 1997.

Salvatore, Armando. "The Exit from a Westphalian Framing of Political Space and the Emergence of a Transnational Islamic Public." *Theory, Culture & Society* 24, no. 4 (2007): 45–52. doi.org/10.1177/0263276407080092.

Schaap, Andrew. "Aboriginal Sovereignty and the Democratic Paradox." In *The Politics of Radical Democracy*. Edited by Adrian Little and Mona Lloyd. Edinburgh: Edinburgh University Press, 2009.

Schbley, Ayla, and Clark McCauley. "Political, Religious, and Psychological Characteristics of Muslim Protest Marchers in Eight European Cities: Jerusalem Day 2002." *Terrorism and Political Violence* 17, no. 4 (2005): 551–72. dx.doi.org/10.1080/09546550500174921.

Schechner, Richard. *Performance Studies: An Introduction*, 3rd edition. London: Routledge, 2006.

Von Schlosser, Julius. "History of Portraiture in Wax." In *Ephemeral Bodies: Wax Sculpture and the Human Figure*. Edited by Roberta Panzanelli. Los Angeles: Getty Publications, 2008. 171–314.

Sharlow, Carrie. "Michigan Lawyers in History: Roth, Stephen J." *Michigan Bar Journal*, 2012. michbar.org/file/journal/pdf/pdf4article2106.pdf.

Shehab, Shaden. "Effigy Burning Ban." *Al-Ahram Weekly* 585, May 9–15, 2002. http://weekly.ahram.org.eg/2002/585/eg7.htm.

Shepard, Benjamin. *Queer Political Performance and Protest.* New York: Routledge, 2010.

Sinha, Manisha. "The Caning of Charles Sumner: Slavery, Race, and Ideology in the Age of the Civil War." *Journal of the Early Republic* 23, no. 2 (2003): 233–62. jstor.org/stable/3125037.

Sreberny, Annabelle, and Ali Mohammadi. *Small Media, Big Revolution: Communication, Culture, and the Iranian Revolution.* Minneapolis: University of Minnesota Press, 1994.

Stallybrass, Peter, and Allon White. *The Politics and Poetics of Transgression.* New York: Cornell University Press, 1986.

State Historical Society of North Dakota (website). "Education > Lesson Plans > Visual Evidence." http://history.nd.gov/historicsites/chateau/chateauLesson/visual_photographs.html.

Stewart, Peter. *Statues in Roman Society: Representation and Response.* Oxford: Oxford University Press, 2003.

Steyerl, Hito. "In Defense of the Poor Image." *e-flux journal* 10 (2009). e-flux.com/journal/10/61362/in-defense-of-the-poor-image/.

"Students Burn Weyler in Effigy." *New York Times*, April 22, 1898. nyti.ms/2zNg1Sx.

Tager, Jack. *Boston Riots: Three Centuries of Social Violence.* Boston: Northeastern University Press, 2001.

Tancons, Claire. "Occupy Wall Street: Carnival Against Capital? Carnivalesque as Protest Sensibility." *e-flux journal* 30, no. 12 (2011). e-flux.com/journal/30/68148/occupy-wall-street-carnival-against-capital-carnivalesque-as-protest-sensibility/.

Tapper, R. "Azerbaïjan: Population and its Occupations and Culture." *Encyclopaedia Iranica Online.* 1996. www.iranicaonline.org/articles/azerbaïjan-vi.

Taylor, Diana. *The Archive and the Repertoire: Performing Cultural Memory in the Americas.* Durham and London: Duke University Press, 2003.

———. "Performance and Politics." *Identities* 21, no. 4 (2014): 337–43. dx.doi.org/10.1080/1070289X.2014.874349.

———. *Performance.* Durham, NC: Duke University Press, 2016.

Taylor, Isaac. "Riding the Stang at Welburn." *The Folk-Lore Journal* 1, no. 9 (1883): 297–302. jstor.org/stable/1252796.

Thompson, E. P. "Rough Music Reconsidered." *Folklore* 103, no. 1 (1992): 3jstor.org/stable/1261031.

"Three De Autremonts Are Hanged in Effigy." *New York Times*, June 25, 1927. nyti.ms/2zN6WZX.

Tilly, Charles. *Contentious Performances.* Cambridge: Cambridge University Press, 2008.

Torab, Azam. *Performing Islam: Gender and Ritual in Islam.* Leiden and Boston: Brill, 2007.

Turner, Victor. *The Ritual Process.* Ithaca, NY: Cornell University Press, 1969.

"A Unique Story in the Public Spaces of Port Said." *RHET201-Research* (blog). May 21, 2010. abougendy.wordpress.com/2010/05/21/a-unique-story-in-the-public-spaces-of-port-said/.

"The 'Waiheathens' at Gallipoli: Diary and Letters of a Waihi Soldier Gerald (Tad) Morpeth One of the Six Morpeth Brothers from Waihi Who Served in WW1." *Tauranga Memories: Remembering War* (website). tauranga.kete.net.nz/remembering_war/documents/show/426-the-waiheathens-at-gallipoli.

Warburg, Aby. *The Renewal of Pagan Antiquity: Contributions to the Cultural History of the European Renaissance.* Translated by David Britt. Los Angeles: Getty Research Institute, 1999.

———. "Dürer und die italienische Antike." In *Aby Warburg. Gesammelte Schriften.* 2 vols. Leipzig: B.G. Teubner, 1932.

Wells, Ida B. *Lynch Law in Georgia.* Chicago: Chicago Colored Citizens, 1899.

Weiss, Allen S. "Impossible Sovereignty: Between The Will to Power and The Will to Chance." *October* 36 (1986), 129–46.

Werbner, Pnina. "Divided Loyalties, Empowered Citizenship? Muslims in Britain." *Citizenship Studies* 4, no. 3 (2000): 307–24. dx.doi.org/10.1080/713658798.

———, Martin Webb, and Kathryn Spellman-Poots, eds. "Introduction." *The Political Aesthetics of Global Protest: The Arab Spring and Beyond.* Edinburgh: Edinburgh University Press 2014.

"Who's Behind Egypt's Rampage Against Palestinians?" *Executive Intellingence Review* 5, no. 8 (1978): 6–7.

Wilf, Steven. *Law's Imagined Republic: Popular Politics and Criminal Justice in Revolutionary America.* Cambridge: Cambridge University Press, 2010.

Wing, Nick. "Secret Service Visits Man Who Hung Obama Effigy From Tree As 'Spooky' Halloween Decoration." *Huffington Post*, October 25, 2012. huffingtonpost.com/2012/10/25/secret-service-obama-effigy_n_2018851.html.

Yates, Christopher. "Introduction." In *Philosophy and the Return of Violence Studies from this Widening Gyre.* Edited by Nathan Eckstrand and Christopher Yates. New York: Continuum Books, 2011.

Young, Iris Marion. *Justice and the Politics of Difference.* Princeton: Princeton University Press, 2011.

"Youths Stage Mocktrial, Hang Jane Fonda in Effigy." *Lakeland Ledger*, October 9, 1979. news.google.com/newspapers?id=0NsvAAAAIBAJ&sjid=DPsDAAAAIBAJ&pg=3764%2C2680723.

Yuenger, James. "U.S. Embassy: Where It All Started." *Chicago Tribune*, January 21, 1981. archives.chicagotribune.com/1981/01/21/page/4/article/u-s-embassy-where-it-all-started.

Zangl, Veronika, and Sruti Bala. "Editorial: Humour in Art and Activism." *European Journal of Humour Research* 3 (2016): 1–6. dx.doi.org/10.7592/EJHR2015.3.2.3.zangl.

Descriptor	Page	Credits / Source	Caption
1765_08_00_ USA-MA: tory	67, 91	Goodrich, Ch. A. *The Child's History of the United States*. Boston: American Stationers' Company, 1836. p. 64.	The inhabitants of Boston hanging the Tory image.
1765_08_14_ USA-MA: stamp master Oliver	17, 91	*HathiTrust Digital Library* (hathitrust.org).	The Colonists Under Liberty Tree. In: Ollier, Edmund. *Cassell's Illustrated History of England*. London: Cassell, Petter & Galpin, 1873–1874. 109.
1765_09_12_ USA-NH: stamp master Meserve	83, 91	*The Robinson Library* (robinson library.com).	New Hampshire: Stamp Master in Effigy
1765_11_01_ USA-MA: British MP Huske	87–88	Paul Revere/Massachusetts Historical Society (masshist.org).	Revere, Paul. "A View of the Year 1765." Boston, 1765. Political cartoon depicting the American colonies' opposition to the Stamp Act of 1765.
1774_00_00_ USA-MA: Governor Hutchinson	99	After Felix O.D. Darley/ *U.S.History* (ushistory.org).	Engraving late 19th century.
1775_04_00_ USA-NY: publisher Rivington	99	*Journal of the American Revolution* (allthingsliberty. com). 3 Mar 2014.	Woodcut depicting James Rivington being hung in effigy as it appeared in Rivington's *New-York Gazetteer*, April 20, 1775.
1780_09_30_ USA-PA: General Arnold	97, 224	Historical Society of Pennsylvania (digitallibrary.hsp. org).	A Presentation of the Figures exhibited and paraded through the streets of Philadelphia on Saturday the 30th of September, 1780.
1795_08_00_ USA: Chief Justice Jay	99	Albert Bobbett/The New York Public Library.	John Jay burned in effigy. 1905.
1861_12_25_ USA-MD: Confederacy President Davis	115	Alfred R. Waud/Library of Congress (Wash., DC).	Alfred R. Waud, "Holiday in the camp of the 23 Pennsylvania Volunteers near Bladensburg, Maryland." *New York Illustrated News*, January 11, 1862.
1887_06_03_Ireland: Sherriff McMahon	61	Henry Norman/*Pall Mall Gazette*/Eblana Photograph Collection, National Library of Ireland.	The Fire Brands, Bodyke, County Clare, 3 June 1887: The sign on the effigy reads: PRAISE THE LORD / FOR HERE / THE TYRANT'S ARM WAS / PARALYSED. Taken the day after Widow McNamara's eviction. Sheriff McMahon had turned up with a large force several days earlier but had an epileptic fit and withdrew. The tenants saw this as divine intervention and made this effigy of him.
1892_00_00_ USA-PA: steel factory manager	102	The Battle of Homestead Foundation (battleofhomestead.org).	Homestead Strike of 1892: Effigies of managers were hung from telephone poles before the Strike of Amalgamated Association of Iron and Steel Workers against Carnegie Steel Corporation in Pittsburg.

Descriptor	Page	Credits / Source	Caption
1896_01_09_ USA-ND: members of a jury	109	State Historical Society of North Dakota (history.nd.gov).	The jury in the trial of Mr. and Mrs. Mark Wadsworth in Bismarck, Burleigh County, found the defendants not guilty in the killing of Ed Severson. Medora residents expressed rage at the verdict by hanging the jury in effigy and displaying a large banner on the side of the de Mores Hotel.
1903_11_19_ USA-IL: strike breaker Frank Curry	18, 102	The Chicago Daily News collection/Chicago History Museum/Getty Images (chicagocollections.org).	Effigy of strike breaker Frank Curry hanging over 42nd Street and Wentworth Avenue during the Chicago Railway Strike of 1903.
1907_12_27_ USA-NY: landlord (rent-strike)	102	The New York Public Library (libcom.org).	New York, December 1907: A group of children on the Lower East Side hangs a landlord in effigy, *The Independent*, January 1908. In Lawson, Ronald. "The tenant movement in New York City, 1904–1984." New Brunswick: Rutgers University Press, 1986.
1911_03_00_ France: Council President Monis (a)	67	Médiathèque Municipale de Troyes, France (journals.openedition.org).	March 1903: Manifestation de vignerons a Bar-sur-Aube. Le mannequin représentant M. Monis promené en tête de cortège à travers la ville. In: Lynch. Édouard. "Mobilisations paysannes et antiparlementarisme dans la première moitié du XXe siècle." *Siècles* 32 (2010).
1911_03_19_ France: Council President Monis (b)	76		Vine-growers of the Marne and the Aube protest legislation protecting the viticulture of the South. They accuse the president of the Council, Ernest Monis of treason and burn him in effigy in Bar-sur-Aube.
1914_00_00_ USA-CO: mine owner	102	Denver Public Library (denverlibrary.org).	Ludlow, CO, USA, 1914: View of the United Mine Workers of America camp for coal miners on strike against the Colorado Fuel and Iron Company.
		Bain News Service/Library of Congress (Wash., DC).	Effigy of Kaiser Wilhelm II hung in Paris, France, at the beginning of World War I.
1915_11_05_UK: German Kaiser Wilhelm II	142	*Picturing the Great War: The First World War Blog from Mary Evans Picture Library* (blog.maryevans.com), 5 Nov 2013.	Gosling, Luci. "'Guy-ser' Bill – Remember, remember, the Fifth of November."
1917_10_17_ USA-WI: German Kaiser Wilhelm II	103, 215	*Milwaukee Journal* (WI), 21 Oct 1917.	At the land clearing demonstration recently, after stumps had been pulled, blasted and piled in one huge pile, the effigy of the kaiser was burned. His head consisted of a pumpkin his helmet a tin pan, the spike of his helmet a nail covered with tinfoil, his mustache, a frayed piece of rope: the iron cross, tow railroad spikes fastened together, his badges, numerous pieces of tin; and his sword a piece of lath, was designed and constructed by Lawrence Livingston. The effigy was elevated to the top of the pile and fastened there, with the sword pointing directly upwards. In a very few minutes the roaring flames reached the kaiser. The most spectacular feature was when the right arm, holding the sword, dropped in a most lifelike manner, the sword falling into the flames.
1918_04_16_USA-WI: German Kaiser Wilhelm II + McElroy (a)	104	McKill op & Ruud/University of Wisconsin (digicoll.library.wisc.edu).	During World War I, a large crowd burns McElroy and Kaiser Bill [Wilhelm] in effigy on the Lower Campus (now Library Mall) at night.
1918_04_16_ USA-WI: German Kaiser Wilhelm II + McElroy (b)	104	McKill op & Ruud/University of Wisconsin (digicoll.library.wisc.edu).	University of Wisconsin, 16 Apr 1918: Representative of the National Security League, Robert McNutt McElroy, gave a speech on April 6, after which he dismissed the University as "a bunch of damned traitors". Students reacted strongly burning effigies of McElroy and Kaiser Wilhelm.
1918_11_11_ USA-ID: German Kaiser Wilhelm II	104	University of Idaho Library (digital.lib.uidaho.edu).	Hanging the Kaiser in effigy in Challis, Idaho.
1918_11_11_UK: German Kaiser Wilhelm II + Little Willie	215	Bob Thomas/Popper-foto/Getty Images, Seattle (WA).	Effigies of the Kaiser and "Little Willie" hang at Brackley, Northamptonshire, as a crowd gathers on Armistice Day, November 11th 1918
1918_11_11_ USA-IL: German Kaiser Wilhelm II	104	*Chicago Daily News*/ Chicago Collections (chicagocollections.org).	Image of men carrying an effigy of Kaiser Wilhelm II hanging from a noose for the Armistice Day peace celebration parade. They are standing on the intersection of East Madison Street and on South Michigan Avenue in the Loop community area of Chicago, IL.
1918_11_11_ USA-MI: German Kaiser Wilhelm II	104	Detroit News Staff/Walter P. Reuther Library, Wayne State University (MI) (reuther.wayne.edu).	An effigy of Kaiser Wilhelm II is carried through the streets of Detroit in celebration of the end of the First World War.

Descriptor	Page	Credits / Source	Caption
1918_11_12_ France: German Kaiser Wilhelm II burned in effigy by Australian soldiers	143	Arthur Streeton/Australian War Memorial, Campbell (awm.gov.au).	Australians burning effigy of Kaiser Wilhelm in square on Armistice Day.
1918_11_12_ USA-NY: German Kaiser Wilhelm II	104	George W. Fenner/New York Heritage Digital Collections (nyheritag.org).	A man in costume mocks the Kaiser during the Peace Day Parade in Syracuse. (*Syracuse Herald* (NY), 12 Nov 1918, 3).
1919_00_00_ USA-CA: member of anarchist union	102	Online Archive of California (oac.cdlib.org).	Mock hanging of an IWW (Industrial Workers of the World) figure during protest in Banning, California.
1920_09_06_Belfast, Northern Ireland: Nationalist residents	250	British Pathé (UK).	"Grave Riots In Belfast 1920." Intertitle: "Situation in Ireland grows more tense every day – ruins resulting from war between revolutionists and British troops." Intertitle: "Effigies dangling from windows are familiar sights in the streets of Belfast." Low angle M/S of a terrace house – the Union Jack is flying from the window, two scarecrow-like dummies hang by their necks from the guttering – obviously effigies of Nationalists, very gruesome.
1930_06_25_ India: British Home Secretary Simon	17	*The Times* (UK), 25 Jun 1930.	An effigy of Sir John Simon was taken through the streets on the roof of a motor-car and, together with a quantity of foreign clothing, was burnt on the river bank at Surat.
1934_05_01_ USA-NY: Hitler	106	Acme Photo/National Library of Israel, Historical Jewish Press (www.jpress.nli.org.il).	The prize for the most striking presentation of how the cracked chancellor is regarded universally, goes to the Socialists of New York City who carried the remarkably vivid effigy, shown above, of the most contemptible tyrant the world has ever known, in their May Day parade that culminated in a demonstration in Madison Square in which 100,000 participated. Sentinel, Chicago, 17 May 1934.
1935_01_22_ Germany: editor Max Braun	77, 250	Bettmann/Corbis, Seattle, WA.	Celebrating the result of the plebiscite which returned the Saar to Germany, jubilation reached fever heat in the streets of Saarbrucken, a day after the vote. This truck, loaded with ecstatic Nazis, is seen pushing through the throng with an effigy of Max Braun, Saarland Socialist leader, hanging from the tailboard.
1935_05_01_ USA-NY: Hitler	106	Ed Jackson/NY Daily News Archive via Getty Images	A Hitler effigy is hung by the Ladies' Neckwear Union during May Day celebrations in New York.
1935_Rome, Italy: Mussolini in front of a statue of Julius Caesar	34	The Hawaii Times Photo Archives Foundation (ddr.densho.org).	Rome, 18 Sep 1935. Mussolini giving a salute next to a statue of Caesar.
	72	J. Berkley Green Photo Collection (patch.com).	Herndon, Virginia, 1936: Three town council members hung in effigy after a vote about town liquor sales.
1937_01_00_ USA-MI: strike breakers	102	Time Life Pictures/Getty Images	A group of sitdown strikers peer from the windows of the Chevrolet Plant in Flint, Michigan in December of 1936 after the start of a 43 day strike of General Motors auto workers. The workers hold up signs and an dummy with a sign on it.
1938_10_02_ USA-NJ: Hitler	105	Charles Hoff/NY Daily News Archive via Getty Images	Anti-Nazi protestors burn an effigy of Hitler during a demonstration in Union City, N.J. where Nazis were attempting to hold a Bund meeting.
1939_00_00_ Lithuania: Hitler + Stalin	224	V. Kapočius/*Lithuanian Quarterly Journal of Arts and Sciences* 36, no.2 (1990), (lituanus.org).	Effigy of Stalin and Hitler, denouncing the Molotov-Ribbentrop Pact.
1939_05_01_ USA-FL: African-American voter (a)	116	AP Photo	Miami, FL, 1 May 1939: A dummy is hanging from a lamp post in an attempt to intimidate African-Americans and keep them away from the voting polls in the municipal primary election. The sign on the dummy reads, "This n..... voted."
1939_05_03_ USA-FL: African-American voter	216	Bettmann/Corbis, Seattle (WA).	The waning power of the Ku Klux Klan was demonstrated at Miami, FL, where, despite a "scare parade" designed to frighten Negro voters, they found that more Negroes turned out to vote than ever before in the history of the city. This effigy hung from a telephone pole, shows the extremes to which the terroristic Klan went to achieve it's hoped for ends. Other Klansmen carried nooses.
1940_00_00_ USA-MA: Hitler	105	Leslie Jones/Digital Commonwealth, Massachusetts Collections Online (ark.digitalcomm onwealth.org).	"Help hang Hitler – scrap will do it" Ready to hang Hitler in effigy.

Descriptor	Page	Credits / Source	Caption
1941_01_22_ USA-MD: Hitler	106	Thomas McAvoy/*Time Life* (New York). 5 Mar 2014.	A Hitler hex party, 1941: The ritual prepared by Mr. Seabrook, began with the naming of the image: "You are Hitler; Hitler is you!" Next the chief hexer intoned: "The woes that come to you, let it come to him! Decapitation, the brief life span of Adolf Hitler's dummy."
1941_07_00_ USA-CA: Walt Disney (a)	102	Kosti Ruohomaa/Rob Cowan/*Stuff from the Park* (matterhorn1959.blogspot. nl). 26 Apr 2008.	
1941_07_00_ USA-CA: Walt Disney (b)	75, 102	Kosti Ruohomaa/Rob Cowan/*Stuff from the Park* (matterhorn1959.blogspot. nl). 26 Apr 2008.	The image is of an effigy. It may be of Walt or of Gunther Lessing, the Disney legal rep. Walt Disney Studio in 1941. The strike is one of the defining moments for Walt Disney and the Disney company.
1942_00_00_ USA: Japanese Emperor Hirohito	106	The Monti- fraulo Collection/Getty Images, Seattle (WA).	Three people sitting on the bonnet of a motorcar on a busy American street next to a lamp post with a hanging effigy of the Japanese Emperor Hirohito with a painted note "Here hangs Hirohito," buildings and the framework of a large iron bridge in the background, America 1940s.
1942_04_04_ Brazil: Hitler + Japanese Emperor Hirohito as Judas	45	*Palestine Post* (Jerusalem), 5 Apr 1942 (www.jpress.nli. org.il).	
1942_04_20_ USA-NY: Hitler	105	Weegee (Arthur Fellig)/ International Center of Photography (New York)/ Getty Images.	New York, 21 April 1942: Photo originally entitled "Der Fuehrer's Birthday," depicts a group of revellers as they hang Nazi dictator Adolf Hitler in effigy. They clog the street in front of the RKO Palace and Embassy movie theatres.
1943_05_10_ USA-WA: Japanese Emperor Hirohito	106	Seattle Post-Intelligencer Collection; Museum of History and Industry/Corbis Images, Seattle (WA).	Seattle, WA, May 1943: Hundreds of workers at a Seatac shipyard gather to hang Emperor Hirohito in effigy.
1945_00_00_ USA-OH: African-American man	117, 216	Allan Grant//Time Life Pictures/Getty Images	An effigy of a boy that has spoken to a woman.
1945_05_02_ Canada: Hitler	77, 239	Toronto Star Archives (torontopublic library.ca).	Canada, 2 May 1945: Burning of the effigy draws an hilarious crowd to the scene. Some of them have just heard the news and quickly pass it on to others who join in the general celebration.
1945_05_08_ USA-IN: Hitler	70, 106	*IndyStar* (Indianapolis) (photos.indystar. com).	Indianapolis, 8 May 1945: A trio of Indianapolis women booting around an effigy of German dictator Adolf Hitler. When Pvt. James Millay of Indianapolis sent his wife a swastika armband from Europe, she fashioned a dummy of Hitler, affixed the armband to it then laid it aside for V-E Day. With the proclamation of surrender Mrs. Millay tied the effigy to the back of an automobile and dragged the effigy throughout Downtown.
1945_05_08_ USA-NY: Hitler	221	Tony Linck/Time Life Pictures/Getty Images	Hitler mask on crude effigy, which jubilant celebrants are about to string up as man holds up sign that reads "WANTED FOR MILLIONS OF MURDERS/ DEAD OR ALIVE" during end of war in Europe celebration on street.
1945_05_08_ USA-OH: Hitler	106	CSU Archives/Everett Collection/Alamy Stock Photo (UK).	A crowd in Ohio celebrating VE Day and the end of World War II.
1948_12_00_ USA-GA: member of the KKK	121		Robed Klansmen attending a Southwide rally in Macon, GA, were angered when they saw this figure dangling from the YMCA window. It was hung by Afro special correspondent, Stetson Kennedy.
1949_04_09_ USA-NY: actor and activist Paul Robeson	117, 217	Bettmann/Corbis/Perucci, Toni. "The Red Mask of Sanity: Paul Robeson, HUAC, and the Sound of Cold War Performance" *TDR: The Drama Review* 53, no. 4 (2009).	An effigy of Paul Robeson hangs from rear of tow truck in Oregon Corners, Peekskill, NY, echoing the sentiments of the town's residents. Paul Robeson, black actor, civil rights activist (demanded anti-lynching legislation from Pres. Truman), communist: "The artist must take sides. He must elect to fight for freedom or slavery. I have made my choice. I had no alternative."
1952_01_03_ Egypt: British soldier	144	Bettmann/ Corbis	Effigy of British Soldier hung in Cairo.
1953_05_00_ Cuba: President Batista	69	*MensPulpMags* (menspulpmags.com). 13 May 2015.	*HIS* magazine, May–June 1953.

Descriptor	Page	Credits / Source	Caption
1956_08_06_ USA-AL: NAACP activists	119	*Africanafrican* (blog). (site discontinued)	NAACP and white integrationists were hanged in effigy in Montgomery in 1956. "Built by Union Labor" sign was meant to support stand taken by some Southern locals against the integration policies of the national AFL-CIO.
1956_08_30_ USA-TX: African-American student (b)	247	Wilburn Davis/University of Texas at Arlington Libraries (library.uta.edu).	Crowd of Mansfield residents gathered on school grounds during attempt to desegregate Mansfield High School.
1956_08_30_ USA-TX: African-American student (d)	248	University of Texas at Arlington Libraries.	School girls around a Texas Ranger.
1956_08_31_ USA-TX: African-American student (a)	236	Texas State Library and Archives Commission (mansfieldcrisis.omeka.net).	Texas Rangers pose in front of effigy at Mansfield High School.
1956_08_29_ USA-TX: African-American student (c)	248	University of Texas at Arlington Libraries. (library.uta.edu)	Patrolmen R.W. Cole, left, and Delbert Giles with effigy of Negro found hanging from W. Lancaster bridge in Trinity Park in reaction to federal court order permitting enrollment of Negro students to Mansfield High School.
1956_08_29_ USA-TX: African-American student (e)	248	University of Texas at Arlington Libraries (library.uta.edu).	Fort Worth Sheriff Harlon Wright looks at effigy of Negro found hanging across Mansfield's Main St. in protest to federal desegregation order to allow minorities to attend public schools.
1956_09_03_ USA-TX: African-American home-owner	117	*KXAS-TV/NBC-5* (TX).	"New Racial Strife in Fort Worth."
1956_09_15_ USA-TX: African-American home-owner	117	*Illustrated London News*, 15 Sep 1956. p. 425 (nationalarchives.gov.uk).	Strung up outside the negro family's home in the "all-white" section of Fort Worth: an effigy of a murdered negro.
1956_12_21_ Egypt: UK Premier Eden	144	AP Photo/*Montreal Gazette*, 21 Dec 1956.	People milling on street in Port Said, Egypt, point up to an effigy of a British soldier hanging from a wire across the street as British and French continued evacuating the city.
1957_03_14_ Gaza: Israeli Premier Ben-Gurion	144	AP Radiophoto/*New York Times*. 14 Mar 1957.	Demonstrators in Gaza carrying an effigy of David Ben-Gurion yesterday. They hailed the projected return to Egyptian rule.
1957_10_03_ USA-AR: African-American student (a)	118, 122	Associated Press Images (New York).	Little Rock, AR, 3 Oct 1957: An unidentified white student slugs an effigy of a black student outside Central High School in Little Rock, as nearly 75 students of the school walked out to protest integration. Troopers stationed around the school broke up the demonstration.
1957_10_03_ USA-AR: African-American student (b)	142	Bettmann/Corbis, Seattle (WA).	Little Rock, AR, 3 Oct 1957: Photo shows one of the students holding the effigy while another puts a match to the stuffed legs to set it afire.
1957_12_23_ Egypt: British	145	Bibliotheca Alexandrina and the Gamal Abdel Nasser Foundation, President Gamal Abdel Nasser Photo Archive (nasser.bibalex.org).	Egypt, 23 Dec 1957: Abdel Nasser attends Victory Day celebrations in Port Said.
1959_01_00_ Cuba: unknown effigy	243	Lester Cole/Corbis	Havana, Cuba, Jan 1959: Effigy Hanging on a Wall.
1960_04_02_ USA-TX: author John Howard Griffin	69, 235	Bob Bain/Fort Worth Star-Telegram Collection, University of Texas at Arlington Libraries, TX (mansfield-crisis.omeka.net).	Effigy of Mansfield author John Howard Griffin who wrote the book Black Like Me; the effigy was hung over a traffic signal in Mansfield, then removed and taken to the Mansfield dump.
1960_04_02_ USA-TX: author John Howard Griffin with newspaper showing his effigy	119	Fort Worth Star-Telegram Collection, University of Texas at Arlington Libraries, TX (mansfieldcrisis.omeka.net).	Mansfield author John Howard Griffin who wrote the book Black Like Me holds a Fort Worth *Star-Telegram* newspaper, which includes a photo of an effigy someone hung of him. Griffin spent most of his life studying racial equality.

Descriptor	Page	Credits / Source	Caption
1960_07_26_ USA-FL: Cuban President Castro (a)	107	Len Morgan/Harry Ransom Center, University of Texas at Austin (norman.hrc. utexas.edu).	Jack Ruby, in an attempt to assassinate Fidel Castro at Police Headquarters in Miami, before realizing it was just an effigy.
1960_07_26_ USA-FL: Cuban President Castro (b)	240	Bettmann/Corbis, Seattle (WA).	New York, 26 Jul 1960: Members of the White Rose Organization attempted to hang Fidel Castro in effigy in Rockefeller Plaza as their contribution to the 26th of July anniversary but were told they could not. They finally released some of their pent-up energy and emotions by smacking the dummy around.
1960_09_19_ USA-NY: USSR leader Krushchev	107	Photo by Popperfoto/Getty Images	An effigy of Russian Premier Nikita Krushchev swings from a gallows as the Russian liner "Baltika" steams to her berth to bring the Soviet leader to speak at the United Nations General Assembly.
1961_09_18_ UK: pretend effigy protest in army exercise	140	British Pathé.	18 Sep 1961: "Salisbury Plain: Tommy in Fancy Dress." Army Exercises to deal with Middle Eastern Mobs. Combined army-airforce exercise, dressed half of them as orientals, assumed that the ruler of the state had appealed to the British for aid against unfriendly neighbours.
1962_10_03_ USA-MS: African-American student	68, 118	AP Photo/stf/*NewBlackMan (in Exile)* (newblackman. blogspot.com). 17 May 2012.	Oxford, MS, 3 Oct 1962: An effigy of James Meredith, a recently admitted black student, hangs from a dormitory on the campus of Ole Miss.
1963_05_06_ USA-AL: Martin Luther King	119	Bettmann/Corbis, Seattle (WA).	Protesting African American civil rights demonstrations, Dr. Edward R. Fields and James Murray, members of the National States Rights Party, hang an effigy of Martin Luther King, Jr. outside the party's headquarters in Birmingham, Alabama.
1964_07_19_ Vietnam: CPV chairman Hồ Chí Minh + French President DeGaulle	254	in.pinterest.com/explore/ effigy/.	
1966_01_30_ USA-WA: Governor Evans	121	Doug Wilson/Associated Press Images (New York).	Tacoma, WA, 30 Jan 1966: Native American dancers shuffle around fire after burning Washington Gov. Dan Evans in effigy at Franks Landing on the Nisqually River. About 200 Indians and whites, many of them spectators, were on hand at the demonstration held to protest the state's restriction of off-reservation net fishing by Washington Indians.
1967_05_11_ USA-NJ: former Alabama Governor Wallace	253	AP Wirephoto.	Princeton, NJ: Students at Princeton University protest appearance tonight of former Gov. George Wallace of Alabama in hanging of effigy at window of one of the campus halls. The students are rehanging this effigy after campus police ripped down their first one.
1967_06_00_ Lebanon: British Queen Elizabeth	148	Tim Page/Corbis.	Beirut, Lebanon, Jun 1967: An effigy, painted with the Star of David, hangs in a Beirut street during the Six Day War.
1968_02_16_ USA-SC: Governor McNair	cover, 253	Charlotte Mecklenburg Library (NC) (cmstory.org).	Johnson C. Smith students burn an effigy of South Carolina Gov. Robert McNair in a sympathy demonstration. They were protesting the deaths of three students in Orangeburg, SC, killed by law enforcement officials during a demonstration against racial discrimination by a segregated bowling alley.
1969_00_00_ USA-NY: college administrator	120	Ithaka College Archives (NY) (ithaca.edu).	Ithaka College, New York, 1969: The Afro-American Society and the Students for a Democratic Society burn an effigy of an unnamed college administrator during a rally. The rally protested the college's small number of African American students and faculty and the alleged mishandling of the college's Educational Opportunity Program finances, and advocated for the establishment of a black studies program.
1969_04_09_ Palestine: Israeli defense minister Dayan	148	AP Wirephoto	School children cheer as they burn an effigy of Israeli Defense Minister Moshe Dayan, during an anti-Israeli demonstration in the casbah of the town of Nablus, located in the occupied Jordan.
1969_04_21_ USA-NY: "racism"	253	Vincent Riehl/NY Daily News Archive via Getty Images	City College of New York: Waving flag of black liberation and shouting protests, dissidents burn effigy, which symbolizes racism.
1970_03_21_ USA-CO: Indian Affairs Commissioner	253	Dave Buresh/The Denver Post via Getty Images/ *Littleton* (CO) (littletongov. org).	A Group Of American Indians Protesting In Littleton Marches, Chants; Burning in foreground is effigy representing U.S. Commissioner of Indian Affairs.

Descriptor	Page	Credits / Source	Caption
1970_05_00_New Zealand: US President Nixon	73	*Otago Daily Times* (Dunedin, New Zealand). 4 Jun 2012.(odt.co.nz).	University of Otago, New Zealand, May 1970: Gregor Ronald ducks away after setting alight a kerosine soaked effigy of the then-president Richard Nixon swinging from a gibbet.
1970_05_05_USA-LA: US President Nixon	121, 253	AP Wirephoto	Students at Tulane University held a rally near an effigy of President Nixon they hung in protest of the administration's war policy. The demonstration followed an all-night vigil in protest of four Kent State University students.
1970_06_07_USA-NY: NY mayor Lindsay	254	AP Wirephoto	Members of the militant "Young Lords" drag an effigy of New York mayor Lindsay, and burn an American flag, as they pass reviewing stand before New York City's Metropolitan Museum of Art Sunday during a Puerto Rican Day parade.
1971_06_26_USA-NY: Thomas Cuite (gay rights protest)	121	Richard C. Wandel/International Gay Information Center collection, New York Public Library.	GAA street fair, New York, 26 Jun 1971: City Council member Thomas Cuite hung in effigy.
1971_08_05_UK: Judge Argyle	76	Popperfoto/Getty Images	Supporters of *Oz Magazine* sit outside London's Old Bailey court and burn an effigy of Judge Argyle QC who presided over the obscenity trial.
1972_00_00_USA-IL: President Nixon (b)	122	Lawrence Roth/Flickr, user: M. T. Harris.	Southern Illinois University, Spring 1972: Students burn President Nixon in effigy at SIU's "Free Forum" area.
1972_00_00_USA-IL: President Nixon (a)	122	Lawrence Roth/Flickr, user: M. T. Harris.	Southern Illinois University Spring 1972: Students burn President Nixon in effigy at SIU's "Free Forum" area.
1973_01_13_France: Israeli Premier Meir	148	"Students Burn Meir in Effigy at Paris." *Kentucky New Era* (Hopkinsville), 13 Jan 1973.	
1973_06_17_Italy: Premier Andreotti	74	Vittoriano Rasfelli/*New York Times*. 17 Jun 1973.	Striking Roman workers and a hanging effigy of Premier Giulio Andreotti.
1976_00_00_USA-MS: President Ford	254	Ed Hille/Picturedesk	Yippie protesters march in Kansas City, Missouri, during the 1976 Republican Convention. A large paper mache effigy of President Gerald Ford and posters blasting Richard Nixon are carried by the participants.
1976_10_02_USA-DC: publisher Graham	102	Reading/Simpson/*Washington Area Spark* (washington-spark .wordpress.com). 12 Dec 2012.	Over 1,000 striking pressmen and supporters staged a march and rally on the one year anniversary of the strike on October 2, 1976 that culminated with burning *Washington Post* publisher Katherine Graham in effigy in front of the Post headquarters.
1978_11_24_Germany: Iranian Shah Reza Pahlavi	152	AP/*Daily Item* (Sumter, SC). 27 Nov 1978.	Demonstrators drag an effigy of the Shah through downtown Frankfurt during a protest demonstration against the Iranian leader. 7,000 people took part in the demonstration that later erupted in violence, causing hundreds persons to be injured.
1978_12_18_India: Iranian Shah Reza Pahlavi	152	Associated Press Archive (New York).	18 Dec 1978: Demonstration against Shah of Iran by 500 Indian and Iranian students outside the American library in New Delhi.
1979_01_14_USA-GA: President Carter	153	AP Laserphoto/*Ledger* (Lakeland, FL). 15 Jan 1979.	Protesters against US policies in Iran wave a burning effigy of President Carter across the street from Ebenezer Baptist Church in Atlanta Sunday, where Carter received the Dr. Martin Luther King Jr. Non-Violent Peace Prize.
1979_02_18_Iran: Uncle Sam	cover, 153	*Past Daily* (pastdaily.com). 18 Feb 2015.	
1979_11_00_Iran: US President Carter	155	Henri Bureau/Sygma/Corbis	Tehran: Anti-American demonstration during the hostage crisis and the Iranian Revolution.
1979_11_00_USA-PA: Iranian leader Khomeini	108	University of Scranton Archives (PE).	University of Scranton students demonstrating outside of Jefferson Hall. The students were protesting the detention of 49 American hostages in Tehran, Iran. The stuffed figure hanging from the fourth-floor window is an effigy of Ayatollah Khomeini.
1979_11_09_Iran: US President Carter	153	Associated Press Archive (New York).	Scenes outside the United States embassy in Tehran, crowd with effigy of Jimmy Carter dressed as Uncle Sam.

Descriptor	Page	Credits / Source	Caption
1979_11_13_ Iran: Uncle Sam	154	AP Photo	Iranian demonstrators burn an effigy of Uncle Sam, branded with CIA on its right arm outside the U.S. Embassy in Tehran, Nov. 13, 1979, during a demonstration in support of the Iranian militants who took over the embassy November 4. About 60 Americans and 40 other nationals are being held inside the embassy.
1979_11_13_ Philippines: US President Carter	156	AP Photo/*Sumter Daily* (SC). 13 Nov 1979.	Iranian students in Makati, Philippines, burn effigies of President Carter and Egypt's Anwar Sadat at the Iranian Embassy compound. The Iranians are supporting the take-over of the U.S. Embassy in Teheran.
1979_11_15_ USA-ME: Iranian leader Khomeini	157	Jack Loftus/*Bangor Daily News* (ME). 15 Nov 1979.	Student Michael Brooker holds burning effigy of Khomeini at Bangor. They rallied in the rain to chants of "Bring the Americans home" and burned an Iranian flag and an effigy of Iranian leader Ayatollah Khomeini.
1979_11_16_ USA-NY: Iranian leader Khomeini	157	Bettmann/Corbis, Seattle (WA).	Two hundred students on the Syracuse University campus witnessed a demonstration by about 25 activists protesting the Iranian situation. The students in this picture are kicking an effigy of Khomeini which they've just set afire. They also burned a home-made Iranian flag, and carried banners and placards.
1979_11_18_ Iran: Uncle Sam	155	*Radio Free Europe* (Prague, Czech Republic). 4 Nov 2009.	ABŞ-ın Tehrandakı səfirliyi qarşısında nümayiş, 18 noyabr 1979. 1979-cu il noyabrın 4-də tələbə fəalları Amerikanın Tehrandakı sə firliyini tutdular və 90 işçini girov götürdülər. Əsas tələb ABŞ-ın şahı verməsi idi.
1979_11_25_ Iran: US President Carter	155, 229	Bettmann/Corbis	Tehran, 25 Nov 1979: Demonstrators jam street outside the U S. Embassy, where 49 American hostages still being held for the 22nd day, as the militants display cardboard effigy of President Jimmy Carter hung on scaffold and at left a portrait of Ayatollah Khomeini.
1979_12_00_ Iran: US President Carter	134, 160	Postcard, bought on ebay.	In the streets of Teheran, near the Embassy, President Carter is burned in effigy by Iranian revolutionaries.
1979_12_15_ Iran: Shah Reza Pahlavi	155	AP Photo/*BBC News* (London). 17 Jul 2015.	The Shah's authoritarian rule lead to mass protests which eventually forced him into exile. An effigy of the deposed Shah of Iran is burned at a demonstration outside the US
1979_12_23_ Iran: US President Carter	155	AP Photo/*Politico* (USA). 6 Oct 2012.	An effigy is held aloft during a mass demonstration as thousands of factory workers show their support for the students holding hostages inside the U.S. Embassy in Tehran, Dec. 23, 1979.
1979_12_31_ Iran: Afghan President Karmal + USSR leader Brezhnev	166	Associated Press Archive (New York).	"Afghanistan – The Soviet Invasion"
1980_01_06_ Canada: USA-SR leader Brezhnev	167	Erin Combs/Toronto Star Archives (torontopubliclibrary.ca).	Brezhnev burns: Demonstrators at Nathan Phillips Square yesterday shouted anit-Communist slogans as they burned Soviet Premier Leonid Brezhnev in effigy to protest the Soviet invasion of Afghanistan. About 200 took part in the demonstration.
1980_01_11_ Thailand: USSR leader Brezhnev	167	Gary Mangkorn/Associated Press Images (New York).	Bangkok, Thailand, 11 Jan 1980: Thai Muslim demonstrators carry an effigy of Soviet President Leonid Brezhnev in front of the U.S.S.R. embassy in Bangkok. The protesters, denouncing Soviet intervention in Afghanistan, burned the effigy.
1981_01_01_ Iran: Uncle Sam	158, 228	Gamma-Keystone via Getty Images	Iran, 1981: Demonstrations Anti USA, Effigy Of USA.
1981_03_05_NL: Morocco King Hassan II	69, 229	Robert Hartogh/ The Memory of the Netherlands Database (geheugenvannederland.nl).	KMAN-demonstratie (Komittee Marokkaanse Arbeiders in Nederland) tegen het bewind van de Marokkaanse koning Hassan II, Rotterdam, 1981.
1981_12_27_ Iran: USSR leader Brezhnev	167	Canpress/Associated Press Images (New York).	27 Dec 1981: Afghan refugees living in Tehran march through the street on Sunday, carrying an effigy of Soviet President Brezhnev during a demonstration when thousands of Afghans marched in protest burning the Russian flag and chanting anti-Soviet slogans on the second anniversary of the Soviet military intervention of their country.
1982_03_11_ Israel: Premier Begin	149	Beni Tel Or/GPO/Getty Images	Yamit, Sinai desert, 11 Mar 1982: Jewish settlers hang then Israeli Prime Minister Menahem Begin in effigy as they resist forced evacuation from their Sinai Desert settlement of Yamit, as part of Israel's peace treaty with Egypt.

Descriptor	Page	Credits / Source	Caption
1986_12_28_ Pakistan: USSR leader Gorbachov	191	United Press International/*Star News* (Wilmington, NC). 28 Dec 1986.	Afghan demonstrators burn Soviet leader Mikhail Gorbachev in effigy during a protest march by more than 10,000 exiles through the streets of Islamabad, Pakistan. The rally was held to mark the seventh anniversary of the Soviet intervention in Afghanistan.
1987_07_24_ Lebanon: USA + France	81, 171	Maher Attar/Sygma/Corbis	Beirut, Lebanon: Hezbollah supporters burn effigies during an anti-American and anti-French demonstration in the streets of Beirut.
1987_09_29_ Iran: US President Reagan + Iraqi President Saddam Hussein	158	AP Laserphoto/*Chicago Tribune*. 29 Sep 1987 (archives.chicagotribune.com).	An effigy of President Reagan sits among Iraqi prisoners of war listening to a speech in Tehran recently.
1988_03_03_ Netherlands: Minister Braks	73	Rob Bogaerts/Nationaal Archief, Nederland (gahetna.nl).	Protest boeren tegen mestheffing in Assen; demonstratie en verbranden pop die Minister Braks voorstelt.
1989_01_14_UK: author Salman Rushdie	162		Protesters hold up an effigy of author Salman Rushdie in a protest against the publication of his book *The Satanic Verses*, which they considered to be an insult to islam.
1989_01_14_UK: Satanic Verses	162	Garry Clarkson/BMT	*Satanic Verses* Book Burning, Bradford UK, 14 January 1989.
1989_02_19_ India: author Salman Rushdie	69, 162	Ravi Raveen-dran/AFP/ Getty Images/*Spectator* (London), 17 Sep 2012. (blogs.spectator.co.uk)	Indian Moslems burn an effigy of British author Salman Rushdie and shout anti-government slogans during a demonstration 19 February near India's largest mosque in New Delhi. Some 2,000 people protested against the (Hindu nationalist BJP) government's decision to grant Indian-born Rushdie a visa.
1989_02_26_ Pakistan: author Salman Rushdie	163	Moin Bangash/AP/*New York Times*. 18 Sep 2012.	17 Feb 1989: People in Rawalpindi, Pakistan, protest for a second day against the publication of Salman Rushdie's book *The Satanic Verses*. On the day before, six people were killed in Pakistan during a protest over the publication of the book in the United States.
1989_03_05_ Netherlands: author Salman Rushdie	164	ANP/*de Volkskrant*, (Amsterdam). 23 Sep 2012.	Rotterdam, Netherlands, 1989: Demonstraties tegen *De Duivelsverzen van Rushdie*.
1989_03_07_ Thailand: author Salman Rushdie	164	AP Wirephoto/*Haaretz* (Tel Aviv). 14 Oct 2011.	Bangkok, Thailand: An effigy of author Salman Rushdie is burned during a demonstration by more than 300 Thai Muslims at the central mosque. The muslims demand that the Thai Government ban the controversial book *The Satanic Verses*.
1989_05_00_ USA-WI: Native American	251	Loew, Patty and James Thannum. "After the Storm: Ojibwe Treaty Rights Twenty-Five Years after the Voigt Decision." *The American Indian Quarterly* 35, no. 2 (2011): 161–191.	Protestor holding speared head. Photograph taken of anti-treaty protestors at a Wisconsin boat landing during the spring Chippewa spear fishing season.
1989_05_27_UK: author Salman Rushdie	164	amjamjazz/Flickr.	London 27 May 1989: Anti-Rushdie March. Salman Rushdie hanged in effigy in Hyde Park. An estimated 8,000 protestors rallied in the park and marched to Parliament Square. Copies of *The Satanic Verses* were burned. A counter demonstration in Parliament Square by Women Against Fundamentalism was harrassed, but was able to make its point, if only briefly.
1990_00_00_ USA-FL: Iraqi President Saddam Hussein	108	Carl De Keyzer/Magnum Photos (New York).	Tampa, FL, 1990: Pro Gulf War demonstration.
1990_04_19_ India: Pakistani Premier Bhutto (a)	67, 213	Robert Nickelsberg /Time Life Pictures/Getty Images, Seattle (WA).	Anti-Pakistan demonstrators with effigy of PM Benazir Bhutto (for burning) protesting Pakistan's interference in Kashmir, near Pakistani embassy.
1990_04_19_ India: Pakistani Premier Bhutto (b)	68, 213	Robert Nickelsberg /Time Life Pictures/Getty Images/ Alamy Stock Photo (UK).	Anti-Pakistan demonstrators with effigy of PM Benazir Bhutto (for burning) protesting Pakistan's interference in Kashmir, near Pakistani embassy.
1995_02_17_ USA-NY: US banks	225	John Levy/Getty Images, Seattle (WA).	New York, 17 Feb 1995: A New York City Policeman extinguishes a burning effigy representing US banking interests in Mexico outside of the head office of Chase Manhattan Bank. About 100 protesters gathered to show solidarity with the Zapatista rebels in the south of Mexico.

Descriptor	Page	Credits / Source	Caption
1996_10_28_ India: BSP chief Ram	70	Sherwin Crasto/Associated Press Images (New York).	Bombay, India, 28 Oct 1996: Members of Syahi, a literary organisation, spitting on the effigy of Kanshi Ram, chief of the Bahujan Samaj Party, a political party representing the low caste people of India. The mass spitting was to protest the beating up of some reporters and cameramen by Kanshi Ram security guards in New Delhi last week.
1997_12_04_ Germany: Minister Waigel + Minister Rüttgers + Chancellor Kohl	60	DPA/*Der Spiegel* (Hamburg, Germany). 31 Oct 2007.	Düsseldorf, Germany, 4 Dec 1997: Mit drei Stoffpuppen von Theo Waigel, Jürgen Rüttgers und Helmut Kohl (v.l.n.r.) am Galgen marschieren Studenten zum Landtag. Mit der Kundgebung in der Landeshauptstadt wollen die Demonstranten auf das nach ihrer Meinung unzumutbare neue Hochschulrahmengesetz aufmerksam machen.
1998_11_09_Palestine: Premier Netanyahu + US President Clinton	62, 150	Nasser Isstayeh/Associated Press Images (New York).	9 Nov 1998: Palestinian students at the An-Najah university in Nablus hang up effigy's of Israeli Prime Minister Netanyahu, left, and U.S. President Clinton, on a university building during a demonstration against the Wye agreement.
1998_12_18_ India: US President Clinton + British Premier Blair	242	Str/Associated Press Images (New York).	18 Dec 1998: Indian Muslims shout slogans and burn effigies of President Clinton, right, and British Prime Minister Tony Blair outside the Jama Masjid during a demonstration in New Delhi. Throughout the Arab world, the message was that the unleashing of missiles at the heart of Baghdad would do more harm to the Iraqi people than to their President Saddam Hussein.
2000_03_16_ Philipines: President Estrada	71	Luis Liwanag	Manila, the Philippines, 16 Mar 2000: Carmen Deonida, a leader of the militant group of poor urban Filipinos KADAMAY, punches an effigy of Philippines President Joseph Ejercito Estrada. The group is criticizing the inability of Estrada's administration to act on the national crisis of increasing oil prices.
2000_04_14_ India: author Salman Rushdie	164	John MacDougall/AFP Photo/*South China Morning Post* (Hong Kong). 14 Mar 2015.	14 April 2000: Muslim activists beat a burning effigy of *Satanic Verses* author Salman Rushdie during a demonstration near parliament in New Delhi. Hundreds of demonstrators protested against the government's decision to let Rushdie enter India, as one of the nominees of the Commonwealth Writers Prize.
2000_06_22_ Pakistan: Indian Premier Vajpayee	60	K.M. Choudary/Associated Press Images (New York).	Lahore, Pakistan, 22 Jun 2000: Protesters burn an effigy of Indian Prime Minister Atal Behari Vajpayee. They chanted anti-Indian slogans and condemned recent attacks on Christians and their churches in India.
2000_12_00_ Philippines: President Estrada	223	UGATLahi Artist Collective/Facebook	Erapzilla.
2001_02_13_Palestine: Israeli Premier Sharon	150	Mohamed Zatari/Associated Press Images (New York).	February 13, 2001: A Palestinian girl covers an effigy of Israeli Prime Minister-elect Ariel Sharon with an American flag as she prepares for a mock hanging, during a sit-in at Ein el-Hilweh refugee camp on the outskirts of Sidon, south Lebanon, to protest Sharon's hard-line policies. About 300 Palestinians participated in the anti-Sharon protest to mark Tuesday as "a day of rage" called by Palestinians in the West Bank and Gaza Strip.
2001_09_22_ Pakistan: US President Bush	7–8	EPA/*de Volkskrant* (Amsterdam) 22 Sep 2001.	Pro-Taliban-demonstranten in de Pakistaanse hoofdstad Karachi hakken in op een pop die president Bush van de Verenigde Staten voorstelt.
2001_10_12_ Pakistan: US President Bush	62	Chris Hondros/Getty Images, Seattle (WA).	Pakistan, 12 Oct 2001: A pro-Taliban protester sips a drink while looking over an effigy of U.S. President George W. Bush during a rally in Peshawar. The biggest pro-Taliban rallies took place as the U.S.-led air strikes continued against neighboring Afghanistan.
2001_11_04_ Iran: Uncle Sam	158	Keivan/Getty Images, Seattle (WA).	Tehran, 4 Nov 2001: Iranians burn an effigy of Uncle Sam in front of the former US embassy. Thousands of Iranians gathered in front of the former embasssy compound to commemorate the 1979 takeover of the "den of spies" by militant students.
2001_11_09_ Pakistan: US President Bush	223	AP/PTI/*Tribune* (Chandigarh, India). 11 Nov 2001.	Karachi, Pakistan, 9 Nov 2001: Pro-Taliban protesters parade an effigy of US President Bush on the back of a donkey during a protest rally. Pakistani political and religious parties called for a nationwide general strike to protest against the US-led airstrikes on Afghanistan and the Pakistan government support to the US action. The text on the shirt reads "dog".
2001_12_30_ USA-FL: Osama bin Laden	cover, 108	Joe Raedle/Getty Images	Coconut Grove, FL, 30 Dec 2001: A young boy prepares to hit the Osama Pinata during the King Mango Strut parade in. The parade which is in its 20th year of parody and satire pokes fun at everything from local politics to international crisis.

Descriptor	Page	Credits / Source	Caption
2003_04_11_ Bangladesh: US President Bush	189	Rafiqur Rahman/ Reuters/ *Kholamon* (kholamon.tripo d.com). Apr 2003.	3 Apr 2003: Bangladeshi activists burn an effigy of U.S. President George W. Bush during an anti-war protest in Dhaka. Anti-war protests continued in predominantly Muslim Bangladesh as U.S-led forces neared Iraqi capital Baghdad on Thursday.
2004_03_30_ Egypt: US President Bush + British Premier Blair + Israeli Premier Sharon	151	Marcoo Di/AFP/Getty Images, Seattle (WA).	30 March 2004: Egyptian students hangs effigies of British Prime Minister Tony Blair, US President George W. Bush and Israeli Prime Minister Ariel Sharon during a demonstration at the al-Azhar University in Cairo to mark 'Land Day.' Land Day is a yearly gathering of Palestinians to commemorate the death of six people protesting against the confiscation of Arab lands on March 30, 1976, by Israel.
2004_07_29_ USA-MA: President Bush + John Kerry	79	S. Patrick Ouellette/Portland Press Herald/Getty Images, Seattle (WA).	A protester jumps over a burning effigy of a two faced Bush/Kerry outside the Fleet Center in Boston Thursday.
2004_08_25_ Pakistan: US President Bush	69	Aamir Qureshi/AFP Photo/ Getty Images, Seattle (WA).	25 Aug 2004: Activists of Pakistani Muslim religious group Sunni Tehrik hold aflot an effigy of US President George W. Bush while chanting anti-US slogans during a protest rally in Karachi. The demonstrators condemned the US attacks on the Iraqi holy city of Najaf and demanded the immediate withdrawal of US-led coalition forces from Iraq.
2005_03_19_ Brazil: US President Bush	228	Alexandre Meneghini/AP Photo/*Hellblazer* (hellblazer. com). 20 Mar 2005.	Sao Paulo, Brazil, 19 Mar 2005: An effigy of US President George W. Bush is seen during an anti-war protest in downtown Sao Paulo for the second anniversary of the U.S.-led invasion on Iraq.
2005_04_09_ Iraq: Saddam Hussein + US President Bush + British Premier Blair (a)	193	Ali Jasim RCS/Reuters/ *France Info* (Paris). 8 Jul 2014.	Baghdad, 9 Apr 2005: Des milliers d'Irakiens chiites fidèles à Moqtada al-Sadr iman et nouveau leader politique manifestent sur la place Firdos la place du Paradis à Bagdad. Ils réclament le départ des troupes américaines et le procès de l'ancien président Saddam Hussein.
2005_04_09_ Iraq: Saddam Hussein + US President Bush + British Premier Blair (b)	193	*Democratic Underground* (democraticunder ground. com). 14 Apr 2009.	Baghdad, 9 Apr 2005: Effigies of Blair, Hussein, and Bush all wearing chains, nooses and prison jump suits at former location of the famous Saddam statue.
2005_04_09_ Iraq: Saddam Hussein + US President Bush + British Premier Blair (c)	193, 222	Wathiq Khuzaie/Getty Images/*Sfgate* (San Francisco). 10 Apr 2005.	9 Apr 2005: Effigies of U.S. President George W. Bush, former Iraqi President Saddam Hussein and British Prime Minister Tony Blair are seen during a rally in Baghdad, Iraq. Thousands of Iraqi Shiites loyal to the firebrand Shiite cleric Moqtada al-Sadr gathered in Baghdads Firdos square.
2005_05_11_ Afghanistan: US President Bush	170	Akhter Khan/AFP Photo/ Getty Images, Seattle (WA).	Afghanistan, 11 May 2005: Afghan students from the Nangarhar University burn an effigy of US President George Bush during a protest in Jalalabad. Four people were killed and dozens injured in violent protests in the city sparked by reports that US soldiers were desecrating the Koran at Guantanamo Bay, a doctor said.
2006_00_00_ USA-CA: President Bush	123		San Francisco.
2006_02_10_ India: Danish government	171	Raveen-dran/AFP/Getty Images, Seattle (WA).	10 Feb 2006: Indian Muslims burn an effigy of the Danish government during a demonstration outside the Jama Masjid in New Delhi. Thousands of Muslims poured out on the streets of India's capital after Friday prayers in the first such protest in overwhelmingly Hindu India against cartoons depicting Prophet Mohammed.
2006_02_24_ Pakistan: Danish cartoonist	171	Zahid Hussein/Reuters/ *Daily Maverick* (Johannesburg, South Africa). 8 Sep 2010.	24 Feb 2006: Pakistani Muslims beat an effigy of a Danish cartoonist during a rally in Karachi. Passban, a social organisation, held the rally to protest against the publication of cartoons and caricatures depicting the Prophet Mohammad in European newspapers.
2006_03_01_ India: US President Bush	66	Manpreet Romana/AFP/ Getty Images, Seattle (WA).	New Delhi, 1 Mar 2006: An Indian Muslim carries an effigy of US President George W. Bush on his shoulder before burning it during a protest against Bush's visit to India.
2006_12_30_ India: US President Bush	189	Altaf Zargar/*Kashmir Newz*, Sonwar Bagh Srinagar, India, Dec 30 2006.	People setting fire to an effigy of US president George W Bush during a protest demonstration in Srinagar. Angry mob came out on streets at many places in Kashmir raising slogans against USA and its allies, as the news of former Iraqi president Saddam Hussain's execution reached here.

Descriptor	Page	Credits / Source	Caption
2006_12_30_ Iraq: former President Saddam Hussein (a)	67	Wait Khuzaie/Getty Images/*Los Angeles Times*. 17 Dec 2011.	Baghdad, 30 Dec 2006: After hearing news about the execution of the former Iraqi president Saddam Hussein, Iraqi's drive through the streets of Sadr City with an effigy of the executed dictator hanging from a rope.
2006_12_30_ Iraq: former President Saddam Hussein (b)	71	Ahmad Al-Rubaye/AFP/ *Gateway Pundit* (USA). 30 Dec 2006.	Baghdad: An Iraqi uses a shoe to beat an effigy of ousted dictator Saddam Hussein. US President George W. Bush has hailed Saddam's execution as "an important milestone" on the road to building an Iraqi democracy but warned it will not end deadly violence there.
2007_01_04_ India: US President Bush	224	*Novatownhall* (novatownhall. com), 1 Nov 2011.	
2007_05_01_ Afghanistan: US President Bush	74	Rahmat Gul/AP Photo	1 May 2007: Afghan youths look at an effigy of U.S. President George W. Bush after setting it on fire during a protest in Jalalabad, the provincial capital of Nangarhar province, east of Kabul.
2007_06_21_ India: author Salman Rushdie	164	*Hindustan Times* (Pakistan). 21 Jun 2007. (page discontinued).	Kashmiri protesters burn an effigy of British author Salman Rushdie during a protest in Srinagar on June 21, 2007. Angry protesters took to the streets in Srinagar on Thursday to denounce a British knighthood for Rushdie, whose novel *Satanic Verses* outraged Muslims worldwide. The placard on effigy reads "Hang apostate Salman Rushdie".
2007_08_24_ USA-DC: President Bush	67, 111	"Democratic Mob Censure Bush in Effigy." *The Onion* (Madison, WI). 24 Aug 2007.	The Bush effigy, a surprisingly accurate likeness outfitted in a blue suit and red power tie, was originally to be taken to the steps of the Capitol Building for the censure proceedings. The mob turned back, however, when one among the rabble called a point of order and explained that the president would not be present if Congress were actually to pass censure. When the measure finally passed, the news was officially delivered to the effigy and a large banner reading "CENSURED!" was hung above it.
2008_02_15_ Pakistan: Danish Premier Rasmussen	170	EPA/MK Chaudhry	Multan, Pakistan 15 Feb 2008: Supporters of Islamic party Jamiat Tulba-e-Arabia burn an effigy of Danish Prime Minister Anders Fogh Rasmussen during a protest to condemn the republication of a controversial caricatures depicting the Prophet Mohammed.
2008_03_21_ Afghanistan: Dutch politician Wilders	170	Novum/AP	21 Mar 2008: Duizenden Afghanen hebben vrijdag in de hoofdstad Kabul Nederlandse en Deense vlaggen in brand gestoken en een pop die Geert Wilders moest voorstellen verbrand.
2008_03_30_ Pakistan: Dutch politician Wilders	170, 239	Fareed Khan/AP Photo	Karachi, Pakistan, 30 Mar 2008: A Pakistani woman gestures next to a burning effigy of Dutch lawmaker Geert Wilders during a protest against a recent Dutch film that portrays Islam as a ticking time bomb aimed at the West.
2008_04_03_ Zimbabwe: President Mugabe	223	AP Photo/*The Age* (Fairfax, Australia). 4 Apr 2008.	Harare, Zimbabwe, 2 Apr 2008: Mocked: An election poster of Zimbabwe's President Robert Mugabe pinned to an effigy.
2008_06_09_ Pakistan: President Musharraf	73, 214	Khalid Tanveer/AP Photo/ *Militaryphotos* (militaryph otos.net). 9 Jun 2008.	Multan, Pakistan, 9 Jun 2008: Supporters of deposed Pakistani judges burn an effigy of President Pervez Musharraf. Thousands of Pakistani activists and lawyers gathered in major cities Monday to kick off a series of protests aimed at pressuring the new government to restore judges sacked by Musharraf.
2008_10_18_ Iraq: US President Bush + US Secretary of State Rice (a)	194	Wathiq Khuzaie/Getty Images, Seattle (WA).	Baghdad, 18 Oct 2008: Iraqi Shiite demonstrators burn effigies of U.S. President George W. Bush and U.S. Secretary of State Condoleezza Rice during a protest against a proposed U.S.-Iraqi security pact.
2008_10_18_ Iraq: US President Bush + US Secretary of State Rice (b)	195	Karim Kadim/AP Photo	Baghdad, 18 Oct 2008: Followers of Shiite cleric Muqtada al-Sadr burn effigies of U.S. President George W. Bush, right and Secretary of State Condoleezza Rice, during a rally to protest a draft U.S.-Iraqi security agreement.
2008_10_18_ Iraq: US President Bush + US Secretary of State Rice (c)	195	*Monsters and Critics* (media. monster sandcritics.com).	
2008_10_18_ Iraq: US President Bush + US Secretary of State Rice (d)	195	Wathiq Khuzaie/Getty Images, Seattle (WA).	Baghdad, 18 Oct 2008: Shiite demonstrators take part in a protest against a proposed U.S.-Iraqi security pact. Supporters of radical Shiite cleric Moqtada al-Sadr protested against the agreement which would replace the existing U.N. mandate authorizing the U.S.-led forces in Iraq.

Descriptor	Page	Credits / Source	Caption
2008_10_18_ Iraq: US President Bush + US Secretary of State Rice (e)	195	Wathiq Khuzaie/Getty Images/*Sfgate* (San Francisco). 19 Oct 2008.	Baghdad, 18 Oct 2008: Iraqi Shiite demonstrators burn effigies of U.S. President George W. Bush and U.S. Secretary of State Condoleezza Rice during a protest against a proposed U.S.-Iraqi security pact.
2008_10_18_ Iraq: US President Bush + US Secretary of State Rice (f)	78, 195	Hadi Mizban/AP Photo/ *Cleveland.com (OH)*. 19 Oct 2008 (page deleted).	Baghdad, 18 Oct 2008: Followers of Shiite cleric Muqtada al-Sadr burn effigies of U.S. President George W. Bush, right and Secretary of State Condoleezza Rice, during a rally to protest a draft U.S.-Iraqi security agreement.
2008_10_19_ USA-OH: presidential candidate Obama (a)	228	*HuffPost* (USA). 19 Nov 2008.	
2008_10_19_ USA-OH: presidential candidate Obama (b)	228	CNN	
2008_10_29_ USA-CA: Sarah Palin	94	Francine Orr/*Los Angeles Times*	West Hollywood, CA, 28 Oct 2008: A portrait of Mito Aviles (left) and Chad-Michael Morrisette in front of their Halloween decoration which includes a caricature of VP candidate Sarah Palin hanging with a noose around her neck and Presidential candidate John McCain coming out of a flaming fire place.
2008_10_29_ USA-CA: Sarah Palin guard	94	Stewart Cook/Rex Features	
2008_10_31_ USA-CA: Sarah Palin + Chad	94	Lesley O'Toole/*The Guardian* (UK). 30 Oct 2008.	Creator of the Palin effigy gets a taste of his own medicine.
2008_11_21_ Iraq: US President Bush (a)	196	Karim Kadim/AP /*The Immelman Turn* (immelman.us), 25 Feb 2010.	Baghdad, 21 Nov 2008: A protester uses his shoe to strike an effigy of President Bush, as thousands of followers of Shiite cleric Muqtada al-Sadr converge on Firdous Square in central Baghdad for a protest against a proposed U.S.-Iraqi security pact.
2008_11_21_ Iraq: US President Bush (b)	196	Ali Jasim/United Press International (USA). 21 Nov 2008.	Thousands of demonstrators hang an effigy of U.S. President George W. Bush during a rally at Firdos Square in Baghdad. The followers of Shiite cleric Moqtada al-Sadr marched against a pact letting U.S. forces stay in Iraq until 2011.
2008_11_21_ Iraq: US President Bush (c)	197	Ali Jasim/United Press International (USA). 21 Nov 2008.	Ibid.
2008_11_21_ Iraq: US President Bush (d)	197	Ali Jasim/United Press International (USA). 21 Nov 2008.	Ibid.
2008_11_21_ Iraq: US President Bush (e)	197	Ali Jasim/United Press International (USA). 21 Nov 2008.	Ibid.
2008_11_21_ Iraq: US President Bush (g)	197	Ali Jasim/United Press International (USA). 21 Nov 2008.	21 Nov 2008: Thousands of demonstrators hang an effigy of U.S. President George W. Bush during a rally at Firdos Square in Baghdad.
2008_11_21_ Iraq: US President Bush (f)	197	*Asadandtiger's name* (thetigris.blog.over-blog.com), 6 Dec 2008.	Baghdad, 21 Nov 2008: At the spot where U.S. forces helped Iraqis topple a statue of Saddam Hussein in 2003, protesters Friday tore down an effigy of President Bush and set it afire during a demonstration over plans to keep American troops in Iraq through 2011.
2009_01_18_Lebanon: US Presidents Bush + Obama	151, 225	Ali Hashisho/Reuters/*First Things Test* (gatewaypundit.wordpress.com), 18 Jan 2009.	18 Jan 2009: Leftist protestors burn an effigy of U.S. President George W. Bush and U.S. President-elect Barack Obama during a demonstration displaying solidarity with the Palestinians in Gaza, near the US embassy building in Awkar, north of Beirut.
2009_03_10_ Egypt: company lawyer Al Dossuqi	200	Per Bjorklund/Flickr, 9 Mar 2009.	Egypt, 9 Mar 2009: Just inside the main gates striking workers had hung an effigy of company lawyer Ali al-Dossuqi, who apparently had described them as baltagiyya, or a bunch of thugs, in an interview on private TV-channel el-Mehwar last night.
2009_04_07_ Iraq: former US President Bush (b)	198		A follower of radical Shiite cleric Muqtada al-Sadr was pictured preparing an effigy of the former U.S. President in the Sadr City neighborhood of Baghdad.

Descriptor	Page	Credits / Source	Caption
2009_04_07_ Iraq: former US President Bush (a)	198	Ali Al-Saadi/AFP/Getty Images/*Washington Post*. 7 Apr 2009.	7 Apr 2009: Followers of radical Iraqi Shiite cleric Moqtada al-Sadr work on an effigie of former US President George W. Bush in Baghdad's Sadr City. The Sadr movement is planning a huge protest in Baghdad on April 9 to mark the sixth anniversary of the fall of Saddam Hussein's regime and call for the immediate withdrawal of US troops from Iraq.
2009_04_09_ Iraq: former US President Bush (a)	198	Karim Kadim/AP/*CTV News*, Canada. 9 Apr 2009	Baghdad, 9 Apr 2009: Supporters of anti-U.S. Shiite cleric Muqtada al-Sadr burn an effigy of former U.S. President George W. Bush in central Baghdad, for a rally marking the sixth anniversary of the fall of the Iraqi capital to American troops.
2009_04_09_ Iraq: former US President Bush (b)	201	Karim Kadim/AP/*Le Monde International* (Paris). 9 Apr 2009.	Les manifestants ont également brûlé des posters et des mannequins à l'effigie de l'ancien président américain George W Bush.
2009_04_09_ Iraq: Saddam Hussein	198	Ali AlSaadi/AFP/*Le Monde International* (Paris). 9 Apr 2009.	Des portraits de Saddam Hussein, qui dirigeait le pays depuis 1979 et a été renversé dans la foulée de l'entrée des troupes américaines dans Bagdad le 9 avril 2003, étaient également visibles dans la foule.
2009_06_00_UK: Premier Brown	243	Demotix Photo Agency (London).	The Government of the Dead zombies rip apart and pretended to eat an effigy of Gordon Brown outside of the Labour Party HQ in Victoria Street, central London. They sprayed fake blood on the pavement, and performed undead street theatre. The protesters highlighted the Labour Party involvement in the recent MP's expenses scandal, and called for the Prime Minister to step down as he was in their words "already dead".
2009_09_18_ Pakistan: US Presidents Bush + Obama	225	Shakil Adil/AP Photo	Karachi, Pakistan, 18 Sep 2009: Pakistanis hold up an effigy of former U.S. President George W. Bush during a rally to mark Quds Day, an annual anti-Israel commemoration that reflects Pakistan's sympathy with the Palestinians.
2009_10_25_ Afganistan: US President Obama	187	Shah Marai/AFP/Getty Images, Seattle (WA).	Kabul, Afghanistan, 25 Oct 2009: Furious Afghans on torched an effigy of US President Barack Obama at a mass protest over allegations that Western troops fighting the Taliban had set fire to a copy of the Koran. Afghan university students shout anti-US slogans and hold a banner reading 'No Democracy; We want just Islam!' during a demonstration in Kabul.
2010_02_23_ India: Taliban	63	photogallery. sandesh.com	Activists of Indian Sikh community shout slogans as they burn an effigy of Pakistan-based Taliban militants during a protest against the Taliban militants who beheaded a Sikh in Pakistan during a demonstration in Amritsar on February 23, 2010.
2010_03_02_ Yemen: President Saleh (a)	184	*Mareb Press* (Sana, Yemen), 2 Mar 2010.	On Sunday, al Yafie burned an effigy of Yemeni President Ali Abdullah Saleh during an anti-government rally in Zinjibar, Abyan.
2010_05_00_ Pakistan: US President Obama	240	AFP/*Radio Free Europe* (Prague, Czech Republic). 14 Jun 2012.	Pakistani protesters burn an effigy of Obama in Lahore in May 2010.
2010_05_01_UK: Premier Brown	48, 65	Paul Hackett/In Pictures/ Corbis	London, UK, 1 May 2010: Effigies of British Political leaders, Nick Clegg, Gordon Brown and David Cameron are placed in Parliament Square during a May Day demonstration, London.
2010_05_12_ Egypt: Governor Labib (a)	178	Flickr, user: ESFBN.	12 May 2010: Mock funeral of Adel Labib, governor of Alexandria. The residents of Tousson mark the second anniversary of the demolition of their homes at their sit-in in front of the Dokki Ministry. Sign reading: Death to all those who have caused the misery of Toussoon's people.
2010_05_12_ Egypt: Governor Labib (b)	260	Flickr, user: ESFBN.	Mock funeral of Adel Labib, governor of Alexandria.
2010_06_07_ Malaysia: Israeli Premier Netanyahu	242	Lai Seng Sin/AP Photo/ *Think Israel* (think-israel. org). Shulman, Richard H. 11 Jun 2010.	Kuala Lumpur, Malaysia, 7 Jun 2010: Muslim protesters hit an effigy of Israeli Prime Minister Benjamin Netanyahu during a demonstration against Israel's naval commando raid on a flotilla of ships carrying aid and hundreds of pro-Palestinian activists to the Gaza Strip.
2010_07_06_Sri Lanka: UN Secretary General Ban Ki-moon	64	Lakruwan Wannia- rachchi/ AFP/*ABC News* (Australia). 6 Jul 2010.	Activists burn an effigy of UN secretary-general Ban Ki-moon

Descriptor	Page	Credits / Source	Caption
2010_08_24_ India: Osama bin Laden	62	*Hindustan Times* (Pakistan). 24 Aug 2010.	BJP workers burn an effigy of terror king Osama Bin Laden during a demonstration blaming him responsible for Kashmir terrorism issue in Bhopal.
2010_09_06_ Afghanistan: US pastor Jones	172	RT News Channel/*Daily Motion* (New York).	Scores of people have gathered in Afghanistan's capital Kabul on Monday to denounce a U.S. church's plan to burn the Islamic holy book, the Quran. The crowd in Kabul, numbering as many as 500, chanted "Long live Islam" and "Death to America". Pastor Terry Jones, of the Dove World Outreach Center in Gainesville, a non-denominational Christian church, said he planned to burn the Quran on Saturday, 11 September, to mark the ninth anniversary of the 9/11 attacks.
2010_11_08_ India: US President Obama	cover	Bikas Das/AP Photo	8 Nov 2010, Calcutta: Activists of Socialist Unity Center of India burn an effigy of U.S. President Barack Obama to protest against his visit to India.
2011_01_31_ Egypt: President Mubarak	178	John Rees/Flickr, user: Counterfire.	31 Jan 2011: Mubarak effigy hangs in Tahrir Square.
2011_02_01_ Egypt: President Mubarak and government members (a-d)	54/ 55	Associated Press Archive (New York).	Effigies of Egyptian President Hosni Mubarak with images of the Pyramids Star of David and the US Capitol Building drawn on. A protester speaking, name not given: "The ousted President is subjected to a civilian tribunal because of the 30 years of oppressing the people and killing the Egyptian people." Man wearing judges' gown writing down a note. Protester's face with slogan on his face reading (Arabic) "Step Down." Various protesters hanging effigies.
2011_02_02_ Egypt: President Mubarak	179	Lefteris Pitarakis/AP Photo/*Israeli Defense* (Kfar Saba, Israel). 27 Mar 2018.	2 Feb 2011: Effigies of Egyptian President Hosni Mubarak can be seen hanging from traffic lights, as Egyptian anti-government protesters gathered in Tahrir (Liberation) Square, watch U.S. President Barack Obama, not seen, live on a TV broadcast from Washington, speaking about the situation in Egypt. Egyptian President Hosni Mubarak announced he will not run for a new term in September elections but rejected protesters' demands he step down immediately and leave the country.
2011_02_03_ Egypt: President Mubarak	179	ghazalairshad/ Flickr.	
2011_02_04_ Egypt: President Mubarak	179	Zeinab Mohammed/Flickr.	4 Feb 2011: One of the hanged Effigies representing Mubarak at the Tahrir square.
2011_02_07_ Egypt: President Mubarak	179	Asmaa Waguih/Reuters/ BeBo OpaA /Flickr.	Cairo 7 Feb 2011: A protester rips apart an effigy of Egyptian President Hosni Mubarak after a mock funeral at Tahrir Square. Protesters dug in for a long fight on Monday, pressing their demand for an overhaul of the political system and the resignation of President Hosni Mubarak.
2011_02_24_ Libya: Colonel Gaddafi (a)	75	Luis Sinco/*Los Angeles Times*, 25 Feb 2011.	Libya, 24 Feb 2011: A young man stabs an effigy of Libyan dictator Muammar Khadafi along the waterfront in Benghazi.
2011_02_24_ Libya: Colonel Gaddafi (b)	184	Reuters/*Daily Mail* (UK), 24 Feb 2011.; *Cryptome.* 24 Feb 2011.	Libya, 24 Feb 2011: Effigies of Muammar Gaddafi and his son Seif are hung from a burnt state security building in Benghazi. After a week of violence in which it threw off government control, this elegant port of about 700,000 is being run by committees of citizens as the dust of rebellion settles.
2011_04_03_ Afghanistan: US President Obama (a)	172	Rahmat Gul/AP Photo/ *Die Welt* (Germany), 3 Apr 2011.	Afghanen protestieren mit einem Kreuz und einer Puppe, die US-Präsident Barack Obama darstellen soll, gegen die Koran-verbrennung
2011_04_03_ Afghanistan: US President Obama (b)	172	AP/*Fox News* (USA). 3 April 2011.	3 Apr 2011: An Afghan protestor beats a burning effigy of U.S. President Barack Obama during a rally in Jalalabad, Afghanistan. Afghan protests against the burning of a Quran in Florida entered a third day with a demonstration in the major eastern city Sunday, while the Taliban called on people to rise up, blaming government forces for any violence.
2011_04_08_UK: Nick Clegg	67	AP/*Daily Mail* (London). 8 Apr 2011.	Unrepentant: Clegg's decision to back plans to raise university tuition fees, despite a pledge not to, sparked protests; right, an effigy of Clegg is hanged by activists
2011_04_09_ Iraq: former US President Bush	200	Khalid Mohammed/AP Photo/*Times Union* (Albany, NY). 9 Apr 2011.	Iraq 9 Apr 2011: Followers of radical Shiite cleric Muqtada al-Sadr wave Iraqi flags as they burn an effigy of former U.S. President George W. Bush and U.S. flags during a rally marking the eighth anniversary of the fall of the Iraqi capital to American troops in Baghdad.

Descriptor	Page	Credits / Source	Caption
2011_05_08_ Libya: effigy	217	Thomas Dworzak/Magnum Photos (New York).	Libya, 2011.
2011_05_23_ Pakistan: US pastor Jones	172	Mohsin Raza/Reuters/*Daily Mail* (UK). 4 Apr 2011.	23 Mar 2011: Pakistani Christians burn an effigy depicting U.S. pastor Terry Jones during a protest in Lahore. Jones supervised the burning of a copy of the Koran in front of a crowd of about 50 people at an obscure church in Florida on Sunday, according to his website.
2011_06_24_ Turkey: Syrian President Assad	70	Reuters/*International Business Times* (New York). 24 Jun 2011.	24 Jun 2011: A demonstrator poses with an effigy of Syria's President Bashar al-Assad during a protest at the courtyard of Fatih mosque in Istanbul.
2011_06_28_ Libya: Colonel Gaddafi	75	Mohamed Abd el-Ghany/ Reuters/*Telegraph* (UK). 28 Jun 2011.	27 Jun 2011: A Libyan woman drags an effigy of Libyan leader Muammar Gaddafi after receiving news of an arrest warrant issued against him, at the courthouse in Benghazi.
	88, 248	Reuters/*Express Tribune* (Pakistan). 15 Jul 2011.	14 Jul 2011: Supporters of MQM burn an effigy representing Zulfiqar Mirza during a protest in Karachi. Tempers flared in the aftermath of Zulfiqar Mirza's statements late Wednesday night.
2011_07_22_ Syria: President Assad	64	HO/Reuters/*Washington Post*. 22 Jul 2011.	An effigy of Syrian President Bashar al-Assad is raised during a protest against him in the tribal province of Deir al-Zor, Syria.
2011_08_01_ India: Om Parkash Chautala	23, 211	Amar Singh Jyani/GS Mann/*Sirsa News* (India). 1 Aug 2011.	Congress leaders and party supporters carried an effigy of Om Parkash Chautala from Congress Bhawan through the main bazaars and burnt it at Subhash Chowk after the news of indictment of the Chautalas in JBT scam by a Delhi Court and in cases of "income in excess to known sources."
2011_08_24_ India: "corruption"	221, 242	Ajit Solanki/AP/*Washington Post*. 25 Aug 2011.	Supporters of anti-corruption activist Anna Hazare beat an effigy representing corruption during a rally in Ahmedabad India.
2011_09_27_ Pakistan: US President Obama + US Vice President Biden (b)	211	Akram Shahid/Reuters/ *International Herald Tribun* (New York). 27 Sep 2011.	Supporters of a religious political party burned an effigy of President Obama at a rally in Hyderabad, Pakistan, on Tuesday.
2011_09_27_ Pakistan: US President Obama + US Vice President Biden ()	77	Akram Shahid/Reuters	Supporters of a religious political party burned an effigy of President Obama at a rally in Hyderabad, Pakistan, on Tuesday.
2011_10_07_Lebanon: Syrian President Assad	93	Bilal Hussein/AP/National Public Radio (Washington, DC), 7 Oct 2011.	7 Oct 2011: Protesters opposed to Syrian President Bashar Assad burn an effigy of him during Friday prayers in Tripoli, Lebanon.
2011_10_10_ Pakistan: PPP leader Mirza	220	Aftab Ahmed/PPI Images	Hyderabad, Pakistan: Angry residents of Hyderabad hold burning effigy as they are protesting against Dr.Zulfiqar Mirza on Monday
2011_12_16_ Syria: President Assad and ministers	184	Sameh Jabbouli/Youtube.	16 Dec 2011: According to the Syrian Observatory for Human Rights, more than 200,000 people hit the streets in Syria's flashpoint city of Homs on Friday, December 16, where anti-government protesters staged a mock trial of President Bashar al-Assad. The verdict? Death penalty. Assad and four of his close allies were quickly strung up and hanged in effigy.
2012_02_02_ Egypt: Field Marshall Tantawi	60, 180	Zadokite (Omar Kamel)/ Flickr.	2 Feb 2012: Effigy of Tantawi in Tahrir.
2012_02_22_ Afghanistan: US President Obama (a)	211	AFP/Getty Images/*Daily Mail* (UK), 23 Feb 2012.	Anger: Effigies of Barack Obama are paraded through the streets of Afghanistan in response to the Koran being burned by U.S. troops.
2012_02_23_ Afghanistan: US President Obama	65, 172, 212	Rahmat Gul/AP Photo/ *Daily Mail* (UK), 23 Feb 2012.	22 Feb 2012: Afghans shout slogans during an anti-US demonstration in Jalalabad, east of Kabul. Anti-American demonstrations continued for a second day Wednesday in Afghanistan over what the U.S. has said was the inadvertent burning of Muslim holy books at a NATO military base. The effigy depicts U.S. President Barack Obama.

Descriptor	Page	Credits / Source	Caption
2012_03_13_ Afghanistan: US President Obama (a)	70	Rahmat Gul/AP Photo/ *Anorak* (Middlesex, UK). 16 Sep 2012.	13 Mar 2012: Afghans chant anti U.S. slogans as they carry an effigy depicting U.S. President Barack Obama following Sunday's killing of civilians in Panjwai, Kandahar by a U.S. soldier during a protest in Jalalabad east of Kabul.
2012_03_13_ Afghanistan: US President Obama (b)	71	Rahmat Gul/AP Photo/ *Deseret News* (Salt Lake City, USA), 13 Mar 2012.	13 Mar 2012: A demonstrator writes on an effigy depicting U.S. President Barack Obama before setting it on fire following Sunday's killing of civilians in Panjwai, Kandahar by a U.S. soldier during a protest in Jalalabad east of Kabul.
2012_03_13_ Afghanistan: US President Obama (c)	71	Khan/Afghan Eyes/*Deutsche Welle* (Germany), Haussa edition.	Birnin Jalalabad na cikin inda zanga-zangar ta fi kamari.
2012_03_13_ Afghanistan: US President Obama (d)	71	*Midnight Watcher's Blogspot* (midnightwatcher. wordpress.com). 13 Mar 2012.	
2012_03_20_ SouthKorea: North Korean leader Kim Jong-un	219	Lee Jinman/AP/*Globe and Mail* (Toronto). 23 Mar 2012.	An effigy of North Korean leader Kim Jong-un is put on a mock North Korean missile during an anti-North Korea rally denouncing North's plan to launch a long-range rocket in Seoul.
2012_04_26_ Egypt: intelligence chief Suleiman	179	MaryAnn Moore, futurity-times/Flickr.	26 Apr 2012: Tahrir Square, Mubarak Effigy.
2012_04_26_ North Korea: South Korean President Lee	75	*Sino NK* (UK). 5 May 2012.	Rodong Sinmun, DPRK, 26 Apr 2012: Just Another Day in Nampo. How can depicting the head of a president on a rat's body tied to a pole surrounded by burning flames not attract attention?
2012_04_28_ North Korea: South Korean President Lee (a)	219	*Telegraph* (UK). 28 Apr 2012.	28 Apr 2012: An outpouring of anti-South Korean feeling culminates in a lifelike effigy of Lee Myung-bak being attacked by a dog, run over by a tank and stoned by protesters.
2012_04_28_ NorthKorea: South Korean President Lee (b)	219, 243	*On Demand News* (UK)/ Youtube, 28 Apr 2012.	Attack dogs tanks and rocks used by North Koreans to destroy an effigy of South Korean President Lee Myung-bak.
2012_05_00_ Syria: President Assad	225	tiny.cc/SyriaFreedom/www. almaara.com.	
2012_05_01_ Pakistan: World Bank	66	Demotix Photo Agency (London).	Members of Sindh Sugar miles workers federation Burning world bank effigy in Hyderabad during international labor day.
2012_06_03_ Egypt: former President Mubarak	180	Young Shanahan/Flickr.	In the week leading up to the presidential run-off between Mursi and Shafiq, the square is full every night. Tense and expectant but peaceful, for the most part. Effigy of Mubarak swings from the taffic lights.
2012_06_07_ Egypt: former President Mubarak	181	*Odd Stuff Magazine* (oddstuffmagazine.com).	Cairo, 7 Jun 2012: A protester carries symbolic heads depicting ousted President Hosni Mubarak, his son Alaa, his interior minister Habib al-Adly, wife Suzanne and son Gamal during a rally protesting the outcome of the Mubarak trial at Tahrir Square.
2012_06_07_ Egypt: former President Mubarak and government members	74, 182	*Laselvaoscura* (laselvaoscura.wordpress. com). 7 Jun 2012.	7 Jun 2012: Mubarak and Co-Defendants hanged in effigy, each branded with the Star of David on their foreheads (for allegedly selling Egyptian natural gas to Israel at below-market prices and reaping the rewards themselves).
2012_06_09_ USA-FL: President Obama	124	Broward-Palm Beach New Times/*The Blaze*, 9 Jun 2012.	Florida pastor Terry Jones, whose Koran-burning activities have gained worldwide attention, is in the news again, this time for hanging President Barack Obama in effigy in front of his church.
2012_06_12_ Pakistan: electricity company	76	Jamal Da-woodpoto/ Demotix/Corbis Images, Seattle (WA).	Larkana, Pakistan: 27 Traders Associations of Larkana conduct a large rally, held a protest demonstration, staged a sit-in, burnt tyres and burnt effigies against frequent electricity load shedding to demand that it ends.

Descriptor	Page	Credits / Source	Caption
2012_06_20_ Iraq: "statue" of Muqtada al Sadr	205	Ahmad al-Rubaye/AFP Photo/Getty Images, Seattle (WA).	20 Jun 2012: An Iraqi protester holds up a portrait of Shiite Muslim cleric Muqtada al-Sadr next to a pinned national flag on a monument pedestal in Fardous Square during a demonstration in Baghdad to protest against the action by the government after shutting down the offices of Al-Baghdadia a Cairo based independent Iraqi-owned Arabic-language satellite channel in Iraq.
2012_09_11_ Pakistan: US pastor Jones	65, 220	Arif Ali/AFP/GettyImages/ *Baltimore Sun* (PE), 9 Sep 2012.	24 Sep 2012: A Pakistani demonstrator holds a burning effigy of Florida pastor Terry Jones during a protest against an anti-Islam film in Lahore. More than 50 people have died around the world in violence linked to the low-budget movie, which mocks Islam and the Prophet Mohammed, since the first demonstrations erupted on September 11.
2012_09_14_Lebanon: US President Obama	173	AFP/Getty Images, Seattle (WA).	14 Sep 2012: Palestinian protesters burn an effigy covered in the US flag during a demonstration against an amateur film mocking Islam in the Palestinian refugee camp of Ain el-Helweh near the southern Lebanese city of Sidon.
2012_09_14_Palestine: US President Obama	174	AP Photo/Hatem Moussa	14 Sep 2012: Palestinian Hamas supporters burn U.S. and Israeli flags plus an effigy of Morris Sadek during a protest in Gaza City, as part of widespread anger across the Muslim world about a film ridiculing Islam's Prophet Muhammad.
2012_09_15_ Pakistan: US President Obama	64	Fareed Khan/AP Photo/ *Washington Times*, 15 Sep 2012.	15 Sep 2012: Supporters of a Insaf Student Federation burn an effigy of U.S. President Barack Obama and a representation of a U.S. flag demonstration in Karachi, Pakistan, as part of widespread anger across the Muslim world about a film ridiculing Islam's Prophet Muhammad.
2012_09_16_ Pakistan: effigy	173	Janali Laghari/Demotix/ Corbis Images, Seattle (WA).	Hyderabad, Pakistan,16 Sep 2012: Residents of different areas and members of different political and religious parties take part in the rally against the US film. They also burn an effigy during the protest outside the press club.
2012_09_18_ Pakistan: US President Obama	240	Rizwan Tabassum/AFP Photo/*RT News* (Moscow), 21 Sep 2012.	18 Sep 2012: Pakistani Sunni Muslims protesters beat an effigy of the US President Barack Obama during a protest against an anti-Islam movie in Peshawar.
2012_09_19_ Afghanistan: US President Obama	67, 174	Noorullah Shirzada/AFP/ Getty Images/Corbis Images, Seattle (WA).	19 Sep 2012: Afghan university students shout slogans during an anti-US demonstration in Jalalabad, capital of Nangarhar province. Hundreds of Afghan protesters took to the streets, setting fire to an effigy of US President Barack Obama and demanding the death of the film-maker who they say insulted the Prophet Mohammed.
2012_09_21_ Afghanistan: US President Obama	222	Massoud Hossaini/AFP Photo/Getty Images, Seattle (WA).	21 Sep 2012: Afghan parade an effigy representing US President Obama during a protest, against an anti-Islam movie and a French Magazine which published Muhammad Prophet's cartoons, in Kabul.
2012_09_21_ Bangladesh: US President Obama	174	Munir Uz Zaman/AFP/ Getty Images, Seattle (WA).	21 Sep 2012: Demonstrators set fire to an effigy of US President Barack Obama during a protest against an internet film mocking Islam in Dhaka. More than 30 people have been killed around the world during more than a week of attacks and violent protests linked to the controversial film, seen as insulting to the Prophet Mohammed.
2012_09_27_ India: US President Obama	174	Bikas Das/AP Photo	27 Sep 2012: Indian Muslims burn an effigy of U.S. President Barack Obama during a protest rally in Kolkata against an anti-Islam film produced in the U.S. called *Innocence of Muslims*.
2012_10_05_ India: filmproducer Roberts	61, 174, 232	Ibyangshu Sarkar/AFP/ GettyImages	5 Oct 2012: Indian Muslim protestors burn an effigy of Alan Roberts, the alleged director of an anti-Islam video, during a protest against the film in Kolkata.
2012_10_29_ USA-UT: President Obama + Mitt Romney	125	*KSL.com* (Salt Lake City, UT). 29 Oct 2012.	Orangeville, Utah, 29 Oct 2012: This effigy depicting Republican presidential candidate Mitt Romney hanging President Barack Obama drew enough attention for the Secret Service to pay the Orangeville man a visit.
2012_11_00_ USA-NC: President Obama	110	*KHOU11 News* (CA), 5 Nov 2012.	Sep 2012: He said that's why President Obama's effigy is hanging in the gallows.

Descriptor	Page	Credits / Source	Caption
2012_11_05_ Lewes, UK: German chanc Merkel as Guy Fawkes	45	Dan Kitwood/Getty Images/ *Baltimore Sun* (PE), 6 Nov 2012.	An effigy of German Chancellor Angela Merkel is paraded as bonfire societies process through the streets during the Bonfire Night celebrations on November 5, 2012 in Lewes, Sussex in England. Bonfire Thousands of people attend the parade as Bonfire Societies parade through the narrow streets until the evening comes to an end with the burning of an effigy, or "guy," usually representing Guy Fawkes, who died in 1605 after an unsuccessful attempt to blow up The Houses of Parliament.
2012_11_15_ Portugal: German Chancellor Merkel	228	Action Press/Rex Features/ *Daily Mail* (London), 15 Nov 2012.	Protesters with an effigy of German Chancellor Angela Merkel in Lisbon, Portugal.
2012_12_28_ Malaysia: FELDA chairman Samad	68, 212	Choo Choy May/*The Malaysia Insider* (themalaysian insider.com), 28 Dec 2012.	Settlers carry an effigy with a photo of FELDA chairman Tan Sri Isa Samad on it. Over a thousand settlers today gathered at the national capital here to protest against Tan Sri Isa Samad urging him to step down as the Federal Land Authority (FELDA) chairman.
2012_12_28_ USA-KY: President Obama	125	www.lex18.com/*New York Daily News*, 28 Dec 2012.	Kentucky man defends his racist roadside effigy of a watermelon-holding Obama.
2012_12_30_ Ecuador: Central Bank gov Delgado as Ano Viejo	63	Theresa McGarry/Tim McDowell/*ecuadorfulbright-gua-randa* (ecuadorfulbright guaranda.wordpress.com), 3 Jan 2013.	Making a large Año Viejo effigy-doll. This one will be the disgraced political figure Pedro Delgado.
2012_12_30_ Peru: various politicians as Ano Viejo	45	*DePeru*, 2 Jan 2012.	
2013_01_02_ Iraq	200	*Wolves in the City* (neoclassics.blogspot.nl), 2 Jan 2013.	1 Feb 2013: Shiite cleric predicts "Iraqi Spring" as Sunnis continue to protest in the western desert province of Anbar and other Sunni strongholds for more than a week.The demonstrations follow the arrest of bodyguards assigned to the Sunni finance minister Rafia al-Issawi, though they tap into deeper Sunni grievances of perceived discrimination by the government of Shiite Prime Minister Nouri al-Maliki.
2013_01_16_ India: US President Obama	221	*Deccan Chronicle* (Secunderabad, India). 16 Jan 2013.	Muslims carry an effigy of US President Barack Obama during a rally in Kolkata to press for their various demands.
2013_01_28_ USA-FL: Presidents Obama + Clinton	73, 241	*HuffPost* (USA), 28 Jan 2013.	Pastor Terry Jones Burns Obama, Clinton Effigies In Response To Gay Rights Support: The infamous Quran-burning pastor expressed his disdain for President Barack Obama's support of the LGBT community by blitzing an effigy. Terry Jones, who has previously condemned Islam, cited Obama's promotion of "the gay-lesbian agenda" and abortion as incentive for the spectacle. Also burned alongside the Obama effigy was a Clinton counterpart, in response to the former president's support of the Obama administration.
2013_02_03_ Egypt: President Morsi	181	Lora A. Lucero/*Why Gaza?* (loralucero.word press.com), 3 Feb. 2013.	Even without the language, I understand two messages clearly. President Morsi is hung in effigy. And U.S. Ambassador Anne Patterson is warned to "GO BACK TO HELL"
2013_02_08_ India: Rajya Sabha chairman Kurien	70, 211	Express photo/*The New Indian Express*, 8 Feb 2013.	Members of various women's organisations in Kerala pouring black oil on the effigy of P J Kurien demanding reinvestigation into his involvement in the Suryanelli case.
2013_02_24_ Bangladesh: "atheist blogger"	79, 251	Monirul Alam/ZUMA Press/Corbis Images, Seattle (WA).	Dhaka, Bangladesh, 24 Feb 2013: A Madrasa student's burns blogger effigy during the country wide down-to-dusk strike in the Kamrangir Char, Dhaka. The eight Islamist parties enforced today's strike protesting attacks on their Friday's demonstrations, and demanding punishment to "atheist" bloggers.
2013_03_07_ Czech Republic: President Klaus as Morena	47, 257	AFP Photo/Michal Cizek	Czech Republic, Prague, 7 Mar 2013: People hold a burning effigy of Czech President Vaclav Klaus symbolizing the end of his presidency, at the Charles Bridge in Prague.
2013_04_10_ India: Russian President Putin	68, 212	*News Track India* (New Delhi), 10 Apr 2013.	Social activists under the leadership of Subash Gupta, President of Human Rights Commission carried out a protest and burnt an effigy of Russian President Vladimir Putin against the heinous crime and atrocities being committed against Indian businessmen in Russia by misusing section 165 on Russian constitution.

Descriptor	Page	Credits / Source	Caption
2013_04_16_ South Korea: North Korean leader Kim Jong-il	219	Kin Cheung/AP/*Times of Israel*, 17 April 2013.	16 Apr 2013: South Korean protesters burn effigies of North Korean leader Kim Jong-un, and late leaders Kim Jong-il and Kim Il-sung, at an anti-North Korea protest on the birthday of Kim Il-sung in Seoul. North Korea lashed out anew at South Korea over the small public protest, saying it would not hold talks with its southern neighbor unless it apologized for anti-North Korean actions "big and small" and warning that it could take retaliatory measures at any time.
2013_04_17_UK: Premier Thatcher	239	WENN.com/*Daily Mail* (London), 17 Apr 2013.	Residents of Goldthorpe drink to Lady Thatcher's death as they hold a sign reading "Thatcher the scab".
2013_05_09_ India: UPA government as Ravana	47	*Deccan Chronicle* (Secunderabad, India), 9 May 2013.	India, 9 May 2013: BJP workers carry an effigy during a protest against UPA government over corruption and scams in Jaipur.
2013_05_11_ Egypt: former President Mubarak	181	Amr Nabil/AP/*Deseret News* (Salt Lake City, UT), 11 May 2013.	11 May 2013: Egyptian anti-Mubarak protesters hold effigies representing former Egyptian President Hosni Mubarak, center, his wife Suzanne, fourth left, and his sons Gamal, third left, and Alaa, second left, outside a court in Cairo. Egyptian prosecutors say they are presenting new evidence in the retrial of former President Hosni Mubarak for failing to stop the killing of 900 protestors in the 2011 unrest that ousted him. The sons face corruption charges.
2013_06_26_ Egypt: President al-Sisi	181	STR/AFP/Getty Images, Seattle (WA).	26 Jul 2013: Supporters of the Muslim Brotherhood and Egypt's ousted president Mohamed Morsi hold up a dummy decorated with a portrait of Egyptian Army chief who ousted Morsi, Abdel Fattah al-Sisi, and the Israeli and US flags, during a demonstration in the Mediterranean city of Alexandria.
2013_07_22_ Brazil: Governor Cabral	72	AFP/*News That Matters* (ivarfjeld.com). 25 Jul 2013.; *Fox News* (New York). 23 Jul 2013.	22 Jul 2013: People burn an effigy of Rio de Janeiro's state Governor Sergio Cabral as atheists and the Anonymous protest group demonstrate against the money spent on the pope's visit, while Brazilian President Dilma Rousseff offers a welcoming ceremony for Pope Francis at the Guanabara Palace, seat of the city's government, in Rio de Janeiro.
2013_08_01_ India: INC president Sonia Gandhi	70	PTI/*India Today* (New Delhi). 1 Aug 2013.	Women activists with an effigy of AICC President Sonia Gandhi protest against the creation of Telangana in Chittoor on Thursday.
2013_08_01_ India: Potti Sriramulu (anointing the statue by pouring milk)	211	*Deccan Chronicle* (Secunderabad, India). 1 Aug 2013.	1 Aug 2013: Members of Chamber of Commerce pour milk to 'cleanse' the statue of Potti Sriramulu to protest against the CWC's decision to announce formation of Telangana in Rajahmundry.
2013_09_11_ Poland: government of Premier Tusk	62	Patryk Wasilewski/*Wall Street Journal* (New York), 11 Sep 2013.	11 Sep 2013: Polish Prime Minister Donald Tusk is burned in effigy by protesters in Warsaw.
2013_09_27_ India: Pakistani Premier Sharif	230	Mukesh Gupta/Thomson Reuters Foundation News (London). 27 Sep 2013.	27 Sep 2013: Supporters of Shiv Sena, a Hindu hardline group, burn an effigy of Pakistan's Prime Minister Nawaz Sharif during a protest against Thursday's militant attacks in Jammu.
2013_11_19_ Afghanistan: US President Obama	71	Reuters/*Dawn* (Karachi, Pakistan). 19 Nov 2013.	Students shout anti-government and anti-US slogans as they punch an effigy of US President Barack Obama during a protest against the upcoming national gathering called a "loya jirga", in Jalalabad, eastern Afghanistan. The students expressed their concern about a proposed bilateral security agreement between Afghanistan and the U.S.
2013_12_03_ India: Union Carbide CEO Anderson (a)	227	*Two Circles* (Cambridge, MA). 4 Dec 2013.	3 Dec 2013: Effigy of Dow Chemical which the survivors hold responsible for their plight as it refuses to own responsibility to clean up toxic chemicals which has seeped into the soil contaminating the underground water used for drinking by residents living around the abandoned Union Carbide factory.
2013_12_03_ India: Union Carbide CEO Anderson (b)	227	IANS/*Prokerala* (Manganam, India). 3 Dec 2013.	Bhopal, India, 3 Dec 2013: Survivors of Bhopal gas tragedy burn effigies of Union Carbide chairman Warren Anderson as they demonstrate on the 29th anniversary of the tragedy outside abandoned factory of Union Carbide.
2013_12_03_ India: Union Carbide CEO Anderson (c)	227	IANS/*Prokerala* (Manganam, India). 3 Dec 2013.	Ibid.

Descriptor	Page	Credits / Source	Caption
2014_04_28_ Philippines: President Aquino + US President Obama (c)	223	EPA/*Vos Iz Neias* (New York). 29 Apr 2014.	28 Apr 2014: Filipino protesters pull an effigy of US President Barack Obama (Top) and Philippines President Benigno Aquino III (Bottom) during a protest rally against the visit of US President Barack Obama heading towards Malacanang presidential palace in Manila, Philippines.
2014_04_28_ Philippines: President Aquino + US President Obama (b)	78	Noel Celis/AFP/Getty Images/*NBC News* (New York). 28 Apr 2014.	28 Apr 2014: Protesters burn an effigy of President Barack Obama during an anti-U.S. protest near Malacanang palace in Manila.
2014_10_09_ USA-VA: pretend effigy protest in US army exercise	139	Pablo Martinez Monsivais/ AP Photo/*Sputnik International News Agency* (Moscow). 11 Nov 2014.; *WJLA* (Arlington, TX). 11 Nov 2014.	9 Oct 2014: Participants playing the roles of anti-American demonstrators burn a effigy outside a fake US Consulate during a US Diplomatic Security Service High Threat training program held at a mock town named Erehwon, "nowhere" spelled backwards, on a rural Virginia military base. Two years after the deadly attack on a U.S. facility in Benghazi, Libya, the Diplomatic Security Service that is responsible for protecting some 100,000 Americans around the world has dramatically expanded training.
2015_01_16_ Pakistan: French President Hollande	174	EPA/*Daily Mail* (London). 16 Jan 2015.	16 Jan 2015: Violent and bloody protests have erupted around the world as furious Muslims react to *Charlie Hebdo*'s "survivor" edition—again featuring the holy Prophet Muhammad on its front cover. Supporters of banned Islamic charity Jamatud Dawa burn an effigy of the French President during protests.
2015_01_17_ Somalia: Charlie Hebdo Protest	175	AP/*Blazingcatfur* (blazingcatfur.ca), 17 Jan 2015.	Protests against *Charlie Hebdo*'s front cover have seen thousands more take to the streets—with students in Somalia declaring "Je Suis Muslim"—and "I love my Prophet." Students marched through Mogadishu on Saturday morning three days after the commemorative edition of the satirical magazine went on sale.
2015_01_23_ India: Charlie Hebdo director Charb	174	authintma il.com	23 Jan 2015: The effigy of *Charlie Hebdo* cartoonist who sketched blasphemous cartoons of Prophet Mohammad. A shutdown was observed on Friday in Indian administered Kashmir to protest the publication of blasphemous cartoons carried by French magazine, *Charlie Hebdo*.
2015_07_29_ Philippines: President Aquino (a)	64	Raymund B. Villanueva/ *Bulatlat* (Manila, Philippines). 29 Jul 2015.	Effigies have been featured and written about through the years that they have been made the centerpieces of the main protest rallies when the Philippine president delivers his or her State of the Nation Address. Some even ask should effigies be replaced already as a main symbol of these protests.
2015_07_29_ Philippines: President Aquino (b)	258	Raymund B. Villanueva/ *Bulatlat* (Manila, Philippines). 29 Jul 2015.	The throng, for its part, shows it respect–not to the person who the image represents, but the artists who built it. They help protect it from the police and firefighters who may wish it ill. They have their pictures taken with it, happy that it was, as always, finished on time and that it joins them again in one of this country's biggest annual political exercise.
2015_09_13_ USA-LA: President Trump	126	Jim Hoft/*Gateway Pundit* (USA). 13 Sep 2015.	The masses turned out to destroy El Trumpo. St. Louis Leftists Hang Donald Trump Effigy at Hispanic Festival. This weekend Cherokee Street in South St. Louis celebrated Mexican Independence Day. The Cherokee neighborhood has several Mexican restaurants and shops.
2015_11_17_ India: ISIS	189	AP/*Samakal* (Bangladesh), 17 Nov 2015.	Indian Muslims carry an effigy of the Islamic State group and shout slogans condemning Friday's attacks in Paris and expressing solidarity with France during a protest in Mumbai, India.
2015_11_23_ South Korea: North Korean leader Kim Yong Un	75	Chung Sung-Jun/Getty Images, Seattle (WA).	23 Nov 2015: A South Korean protester hits a effigy of North Korean leader Kim Jong-un during a anti-North Korea rally in Seoul, South Korea. Today marks the fifth anniversary of the shelling of border island by North Korea.
2016_01_14_ Iran: US President Obama	159	Amir Harirchi / ISNA/ *Nameh News* (Iran), 16 Jan 2014.	Protest in front of the Saudi consulate in Mashhad, Iran, burn effigies of US President Obama and Saudi King Salman burned in response to the execution of Shia cleric Sheikh Nimr in Saudi Arabia.
2016_01_30_ USA-TX: presidential candidate Trump	126	Edward A. Ornelas/*San Antonio Express News* (TX). 30 Jan 2016.	30 Jan 2016: Bexar County Democratic Party Chairman Manuel Medina hits a Donald Trump pinata during the "Bernie Beats Trump on the West Side" event held.
2016_02_10_ Iran: US President Obama	158	Thomas Erdbrink/twitter.	10 Feb 2016: Effigy of president Obama, at annual revolution anniversary rallies in Tehran. Louis Farakkhan is prominent guest.

Descriptor	Page	Credits / Source	Caption
2016_03_27_ Mexico: US presidential candidate Trump as Ano Viejo	63	*The News* (Nigeria). 27 Mar 2016.	Donald Trump effigy in the making: In Mexico City's poor La Merced neighborhood hundreds of cheering residents yelled "death" and various insults as they watched the explosion of the grinning papier-mâché mock-up of the real estate tycoon, replete with blue blazer, red tie and his trademark tuft of blond hair.
2016_09_15_ USA-OH: presidential candidate Hillary Clinton	74	Ashley Honea/SBG/*Komo News* (Seattle, WA).	11 Sep 2016: A black, rubber wet-suit sporting women's clothing and a blonde wig hangs from a noose attached to a crane.
2016_11_09_ USA-CA: President elect Trump	cover, 146	Marcus Yam/*Los Angeles Times*/Getty/*Newsweek* (New York). 23 Nov 2016.	9 Nov 2016: Anti-Trump protesters burn an effigy of the president-elect, Donald Trump, outside City Hall in Los Angeles.
2016_12_28_ Colombia: US President elect Trump as Ano Viejo	32	*Canal CNC Cali* (Colombia)/Youtube, 28 Dec 2016.	Donald Trump, el año viejo más vendido para quemar en fin de año.
2017_01_20_ Netherlands: US President Trump + Geert Wilders	61	Florian Göttke	Protesters burn effigies of US President Trump and Dutch right-wing politician Geert Wilders in a demonstration in Amsterdam.
2017_05_10_ USA-DC: President Trump	126	Chip Somo-devilla/Getty Images/*Breitbart News* (USA), 11 May 2017	Demonstrators Protest Outside White House Over President Trump's Firing Of FBI Director James Comey.
2017_05_23_ Palestine: US President Trump	71	Arab Media/*Jerusalem Post*. 23 May 2017.	23 May 2017: Armed men point machine guns at effigy of Donald Trump in Gaza. Thousands of supporters of the Popular Front for the Liberation of Palestine (PFLP) in Gaza protested US President Donald Trump's visit to Bethlehem on Tuesday.
2017_08_30_ Pakistan: Indian Premier Modi + US President Trump	60	Muhammad Sajjad/AP Photo/Sputnik International News Agency (Moscow). 30 Aug 2017.	Thousands of Pakistanis Rally to "Reject the Rhetoric," Burn Trump Effigy, Pakistanis in a major rally in Quetta have responded forcefully to US President Donald Trump's suggestion that their government has harbored jihadist elements within its borders.
2017_11_08_Brazil: philosopher Judith Butler	251	*Words and what not* (ultimategerardm.blogspot.com). 9 Nov 2017.	The hullabaloo was organized by a few small conservative groups, like the TFP (Tradition, Family and Property)—a far-right group founded in 1960—and a group led by former D-list actor Alexandre Frota, which has a strong online presence. On the other side, supporting Butler in greater numbers, were leftist groups, some of them carrying antifa flags.
al-Limby: 1990s_ Port Said, Egypt	146	*Youm 7*, Cairo, Egypt/Dessouki, Mohamed Adel. "The Interrelationship between Urban Space and Collective Memory." (Bachelor Thesis, Cairo University. 2012): 95.	Allenby effigies before being burnt.
al limby: 2012_11_28_ Egypt (President Morsi)	182	Ahmed Fahmy/Facebook.	مـرسـى أتحـــرق يا رجالة: فى التاريخ عندما ألقى البورسعيدية باللورد (لمبى) فى النيران وأصبح ذلك موروثا" شعبيا" يحرق من خلاله الدمى الطغاه كل عام بالمدينة الحرة و كان ذلك الشرارة الأولى تاريخيا" لبداية طرد الأحتلال الأنجليزى من مصر سيكتب التاريخ أيضا" بحروف من نور الوطنية أن حرق دمية (الرئيس اللمبى) أمس ببورسعيد ستكون الشرارة الأولى لسقوط الرئيس قاتل شعبة وتحرير مصر من الأحتلال الأخوانى.
al-Limby: 2014_04_19_ Egypt: Turkish President Erdoğan + US President Obama + Qatari royal family + others	182	As Masry Al Youm/Youtube, 19 Apr 2014.	بدأت بورسعيد، الاحتفالات بأعياد الربيع وشم النسيم على طريقتها الخاصة، وذلك بظهور عرائس الألمبي في المدينة. وعرائس الألمبي تقليد برسعيدي بدأ عندما صنع أهل المدينة عروسة على شكل اللورد اللمبي و، في فترة الاختلال البريطاني، وأحرقوها اعتراضا على ظلمه.
Carnival: 2010_ Keratea, Greece	42	*The Long Road to Greece* (thelongroadtogreece.wordpress.com), 25 Feb 2010.	
damnatio memoriae on a coin: 64_Rome (Emperor Nero)	35	*Romae Aeternis Numismatics* (www.vcoins.com).	Nero AE AS. Rome Mint 64 AD. Obverse: NERO. CLAVDIVS CAESAR AVG GERMANIC, eradicated head of Nero right; Damnatio Memoriae scratches all over bust.

Descriptor	Page	Credits / Source	Caption
demon Narkasur: 2014_Panjim, India	43	Bharne, Vinayak. "Diwali Urbanism." *The Indian Cities* (theindiancities.com), 28 Oct 2014.	In Panjim during Diwali, each neighborhood, precinct, locality, complex or micro-community is represented by a Narakasura or a demon effigy.
formal effigy punishment: 1789_Netherlands (Pensionary of Brabant De Cock)	39	Rijksmuseum Amsterdam, Netherlands.	Spotprent op E.M. de Cock, pensionaris van de Staten van Brabant, veroordeeld als landverrader en op 14 mei 1789 in effigie opgehangen aan de galg. Aan de voet van de galg staat Vrouw Wereld. Rechts wordt een jongeman door een groep vrouwen weggejaagd, op de achtergrond verkoopt een kramer pamfletten.
funeral effigy: 1685_UK (King Charles II)	37	Sir Benjamin Stone/Victoria and Albert Museum (London).	The funeral effigy of King Charles II, Westminster Abbey, 1896.
gold 50 dinars: 1980_Iraq (Saddam Hussein)	192	Numista (en.numista.com).	Commemorative issue: 1st Anniversary of the Inauguration of President Saddam Hussein.
Guy Fawkes: 1877_UK	44	John Thomson/J Paul Getty Museum (Los Angeles).	London, 1 Nov, 1877: November Effigies.
Guy Fawkes: 1900_New Zealand	44	Edward George Child/Alexander Turnbull Library (Wellington, New Zealand).	Unidentified children with rival guys, on Guy Fawkes day at Ohingaiti, circa 1900. Shows a group of children, standing by two effigies of Guy Fox in wheelbarrows. The four boys in the foreground wear suits and hats.
1946_03_00_Germany: Hitler as Haman	54	Ghetto Fighters' House Museum (infocenters.co.il/gfh).	A Purim parade in the Landsberg Deplaced Persons camp celebrating the holiday in March 1946. An open car with placards and men riding on the front bumper, and in the back seat, a prop representing a gallows with an effigy of Hitler hanging from it, and a man wearing camp inmates' garb.
Haman: 2011_Israel	43	*Haaretz* (Tel Aviv). 2 Mar 2015.	
inquisition effigy: 1544_Majorca, Spain	39	The Magnes Collection of Jewish Art and Life, University of California, Berkeley.	Inquisition Effigy Doll, Majorca, Spain, 15th Century: Wooden and cloth, black cloth covering wooden doll, face has red dye at neck and mouth, white dye for eyes, and black dye to depict hair, boots and hands. Clothes resemble a black robe with belt. Leather arms. According to Cecil Roth in *A History of the Marranos* such figures were representative of fugitives or those who had escaped justice by dying prior to trial.
Judas: 2003_Pruchnik, Poland	43	*Sven-Mueller* (sven-mueller.info).	Sven Müller. "Pruchnik: Die Verurteilung, Bestrafung, Verbrennung und Ertränkung des Judas."
Judas: 2010_Pampanga, Philippines	43	*Ivan about Town* (ivanhenares.com). 4 Apr 2010.	Pampanga: Easter Sunday Pakbung Hudas tradition in Minalin and Santo Tomas, Pampanga. Pakbung Hudas is an event wherein an effigy of Judas Iscariot, stuffed with firecrackers, is lit up in front of the church patio for a big bang to start the Easter Season. The firecrackers are so positioned so that the effigy moves horizontally counter-clockwise then clockwise, then vertically clockwise and counter-clockwise before finally exploding.
Judas: 2010_Valparaiso, Chile	43	Lydia/*Just smile and nod* (mnlydia.blogspot.com), 4 Apr 2010.	
Judas: 2016_Cordoba, Spain	43	Salas (EFE)/*Diario Cordoba* (Spain), 27 Mar 2016.	Vecinos de Espiel disparan a uno de los muñecos. El municipio minero de Espiel, en pleno del valle del Guadiato cordobés, el Domingo de Resurrección amanece con disparos de trabucos "matando" a los Judas, unos muñecos de paja y ropa vieja que cuelgan de las encaladas casas, para celebrar el triunfo del bien sobre el mal.
Leviathan (frontispice), Thomas Hobbes, 1651	38	Abraham Bosse/College of St. George (Windsor, UK). Archives Blog. 7 Jan 2009.	*Leviathan*, frontispiece to the 1651 edition. The impressive frontispiece shows earthly power represented by the castle, battlefield and crown on the left, spiritual power represented by the church, court and Bishop's mitre on the right. The sovereign is shown as a giant rising above, ruler over both.
Maslenitsa: 2015_Belgorod, Russia	42	Лобачев Владимир/Wikimedia Commons, 24 Feb 2015.	In some regions, each day of Maslenitsa had its traditional activity. The community builds the Maslenitsa effigy out of straw, decorated with pieces of rags, and fixed to a pole formerly known as Kostroma. It is paraded around and the first pancakes may be made and offered to the poor. As the culmination of the celebration people gather to "strip Lady Maslenitsa of her finery" and burn her in a bonfire. Lady Mas-lenitsa's ashes are buried in the snow to "fertilize the crops."

Descriptor	Page	Credits / Source	Caption
Mere-Folle: 1935_ Dijon, France	42	*Collaborative Media International* (collaborativemedia. blogspot.nl).	L'effigie de la Mère-Folle en train de brûler, pendant le Carnival de Dijon de 1935. Whalen, Phillip. "The Return of Crazy Mother: The Cultural Politics of Carnival in 1930s Dijon." *Social Identities* 16, no.4 (2010): 471–496.
Pope Day: 1768_ Boston, USMA	44, 96	Library of Congress (Washington, DC).	"South End Forever — North End Forever, Extraordinary Verses on Pope-Night. Or, a Commemoration of the Fifth of November, giving a history of the attempt made by the papists to blow up King and Parliament, A. D. 1588." Boston: The Printers Boys, 1768.
Ravana: 2010_ Edinburgh, UK	44	stevefaeembra/Flickr.	
revolutionary mob practice: "The Tory's Day of Judgement"	92	Elkanah Tisdale/Trumbull, Jon. *M'Fingal: A Modern Epic Poem.* New York: John Buel, 1795. 85.	"The Tory's day of judgment." Illustration shows colonists preparing to tar and feather a loyalist seated on the ground as another loyalist hangs from from a gallows with a rope around his waist.
revolutionary mob practice: tar and feather	92	The British Museum	Two Bostonians tarring and feathering a customs officer. Printed for Carrington Bowles, London, 12 Oct 1774.
rough music: 1727_UK ("The skimmington: rough music that mocked cuckolds, hen-pecked husbands and shrewish wives")	40	William Hogarth/*The Archives and Old Library at Trinity Hall* (oldlibrary trinityhall.wordpress.com), 16 Dec 2011.	William Hogarth, "The skimmington: rough music that mocked cuckolds, hen-pecked husbands and shrewish wives." 1727.
rough music: 1930_Netherlands (wedding couple)	40	*Algemeen Handelsblad* (Amsterdam). 18 Jan 1930.	In effigie terecht gesteld: Te Middelrode (N.B.) is het gewoonte dat op een trouwlustig paar op een huwelijksdag voor de buurtgenoten een vat bier beschikbaar stelt. Wee degenen die dit gebruik niet eren. Tot hun schande worden twee poppen, een getrouwe nabootsing van het paartje, in de bomen opgehangen, terwijl op een der stammen het "vonnis" wordt aangebracht.
rough music: 1952_Netherlands (unfaithful suitor)	40	Museum t'Oude Slot, Veldhoven, NL/Rooijackers, Geraard. *Eer en schande – Volksgebruiken van het oude Brabant.* Nijmegen: SUN, 1995.	The morning after van een tafelpartij in de Kempen (Zandoerle, 1952). In de dakgoot van de boerderij is onder grote hilariteit zaterdag s'nachts een ledikant geplaatst met een pop, liggend op een strooien matras ten teken dat dit volksgericht doelt op overtredingen betreffende de moraal inzake huwelijk en seksualiteit, in dit geval een minnaar die zijn meisje heeft 'laten zitten' door op het laatste moment de trouwbelofte te verbreken.
"The Death of Orpheus," Venice, 1501	242	Jacob of Strasbourg/The Metropolitan Museum (New York).	"Death of Orpheus," woodcut from Ovid. *Metamorphoses.* Venice, 1501.
tomb effigy: 1603_ UK (Elizabeth I)	37	*Tudor England* (landoflegendslv.com).	Effigy from Elizabeth I tomb in Westminster Abbey, London.

Index of
Geographical Locations

Florian Göttke (Gelsenkirchen-Buer, DE, 1965) is a visual artist, researcher, and writer based in Amsterdam. He combines visual modes of research (collecting, close reading, and image montage) with academic research to investigate the functioning of public images and their relationship to social memory and politics. Göttke has exhibited internationally, has written articles for academic journals and art publications. His book *Toppled* (Rotterdam, 2010), an iconological study of the toppled statues of Saddam Hussein, was nominated for the Dutch Doc Award 2011.

Göttke studied at the Gerrit Rietveld Academie and the Sandberg Instituut, both in Amsterdam. He obtained a PhD Artistic Research at the University of Amsterdam and the Dutch Art Institute in 2019. His dissertation entitled *Burning Images: Performing Effigies as Political Protest* (Amsterdam, 2019, self-published) investigates the peculiar practice to hang or burn effigies as a form of political protest. The book you now hold in your hands is a reworked and revised version of this dissertation.

floriangoettke.com

Earlier Publications

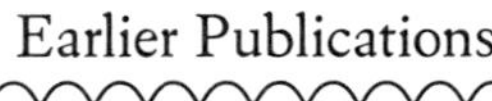

This publication is a revised version of Florian Göttke's dissertation *Burning Images: Performing Effigies as Political Protest*, Universiteit van Amsterdam, 2019.

An early outline of this study has been published under the title "Burning Effigies with Bakhtinian Laughter" in the *European Journal of Humour Research* in 2015. Chapter 6 forms the starting point for the article "Plaatsvervangende Lichamen: Het tragische lot van de effigie" published in the Dutch art magazine *Metropolis M* in 2017. An essay entitled "Of Falling Statues: Destabilizing a Media Icon" that builds on the arguments put forth in chapter 5, has been published in the book *Decoding Dictatorial Statues* by Ted Hyunhak Yoon in 2019.

Author: Florian Göttke
Editing: Janine Armin
Proofreading: Els Brinkman
Index: Florian Göttke, Rosie Haward
Design: Sam de Groot
Layout assistance: Boldizsár Tóth
Typefaces: Eldorado (William Addison Dwiggins, 1953),
    Computer Modern (Donald Knuth, 1984),
    SKI DATA (Tariq Heijboer, 2014)
Lithography: Mariska Bijl, Wilco Art Books
Paper: Munken Print White, 100 grs 1.5 (inside),
    Munken Lynx Rough, 300 grs (cover)
Printing and binding: Wilco Art Books, Amersfoort
Publisher: Valiz, Amsterdam, 2021, www.valiz.nl
    Astrid Vorstermans & Pia Pol

This publication has been printed on FSC-certified paper by an FSC-certified printer. The FSC, Forest Stewardship Council promotes environmentally appropriate, socially beneficial, and economically viable management of the world's forests. fsc.org

Distribution
BE/NL/LU: Centraal Boekhuis, www.cb.nl
Europe/Asia: Idea Books, www.ideabooks.nl
GB/IE: Anagram Books, www.anagrambooks.com
USA/Canada/Latin America: D.A.P., www.artbook.com
Australia: Perimeter Books, www.perimeterbooks.com
Individual orders: www.valiz.nl; info@valiz.nl

This book has been generously supported by
Mondriaan Fund
Prins Bernhard Cultuurfonds

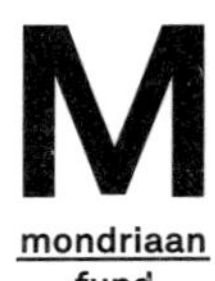 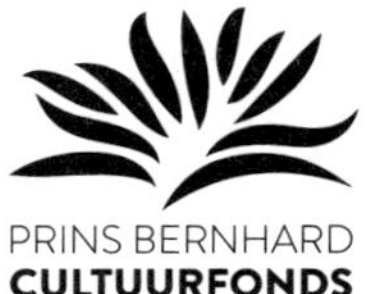

Amsterdam, 2021
ISBN 978-94-92095-96-1
Printed and bound in the EU

v i s - à - v i s

The vis-à-vis series provides a platform to stimulating and relevant subjects in recent and emerging visual arts, architecture and design. The authors relate to history and art history, to other authors, to recent topics and to the reader. Most are academic researchers. What binds them is a visual way of thinking, an undaunted treatment of the subject matter and a skilful, creative style of writing.

Series design by Sam de Groot, www.samdegroot.nl.

2015

Sophie Berrebi, *The Shape of Evidence: Contemporary Art and the Document*, ISBN 978-90-78088-98-1

Janneke Wesseling, *De volmaakte beschouwer: De ervaring van het kunstwerk en receptie-esthetica*, ISBN 978-94-92095-09-1 (e-book)

2016

Janneke Wesseling, *Of Sponge, Stone and the Intertwinement with the Here and Now: A Methodology of Artistic Research*, ISBN 78-94-92095-21-3

2017

Janneke Wesseling, *The Perfect Spectator: The Experience of the Art Work and Reception Aesthetics*, ISBN 978-90-80818-50-7

Wouter Davidts, *Triple Bond: Essays on Art, Architecture, and Museums*, ISBN 978-90-78088-49-3

Sandra Kisters, *The Lure of the Biographical: On the (Self-)Representation of Artists*, ISBN 978-94-92095-25-1

Christa-Maria Lerm Hayes (ed.), *Brian O'Doherty/Patrick Ireland:
Word, Image and Institutional Critique*, ISBN 978-94-92095-24-4

2018
John Macarthur, Susan Holden, Ashley Paine, Wouter Davidts,
Pavilion Propositions: Nine Points on an Architectural Phenomenon,
ISBN 978-94-92095-50-3
Jeroen Lutters, *The Trade of the Teacher: Visual Thinking with Mieke Bal*,
ISBN 978-94-92095-56-5
Ernst van Alphen, *Failed Images: Photography and its Counter-Practices*,
ISBN 978-94-92095-45-9
Paul Kempers, *'Het gaat om heel eenvoudige dingen': Jean Leering en
de kunst*, ISBN 978-94-92095-07-7
Eva Wittocx, Ann Demeester, Melanie Bühler, *The Transhistorical
Museum: Mapping the Field*, ISBN 978-94-92095-52-7

2019
Nathalie Zonnenberg, *Conceptual Art in a Curatorial Perspective: Between
Dematerialization and Documentation*, ISBN 978-90-78088-76-9
Wouter Davidts, Susan Holden, Ashley Paine (eds.), *Trading between
Architecture and Art: Strategies and Practices of Exchange*,
ISBN 978-94-92095-67-1
Jeroen Lutters, *In the Shadow of the Art Work: Art-Based Learning in
Practice*, ISBN 978-94-92095-66-4

2020
Jeroen Lutters, *Creative Theories of (Just About) Everything: A Journey
into Origins and Imaginations*, ISBN 978-94-92095-74-9
Ashley Paine, Susan Holden, John Macarthur (eds.), *Valuing Architecture:
Heritage and the Economics of Culture*, ISBN 978-94-92095-93-0